Failure of a Dream?
Essays in the History of American Socialism

JOHN H. M. LASLETT, who was born in England and educated at Oxford University, is Associate Professor of American History at UCLA. In this country he taught previously at the University of Chicago. Among his other works are *Labor and the Left: A Study of Socialist and Radical Influences in the American Labor Movement, 1881–1924,* and *A Short Comparative History of American Socialism (With Proposals for a New Theory of the Labor Movement)*, forthcoming from Harper & Row. He is currently Visiting Professor of American Labour History at the Centre for the Study of Social History at the University of Warwick in England. He is married to a sociologist, and has two children.

SEYMOUR MARTIN LIPSET is Professor of Government and Sociology and a member of the Executive Committee of the Center for International Affairs at Harvard University. He has held fellowships from the Social Science Research Council, the Ford Foundation, the Guggenheim Foundation, and the Center for Advanced Study in the Behavioral Sciences. He has been elected to the American Academy of Arts and Sciences, the National Academy of Education, and the National Academy of Sciences. His authored or co-authored books include: *Agrarian Socialism, Union Democracy, Social Mobility in Industrial Society, The First New Nation, Revolution and Counter-Revolution, Rebellion in the University, Academics, Politics and the 1972 Election,* and *Professors, Unions and American Higher Education.* Two of his works have received awards, *Political Man* (the MacIver Award) and *The Politics of Unreason* (the Myrdal Prize). His books have appeared in eighteen languages.

Failure of a Dream?

Essays in the History of American Socialism

☆

Edited by
John H. M. Laslett
and
Seymour Martin Lipset

Anchor Books
Anchor Press/Doubleday
GARDEN CITY, NEW YORK
1974

Grateful acknowledgment is made for the use of the following:

Portions of *The End of Ideology: On the Exhaustion of Political Ideas in the Fifties* by Daniel Bell. Reprinted by permission of the author.
"The Socialist Party, Its Roots and Hidden Strengths, 1912–1919," by James Weinstein. Reprinted by permission of the author.
From *Utopia and Reality* by Betty Yorburg. Published by Columbia University Press, 1969. Reprinted by permission of author and publisher.
From *Toward a United Front* by Leon Samson. All Rights Reserved. Reprinted by permission of Holt, Rinehart & Winston, Inc.
From *Marxism: The View from America.* Copyright © 1960 by Clinton Rossiter. Reprinted by permission of Harcourt Brace Jovanovich, Inc.
From *The Liberal Tradition in America,* copyright © 1955 by Louis Hartz. Reprinted by permission of Harcourt Brace Jovanovich, Inc.
"Comments on Selig Perlman's *A Theory of the Labor Movement,*" by Adolf Sturmthal. Reprinted from the *Industrial and Labor Relations Review,* Vol. 4, No. 4, July 1951. Copyright © 1951 by Cornell University. All rights reserved.
"The Catholic Church and the Political Development of American Trade Unionism (1900–1918)," by Marc Karson. Reprinted from the *Industrial and Labor Relations Review,* Vol. 4, No. 4, July 1951. Copyright © 1951 by Cornell University. All rights reserved.
Portions of *Socialism Re-examined.* Reprinted from *Socialism Re-examined* by Norman Thomas. By permission of W. W. Norton & Company, Inc. Copyright © 1963 by Norman Thomas.
"Working Class Social Mobility in Industrial America" by Stephan Thernstrom. Reprinted by permission of the publishers from Melvin Richter, ed., *Essays in Theory and History: An Approach to the Social Sciences.* Cambridge, Mass.: Harvard University Press, Copyright, 1970, by the President and Fellows of Harvard College.
Portions of *We Shall Be All: A History of the Industrial Workers of the World.* Reprinted by permission of Quadrangle Books from *We Shall Be All: A History of the Industrial Workers of the World* by Melvyn Dubofsky, copyright © 1969 by Melvyn Dubofsky.

CONTENTS

PART THREE: EXTERNAL FACTORS: AMERICAN SOCIETY AND AMERICAN SOCIALISM

PREFACE

Contrary to most popular beliefs, the United States has an indigenous socialist tradition, if only a small one by European standards, which exerted a significant influence both in the labor movement and in American politics in the years before the First World War. In 1912, the Socialist Party of America had more than a thousand of its members in public office as mayors, state assemblymen, and other elected officials, and Eugene V. Debs received nearly a million votes in his campaign for the presidency that year. Yet by 1919, with the reforms of the Progressive movement, the Red Scare, and the split over Bolshevism, the American socialist movement received a setback from which it never recovered, not even during the Depression of the 1930s.

The purpose of this book is to examine the reasons for the relative weakness of American socialism with respect to the internal problems of the party and the movement in matters of tactics, ideology, and leadership. It also deals with the negative effects on socialism stemming from the nature of American society itself —for example, the relatively high degree of social fluidity, the pervasive character of American liberalism, or the nature of the political system. Part Two addresses itself largely to the first of these two sets of factors, and Part Three to the second. Part One consists of two chapters providing a general overview of the subject, with which the non-specialist reader is urged to begin. Chapter One represents, in summary form, portions of a series of interviews with old socialists giving their views of why the Socialist Party of America failed to attract more than a very small number of American voters to its banner. Chapter Two takes the form of a dialogue between the two editors, giving their respective views as students of the subject. Though they disagree over specific areas of interpretation, both authors consider the extent to which American society has differed from other societies in those elements which make for the growth of a strong socialist tradition crucial to an understanding of the problem.

The question "Why is there no socialism in the United States?" —the title of a famous essay published in 1906 by the German sociologist Werner Sombart, parts of which are reproduced in this volume in English for the first time—is not simply an academic one. In the 1840s Karl Marx and Friedrich Engels were only the first in what has since become a long line of foreign and domestic observers who still continue to discuss the absence of a strong socialist movement in what is by now by far the most advanced capitalist country in the world. This phenomenon has also been used by scholars as one of their major arguments in the continuing debate over America's alleged "exceptionalism"—how far, that is to say, American development has differed from that of other industrial societies in the West. Given the immense contemporary influence of the United States in other parts of the world, the question also has important consequences which go beyond understanding America's own history. It affects our judgment of what may happen elsewhere, as both Europe and Japan appear to take as many of the characteristics of mass industrial society which first appeared in the United States.

The issue has taken on added interest and importance with the rise of the New Left, both in the United States and abroad. When the idea for this book was first conceived, in 1969, it appeared for a time as though the American independent Left might break out of the mold of frustration, cooptation, repression, and failure which has so often dogged its footsteps in the past; and perhaps even establish a mass movement which would belie the terms in which Sombart's original question had been posed. Since then the New Left has failed to maintain its momentum. In our view, however, its collapse has increased, instead of diminished, the need for the kind of symposium presented here. Part Four of the work consists, therefore, of two essays by prominent representatives of the New Left which discuss both the differences between the Old Left and the New in American society, and the prospects for the New Left at the present time. Taken in conjunction with the largely historical materials presented in Parts Two and Three, they should enable the general reader, as well as the specialist, to form a clearer judgment about the past character and likely direction of American radicalism as a whole.

Previously published material which in our judgment incorporates a significant proportion of the important scholarly work which has hitherto been done on the subject constitutes only about half of the essays included in this book. The remainder consists of invited essays of Comment on these writings by distinguished scholars presently working in the field, followed by Replies from the original authors where they are still living, or by a second essay of Comment where they are not.

A deliberate effort has been made to solicit contributions both from scholars who have written on the subject, and from activists presently involved in the New Left movement, as well as to include representatives of different generational and ideological points of view. Inevitably, however, in dealing with so large a subject the collection is not wholly comprehensive. Some of the invited contributors were unable to participate in the symposium, and some previously published material could not be reproduced. Constraints of space have also meant that a number of important questions are not explored as fully as they might be. These include the issue of the frontier as a "safety valve" for working-class discontent, ethnic fragmentation as a problem in American working-class consciousness, and the role of blacks and other oppressed racial minorities as an "absentee proletariat" in the nineteenth-century American economy.

There are also a number of deliberate omissions. No attempt, for example, has been made to deal comprehensively with the issue of communism—even though many of the arguments made by the contributors to the symposium concerning the weakness of American socialism can equally be made with respect to American communism. Our central focus has been upon socialism and the Socialist Party; to deal with communism in detail would require another volume. We have largely found it necessary to ignore other radical tendencies as well.

Despite these limitations, these essays are offered in the belief that they represent the most comprehensive collection of scholarly work on the subject now available. For the general reader, we hope that they will satisfy at least part of his curiosity about the historical background which lies behind the present ferment on the American Left. For the student and the scholar we hope that they will stimulate further study and research into a question which has always been at the center of American historical and political debate.

One further point should be made. Although some scholars would undoubtedly argue to the contrary, as Betty Yorburg implies at the beginning of Chapter One, the reasons which they have chosen to emphasize in their explanations for the relative absence of socialism from America often reflect, either directly or indirectly, their own value judgments concerning both the nature and purposes of socialism as an ideology, and the merits or defects of American society itself. Many on the political Left, for example, regard the weakness of socialism in America as a regrettable but by no means inevitable occurrence which resulted from oppression, corruption, or inefficient leadership, or from the idiosyncrasies of the American electoral system or of American historical development generally. Others, usually associated of course with the political Right, regard it as a generally beneficent development which grew out of the generally successful character of the United States as an equalitarian society, or perhaps out of the virtually inevitable triumph of a liberal (as opposed to a Marxist or a conservative) form of political consensus.

A wide variety of other, more or less conscious, value judgments concerning this issue are embedded at various places in the scholarship which has been carried out on this topic, as the reader will soon discover for himself. The use of the word "failure" in the title of this volume, as elsewhere in its pages, should not be taken to imply either a pejorative or a deterministic judgment concerning the past performance or present fortunes of the American Left. Our opinions concerning the reasons for the weakness of the American socialist movement are made clear in various of our own contributions to this symposium, revealing along with them, of course, our own particular political points of view. The use of the word "failure" is a shorthand way of stating what seems to us the obvious fact that neither in America nor in Europe (or in any other part of the world, for that matter) have either the socialists, the Communists, or any other ideological grouping of revolutionary radicals yet succeeded in implementing even the most obvious of those common characteristics of a future society which are advocated by all socialists alike. For a further critique of the deterministic and ahistorical position which in Laslett's view both vulgar liberals and vulgar Marxists in America have been guilty of taking up in their writings on this subject, as well as a more extensive theoretical presentation of his own views, see the first chapter of his *A Short Comparative History of American Socialism (With Proposals for a New Theory of the Labor Movement)*, which is shortly to be published by Harper & Row. For a further elaboration of Lipset's views on this and similar questions, see his *Revolution and Counterrevolution: Change and Persistence in Social Structures* (Anchor Books, 1970), especially Chapter One.

September 1973.
John H. M. Laslett, U.C.L.A.
Seymour Martin Lipset, Harvard.

Part One

☆

The Problem of Socialism
in America

Chapter 1

SOCIALISTS VIEW THE PROBLEM*

Betty Yorburg

1. *Questions Raised by the Old Left*

A final and incontestable answer to the question of why socialism and the Socialist Party failed in this country is not possible.
The very question calls forth protests such as: "The Socialist Party
failed, but socialism did not fail in America," or "Socialism failed
everywhere in the West, no more so here than in Britain and the
Scandinavian countries, which have only nominal socialism." Or,
"The Party failed politically, but not personally—it served many
valuable functions for its members."

The question of the failure of socialism in America is an exceedingly difficult one to answer, bound up as it is with values
and with present-day confusions with regard to what socialism is
as an economic system, what its goals are, and what methods should
be used for obtaining these goals, [as the response of one old
Socialist Party member makes clear]:

Well, what's socialism today? So long as you don't have socialism,
it's pretty clear what you want. But once you have a little bit of socialism, it's not so clear what you want because clarity is much easier
when you are at a distance from the thing. The outline is clearer when
you don't take in the details of what you want, and how you are
going to get it, and how you are going to manage it.

Socialism is collective ownership as opposed to private ownership,
period. What's so complicated about that? And, in the 1920s, that was
it. And into the 1930s, that was it.

* Chapter 3 from Betty Yorburg, *Utopia and Reality: A Collective Portrait
of American Socialists* (New York: Columbia University Press, 1969), originally entitled "The Failure of Socialism in America." The remaining chapters of this book analyze generational differences among old Socialist Party of
America members concerning their ideological beliefs, their reasons for joining the Socialist Party, and their views on the prospects for socialism in
America in the future.

Of course, the Soviet Union had their system collectivized, but we said that's a strange animal anyhow because they had no right to make a socialist revolution in Russia. Russia was an agricultural country, and socialism is not for pigs. Socialism is for industrial workers. So, okay, that was an accident of history.

But then, as the years have gone by, the concept of socialism was picked up all over the earth. And the use of the phrase is now universal except in the United States.

The Soviet Union has socialism. And China has socialism. But that's different. And the Scandinavian countries have socialism. That's still more different. The Labour Party of Britain is for socialism. It is the Socialist Party of Great Britain. And their socialism is a completely different animal. I am not quite sure whether they have nationalized steel or not, at this moment.

And even when the fairly conservative Catholic parties of central Europe take over, they refer to themselves as Christian Socialists.

Then Nasser is for Arab socialism. And when Castro made the revolution in Cuba, he said: "We are the first socialist republic in the Western hemisphere." And Trujillo said, "No, the Dominican Republic is."

And then you go into Southeast Asia and you have a collection of feudal lords who talk about feudal socialism. And you have a monarchic socialism and a military socialism. And you have a Socialist Party in the United States.

But we are beyond the point where it's all so clear: collectivism *vs.* private ownership. Actually, we live in a world where I suppose the majority of the peoples are living under some form of government that describes itself as more or less socialist.

So it's no longer quite so simple. And when you ask me am I still a socialist—that's a good question.

What are the basic tenets of socialism? In the final analysis, it's collectivism *vs.* private ownership. But if you were to examine any one of the societies on the face of the earth today, there is a high degree of collective action, a high degree of it.

And that includes the United States. We do it in a sneaky way in the United States, but the United States does not reject the collective action that it rejected in the early 1930s and would not even consider in the 1920s.

Given the current intricacy and complexity of economic systems, and to avoid compounding confusion, before attempting to discuss the failure of socialism in the United States, we might attempt to answer two questions. Is the United States approaching a socialist economic system? Given certain standards, how close is this country to socialism compared to other industrialized, democratic countries?

Socialism can be defined as an economic system in which there is nationalization of basic industries, a dominant public sector, equal income distribution, a total welfare state, and central economic planning. This is an ideal-typical construction. No society in existence today, whether or not it defines itself as socialist, has an economic system which meets all of the above criteria. The definition is an exaggeration of reality, containing the essential features of socialism in pure form.

Using this model as a yardstick, we must conclude that the United States is certainly not a socialist state, and whether or not it is approaching socialism is problematic.

Widespread nationalization of basic industries has not taken place in this country; floundering industries are usually subsidized, not nationalized.[1] Government policy in this country has followed the principle of encouraging private industry to undertake the production of new goods and services, rather than expand the public sector. The implementation of urban renewal programs, in which private industry has provided private housing units for middle-income groups, for the most part, is an example of the operation of this policy. The public sector is smaller in the United States than in most other industrial nations in the West. Utilities such as telephones and railways, which are state-owned in most countries, are privately owned and subject only to moderate government regulation in the United States.

Social scientists disagree in their conclusions about current trends in income distribution in the United States. A major difficulty in making accurate assessments of these trends is that data are based on reported income figures. Real income consists of actual command over goods and services by various categories of people in a society. Reported income figures do not include illegal income, intrafamilial transfers of income, and fringe benefits such as hospitalization, pension benefits, deferred income payments, undistributed profits, expense accounts, etc. Higher-income groups share disproportionately in these benefits.

Given these difficulties in ascertaining real income, it is not surprising that there is disagreement among social scientists regarding trends in income distribution. Gabriel Kolko,[2] using census data on reported income, found a long-range decline in the percentage of income going to the bottom 20 per cent of American families from the years 1910 to 1959. Herman P. Miller[3] found that the percentage of national income going to the bottom 20 per cent increased up to 1944, then remained stable to 1961.

Regardless of their differences, both writers agree that the reduced income of upper-income groups, by means of progressive taxation, has been redistributed largely to middle-income groups in our society. Miller, in his cross-sectional view of national income, found that the upper 5 per cent of American families received 30 per cent of all family income in 1929 and 20 per cent of all family income in 1961. The latter figure indicates a continued substantial differential in the distribution of reported income. It should be emphasized that actual purchasing power has increased enormously within the lower strata in America over the years. However, tax cuts and loopholes, and differential access to fringe benefits have blunted the possible redistributive effects of progressive taxation considerably.

As for the other aspects of socialism, we do not have compulsory central planning or even the voluntary type of planning used in such countries as France and Belgium. Planning, by the automobile industry, for example, is short-term and is oriented toward the goals of the particular industry.

Finally, the United States has a very limited welfare state compared with many European countries which have more comprehensive social security and public housing measures.

If we utilize a precise and ideal-typical definition of socialism, therefore, the question of the failure of socialism in America is a legitimate one. The literature on this question is voluminous, but agreement on the weight which should be given to various factors is rare. Reasons given for the failure of socialism range from the purely economic (the wealth of the country) to the purely ideological (the American Dream) with the purely political (the two-party electoral system) somewhere in the middle. Most analyses are multi-causal in approach, but they attempt to distinguish, arbitrarily by necessity, between primary or ultimate and secondary or contributing factors.

Occasionally in the literature, one encounters an explanation resting on a single and predominant factor. Harvey Goldberg[4] and Seymour M. Lipset and Reinhard Bendix[5] cite the American

Dream as an all-important element in the failure of the socialist movement in this country. Lipset and Bendix argue that while the rate of intergenerational mobility from the working class into the middle class since the turn of the century has actually been approximately the same in various Western industrialized countries, the belief in the possibility of unlimited success for everyone has tended, in the United States, to deflect potential radical protest into transvaluational religions or into hopes for one's children. In other words, as W. I. Thomas observed, if men define situations as real, they are real in their consequences.[6]

Other examples of monistic emphasis are: the desire of immigrants in this country to become acculturated and, thus, to accept the status quo;[7] factionalism—particularly the splitting off from the Socialist Party of the militant Haywood group in 1912;[8] the individualism of the American national character, which was incompatible with socialist goals of collective existence;[9] the inability of the Socialist Party to reconcile its ethics with the demands of political expediency—it was "in but was not of the world";[10] and the preemption of socialist ideas by the New Deal.[11]

Examples of more complex analyses go back at least to Werner Sombart's question at the turn of the century, "Why is there no socialism in the United States?" Previously, of course, the question was phrased in terms of when socialism would arrive in the United States rather than why it did not. Karl Marx and Frederick Engels shared the unrestrained enthusiasm of the early socialists for the prospects of socialism in this country. In a letter to Friedrich Sorge, written in 1893, Engels[12] predicted that if Americans were properly informed of European theoretical knowledge of the laws of social change, their extraordinary vitality and energy could lead to victory for socialism within ten years.

Werner Sombart, writing some ten years later, anticipated the thousands of pages which were to be written in the years to follow on the question of why socialism did not arrive in the United States. Sombart[13] attributed the failure of the movement, up to that time, to the fluidity of the class structure in the United States, to the open frontier which contributed to this fluidity, and to the economic wealth and rising standards of living in this country.

Selig Perlman attributed the failure of cooperative movements in the United States to the fluidity of the class structure—"the opportunity for the exceptional workman to desert his class and set up in business for himself,"[14] to the ethnic and racial cleavages which prevented class solidarity and consciousness of kind from developing in this country, and to certain aspects of American national character which were incompatible with cooperative social organization: the traditional individualism in this country and the heritage of puritanism with its emphasis on individual achievement.

More recently, G. D. H. Cole[15] singled out the political democracy which existed in this country in contrast to Europe, where workers found a common rallying ground in opposition to autocracy and militarism. He believed that a second factor preventing the continued growth of the movement in America was the cleavage, reinforced by ethnic differences, between skilled and unskilled workers.

Typically, those analysts who maintain a traditional Marxist orientation attribute the failure of the socialist movement in this country to economic factors—next to which all other factors are viewed as secondary or derivative.[16]

2. Reasons for Failure

When our respondents were asked to give their opinion on this problem, they replied with lengthy and often scholarly arguments, indicating in many instances an extraordinary memory for facts and figures and a thorough familiarity with the history of the movement. Those leaders who have written about the socialist movement and its failures in this country tend to repeat the arguments which have already appeared in print. There have been no major changes in the thinking of these leaders about the problem.

Content analysis of the data indicates only the relative frequencies with which certain factors are mentioned. It does not reveal the relative emphasis or weighting given to these factors nor does it reveal the evaluation of these factors by our respondents. For example, the New Deal economic reforms mentioned by two respondents as a factor in the failure of the movement can, in one case, be viewed as the realization of the goals of the Socialist Party (at least in terms of its immediate goals) or, in another case, as a conservative holding action on the part of the ruling class in this country.

In general, patterns in the thinking of the leaders about the problem of the failure of socialism in America do not coincide with generational categories in that no one factor is cited more frequently by one generation than another. However, there is a tendency for certain factors to be given more weight in particular generations. All of the leaders give multiple reasons for the failure of the movement.

The most frequently mentioned reason for the failure of the movement and the Party in this country is the New Deal reforms and other economic reforms that have been introduced over the past fifty years. In descending order, other frequently cited reasons are: factionalism and splitting within the Party; the failure to capture the imagination of the labor movement, or stated in another way, the inapplicability of socialist ideology to the goals and desires of the working class in this country; the fluidity of the class structure and the relative weakness of the class struggle in this country; the two-party electoral system; ethnic differences and cleavages; and the fact that the ideology was imported from Europe.

Causes mentioned infrequently but with about equal frequency are: the wealth of the nation; the American Dream; the poor leadership of the Party; governmental repression of the Party and its pacifist stand on war.

Significantly, there are a large number of miscellaneous and infrequent responses such as: Americans like to remain with the winner; the Party did not have enough morale; the American Labor Party outmaneuvered the Party; confusion existed in the public mind between communism and socialism; and socialism was a Jewish movement, and in the United States Jewish political movements are not subject to great growth.

3. *Evaluations of Failure*

At least since the time of Edmund Burke, in the realm of political theory, and at least since the time of Otto von Bismarck, in the realm of political action, it has been recognized that the essence of conservatism is timely reform. Our respondents tend to affirm this, although not consistently in those terms. Almost all of the leaders, with very few exceptions, list the New Deal reforms and other economic reforms, going back to the Progressive Era, as a decisive factor in the failure of the socialist movement in this country. The evaluation of the adequacy of these reforms varies, however, and usually it tends to coincide with the present relationship of our respondents to the Socialist Party.

Leaders who left the Party many years ago tend to emphasize the material and moral gains that have been achieved in this country since the days of early, unregulated capitalism:

We are not satisfied, naturally, and we want more change and more rapid change. But you must remember how things *have* changed.

There is less corruption and graft in government. There is less violence against minority groups and against labor. There is less flagrant bias in the newspapers (people are smarter). And business methods, while they leave much to be desired, are certainly less ruthless than they were.

* * *

In the new countries all over the world, socialism is taken for granted. In this country, there has been a conscious campaign, a concerted effort of all the opinion makers to isolate America from Europe. They don't want to share this European general acceptance of the ideals of socialism.

However, as far as the practical development of socialist measures is concerned, America is an advanced socialist country. In terms of national control—national, government control of the direction of the economy and the practical distribution of its fruits, the increasing distribution of profits to the masses—socialism is here.

* * *

Basically, socialism means collectivism versus private ownership. Well, today we have a high degree of collectivism in the United States.

First of all, we have collective restraints on industry. The minimum wage law is a collective restraint, so that you may not pay a wage below a certain level. Now, it's private ownership and it's called private ownership, but it's no longer the private ownership in the sense that it once was, when you could do any damn thing you wanted to do with your property. That's no longer valid.

The fact that you now have a National Labor Relations Act that says that when the majority of your workers want to join the union, you *must* bargain with them, you must recognize them is a tremendous restraint on ownership. It means that you own it, but you are limited.

And there are other forms of collective action—unemployment insurance, workmen's compensation, social security, and, now, we're moving into the whole field of medicine.

The original socialist concept didn't *just* mean governmental ownership; it called for a variety of collective activities whereby people co-
operatively would pool their funds and their knowhow in order to
accomplish certain purposes.

In the 1930s, the Union Health Center was a freak. It was a form
of third-party medicine run by the ILGWU. Today, third-party medicine probably covers the majority of the people in this country. You
either have Group Health or HIP or Blue Shield or Blue Cross, or
you are under some veterans' plan or under some military plan, or
under some other municipal or governmental employees plan, or under
some union-run plan. Well, this is a form of collective protection for
the community; it's a form of collectivism.

But we really go much beyond that. You take housing in the United
States. You take the whole FHA program, the whole GI housing program, the whole Title One program, and federal and state and municipal monies for low-cost housing. Government housing—it runs into
billions of dollars in the United States. It's government *housing*.

Once, housing was something that belonged to landlords exclusively.
And now there's huge government housing, even though it may appear
to be private. For instance, if you have an FHA mortgage, it's government underwritten. Fundamentally, it's the government that's financ-
ing the housing except that the government says to you, "If you get
an FHA mortgage, you may go to the bank and the bank will lend
you the money at a given rate of interest. And we will insure that
mortgage. In other words, if you can't pay, we will pay."

Now really, this is the government saying, "We are putting up the
housing. We stand behind it." It's socialism at six per cent, and the
bank gets its cut of this kind of socialism.

The socialists also believed that there should be a program enacted
immediately short of socialism that would provide a whole series of
social insurances and securities. And the socialists, when they used to
campaign everywhere in the world, didn't just talk about socialism,
they spoke about minimum wages and social security and the rest of
it.

Well, that we have. We got it in what was called the New Deal.
It's an expanding concept however. It isn't just the original New Deal.
It's the New Deal plus everything that's come along on top of the
New Deal. All the other things.

So this aspect of socialism we've accepted, even in the United States.
What else was socialism? Socialism was a concept of the role of labor
in society. This was the whole notion of industrial democracy. That
is, the working man should have a voice, an important voice, in (a)
the economy and in (b) the government of the nation.

And the old socialist concept was very simple. A government was a class government. The capitalists owned and called all the industrial shots, and the capitalists also owned the government. It was their government, and, therefore, you had to have a class party to dispossess it.

Well, you cannot say that the American worker does not have a sizable voice, a dominant voice—surely it's not the only voice and I'm not sure that it's the major voice, but it's a sizable voice in determining the nature of the economy. Surely, this is true in the area of wages, but more than that in many other areas.

And politically, it's no longer possible to say that this is simply the government of the capitalists and that the working man has no voice in the government of the nation. Of course, he has a voice. It's perfectly obvious.

We are constantly being told by right-wing critics that Johnson is nothing but the tool of labor, and so was Truman and so was Roosevelt. It's not true. They are not the tool of labor. And it's not true—as some of them charge—that the moment the labor bosses speak, all the congressmen jump. It's not true.

However, labor has a very important political voice in the United States at the present time, and, more important in terms of the future, labor can have a *greater* political voice. As a matter of fact, it's just a matter of educating its own ranks and organizing to do a better job.

So the old socialist notion that it's important to have an industrial democracy—I think it's happening. I don't think we have *the* industrial democracy, but we have been moving every year in the direction of industrial democracy in the United States *and* in the direction of political democracy.

We have not achieved a full victory. We may not achieve a full victory ever. I'm not sure we want a full victory. But certainly this has been the direction. This is clear. . . .

In a general sense, the acceptance by the society of responsibility for the economic well-being of the individual—there is no country on the face of the earth today that does not accept this to a greater or to a lesser degree. We have really turned our back completely on the notion of everybody for himself.

Now, is this socialism? Well, it's socialism of a sort. But who has the other kind of socialism, except in the Soviet-run countries? Otherwise you don't have it. Hitler, in a sense, had it, and he practically took over the whole show. And Peron came mighty close to it.

If you just see socialism as a diagram, that is, government ownership, it only exists really in the Soviet countries. In other countries, we have socialism or semi-socialism in the form of collectivism. And the old concept of what socialism is today is *out*.

Socialism, we see again, now means many different things to different people.

The leaders who are still members of the Socialist Party tend to evaluate welfare state measures in this country and governmental regulations of industry as inadequate—too little, if not too late:

As far as socialism and socialist ideas are concerned, there certainly was a different attitude toward a good many things that the socialists preached in the early days than you find at present.

When the Socialist Party was first born, only a minority of Americans was in favor of social legislation—of unemployment insurance, old-age pensions, health insurance. Only a minority felt that the government had any interest in doing anything about the elimination of the slums and in the bringing about of decent housing.

There was much less emphasis on education, particularly on higher education. There was much less control and regulation of the great industries of the country. We just didn't have the public ownership that we have at the present time—in the TVA and the electrical industry. And the concept of the welfare state was a concept which seemed to be alien to the American people.

I remember in 1929 coming back from Vienna after having seen any number of very fine homes for the workers in Vienna, and the slums disappearing, and urging that we do the same thing in the United States. And my audiences said, "Well, that's a fine thing, but it's not a function of government."

Well, in 1936 and 1937, it became a function of government, and we have advanced quite a distance, although the great problem is still to be solved.

If you go down to Washington now and hear what they say about its being a government job to eliminate poverty—that's a far cry from what one heard at the beginning of the century.

The trade union movement has grown from two or three million to about seventeen million. And now there are any number of laws protecting the movement, whereas at the turn of the century, one heard simply of injunctions and police brutality, and so forth, preventing the legitimate activities of the labor movement.

So there has been quite a different attitude toward what a community should do in protecting the workers, in abolishing poverty, in developing public agencies, education, recreation, and things of that sort.

However, we socialists would say that *still* you find the great and unjust inequality of wealth that one found at the beginning of the century. *Still* you find tremendous concentration of control in American industry—the development of monopolies and oligarchies and so forth.

Still you find, on the whole, the motive of success is that of becoming rich rather than serving the community. *Still* you find five million people unemployed. *Still* you find one-fifth of the people in bad homes.

Still you find, with the tremendous development of technology, that social legislation has not kept pace. *Still* you find our natural resources are being wasted. We are not doing the job in preserving our resources —our forests, our waterways. *Still* you find billions of dollars lost every year for lack of flood control.

Still you find, say in communications, the great cities of the country are lacking railroad communications because the private railroads don't find it profitable to have proper commuter services. *Still* you find chaos as far as transportation and communication is concerned, and so forth.

Of course, the socialists were incorrect in timing social change. They were incorrect in feeling that the capitalist system did not have before it the opportunity to expand as it has expanded. They had little idea of the tremendous development of productivity as a result of our greatly advanced technology. And they probably had little concept of what taxation could do in giving a tremendous resource to the government through income and inheritance taxes, and so forth.

But with the development of technology, it becomes more and more necessary to have national economic planning. And we have only the beginning of national economic planning.

And the need for democratic social planning, which the socialists have urged, is as great if not greater than before.

4. *Generational Perspectives*

As I have pointed out, no striking differences arise between the generations in the relative frequency with which particular reasons for the failure of the Party or the movement are singled out. However, there is a tendency for emphasis on particular factors to vary. Those which are emphasized tend to be related to the social conditions prevailing in America at the time of most active participation in the movement by the different generations.

The World War I Generation, particularly those who were born in Europe, tend to stress the fluidity of the class structure, and the ease of vertical social mobility in this country:

When I used to teach history classes, I would say, "Look, if you want to see the difference between the labor movement in the United Kingdom and here, there are two points that you must understand."

The worker, the dissatisfied worker in the city, dissatisfied with his treatment as a worker, had an alternative in America. He could take off. The brainy worker went West instead of going into socialism. "Go West, young man." There was land here, you see.

There was opportunity here. Education wasn't so caste bound. Here you didn't get the whole caste system that you had in England.

I don't know whether I sound ancient, but in England when I was a child in the early 1900s, we used to sing in our church school, "The Rich Man in His Castle, The Poor Man at His Gate, God Made Them, High or Lowly, and Ordered Their Estate."

That is, you were born there and you would *stay* there. And this caste system in Europe was not present here. After the Americans destroyed the American Indians—bumped them off, or put them up safely in reservations—there was no "squirearchy" here.

As a matter of fact, the attempt to introduce the feudal system down in Virginia failed because the people they brought over to be serfs went off and got land for themselves. There was always the frontier factor present here.

I'm not suggesting that people went out and picked up the Kohinoor diamond or things of that sort, although some people actually did that. But there were opportunities here. There was almost a blank tablet on which people could write.

And so, the vigorous, militant worker—he found satisfaction in going out and becoming Andrew Carnegie rather than being Eugene Debs.

That is the American Dream. You can call anybody by his first name after you've known them for a few days. You do not bow or curtsy because this guy supposedly has got blue blood or he is a lord or a lady or something of that sort.

That is the essence of the American Dream: that a man can stand upright and be a man and not have to "kowtow" to his superiors.

If a man felt irreligious, he could be irreligious—like Ingersoll. If he wanted to talk like Walt Whitman, he could do it. You were away from your cultured, manicured, ancient traditional society.

These are all circumstances which were more important than the socialist idealism that the immigrants brought, because even if they still held to it as a sort of nostalgic dream, their sons and daughters didn't.

Their sons and daughters went to college. They got better jobs and they engaged in businesses of their own or they found employment in the corporations—and things of that sort.

The Interwar Generation tends to regard New Deal Reforms and the electoral difficulties of third parties in this country as basic factors in the failure of the Party:

I would say that the socialist movement found a number of obstacles in its path as a result of the political system in this country. This was particularly a result of the fact that every four years you were fighting primarily for the election of a president rather than concentrating more on the election of various congressmen from various parts of the country.

This is what you have in Great Britain and some other countries. In Great Britain, for instance, the Prime Minister is elected by members of the Party who are members of Parliament and not by the people as a whole.

In the United States, every four years, it seems to be largely a contest between say Kennedy on the one hand, Goldwater on the other—between presidential candidates—and in many states, a few votes might mean a difference in a large number of electoral votes.

In New York, for instance, a few votes for the Republicans or the Democrats might mean that—what is it, seventy-two votes—seventy-two electoral votes might swing one way or another.

Consequently, throughout the history of political parties in the United States you find that people in every state were saying, "Now, shall I throw my vote away on a minority party, a minority candidate? If I do, I might be instrumental in electing the worst of the two candidates."

They would say, "Yes, I believe in socialism and I don't think there is much difference between the Republican and Democratic Party, but there is some difference, and I want to cast my vote in such a way as to make it possible for the more liberal or the less illiberal of the two major candidates to be elected rather than to increase the vote of the socialist candidates."

Therefore, when there has been such a concentration on presidential candidates in the two parties, it has been difficult oftentimes for a socialist candidate to get a vote that is in proportion to his real acceptance by the American people.

It was so in the case of Norman Thomas, time and time again. People said, "Well, Norman Thomas is the best candidate among the three, but if I vote for him it may be that the Republicans will get in, will obtain the electoral votes in my particular state. Therefore, I will not take a chance. I will vote for the lesser of two evils instead."

That has been to a considerable extent, I think, responsible for the many thousands of votes that the socialists have lost in presidential campaigns.

* * *

I would say that the fact of the two-party electoral system in this country was first in importance in the failure of the Party. I'd say that even if Roosevelt had *not* taken our policies, we would not have been successful in becoming a mass party.

No third party can succeed. Even the Republican Party when it started out was a second party. It was built on the collapse of the Whigs.

And this is something about the American political scene that I think a lot of historians have not really recognized. For instance, Danny Bell, in his analysis of the decline of the Socialist Party, talks about the "program was in but not of this world."

Well, it's nonsense because everything that he said about the Socialist Party in the United States applied equally to the Socialist Party in France, in the Scandinavian countries, the labor parties or social democratic parties, the British Labour Party. The same kinds of compromises had to be made there. You had the same problems of factionalism within the parties. You had the right wings and the left wings.

The difference is that in a party in those countries where, by use of the parliamentary system, there was a chance of victory, that chance of victory is a cementing force that keeps these factional disputes from becoming splits.

In a situation where there is no possibility of electoral victory in that way, then doctrinal purity becomes the *sine qua non* and you have splits.

The World War II Generation, having come of political age in a period of prosperity, tends to stress the economic wealth of the United States—its natural resources and the great pace and scope of industrial expansion:

That's a very big question. So far as I'm concerned, I'm never satisfied that I know the answer to the question of why socialism failed in America.

I think there can be no question that the basic objective answer or the basic answer lies in objective circumstances rather than in party tactics.

And that objective factor has been the phenomenal capacity of capitalism in America to satisfy human wants and needs. I think we socialists vastly underestimated the ability of capitalism to be as productive, as flexible, as successful as it has been, whether you look at the classical Marxian analysis or the non-Marxian socialists.

You pick up the old socialist material from pre-World War I days, and you will find that inevitably all of them took the position that the doom of capitalism was around the corner. Capitalism simply could not survive. It couldn't meet the needs of the people. It couldn't expand.

18 / BETTY YORBURG

It was doomed and its end was only a matter of a short number of years. Debs repeated this over and over again in his speeches.

Well, I think history has proved that they were absolutely wrong in this respect. This is not my own theory. Obviously, it's a very common one. And I think that's the most important factor to understand in the failure of socialism as a political force in the United States.

Workers were not convinced that a change in the system was necessary in order to provide them with the things that they needed. On the contrary, they were convinced that within the system they could get the things that they needed, and from the standpoint of what they thought they needed they were *right*.

After all, as a democrat, I can't impose my view of what they need on theirs. They were right and the socialists were wrong.

The workers said, when it comes to pork chops, they could get everything they wanted from their own standpoint—which I regard as a narrow and limited one—under the capitalist system, through their unions, through the old American Federation of Labor, and its business unionism.

And history proves that they were right. That doesn't mean that my socialist goal is not a valid one—that it's not a correct ideal toward which to work. But it does prove that the socialist economic analysis of those days was an incorrect one.

Now you can't build a powerful mass movement based only on putting forward the ideals of a finer, more moral, or more upright social order.

The fact is, as far as I know, never in history has a mass movement that has involved tens of thousands and millions of people been based simply on a vision of a better society without the prod of misery behind it.

And workers in America weren't miserable, although it's true there were ups and downs. Still, each subsequent up was higher than the previous up. So they always had the feeling that with a little more effort, with some more savings, with some breaks, they would be able to make out. And by and large, they did.

This is what basically accounts for the difference between the socialist movement in this country, politically, and the European socialist movements.

Incidentally, if you look at the Socialist Party in the United States before World War I and compare it with the Labour Party in Britain, you'll find they were pretty much the same.

In 1912, we had over a thousand elected public officials, a couple of members in Congress, members in state legislatures, city councils, and so on; and the British Labour Party wasn't much ahead of us.

Likewise, in terms of our influence in the trade union movement. In 1912, we got one-third of the vote of the delegates to the AFL convention, and the trade unions of Britain had not yet fully endorsed the Labour Party or socialism. That didn't come actually until the end of World War I.

But the United States benefited economically from World War I. Britain was hurt by it, although not as much as by the Second World War. We proved in World War I that American capitalism could produce guns and butter in increasing quantities. There was no conflict between the two. It could produce more and more butter, and more and more guns at the same time.

And that, in my opinion, was the basic historical factor—the objective factor.

5. It Did Not Fail

Expectations that the Socialist Party would be successful were never high in the World War II Generation, and belief in the inevitability of socialism was no longer the all-encompassing faith that it had been for members of the older generations, particularly the World War I Generation. Leon Festinger, in his study of a social movement, found that an individual with a strong belief, who has taken irrevocable actions because of it, when presented with undeniable and unequivocal evidence that his belief is wrong, will emerge not only unshaken but even more convinced of his beliefs than ever before.[17]

Over half of the leaders in the World War I Generation believe that socialism as a social movement did not fail in this country. A few leaders in the Interwar Generation also have this belief. No leader in the World War II Generation expresses this conviction. There would seem to be a relationship between the strength of the initial belief in inevitability and the need to claim success for these beliefs and goals by the different generations. One way to reduce the dissonance of an awareness of a disparity between goals sought and goals achieved is to emphasize the latter.

The failure of socialism in this country is viewed by many of the older leaders as a matter of degree and a matter of definition. No one denies the failure of the Socialist Party as a political organization, but there are varying estimates of the Party's effect on the centers of political power in this country and on the general moral climate in America. The older leaders argue that the

New Deal utilized Socialist Party platforms as a source for its measures of economic reform. But, as I remarked earlier, those who are still members of the Party are more indignant about what remains to be done:

I've been addressing myself to the question of the failure of the Socialist Party organizationally. But, you see, one of the things that damaged the Party organizationally was the fact that much of its ideology—at least the tone and temper of its ideology—finally prevailed.

The key element that attracted me into the Socialist Party—the idea of social responsibility for the welfare of the individual in a society in which such interdependence exists that no man's success is wholly of his own making, and no man's defeat is wholly his own defeat—that idea of social responsibility became the singularly attractive thing about the socialist movement. And that idea *did* prevail.

One of the premises of the socialist movement—namely that economic conditions would produce changes in attitudes—proved to be true. The depression had a remarkable effect on the American outlook.

And there is no doubt that the New Deal administration came into office with no program. All you've got to do is look at the platform of the Democratic Party in 1932.

The Democratic Party had no program, but it cast around for a program and the only program that was available was the Socialist Party platform.

I think it would be a very interesting part of your study to look at the legislation that was adopted in the 1930s and stack it up against the program of immediate demands contained in the Socialist Party platform of 1928 for example, or '32.

Now, having proved successful to this extent, if I were a young fellow coming on the scene in 1936 or in 1944, when my political judgments were being formed for the first time, and if my initial motivation was the acceptance by society of social responsibility, I would have been attracted to the New Deal.

But, I think there is more to be added. The New Deal, while it adopted these things and helped to cushion the shocks of the depression by meeting the socialist immediate demands, actually failed as an economic program. It did not solve the unemployment problem. The war did.

Now, that's a hell of an alternative solution to the solution that socialists were offering for solving the unemployment problem.

Not only the acceptance of the principle of social responsibility and the enactment of specific measures of economic reform but other, less tangible benefits are believed by some of the older leaders to be directly attributable to the efforts of the Socialist Party in this country:

The idea of human solidarity is something with which I think the socialists are still ahead of their time. I go around talking, these days, when I'm invited, about one world or none. If we don't hang together, we will hang separately.

That was as good an argument for this country in 1776 as it is in the world of 1970, and with all the economic implications that it involves.

And this is why I am, to a certain extent, an unreconstructed socialist—as far as the basic ideals go. I still think that what the socialist movement did was a wonderful educational job. It built up ideals. It did not achieve electoral success, but the ideas that it developed, the methods of tackling social problems that it developed, have become part and parcel of the system of our time.

So is that failure? I don't think so. And it is just gross miseducation and misunderstanding that prevents the ordinary people from seeing this.

Others argue that the Party served as a valuable training ground for many people who went on to become important figures in public life:

I have come to the conclusion that in some mysterious way, our movement developed talent in a way which was fantastically out of proportion to its size; or else we drew to ourselves people who were, by their personal abilities, destined to play important roles.

Let me put it this way. In my present job I have the opportunity of meeting many times with the representatives of community and national groups interested in—well it starts with civil rights, but it spreads from that to many social and community issues.

Cutting across the whole range from trade union representatives to Protestant and Catholic church representatives, we can pick out maybe half the people participating as people whom we knew personally—knew as part of that infinitesimal socialist group. People that participated.

Oh, and I want to say, cutting across from labor to religion, I left out the academic world where this is equally true.

Recently I went to a certain well-known graduate school, and I met the new dean. And I knew him, by God. He was one of the best street corner orators we had in our Socialist Party branch.

The leaders recognize a disparity between the ethical ideals of the movement and the conditions which exist in contemporary society but:

As far as the ideals that we preached, I think they had great success in America. Look what's happening. Look what's happened in fifty years.

People eventually find out what their interests are. I must say that socialist ideals didn't come the way we expected. Nothing comes the way founders expect, not even religion.

Moses couldn't get into Israel or Palestine. Things switch. Things have a terrific way of being different from expectations. Christ had the same experience.

Every preacher of high ideals finds that when an ideal becomes part of the mass, it changes in form. But if you look at it sensibly, part of your heritage is included.

So I wouldn't say that socialism was a failure. The role of liberalism comes from our people—people who were trained by us, first, second, and third generation. Somehow or other it has a way of sticking. It comes down from the father.

And yet:

The immediate demands of the Socialist Party platform consisted of what we already have today. And I don't think it would be out of place to say that we have left our contribution—the contribution of the Socialist Party toward the realization of social security and things like that.

The workers earn a decent wage and they have comforts—good housing. In my day, bathroom facilities were down in the yard. The bedrooms had no windows. And one room served as dining room, living room, and additional sleeping space.

The workers don't have this kind of world today. That was something we had to work for and fight for and bleed for. They don't have to do it today. They have it on a silver platter—without fighting, without striking, without being sent to jail, without policemen's clubs. They get the things they need and want without any struggle.

Well, we didn't. We had to fight for these things and fight hard, and, therefore . . . as I said in the beginning, it's a different world. I think we gained materially enormously . . . but maybe we lost something spiritually, too.

What has been lost spiritually, perhaps, is the belief in unlimited progress and the perfectibility of man. This belief is dead now, and this is the broader, symbolic meaning of the "God is Dead" thesis.

With the possible exception of a few idiosyncratic responses, each of the various factors mentioned by the leaders as contributing to the failure of the socialist movement in this country undoubtedly had an important effect. They can all be subsumed under the three general categories of explanation mentioned in the beginning of this chapter: the economic, the political, and the ideological. In reality, these three types of explanatory factors have operated inseparably, reinforcing and reacting upon each other; in retrospect, they cannot be assigned ultimate, intermediate, and immediate causal significance with any degree of assurance.

Regardless of how they feel about the success or failure of socialism in America, almost all of our respondents continue to define themselves as socialists. Even those who are most enthusiastic about the economic changes that have occurred in this country are not quite satisfied. What is it that they still desire, and do they feel it can be achieved?

NOTES

1. Some social critics have labeled this phenomenon "Socialism for Private Profit," or "The Rich Man's Welfare State."

2. Gabriel Kolko, *Wealth and Power in America* (New York: Praeger, 1962), p. 14.

3. Herman P. Miller, *Rich Man, Poor Man* (New York: Signet Books, 1965), pp. 35–36.

4. Harvey Goldberg, *American Radicals* (New York: Monthly Review Press, 1967).

5. Seymour M. Lipset and Reinhard Bendix, *Social Mobility in Industrial Society* (Berkeley, California: University of California Press, 1960), p. 263.

6. W. I. Thomas and Dorothy S. Thomas, *The Child in America* (New York: Alfred A. Knopf, 1928).

7. Wayne H. Morgan, ed., *American Socialism: 1900–1960* (New Jersey: Prentice-Hall, 1964).

8. Ira Kipnis, *The American Socialist Movement: 1897–1912* (New York: Columbia University Press, 1952).

9. Donald Drew Egbert, "Socialism and American Art," in Donald D. Egbert and Stow Persons, eds., *Socialism and American Life* (Princeton, New Jersey: Princeton University Press, 1952), p. 621.

10. Daniel Bell, "Marxian Socialism in American Life," Ibid., p. 217.

11. Ralph Milliband and John Saville, *The Socialist Register* (New York: Monthly Review Press, 1964).

12. Karl Marx and Frederick Engels, *Letters to Americans* (New York: International Publishers, 1953), p. 141.

13. Werner Sombart, *Why Is There No Socialism in the United States?* (Tübingen, Germany: J. C. B. Mohr [Paul Siebeck], 1906).

14. Selig Perlman, *A History of Trade Unionism in the United States* (New York: The Macmillan Co., 1922), p. 65.

15. G. D. H. Cole, *The History of Socialist Thought* (London: Macmillan and Co., 1955).

16. Paul M. Sweezey, "The Influence of Marxian Economics on American Thought and Practice," Donald D. Egbert and Stow Persons, eds., *Socialism and American Life*, p. 453.

17. Leon Festinger, Henry W. Riecken, and Stanley Schachter, *When Prophecy Fails* (New York: Harper & Row, 1964), p. 3.

Chapter 2

SOCIAL SCIENTISTS VIEW THE PROBLEM*

John H. M. Laslett and Seymour Martin Lipset

1. The 1960s: Structural Crisis, or Transitional Discontent?

Laslett: At the end of Chapter One Betty Yorburg raised the questions of what changes, in the late 1960s, Old Left socialists still wanted to see made in contemporary American society, and of whether the reforms which they favored could be secured. Because of the virtual death of the Old Left in this country this issue has, temporarily at least, been transcended by the much more problematical question of what it is that the New Left has been seeking to achieve in American society, and of whether its more utopian (but at the same time much more radical) aims have any chance of being secured. In turn, this raises issues both about the nature and purposes of the New Left, and about how much it has learned from the difficulties and weaknesses of the Old.

In the 1968–71 period many young people felt that the American New Left movement, growing as it did out of the civil rights movement of the early 1960s, out of student disaffection with what they felt to be a corrupt, self-serving bourgeois society, and out of bitter hostility toward the Vietnam war, had at last created the potential for a mass radical movement which would be able to affect powerfully, and perhaps even to reshape, the future course of American politics in a way that the Old Left in this country had never been able to do. In the past three years, however, the New

---

* Dialogue taped at Cambridge, Massachusetts, between John H. M. Laslett and Seymour Martin Lipset, and subsequently revised by both authors. Not all of the issues described in greater detail in subsequent chapters are examined here, nor is a definitive analysis claimed for those that are discussed. But two contrasting views of a possible framework in which to interpret the weakness of socialism in America are presented here which refer to many of the arguments made by the other contributors to this volume, and with which the general reader might find it helpful to begin.

Left appears to have collapsed almost as dramatically as it first came into being. It seems to me that the attempt to explain why raises a whole series of extremely interesting and important questions about the character and fortunes of the American Left, generally, many of which can be asked about the socialist and communist movements at earlier periods of American history, and some of which are relevant to the study of the social democratic movement as a whole.

Among them are the following: Did the breakup of Students for a Democratic Society in 1969, which was in many ways the core of the late-1960s student Left, reflect a penchant for fissiparousness which is an endemic disease in all American left-wing movements, or was it simply the result of inexperience and the transitional nature of student politics? What did the role of the Vietnam war as an issue in American politics tell us about the role of wars in general as catalysts for revolutionary or radical change? And what did the victimization of the Black Panthers by the police (who were extremely small and could not be thought of except by the far Right as posing any real threat to the security of the state) tell us about the existence of a Red Scare syndrome in American history as a perennial source of weakness in the American Left as a whole?

All these, and many other issues, can fruitfully be discussed. But to my mind the most interesting issue raised by the collapse—even though it may be only temporary—of the American New Left is this. Was it, potentially at least, a deep-seated movement for social change which was, even if the movement itself was ephemeral, able to expose major structural weaknesses in American society which were analogous to the structural weaknesses of older capitalist societies and which, if only by its emergence on so large a scale, undermind the "end of ideology" thesis about modern industrial societies which you, along with Daniel Bell, Raymond Aron, and others put forward in the 1950s?[1] Or was it little more than the expression of certain local, temporary, and limited discontents which sooner or later can and will be dealt with within the framework of what is often acclaimed as America's uniquely flexible and democratic industrial society?

Lipset: Much of what you say raises the issue of the relationship between explanations at the level of structural forces and trends, and the specific historical factors which enter into any given situation at a moment in time. Both Marx and Engels strongly criticized various young "Marxist" intellectuals for assuming that they could account for particular events or behavior by reference to the materialist interpretation of history. Rather, they argued, any single major happening, such as a war or a revolution, might result from a fortuitous circumstance, including the presence or absence of a particular type of political leader, the ambitions of some individual, a mistake, and the like. Marx was well aware that much of the history of Europe in his lifetime, including the prospects for revolution, was decisively affected by Napoleon III, whose position was made possible by his relationship to Napoleon I. Trotsky was later to argue effectively that without Lenin, the Bolshevik Party would have followed policies with respect to the Kerensky government and the possibility of a second Russian Revolution not very different from those of the Mensheviks. Presumably, they all agreed that "in the long run," decisive outcomes, e.g., the movement toward socialism, were consequences of endemic structural factors, but how long it took for such outcomes to occur, and the form that they took, could not be accounted for by a structural trend analysis.

However, to take up the issue which you first raised, it is certainly true that many people on the Left have attributed responsibility for stressing the "end of ideology" as a necessary outcome of contemporary society largely to Dan Bell, Raymond Aron, and myself. But actually if they will go back and read my statement in the last chapter "The End of Ideology?"[2] in *Political Man*, it is presented in part as an argument against much more extreme statements taking such a position by people who were much further to the Left, such as Barrington Moore, Herbert Marcuse, or Stuart Hughes.[3] Hughes, who was a supporter of Henry Wallace in 1948, and ran for senator as a third party peace candidate in 1962, was the first person to use the phrase "end of ideology" in an article published in 1951.[4] Essentially what most of us from Marcuse to Moore to Aron and Bell were arguing—although from different perspectives, of course—was that the consequences of affluence, of reductions in the hours of work, and of the spread of political democracy and the like had undercut many of the conditions which earlier had led workers to support different forms of class-conscious radical ideology.

In fact, putting this discussion in terms of the structural versus specific event issue, it is interesting to note that in the early 1960s Marcuse, who has often been credited with having the greatest impact on New Left students around the world, himself argued that structural factors in American society precluded the possibility of organized opposition from any group. In the preface to his book *One Dimensional Man,* published in 1964, which was subtitled "Society Without Opposition," Marcuse argued that even though American man was basically alienated man, structural factors in American capitalism such as affluence, the media, entertainment, increases in the amount of leisure, etc. made revolt impossible. At a symposium at Rutgers University in 1965, he added that blacks could not be a source of opposition, that they were essentially brainwashed, that all they wanted was to enter the bourgeois society. When asked during the question period whether, if that was the case, was there any point in fighting for civil rights for blacks, Marcuse said that he didn't think so, and that he would go "out on a limb" and agree that there was no point in blacks gaining the right to vote.[5] As late as April 1968 he even said that students everywhere and always were a conservative stratum, that the slogan of student power, therefore, was a reactionary slogan.[6]

And yet in his essay on *Liberation,* in 1969, Marcuse changed his mind, and talked about students and blacks as a source of *opposition.* Marcuse and Moore, two extremely sophisticated Marxist or revisionist-Marxist analysts, clearly took a pessimistic view of long-term American structural trends, but when the New Left came along (which they didn't anticipate), they, like others, adapted their analysis to new events.

Similarly at earlier periods in American history also characterized by the rise of mass protest movements of the Right or the Left —e.g., the Know-Nothings (1853–57), the American Protective Association (1890–95), and the Ku Klux Klan (1920–25) on the Right, or the Populists (1890–96), the Socialist Party (1904–14), the Wobblies (1905–17), etc. on the Left—contemporary commentators, as during the late 1960s, tended to explain them as a reflection of underlying structural weaknesses in the society. But each petered out.[7] In fact, more often than not, mass movements— periods of bitter crisis—appear to last only about half a decade. This is obviously not an absolute statistical judgment, but many major crises of confidence and authority in the United States have been short-lived.

This history suggests the need to be very careful about drawing long-term structural conclusions from the fact of any given crisis. Anyone concerned with American politics should try to understand this four- to five-year protest pattern. Among other factors, I would suggest, first, that the major source of the crisis event usually gets resolved as a result of adaptations by the system, policy changes, shifts in the ideology of one of the major parties, and the like. But another factor, to state a kind of tautology, is that a period of severe political conflict is simply too tense for most people to endure for a long time. It has to end fairly quickly. One way it can end, of course, is by revolution; another is by repression. But a third way, which is more common than either, is simply for people to withdraw from politics, to withdraw from the situation which makes life miserable for them personally. Most people are not political men in the sense that they can stand long-term political tension and unrest. I think we are now seeing this in the universities. In recent years, many faculty—including a great number of radical ones who initially welcomed the student movement with great enthusiasm—began to turn against the movement or to withdraw their support because their personal lives, their work and living environment were disturbed by the situation. They dropped out as they recognized that encouragement of student activism meant that politics would undercut scholarship, that the campus was going to go on being disturbed year after year. Although students were less affected in this way than faculty, as a group they also lost their enthusiasm for politics.

Laslett: Yes, but you know, the fact that it was not you or Bell but Stuart Hughes, or Marcuse, or someone else on the Left who first used the phrase "end of ideology" evades what I would regard as the self-evident fact that that mode of analysis, even if it appeared temporarily plausible in the 1950s, has clearly been overtaken by the course of events. Anyone with a sense of history should, I think, immediately recognize that ideology, even taken simply as a world view on the basis of which one charts one's conduct, is a constant in human affairs; and the fact that *one kind* of radical ideology, namely Marxism, appears now to have less appeal than it did, or that one *particular class,* namely the urban working class, does not appear for the time being to give it their wholehearted support, should not lead us to abandon the concept of ideology altogether. In fact, it is precisely because Bell discusses the so-called failure of the American Socialist Party too exclusively in terms of the general failure of Marxism that I would challenge his interpretation of the failure of American socialism as a whole (see Chapter Three, below). From this point of view all that the rise of the New Left shows us, is that radical discontent is not simply a response to material deprivation (i.e., poverty, the absence of leisure, or long hours of work, to put it in your terms), but that it results from a much more complicated set of factors, some cultural, some political, and some economic, which we all should have known in the first place.

Nor does the fact that certain left-wing intellectuals changed their minds about the role of structural factors relieve us of the responsibility for assigning relative degrees of responsibility to these, as opposed to specific event factors, in assessing the reasons for the difficulties encountered either by the Old Left or by the New. This issue is, as you say, extremely complicated. I would of course agree that good fortune, determined leadership, and a particular combination of circumstances play a crucial role in transforming a potentially revolutionary situation into an actual one. The point is, however, that while human agency clearly plays the final role in the chain of events that leads to revolution, its ability to play that role is clearly limited by the nature of the society in which it chooses to operate. In this sense the United States in 1968 clearly had not satisfied the preconditions for the growth of a major left-wing movement, still less those for a successful revolution. France, on the other hand, due to a wholly different set of "givens" (among them a metropolitan-intellectual culture, a theoretical if not a practical tradition of general strikes, and the fact that the stability of the regime rested largely on the shoulders of General de Gaulle, instead of being dissipated throughout a federal system as it was in the United States), may have been on the verge of developing a revolutionary situation, even if the revolution itself remained unconsummated.[8]

On your other point, I agree that there tends to be a periodic character about the rise and fall both of American right- and left-wing movements. But I cannot agree that this periodicity is explained simply by the desire for a return to normalcy, or by the fact that within that time period most problems are "resolved." It is not quietism as such which makes for the failure of revolutionary movements—indeed, as an explanation for social change this theory seems to me to have remarkably little explanatory power. It is the absence of a combination of events and men that can prevent these tendencies from taking hold, as, for example, Lenin and the Bolsheviks succeeded brilliantly in seeing that they did in Russia between April and October 1917.

On this issue it is also worth pointing out the crucial importance of who, and when, and in what order the discontented elements in a society are aroused. It was the unique *combination* of discontent among blacks, students, anti-war liberals, and other elements that gave the New Left its potential power. Unfortunately, it is now becoming clear that it was opposition to American involvement in Vietnam which provided the common denominator for action among these groups, rather than a sense of common grievance against the society as a whole; and although new groups are now showing militancy who have as great, if not greater, cause for grievance against the society generally (women, Chicanos, Indians) than their predecessors, none of these—save perhaps women, who are notoriously the victims of "false consciousness" —play the same strategic role in the economy that either students or blacks do. Once the Vietnam war was pushed into the background as a major issue, in other words, each of these groups has tended to lapse into the more common American pluralist pattern of pressure group activity on behalf of a limited constituency, rather than that of general action on behalf of an aggrieved class.

However—if this is indeed what you intended—it is taking an extremely simplistic, as well as disjointed and ahistorical view of American history to argue that the issues which give rise to crises are usually "resolved" within a five-year period. Few deep historical problems are ever "solved"—certainly not those of the complexity and dimensions of civil rights, the role of war as an arm of foreign policy, or the issue of equality for women. After efforts have been made, either by legislation or by other means, to alleviate them, they go underground to reappear in different forms, or with different degrees of intensity, later on. As I'm sure you are aware, there's a whole literature on how far the Populist, Progressive, and New Deal reform movements were antecedents one for the other and how far each of them, either within its own time span or sequentially, attempted to deal with the same or similar problems as those with which their predecessors had been faced.[9] But no self-respecting historian would argue that the problems created by agrarian discontent, business corruption, or fluctuations in the business cycle have in any final sense been "solved."

And yet the question of periodicity—of why it is that in situations of severe crisis America has not moved from protest movements which have national dimensions but which remain within the system to those which precipitate fundamental challenges to the society from without—remains an interesting one. It seems to me clear that there is only one case in American history, that of the Civil War, in which the society was so disrupted that profound changes did occur in the party system, in the economy, and in other areas. But one does not have to get into the old Beardian argument of how far the Civil War was or was not a bourgeois revolution in the Marxist sense in order to acknowledge that it clearly was not—and, given the nature of the American polity in the 1860s could not have been—in any sense a socialist one.[10] More relevant, because by this time you do have a mass industrial economy, is the Depression decade of the 1930s. The central point here, I think —and also, from a socialist's point of view, the most depressing one —is that despite what I think one can confidently call the most serious economic crisis in the history of modern capitalism (a crisis, that is to say, which took place on a scale equal or greater than in Europe and which was so prolonged it might well have been expected to deal an extremely serious blow to a society which had such confident expectations about the future), you really get a very minor expression of radical discontent defined as an attack on the capitalist system as such. You do get a major radicalization of the trade union movement; you do get a major shift in the ideology of one of the two major parties. But on the whole the system seems able to cope with the crisis with relative ease, without even bringing about the degree of structural change that resulted in western Europe.

Now why is this? The obvious answer (which Diamond and Johnpoll debate in Chapter Eight) is whether it is right to blame the New Deal wholly for the socialist and communist failure, or whether other factors are relevant as well. In other words, whether the central problem was defects in the Old Left's strategy, or whether—and this would be an argument in favor of a structural interpretation—the system was flexible enough to deal with a crisis even of this magnitude.[11]

Lipset: I do not think we should get sidetracked with a discussion of the meaning of the "end of ideology" debate. There are two collections of articles reflecting various interpretations of this issue, and our readers can look at these, if they so choose.[12] I would note, however, that in some measure the discussion is terminological. I, for one, never argued that ideology was over. In *Political Man*, I specifically interpreted the relative quiescence or moderation of critical views among intellectuals in the 1950s as a consequence of a specific historical event, Stalinism and the Cold War, not as part of the structural processes, which I thought reduced the potential for revolutionary politics among the workers.[13] And although our formulations about the intellectuals differed somewhat I should note also that C. Wright Mills, in his writings on and to the New Left in 1959–60, concluded unequivocally that structural changes had outmoded the revolutionary potential of the industrial working class in advanced industrial societies.[14]

With respect to another of your comments that the past American crises did not end because they were "solved," I would, of course, completely agree. But as I see it, problems are never "solved." There is no solution to the punitive consequences of stratification, of inequality. The "old crap," to use Marx's phrase, always returns, since those who are privileged and powerful always seek to institutionalize and enhance their advantages. The changes made to react to or "buy off" protest are always too little, sometimes very little. But the historical fact seems to be that by yielding in some degree, protest may be reduced, only to reappear again when trends or specific events create the conditions for its revival. And, up to now, the American system has been remarkably successful in adjusting to protest. With the major exception of the slavery issue, the two-party system, particularly, has repeatedly adapted to reinclude groups which have moved out of it. I would like to go into a discussion of the role of the American party system in a comparative context, since I feel it is extremely important.

2. Ideology and the Role of the Electoral System

Lipset: As I have indicated in various of my writings, the American party system, which differs greatly from those in most of Europe, has permitted the country to endure severe crises such as that of the Great Depression without experiencing major political changes, i.e., new institutionalized radical parties of the Right or

Left. In comparing the American political system with that of Europe it is important to recognize that party in the United States means a very different thing from what it implies in much of Europe. Parties in the United States, unlike the Christian Democrats, the Social Democrats, or the Communist parties in Europe, are loose coalitions of diverse groups or factions, which in most other countries of the world would be separate parties. On the European continent, these groups, called parties, form coalitions *after* the election, while still retaining their separate identity, as in Italy, where Left Socialists, Social Democrats, and Christian Democrats have cooperated in the same government. In the United States such disparate groups form coalitions *before* the election, by working through the framework of one or the other of the two major existing (alliance) parties. The U. S. Constitution also *requires* a focus on the presidency, on electing one man as the leader of the government, to whom all members of the Cabinet are personally responsible. It does not permit a coalition multi-party government responsible to parliament.[15] The electoral system presses the factions to form a coalition behind a presidential nominee under either the Republican or the Democratic label. A third candidacy almost always seems hopeless. And repeatedly most potential third-party voters wind up making a choice between one of the two major party candidates, as the lesser evil.

This does not, of course, prevent the occasional emergence of massive third parties, of which the George Wallace 1968 movement was the most recent example. But significant third-party movements only arise in this country in periods when there is an issue with substantial appeal to which the two major parties, for one reason or another, do not respond. Thus, I think the Wallace third-party appeal is to be understood by the fact that in the climate of American opinion in the 1960s neither major party felt it could afford to make the kind of racist appeal that some whites, mainly Southerners, were seeking. The strong racist sentiment had to go outside the two-party system in 1968. Wallace's success resulted in concessions being made to his issues, as, say, Vice-President Agnew did in the 1970 congressional elections. But since most Democrats and Republicans would be outraged by explicit racism, the concessions had to be moderated, thus leaving a basis for the Wallace movement. In 1972, as Wallace demonstrated his considerable support in the Democratic primaries, politicians from

Nixon to McGovern increasingly moved over to his position on busing and accepted him personally as a legitimate actor within the political system. This illustrates a process which occurred with respect to assorted third-party efforts since the Anti-Masonic Party. When an issue appears during a period of unrest which gives rise to a third party, some major group within one or both of the two major parties in effect takes over the issue as its own. This happened to the Left in 1968. It is possible that there was more left-wing discontent in 1968 than right-wing, but the Right rather than the Left went the independent party route. The reason the Left did not do so was the candidacies of Senators Eugene McCarthy and Robert Kennedy; that is, the Left anti-war groups were coopted by these candidacies, much as again occurred more successfully with McGovern in 1972.

Laslett: If I may interrupt you on this point, this is exactly the argument that Weinstein makes in his Old Left-New Left essay (in Chapter Seventeen), because one of the things he argues there is that in 1968 it was a disaster for the Left that Eugene McCarthy ran for the presidency, and that Bobby Kennedy then entered the race and stole the Left's thunder. I think this brings us back to the traditional explanation that a major reason for the weakness of the American Left has been the flexibility of the two-party system, with which I have no quarrel and which, of course, reinforces the structural position which I argued earlier.

Lipset: But, you know, it is more than simply the flexibility of the electoral system; this speaks to the old issue of what tactics the socialists should pursue that has been debated ever since there has been a socialist movement in this country. One group has tended to argue for an independent radical or revolutionary socialist party, that this is the only way for socialists to really present what they believe and to build a movement that will accomplish structural change; whereas others in effect have argued, sometimes with sophistication and sometimes not, that since American parties are not parties in the European sense, the best way for American radicals to operate is as an organized faction within one of the two parties. There have been successful electoral examples of this strategy, of which the most noteworthy was the Nonpartisan League in North Dakota. The NPL was started by socialists before World War I who felt on the basis of campaign experience that they couldn't get very much support for the Socialist Party but that as a socialist group within the Republican Party, the dominant party in that area, they could win primaries and elections—and they did. In North Dakota, where the Nonpartisan League held office for many years, it legislated government-owned banks, government-owned flour mills, support for cooperatives, assorted welfare measures, etc., much the same program on a state level that a Socialist Party government would have implemented.

In my book *Agrarian Socialism* I concluded that in North Dakota and Saskatchewan, which border each other and are structurally identical—wheat economies, similar populations, and the like—NPL and CCF (socialist) governments passed the same kind of social democratic legislation.[16] They were each backed by an extremely strong rural cooperative movement. But in Canada, given a parliamentary system of government, the agrarian radicals used the third-party route, whereas in the United States, the same kind of people and social forces worked as an electoral faction within the Republican Party. The sheer electoral mechanics suggest different tactics for a socialist movement; to simply then say, as Weinstein does, that Eugene McCarthy or Robert Kennedy were disasters for the Left in 1968 is in one sense true. But they weren't accidents, and the behavior of the American Left was not simply a mistake. It just didn't happen that someone named Gene McCarthy came along and stole the Left's thunder. The *system* was behaving typically. If it hadn't been McCarthy or Kennedy it would have been someone else. And in 1972 his name was George McGovern. The system encourages such behavior; it is not just idiosyncratic behavior.[17]

Laslett: I agree that the nature of the electoral system makes an important difference to the choices which socialists are forced to make; and one could document this argument further by referring to Upton Sinclair's superior performance as Democratic candidate for governor of California in 1934, even though he spoke to many of the same issues as a Democrat which he had upheld as a socialist only a few months earlier.[18] Or to the contemporary role of the Liberal (earlier American Labor) Party in New York, which contains many Jewish voters who formerly voted socialist but who found the Socialist Party increasingly inadequate as a vehicle for expressing their views.

The problem of the relative weakness of socialism in the United States cannot be explained simply by reference to differences between parliamentary and non-parliamentary electoral systems, however. Otherwise, one might expect Canada to have developed a socialist movement of European proportions, which clearly it has not although its movement is somewhat larger than that of the United States. In my view, the question of whether Canadian or American socialists should follow an independent line or seek to exert pressure within one or other of the existing political parties— "reward your friends, punish your enemies," as Samuel Gompers used to call it—reflects also one aspect of the Parliamentary dilemma which afflicted virtually all social democratic movements at the end of the nineteenth century, irrespective of electoral systems. This was whether the aims of the movement were best advanced by giving support to liberal elements within existing regimes, ultimately by joining progressive governments as a means of securing recognition, for example, as Alexandre Millerand did in the 1899 Waldeck-Rousseau cabinet in France; or whether to avoid contamination by remaining aloof from the affairs of an ongoing capitalist society, as the German Social Democrats (although with an increasing air of unreality) tried to do in the years before 1914.[19]

Fundamentally, this is an ideological as well as an electoral issue. In its heyday before the First World War (as David Shannon notes in his *Socialist Party of America* but which Bell and Hartz do not[20]) the American Socialist Party was a genuine American political party, a coalition party, that is to say, which included farmers, trade unionists, intellectuals, and different types of ethnic groups, many of them native-born Americans, which for a time maintained quite a high level of militancy while at the same time speaking to a genuine constituency of its own. It did not, in other words, simply arise in response to grievances to which the major parties were unwilling to respond. And yet by the 1930s, or even by 1920 or 1924, this Socialist Party—although when asked, it would trot out its Marxist credentials—had, like most of the social democratic parties of Western Europe, compromised its revolutionary purpose to such an extent as to have become little more than a party of liberal reform. It remained, in other words, unable to build up the support of a mass coalition while at the same time remaining free of the kind of ideological emasculation which has now turned virtually all Western socialist parties into reformist defenders of bourgeois democracy.

In addition, if you argue that the crucial difference between

America and Europe (or between America and Canada) as regards the potential for a socialist movement is the electoral system, this still leaves open the question of whether there were not common economic or other types of social grievances present in both New and Old World societies which one type of electoral system can assuage or dissipate, but which the other one cannot. Indeed, if by your remark that the situation of North Dakotan and Saskatchewan farmers was "structurally identical" you meant that they had similar economic grievances—arising, presumably, essentially out of the price of wheat—the implication would clearly be that the electoral system did indeed constitute the essential difference between the two situations, resting, however, upon a common set of economic grievances which in both societies were severe.

3. Ethnicity, Trade Unionism, and the Idea of a Labor Party

Lipset: Going back now to the issue of the Socialist Party of America as a coalition of disparate elements—and I agree that at its height in the pre-1914 period this is how the party should be viewed —one of the questions we have to confront, which we have not yet done, is not so much why the party ultimately failed in its objectives, but why, for a time at least, it was so successful. What was it about the nature of American society at that time that impelled people to withhold their support from one of the two old parties, and to go to the Socialist Party instead?

One of the reasons, of course, is the obvious fact that American employers were resisting unionization at this time, and this drew a lot of union leaders and pro-unionists to the socialist cause. At the AF of L conventions during this period the socialists received about a third of the convention vote; and while this does not mean that all the members of the unions whose delegates voted for socialist resolutions were socialists themselves, it does show that there were big socialist minorities in several of the most important unions, such as the Printers, the Carpenters, the Butchers, and the United Mine Workers.[21]

Another important factor was the special role of ethnic groups, some of which brought socialism over with them from Europe, such as the Germans in Milwaukee, or the Jews in New York. A number of these ethnic groups were also fighting the struggle for admittance to the system. They were being discriminated against. The Irish still could see signs saying "No Irish Need Apply." Overt discrimination against various recent immigrant groups pressed them to be sympathetic to Left causes as out groups.

But the fact remains the Socialist Party never received more than six per cent of the vote in a presidential contest (1912), although it was often much stronger in local elections. The question must be raised as to whether it would have been more successful if it had turned itself into a labor party, i.e., a Lib-Lab rather than a specifically socialist type of party, on the model of the Labour Party—or, rather, at first at least, the Independent Labour Party (1893)— in Great Britain. In some of the international literature on the socialist movement around the turn of the century, the American Socialist Party was considered relatively stronger than the ILP; there was even a sense that socialism generally was stronger in America circa 1900 and 1903–4 than it was in England. Eugene Debs was considered as important a figure on the American scene as, say, Keir Hardie was in England. However, it was the British Labour Party which finally emerged as a major political party, of course, not the Socialist Party of America. After 1905 there was a lot of debate within the American labor movement as to whether it should go the Labour Party route as well. There were many people in the AF of L, as there were in British unions, who were for a labor party but not a socialist labor party, even though many of the socialists themselves did not go along with that view. Now whether that would have made any difference or not is questionable, but we have an interesting comparison that in much of the Continent and in Britain mass social democratic labor parties—the British Labour Party, the Swedish Social Democrats, and suchlike —eventually emerged, whereas this did not happen in the United States. This is what people mean when they say "why no socialism in the United States?" I.e., not why don't we have a revolutionary Marxist party like the Bolsheviks in Russia, but why don't we have the equivalent of the Swedish Social Democratic Party or the British Labour Party, instead of the American Democratic Party?

It can be argued that the coalition flexibility that we have discussed in the American system prevented a new labor party since the Democratic Party always has been ready to move as far toward the Left as it has to go to keep the votes. It is prepared to become a social democratic party, as Edward Flynn, the New York Democratic chief, once noted. And since the 1930s it has become committed to the welfare state and the trade unions, whereas conversely, the European social democratic parties have moved in the direction of becoming Democratic-type parties in order to secure and retain the growing number of middle-class non-radical votes. The ability of the Swedish Socialists or of the British Labourites to form a majority government is to some degree a function of their being coalition parties, coalitions which include many whom in America we would consider liberals, even relatively moderate ones. There are clearly a number of Labourites in the House of Commons, for example, who would be much more at home in the Democratic Party than they would be in a class-conscious socialist party.[22]

Many of the New Left people in America would of course argue that the Swedish Social Democrats or the British Labourites are not really socialists (in terms of some conception of socialism meaning a fundamental reorganization of society, which among other things involves doing away totally with the private basis of ownership). But by their criteria it can be argued that there is *no* truly socialist movement of any significance in any advanced industrial country. That is to say, if it is true that the policies of the American Democratic Party are similar to those of the Swedish, British, or German Labour or Social Democratic parties, and one says that these parties are not socialist, then there is no mass socialist party in any advanced industrial country, unless the communists are counted as "real" socialists and the Latin countries of Europe are considered as fully industrialized. But leaving these issues aside, the question becomes not "why no socialism in the United States, and yet socialism in Europe?," but "why has the form of labor representation taken an explicitly class form in northern Europe, and a 'populist' multi-class one in the United States?"

Once the question is put in that way, then its links to the Hartzian issue (see Chapter Nine) become very clear: that in Europe generally there is more aristocracy, more of a feudal tradition, and a society organized more explicitly on class or status lines, quite differently from North America's. Viewed this way the differences between the North American and the northern European systems really get minimized; and the question "why socialism in Europe, and why no socialism in America?" *as such* is not really the big issue that much discussion once made it.

Laslett: The question you have just raised—of how socialist the contemporary social democratic parties in Europe really are—is an extremely interesting one; and I of course agree with you that many radicals (including most of those on the New Left) quite rightly no longer see them as socialist, but as liberal bourgeois reform parties which have been so seduced by the rewards of office, or so traumatized by the 1919 socialist-communist split, that they hardly can be called socialist in any revolutionary sense at all. But again, in making this argument there is a danger in reading back the alternatives faced by the Left today to a time period where the issues were quite different. It may well be true that the Democratic Party today more nearly resembles the welfare-oriented social democratic parties of northern Europe than it does the individualistic, largely laissez-faire Democratic Party of Thomas Jefferson's or Andrew Jackson's day; just as it may well be true that the northern European socialist parties (even including, after 1959, the German Social Democratic Party) more nearly resemble the American Democratic Party of today than they do the classical Marxist parties of pre-1914.

But this development is due to a whole set of factors—the rise of the welfare state, socialist identification with the defense of liberalism against communism, the impact of the New Deal on the Democratic Party, and Keynes's discovery that it is possible to modify major swings in the capitalist business cycle without changing the basis of ownership—that were simply not present in the period before 1914.

And when one considers the issue of a labor versus a socialist party, the real question which the American Socialist Party had to face in the decade before the First World War was not whether its members would have been more comfortable if they had joined the Democratic Party (which most of them ultimately did anyway), but whether the risks it would run in alienating moderate opinion by moving to the Left were not greater than those it would run in alienating IWW members or De Leonite revolutionaries by moving to the Right. In practice, of course, it chose the latter course; and although it is possible to point to its successes in the municipal field, where it espoused "gas and water socialism" and greater democracy rather than revolution, as evidence for the view that it was most successful when it was most Progressivist, it can equally well be claimed (and with increasing frequency has been, by radical historians) that this policy left much of its potential constituency on the Left disillusioned and dissatisfied—among western farmers and miners, exploited immigrants, or blacks working in northern industry, and that by doing so it failed to establish itself as a viable alternative to existing movements for reform.[23]

In addition, I am very skeptical as to whether there was ever really a willingness in either the AF of L or the Socialist Party itself to support the idea of a labor party in America before the First World War. Certainly, before 1914 even the more liberal elements within the AF of L hierarchy were just as strongly opposed to the idea of a labor party as they were to supporting a socialist party as such. There was hope, you know, among the moderate trade union wing of the Socialist Party when neither President Theodore Roosevelt nor Congress did anything to respond to the AF of L's 1906 Bill of Grievances, that the more radical trade unionists would turn toward the idea of a labor party on the British model as the only way out.[24] But, as I think Philip Foner points out (in Chapter Six of this book), this was an illusory hope. The policy of "reward your friends, punish your enemies" was too deeply ingrained, and the opposition of the Executive Council of the AF of L to independent party politics was too influential for a labor party to emerge at that time.

As for the Socialist Party—and this is perhaps the more interesting question—it too was opposed to converting itself into a labor party in this period, partly because it was afraid of betraying its supposedly revolutionary ideology by entering a more moderate Lib-Lab coalition, and partly because there was no such coalition, short of the Progressive Party itself, for it to enter. After the First World War, in 1919, when the Socialist Party had split over the issue of communism and the Progressives were disillusioned with the collapse of Wilsonian liberalism, the situation was quite different. Indeed, in 1924 the socialists did reluctantly enter the Conference for Progressive Political Action, which nominated Senator Robert La Follette for the presidency. However, there is much dispute among historians about whether this did not do the party more harm than good, for the failure of the La Follette Progressives to reorient the course of American politics severely disillusioned many, who believed that the Socialist Party had permanently compromised its sense of separate identity by collaborating with a much larger group over which it could not exert any direct control.[25]

On the question of ethnicity, again one has to tread extremely carefully. It is certainly true that there were some ethnic groups, such as the Jews, who brought their socialism with them from Europe but whose interest in it long outlasted their acceptance into the property-owning middle class. Nevertheless there were also others, such as most of the Germans, who after a relatively short period of time seemed willing to abandon their support for revolutionary politics in the New World, despite the fact almost as large a proportion of them had come over here with such beliefs. One thinks, for example, of the former Forty-Eighter Carl Schurz serving in Lincoln's Cabinet during the Civil War. In addition, there are some among still other ethnic groups, such as the Irish (who Marc Karson asserts in Chapter Five, I think erroneously, to have been almost one hundred per cent opposed to socialism because of their Catholic faith) who adopted socialism *after* they arrived on these shores.

And then, of course, there is the opposite hypothesis developed by Oscar Handlin and others some years ago, concerning Slavic, Italian, and other southern and eastern European peasant immigrants to this country, that their peasant mentality predisposed them favorably toward patriarchical, machine-type politics, and against abstract reform or revolutionary ideas. This in turn leads into the whole argument about ethnic fragmentation as a *deterrent* to socialist advance. Even on this point, however, there are now revisionist views. A recent book by Victor R. Greene, entitled *The Slavic Community on Strike,* which is a study of the behavior of immigrant Slavs during certain major strikes in the anthracite area of Pennsylvania in the 1890s and early 1900s, shows that contrary to received opinion these immigrants loyally supported their union during strikes, and hence were not necessarily more likely to be predisposed against demonstrations of working-class solidarity than other ethnic groups.[26]

4. *The Role of Wars in Socialist Revolutions*

Lipset: I would like to turn now to the general topic of the New Left. I would argue that the most important single thing that made a mass, alienated protest movement possible in the 1960s was the Vietnam war. Throughout modern history, wars which are viewed as failures from a military or political standpoint have brought about a crisis of authority, a failure of legitimacy, or even a revolutionary situation. From that perspective, it was the opposition movement to American involvement in Vietnam which made possible the rise of an important New Left. It should be noted, though, in addition—something which I think many American radicals and others often forget—that wars have almost always given rise to major anti-war movements in America. Every war in American history, except for World War II, has seen a large-scale anti-war movement. There was one against the War of 1812. In the Mexican War there were actually battalions of American deserters fighting with the Mexican Army against the United States. During the Civil War there was massive opposition to the draft, much as over Vietnam. The Spanish-American War faced great antagonism. And, of course, the socialists along with many other groups continued to oppose American participation in World War I long after we entered it. The Socialist Party received upward of twenty per cent of the vote in city elections in 1917.[27]

The growth of opposition to the Vietnam war must be seen in the context of a felt obligation to obey one's conscience rather than one's country—a doctrine inherent in the teachings of many of the Protestant sects, which in turn represent the predominant American religious tradition. And given a prolonged war against a small country in which the United States clearly failed militarily regardless of what perspectives on the war people started out with, the escalation of overt anti-war sentiment is not surprising. Being opposed to an ongoing war is different from being opposed to any other policy of a government. It can't be handled in the same category. Inherently, if you oppose a war during wartime you are engaged in activities which come close to being rebellious. In the eyes of the supporters of the war you are treacherous. No other American war lasted as long as this one, so that anti-war feelings could turn into a general mood of resentment or opposition to the society. The spread of New Left radicalism reflected this process. Beyond that, however, as Sam Brown, the Harvard divinity student who started the "Dump Johnson Campaign" and who led the 1969 Moratorium movement, pointed out, the special militant confrontationist character of the contemporary anti-war movement was very much affected by the fact that it emerged at the tail end of the civil rights movement of the early 1960s, which had socialized many young Americans into regarding civil disobedience as an appropriate tactic. The tactics of the civil rights struggle were then carried over into the fight against the war, making the anti-Vietnam war movement a much more militant one than those in previous wars.[28]

So that generally, to reiterate what I said earlier, the growth of the kind of massive alienation from American society that occurred in the late 1960s would not have occurred simply as a result of the basic structural characteristics of American capitalism, in the absence of the Vietnam war. This is not to say that there wouldn't have been a revival of a much larger radical movement than existed in the 1940s and 1950s. Here I would suggest that de-Stalinization played a crucial role in opening the door to a revival of radical criticism and action, a matter which I hope to develop at greater length later on. It became possible to redirect energies toward internal reform. But the massive character of the New Left movement was, I think, very much a function of a specific and unique historical event that did not have to happen.

Laslett: I would, of course, agree, as I indicated earlier, that opposition to the Vietnam war acted as a catalyst for certain elements in the New Left's ideology. Its hostility toward the neo-colonialist attributes of the Vietnam adventure, for example, undoubtedly enabled it to strengthen its critique of American treatment of blacks, Mexican-Americans, and other elements back home. More generally, anti-war sentiment performed an invaluable role as a kind of cement, or glue, which helped to keep together disparate elements of a movement which might not otherwise have secured even the limited degree of coherence that it did achieve. The evidence for this is that in 1971 and 1972 when President Nixon ended the draft, withdrew the bulk of American forces from Vietnam, and negotiated a cease-fire with the North Vietnamese the New Left began to disintegrate at an even more rapid pace than it had before.

But I would also argue that to suggest that Vietnam was the sole (or even the most important, aside from de-Stalinization) reason for the resurgence of radicalism in the 1960s is to ignore serious and long-standing grievances on the part of numerous elements in American society which in their origins had nothing whatsoever to do with the Vietnam venture, and which can only be properly explained by some kind of structural analysis of the reasons for the profound disaffection which many minority groups and other

Americans feel toward the system. The most obvious manifestation of this, of course, is the civil rights movement and the black revolution, which had already assumed significant proportions before President Johnson escalated the Vietnam conflict in 1964, and which stemmed essentially from the deeply racist character of the majority of the American white community, not from the Vietnam conflict. Much the same thing can be said about the student movement, which began with the free speech movement in Berkeley in 1964 (again predating the Vietnam escalation), and which has been concerned mainly to protest the excessively bureaucratic and impersonal nature of the large-scale educational institutions which have grown up since the Second World War. Similarly also with the women's liberation movement, which has deep historical roots in male domination of family, employment, and other social and economic relationships. And the same goes also for the new wave of militancy and unofficial protest in the labor movement, which results from inflation, automation, and undemocratic procedures in the trade union movement, and which in its fundamental note has nothing to do with opposition to the Vietnam war. Indeed, as you know, many union members, although discontented with other developments in American society, gave stronger support to the American position in Vietnam than most other elements in the community.

Placing too much emphasis upon Vietnam as the major cause of the rise of the New Left also makes it extremely difficult to explain the concurrent revival of radicalism in countries where the Vietnam war was *not* an issue, or not to anything like the same extent, such as France or Germany. None of this means, in my opinion, that the American New Left ever came near to building a revolutionary movement which had a chance of precipitating a far-reaching reorganization of society. It does mean, however, that it should be viewed as a genuine social movement expressing fundamental social grievances which are still capable of precipitating a major social crisis.

Commenting now on your point about the relationship between wars and radical social movements, I would argue that although foreign adventurism or imperialism can serve to exacerbate domestic social tensions, or to provide the occasion for revolutionary movements, they cannot in themselves form the basis of a permanent or long-lived revolutionary movement. This is in contradistinction to civil wars, or wars in which a nation's territorial integrity is threatened, which of course can and do have that effect. Nearly all the major revolutions in European history have been associated with that kind of phenomenon. But the interesting thing from this point of view, again, is that the Civil War is the only war in American history which had that internal characteristic. It was the only major domestic crisis which really did produce a basic reorientation in the party system and in the economy without, of course, as I said earlier, becoming a full-blown bourgeois revolution capable of pushing American society more than a few steps down the road toward the creation of a full-scale revolutionary proletariat.

Indeed, upon reflection I would go beyond this and add that moral concern about injustices in society (and it was essentially the immorality of the Vietnam war which shocked most Americans), although it can certainly provide one of the most important ingredients for a socialist movement—as, for example, with the nonconformist religious tradition in the British Labour Party, or the French Socialist Party under Jean Jaurès—it cannot, *in itself,* provide a sufficient basis for any general movement of fundamental social change. In a book which he published in 1968, for example, called *Intellectual Origins of American Radicalism,* Staughton Lynd argued that you can extrapolate from Tom Paine, Thoreau, Garrison, and Debs, as well as from some of the more radical pamphleteers at the time of the American Revolution a specifically American tradition of radical reform which provides at least some of the rationale of the contemporary New Left. I agree with him in part, but with opposite implications for our topic in this debate.

The trouble with Lynd's analysis is, as Eugene Genovese pointed out in a review of his book, that although this type of moral protest tradition may indeed serve as the source for a purely reformist Progressivist type of movement such as one had in America before the First World War, it will not serve as the basis for a reformist socialist, still less a Marxist, political party.[29] This is partly because it was precisely this kind of moral appeal which characterized early twentieth-century liberal parties—to whose siren calls the American radical movement will again succumb if it stands upon that leg alone—and partly because such an appeal does not provide any vigorous or coherent alternative mode of economic or political analysis on the basis of which a new society can be built.

Lastly, on the issue of war, I would like to suggest that although both in Europe and America during the course of a war you get the build-up of nationalism and of a patriotic fervor which is intolerant of dissent when opposition to the war is associated with movements of radical protest in America, you get, in addition, the disproportionate invocation of what I call the "Red Scare syndrome," which seeks not merely to protect the nation's security, but also to stamp out all signs of opposition and even to throw doubt upon the loyalty of those who suggest alternative ways of prosecuting it. You can go forward in American history from the Alien and Sedition Acts of 1799 and 1800 right up to the Vietnam war, and find—in differing forms and with differing content but almost always with extremely damaging consequences for the Left— a nativist, anti-intellectual, anti-immigrant hysteria which begins by pointing an accusing finger at all those who presumed to dissent from the policies of their government and ends up by shouting "off with their heads!"[30]

The association between nativist hysteria and anti-radical sentiments in American history is of course well known. What I think is less well known but much more interesting is that although suppression of dissent in wartime is a universal phenomenon, in America even though you may sometimes get a significant Left movement rising up in opposition to the war, compared to Europe you nearly always get a much larger and much more disproportionately massive response from the far Right.

5. Repression as a Cause of Failure

Laslett: Discussion of the Red Scare syndrome leads us to another factor which helps to account for the weakness of American socialism, and that is the role of repression.

A lot of people like to believe, I think, that America is a tolerant, open society in which suppression of unpopular causes is not usual. Given the long history of repressive acts undertaken against radicals and Marxists, however, going back at least to the Haymarket Red Scare of 1886, and forward to the Hatch Act and other repressive legislation enacted against the communists in the 1940s and the 1950s—and expressed most classically, perhaps, in the 1919 Wobbly trials, when the police broke into the IWW national headquarters, stole their documents, and arrested large numbers of IWW members simply because of their membership in that organization—I am surprised that so many commentators have dismissed this issue so cavalierly. The most interesting contemporary analogue to the IWW experience, of course—although the context is in other respects quite different—is the way the police have treated the Black Panthers, using possession of guns or some other relatively minor excuse to break into their homes and offices, and to precipitate gun battles, if not actually to commit murder, in the name of an alleged conspiracy threat which has consistently served as a justification for the persecution of radicals in the United States.

I think there are two ways in which this intolerance is expressed. One is in the formal manifestation of public opinion expressed in law (the Espionage Act of 1917, for example, or the statewide criminal syndicalist acts of the post-World War I period) which in terms of the actual size of the American communist or other kinds of revolutionary movement unquestionably represents overreaction of a very marked kind. More important, however, and at the same time more insidious and widespread, is the informal expression of public opinion, expressed on the one hand in the social unrespectability of Marxism, which has deep roots in American political culture, and on the other hand in a readiness to resort to intimidation or violence (sometimes sanctioned by law, but more often not) to suppress popular movements. This is a factor which, it seems to me, may well inhibit the development of radical sentiments *before* they reach the level of public manifestation, and which stems in part from the absence of a sense of restraint which is often to be found in more aristocratic societies. Whatever the reason, I think there is a strong case to be made for the view that there has been a systematic attempt either to destroy or to so inhibit the functioning of the Black Panthers as a movement (like the old IWW, the Communist Party, and numerous other radical segments) so that to the extent they were really the core of the radical element within the black Left, this has had an extraordinarily inhibiting effect on the radical wing of the New Left movement as a whole.[31]

Lipset: Well, the issue of repression is, of course, an important one because a lot of people are convinced, I believe in exaggerated form, of the extent of repression in the current period. But first I'd like to say that I agree with you about the 1919–20 period. In fact, as discussed in my book (with Earl Raab) on the American right wing, *The Politics of Unreason,* I would say the most re-

pressive right-wing period in America, culturally, politically, and
governmentally, was the early 1920s, i.e., the post-World War I
period up to 1924 or 1925, when there was mass support for the
Ku Klux Klan and a wide variety of other repressive movements.
During that time the federal government deported thousands of
people for radical activity. There were also mass arrests, the beating up and even killing of Wobblies, and the passage of repressive
legislation.

In fact, compared to the 1920s, even the McCarthy period of the
1950s was nowhere as bad. I remember, in the early 1950s, Bern-
hard Stern, then editor of *Science and Society* and a communist,
came running into my office one day at Columbia to ask me to take
some of his classes because he had to go down and testify before
McCarthy. When I began to commiserate with him, he looked up
and said, "Oh, don't worry, this is really nothing. If you'd been
around in the 1920s, you would know what was really bad. Mc-
Carthy is doing little compared to the government then. But this
will pass. The 1920s went away, this will go too." And the Vietnam war situation, i.e., 1965–72, was much less repressive than
the McCarthy period. There's no question that there have been
various acts of repression in the past few years, but as compared
to other wartime periods, the rights allowed to foes of the war and
radicals generally were amazing. Overt radical anti-war activists, as
journalists, were allowed to go to Vietnam and were taken around
by the Army, sometimes in Army helicopters. They were even allowed to go to and from Hanoi, which was, after all, the capital of
an enemy state. I doubt that there has ever been a war anywhere
whose opponents had as much civil liberties.

In fact, I would even go so far as to say that in the 1950s the
Communist Party contributed to the strength of McCarthyism by
stressing we were in a near-fascist period, that any liberal, or opponent of American foreign policy, was in danger of losing his job,
or of being tossed in jail. Now this was just untrue, though some
were victimized. What happened, however, is that hundreds of
thousands of people began to believe that it could happen to
them.

The issue as to the actual situation with respect to repression is
not simply an academic question to be evaluated at some future
date by historians. Those who exaggerate the pressure, as the communists did in the early 1950s, when in order to get liberals to iden-

tify with their tactic of "taking the Fifth Amendment" they stated that progressives who had never been associated with the party were being indiscriminately harassed by investigative committees, help to intimidate many who might have otherwise spoken up more vigorously. Overemphasizing for propagandistic reasons the threats to civil liberties at a given moment in time can harm the radical movement much more than the Establishment. Many will be afraid to participate if they think they will run a risk of penal sanctions. In his book on the French student movement, Daniel Cohn-Bendit, the leader of the 1968 French revolt, argues just the opposite in his effort to encourage students to be political activists. That is, he says that because of age-old norms giving free license to university students, they run little risk if they engage in radical activities. Therefore, they have little excuse, in his judgment, for not participating.[32]

Much more important than repression, or even the fear of repression, in undermining the American Left, however, has been its propensity for internecine warfare. As you know, the various militant black groups fight each other bitterly, and as in the case of the Panthers, split and then denounce the other side for betrayal. In your own university, UCLA, two Panthers were killed on campus by other militant blacks. Stokely Carmichael was attacked by the Panthers for giving up the struggle, and more recently Eldridge Cleaver and Huey Newton have each used vitriolic language against the other. SDS, perhaps the most successful radical student movement in American history, which briefly stood out as the leading organization in the large amorphous movement, divided and subdivided, so that today it is a small, uninfluential organization, largely the student section of the ex-Maoist Progressive Labor Party. Other groups have subdivided further. The SDS caucus which called itself the National Labor Committee is now two bitterly hostile organizations. The majority of the International Socialists, founded by the ex-Trotskyist Hal Draper, split with their leader. In addition to the main Trotskyist group, the Socialist Workers Party and the Young Socialist Alliance, there are now a number of dissident groupings, Spartacus, Youth Against War and Fascism, and others.

When groups divide and start throwing mud at each other, they usually help create a third segment, often the largest one, derivative from the once unified tendency, the camp of apathy or withdrawal. The less committed, when faced with charges and countercharges, or with debates about esoteric points of revolutionary doctrine, drop out in despair and disgust.

I doubt that the decline of the radical New Left since 1969 can be explained as a consequence of repression or the lack of a mass base within which to operate. In relating its weakness to the propensity for internal conflict, it is interesting to note that Morris Janowitz a quarter of a century ago accounted for the failure of the American extreme Right to capitalize on widespread potential support in the 1930s on similar grounds. Unlike the situation in most European countries, in which one major fascist party emerged on the Right, Janowitz noted the various American fascist and extreme rightist groups spent much of their time fighting each other.[33] This pattern still continues among the much smaller rightwing sects today. I would not attempt to explain this, except perhaps to suggest that such behavior may be another phenomenon derivative from the same Protestant sectarian moralism which, I earlier suggested, has repeatedly encouraged conscientious opposition to wars and social movements. Moralistic Americans, even when secular or irreligious, have the need to purify themselves, not to compromise their version of holy or political truth. But then, I suppose, as Engels noted long ago in *On Religion,* there are strong resemblances between radical politics and Christian sectarian behavior in many environments.

Laslett: I agree with you in part about the exaggeration of repression, but I think it is misleading to suggest that fear of repression (although unquestionably recognizable as a separate issue) has been a more important inhibiting factor in the growth of the Left than repression itself. Intelligent people, after all, do not willfully commit suicide by deliberately provoking their would-be oppressors—unless, that is, you take a pathological view of dissenting behavior.[34] This is a view which I do not share. Indeed, I would argue that if evidence of pathological behavior is needed, it is to be found in the irrational fear of conspiracy displayed by right-wing leaders, much more frequently than among people on the Left. I would reiterate—and one could cite a very large number of cases in American history to establish the point, of which the Mooney case in 1916, Sacco and Vanzetti in the 1920s, the Communist witch hunt trials of the 1950s, or the Angela Davis case in 1970–71 are only a few of the more recent examples—that in America repression of radical movements has not taken the form of deliberate murder or destruction as often as it has in a number of European countries. Instead, it has taken the form of mobilizing public opinion in such a way as to make it impossible for a radical group to act, or of undermining its sources of financial support by means of court cases so as to make continuation of its activities virtually impossible.

In fact, if you accept my argument, not that repression has been greater here than in Europe (which is of course untrue) but that in relation to the actual or presumed threat the Right has been invoked *proportionately* much more massively here than there, I think this helps to account for the fact that at crucial periods in the history of the Left—1919 being the most notable example—repression has been relatively successful in this country, whereas in most European countries it has generally only either halted or stilled a socialist movement temporarily, or has even actively advanced it by driving it underground in such a manner as to increase its revolutionary zeal. The most notable examples of the latter phenomenon perhaps are the pre-Bolshevik movements in Russia and the failure of Bismarck's anti-socialist legislation in Germany in the 1880s.

Now, this disparity between relatively successful movements of repression in the United States compared to relatively unsuccessful movements of suppression in Russia or in Germany (at least in the pre-1914 period: the 1930s are a different story) has to be explained. I would suggest that part of the explanation is to be found in the fact that where you have a highly stratified society in which crucial elements of either the peasantry or the proletariat are already predisposed against constituted authority and at a time of crisis are willing to follow class leaders or otherwise to act in a class way, then repression simply drives the movement underground, from where it will reemerge, strengthened, at a suitable moment. On the other hand, if you have a society in which either the agrarian element or the urban working class lacks any coherent sense of class loyalty and is predisposed instead toward acculturation or assimilation, as in the United States, then repression will have the opposite effect. Instead of nourishing rebellion, in other words, it will induce its followers to draw back from any fundamental challenge to the society, and to accept their place instead in what may continue to be an unjust social system. This, in my opinion, is what happened to the American Left in 1919.

I am aware, of course, in making this argument, both of the complexity of the problem and of the wide variety of different contexts in which repression has been called upon to act. But it seems to me that Edward Shils's book, *The Torment of Secrecy,* which was an attempt to explain the phenomenon of McCarthyism in the 1950s, makes a great deal of sense if looked at in this way. Shils argues that elements in each immigrant group as it has come to this country have, in order to establish their credentials in the society, at times of crisis (and 1917–19 would be a conspicuous example of this) deliberately accentuated their Americanism, and have sometimes turned against subsequently arriving or less obviously assimilated ethnic groups as a means of demonstrating their loyalty to the system.[35] Although I disagree with much of the rest of the argument put forward in Shils's book (that McCarthyism can best be explained as some sort of "Populism gone to the right"), if you look at the way in which public opinion almost universally condemned the Socialist Party in 1919 as pro-German, even though its argument against the war was predicated upon orthodox Marxist antagonism toward capitalist wars in general, and only a relatively small minority of its members were actually German-born at the time, this part of Shils's argument makes good sense.

Lipset: The notion of one hundred per cent Americanism, and the fact that pressure for it is intensified by the problem of assimilation of new ethnic groups, is, I think, a valid one. But there is another aspect to it which you might say reinforces this factor, and that is the impact of the American tradition of Protestant moralism to which I referred. Given the fact that a majority of Americans stem from religious roots linked to the Protestant sects, the need has developed to see the social rebel as a Satan, or as an evildoer who must be cast out from society's midst. And what happens, I think, is that when groups such as the Catholic Church, foreigners, communists, or radicals generally are defined by public opinion (or by an important segment of it) as evil, people do not just regard them as mistaken people (which a traditional conservative might be expected to do) but as morally wicked and dangerous elements which must be eliminated from the system. When some cast out the socialist as un-American, they cast out the agent of Satan. But given this perspective what is truly astonishing is not the amount of repression in the recent period, which was after all also a state of war, in which almost fifty thousand Americans were killed, but the opposite—the lack of popular support for repression of anti-war or radical activity.

A comparative view also challenges the argument that the decline of New Left and black nationalist militancy during the Nixon years reflects the increased use of repressive measures by the American government. The rise of the New Left in the 1960s occurred throughout most of Europe, often following the tactical lead of the American movement. Confrontationist tactics based on student movements occurred in many countries. And these were followed in many of them by the growth of conservative political tendencies among the electorate, and internecine conflict within the New Left. In Europe, Germany apart, and in Japan and Canada, the campus-based radical movements have declined greatly. They all still exist, stronger than comparable tendencies of the 1950s, but generally with much less support and élan than in the late 1960s.[86] They exhibit the major weaknesses of youth and student-based movements throughout history—their lack of a time perspective, their sense of urgency, their desire to resolve the struggle now, to press for the revolution even though a revolutionary situation does not exist. And discouragement at their failures to build a major mass movement in a few years leads to the internal splits we discussed earlier, and to the increased reliance by a small minority of Blanquist terrorist tactics, which in the absence of major delegitimating crises only serve to further weaken the appeal of the movement.

6. Social Mobility and the Role of Myth

Laslett: There is another issue raised by our discussion of repression which you touched on earlier, which I would now like to confront directly. That is the general question of the role of myth versus reality in American history, or of what people have believed American society to have been like in the past, compared to what it actually was. By belief here I do not mean deference to tradition, Constitution, and flag, although these too play an important part in American culture. Instead I mean the consequences for political behavior among a largely immigrant nineteenth-century work force of the optimistic psychology bred by the Horatio Alger myth, or the notion that in leaving Europe one also left behind the restraints imposed by poverty, monarchy, and a rigid social hierarchy, and entered instead a society characterized by equal opportunity.[87]

Of course, few immigrants can be expected to have taken these beliefs literally. But it seems to me that assessing the relative impact of the actual circumstances in which a working-class group might find itself and comparing it with some idealized notion of what it had been led to hope for, either for itself or (more likely) for its children—and, of course, the nature of these hopes when they can be identified at all, varied enormously according to generation, ethnic affiliation, occupation, and a whole host of other factors —creates uniquely difficult problems for the American social historian, as well as presenting equal temptations to both Marxist (or pessimistic) and liberal (or optimistic) historians alike in the way they describe social reality. Who is to say, for example, what the relative significance has been of presumptions about the availability of "free land" in the West, compared to the frontier's *actual* role as a nineteenth-century safety valve? How do we interpret widespread belief in open access to entrepreneurial advancement, when contrasted with high bankruptcy rates among small business starts?

One of the most interesting aspects of this question, which is touched on by Stephan Thernstrom's and your discussion of social mobility (Chapter Twelve), is the implication for class formation, and hence for the socialist movement, of the belief that there were unique opportunities for upward occupational mobility among the mass of working-class immigrants entering the United States in the nineteenth century, compared to suggestions in the literature that in reality mobility rates in America were not uniquely high, but were fairly similar to those in most rapidly industrializing nations.

Now we still know very little about what actual social mobility rates were for any society in the nineteenth century, or still less for earlier centuries; and in my judgment there is considerable danger in implying, as I believe both you and Reinhard Bendix do in your collaborative book *Social Mobility in Industrial Society*, that one can extrapolate post-World War II comparative social mobility tables back into the crucial decades between 1875 and 1914 when the modern socialist movement came into being. But leaving aside the question of the reality of the situation (as also the problem, which for me is an important one, of whether a knowledge of mobility rates in itself is likely to tell us very much about the determinants of socialist ideology), the question still remains of *belief* in unique mobility opportunities in America as a deterrent to class politics, and of whether what people believed to be the case (as opposed to what it really was) is researchable. On this score we have so far gone little further than the rather simple proposition presented in your and Bendix's study that even if mobility rates differed little between Europe and America in the nineteenth century, American belief in high rates in itself may have had important implications for the development of the social system.[38] I would argue, however, that before we can draw any conclusions of this kind we must take into account the social composition, ethnic character, and a whole host of other characteristics of the particular element in the labor force we are dealing with. Were the most discontented elements in the society immigrants whose expectations were of a certain kind—skilled English artisans, for example, who were disturbed by the even greater skill dilution which they found on this side of the Atlantic compared to that in England, as I suggested (although on the basis so far of limited evidence) in certain chapters of my *Labor and the Left?*[39] Did they come from a particular ethnic group, ex-coolies from southern China, or Irish peasants, for example, whose high piece rates may have outweighed the dangers and isolation of building America's railroads? Or were they second-generation ethnics who had been in this country for some time and had "horizons" or expectations different from those of both their parents and their children? Although these are extremely difficult matters for the historian to research, I am convinced that without some knowledge of them a simple analysis of social, occupational geographical mobility rates is not likely to tell us very much.

Lipset: Yes, the belief or myth problem is an important one and, of course, as you say, there are two historical questions here, one of which can be answered (hopefully), which is how much mobility there was, or how much inequality of income existed over a given period of time? But it will be very difficult to get answers to how people felt about it, particularly in the past.

In this respect the general emphasis in American ideology going back to the Revolutionary period, which deepened as time moved on, that the dominant "political religion" (as Lincoln called it) was equality, and the belief that there was more equality here than there was in Europe, had an extremely important influence. It strikes me that very many Americans were convinced of this; and your point, that many immigrants even though they were at the bottom of the system were objectively better off than they had been in Europe, and hence felt that the situation had improved for them, or that that of their children would improve still more, is, I think, well taken. But, to go back to the myth issue, it is still further complicated, for example, by the attitude of the blacks toward their situation in America today. As Coretta King and Bayard Rustin have noted, if you look at the statistical data on blacks, there is no question that the objective situation of blacks today is much better than that of preceding generations. For example, during the decade of the 1960s, as a whole, there has been an enormous increase in the proportion of blacks entering university. (It is now well over forty per cent, almost the same as for whites.) Seventy per cent of them now graduate from high school. Occupational statistics indicate about a third more are in white-collar and professional jobs than in the 1950s, and so forth. All of these gains are reflected in changes in income, in that the percentage gain (though not the absolute dollar amount) among blacks was more than that among whites. So that one can point to the 1960s, on the one hand, as a period of improvement in the situation of blacks. But if you look at the opinion polls, their subjective evaluation of American society and politics is worse, because—and here the blacks have reacted to the same thing that everybody else has—the society seems to be in more trouble, and there is more criticism of the system; this is taken on a personal level by them to mean that their situation has declined, instead of improving.

Laslett: Two quick points in response to that. One is that if you look at the figures for the 1960s (which now show signs of reversing themselves), it does indeed seem clear that in relative terms the position of blacks was improving, in terms of education and training, and in other areas. But one must remember that tremendous amounts of money, publicity, and federal support were required to improve the relative position of blacks even to the limited extent it was improved during that decade, wholly apart from the difficulty, which Betty Yorburg points to in her Chapter One discussion of the differing conclusions reached by Gabriel Kolko and Herman Miller on this issue, of how you measure real versus money income in relation to this problem.[40]

And secondly, one must take into account Tocqueville's famous remark that revolutions are made, not by a *Lumpenproletariat,* but by those with rising expectations, a view which complicates the situation still further for American historians, partly because of the highly diverse character of the American labor force, and partly because of the myth versus reality problem which we have just discussed. It seems to me, as indicated before, that if one is to make a proper approach to this question one has to take into account the generation from which the workingman comes—meaning by this both European and Oriental immigrants, and blacks from the rural South. One has to look at his color; one has to look at his attitudes toward the country or area from which he originated; and one has to look at his reference points or "horizons," in relation both to previous employment experience and to current peer groups. All of this represents an extremely difficult kind of research to carry out. But if we are to make progress with this issue it is an effort which must be made.

7. Intellectuals as a New Working Class?

Lipset: Turning back now in more detail to the sources for support for the New Left, it seems clear to me at least that all countries in which it has developed—or at least in all industrialized countries—much of the movement has expressed primarily the resentments of certain upper segments in society, the intelligentsia and upper-middle-class groups involved in what Richard Flacks has called the welfare and intellectual occupations.[41] To these must be added, of course, less privileged groups who felt themselves denied equal rights, such as minority ethnic groups like the blacks in this country, the Catholics in Ulster, or the French Canadians, and who supported protest movements with their own cultural or political demands.

In effect, the "movement" has consisted of on one hand, the intelligentsia and the students, and on the other hand, the excluded minorities. But throughout the 1960s the workers and farmers remained loyal on the whole to their traditional politics, again with the usual special exceptions to any broad generalization of this kind. Moreover, these groups also remained more or less committed to the ongoing social system. Of course, the politics to which they stayed loyal varied a great deal. It was Democratic here, Labour in England, Social Democratic in Germany and Scandinavia, and Communist in France and Italy.

All the agitation stemming primarily from the upper middle class, supported by segments of the excluded ethnic groups, had relatively little impact on the stratum which Herbert Marcuse, Barrington Moore, C. Wright Mills, and the "end of ideology" writers of the 1950s predicted would remain loyal (or brainwashed as the case may be), i.e., the manual workers. From this perspective it is possible to argue that nothing that happened in the late 1960s

discredited the thesis that conditions no longer existed to produce revolutionary class-conscious politics among the vast masses
of urban workers; or, to put the conclusion somewhat differently,
the history of the New Left as a movement does not validate the
Marxist expectation that an industrial society is likely to be effectively challenged by its workers.

Of course, this did not mean that the writers of the 1950s assumed the society would not be under renewed attack from other
strata. C. Wright Mills in his celebrated "Letter to the New Left"
in 1960 suggested explicitly that intellectuals can be expected to
be an endemic source of revolutionary change even in countries
where the traditional working class is more or less satisfied. In
that letter Mills argued that belief in the revolutionary potential
of the working class was a Victorian hangover, that the working
class which had been revolutionary in the early days of capitalism
no longer was, and that the new revolutionary classes were the
intellectuals and the students. He saw the new radical movement
as based on these groups.[42] Edward Shils also had anticipated a
revived radical potential among students in his 1955 *Encounter*
article on "The End of Ideology."

To develop this idea somewhat more fully, it should be recognized that contemporary society is based on an economy which is
increasingly dependent upon research and development, on engineers, on scientists and scholars, and is much less dependent upon
manual labor. And various writers such as Thorstein Veblen,
Joseph Schumpeter, Jean Paul Sartre, C. P. Snow, and others have
suggested that intellectuals by virtue of their emphasis on creativity, on originality, inherently tend to reject what is traditional,
and thus have a higher propensity to be alienated, to be critical
of the Establishment, and to be at war with the dominant values
of the system than any other stratum of the society.[43] And increasingly in recent decades, intellectuals have, by virtue of both
the greater need for their skills and their increased numbers, also
become much more powerful politically. The tremendous growth
of students (nine million in the United States) who are directly influenced by the values of the intellectual community is the most
visible relevant development. But even more important may be
the changed attitudes of other elite groups in the intelligentsia:
the reporters, the TV people, theologians, and civil servants, who
look to intellectuals for leadership, for whom the critical intellectuals have become a significant reference group. Even more numer-

ous within the intelligentsia is a more amorphous group of people with various kinds of intellectual pretensions—the people in the welfare industries, those who read widely or who are exposed to the intellectual organs. Viewed in this context the structural trends of advanced industrial societies tend to make intellectuals more important rather than less. And I would suggest whenever post-industrial society finds itself in a crisis—whenever it manifestly fails to live up to the egalitarian values which are accepted as the legitimating ones in most societies today, in the Soviet Union and in China as well as in the U.S.A., France, or Britain—these allied groupings of intellectuals, intelligentsia, and students will turn against the system to a greater or lesser degree.

And I would argue that the basic contradiction of post-industrial society—in the Marxist-Hegelian sense of contradiction—may well turn out to be, not the growth of a manual working class that is potentially alienated, which Marx saw as the central contradiction of the nineteenth-century capitalist system, but the increase of an inherently alienated new leading stratum, namely the intellectuals. So that when one evaluates the protest wave of the late 1960s in order to come to some conclusion about it (and the evidence is far from all in) it will be necessary to answer various questions, first, as to whether and to what extent the traditional Marxist protesting strata were involved, and if relatively few were, why not; secondly, whether Mills and others are correct in suggesting that there can be a revolutionary movement in an advanced industrial society which is based largely on some upper levels of the new middle classes, namely on the intellectuals and the students. If Mills and others who have written on the inherent protest potential of these strata are right, then this would suggest that the New Left phenomenon which we have just experienced may be only the first of a series of comparable phenomena occurring whenever post-industrial society faces a crisis.

Laslett: Well, first let me say that in making this argument you have come near to conceding two of the major points I have been insisting on throughout our conversation. First, that insofar as the New Left expressed the grievances of groups—and one should add blacks, Chicanos, women, and other elements to students and intellectuals—who had major grievances which long preceded the Vietnam war, and who were essentially caught up in the transition from one kind of society to another (industrial to post-industrial, although the precise meaning of that transition has to be examined[44]), it reflected structural and not surface or ephemeral discontents. And secondly, that insofar as the "end of ideology" argument was predicated on the decline of radical ideology as a whole in industrial societies, the resurgence of a recognizable revolutionary ideology among elements of the New Left—even though that ideology is anarcho-syndicalist rather than Marxist, and is often hard to pin down—you have acknowledged the view that the original "end of ideology" argument either anticipated far too much, or that it was simply false.

I would also want to be much more careful than you evidently are about implying that the traditional Marxist working class was almost wholly uninvolved in the New Left. Catholic shipwrights in Ulster, for example, blacks in DRUM in the Detroit UAW, or even Chicanos on the California fruit ranches are often urban workers in disguise. And even though in America many of these groups appeared to be indifferent or even hostile to the student movement—or to be preoccupied with racial advancement rather than with class strife—the role of the Renault or the Sud-Aviation workers in the near-general strike in France in 1968, the 1972 British coal miners' strike, or numerous other labor groups who have recently been involved with white-collar elements in official or in unofficial strikes should make us extremely wary of such broad generalizations such as these.

Nevertheless, I would agree that middle-class students and intellectuals formed the central core for the New Left movement. And the most interesting question, as you suggest, is whether from now on we are going to have a post-industrial society in America in which this new class will play the inherently alienated role which the urban working class failed to play in any massive way in nineteenth- and early twentieth-century capitalism. If it does, then a number of interesting consequences might follow for the American Left. The most tantalizing of these, to pursue your own line of thought for a moment, is that since America is the first society which can in any proper sense be called post-industrial— in which, that is to say, such problems of post-industrial capitalism as pollution, fragmentation of interpersonal relations, or alienation resulting from conspicuous consumption have appeared on any scale—this new alienated class might conceivably become sufficiently influential that the new American Left might be able to reverse its traditional weakness compared to the European Left, and play a much more influential role in the general movement of social democracy than it has hitherto done.

There are solid reasons for arguing, unfortunately, not only that these predictions are premature, but that at present they may amount to little more than hogwash. Not only do they leave out of account the immensely resourceful, assimilative, or socializing function of American political parties which we looked at earlier, they also make the unwarranted assumption that the new intelligentsia will be more willing to carry out its assigned revolutionary role than the nineteenth-century working class. In its own literature the New Left has made numerous attempts to see the student movement, not in terms of generational conflict, but as a class-conscious movement whose ultimate interest was in remodeling the system as a whole. In an interesting 1968 pamphlet, for example, John and Margaret Rowntree argued that since 1950 American capitalism had become increasingly dependent on the education and defense ("war and knowledge") industries, which absorbed surplus manpower at lower than market wages, forcing wives to work at poorly paying jobs also, in order to support their husbands throughout college.[45]

Now, I do not believe that this is a wholly chimerical analysis. Indeed, the moderate recession which occurred between 1969 and 1972, and which again seems pending, this time in a more serious form, in 1973 lends it at least a temporary credibility. But it also ignores a number of very obvious facts. First, there is the simple point that as students grow up and grow older their politics tend to change, so that any strategy which looks to students (and they would form much the largest element in the new class) as a base of operations relies upon an unstable (although certainly self-perpetuating) class which, as Lenin saw long ago, is unlikely to be capable of the stern self-discipline necessary for carrying out fundamental social change.[46] Secondly, as Kim Moody pointed out in a more recent New Left pamphlet, although in a sense the rise in the number of clerical, professional, and scientific employees in recent years implies a trend toward white-collar proletarianization inasmuch as some of these groups now sell their labor power, instead of being self-employed, attempts at unionization of these white-collar groups, still less at converting them to radical politics, have so far met with only limited success. Although there are some recent hopeful signs, professional and technical workers have so far largely resisted attempts to unionize them into the IUE, the

UAW, or the AFTE, and among teachers—much the largest group among the new intelligentsia—the problem of a status rather than a class orientation remains a powerful stumbling block.[47]

Thirdly, we must remember that although some of the groups in this new white-collar intelligentsia—clerks, perhaps, and some teachers—are now less well paid than skilled blue-collar workers, most are paid quite a lot more. And even if it is relative deprivation rather than poverty as such which counts in the forming of revolutionary movements, in my view it is extremely unlikely in the near or even the middle-range future that a sufficiently large number of these groups will become sufficiently alienated that a viable analogy can be drawn between them and the early Victorian working class.

Most important of all, in liberal-democratic societies (or even in autocratic societies, as Michael Confino recently suggested in an article showing that most intellectuals in Czarist Russia remained servants of the state until well into the 1840s), it is simplistic to argue that intellectuals have an inherent tendency to be at war with the system. Even in imperial Germany, as Adolph Sturmthal points out in his critique of Perlman's *A Theory of the Labor Movement* (see Chapter Fifteen), many of the intellectuals in the German Social Democratic Party tended to take the conservative or moderate position in the debate over revisionism in the 1890s. In England, one has the continuing problem of the Tory intellectual, as, indeed, of the Tory worker.[48] And in the United States, one of the initial sources of support for the contemporary New Left has been a deep division between the present generation of student intellectuals and their former teachers over what the proper role of the university, of social science research, and of the scientific community should be.

In addition, as you know, there has been great bitterness in the present generation against the intellectuals of the 1930s, 1940s, and 1950s generation—including yourself—not only because of their unwillingness to ally themselves with the New Left and its protests over what the student generation considers to be deep injustices in the society, but also because of their hostile and even contemptuous attitude toward it.[49] Disappointment that intellectuals who were associated with the social democratic Left before the Second World War have not been willing to align themselves with the New Left, in other words, has been one of the things which has separated it from the Old Left; and it has also been a source of weakness to the New Left itself in the sense that it has failed to secure leadership from an older generation to whom it thought it could turn for support. The same thing has been true to a greater or lesser degree in both eastern and western Europe. So I think that generalizations about the inherently alienated behavior of intellectuals as a group in the future will have to be treated just as carefully as generalizations about the supposedly alienated behavior of the working class in the past.

Lipset: On this question, first I think there is no question about the existence of this generation gap or cleavage that you speak of, but I would attribute the split primarily to the impact of the Second World War, and then of the Cold War. The period from approximately 1940 to, I would say, the late 1950s was one in which intellectuals as a group were much less critical of the larger social system than they had been in earlier periods throughout modern history, or than they have been since this period came to an end. The reason for this, I believe, is that throughout this period the so-called Western democracies viewed themselves as being at war with aggressive totalitarian systems which were threatening the societies from an autocratic, totalitarian point of view, and which, if successful, would seemingly have made them much worse. The defensive posture on the part of the social democratic Left began in the 1930s, first against fascism, when the communists themselves played a major role in fostering the Popular Front days, arguing strenuously that intellectuals and others shouldn't be critical of America or other Western societies because that played into the hands of the Nazis. And then, after 1945, this Popular Front ideology was projected against the Stalinist threat.

When the New Left appeared, particularly in the United States, a cleavage occurred between these two generations over means and ends in politics which again has to be understood in terms of the different historical experience of the two generations. Generation conflict does not only result, as some young radicals think, because older people are more conservative (since they have lived longer, or have more of the goods of the society, or have more to lose), but also because older generations react differently from younger since they have had a greater variety of experiences to which, rightly or wrongly, they react. In this case, it is important to recognize that many in the older Left have continued to respond to their experience with Stalinism. They saw how the Bolsheviks had paved the way for Stalinism by using tactics which were incompatible with the objectives of a democratic egalitarian socialism. They witnessed a movement dedicated to justice, equality, and democracy turn into a monstrous totalitarian system which was explicitly racist, killed millions of innocent people, and justified the use of any means in the attainment of the ends of power. They argued that the overthrowal of capitalism would result in a *worse* system if the revolution also eliminated the institutional protections for democracy, and for conflict with those who hold state power. The experiences of fascism and Stalinism indicated that these protections are even more necessary in a society without private ownership or control of the economy than in a system in which economy and state are somewhat separate.

Then along came the New Left without any direct experience with Stalinism—not that it did not regard Stalinism as bad, but it did not have the same visceral attitude toward it. Intent on destroying the capitalist system, it developed anew the belief that the ends justify the means, that anything which would weaken a bad society was justified. New Leftists rejected and failed to understand the position that many older Leftists took, that the norms and institutions which had emerged under capitalism to protect due process, minority rights, free speech, opposition movements, independent unions, etc. are good, are in fact not bourgeois but proto-socialist. The ideologies of anti-fascism and anti-Stalinism emphasized protection of these norms, and pointed to the difficulties of reestablishing them, once destroyed.

This generational variation in perspective has been especially great in affecting the variations among the different estates of the university, the professoriate, and the students. The university is one of the best institutions of capitalism, or as Marcuse once put it, the least bad one. Many older intellectuals have pointed to its role of the principal center of political criticism, to the protection which the concept of academic freedom for all points of view gives to radical critics. They therefore believe that it should be defended rather than destroyed. When New Left students attacked the university as a fundamentally bad institution, as a bulwark of the society, many older intellectuals, some of whom rightly or wrongly still thought of themselves as radicals, felt that the student militants were often challenging the conditions which made the university possible, that many students had been seduced into taking the wrong position on the classic problem of means versus ends.

The basis for this argument, however, rested in the concern of the older Left over Stalinism and Nazism, which was never properly communicated to the younger generation. As a result, many elements in the New Left simply looked at the Cold War period as a period in which their professors, those liberal Left intellectuals who went along with it, were either stupid, hypocrites, or had sold out.

Laslett: What you say provides a perfectly good justification for the attitude of the old social democratic Left toward the need to defend liberal democracy in the 1940s and the late 1950s, as well as expressing a legitimate criticism of some of the more mindless attacks of extreme Left students upon the universities, which did indeed run into the problem of ends versus means, although not, in my judgment, to anything like the degree which you suggest. The important point, however, is that de-Stalinization began in 1956, at least in Russia, almost twenty years ago; and although in my view communism is now hardly less brutal and dehumanizing than it was then (intellectually, for much of the new generation, it is simply irrelevant), it seems to me that many of the New Left critics of your generation are correct when they argue that the old social democratic Left became so preoccupied with anti-communism, and then so dazzled by its acceptance as part of the Establishment, from the New Deal Brains Trust to the inner cabinet of the Kennedy years, that it is no longer either willing or able to commit itself to courses which would involve far-reaching social change. It may well be argued (indeed I would probably argue it myself, however appalling the prospect!) that the Democratic Party is the nearest thing we are likely to get to a radical party in this country, at least in the foreseeable future. But this does not in itself justify the bitterly hostile reaction of many Old Leftists toward a New Left movement which was just as anti-communist as the old social democratic Left, but which was in addition, however naïvely, concerned to bring about genuine social change.

However, all of this also begs the more fundamental question of whether the conflict between Old and New Left generations of intellectuals, both in Europe and America, is a problem of these particular generations, or of whether, as I would continue to argue, it reflects the more general problem of the intellectual as a conservative which Michael Confino analyzed in his discussion of intellectuals under Peter the Great.[50]

8. *Value Analysis and the Dangers of Ahistoricism*

Laslett: Earlier I suggested the need for a structural or societal rather than a "transitional discontent" explanation for the rise of both the New and Old Left movements in this country; and then appeared to qualify it by insisting on the need to take unique and unrepeated historical circumstances into account. You, on the other hand, appeared to begin taking a "specific event" position which, as I see it, you have since qualified—over the alienated response of a new intelligentsia to post-industrial society, for example—by adopting a more structural stance.

I would like to make my position on this point clear. Let me say, first, that I do not believe that any basic difficulty for the structuralist position is posed by urging the need to take specific or unrepeated historical circumstances into account. As I said earlier, in assessing the radical potential of any given situation it would clearly be absurd to suppose that long-term structural factors (the extent of poverty, the character of the labor force, a tradition of revolt) can *in themselves* make a revolution. Human agency alone can do that. What I would argue, however, is that explanations for the weakness of American socialism which limit themselves to a "transitional discontent" type of analysis, or which concentrate solely either upon the internal ideology and tactics of the American socialist movement or upon what I think you would call the general character of the American value system, are inherently flawed because they do not attempt to take the particular nature of American social reality into account. For example, Daniel Bell's argument in his *Marxian Socialism in the United States* that the socialist movement failed in America because it was "in, but not of the world" (i.e., that it could not cope as a revolutionary movement with being part of the world which it was trying to change) seems to me to be unsatisfactory because it is put forward as an argument for explaining the difficulties which the socialist movement experienced in Europe as well as in this country, and because it makes no attempt to point out those features of the American experience which rendered this ideological problem particularly difficult to overcome.[51]

Or take Hartz's essentially dialectical argument about the absence of a feudal heritage as a reason for the absence of socialism in America—an argument which he has also applied, with considerable effect, to other countries in his *Founding of New Societies*.[52] Traditionally, this argument has rightly been accepted as a very important part of the explanation for the relative mildness of the American Revolution; and it can sometimes throw illuminating light on other areas of American history also. But in Hartz's hands it becomes essentially an argument about political theory and social mythology, not about social reality; and without discounting the importance of myths, Hartz's analysis lacks any rigorous attempt to examine in detail how they applied to any specific historical situation. Taken seriously as a piece of social analysis, for example, Hartz's theory would lead one to suppose that Americans have always lived in a relatively unchanging form of liberal capitalism, which derived most of its values and much of its economic apparatus from the Enlightenment. In practice, of course, it has changed a very great deal, and (which is crucially important for our purposes) in ways which have had an enormous impact—both positively and negatively—upon the fortunes of American socialism: from rural to urban, from frontier to non-frontier, from agrarian to industrial, and from slave to free.

In addition, Hartz's theory leaves one with the misleading impression that socialism arises primarily in response to the presence or absence of aristocratic or feudal remnants in a society, which in part, of course, it does do. But to argue this in isolation implies that the character and type of capitalist economy under which one lives—and which, in nineteenth-century America, was undoubtedly as exploitative and unbridled as it was anywhere—is of only secondary importance, when it is primary. Friedrich Engels, for example, when he came to look at American society in the 1880s, rejoiced that the potential for a revolutionary movement was greater here than it was in Europe precisely because America had skipped the feudal stage and was characterized by a purer form of capitalism than in Europe. Engels' view in the end turned out to be just as misleading as Hartz's. But it nevertheless drew precisely the opposite conclusion from the same kind of evidence.[53]

So that it seems to me that the danger of confining oneself to this broad, value-oriented, absence-of-feudalism type of analysis is that it involves one in an essentially ahistorical, deterministic, and oversimplistic kind of history which is just as misleading as the more traditional, narrative, or "internal to the movement" type of analysis. What one needs, of course, is an approach which seeks to combine the virtues of both.

Lipset: Yes, there is no question that value analysis can do that, and I suppose in a number of cases it has actually done so. But I would argue that Hartz, myself, or the other people whom you mentioned—including Marx, in discussing this problem—have all in a certain sense echoed Tocqueville's classic statement about the American equalitarian value system: that America was born modern, whereas other societies have become so.[54] That is, that America idealized the future as already here, as part of its basic value system before the future existed. As many people, such as David Riesman, have pointed out, Tocqueville's description of America in the 1830s is in a sense a more accurate description of the United States in the 1960s than it was of the 1830s.[55] The ideal of a universalistic, egalitarian, achievement-oriented society was then seen by various forces in America as the legitimate goal of the society; whereas in Europe, whose long history of alliances between royalty, Church, and aristocracy legitimated an ascriptive, hereditary type of status system, the Left, including the bourgeois Left, had to spend much of its energy challenging this older aristocratic system. The European socialist movement arose in opposition to the values of aristocracy, to a fixed status system. I certainly would not argue—in fact, just the opposite—that institutional relationships have remained the same, but rather that in America the anti-aristocratic Enlightenment value system informed and legitimated a kind of Left tradition from the start. Consequently, it was difficult to build a new Left movement in the European tradition, as many American socialists tried to do.

You know I've often made the point, which a number of radicals have attacked me for, that the values of America are Left values. This is Samson's argument (in Chapter Ten), i.e., that, property relations apart, American values are akin to the values of socialism. What Samson is saying is that in America socialists have to convince Americans that they do not have such values in practice when—to get back to the role of myth—they think (erroneously) that they already have them. Europeans, on the other hand, were not told by their elites that they should have (and do have) a society characterized by equality of opportunity. (Samson, of course, did not believe that the underlying American economic reality was very different from that of Europe. He believed the European socialist parties grew in strength as opponents to the rigidly defined class system, not simply to capitalism.)

I have also argued that it is much easier to build a socialist movement in a society that has ascriptive conservative traditions than in one that has egalitarian liberal traditions, not only because there is an opponent in the former that is easy to recognize, but also because there is a similarity between conservative, aristocratic values, which accept the legitimacy of the state, on the one hand, and the statist values of socialism, on the other. In America, as I suggest in my essay in this book (Chapter Thirteen), the equalitarian tradition is linked to the idea of individualism and anti-statism, not to the idea of collectivism or planning; and therefore, the attempt to impose statism on the egalitarian liberal tradition has seemed to many Americans to be introducing a kind of reactionary European principle.

All of this is not to deny the constant presence of structural changes, but instead to argue that these changes have varying political consequences depending on national differences in value systems. In saying this I would not of course argue that value systems remain intact, that what we think we believe today is what people thought they believed in 1790 or in 1810. Obviously the content, the words, the symbolic meaning have changed. But although the value gap between the United States and Europe has narrowed greatly in the twentieth century, there is still a great difference between the respective value systems.

Laslett: Yes, but that argument not only acknowledges that despite the presence of these presumed Left values in American society there are important gaps between myth and reality in the society which in themselves may act as motives for radical action—and which may, paradoxically, have an even greater effect here than in the communist countries because of the nature of American expectations about human nature. It also leaves out of account a recognition of the need to determine what the nature of social reality in any given society actually *is;* and my point was, not that value systems are not important and influential, but that taken by themselves they tell us very little about the determinants of social change. It is the causal relationship between values, or myths, on the one hand, and actual life situations, on the other, which is interesting and important, not the myths themselves, as I argued in the case of the kind of needed research into the position of immigrants in American society. And without examining that relationship in a concrete historical context we are in danger of retreating simply into unsubstantiated assertions about what people may have believed, as I suggested about your and Bendix's argument concerning the role of belief in relation to rapid upward mobility rates, instead of engaging in hard-nosed empirical research. For example, for me it is simply an ingenious but intellectually dishonest sleight of hand for Samson to argue that in some sense the United States has already achieved some of the goals of socialism simply by describing elements of the American belief system.

Moreover, the extremely heuristic terms in which both you (in Chapter Thirteen), Clinton Rossiter (in Chapter Eleven), Louis Hartz (in Chapter Nine), and other social theorists of this type have chosen to describe American society tend to predispose the unsuspecting reader into accepting an often largely unsubstantiated version of social reality simply by the way in which the ideology of an extremely limited number of elements in the community is described. Despite his brilliant insights not even Tocqueville, as you say, was always a reliable historian—in his descriptions of slavery, for instance—and part of the reason for that, I believe, is that his primary interest lay in expressing concern over the likely prospects for the first popular model of democracy the world had until that day seen, not mainly with accurate social *reportage.* Similarly the main purpose of your *First New Nation,* as I understand it, is to describe how an ex-colonial society achieves stability and identity, and on that level I find it an extremely interesting and suggestive book. But this approach in itself implies acceptance of an enormous number of "givens" about American society from the eighteenth century to the present without examining in detail how they have changed over time, or even how accurate they were then. As Andrew Gundar Frank pointed out some years ago, functional sociology only "ask[s] of the whole how it explains the part. Of the whole itself they ask no questions at all. They do not ask why it exists or how, where it comes from or what is happening to it. . . . They simply accept the whole system as it is."

9. *Uses and Abuses of the Comparative Method*

Lipset: Well, you cannot argue with methodological statements which urge virtue and complain about specific or general acts of sin. But to talk about value systems, or the consequences of the absence of feudalism, or the nature of the status system, has no meaning except in a comparative context. Few who discuss the presumed consequences of an equalitarian value system deny the existence of a steeply stratified system of inequality with respect to economic position or power in America or the Soviet Union. When Tocqueville was writing about equality in America he was discussing, as he well knew, a society with slavery. When Harriet Martineau, who was a radical socialist, an ardent abolitionist, and a strong feminist, also wrote enthusiastically about equalitarian America, she knew it was a society with slavery and private property. But what Tocqueville and Martineau were doing was to compare the (white) United States to the Europe or France and England of their day. Their emphasis of more-egalitarian-values-or-less only makes sense in relation to comparative judgments.

There is indeed the problem that all these social systems have changed and do change constantly. This also raises the question of changes in meaning and language over time: the meaning of equality in 1830 was surely very different from what is meant by equality today. One of the great dangers in writing history, or even in reading historical materials, is that we read back concepts of the present into the past. These present enormous difficulties, as you know better than I, being a historian.

Nevertheless, I would still maintain that in order to understand American political behavior, in relation to the periods of strength as well as to the periods of weakness of American socialism, the notion of America's being "born modern" is important. Or, to put it the other way around, societies "born traditional," so to speak, with a greater degree of overt class stratification, can more readily develop systems of class-conscious politics than those which are not. Some years ago Stein Rokkan, a Norwegian political sociologist, and I attempted to systematize the bases of difference among political parties—all types of parties, not just socialist and non-socialist. The most striking thing we noted was the way in which political parties institutionalized basic cleavages that arose in different countries at the *beginning* of their modern political history.[56] In some countries the religious issue became a major determinant of the party system, e.g., the Protestant-Catholic party separatism, or the clerical-anti-clerical struggle. Attitudes to the French Revolution have remained part of the party system in parts of Europe. What is most interesting, however, is the extent to which these institutionalized cleavages have persisted over one hundred or even one hundred and fifty years. They have taken on different meanings, but as the divisions into different tendencies continued, people acquired a vested interest in maintaining them.

The name of the Dutch Anti-Revolutionary Party does not refer to the Bolshevik Revolution of 1917, but to the French Revolution of 1789.

Laslett: But "What's in a name?" Parties change, and unless we look beyond some vague and generalized set of national values to examine the policies and bases of support of the Dutch Anti-Revolutionary Party *over time,* how can we possibly know whether it still represents the same conservative tendencies in Dutch life that it did a hundred years ago? It would be extremely misleading, for example, to argue that either of the two major American political parties still stands for the same things that it did at the time of the American Revolution. Indeed, one might argue that in many respects they have reversed their former roles: the libertarian, anti-statist Democratic Party of Jefferson now welcomes semi-collectivist measures in the name of an increasingly powerful welfare state, while the mercantilist Hamiltonian Federalists (Republicans) espouse the cause of anti-statism and laissez faire. It may be, in other words, that the Dutch Anti-Revolutionary Party of which you speak now secures support for reasons which have very little to do with its origins; and I think this again points to the danger of obscuring the whole nature of the historical process by thinking of change simply in terms of broad and general propositions.

But I agree entirely (or almost entirely) with the point you make about the need for comparative analysis; and I think we might conclude our dialogue by reiterating a point that has been symptomatic throughout our discussion—which I tried to make concerning Bell's *Marxian Socialism in the United States,* and which I think could be made concerning many other purely internal analyses of American socialism, but which we have not yet said openly —and that is that in my view the only way one can possibly hope to get a satisfactory answer to the question of "why is there no socialism in America?" is by means of rigorous, localized, and detailed comparative analysis. Socialism, like slavery, was either defined by its founders as an international phenomenon or became so because of historical accident; and its relative absence in what is now by far the most advanced capitalist society in the world provides one of the best opportunities we have of studying America's alleged "exceptionalism" within Western society as a whole.

In fact, since comparative analysis is now so fashionable among historians, it may be important to point out its dangers as well as its virtues in relation to our subject. Intellectual fashion, degrees of cosmopolitanism, and—I think especially in America—responses to periods of nationalism or to the question of national self-confidence have affected liberal scholars as varied and distinguished as Charles A. Beard, Frederick Jackson Turner, and Vernon Parrington in their general writing of history; and it has sometimes led conservative social historians (perhaps most recently Daniel Boorstin)[57] to emphasize the differences between America and Europe as a means of expressing their personal approval of the society in which they live, or even of demonstrating its superiority over others.[58] Radical or Marxist historians, on the other hand—reflecting the twin stigma which being both a Marxist and an intellectual used to bring upon American academics—have sometimes erred in the opposite direction by emphasizing America's lack of difference from other industrial societies, while at the same time pointing to its cultural inferiority.

These dangers are especially great in treating the topic of American socialism, where practitioners and recorders alike are usually *engagé,* and whose predispositions therefore inevitably affect their judgment. I would argue, for example, that to acknowledge the presence of inequities with respect to income, wealth, and power in American society, which you did just now, but then to invoke Tocqueville's comparative purpose as a means of implying that relatively speaking Americans were much better off than Europeans (which of course they were), begs the question of what American society, internally speaking, was really like.

The point here is an old one: not that history can ever be wholly objective—no good history ever is—but that it should be written in the full light of the historical record. And at this stage my own tendency, given the present state of our knowledge about this subject, is to say—in a manner which will no doubt strike both radicals and conservatives as infuriatingly mealymouthed—that in the crucial decades of the late nineteenth century when socialism developed as an international movement, American industrial society in certain respects resembled, or was very much like, that of a number of European countries, but was in other respects rather different. If I am right about Bell's argument over ideological rigidity, for example (that is, that the problems of the British Labour Party or of the German Social Democratic Party were very similar to those of the American Socialist Party in the years before the First World War), then comparative analysis will have shown us that from the point of view of ideology there are very important *similarities* to the problems faced by socialists in Europe and America. On the other hand, preliminary evidence suggests that the kind of research which I am doing into the political behavior of coal miners in Britain and America—who were a large and highly politicized element in the labor force in both countries, and who played an important role in determining the presence of a labor party in Great Britain and the absence of one here—may show that the political behavior of a labor force in an immigrant and highly mobile society such as the United States was really quite *different* from that of an ethnically and culturally diverse but still far more homogeneous and settled labor force in the same industry in Great Britain. Whatever the truth of this, I am convinced that the best way ahead is both to carry out local case studies comparing the behavior of elements *within* American society and also to compare the behavior of elements within American society with that of elements in a number of carefully selected European countries, as well as elsewhere.

Lipset: I agree; and let me conclude with an old hobbyhorse of my own, that not only does Europe and America, or England and America, make for a fruitful comparison, but that when dealing with the issue of labor and socialism comparisons between the United States and Canada are also valuable. Since the 1930s Canada has had a relatively important socialist party, now called the New Democratic Party, which judging from recent elections has taken a new lease on life. It now governs three western provinces, and is the official opposition in Ontario. The Canadian labor movement, part of the AFL-CIO for certain purposes, officially supports the New Democratic Party in Canada. In a long essay in my book *Revolution and Counterrevolution,* I have tried to trace through some of the reasons for the differences between Canada and the United States that tie in with some of the points made here.[59]

But regardless of what I've said, I think anyone interested—as you are—in the coal miners or workers in different industries, and the consequences of having a different conception of the role of labor within the political system, can, by comparing the same groups in Canada and the United States over time, or contemporaneously, shed a great deal of light on the forces in American society which stabilize or destabilize certain tendencies.

NOTES

1. For a discussion of the "end of ideology" as a major theme in social science and political literature presenting a variety of points of view, see Chaim I. Waxman, ed., *The End of Ideology Debate* (New York: Funk & Wagnalls, 1968), and M. Rejai, ed., *Decline of Ideology?* (Chicago: Aldine, Atherton, 1971).

2. S. M. Lipset, *Political Man* (Garden City, N.Y.: Doubleday, 1960), pp. 403–17. My most comprehensive statement on the subject is in "The Changing Class Structure and Contemporary European Politics," *Daedalus*, 93 (Winter 1964), pp. 271–303, which is reprinted in slightly revised and updated form in my book *Revolution and Counterrevolution* (Garden City, N.Y.: Doubleday, Anchor Books, 1970, rev. ed.), pp. 267–304.

3. H. Stuart Hughes, "The End of Political Ideology," *Measure*, 2 (Spring 1951), pp. 146–58. For a discussion of these varying approaches, see S. M. Lipset, "Ideology—And No End," *Encounter*, 39 (December 1972), pp. 17–22.

4. "Left-wing" versions of the "end of ideology" thesis which go much further than Aron, Bell, or Lipset in asserting that the basis for "conflict" is also gone may be found in Barrington Moore, Jr., *Political Power and Social Theory* (Cambridge: Harvard University Press, 1958), p. 183; and Herbert Marcuse, *One Dimensional Man* (Boston: Beacon Press, 1964), pp. xii–xiii. For a critique of Marcuse's position see Lucien Goldman, "Understanding Marcuse," *Partisan Review*, 38, no. 3 (1971), p. 258.

5. See Leo Rosten, *A Trumpet for Reason* (Garden City, N.Y.: Doubleday, 1970), pp. 64–65.

6. Herbert Marcuse, *An Essay on Liberation* (Boston: Beacon Press, 1969), pp. 51–52. In an interview with *Le Monde* on April 11, 1968, Marcuse had opposed "student power" as "conservative or even reactionary" on the ground that "everywhere and at all times, the overwhelming majority of students are conservative and even reactionary." See "Upsurge of the Youth Movement in Capitalist Countries," *World Marxist Review*, 11 (July 1968), p. 8.

7. For an account of the various American right-wing movements see S. M. Lipset and Earl Raab, *The Politics of Unreason: Right-Wing Extremism in America, 1790–1970* (New York: Harper & Row, 1970).

8. Some of the more important accounts in the now burgeoning literature on the French "May 1968" may be found in Gabriel and Daniel Cohn-Bendit, *Obsolete Communism: The Left-Wing Alternative* (New York: McGraw-Hill, 1969); Henri LeFebvre, *The Explosion: Marxism and the French Upheaval* (New York: Monthly Review Press, 1969); and *Revolt in France, May–June: A Contemporary*

Record (compiled from *Intercontinental Press* and *The Militant*) (New York: 1968).

9. See, for example, Arthur Mann (ed.), *The Progressive Era, Liberal Renaissance or Liberal Failure?*, American Problem Studies (New York: Holt, Rinehart, 1963); or Edward C. Rozwence (ed.), *The New Deal, Revolution or Evolution?*, Problems in American Civilization (Boston: Heath, 1959).

10. See, for example, Eugene D. Genovese, "Materialism and Idealism in the History of Negro Slavery in the Americas," in *Journal of Social History* (Summer 1968), pp. 371–94; Staughton Lynd, *Class Conflict, Slavery, and the United States Constitution* (Indianapolis: Bobbs-Merrill, 1967), especially Chapter One.

11. Bernard Johnpoll's recent book, *Pacifist's Progress, Norman Thomas and the Decline of American Socialism* (Chicago: Quadrangle Books, 1970), Chapters Four through Six, has an extensive discussion of these issues.

12. See note 1 for references.

13. See Lipset, *Political Man*, op. cit., pp. 310–23, 340–43.

14. C. Wright Mills, "Letter to the New Left," reprinted in Mills, *Power, Politics and People* (New York: Ballantine Books, 1963), pp. 256–57.

15. For an analysis of the particular problems of third parties in the American two-party system, see E. E. Schattschneider, *Party Government* (New York: Holt, 1942), pp. 65–98; William B. Hesseltine, *The Rise and Fall of Third Parties* (Washington, D.C.: Public Affairs Press, 1948). For a discussion of the way in which electoral mechanics affect the propensity for the two-party or multi-party outcomes of different political systems, see S. M. Lipset, *The First New Nation* (Garden City, N.Y.: Doubleday, Anchor Books, 1967), pp. 327–65.

16. S. M. Lipset, *Agrarian Socialism* (Berkeley: University of California Press, 1971, rev. ed.).

17. These patterns of behavior are discussed in S. M. Lipset and Carl Sheingold, "Values and Political Structure: An Interpretation of the Sources of Extremism and Violence in American Society," in William J. Crotty, ed., *Assassinations and the Political Order* (New York: Harper & Row, 1971), pp. 388–414.

18. On this, see Johnpoll, op. cit., pp. 135–37.

19. A useful summary of the revisionist debate in various European countries is to be found in Carl Landauer, *European Socialism: A History of Ideas and Movements* (Berkeley: University of California Press, 1959), Vol. I, pp. 298–339, 356–83.

20. Compare David Shannon, *The Socialist Party of America, A History* (New York: Macmillan, 1955), pp. 1–61, with Daniel Bell, *Marxian Socialism in the United States* (Princeton: Princeton University Press, 1967), pp. 45–90, or with Louis Hartz, *The Liberal Tradition in America: An Interpretation of American Political Thought Since the Revolution* (New York: Harcourt, Brace, 1955), paper ed., pp. 244–48, 277–83.

21. Lewis L. Lorwin, *The American Federation of Labor: History, Policies, and Prospects* (Washington, D.C.: Brookings Institution, 1933).

22. For general discussions of the relationship between the labor movement and the Socialist and Democratic parties in America, on the one hand, compared to their relationship with the Liberal and Labour parties in England, see Laslett, *Labor and the Left: A Study of Radical and Socialist Influences in the American Labor Movement, 1881–1924* (New York: Basic Books, 1970), Chapter Six; Roy Gregory, *The Miners and British Politics, 1906–1914* (London: Oxford University Press, 1968); Marc Karson, *American Labor Unions and Politics, 1900–1918* (Carbondale, Ill.: Southern Illinois University Press, 1958); Gerald Grob, *Workers and Utopia: A Study of Ideological Conflict in the American Labor Movement, 1865–1900* (Evanston, Ill.: Northwestern University Press, 1961); Henry Pelling, *The Origins of the Labour Party, 1880–1900* (London: Macmillan, 1954); and Frank Bealey and Henry Pelling, *Labour and Politics, 1900–1906* (London: Macmillan, 1958).

23. For example, James Weinstein, "The IWW and American Socialism," in *Socialist Revolution*, 1 (September–October 1970), pp. 3–41; Sally Miller, "The Socialist Party and the Negro, 1901–1920," in *Journal of Negro History*, 56 (July 1971), pp. 220–29.

24. See, for example, the speech made by Max Hayes at the November 1906 AF of L convention in Minneapolis, in which he argued that "the socialists who have steadfastly fought in conventions in favor of political action have been vindicated," and that if they persisted in their efforts an independent labor party would be the result. *Proceedings, Twenty-Sixth Annual Convention of the A.F. of L.* (Washington, 1906), pp. 183–204. See also Harry Sell, "The A.F. of L. and the Labor Party Movement of 1918–1920" (unpublished M.A. Thesis, University of Chicago, 1922), pp. 95–117.

25. For discussions of the Socialist Party's attitude toward the idea of a labor party, see Shannon, op. cit., pp. 63–66, 168–81; James Weinstein, *The Decline of Socialism in America, 1912–1925* (New York: Monthly Review Press, 1967), pp. 222–29, 278–79; and Kenneth McKay, *The Progressive Movement of 1924* (New York: Columbia University Press, 1947), pp. 22–155.

26. See Oscar Handlin, *The Uprooted* (Boston: Little, Brown, 1951), pp. 217–18ff.; J. Joseph Hutmacher, "Urban Liberalism and the Age of Reform," *Mississippi Valley Historical Review*, 49 (September 1962), pp. 231–41; Melvyn Dubofsky, "Success and Failure of Socialism in New York City, 1900–1918," *Labor History*, 9 (Fall 1968), pp. 361–75; Victor Greene, *The Slavic Community on Strike: Immigrant Labor in Pennsylvania Anthracite* (Notre Dame: University of Notre Dame Press, 1968).

27. See Lipset, *The First New Nation*, op. cit., pp. 159–92; S. M. Lipset, *Rebellion in the University* (Boston: Little, Brown, 1972), pp. 12–14.

28. Sam Brown, "The Politics of Peace," *The Washington Monthly*, 2 (August 1970), pp. 24–46.

29. Staughton Lynd, *Intellectual Origins of American Radicalism* (New York: Pantheon Books, 1968); Eugene D. Genovese, "Abolitionist," in *New York Review of Books* (September 26, 1968), pp. 69–74.

30. For a recent study of this phenomenon which covers the whole period, see Lipset and Raab, *The Politics of Unreason: Right-Wing Extremism in America, 1790–1970*, op. cit.

31. For suggestive accounts of violence in America and its relationship to the repression issue, see the essays by Frantz, Brown, Brooks, and Tanter in Hugh D. Graham and Ted R. Gurr, eds., *The History of Violence in America* (New York: Bantam Books, 1969).

32. Daniel and Gabriel Cohn-Bendit, *Obsolete Communism*, op. cit., p. 47.

33. Morris Janowitz, "Native Fascism in the 1930s," in his *Political Conflict* (Chicago: Quadrangle Books, 1970), pp. 149–70.

34. The most authoritative account of the New Left student movement which describes it in psychological terms is Lewis S. Feuer, *The Conflict of Generations: The Character and Significance of Student Movements* (New York: Basic Books, 1969). For a different approach, see Richard Flacks's essay review of Feuer's book in the *Journal of Social History*, 4 (Winter 1970–71), pp. 141–53.

35. Edward Shils, *The Torment of Secrecy: The Background and Consequences of American Security Policies* (Glencoe: The Free Press, 1956), pp. 77–104.

36. Lipset, *Rebellion in the University*, op. cit., pp. 248–49.

37. For an interesting account of the Horatio Alger myth as part of American cultural history, see Richard Weiss, *The American Myth of Success, From Horatio Alger to Norman Vincent Peale* (New York: Basic Books, 1970).

38. See, esp., Seymour Martin Lipset and Reinhard Bendix, *Social Mobility in Industrial Society* (Berkeley: University of California Press, 1959), Chapter 3.

39. Laslett, *Labor and the Left*, op. cit., pp. 59–62, 151–53ff.

40. See above, pp. 5–6.

41. Richard Flacks, "On the New Working Class and Strategies for Social Change," in Philip G. Altbach and Robert S. Laufer (eds.), *The New Pilgrims: Youth Protest in Transition* (New York: David McKay, 1972), pp. 85–98.

42. Mills, op. cit.

43. See S. M. Lipset and Richard Dobson, "The Intellectual as Critic and Rebel: With Special Reference to the United States and the Soviet Union," *Daedalus*, 101 (Summer 1972), pp. 137–98, for a detailed statement of the thesis and recent evidence.

44. One of the most rigorous and thought-provoking attempts to describe both the content and character of this transition may be found

in Daniel Bell (ed.), *Toward the Year 2000: Work in Progress* (Boston: Houghton Mifflin, 1968), partially reformulated in his article "Unstable America: Transitory and Permanent Factors in a National Crisis," in *Encounter*, 34 (June 1970), pp. 11–26.

45. John and Margaret Rowntree, "Political Economy of Youth (Youth as a Class)," Radical Education Project pamphlet, from *Our Generation*, 6 (1968).

46. In his attack on "spontaneity," and his call for a unified Russian Social Democratic Party led by professional revolutionaries in *What Is to Be Done?* (1902), Lenin criticized the "second period" of Russian Social Democracy, between 1894 and 1898, when the party was largely led by young people under thirty-five. "Owing to their youth," Lenin wrote, "they proved to be untrained for practical work and they left the scene with astonishing rapidity." (New York: International Publishers, 1929), p. 175.

47. Kim Moody, *The American Working Class in Transition* (International Socialists, 1969). See also Herbert Gintis, "The New Working Class and Revolutionary Youth," *Socialist Revolution*, 1 (May–June 1970), pp. 13–43; and Donald Clark Hodges, "Old and New Working Classes," *Radical America*, 5 (January–February 1971), pp. 11–32.

48. Michael Confino, "On Intellectuals and Intellectual Traditions in Eighteenth and Nineteenth Century Russia," *Daedalus*, 101 (Spring 1972), pp. 117–49; Selig Perlman, *A Theory of the Labor Movement* (New York: Macmillan, 1928), pp. 49–65, 74–94, 176–82, 280–303; Eric A. Nordlinger, *The Working Class Tories: Authority, Deference and Stable Democracy* (London: MacGibbon & Kee, 1967). See also J. P. Nettl, "Ideas, Intellectuals, and Structures of Dissent," in Philip Rieff (ed.), *On Intellectuals* (Garden City, N.Y.: Doubleday, 1969), pp. 53–122.

49. Evidence of this hostility can be found in the work of Feuer cited above, and in various essays in *Encounter* in the period 1968–70. It can be seen perhaps in its most characteristic form in Robert Nisbet's "Who Killed the Student Revolution?", in *Encounter*, 34 (February 1970), pp. 10–18.

50. For a further highly provocative discussion of these issues, see Noam Chomsky's essays on "Objectivity and Liberal Scholarship" and "The Responsibility of Intellectuals," in his *American Power and the New Mandarins* (New York: Vintage, 1969), pp. 23–158, 323–66.

51. Bell, *Marxian Socialism*, op. cit., esp. pp. vii–xiii.

52. Louis Hartz, *The Founding of New Societies: Studies in the History of the United States, Latin America, South Africa, Canada and Australia* (New York: Harcourt, Brace, 1964), esp. pp. 1–65.

53. Preface to the American edition of *The Condition of the Working Class in England* (1887), reproduced in *Marx & Engels, Letters to Americans, 1848–1895: A Selection* (New York: International Publishers, 1953), pp. 285–91.

54. On the influence of analysts of America on Karl Marx, see Lewis S. Feuer, *Marx and the Intellectuals* (Garden City, N.Y.: Doubleday, Anchor Books, 1969), pp. 164–215.

55. See David Riesman, *The Lonely Crowd* (New Haven: Yale University Press, 1950), pp. 19–20.

56. See S. M. Lipset and Stein Rokkan, "Cleavage Structure, Party Systems and Voter Alignments," in Lipset and Rokkan (eds.), *Party Systems and Voter Alignments* (New York: The Free Press, 1967), pp. 1–64.

57. As in his *The Genius of American Politics* (Chicago: University of Chicago Press, 1953).

58. See C. Vann Woodward's interesting discussion of this issue in the first chapter of his edited volume *The Comparative Approach to American History* (New York: Basic Books, 1968).

59. Lipset, *Revolution and Counterrevolution*, op. cit., pp. 37–75.

Part Two

☆

Internal Factors: The
Socialist Movement and
American Socialism

Chapter 3

THE PROBLEM OF IDEOLOGICAL RIGIDITY*

Daniel Bell

> The Rabbi of Zans used to tell this story about himself:
> "In my youth when I was fired with the love of God, I thought I would convert the whole world to God. But soon I discovered that it would be quite enough to convert the people who lived in my town, and I tried for a long time, but did not succeed. Then I realized that my program was too ambitious, and I concentrated on the persons in my own household. But I could not convert them either. Finally it dawned upon me: I must work upon myself, so that I may give true service to God. But I did not accomplish even this."
>
> Hasidic Tale

> He who seeks the salvation of souls, his own as well as others, should not seek it along the avenue of politics.
>
> Max Weber

Socialism was an unbounded dream. Fourier promised that under socialism people would be at least "ten feet tall." Karl Kautsky, the embodiment of didacticism, proclaimed that the average citizen of the socialist society would be a superman. The flamboyant Antonio Labriola told his Italian followers that their socialist-bred children would all be Galileos and Giordano Brunos. And the

---

* Chapter 12 from Daniel Bell, *The End of Ideology: On the Exhaustion of Political Ideas in the Fifties* (Glencoe: Free Press, 1960), originally entitled "The Failure of American Socialism: The Tension of Ethics and Politics."

high-flown, grandiloquent Trotsky described the socialist millennium as one in which "man would become immeasurably stronger, wiser, freer, his body more harmoniously proportioned, his movements more rhythmic, his voice more musical, and the forms of his existence permeated with dramatic dynamism."

America, too, was an unbounded dream. When the American colonies broke away from England, they inscribed upon the back of the great seal authorized by Congress *Novus Ordo Seclorum*— we are "the new order of the ages," the beginning of the American era. The American continent, with its vast lands and mighty riches, was destined to be a great social laboratory. Here the unfolding design of "God, Master Workman," would be manifest. Such a disguised deism, emphasizing the aspect of God as a craftsman rather than as a fixed revelation, was congenial to the growth of a pragmatic temper. It was a society which, if it did not welcome, would at least abide without scorn the efforts of small bands to explore the design of the millennium. And if in places the response was hostile, there was the Icarian wilderness, stretching from Texas to Iowa, in which Utopian colonies might find refuge, safe from prying eyes, to continue their chiliastic search. Small wonder then that such colonies arose in prodigal number.

Here, too, it seemed as if socialism would have its finest hour. Inspired, perhaps, by the expanse of the virgin wilderness, Marx and Engels felt a boundless optimism. In 1879 Marx wrote, "the United States have at present overtaken England in the rapidity of economical progress, though they lag still behind in the extent of acquired wealth; but at the same time, the masses are quicker and have greater political means in their hands to resent the form of a progress accomplished at this expense." Engels, who wrote a score of letters on the American scene in the late 1880's and early nineties, repeated this prediction time and again. In his introduction to the American edition of *The Conditions of the Working Class in England,* written at the height of enthusiasm over the events of 1886—notably the spectacular rise of the Knights of Labor and the Henry George campaign in New York—he exulted: "On the more favored soil of America, where no medieval ruins bar the way, where history begins with the elements of modern bourgeois society, as evolved in the seventeenth century, the working class passed through these two stages of its development [a national trade-union movement and an independent labor party] within ten months." And five years later, his optimism undiminished by the sorry turn of events, Engels wrote to Schleuter: ". . . continually renewed waves of advance followed by equally certain set-backs are inevitable. Only the advancing waves are becoming more powerful, the setbacks less paralyzing. . . . Once the Americans get started it will be with an energy and violence compared with which we in Europe shall be mere children."[1]

But there still hovers the melancholy question posed by Werner Sombart at the turn of the century in the title of a book, *Why Is There No Socialism in the United States?* To this Sombart supplied one set of answers. He pointed to the open frontiers, the many opportunities for social ascent through individual effort and the rising standard of living. Other writers have expanded these considerations. Selig Perlman, in his *Theory of the Labor Movement,* advanced three reasons for the lack of class consciousness in the United States: the absence of a "settled" wage-earner class; the "free gift" of the ballot (workers in other countries who were denied such rights—for example, the Chartists in England—developed political rather than economic motivation); and third, the impact of successive waves of immigration. It was immigration, said Perlman, which gave rise to the ethnic, linguistic, religious, and cultural heterogeneity of American labor and to the heightened ambitions of immigrants' sons to escape their inferior status. Count Keyserling, a traveler here in the twenties, observed that Americanism, with its creed of egalitarianism, was a surrogate for socialism; and the "conversions" of many German socialists who came here in the late nineteenth century attests to the acuity of this remark. Some writers have stressed the agrarian basis of American life, with the farmer seesawing to radicalism and conservatism in tune to the business cycle. Others have pointed to the basically sectional rather than functional organization of the two-party system, with its emphasis on patronage, its opportunism, and its vacuity of rhetoric as the mode of political discourse; hence compromise, rather than rigid principle, becomes the trading concern of the interest-oriented political bloc. In the end, all such explanations have fallen back on the natural resources and material vastness of America. In awe of the fact that the Yankee worker consumed almost three times as much bread and meat, and four times as much sugar, as his German counterpart, Sombart exclaimed: "On the reefs of roast beef and apple pie, socialistic Utopias of every sort are sent to their doom."[2]

Implicit in many of these analyses was the notion, however, that such conditions were but temporary. Capitalism as an evolving social system would of necessity "mature," crisis would follow crisis, and a large, self-conscious wage-earner class and a socialist movement on the European pattern would emerge. The great depression was such a crisis—an emotional jolt which shook the self-confidence of the entire society. It left scar tissue on the minds of American workers. It spurred the organization of a giant trade-union movement which, in ten years, grew from less than three million to over fifteen million workers, or almost 30 per cent of the wage and salaried force of the country. It brought in its train smoking-hot organizing drives and sit-downs in the Ohio industrial valley which gave the country a strong whiff of class warfare. It spawned strong anticapitalistic and antiplutocratic populist movements (e.g., Huey Long's share-the-wealth, Father Coughlin's social justice, Dr. Townsend's old-age pension scheme). Here, seemingly, was the fertile soil which socialist theorists had long awaited.

Yet no socialist movement emerged, nor did a coherent socialist ideology take seed either in the labor movement or in government. It would seem that the general reasons adduced earlier simply held —and that the New Deal, like the earlier ideology of Americanism, had become a somewhat different surrogate for socialism. But all such explanations are "external," so to speak, to the radical movement, and, even if true, are simply one side of the coin. The other is: How did the socialist see the world, and, because of that vision, why did the movement fail to adapt to the American scene? Why was it incapable of rational choice?

A general answer why the socialist movement did not face up to the real situation—and these judgments are always after the fact —involves *the interplay of social character* (i.e., the social composition of the movement and the kind of allegiance it demanded of its members), *the degree of "access" to other institutions,* and *the nature of its ideology.*[3] A full explanation of the failure—or success—of a social movement would have to describe how these three elements affect each other. Thus, a movement completely alienated from the society, for ethnic or emotional reasons, would find it harder to make compromises with an existing order; in such cases, the social character of the movement might be the decisive explanation for its failure to adapt to changing reality. A social movement with a high proportion of union members, one with a high proportion of professional persons, might have an easier "bridge" to other political groups; hence, "degree of access" might be the important factor. In other instances, the nature of the ideology might be the agent that creates the dilemma of action. For some movements, ideology is a pose, easily dropped; for others it is a bind.

This chapter concerns itself with the ideology of socialism. It is my argument that the failure of the socialist movement in the United States was rooted in its inability to resolve a basic dilemma of ethics and politics: the socialist movement, by the way in which it stated its goal, and by the way in which it rejected the capitalist order as a whole, could not relate itself to the specific problems of social action in the here-and-now, give-and-take political world. In sum: it was trapped by the unhappy problem of living *in* but not *of* the world; it could only act, and then inadequately, as the moral, but not political, man in immoral society. It could never resolve, but only straddle, the basic issue of either accepting capitalist society and seeking to transform it from within, as the labor movement did, or of becoming the sworn enemy of that society, like the Communists. A religious movement can split its allegiances and (like Lutheranism) live *in* but not *of* the world (after all, it is not concerned with this life but the after-life); a political movement cannot.

The Two Ethics

In the largest sense, society is an organized system for the distribution of rewards and privileges, the imposition of obligations and duties. Within that frame, ethics deals with the *ought* of distribution, implying a theory of justice. Politics is the concrete *mode* of distribution, involving a power struggle between organized groups to determine the allocation of privilege. In social action there is an ineluctable tension between ethics and politics. Lord Acton posed the problem in a note: "Are politics an attempt to realize ideals, or an endeavour to get advantages, within the limits of ethics?" More succinctly, "are ethics a purpose or a limit?"[4]

In some periods of history, generally in closed societies, ethics and politics have gone hand in hand. There, in theory, the moral law and the just price rule, and each stratum receives its privileges according to fixed status. But a distinguishing feature of modern society is the separation of ethics and politics—since no group can, through the civil arm, impose its moral conceptions on the whole society; and ideology—the façade of general interest and universal values which masks specific self-interest—replaces ethics. The redivision of the rewards and privileges of society can only be accomplished in the political arena. But in that fateful entry into politics, an ethic stated as purpose (or end), rather than as a limit (or simply the rules of the game), becomes a far-reaching goal which demands a radical commitment that necessarily transforms politics into an all-or-none battle.

Acton's dilemma was most clearly reformulated by Max Weber in his discussion of politics as a way of life. One can see the political game, he said, as an "ethic of responsibility" (or the acceptance of limits), or as an "ethic of conscience" (or the dedication to absolute ends). The former is the pragmatic view which seeks reconciliation as its goal. The latter creates "true believers" who burn with pure, unquenchable flame and can accept no compromise with faith.

Weber, arguing that only the ethic of responsibility is possible in politics if civil peace is to be maintained, writes: "The matter does not appear to me so desperate if one does not ask exclusively who is morally right and who is morally wrong, but if one rather asks: Given the existing conflict how can I solve it with the least internal and external danger for all concerned?"[5]

Such a view of politics, rather than the dedication to some absolute (whether it be Bolshevism as an active, disruptive force of society or religious pacifism as a passive withdrawal from society) is possible, however, only when there is a basic consensus among contending groups to respect each other's rights to continue in the society. The foundation of a pluralist society rests, therefore, on this separation of ethics and politics and on the limiting of ethics to the formal rules of the game. In practice, the socialists accepted this fact; in theory, because of its root rejection of the society, the socialist movement could never wholeheartedly accept this basic approach, and on crucial doctrinal issues it found itself stymied.

The question of which ethic one accepts becomes crucial, for the distinctive character of "modern" politics is the involvement of *all* strata of society in movements of social change, rather than, as in feudal or peasant or backward societies, the fatalistic acceptance of events as they are. The starting point was, as Karl Mannheim elegantly put it, the "orgiastic chiliasm" of the Anabaptists, their ecstatic effort to realize the Millennium at once. Martin Luther had torn down the monastery walls which separated the sacred from the profane life. Each man now stood alone, in the "equality of believers," forced to make his affirmation and to realize the Christian life himself, directly, rather than through the vicarious atonement of the saints. But if all men were equal, how could there be master and servant? If all men stood naked before God in the matter of salvation, should they not be equal in sharing the material goods of the worldly life? These were the disturbing questions asked by Thomas Munzer and the radical Anabaptists. Suddenly, other-worldly religious quietism became transformed into a revolutionary activism to realize the Millennium in the *here and now*. Thus the religious frenzy of the chiliasts which burst the bonds of the old religious order threatened to buckle the social order as well; for unlike previous revolutions, which aimed at single oppressors, chiliasm sought to overthrow the entire existing social order.†

The characteristic psychological fact about the chiliast is that for him "there is no inner articulation of time"; there is only "absolute presentness." "Orgiastic energies and ecstatic outbursts began to operate in a worldly setting and tensions previously transcending day to day life became explosive agents within it."[6] The chiliast is neither in the world nor of it. He stands outside of it and against it because salvation, the Millennium, is immediately at hand.

Where such a hope is possible, where such a social movement can transform society in a cataclysmic flash, the "leap" is made, and in the pillar of fire the fusion of ethics and politics is possible. But where societies are stable and social change can only come piecemeal, the pure chiliast, in despair, turns nihilist, rather than

---

† Munzer's millenarian dreams kindled the literary utopias, more than a century later, of Robert Burton's idyllic land, in his preface to the *Anatomy of Melancholy*, and the technological paradise of Bacon's New Atlantis, and found political expression in the egalitarian demands of the Levellers and Diggers during the Cromwell rebellion. A century and a half later, the same impulses flickered strongly, during the French Revolution, in Gracchus Babeuf's "conspiracy of the equals," and passed into the common currency of the revolutionary movements of the nineteenth century.

make the bitter-tasting compromises with the established hierarchical order. "When this spirit ebbs and deserts these movements," writes Mannheim, "there remains behind in the world a naked mass-frenzy and despiritualized fury." In a later and secularized form, this attitude found its expression in Russian anarchism. So Bakunin could write: "The desire for destruction is at the same time a creative desire."

Yet not only the anarchist, but every socialist, every convert to political messianism, is in the beginning something of a chiliast. In the newly found enthusiasms, in the identification with an oppressed group, there is the unsuppressed urgency and hope that the "final conflict" might soon be in sight. ("Socialism in our time" was the banner which Norman Thomas raised for the new recruits to the Socialist party in the 1930's.) But the "revolution" is not always nigh, and the question of how to discipline this chiliastic zeal and hold it in readiness has always been the basic problem of radical strategy.

The anarchist had the vision of *die Tat*, "the deed." Like Paul Munnumit, in Henry James's *Princess Casamassima*, he could live a drab, humdrum life because of his secret, omnipotent conviction that "a shot" could transform the world in a flash and that he could command the moment when the shot would come. Powerful as the image was, its believers could only live, like sleepwalkers, in a fantasy world. Yet only through fantasy could the anarchists keep the believer from becoming tired or dispirited. The most radical approach was that of Georges Sorel, with his concept of the revolutionary myth (*images de batailles*), a myth which, for the anarcho-syndicalists, functioned as a bastardized version of the doctrine of salvation. These unifying images, Sorel wrote, can neither be proved nor disproved; thus they are "capable of evoking an undivided whole" from the mass of diverse sentiments which exist in society. "The syndicalists solve this problem perfectly by concentrating the whole of socialism in the drama of the general strike; thus there is no longer any place for the reconciliation of contraries in the equivocations of the professors; everything is clearly mapped out so that only one interpretation of socialism is possible." In this "catastrophic conception" of socialism, as Sorel called it, "*it is the myth in its entirety which is alone important.*"[7]

But how long can a myth sustain, when the reality constantly belies it?

The Veils of the Proletariat

What of the proletariat itself? What is its role in the socialist drama of history? How does the proletariat see through the veils of obscurity and come to self-awareness? Marx could say with Jesus, "I have come to end all mysteries, not to perpetuate them." His role, in his own self-image, was to lay bare the fetishes which enslave modern man and thus to confute Hegel's claim that freedom and rationality had already been achieved. But, like his old master, he could only deal with "immanent" forces of history, not the mechanics of social action.[8]

All political movements, Marx wrote, have been slaves to the symbols of the past. ("Thus Luther donned the mask of the Apostle Paul, the Revolution of 1789 to 1814 draped itself alternately as the Roman Republic and the Roman Empire," he wrote in *The Eighteenth Brumaire*.) But history is the process of progressive disenchantment; men are no longer bound to the river gods and anthropomorphic deities of the agricultural societies; nor need they be bound to the abstract impersonal deity of bourgeois Protestantism. Man was potential. But how to realize his potentiality? The intellectual was, in part, capable of self-emancipation because he possessed the imagination to transcend his origins. But the proletariat, as a class, could develop only to the extent that the social relations of society itself revealed to the slave the thongs that bind him. Man is not freer, said Marx in *Das Kapital*, because he can sell his labor power to whom he wishes. Exploitation is implicit in the very structure of capitalist society, which, in order to live, must constantly expand by extracting surplus value and accumulating new capital. In the process, the proletarian would be reduced to the barest minimum of human existence (the law of increasing misery) and thus be robbed of any mark of distinction. In the agony of alienation he would realize a sense of identity which would unite him with others and create a cohesive social movement of revolution. In action he would no longer be manipulated but would "make" himself.[9]

Thus the scene is set for the grand drama. Out of the immanent, convulsive contradictions of capitalism, conflict would spread. The proletariat, neither in nor of the world, would inherit the world.

But History (to use these personifications) confounded Marx's prophecy, at least in the West. The law of increasing misery was refuted by the tremendous advances of technology. The trade-union began bettering the workers' lot, and, in the political struggles that followed, the proletariat found that it could sustain itself not by becoming a revolutionary instrument against society but by accepting a place within society.

A Place in the Sun

In the America of the nineteenth century, almost every social movement had involved an effort by the worker to escape his lot as a worker. At times the solution was free land, cheap money, producer's co-operatives, or some other chimera from the gaudy bag of utopian dreams. The rise of the American Federation of Labor signaled the end of this search for the land of Prester John. "The working people," said Gompers, "are in too great need of immediate improvement[s] in their condition to allow them to forego them in their endeavour to devote their entire energies to an end however beautiful to contemplate. . . . The way out of the wage system is through higher wages."[10]

It was the obstinate manner in which the sectarians ignored the bread-and-butter aspect of the situation that soured him completely on the political socialists. In the 1880's, the cigarmakers union, headed by Gompers, sought legislation outlawing the manufacture of cigars in tenement homes. He marked for reprisal those legislators who voted against the measure and called for support of those who voted for the bill. But the political socialists were dead-set against voting for old-party candidates, even the pro-labor ones, charging that such a move might provide temporary gains for the cigarmakers but would "corrupt" the labor movement. Even when the first tenement-house bill was enacted, the socialists refused to support for re-election Gompers' man, Edward Grosse, who had been instrumental in pushing through the measure. It was a lesson that Gompers never forgot.

But there was another side to the seeking a place in the world to which Gompers was no less sensitive, though he was more masked in his statement of the case. Gompers, the son of Dutch-Jewish parents, came to the United States at the age of thirteen and, for most of his life, was acutely aware of his foreign birth. Most of the leaders of American labor have been immigrants or close to immigrant stock, and the desire to be accepted, as Marcus Lee Hansen has noted, was part of the intense status drive of most immigrants. In effect, the immigrant has not been a radical force in American life; on the contrary, the immigrant generation has tended to be conservative. When in the early 1900's the AFL took the much debated step of entering the National Civic Foundation, an organization headed by Republican political boss and president-maker Mark Hanna, Gompers explained the move in the following terms: "It helped to establish the practice," he wrote, "of accepting labor unions as an integral social element and logically of including their representatives in groups to discuss policies."[11] This was labor's single ambition: to win acceptance as a "legitimate" social group, equal with business and the church as an established institution of American life. For Gompers, the immigrant boy, it was a personal crusade as well. He sought to win recognition for labor in all civic aspects of American life: an entry and a hearing at the White House, an official voice in government, and acceptance in the community at large. To become respectable—this was Gompers' and labor's aim. And, by the mid-century, labor had indeed become the new parvenu force of American life.

Waiting for Socialism

Neither nineteenth-century American radicals nor the American socialists faced up to this problem of social compromise. The utopias that were spun so profusely in the nineteenth century assumed that in the course of evolution, "reason" would find its way and the perfect society would emerge. But so mechanical were the manikin visions of human delights in such utopias that a modern reading of Bellamy, for example, with its plan for conscript armies of labor ("a horrible cockney dream," William Morris called *Looking Backward*), only produces revulsion.

The "scientific socialist" movement that emerged at the turn of the century mocked these utopian unrealities. Only the organization of the proletariat could bring a better world. But this apparent relatedness to the world was itself a delusion. The socialist dilemma was still how to face the problem of "in the world and of it," and in practice the early socialist movement "rejected" the world; it simply waited for the new. Although the American Socialist party sought to function politically by making "immediate demands" and pressing for needed social reforms, it rarely took a stand on the actual political problems that emerged from the everyday functioning of society. "What but meaningless phrases are 'imperialism,' 'expansion,' 'free silver,' 'gold standard,' etc., to the wage worker?" asked Eugene V. Debs in 1900. "The large capitalists represented by Mr. McKinley and the small capitalists represented by Mr. Bryan are interested in these 'issues' but they do not concern the working class."

These "issues" were beside the point, said Debs, because the worker stood outside society. Thus Debs and the socialist movement as a whole would have no traffic with the capitalist parties. Even on local municipal issues the party would not compromise. The socialist movement could "afford" this purity because of its supreme confidence about the future. "The socialist program is not a theory imposed upon society for its acceptance or rejection. It is but the interpretation of what is, sooner or later, inevitable. Capitalism is already struggling to its destruction." So proclaimed the Socialist national platform of 1904, the first issued by the Socialist party.

And the Socialist party and its leader, Gene Debs, waited. To the extent that any one person can embody the fantastic contradictions inherent in the history of the socialist movement—its deep emotional visions, its quixotic, self-numbing political behavior, its sulky, pettish outbursts—it is Eugene Debs. Debs had what the theologians call charisma, the inner light of grace, or, as put by a laconic southerner, "kindlin' power." "He was a tall shamblefooted man, had a sort of gusty rhetoric that set on fire the railroad workers in their pine-boarded halls . . . made them want the world he wanted, a world brothers might own where everybody would split even," wrote Dos Passos.

Yet while Debs fully *realized* the messianic role of the prophet, he lacked the hard-headedness of the politician, the ability to take the moral absolutes and break them down to the particulars with the fewest necessary compromises. He lacked, too, the awareness that a socialist leader must play both of these roles and that in this tension there arise two risks—the corruption of the prophet and the ineffectuality of the politician. But Debs never even had the strength to *act* to the hilt the role of the prophet. A shallow dogmatism gave him the illusion of an inflexible morality. "If his mind failed to grasp a direct connection between a proposed reform and socialism," writes a sympathetic biographer, "he refused to waste time with reform. Then argument became futile; he could not be swayed."[12]

This dogmatism had its roots not in an iron revolutionary will, as with Lenin, but in an almost compulsive desire to be "left" of orthodox labor opinion. Nor did this thick streak of perpetual dissidence flow from the spirit of a dispossessed rebel, like Haywood. Its wellspring was a sentimental nineteenth-century romanticism. He had been named for Eugene Sue and Victor Hugo, and their concern for the underdog, as well as the naive optimism of a Rousseau, soared in him. Yet in his personal life, manner, and habits (except for a later private addiction to drink), Debs was respectable and almost bourgeois; his wife Kate was even more so. His literary tastes were prosaic: his favorite poet was Elbert Hubbard. But in his politics Debs wore romanticism like a cloak—and this was his strength as well as his weakness. It allowed him to be rhetorical and emotional, touching people at the ragged edge of their desire for a purpose outside themselves. But it also caused him to shun the practical and to shirk the obligations of day-to-day political decision. His fiercest shafts were reserved for the bureaucrat and party boss; his warmth and affection for those who led turbulent and dissident careers like his own. But, at bottom, it was the easiest path.

Withal, the lonely figure of Debs, his sagging, pleading gauntness, pierced all who beheld him. It was perhaps because, in a final sense, he was the true protestant. Debs stood at the end of the long road of the Reformation. He had an almost mystical— at times omniscient—faith in the dictates of his inner self. Like the Anabaptists of old, all issues were resolved by private conscience. From the priesthood of all believers he had become the solitary individual, carrying on his shoulders the burdens of humanity. That sense of loneliness—and grandeur—touched others who were equally afflicted with the terrible sense of isolation. By his standing alone, he emphasized the individual and his rights, and at best, such an attitude of "autonomy" provides a unique defense of the dignity of the person. But in its extreme antinomianism, in its romantic defiance of rational and traditional norms, it shirks the more difficult problem of living in the world, of seeking, as one must in politics, relative standards of social virtue and political justice instead of abstract absolutes. It is but one pole—a necessary one—in creating standards of action. But as the isolated protestant refuses to join the community of "sinners," so the isolated prophet evades the responsibility of political life. The prophet, Max Scheler once said, stands on the mountain as a sign-post; he points the way but cannot go, for if he did, there would no longer be a sign. The politician, one might add, carries the sign into the valley with him.

Straddling for Socialism

Unlike the other-worldly movements toward salvation, which can always postpone the date of the resurrection, the Socialist party, living in the here and now, had to show results. It was a movement based on a belief in "history"; but it found itself outside of "time." World War I finally broke through the façade. For the first time, the party had to face a stand on a realistic issue of the day. And on that issue almost the entire intellectual leadership of the party deserted; and, as a result, the back of American socialism was broken.

The socialist movement of the 1930's, the socialism of Norman Thomas, could not afford the luxury of the earlier belief in the inevitable course of history. It was forced to take stands on the particular issues of the day. But it too rejected completely the premises of the society which shaped these issues. In effect, the Socialist party acknowledged the fact that it lived "in" the world, but refused the responsibility of becoming a part "of" it.

But such a straddle is impossible for a *political* movement. It was as if it consented to a duel, with no choice regarding weapons, place, amount of preparation, etc. Politically, the consequences were disastrous. Each issue could only be met by an ambiguous political formula which would satisfy neither the purist nor the activist, who lived with the daily problem of choice. When the Loyalists in Spain demanded arms, for example, the Socialist party could only respond with a feeble policy of "workers aid," not (cap-italist) government aid; but to the Spaniard, arms, not theoretical niceties, were the need of the moment. When the young trade-unionists, whom the socialists seeded into the labor movement, faced the necessity of going along politically with Roosevelt and the New Deal in order to safeguard progressive legislative gains, the socialists proposed a "labor party," rather than work with the

Democrats, and so the Socialist party lost almost its entire trade-union base. The threat of fascism and World War II finally proved to be the clashing rocks through which the socialist argonauts could not row safely. How to defeat Hitler without supporting capitalist society? Some socialists raised the slogan of a "third force." The Socialist party, however, realized the futility of that effort; in characteristic form, it chose abnegation. The best way to stem fascism, it stated, "is to make democracy work at home." But could the issue be resolved other than militarily? The main concern of the anti-fascist movement had to be with the political center of fascist power, Hitler's Berlin, and any other concern was peripheral.

In still another way the religious, chiliastic origin of modern socialism revealed itself: in the multiplication of splits, in the constant formation of sectarian splinter groups, each hotly disputing the other regarding the true road to power. Socialism is an eschatological movement; it is sure of its destiny, because "history" leads it to its goal. But though sure of its final ends, there is never a standard for testing the immediate means. The result is a constant fractiousness in socialist life. Each position taken is always open to challenge by those who feel that it would only swerve the movement from its final goal and lead it up some blind alley. And because it is an ideological movement, embracing all the realm of the human polity, the Socialist party is always challenged to take a stand on every problem from Vietnam to Finland, from prohibition to pacifism. And, since for every two socialists there are always three political opinions, the consequence has been that in its inner life the Socialist party has never, even for a single year, been without some issue which threatened to split the party and which forced it to spend much of its time on the problem of reconciliation or rupture. In this fact lies one of the chief clues to the fecklessness of American socialism as a *political movement* in the last thirty years.‡ But if in politics it proved to be impotent, it remained a moral force, and in Norman Thomas it had a new signpost.

‡ Beyond the reaches of this essay is the problem of the psychological types who are attracted by a sectarian existence. Yet one might say that the illusion of settling the fate of history, the mimetic combat on the plains of destiny, and the vicarious sense of power in demolishing opponents all provide a sure sense of gratification which makes the continuance of sectarian life desirable. The many leadership complexes, the intense aggressiveness through gossip, the strong clique group formations, all attest to a particular set of psychological needs and satisfactions which are filled in these opaque, molecular worlds.

If Debs was, at bottom, the sentimentalist of American socialism, Norman Thomas has been its moral figure. A communist critic once sneered at Norman Thomas for entitling his study of poverty in the United States *Human Exploitation* rather than *Capitalist Exploitation*. The critic, unwittingly, had a point, for what aroused Thomas was not the analytical and sociological but the ethical and emotional. Intellectually, Thomas would know that "the system" is to blame; but such abstractions rarely held meaning for him. His interest had always been the personal *fact* of injustice, committed by individuals; and while socialism might analyze the impersonal "basic" causes, he was always happiest when he could *act* where the issue was immediate and personal. In speaking out against sharecropper terror in Birdsong, Arkansas; in defying martial law in Terre Haute, Indiana; in exposing the Klan in Tampa; in uncovering the municipal corruption of Jimmy Walker's New York; in combating the anti-free-speech ordinances of Jersey's Boss Hague—in all these instances, Thomas' voice rang out with the eloquent wrath of an Elijah Lovejoy or of a William Lloyd Garrison.

These impulses came naturally to Norman Mattoon Thomas. Religion, orthodox Presbyterianism, was the center of his boyhood home. His father was a minister, as was his Welsh-born grandfather. He was raised in a strict sabbatarian code, but the harshness of his ancestral Calvinism was modified by the kindness of his parents. "My father who believed theoretically in eternal damnation," wrote Thomas, "would never say of any one that he was damned."[13]

Thomas, born in Marion, Ohio, in 1884, was a sickly little boy who grew too fast, became an awkward, skinny kid, shy with his peers and talkative with his elders, and who found his main satisfaction in reading. Norman was the eldest of six children, and the family was always busy with household chores and other activities of small-town middle-class life. Of the parents, Emma Mattoon was the more outstanding personality, and "father was content to have it so." In thinking back on his boyhood in the small Ohio town, Thomas remarked: "What a set-up for the modern psychologically-minded biographer or novelist. A study in revolt born of reaction from Presbyterian orthodoxy and the Victorian brand of Puritanism in a midwest setting. The only trouble is that this isn't what happened."

With the financial help of an uncle, Thomas satisfied a boyhood dream and entered Princeton, graduating in 1905 as class valedictorian. Entering the ministry was a more or less destined fact. But in the age of genteel faith in progress, acceptance of the old orthodoxies seemed out of place. As with many social-minded ministers of the day, the modernist and liberal gospel of Walter Rauschenbusch had its appeal. But it was the filth and poverty of the coldwater flats of the Spring Street slums on New York's west side that turned Thomas actively to social reform. And it was World War I and the influence of the Fellowship of Reconciliation, a religious pacifist organization, that made him a socialist. "God, I felt, was certainly not the 'God and Father of Our Lord Jesus Christ' if his servants could only serve him and the cause of righteousness by the diabolic means of war." Thomas' stand took him from the ministry into politics and journalism. (Rather than endanger the financial support his church received, he resigned the pastorate.) A tall handsome man with strongly-etched patrician features, rich resonant voice, and fine American credentials, he quickly became an outstanding leader in a party depleted of public figures. In 1924 he was nominated for governor of New York; four years later—because the two veteran party leaders, Morris Hillquit and Victor Berger, were European-born and because Dan Hoan was busy being mayor of Milwaukee—Thomas was nominated for the presidency.

As a party leader, Thomas had two serious flaws. For one, he strikingly distrusted his own generation and surrounded himself with considerably younger men who stood in an admiring and uncritical relation to him. The other was a profound fear of being manipulated, so that every political attack was taken personally. Unlike Debs, Thomas was intent on being party leader. Often a situation would develop—particularly in the late thirties—when, if party policy tended in a direction other than his, Thomas would threaten to resign (otherwise how could he speak on an issue with pure conscience?). Yet many of Thomas' decisions were made not with an eye to the political results but to the moral consequences as he saw them. Moreover, by background and temperament, Thomas was concerned largely with issues rather than ideas. In a party whose main preoccupation has been the refinement of "theory" even at the cost of interminable factional divisions, Thomas' interest in specific issues often meant shifting alliances with different factions while maintaining aloofness from the jesuitical debates that gave rise to these groups. Thus in the late thirties Thomas was with the right wing on the labor-party issue and shifted to the pacifist and left wing on the war problem. Thomas was probably most unhappy during the early and middle thirties, when, as a professed non-Marxist, he was involved in the conflicts of fifty-seven varieties of claims to revolutionary orthodoxy.

As a man whose instincts were primarily ethical, Thomas was the genuine moral man in the immoral society. But as a political man he was caught inextricably in the dilemmas of expediency, the relevant alternatives, and the lesser evil. As a sophisticated modern man, Thomas was acutely aware of his ambiguous role and felt he made the political choice. "One is obliged," he wrote in 1947, "to weigh one's actions in terms of relative social consequences . . . and the tragedy is that no choice can be positively good. . . . Positively [the pacifists] had nothing to offer in the problem of stopping Nazism before its triumph could not only enslave but corrupt the world. Nothing, that is, except for a religious faith in the power of God, a faith stronger if it could include a belief in immortality. It was something but not enough to affirm that the method of war was self-defeating for good ends. It was not enough to say 'if all Americans would act like Gandhi' we should more surely defeat avowed fascism. Possibly, but since almost no Americans would thus act the question remained of the lesser evil." Thomas did learn the lesson of the lesser evil: instead of being an absolute pacifist, however, he became an indecisive one. When the Franco rebellion broke out, Thomas gave up his religious pacifism, but was led to an ambiguous distinction whereby he supported the right of individuals to volunteer and fight but not "American official intervention by war which would involve conscription." After Pearl Harbor, Thomas came out in "critical support" of the United States government, a position which consisted in the first years largely of ignoring foreign policy and of speaking out against injustices on the home front. Fearful of another split, the Socialist party adopted a formula sufficiently elastic and ambiguous to permit pacifists, anti-war socialists, and pro-war socialists to continue together inside the party.[14] But to little avail. No one was satisfied with the compromise, and since factions were robbed of the incentive to split, the members simply resigned. From that point on, the Socialist party simply wasted away.

The Alien Outsider

For the twentieth-century Communist, there are none of these agonizing problems of ethics and politics. He is the perpetual alien living in the hostile enemy land. Any gestures of support, any pressure for social reforms, are simply tactics, a set of Potemkin villages, the façades to be torn down after the necessary moment for deception has passed. His is the ethic of "ultimate ends"; only the goal counts, the means are inconsequential.[15] Bolshevism thus is neither in the world nor of it, but stands outside. It takes no responsibility for the consequences of any act within the society nor does it suffer the tension of acquiescence or rejection. But the Socialist, unlike the Communist, lacks that fanatical vision, and so faces the daily anguish of participating in and sharing responsibility for the day-to-day problems of the society.

It is this commitment to the "absolute" that gives Bolshevism its religious strength. It is this commitment which sustains one of the great political myths of the century, the myth of the iron-willed Bolshevik. Selfless, devoted, resourceful, a man with a cause, he is the modern Hero. He alone, a man of action, a soldier for the future, continues the tradition of courage which is the aristocratic heritage bestowed on Western culture and which has been devitalized by the narrow, monetary calculus of the bourgeoisie. (Can the businessman be the Hero?) Such is the peculiar myth which has taken deep hold among many intellectuals. It is a myth which is also responsible for the deep emotional hatred and almost pathologic resentment felt most keenly by the ex-communist intellectual, the "defrocked priest," toward the party. For the "Bolshevik," through the myth of absolute selflessness, claims to be the "extreme man," the man of no compromise, the man of purity. The intellectual, driven to be moral, fears the comparison and resents the claim. Thus he bears either a sense of guilt or a psychological wound.

In addition to the myth of the Bolshevik as iron-willed Hero, twentieth-century communism has made several other distinctive contributions to the theory and practice of modern politics. Like so many other social doctrines, these were never put down systematically in a fully self-conscious fashion; yet over the years they have emerged as a coherent philosophy. Of these contributions some five can be linked schematically. These are central for understanding the history of the Communist party in this country.

One of the major innovations of the Bolsheviks is their theory of power. Against the nineteenth-century liberal view which saw social decisions as a reconciliation of diverse interests through compromise and consensus—this was a theory which social democracy gradually began to accept after World War I, when it was called upon to take responsibility for governments—power was defined as a monopoly of the means of coercion. Power was thought of almost in terms of physics, its equation being almost literally "mass times force equals power." The individual, central to the liberal theory of a market society, was for the Bolshevik a helpless entity. Only the organized group counted, and only a mass base could exert social leverage in society.

But a mass requires leadership. The great unresolved dilemma of Marxian sociology was the question of how the proletariat achieves the consciousness of its role. To await the immanent development of history was to rely on the fallacy of misplaced abstraction. "Spontaneity" was not for Lenin a reality in mass politics; nor was the trade-union an effective instrument. His answer, the most significant addition to revolutionary theory, was the vanguard role of the party.

Against the "economism" which glorified the role of the trade-union, Lenin argued that the mere organization of society on a trade-union basis could only lead to wage consciousness, not revolutionary consciousness; against the spontaneity theories of Rosa Luxemburg he argued that the masses, by nature, were backward. Only the vanguard party, aware of the precarious balance of social forces, could assess the play and correctly tip the scales in the revolutionary direction. This was the classic formulation of revolutionary avant-gardism which Lenin outlined in his *What Is to Be Done?*

In it he wrote that without the "dozen" tried and talented leaders —and talented men are not born by the hundred—professionally trained, schooled by long experience, and working in perfect harmony, no class in modern society is capable of conducting a determined struggle. "I assert," said Lenin, "(1) that no movement can be durable without a stable organization of leaders to maintain continuity; (2) that the more widely the masses are spontaneously drawn into the struggle and form the basis of the movement, the more necessary it is to have such an organization and the more stable must it be (for it is much easier for demagogues to sidetrack the more backward sections of the masses); (3) that the organization must consist chiefly of persons engaged in revolution as a profession."[16]

If the party were to become a vanguard, it needed discipline in action, and thus there arose the principle of party hierarchy and "centralism." A line was laid down by the leadership which was binding on all. Lenin's promulgation of these doctrines in 1903 split Russian socialism and brought about the emergence of the Bolshevik and Menshevik factions. In the beginning Trotsky opposed Lenin's ideas, but later he capitulated. As he wrote in his autobiography: ". . . there is no doubt that at that time I did not fully realize what an intense and imperious centralism the revolutionary party would need to lead millions of people in a war against the old order. . . . Revolutionary centralism is a harsh, imperative and exacting principle. It often takes the guise of absolute ruthlessness in its relation to individual members, to whole groups of former associates. It is not without significance that the words 'irreconcilable' and 'relentless' are among Lenin's favorites."[17]

From the principle of power and the theory of party organization rose two other key tenets of Bolshevism. One was the polarization of classes. Because it looked only toward the "final conflict," Bolshevism split society into two classes, the proletariat and the bourgeoisie. But the proletariat could only be emancipated by the vanguard party; hence anyone resisting the party must belong to the enemy. For Lenin, the maxim of the absolute ethic meant that "those who are not for me are against me." Hence, too, a formulation of the theory of "social fascism," which in the early 1930's branded the Social Democrats rather than Hitler as the chief enemy and led the Communists to unite, in several instances, with the Nazis in order to overthrow the German Republic.

The second tenet, deriving from the backward nature of the masses, was the key psychological tactic of formulating all policy into forceful slogans. Slogans dramatize events, make issues simple, and wipe out the qualifications, nuances, and subtleties which accompany democratic political action. In his chapter on slogans[18] Lenin wrote one of the first manuals on modern mass psychology. During the Revolution, the Bolsheviks achieved a flexibility of tactic by using such slogans as "All Power to the Soviets," "Land, Peace, and Bread," etc. The basic political tactic of all Communist parties everywhere is to formulate policy primarily through the use of key slogans which are transmitted first to the party rank and file and then to the masses.

The consequence of the theory of the vanguard party and its relation to the masses is a system of "two truths," the *consilia evangelica,* or special ethics endowed for those whose lives are dedicated to the revolutionary ends, and another truth for the masses. Out of this belief grew Lenin's famous admonition: one can lie, steal, or cheat, for the cause itself has a higher truth.

Except for the period from 1935 to 1945, the decade of fascism and war, the Communist party did not achieve any sizable following in the United States. In the misnamed "Red Decade," the Communist party, though never a national political force, did achieve important influence in the CIO (controlling at one time unions with about 20 per cent of the membership of the Congress, but, more important, holding almost all the major staff positions in the national CIO and running the large state and city CIO councils in New York, Illinois, California, and other key states) and did attain a position of respectability in the liberal and cultural community of the country.

The greatest triumph of Communist propaganda—the fifth innovation—was the creation of the papier-mâché front organizations. These fronts, sought to "hook" famous names and exploit them for Communist causes by means of manifestoes, open letters, petitions, declarations, statements, pronouncements, protests, and other illusions of opinion ground-swells in the land. The viciousness of the front technique was that it encouraged a herd spirit whereby only "collective opinion" carried weight; and if a critic dared challenge a tenet of Soviet faith, he was drowned out by the mass chorus of several score voices. As Eugene Lyons put it: "Did rumor-mongers charge that a horrifying famine had been enforced by the Kremlin to 'punish' forty million Soviet citizens in an area as large as the United States? Half a hundred experts on nutrition and agronomy, all the way from Beverly Hills to Park Avenue penthouses, thereupon condemned the capitalists and Trotskyites responsible for the libel, and the famine was liquidated."

The corruption of the front technique was that many poor dupes, imagining that they were the leaders of the great causes, found themselves enslaved by the opium of publicity and became pliable tools of the Communist manipulators behind the scenes. In other instances upper-class matrons and aspiring actresses found in the Communist "causes" a cozy non-conformism to replace their passé conventions. The ultimate betrayal was of the masses of front members who gained a sense of participation which they sadly discovered to be spurious when the party lines changed and they found that they themselves were victims of party manipulations.

But such influence was only possible because the Communist party was, at the time, moving in parallel direction with the liberal community whose emotions had been aroused by Hitler and Franco. Because of its superior organization, the Communist party was able to assume the leadership of many "causes." And yet, curiously enough, its very success was almost a corrupting influence. In the late 1930's, in the days of the Popular Front, the Communists suddenly found themselves accepted in areas (labor movement, Hollywood, urban politics) where they had been ostracized or scorned. But the Popular Front was a tactic. It had been dictated by Moscow as part of its policy of seeking national alliances. The Communists had not given up their belief in revolution or power; the liberals were a force to be manipulated. In 1943, however, in the so-called Teheran phase of national unity, there was a new phase. Browder took the decisive step of dissolving the Communist party as a political party and reconstituting it as a political association. But more than tactics was involved. The previous success in the Popular Front had given the party a new perspective. Browder himself was pleased by the new recognition and respectability of the party. In place of the Socialist party, it was becoming the acknowledged "left," occupying a "legitimate" place in American life. How far this revisionism would have gone is a moot point, for in 1945, abruptly and savagely, Browder was dumped, and the party was ordered into a new, sectarian phase, in accordance with the new, anti-Western aggressive line of Moscow. The Wallace campaign of 1948 was a desperate effort to salvage the old liberal support for the new extreme line. But the effort only resulted in isolating the Communists from the labor and liberal movements and leading to their exclusion.

In sum, the main appeal of the Communist party was to the dispossessed intelligentsia of the depression generation and to the "engineers of the future" who were attracted by the elitist appeal described above. It stirred many Americans to action against injustices and left them with burnt fingers when, for reasons of expediency, the party line changed and the cause was dropped. It provided an unmatched political sophistication to a generation that went through its ranks, and it gave to an easy-going, tolerant, sprawling America a lesson in organizational manipulation and hard-bitten ideological devotion which this country, because of its tradition and temperament, found hard to understand. But most of all, through the seeds of distrust and anxiety it sowed, communism helped spawn a reaction, a hysteria and bitterness that democratic America may find hard to live down in the years ahead.

From the sixteenth-century chiliast, burning with impatient zeal for immediate salvation, to the twentieth-century American labor leader, sunning himself on the sands of Miami Beach, is a long, almost surrealist jump of history. Yet these are antipodal figures of a curving ribbon which binds all movements that have sought to change the hierarchical social order in society.

The chiliast and the anarchist live in crisis, at the edge of History, expecting the world to be changed in a flash. The Bolshevik identifies himself with History and confidently expects that the turn of the wheel will put him forward, replacing the old. For these, then, the questions of social compromise, of the tension of ethics and politics, have had no meaning. But for others, particularly the socialists, the dilemma has been insoluble.

Living in the world, one cannot refuse the responsibility of sharing in the decisions of the society. In the here and now, people do not live at the extreme (in the "entirety" which was Sorel's myth), but they live "in parts," parceling out their lives amidst work, home, neighborhood, fraternal club, etc. Nor does History, as Acton put it, "work with bottled essences." Compromise is the "soul if not the whole of politics . . . and progress is along diagonals." For the socialist movement, living in but not of the world, it was a wisdom which it could not accept. Doctrine remained; but the movement failed.

NOTES

1. Letter to Danielson, No. 169, and Letter to Schleuter, No. 222, in *Karl Marx and Friedrich Engels; Selected Correspondence, 1846–1895* (New York, 1934), pp. 360 and 497.
2. Quoted in Goetz A. Briefs, *The Proletariat* (New York, 1937), p. 193. Communist economists, embarrassed by this situation, have tried to deny this material gain. A statistician, Jurgen Kuczynski (now an official of the East German government), argued, in an effort to defend Marx's proposition of the growing impoverishment of the working class under capitalism, that the living conditions of the American workers in the nineteenth century had actually deteriorated. Confronted from his own evidence with the fact that real wages had increased from 1790 to 1900, Kuczynski fell back on the Leninist theory that capitalism divided the workers into a labor aristocracy that did benefit and that in effect was bribed by higher wages, and a larger group of exploited masses. But this was only a rhetorical rather than a statistical claim. See Jurgen Kuczynski, *A Short History of Labour Conditions under Industrial Capitalism* (Vol. II of *The United States of America, 1789 to the Present Day*) (London, 1943).
3. A general hypothesis, such as the one above, can, however, only suggest an answer. It states conditions; it sensitizes one to questions. But the empirical inquiry into the fate of social movement has to be pinned to the specific questions of time, place, and opportunity. A social movement, like an individual, defines its character in the choices it makes. Therefore, one has to locate the "crisis points," define the alternatives which confronted the movement, and understand the motives for the choices made. In my monograph "The Background and Development of Marxian Socialism in the United States," I have tried to locate such turning points in American Socialism. (See Egbert and Persons [eds.], *Socialism and American Life* [Princeton, 1952], pp. 215–404.)
4. Cited in Gertrude Himmelfarb, "The American Revolution in the Political Theory of Lord Acton," *Journal of Modern History*, December 1949, p. 312.
5. "Politics as a Vocation," in *From Max Weber: Essays in Sociology*, eds. H. H. Gerth and C. W. Mills (New York, 1946), pp. 119ff.; also p. 9.
6. Karl Mannheim, *Ideology and Utopia* (New York, 1936), pp. 190–93.
7. Georges Sorel, *Reflections on Violence* (3d ed.; Glencoe, Ill., 1950), p. 140.
8. In *The German Ideology* Marx poses the question of how self-interest becomes transformed into ideology. "How does it come about," he asks, "that personal interests continually grow, despite the persons, into class-interests, into common interests which win an independent

existence over against individual persons, in this independence take on the shape of general interests, enter as such into opposition with the real individuals, and in this opposition, according to which they are defined as general interests, can be conceived by the consciousness as ideal, even as religious, sacred interests?" But Marx, exasperatingly, never goes on to answer the question. (See *The German Ideology* [New York, 1939], p. 203.) Sidney Hook, in his article on "Materialism" in the *Encyclopedia of the Social Sciences* (New York, 1933), X, p. 219, sought to rephrase the problem of consciousness in these terms: "What are the specific mechanisms by which the economic conditions influence the habits and motives of classes, granted that individuals are actuated by motives that are not always a function of individual self-interest? Since classes are composed of individuals, how are class interests furthered by the non-economic motives of individuals?" But having phrased it more sharply, he too left it as a question. So far no Marxist theoretician has yet detailed the crucial psychological and institutional nexuses which show how the "personifications" or masks of class role are donned by the individual as self-identity.

9. The question of how the proletariat achieves self-consciousness, and of the role of the intellectual, a person from another class, as the leader of the proletariat, long bedeviled the radical movement. In Marx's writings there are three different conceptions of class. In the *Communist Manifesto* there is the eschatological view in which the *Götterdämmerung* of history polarizes society into two classes and awareness of class position arises from beholding the widening abyss. In the conclusion to *Das Kapital,* Marx begins a simplified analysis of "essential" class division (i.e., as ideal types, rather than as reality) on the basis of source of income; but the conversion of income groups into congruent categories still begs the question of what the mechanisms of self-awareness are. Marx's actual historical analyses, as in *The Eighteenth Brumaire,* show a subtle awareness of the complex shadings of social divisions, which in action give rise to many varied social categories and diverse political interest groups. It is only, then, in "final" instances, rather than day-to-day politics, that class division and identity become crucial for Marxist politics. (For a discussion of Marx's theory of class, see Raymond Aron, "Social Structure and the Ruling Class," *British Journal of Sociology,* March 1950.)

10. It was in this statement, in the course of a debate with the Socialists, that Gompers first used the phrase, which later was to become the common description of the AFL, of unionism pure and simple. See Samuel Gompers, *Seventy Years of Labor,* I, pp. 286–87.

11. Ibid., II, p. 105.

12. Ray Ginger, *The Bending Cross* (New Brunswick, N.J., 1949).

13. Thomas made some autobiographical references in his *As I See It* (New York, 1932). The above questions, as well as some description of Thomas' beliefs, are from an unpublished memoir which Thomas wrote for his family in 1944 and to which this author had access.

14. A situation which provoked from Dwight Macdonald the comment: "The failure to split on the war issue has always seemed to me an indication of a certain lack of political seriousness in all the S.P. factions" ("Why I Will Not Support Norman Thomas," *Politics,* October 1944, p. 279).

15. "The believer in an ethic of ultimate ends," wrote Max Weber, "feels 'responsible' only for seeing to it that the flame of pure intention is not quenched."

16. V. I. Lenin, *What Is to Be Done?* (New York, 1929), p. 116.

17. Leon Trotsky, *My Life* (New York, 1930), pp. 161–62.

18. V. I. Lenin, "On Slogans," in *Toward the Seizure of Power, Collected Works* (New York, 1932), XXI, Book I, pp. 43–50.

COMMENT
John H. M. Laslett

Bell's major argument in this essay, which is probably the most influential attempt to explain the failure of American socialism to appear in the last twenty years, is that socialism failed in the United States because of its excessively dogmatic and chiliastic ideology, and because of continuing internal disagreements over the nature and purposes of the movement, which prevented it from translating its essentially revolutionary ideology into meaningful political action.[1]

In making this argument Bell aligns himself with those, on both the left and right wings of the political spectrum, who find the explanation for the difficulties which the socialist movement has always experienced in America in the internal dynamics of the movement, not in the exceptionalist character of American society.[2] Structural factors in the society which may have inhibited the growth of a strong socialist movement, such as those described by Sombart or Perlman in Part Three of this book, are dismissed by Bell as "conditions," not "causes," or "even if true, . . . [as] simply one side of the coin." The root cause of the problem, he argues in a much quoted passage, was that the socialist movement (although not the trade union movement, which made the necessary adjustments to American life) "was trapped by the unhappy problem of living *in* but not *of* the world: it could only act, and then inadequately, as the moral, but not the political man in an immoral society."[3] In the preface to a later version of his essay, Bell expands his theory (like Perlman attempting to generalize the presumed exclusive "job consciousness" of the American worker to include British, German, and Russian workers as well) to explain not simply the failure of the Old Left in America but also the difficulties faced by European socialism, and by the New Left, on both continents.[4] It was the ideological rigidity imposed by

Marxist theory, he argues, which prevented the German Social Democratic Minister of Finance, Rudolf Hilferding, from solving the economic problems of the Weimar Republic, because of the lack of sound Marxist teaching on remedying the shortcomings of a capitalist economy in the short run.[5]

Although the original "in" "of" metaphor derives from Martin Luther, the essential framework for this argument comes, as Bell acknowledges, from Max Weber's discussion of politics as a way of life. This is an important matter, since in the essay of Weber which Bell cites, Weber appears at first to confine legitimate politics to those which are limited to an "ethic of responsibility" (i.e., to "is" or present-oriented politics), and to reject those which are devoted to an "ethic of absolute ends" (i.e., "ought" or future-oriented politics), which are unacceptable if civil peace is to be maintained. Bell accepts this distinction, arguing that "the foundation of a pluralist society rests . . . on this separation of ethics and politics and on the limiting of ethics to the formal rules of the game."[6]

Aside from the inherent oversimplifications of this pluralist model, which presents a static, essentially ahistorical view of American society, and which—like the more extreme form of its corollary, the conflict model espoused by radical critics of recent American historiography—runs the risk of avoiding difficult historical questions by the way in which they are posed, this view comes close to imposing a moral imperative upon socialists *not* to interfere with the basic structure of the society, because to do so would run counter to the "rules of the game." It also betrays a major misunderstanding of Max Weber's meaning. Writing in the First World War under the impending chaos of the abortive German revolution of 1918, Weber's purpose was by no means simply to uphold the "ethic of responsibility" (i.e., the politics of minor adjustment and piecemeal change, now espoused by the older generation of American liberals, like Bell himself) as in all cases superior to the "ethic of conscience" (i.e., the politics of passion and commitment, now fashionable among their offspring), but to treat both kinds of politics as complementary to the other, and each as necessary to a dialectical process of social change. Weber certainly chided political chiliasts who ignored social realities, or who failed to take responsibility for their actions. But he disapproved also of political opportunists who sought to enhance their own position in society without any vision of a future world in mind. "Certainly all historical experience," Weber wrote later in the same essay, "confirms the truth—that man would not have attained the possible unless time and again he had reached out for the impossible."[7]

But the major issue is whether Bell's thesis itself is adequate as an historical explanation for the failure of the socialist movement in America, or for its limited success in other countries as well. And on this matter it is possible to have grave doubts.

In the first place, the distinction between "is"- and "ought"-oriented politics is, in the context which Bell is describing, very largely misplaced. All future-oriented social movements, whether political or not, suffer from an inherent tension between "is" and "ought," from feminism, which is semi-political, to the Committee for a More Effective Congress, which is overtly so; and one index of the health of a modern society (perhaps even of modernization itself) is the presence of an institutional framework which provides some means of resolving this tension in a rational way, usually through the medium of political parties. Nowhere is this more true than in the United States, where attempts to resolve the inherent tension between the future-oriented promises of the Declaration of Independence and *de facto* inequalities in the society have for two hundred years provided the major source of ammunition for political debate. (What other country has striven so mightily to translate the moral imperatives of the eighteenth century into twentieth-century political practice? Certainly not Great Britain or France, with their supposedly more ideology-laden revolutionary traditions.[8])

Seen from this point of view, the crucial issue becomes whether or not the American socialist movement, or any other socialist party, has been significantly less able than other future-oriented political movements to state its aspirations in realistic terms, and, when given the opportunity, to pursue them realistically as a matter of political practice. Bell answers this question in the negative, arguing that up until the First World War the American Socialist Party's supposed concern for converting the proletariat and advocating "immediate demands" was not pressed with any real vigor. Instead, the party refused to face up to the realities of the then contemporary political world, and simply "waited for the new." The war itself was the first major issue on which the Socialist Party took a genuine stand, forcing it "in" to the real world, but not yet making it a part "of" it. Thereafter, it "straddled" issues such as the Spanish Civil War and the Second World War, declining feebly into ineffectiveness in the period after 1945.[9]

Many of the assertions contained in this analysis are simply not borne out by the facts. Like the socialist parties of Europe, the Socialist Party of America had a long list of "immediate demands" attached to its Marxist preamble (several of which, like conservation, public ownership of the railroads, employees' compensation, and a graduated income tax, were also included in the platforms of reform-oriented parties such as the Populists, the Progressives, and the Wilsonian Democrats in 1912[10]). Like their European counterparts also, when presented with the opportunity it was these reform measures which the American socialists sought to implement, leaving the revolutionary phraseology of the preamble to rest in the shadows. In his longer essay Bell points to the antipathy displayed by the socialists toward their colleagues who gave support to reform-oriented groups such as the Nonpartisan League in North Dakota. But he ignores the much more widespread and characteristic examples of moderate, reformist activity which the socialists themselves undertook when elected to office. In Milwaukee, for example (the most important city in which the socialists held office), or in Berkeley, California, in Butte, Montana, or in various Massachusetts towns at the turn of the century, the socialists built moderately successful municipal administrations around hostility toward corruption, public works, improved sanitation, and a whole range of "gas and water" reformist measures which were no different from those being enacted in Birmingham or in Bordeaux. Such evidence makes nonsense of Bell's claim that, "Even on local municipal issues the party would not compromise."[11]

Socialist attitudes toward the official trade union movement were indeed somewhat more ambivalent, since Debs and a minority of more radical elements briefly supported revolutionary movements such as the IWW as alternatives to the AFL. Nevertheless, as I have argued in detail elsewhere, despite the attention which has been paid to them by labor historians, in the period before 1914 the influence of the "impossibilists" or extreme left-wing socialists in the labor movement was in fact very small. The IWW did not, unfortunately, secure more than a very limited foothold in any of the industries and trades then being organized by the AFL, with the possible exception of metal mining and coal, even during the period of its greatest strength (1905–17). And its dual-union activities did not prevent very considerable efforts being made—if one is to judge by money collected for union-led strikes, Socialist Party speakers invited to union conventions, and Socialist candidates elected to union office—to secure the support of the existing, frequently conservatively oriented trade unions.[12]

It is true that the First World War was the first important issue on which the American socialists took a virtually unanimous stand (the membership ratified the April 1917 St. Louis Declaration against the war by 21,639 votes to 2,752).[13] But it is wholly misleading to give the impression that the Socialist Party moved from a position of total rejection of American society in the period before 1914 to one of "straddling" it thereafter, and that in the 1930s it "acknowledged the fact that it lived 'in' the world, but refused the responsibility of becoming a part 'of' it." As already indicated, in its pre-1914 municipal and trade union policies the party had already made strenuous efforts to attract reform-minded moderates in the bourgeois world. It also "straddled" political issues just as frequently before the First World War as it did after. It is perfectly true, for example, that on the question of the Spanish Civil War (the touchstone of all left-wing consciences in the 1930s), the socialists "straddled" the issue insofar as they favored voluntary aid to Spain instead of direct government intervention—a position, incidentally, which was similar to that of most European socialist movements. But this was no different from the kind of "straddling" which the party had undertaken before 1917 on such issues as immigration, race, or the agrarian question.[14] In any event, "straddling" in the sense of obscuring ideological differences for the sake of united front is a sign of realism, not of rigidity; and far from being a vice, it is a time-honored American political virtue.

It is hard to escape the conclusion, moreover, that for Bell becoming a "part 'of' the world" in the 1930s would have meant little more for the socialists than becoming a pressure group within the reform wing of the Democratic Party. This was a course of action which by the 1950s the Socialist Party found itself impelled to take because of its continuing weakness—probably rightly if it was to avoid the total futility which remaining independent had brought to the SLP. But throughout the 1930s, with the communists monopolizing the fascism issue, and moderate CIO reformists usurping whatever position the socialists had made for themselves in the labor movement, the party leadership was aware that if it was to have any chance of exploiting the opportunities opened up for it by the Depression, to endorse the New Deal in its entirety—as Norman Thomas showed in his famous pamphlet *A Socialist Looks at the New Deal*[15]—would have meant committing political suicide. The party had come close to doing that once before—when it endorsed Robert M. La Follette for the presidency in 1924—and thereafter it was continually faced with the dilemma of trying to maintain a separate program which would be meaningful to the American electorate, while at the same time trying not to appear irrelevant. It was a dilemma created by attempting to come to terms with the realities of American politics, not by failing to do so.

More fundamentally, it may be argued that most of the difficulties with Bell's argument stem from the fact that he attempts to deal with both the socialist and communist movements in the same analytic framework, seeking to impute to the first of these two movements characteristics which more properly belong to part of—and only to a part of—the second. Throughout his essay Bell makes great play with the view that socialism as a movement originated with the impulse toward a secular form of chiliasm (deriving in turn from the spiritual chiliasm of the Reformation), the inability to find fulfillment for which allegedly leads to nihilism and despair—a final remark which reveals more about the contemporary New Left than it does about the Old. In fact, however, this chiliastic form of millenarianism describes only one psychological dynamic out of many which draw people to socialism (ranging from such apparently contradictory movements as anti-clericalism and Christian humanitarianism, to poverty and an aristocratic distaste for the brutalities of the industrial world), few of which, in themselves, imply the cataclysmic world view which Bell describes.

It may be true—it probably is true—that the communism of the 1930s, like other extreme revolutionary movements, attracted particularly those who had a desire to realize the millennium in the here and now. But by no means all socialists can be characterized in this way. Bell's oversimplifications here, as elsewhere in his book, result from his confusing the demise of the Old Left of the 1930s, and particularly the death of the old CP (i.e., the *End of Ideology*, or the end of the dominant radical impulse for Bell's own particular generation), with the death of socialist idealism generally, which as the rise of the New Left has effectively demonstrated is still very much alive. This confusion goes back, in turn, to Bell's excessively rigid distinction between Weber's "ethic of responsibility" and "ethic of conscience," which makes it difficult for him to recognize any form of politics which goes beyond the first to embrace the second.

In the 1890s, Daniel De Leon's Socialist Labor Party (which in its strict internal discipline and revolutionary commitments strongly resembled the Communist Party of post-1919) did indeed behave in a rigid and doctrinaire manner, repudiating the established labor movement in favor of dual unionism and dismissing "immediate demands" for legislative reform as irrelevant and "infantile." Similarly, the post-1919 Communist Party, acting this time at the bidding of Moscow and the Third International, showed little understanding or regard for the realities of American political life.[16] But in between these two dates, the Socialist Party of America (which was much more important than either of these other two movements) was—Bell's own remarks in the preface to his later essay notwithstanding—in many respects a genuine American political party, a regional and ethnic coalition of Marxists, ex-Populists, Bellamyites, trade unionists, and reformers which responded as pragmatically as could be expected of any future-oriented party, and certainly as pragmatically as most of its European counterparts, to the everyday exigencies of political life.

Bell's discussion of socialist personalities (limited to Debs and Norman Thomas) also reflects the dangers of attempting to encompass an entire movement within a single stereotype. His reference to the messianic character of Debs's rhetoric rings true, but here again his "is"-"ought," present-future dichotomy leads him astray. Most political rhetoric—virtually all American political rhetoric—is in some sense visionary or future-oriented, whatever ideology it purports to represent, and its function is to emphasize vote-catching generalities, not to indicate how a political party would act when once in power. Both Debs's sentimentalism and Thomas' moralism reflected quite different, but effective and respected elements in the American political tradition, the one redolent of William Jennings Bryan, and the other of Woodrow Wilson: both of them great contemporaries whom the two socialist leaders respectively resembled and admired.

It is true that neither Debs nor Thomas was a particularly effective party leader, and both tried to disassociate themselves from the Socialist Party's internal debates. But there were other men in the party, such as the machine-oriented Victor Berger or the practical Morris Hillquit, who were quite different from both Debs and Thomas—and who were in fact considerably more important than either of them in formulating party policy, at least until 1933—both of whom had the requisite "hard-headedness of the politician."[17] It was probably a net advantage to the party to have as its presidential candidates two men who tried to avoid being identified with any particular faction (although both were generally regarded as "left-wing" and after 1933 Thomas did intervene in party disputes, sometimes with disastrous results) around whom the faithful could rally at election time. It is worth adding, moreover, that neither Thomas nor Debs was quite as otherworldly even in their political rhetoric as Bell suggests. For example, Bell cites two or three phrases from a 1900 Debs article to suggest that Debs considered imperialism and the gold standard to be "meaningless phrases," and of no importance to the proletariat. In fact, the remainder of that article is devoted to an extensive attack on McKinley's foreign policy, showing Debs to be fully aware of its importance as an issue.[18] Thomas, by Bell's own admission, was not even a Marxist, but an issue-oriented reformer who was at his best, like the English Fabians, in delineating specific grievances and correcting them—hardly a chiliastic ideologue of the Daniel De Leon or William Z. Foster variety.[19]

It may still be said that even if the Socialist Party of America did resemble other political parties in the looseness of its structure and the diversity of its appeal, it still carried too much intellectual baggage to be a genuine American political party, and that it broke down because it quarreled over issues on which its members could not afford to disagree. There may be something to this, although my own view is that this has far more to do with a lack of access to power—or to influence in "other institutions" in the society, as Bell himself acknowledges, without exploring the idea fully—than it does with the character of socialist beliefs. It was no coincidence, for example, that the major splits in the Socialist Party occurred in the period after 1919, when it had been reduced to political impotence, and not in the period before World War I, when it was growing rapidly and had over a thousand of its members in federal, state, and local office. It is a truism of party theory that sectarianism and factionalism are diseases of political impotence, which diminish with the prospect of office; and it might well be illuminating to inquire more deeply into the influence erected by the Socialist Party's proximity to power upon the character of its ideology. Its conduct when in office, in Milwaukee, Reading, or Lynn, Massachusetts, suggests an ongoing conflict between an almost pusillanimous degree of pragmatism when in power and a narrower form of ideological militancy when out of it—a conflict which in itself may account for many of the party's internal conflicts, but which did not derive from the nature of its ideology as such. European comparisons make an even stronger case for the view that the successful growth of a socialist movement depends far more, as both Perlman and Sombart suggest, upon the presence or absence of certain structural factors in the society than it does upon the character of socialist ideology. (By "structural factors," I mean the nature of the class system, the extent of democracy, the distribution of wealth, and—although this is not usually included in a Marxist definition of structure—the character of the dominant values, as the Italian Marxist Antonio Gramsci, for example, defines them in his recently translated *Prison Notebooks*). Indeed, such comparisons appear to render almost ludicrous any argument which relies upon the nature of that ideology alone. In Germany, for example, the Social Democratic Party grew most rapidly in the first decade of the twentieth century during the period of the great revisionist controversy, which threatened to undermine the whole edifice upon which European Marxism had been built, and made the American socialists' quarrels over tactical and ideological matters seem petty by comparison. In England, the Labour Party took office in 1924 as much because of a split in the Liberal Party and the effects of the Lloyd George coalition upon the general political situation as because of any significant growth in working-class socialist convictions. And in Russia, the Bolsheviks clearly took power because of the collapse of the Czarist regime and the weakness of the Kadets and other liberal elements in the Provisional Government, despite the fact that by 1917 Lenin's doctrinaire (but tactically brilliant) insistence upon a revolutionary putsch had alienated not only the moderate Social Revolutionaries (who were prepared to establish a reformist government along Western political lines) but also many of his former Menshevik and Bolshevik supporters as well.[20]

How socialist parties behave when actually in power at the national level is, of course, a wholly different matter, and one on which the American experience can throw little light above the municipal level—although Victor Berger and Meyer London (the only two Socialists ever elected to Congress, and the nearest the Socialist Party of America ever came to power at the federal level) certainly showed no sign of being paralyzed by being "in" but not "of" the world.[21] Europe is a very different and much more important story, but even here it may be suggested that the inhibitions felt by Hilferding in Germany, by the second Labour government in Britain, or by the Popular Front in France resulted as much from the inherent difficulties of coalition government, from the preoccupation with fascism, and from a lack of political courage as they did from the rigidities or inadequacies of socialist theory.

It is true, as Adolph Sturmthal has pointed out, that in the depression years of the early 1930s the socialist (or socialist-dominated) governments of Britain and Germany (and in 1936 to some extent the Popular Front government in France also) remained prisoners of traditional laissez-faire economics (balanced budgets, stable currency, and reduced government spending), in part because orthodox Marxism provided few guides on how to counteract the cyclical operation of a capitalist economy, believing it necessary to allow the depression to run its course instead.[22] But in Sweden already in the 1930s, and in England and other European countries after the Second World War, once the lessons of Keynes had been fully learned social democratic regimes were able to operate a mixed economy and take steps toward social equality with at least some degree of success, without being caught up in the "in the world, not of it" conflict which Bell appears to believe dooms moderate socialist regimes inevitably to failure.

It can seriously be questioned whether the compromises which Attlee, Blum, or more latterly Brandt found it necessary to make with welfare capitalism in order to remain in power emasculated their earlier radicalism to such a degree that they could no longer be called socialists. In the same way it can be argued that after 1936 a similar rightward drift in the Socialist Party of America made it so reformist as to abandon all serious attempts at socialism—a development which was all the more serious for the American movement, since once Norman Thomas and Michael Harrington had made the American party virtually indistinguishable from the Democrats, they estranged the radicals without winning any new support elsewhere. But it cannot seriously be argued that these socialist leaders were chiliasts who had neither understanding of nor concern for the realities of political life. If anything, of course, precisely the opposite was true; almost to a man, the European so-called socialist statesmen of the 1930s and the 1940s (if they can be dignified with such a contradictory set of terms) were pusillanimous accommodationists who neither knew how to nor basically had any interest in fundamentally altering the capitalist system over which they temporarily exercised control. Even if either of these two qualifications had been present, however, myriads of other factors besides their particular brand of Marxism would have contributed to determining how successful or not they would have been.

Thus, the most serious weakness of Bell's argument is that he gives no satisfactory means of weighing the relative importance of ideology versus structural factors in assessing the reasons for socialism's failure, but simply *assumes* the primacy of ideological rigidity as the "root" cause, with only a passing reference to other possible factors. For the serious historian (and surely also for the serious sociologist) such mono-causal explanations as this must by definition be suspect; and in the absence of overwhelming evidence that ideological rigidity, or the difficulty of translating ideology into practice, *was* the main reason for the failure of socialism in America—which the evidence presented in this brief essay has attempted to refute—other explanations must be brought into play.

None of what has been written above should be taken to imply that the Socialist Party of America did not have a powerful left wing, or that there were not those who pressed it to behave in a more revolutionary way. Sometimes a Right-Center coalition dominated the Socialist Party, and sometimes a Left-Center one (as in the period from 1917 to 1920 or again in the 1930s).[23] But the ideological stand which the party took appeared to bear little relationship—although of course it bore some—to the size of its vote, or to the degree of its acceptance in the society generally. Viewing the American socialist movement as a whole (and including for this purpose both its socialist and communist wings, as Bell does), it is apparent that it went through periods in which "ought" or future-oriented elements were dominant, as well as periods in which "is" or present-oriented factions were in control. Neither approach worked. This surely implies strongly that we must look, not only at the nature of the movement's ideology, but also at the nature of the society in which it operated, if we are to arrive at a full explanation for its lack of success.

NOTES

1. Bell first put forward this thesis in a longer essay, "The Background and Development of Marxian Socialism in the United States," in D. D. Egbert and S. Persons, *Socialism and American Life*, 2 vols. (Princeton: Princeton University Press, 1952), pp. 213–405, the first portion of which constitutes the article under review. The entire essay was republished in book form fifteen years later as *Marxian Socialism in the United States* (Princeton: Princeton University Press, 1967), partly, as Bell rightly says in his preface, because "the theoretical and interpretative framework . . . has influenced many of the subsequent studies in the field" (p. vii). My own comments here are directed to the shorter essay, save where there are specific references to the longer one.

2. On this point (although on little else) Bell agrees with radical historians of American socialism, such as Ira Kipnis, James Weinstein, or Gabriel Kolko, who also espouse the internal dynamics explanation. This shows that arguments over American exceptionalism do not necessarily correspond to arguments between the political Left and Right, although they are often thought to do so.

3. Bell, *End of Ideology*, p. 268.

4. I intend no such blanket statement. By "failure" in this essay, as implied in the Preface to the book as a whole, I mean simply the inability of the Old Left in the United States (the SLP, the IWW, the SP of A, and the CP) to convert any significant number of Americans to the need for overthrowing or seriously modifying the capitalist system. Although I make some interim observations concerning the difficulties encountered by the European social democratic parties later on in this essay, I intend no judgment here as to the ways in which socialist beliefs may have influenced American intellectuals or writers, stimulated social reforms carried out by others, etc., nor as to the past or future prospects of the New Left.

5. Bell, *Marxian Socialism in the United States*, p. viii.

6. Bell, *End of Ideology*, pp. 269–70; Max Weber, "Politics as a Vocation," in H. H. Gerth and C. Wright Mills (eds.), *From Max Weber: Essays in Sociology* (New York, 1958), pp. 120–27.

7. Max Weber's meaning is important, for his distinction (which Bell wrongly erects into a dichotomy) between the "ethic of conscience" and the "ethic of responsibility" is a key element in the current academic debate over the "end of ideology"—and by extension in the debate over the failure of American socialism also, since Bell's interpretations of Weber lead him as if by logic to exclude the "politics and conscience" (including socialist politics) from the realm of the politically possible. See Weber, op. cit., p. 128; Stephen W. Rousseau and James Farganis, "American Politics and the End of Ideology," in *Brit-*

ish Journal of Sociology, XIV, 4 (1963); Chaim Waxman (ed.), *The End of Ideology Debate* (New York, Funk & Wagnalls, 1968).

8. Indeed, it may be argued that future-oriented political parties have a continued guarantee of relevance by virtue of their very future orientation (provided they espouse at least some of the ideals enshrined in their nation's political culture), just as conservative parties do, by virtue of embodying natural traditions. This is less true both of reactionary parties, and of middle-of-the-road parties whose ideology becomes anachronistic or obsolete, such as the British Liberal Party or the French Radical Party.

9. Bell, *End of Ideology,* pp. 274–77.

10. Kirk H. Porter, *National Party Platforms* (New York, Macmillan, 1924), pp. 323, 329, 336–37, 339, 343, 347, 361–68ff. In his longer essay Bell also argues that despite these "immediate demands" the Socialist Party of America rarely took stands on "current issues agitating the American body politic." On this matter, however, the presence or absence of specific demands in the party platform is not a reliable guide. The socialist press, which included over three hundred periodicals at its peak, frequently carried articles discussing issues of national importance, and leading party figures such as Debs, Victor Berger, and Meyer London wrote and spoke out often on agrarian issues, immigration, American foreign policy, the Negro problem, and other matters of contemporary concern. See Bell, *Marxian Socialism in the United States,* pp. 54, 74; Arthur M. Schlesinger, Jr. (ed.), *Writings and Speeches of E. V. Debs* (New York, Macmillan, 1948), pp. 63–73, 271–74, 293–310, 326–28, 337–40ff.; Victor Berger, *Broadsides* (Milwaukee, Social-Democratic Publishing Co., 1912), pp. 54–59, 60–68, 97–114, 121–26, 146–55, 256–63ff.; Melech Epstein, *Profiles of Eleven* (Detroit, Wayne State University Press, 1965), pp. 175–85.

11. Bell, *End of Ideology,* p. 274; Ira Kipnis, *The American Socialist Movement, 1897–1912* (New York, Columbia University Press, 1952), pp. 359–62; Edward Muzik, "Victor L. Berger: Making Marx Respectable," *Wisconsin Magazine of History,* LXVII (Summer 1964), pp. 301–8; Henry Bedford, *Socialism and the Workers in Massachusetts, 1886–1912* (Amherst, University of Massachusetts Press, 1966), pp. 69, 85, 102–4, 121, 131ff.

12. See Laslett, *Labor and the Left, A Study of Socialist and Radical Influences in the American Labor Movement, 1881–1924* (New York, Basic Books, 1970), pp. 289–90ff.

13. James Weinstein, *The Decline of American Socialism, 1912–1925* (New York, Monthly Review Press, 1967), p. 127.

14. Kipnis, op. cit., pp. 127–34, 217–19, 276–88.

15. Norman Thomas, *A Socialist Looks at the New Deal* (New York, pamphlet, Socialist Party of America, 1933), pp. 18–19ff.

16. *Daniel De Leon, The Man and His Work: A Symposium* (New York, Socialist Labor Party, 1919), pp. 26–30, 63ff. For the Communist Party, see I. Howe and L. Coser, *The American Communist*

Party, A Critical History (Boston, Beacon Press, 1957), pp. 73–76, 96–106, 236–72, 319–86ff.

17. For Berger, see Edward Muzik, "Victor Berger: A Biography" (Ph.D. Thesis, Northwestern University, 1960); for Morris Hillquit, see Robert W. Iverson, "Morris Hillquit: American Social Democrat" (Ph.D. Thesis, University of Iowa, 1951).

18. For this, see David Shannon's review of Bell in *Pennsylvania History*, XIX, 4 (October 1952), pp. 511–12.

19. This view of Thomas is sustained by Bernard Johnpoll's recent biography of him, which shows Thomas to have been most successful when he behaved like a liberal Democrat (over civil liberties, Jewish refugees, or the plight of southern sharecroppers) rather than as a third-party leader. Although undoubtedly a sincere social gospeler and democratic socialist in the early part of his career, by 1944 Dwight Macdonald could make a comment on him which still holds true: "My objection to Norman Thomas can be put briefly: he is a liberal, not a socialist. A socialist, as I use the term anyway, is one who has taken the first simple step *at least* of breaking with present-day bourgeois society. . . . His role has always been that of left opposition *within the present society*, the fighting crusader on small matters (like Hague-ism and other civil liberty issues) and the timid conformist in big matters (like the present war)." See Bernard K. Johnpoll, *Pacifist's Progress: Norman Thomas and the Decline of American Socialism* (Chicago, Quadrangle Books, 1970), pp. 146–52, 196–98, 200–4, 218–20; Harry Fleischman, *Norman Thomas, A Biography* (New York, Norton, 1964), p. 303.

20. On this point, see also the interesting remark made by an old socialist (unidentified) to Betty Yorburg in the collective biography of American socialists excerpted in Chapter One, as follows: "Danny Bell, in his analysis of the decline of the Socialist Party, talks about the [sic] 'program was in but not of the world'. Well, it's nonsense because everything that he said about the Socialist Party in the United States applied equally to the Socialist Party in France, in the Scandinavian countries, the labor parties or social democratic parties, the British Labour Party. The same kinds of compromises had to be made there. You had the same problems of factionalism within the parties. You had the right wings and the left wings." Yorburg, *Utopia and Reality: A Collective Portrait of American Socialists* (New York, Columbia University Press, 1969), p. 127.

21. During their congressional terms both Victor Berger and Meyer London pressed vigorously for nationalization of the railroads, a national insurance system, mitigation of unemployment, an end to child labor, and numerous other social reform measures which were also being sought by socialists in Europe. See Muzik, op. cit., pp. 143–68ff.; Harry Rogoff, *An East Side Epic: The Life and Work of Meyer London* (New York, The Vanguard Press, 1930), pp. 85–88, 229, 235ff.

22. Adolph Sturmthal, *The Tragedy of European Labor, 1918–1939* (New York, Columbia University Press, 1943), pp. 83–175.

23. See Weinstein, op. cit., pp. 119–33; David Shannon, *The Socialist Party of America, A History* (New York, Macmillan, 1955), pp. 204–48.

REPLY

Daniel Bell

The limitations of space imposed by the editors forbid a detailed reply. I will cleave, therefore, to the main problem: the Socialist Party "failed" in American life, failed to the extent that it did not have any significant influence *qua* party (I leave aside the influence of its ideas) in the politics of the society. Why?

Mr. Laslett has posed the issue as "ideology versus structural factors," but this is wrongly put, logically and methodologically. Structural conditions can never account for or explain social movements, for they can only specify *contexts* and *constraints;* what they omit is human agency. What my explanation sought to do—accepting the structural conditions—was to locate the failure of American socialism in the human agency, *the character of the party,* and to pose the question: why did not the Socialist Party perceive the structural constraints that are so evident to us now, and why did it fail to adapt to the conditions of American life—as, eventually, the European socialist parties adapted to the circumstances of their societies?

The root of the problem, for all socialist parties, goes back to the historic inevitabilism which was promulgated by Marx himself. As Marx wrote in the author's preface to *Capital:*

In this work I have to examine the capitalist mode of production and the conditions of production and exchange corresponding to that mode. Up to the present time, their classic ground is England. That is the reason why England is used as the chief illustration in the development of my theoretical ideas. If, however, the German reader shrugs his shoulders at the condition of the English industrial and agricultural laborers, or in optimist fashion comforts himself with the thought that in Germany things are not nearly so bad, I must plainly tell him, *'De te fabula narratur.'*

Intrinsically, it is not a question of the higher or lower degree of development of the social antagonisms that result from the natural laws of capitalist production. It is a question of these laws themselves, of these tendencies *working with iron necessity* towards inevitable results. The country that is more developed industrially only shows, to the less developed, the image of its own future.[1]

But history has not been that deterministic and the fate of countries, politically and industrially, has diverged markedly despite a similar capitalist foundation. One has only to compare the diverse fates of England, the United States, Nazi Germany, and imperial Japan.

The second fact is that the labor issue, as a class issue, which Marx thought would become the single overriding issue around which all society would be polarized, has not developed in that direction at all. Again, in *Capital,* Marx wrote:

Along with the constantly diminishing number of the magnates of capital . . . grows the revolt of the working class, a class always increasing in numbers. . . . Centralization of the means of production and socialization of labor at last reach a point where they become incompatible with their capitalist integument. This integument is burst asunder.[2]

But the working class has not grown in numbers but, in fact, relative to the work force has shrunk considerably while the major expansion, since 1910, had been in the professional and technical employments.[3] Equally important, the labor issue, while still rancorous, occasionally, as an *economic* issue, has become institutionalized and encapsulated while the occupational role has lost much of its force in molding the character and desires of the worker.[4] In advanced Western societies, the labor issue is no longer the single overriding issue with the ability to polarize the society and divide it solely into two irremediable and hostile camps. Institutionally, the trade union has become integral to the social structure of industrial society, and, in the process, has also transformed it. Those socialist movements which have been deeply engaged with the labor movements of their countries became transformed as well. (One can see this, finally, in the 1959 Bad Godesberg declaration of the German Social Democratic Party, which, revising the historic declarations from Gotha to Erfurt, declared that it was no longer a class party.)

This has been the main structural transformation of Western industrial society in the last fifty years. Those parties which have been under the compelling myth of Marx's earlier vision, or been seduced by the idea of revolution for the sake of revolution, never could understand the changed reality.

If one looks specifically at the American socialist movement, before 1917, the party was basically a chiliastic party in that it felt, as all socialist movements, that it was on the express track of History. The mood of the party was one of confidence, the confidence of all true believers that they know the path to salvation. It is no accident that a recurrent theme in party conventions was the question whether newcomers would be given the "front seats" in the party pews, since after all the leadership of the party carried with it the tickets to the doors of the future. The fundamental theme was the "purity" of the party and the unthinkability of any compromise with the bourgeois parties. That schisms existed was inevitable; they occur in all sects and churches. That some persons wanted immediate reforms and others only immediate revolution is true. But, at bottom, all factions agreed on this question of socialist purity. Left-wing historians assume that because there was a right wing in the Socialist Party (the extent of its rightism was that *some,* in 1910, wanted a Labor Party!), this right wing was "conservative" and willing to compromise. But that is not true. The right wing was united largely against the use of violence (though there was always the orthodox belief that if the party received "51 per cent" of the vote but was denied peaceful power by the capitalist class it would then resort to arms), but in its own way—on the issue of socialist purity—it was as dogmatic and sectarian as any left-wing group in the party. One has only to consider the views of Victor Berger in this light. He was right-wing, but equally a sectarian. The ideological blinkers were on tight for both groups.

After 1919, the Socialist Party was divided and confused. It now favored a Labor Party, rather than a pure-and-simple Socialist Party, and in 1924 it supported, of course, the La Follette-Wheeler campaign; but the weakness of the trade union movement precluded any labor political party. In the early 1930s, there was a chance for a reorientation of the socialist movement, but the influx of young, inexperienced, unemployed college youths and dispossessed lawyers led to a wholly new confusion. The Depression made it seem as if a revolutionary situation could develop in the United States. Franklin D. Roosevelt was seen as only a stopgap. The sense of *Götterdämmerung* was vivid. Much of Europe was going fascist and the young militants in the Socialist Party assumed, along with the communists, that as a capitalist society America, too, would inevitably go fascist, since fascism was the "last stage" of monopoly capitalism, and that the world had reached the show-down that Marx had predicted. So the party attacked Roosevelt, and went "left."

Again, history was misread and badly so. But the misreading of history was responsible for the split in the Socialist Party in 1935 and the weakening of the movement. From 1936 on, the rapid growth of the CIO led to the development of a progressive wing in the Democratic Party. Ironically, the CIO unions drew some of their strength from the very left-wing elements in the Socialist Party who a few years back had been most vocally "left and revolutionary," men like the Reuthers, Leonard Woodcock, Andrew Biemiller, Paul Porter, Jack Altman, and others. But by that point the Socialist Party had become almost completely sectarian and eventually these men left the party and joined the Democrats.

There is little point in rehearsing, again, this singular fact: at every possible turning point, e.g., the possibility of making a realistic adaptation to the political conditions of American life and joining with the labor movement as a ginger group, the forces of sectarianism won out in the American socialist movement. It is this which the historians have to explain in detail. It is this fact which is the historical puzzle regarding the failure of the American socialist movement, *qua* political party, to become a force in American life.

A note on Weber and the problems of ethics and politics: In Weber's view one could, ethically, adopt a "politics of responsibility," or a "politics of ultimate ends," and under certain situations both are moral stands. Each, pushed to a limit, however, ended in corruption: that of the politics of responsibility in hopeless opportunism, that of ultimate ends in a fanaticism and self-righteousness which results in the totalitarian confusion of means and ends. But central for Weber was the proposition that "the decisive means for politics is violence," and the question, therefore, is under what conditions can violence be justified ethically.

In a democracy, where peaceful means of persuasion are open to all viewpoints, it seems to me that the argument for a "politics of responsibility" is nigh irrefutable. What is important is the "rules of the game," the conditions of freedom which permit the play of all points of view. Where the socialist movement, until about thirty or so years ago, found itself in a profound confusion was the acceptance, from a vulgarized Marxism, of a historicized and relativized view of democracy. Democracy, thus, was seen not as a condition which men have repeatedly struggled for through the ages, and as a condition of the free political life, but as a class instrument and as "bourgeois democracy." In a different sense, Marxists could not believe in the relative autonomies of the economic and political systems and that, historically, political democracy had different roots and traditions in its conceptions of liberty than capitalist economics. For this reason, until quite late, the socialist movements were not prepared to defend democracy as a political fact independent of its economic substructure. The communists, never accepting democracy, were prepared to jettison it, and in the notorious instances in Germany in the 1930s, united with the Nazis to tear down the Weimar Republic. The socialist movements before World War II always faced the ambiguity of not accepting the ethics of ultimate ends but not, wholly, coming to accept the ethics of responsibility either. It was one of the fruits of living so long "in the world, but not of it."

NOTES

1. Karl Marx, *Capital,* Vol. I (Chicago: Charles Kerr, 1906), p. 13. (Emphasis added.)
2. Ibid., pp. 836–37.
3. For an elaboration of this argument and the statistical evidence, see my book, *The Coming of Post-Industrial Society* (New York: Basic Books, 1973).
4. This is a major argument of Ralf Dahrendorf in *Class and Class Conflict in Industrial Society* (Stanford: Stanford University Press, 1959).

Chapter 4

RADICALISM AND THE AGRARIAN TRADITION*

Theodore Saloutos

Agrarian discontent reached a boiling point during the late 1880s and early 1890s because of the sweeping changes that had brought about a downgrading of agriculture as an occupation and the upgrading of the non-agricultural pursuits geared to profit-making. The farmers felt especially grieved because they believed they deserved a better fate than the one wished on them. They reasoned they comprised the bulk of the population, paid most of the taxes, produced most of the food that sustained life and the raw materials that kept the wheels of finance, industry, and commerce going; and furthermore they were convinced they would continue to be the mainstay of American society in the future as they had been in the past. For this reason the economic health of the farmers had to be restored; for farming, in their opinion, was the most fundamental of all occupations, so fundamental that the survival of the nation hinged upon agriculture being elevated to a status of prosperity and prestige commensurate with its contributions to civilization.

Out of the welter of schemes advanced during this period to promote and protect the interests of the farmers, three stand out most conspicuously. The first sought to provide them with more and better social, cultural, and educational opportunities than they had in the past and enable them to enjoy some of the advantages long enjoyed by city people. The second was designed to right the economic imbalance from which the farmers suffered by bringing them higher prices for their goods and lower costs in terms of better marketing facilities, cheaper interest rates, lower taxes, and group buying. And the third was to resort to direct political action that would result in electing farmers, or friends of farmers, to represent them and their interests in public office. Since the main purpose of this volume is to deal with the question of why the

* Previously unpublished essay written for this collection.

American socialist movement failed to develop a major political movement based on all segments of the American working class, it is to the third, a political alternative, that I will address myself here. Each of these approaches was attempted, we shall see, and each of them was found wanting.

At least two courses of action were open to the political agrarians. At first the plan was to agree on a needed reform and then endeavor to persuade each political party to legislate to that effect; and if that failed, to devise some other method aimed to succeed. Although the conviction had grown that reform would have to come through legislative channels, this did not mean that a separate political party would be organized at the very outset. This, of course, was the other alternative.[1] But at first the agrarian politicos refused to attach themselves to either the Republican or Democratic parties, hoping to make both parties serve them.[2]

The agrarians were helped in their efforts by the crop failures and the low prices of the years just prior to 1890, and the existence of branches of farmers' organizations originally established to discuss issues of concern to farmers. Now these groups were being converted into political caucuses that were to aid the political transformation.[3] Many politicians were frightened by the thought of politically aroused farmers. Perhaps the words of a state president of a Farmers' Alliance served as a warning of what the farmers had in mind: "Being Democrats and in the majority, we took possession of the Democratic party. . . ."[4] In the South the farmers worked with the Democratic Party in 1890; but in the western states they worked for the most part outside of both the Republican and Democratic parties, although their strength was drawn more largely from the Republicans. In the general elections of 1890 the farmers elected governors in Georgia, Tennessee, South Dakota, and South Carolina. They also carried state tickets in Kansas, Nebraska, and South Dakota, and sent a total of thirty-eight representatives to the House and several senators to the United States Senate.[5]

Meanwhile the agrarian triumphs of late 1890 opened the floodgates of political action in a manner unprecedented in scope and intensity. Now the question had become not one of trying to get both parties to serve the interests of the farmers, but of whether to try and gain control of the Democratic Party or form a new party of their own. Opinion was badly divided. The southern agrarians for the most part were terrified by the thought of a third party because of the race question, but a small minority was willing to experiment with it; while the Middle Westerners were more favorable, but not overwhelmingly so, to the new party idea. Considerable thought also was given to the role that organized labor would play in such a new alignment. But in the meantime, the more persistent advocates of a new party had grown impatient and arranged for a meeting of the malcontents in Cincinnati on May 19, 1891, who assembled with representatives of organized labor and fired the opening salvo of the campaign of 1892. The net result was the formation of the Populist Party.[6]

The Populist Party, which in fact was the first farmer-labor party of major consequence, was based on the premise that the farmers and laborers had a common foe in monopoly, which had a stranglehold on the Republican and Democratic parties as well as on the arteries of money and banking, manufacturing, transportation, trade, and other facets of American life. Only when the forces of agriculture and labor were aligned into an effective political party could the interests of the farmers and laborers be protected. Naturally the support of the followers of Henry George, Edward Bellamy, the free silver advocates, and other reformist elements was sought in the crusade to wrest control of the government from the special interests and place it in the hands of the people where it belonged. The Populist Party believed that this could be accomplished with a platform asking for the free and unlimited coinage of silver, an increase in the amount of money in circulation, the graduated income tax, the secret ballot, the shorter workday, equality for women, the direct election of United States senators, and other proposals.

The results of the election of 1892 were encouraging, if not spectacular. The most impressive gains were scored in Kansas, where Weaver, the Populist candidate for President, aided by the Democrats, carried the state; and the entire state slate and five of the seven congressional seats were carried by Populists. Half of the votes received by Weaver in 1892 came from the Far West because of the singular interest of the states in this region to silver and not because of any broad commitment to the principles of Populism. One doubts whether the Populist Party would have made much of a dent there if it had not been for silver. In the South the achievements of the Populist ticket at the state level were minimal, and the results in the states east of the Mississippi River were hardly encouraging.

The reasons for the failure of the Populists to make headway in the eastern half of the United States were twofold. The agricultural economies of these states differed from those of the states in the Great Plains, hence their needs were different. The farmers in the older sections of the East had suffered from the expansion of agriculture in the newer sections and were disinclined to support the demands of the farmers of Kansas, Nebraska, and the Dakotas. The eastern farmers diversified their production and did not rely on a single crop such as wheat. Likewise the eastern wage earners continued to support the candidates of the two major parties, despite the special appeal the Populists made to them.[7]

How effective was this effort to achieve a working coalition between the farmers and the wage earners? As a rule the wage earners have been viewed as being more receptive to the farmer-labor ideal than the farmers, but the argument has been made, particularly by Norman Pollack in his book *The Populist Response to Industrial America,* that the Populists failed to develop a viable, long-range national farmer-labor party as a new alternative within the existing two-party system, because labor refused to give them the kind of support which the farmers gave. According to this line of reasoning, historians have erred in assuming that the real barriers to a viable farmer-labor party were the farmers because the favorable response they gave to it in 1891 would refute this. Perhaps the major obstacle in the way of this new alignment, the argument continues, was the lack of full cooperation from organized labor, especially from the American Federation of Labor.[8]

The validity of this thesis is open to serious doubts. The evidence in support of it is flimsy and tends to ignore the effects of the American experience on organized labor and the failures which labor had suffered from in the past when it chose to travel the road of politics; it also presupposes a strength and influence on the part of the American Federation of Labor which it did not have, and exaggerates the willingness on the part of the farmers to coalesce with labor.[9]

The position of the American Federation of Labor, when agitation for the formation of a third party began shaping up late in 1890 and early in 1891, was that of a relatively young and insecure organization seeking to become a fixture on the American trade union scene. For all practical purposes it was still feeling its way. Although the Federation was founded in 1881 it did not begin to get off the ground until 1886. More than anything else the Federation craved a secure footing, for the record of labor in general from the Civil War down to 1886, as its founders knew, had been one of youthful uncertainty, instability, and frustrated ambitions.[10] For one to suggest in the light of this evidence that the farmer-labor coalition failed because the Federation withheld its support is to overlook the impracticality of adopting such a course. It could have been suicidal for the Federation in particular if it had followed this course, and to the cause of the trade union movement in general.

One of the very things that the founding fathers of the Federation wanted to avoid was precisely the kind of entangling political party that the advocates of the third party were proposing. When the Federation was reorganized in 1886, the reorganization proceeded along lines that took cognizance of the prevailing conditions in labor circles and the political climate of the times. The men who helped organize and shape the policies of the Federation in the early years were men of experience. Some had once been members of, or had strongly opposed, the National Labor Union, the Greenback Labor Party, and the largest of the labor organizations prior to the formation of the American Federation of Labor—the Knights of Labor—who were disorganized, bankrupt, and almost extinct after having tried the political formula.[11]

Each of these movements, and the experiences shared by their former members, contributed in one fashion or another to the molding of the philosophy underlying the Federation. They had tasted the bitter fruits of political defeat and wanted to avoid it in the future. From the experiences of the National Labor Union and the Greenback Labor Party, for instance, leaders of the Federation had learned it was futile to try and build a political party based on alliances of farmers and small-business men pitted against the bankers and large-business men. Such alliances flourished in slump periods at best and then dissolved. Labor could not be lifted, and banking and big business could not be defeated, en masse. The immediate targets of the wage earners were the competing employers in the same line of business, and the ones most capable of taking effective aim were the employees of these competing employers, and no others. Finally, the cautious Federation leaders also knew only too well that hitherto no major labor organization had succeeded in surviving a major depression; consequently their primary task was not one of organizing to win political battles by direct political action, but of building a permanent organization capable of withstanding the ups and downs of the business cycle.[12]

The attitudes of the trade unionists, organized and unorganized, hardly lent themselves to the forging of an effective farmer-labor alliance. The trade unionist was interested in higher wages, lower prices on what he bought, and better working conditions today, tomorrow, next week, or next month at the latest, and not in the building of a millennium that would free men from the oppressions of an industrial society. Populism was as much a bread-and-butter proposition to those trade unionists who adhered to its principles as it was to those farmers who believed in it. Why should the trade unionist campaign for the free and unlimited coinage of silver which went to the essence of Populism, when this meant paying more for his food, clothing, and shelter?[13]

Another flaw in the argument that the Federation was a major obstacle to the formation of a farmer-labor coalition is that it exaggerates the importance of the Cincinnati meeting of May 19, 1891. In the first place the role of the farmers and their representation in the Cincinnati conference was minimal. When news of the forthcoming meeting was released the *National Economist,* the official organ of the National Farmers' Alliance and Industrial Union, better known as the Southern Farmers' Alliance, responded that the Cincinnati meeting "had no official sanction whatever from the National Farmers' Alliance and Industrial Union." The *Economist* also complained that the organizers of the meeting made no provisions "to get representation from the rural districts, and when the meeting is opened it will be found to consist of the same old crowd who have been at all times pulling so fast that they have discouraged thousands from joining the move. . . ."[14]

Just how one can imply that sheer attendance at the Cincinnati meeting was *ipso facto* evidence of success in the formation of a farmer-labor alliance is unclear. The Cincinnati meeting was not an Alliance meeting and it never was intended to be that. The Alliance at its last national meeting in Ocala, Florida, had provided for a general conference of all organizations of producers willing to cooperate to secure political reforms to be held in February 1892, agreeing at the time that all delegates from all organizations would meet on an equitable basis of representation, agree upon a set of demands and a method of enforcing them. Whatever action was taken in the February meeting on direct political action was to be taken with the understanding that the Alliance as an organization was to remain non-partisan.[15]

Among the most active advocates of the formation of a new political party, as Pollack points out, were the delegates from Kansas. However, many of these were of dubious agrarian origin, and felt that they were entitled to representation simply because they had left the Northern Farmers' Alliance to join the Southern. It is true that the Kansas delegates were very anxious to get the whole Alliance to support the third-party movement, but the large majority of the southern farmers who comprised the bulk of the membership were unprepared to desert the major party of the South. This reluctance of the Southerners to sever their relations with the Democratic Party did not deter the political ambitions of the third-party advocates from Kansas. The three Vincent brothers, the ones credited with drawing up the call, made the movement appear to have a broader base than it actually had.[16]

Observers substantiated the claim that representation from the South in the Cincinnati meeting was small; according to the *Daily Register* of Mobile, Alabama, the number of delegates in attendance from the entire South was thirty-six. Texas with a delegation of twenty-six had the largest representation by far, while Virginia, South Carolina, North Carolina, and Alabama were without any representation. If anything, the representation was largely Middle Western. The *Clarion Ledger* of Jackson, Mississippi, placed the number of delegates at about fourteen hundred, of which seven hundred were from Kansas and Ohio alone. To the *Times-Democrat* of New Orleans the meeting was more of "a gathering of all the political odds and ends in the country."[17]

The program of the agrarians was appropriated by the third-party people, if not the membership, and the editor of the *Economist,* who was opposed by many inside the Alliance, joined in the chorus of praise this time: ". . . the course pursued by the meeting has been so wise and conservative," he wrote, "that instead of conflicting (with the meeting of February 1892) [it] is destined to prove an actual benefit and supply the link that will unite the farmers with all other occupations in the great approaching conflict." He added that "the reformers of the country have met in mass meeting and unanimously agreed that the platform of the farmers adopted at Ocala, including the sub-treasury plan, shall be the basis of the great and inevitable reform fight which is now on, and that they desire to unite with the farmers and laborers to fight under the banner as a people's party in 1892; . . ."[18]

The Cincinnati meeting was neither the first nor the last of the political meetings attempting to capitalize on the popularity of the farmers' platform and to divert it onto a farmer-labor course. Witness, for instance, the developments in Chicago in the fall of 1894 in which the name of the People's Party was used in the campaign and on the official ballot. "But in all essentials the movement was a labor movement, having its first inception in a labor union, supported throughout by the efforts of organized labor and drawing its principal support at the polls from the manual working classes." Apparently, the aim of the driving forces behind this effort was to give the labor movement "a national character and an enthusiasm it can in no other way attain."[19]

The evidence is all too clear that the Cincinnati meeting, which was heralded as the great opportunity in forming a farmer-labor coalition, was not a farmers' meeting extending the hand of cooperation to laborers to join them in a great crusade. It was dominated by non-farmers with driving political ambitions. The astute reformers, labor leaders, crusaders, and other third-party advocates who sponsored the meeting were prepared to use the farmers, their organization, platform, and any other vehicle at their disposal to achieve their objectives. Some farmers, to be sure, were present but they were unrepresentative of the rank and file, and were too small in number to be significant.[20]

Gompers, in short, in pleading with members of his organization to avoid entangling political alliances, knew of what he spoke. He had no desire of belittling the efforts of the farmers or of withholding sympathy due them in their crusade; he was just looking after what he believed were the best interests of the workingman. He knew the history of the labor movement of this country, its strength and weaknesses, its hopes and frustrations; and he was most anxious to protect what gains had been made in a hostile climate. Future as well as past experiences were to bear out the wisdom of his decision.[21]

Radical analysts of Populism also seek to draw analogies and detect similarities between Populism and Marxism.[22] Unfortunately this analysis is built on shaky foundations. Populism, according to most experts, was an indigenous product, born on American soil and conditioned by the American experience. The European influence on Populism, except that emanating from the small minority residing in urban-industrial centers attracted to it because it was about as well organized and publicized a protest movement as any of its kind at the time, was minimal and found among the more labor-oriented members of the party. If it was radicalism, it was radicalism of the American variety rooted in the traditions of the Grangers, the Farmers' Alliance, the various farmer-labor coalitions formed at the state level, the monetary and bank reformers, and those hell-bent on raising the level of the common folk who for the most part were farmers.[23] To the Marxists this was rank opportunism, compromise, reformism, a sellout, nothing more, nothing less.

If Populism was more than agrarianism, as is claimed, it was only slightly more so, especially beginning in 1891, when non-farmers sought its protective covering and tried to capture the organization lock, stock, and barrel in the name of the farmers. Prior to that the farmers' movement was chiefly agrarian, farmer-oriented, and farmer-directed.

The attempt to view Populism through the eyes of the radical industrial workers of the East and Europe, instead of through the eyes of the disconsolate American farmers of the Middle West, Southwest, and South is tempting, but it is also misleading. This amounts to a certain torturing of the facts. To the more radical industrial elements both Marxism and Populism might have meant the alienation of man from his product, but to the agrarian Populist it was largely alienation from his land, his equipment, his animals, and his personal belongings which made it difficult for him to raise a good crop, market it at a profit, sustain his family, educate his children, and discharge his obligations. One cannot help but believe that the downgrading of the agrarian aspects and elevating of the radical industrial phases of Populism also has caused a number of observers to minimize the importance of the free silver issue, low farm prices, indebtedness, high interest and taxation rates. An understanding of the farmer sentiments on these issues is crucial to any understanding of the farmer-labor relationship that failed to materialize. The farmers might have felt sorry for the workers being exploited by the large corporations, but they also viewed themselves as being a cut or two above the wage earners.[24]

Much is also made in Pollack's book of the creation of tramps and vagabonds who were forced to wander in search of work.[25] That they were a product of the industrial system and a cause of great concern to society is beyond doubt, but others indicate that this has been overstated. Professor Jessy Macy of Iowa College, Grinnell, Iowa, attributed the great attention given to tramps to "the industrious writing of the newspapers," and added that "Iowa has not been greatly afflicted by tramps." J. W. Gleed of Topeka, Kansas, said pretty much the same thing. "Nothing would probably ever have come of the Coxey movement, but the newspapers took it up, and day after day and week after week we had columns of it in the papers all over the West." He also noticed that "the Coxies armies have come almost entirely from large cities and mining country."[26]

A more realistic and immediate concern of the agrarians was not so much the specter of tramps and vagabonds as it was the desertion of the farm, the exchange of the values of rural life for those of the "corrupt" cities, the breakup of the family, and the turning of one's back on the virtuous agrarian way of life. The protests of the more industrial-oriented members of the party that found their way into print in papers carrying the Populist label only after the party had been disappointed elsewhere have been over-emphasized and, as a consequence, left the impression of a party with a greater industrial complexion than the facts justify.

The farmers were genuinely worried about the corporations and monopolies. That there was a growing concentration of wealth is a matter of elementary knowledge. Agrarian suspicions and distrust of the bankers and banks, the railroads, large industrial corporations, the cities, the East, and urban-industrial opposition to the income tax which was designed to lift some of the tax burdens from the land of the farmers and place them on the earnings and profits of those who escaped paying their fair share of the load are traditional but valid arguments.[27]

In effect the third party, or farmer-labor party, failed in 1892 and again in 1896 not because of the unwillingness of labor to give it the support that farmers gave it, but because of certain deep and almost irreconcilable differences. In the first place it was very difficult to bring the farmers of the various sections, let alone of the nation, into an effective political organization because of regional variations and conflicting commodity interests. The race question was a barrier to the third party in the South and the crops produced in the states east of the Mississippi created interests and attitudes different from those of farmers living in the states west of the Mississippi. The farmers in the East suffered in part because of the expansion of agriculture into the West; why should they become a part of a movement designed to bring these farmers more money, cheaper credit, lower transportation rates, greater representation in government, and higher prices for their products?

Finally, the willingness of the farmers to enter into a direct political alliance with the city workers likewise has been overstated. The attitudes of the wage earners, organized and unorganized, hardly lent themselves to the forging of an effective farmer-labor alliance. The wage earners were pragmatists interested in higher wages, lower prices, and better working conditions as soon as possible, and not in building a millennium that would free men from the oppressions of an industrial society. Populism reflected a high degree of idealism, but it also was a bread-and-butter proposition to the rank-and-file farmers supporting it. The wage earner viewed it in the same light. Why should he campaign for the free and unlimited coinage of silver, which went to the essence of Populism, when this meant paying more for his needs?

NOTES

1. *Appleton's Annual Cyclopaedia, 1890,* p. 299.
2. Washington Gladden, "The Embattled Farmers," *Forum,* X (November 1890), p. 319.
3. Fred Emory Haynes, "The New Sectionalism," *Quarterly Journal of Economics,* X (April 1896), p. 271; *Appleton's Annual Cyclopaedia, 1890,* p. 301.
4. *Appleton's Annual Cyclopaedia, 1890,* p. 301.
5. Ibid.
6. William Peffer, *The Farmer's Side* (New York, 1891), pp. 159–60; Helen Blackburn, "The Populist Party in the South, 1890–1898" (M.A. Thesis, Howard University, 1941), pp. 8–9; *Nation,* 52 (May 28, 1891), p. 431.
7. John D. Hicks, *The Populist Revolt* (Minneapolis, 1931), pp. 254–69.
8. See Norman Pollack, *The Populist Response to Industrial America: Midwestern Populist Thought* (Cambridge, 1962), pp. 43–67ff.
9. *Report of the Industrial Commission on the Relations and Conditions of Capital and Labor,* VII (Washington, 1911), pp. 108–10, contains some informative statistical data on the strength of the major labor organizations and their weaknesses.
10. Ibid., VII, p. 108. Gompers pointed out that from 1868, when the National Labor Union held its last convention, until 1881 the country lacked a general labor organization built around a trade union basis.
11. John R. Commons, *History of Labor in the United States,* II (New York, 1918), pp. 482 and 495. See also *Report of the Industrial Commission . . . ,* VII, p. 110, on the mistake made by the Knights of Labor in entering politics. Norman J. Ware, *The Labor Movement in the United States 1860–1895* (New York, 1929), p. 351, points out that "the American Federation of Labor has been the least political of all."
12. Ware, op. cit., pp. 351–52.
13. Ibid., pp. 352–53.
14. *National Economist,* IV (February 21, 1891), p. 357.
15. Ibid., V (May 30, 1891), p. 161.
16. Pollack, op. cit., p. 63; Helen M. Blackburn, "The Populist Party in the South, 1890–1898" (M.A. Thesis, Howard University, 1941), pp. 8–9.
17. Ibid., pp. 15–16.
18. *National Economist,* V (May 30, 1891), p. 161.
19. Willis J. Abbot, "The Chicago Populist Campaign," *Arena,* XI (February 1895), p. 330.
20. Ware erroneously assumes that the Cincinnati meeting of May

19, 1891, was a farmer-dominated meeting (Ware, op. cit., p. 369). See Commons, op. cit., II, p. 494.

21. Samuel Gompers, "Organized Labor in the Campaign," *North American Review*, CLV (July 1892), pp. 93–95.

22. See Pollack, op. cit., pp. 68–84; Anna Rochester, *The Populist Movement in the United States* (New York, 1943).

23. The best analysis of grievances leading to the formation of the Populist Party is still found in John D. Hicks, *The Populist Revolt* (Minneapolis, 1931), pp. 54–95. Walter T. K. Nugent, *The Tolerant Populists* (Chicago, 1963), pp. 167–74, suggests that the foreign-born were receptive to the Populist program, but presents no evidence suggesting that their European experiences influenced it.

24. Theodore Saloutos, "The Agricultural Problem and Nineteenth-Century Industrialism," *Agricultural History*, XXII (July 1948), pp. 169–73; Theodore Saloutos, "The Populists and the Professors," Ibid., XL (October 1966), pp. 245–46.

25. Pollack, op. cit., pp. 25–42.

26. J. W. Gleed, "A Bundle of Western Letters," *Review of Reviews*, X (July 1, 1894), pp. 43 and 46.

27. Theodore Saloutos, *Farmer Movements in the South, 1865–1933* (Berkeley and Los Angeles, 1960), pp. 282–84.

COMMENT

Michael Rogin

Young American historians, seeking to ground the 1960s' radical revival in a usable past, turned to agrarian radicalism. Some offered Populism as an American equivalent for European Marxism.[1] Populism, however, was a movement of farm-owning proprietors, not property-less workers. It attempted to reassert local community control against the economic and political centralization of corporate capitalism.[2] Professor Saloutos, rightly seeing that Populism was not Marxism, has mistakenly read back the triumph of narrow, elitist, interest group politics into the Populist period.

Populism was a radical alternative to the political and economic forces dominating America, and its radicalism had deep and genuine agrarian roots. It did grow out of more moderate, rural efforts at business cooperation and major party pressure politics. But it was a striking departure from those activities. While much of the broad and respectable support mobilized by the Farmers' Alliances, particularly among town merchants, businessmen, and bankers, dropped away from third-party Populism, masses of southern and western farmers adhered to it. If, as Saloutos indicates, the 1891 Cincinnati meeting which pushed for a national third party was dominated by professional reformers rather than farmers, the degree of agrarian support for the third party is all the more significant. In 1892 Populism won more than one third of the vote in eight of the twelve northern states west of the Mississippi, and more than 20 per cent of the vote in every one but California. In 1894 Populist or fusion tickets won 25 per cent of the vote or more in eight of the eleven former Confederate states. Populism was strongly regional; it was weak in the Midwest, and non-existent in the Northeast. Nevertheless, it represented a sharp break with major party traditions and ruling elites in the South and West. In several southern states Populism even overcame the resistance of white farmers to political cooperation with blacks; it remains the only significant example of black and white farmer solidarity in southern history. A radical third party, advocating substantial government ownership and making a powerful attack on finance and industrial capitalist control of the country, evoked enormous grass roots loyalty and participation from southern and western farmers.[3]

It is misleading, moreover, to attribute Populist voting strength primarily to the issue of free silver. While half of the Populist 1892 *electoral* vote came from the western mining states, less than 8 per cent of its total popular vote did.[4] The silver issue did not dominate Populism until the last years of the movement, and even in the mining states, as we shall see, its significance was different than Saloutos suggests.

The Populist image was communal, not Marxist, but it was radical within the American context. Its lack of Marxism hardly alienated American workers. More significantly, many workers were attracted rather than repelled by Populist agrarian appeals. Saloutos believes that the conflict between rural and urban interests— symbolized by the inflationary silver issue—created an impassable gulf between farmers and workers. But the story is more complex. Populism was not a rural interest group simply, but an agrarian crusade. And the traditions of native American workers were agrarian and communal too. The American labor movement had historically aimed at independent producership, even land, for laborers. Like Populism, workers' organizations attacked monopolies in the name of community control. By the same token American workers often shared with Populism a fundamentalist, Protestant mentality, transmuted into movements for social reconstruction— the "holy work" as one southern worker called it.[5] In its religious and fraternal character the pre-industrial labor movement paralleled English developments, although in England the weight lay with workers, in America with farmers. This American working-class tradition culminated in the 1880s with the Knights of Labor.[6]

The Knights had disintegrated by the 1890s, but labor unrest remained widespread. Populism understood the strikes of the 1885–95 decade as worker efforts to reassert popular control over centralizing, capitalist society. In this savage, visible, and prolonged industrial class conflict Populists sided with the working class. They supported the railroad strikes which climaxed in the Pullman boycott of 1894. Local Populist newspapers served as Pullman strike organs, and some Populist clubs collected food for the strikers. Populists sided with workers against the militia in the 1892 Homestead Steel strike and massacre. They supported the coal and metal mining strikes of the 1890s. The Populist governor of Colorado intervened to protect striking miners from a local militia, the reverse of the usual procedure. Populists sympathized with the tramps and vagabonds roaming the country in the wake of the 1893 depression, either alone or in peaceful "armies," seeking redress of grievances. Coxey's Army was the most famous of these, but there were others as well; their presence was more widespread than Saloutos' sources, unsympathetic to Populism, indicate. It is particularly noteworthy that a movement of hard-working Protestant farmers sympathized with men who could not find jobs, and understood, as Kansas Populist governor L. D. Lewelling's Tramp Circular shows, the social causes of their itinerancy. Populists also supported a shorter working day for urban workers. Finally, they attacked the Pinkerton "hireling army" of private strikebreakers employed by capitalists to war on strikers and work in their place.[7]

Both Saloutos on the one hand and Pollack on the other have wrongly minimized the extent to which workers reciprocated Populist support. Yeoman farmers feared that the invasion of powerful, mechanized, external forces would destroy their independent farms and communities. Artisans in several trades faced a similar threat, as the rapid introduction of machinery undermined their autonomy, reduced their income, and devalued their skills. Whether shoe workers in Massachusetts or machinists in the South and West, many such artisans supported Populism. The railroad was perhaps the central Populist symbol of mechanized, external control, and workers in the railway towns of the South and West often voted Populist. Much of the membership of the International Association of Machinists worked in railway shops and supported Populism. The party also received votes in the coal-mining towns of the South and Midwest, and from metal miners in the Rocky Mountain states. The President of the United Mine Workers became a Populist after the disastrous coal strike of 1894. The UMW gave Populism active support, and several miners ran on Populist tickets. The silver issue in the Rocky Mountains, far from splitting farmers from workers, led to a farmer-miner alliance against the silver and copper mineowners. The 1895 convention of the Western Federation of Miners endorsed the Populist Omaha platform. In Montana, Idaho, and

Colorado workers played the most significant role in Populism, and their struggles with the mineowners gave the movement "much more of a revolutionary flavor" than in the non-mining states. In many of the mining and railroad towns of the South and West there were traditions of worker-agrarian radical cooperation going back to the Greenback-Labor Party of the late 1870s, and these bore fruit in Populism.[8]

It is difficult to estimate the actual size of the working-class Populist vote. Among railway workers and miners, particularly in selected areas, the proportions were substantial. Among southern and western artisans as a whole the percentages were much smaller. Even so, Populism received the support of a substantial fraction of organized workers. Moreover, European socialism and syndicalism also began with minority working-class support. What is significant in the Populist case is not the small beginning, but the failure to endure and grow. The Populist-worker alliance was the end of an old tradition, not the beginning of a new one. How is this to be explained?

First of all, leaders of the emerging craft unions represented a new direction in American labor. Instead of resisting the centralizing, bureaucratic tendencies of American society, these craft unionists identified with them. AFL unions organized skilled workers around high-dues, narrow, craft-conscious organizations. These craft unions would cooperate with the "trusts," seeking neither to abolish or regulate them, nor to organize their unskilled workers. The national trades unions would exercise centralized control over local constituent bodies, which had heretofore enjoyed virtually complete autonomy. It was, point by point, the opposite solution to that tried by the Knights of Labor, and implied in a worker-Populist alliance.[9]

These emerging craft leaders opposed not merely Populism but all radical political and industrial action. They claimed to oppose politics, but most had ties to dominant, urban political machines. In part the union leaders were self-serving, but they also believed, with good evidence, that radical political and economic action would continue to decimate labor organizations, as it had in the past. Thus not only was Samuel Gompers hostile to Populism; the president of the International Association of Machinists opposed the Pullman boycott, although most members of the IAM worked in railroad shops, and thousands flocked to the American Railway

Union during the strike. At least one IAM local provided strike-breakers, in a pattern that would become increasingly prevalent in the industrial conflicts of the new century. In Chicago—also a harbinger of things to come—craft union leaders tied to the Democratic machine sought to sabotage a Populist-labor alliance, and opposed the Populist ticket in the elections of 1894 and 1895.[10]

Many of these conservative craft leaders were Irish, which re-enforced their hostility to Populism. They had ties both to the Democratic Party and to the Catholic Church; the Church would shortly begin anti-radical activity in the labor movement. Although the American Irish were not immune to radicalism, the provocation had to be strong, and the commitment was generally short-lived.[11] In addition, the rural Protestant Populist flavor, while congenial to Protestant workers in southern and western towns, had little appeal to urban Irish workers and union leaders in the Northeast.

Craft union leaders erected a barrier between workers and Populism, but their power was hardly overwhelming. AFL unions were tiny in the Populist period, organizing only a small percentage even of the skilled workers prior to 1898. Perhaps Gompers was right that support for Populism would have decimated the labor movement once again. Certainly the AFL unions, hostile to reform, were the first in America to last through a severe depression. But in Europe many abortive efforts preceded successful syndicalist and socialist organizations. The key factor in the survival of AFL unions may well have been not their hostility to reform, but the existence for the first time of a substantial, permanent wage-earning class. Perhaps conservative craft unions were not the only kind that could have survived in America. Perhaps union leaders could have moved into the forefront of a reform-oriented labor movement, which might have survived and grown after 1896, as the AFL unions did. Craft union leaders certainly resisted this possibility, but they alone cannot be blamed for its failure. Populism and its labor allies could not attract any urban, eastern working-class support, skilled or unskilled, union or non-union.

Populism appealed to native artisans, railway workers, and miners, with local community loyalties and visions of social reconstruction. But workers like these could not take the lead in an expanding American labor movement, as happened with French syndicalism.[12] The eastern industrial working class was too immigrant-dominated, too ethnically fragmented, and too demoralized—by the shock of transplantation, by the depression, and by the alliance of state and industry which crushed efforts at revolt. Even in Chicago, where there was significant support for Populism among craft unionists independent of the Democratic machine, workers failed to vote for the party. Of the ten largest American cities, only San Francisco produced a significant Populist working-class vote.[13]

The new European working class emigrating from the country-side to the cities of Europe at least had ties of nationality, local place, and sometimes even political tradition to urban radicalism. In America the ties had to be to agrarian radicalism, and, except for Scandinavian and British immigrants, these ties were absent. Yeoman farmer communal appeals made little sense to the experience of immigrant workers. Eventually, and not without important, temporary exceptions, the immigrant unskilled followed the pattern set by the AFL.

One must not overdo the specifically working-class character of northeastern opposition to Populism. There was simply no Populist electoral or organizational strength here at all, and farmers were no more likely than workers to vote for the party. Populism was born from particular southern and western conditions; the very regional concentration that gave it initial state and local successes doomed it as a national movement. Equally important to the failure of Populism, it lacked staying power in the areas of its greatest strength.

The Populist effort to reassert community control could not embody itself in lasting institutions. Marxism in Europe, as Adam Ulam has written, tapped the anti-industrial emotion accompanying capitalism to industrial logic; workers did not destroy the machines and factories they hated, but organized and voted to overthrow the capitalist system instead.[14] But in America the forces of local control did not transmute themselves through Populism into a permanent, centralized, powerful socialist movement. With its program of nationalization and social control, and with its support for industrial labor, Populism took steps in this direction. But the external forces of resistance and the anti-monopoly, localistic agrarian traditions were too strong. Industrial logic, split from anti-industrial emotion, became embodied in the AFL and parallel farm organizations like the American Farm Bureau Federation. In Europe Marxian socialism emerged as the working class and its leaders recognized the permanence of an industrial capitalist system, until ended by seizure of state power. But in America that recognition led to accepting and working within the industrial capitalist structures, not seeking their overthrow. The dialogue in America—as the 1960s showed—remained one between a dominant, centralizing conservatism and sporadic reassertions of utopian communitarianism.

Less industrialized European countries offered a radical alternative to social democracy. Spain, Italy, and France produced lasting anarcho-syndicalist movements, sustained by rural workers, or workers with powerful local ties.[15] But American agrarian communities could not generate lasting organizations of this sort either. American farmers, sustained in part by cooperative frontier traditions, had produced a long tradition of agrarian protest. As Marx insisted, however, it was more difficult for farmers than for workers to form themselves into cohesive, independent organizations. In addition, industrial giants dominated society far more in America than in France or Spain. The European communities, finally, were in irrevocable opposition to centralizing tendencies within their societies; American rural communities were badly ambivalent. Western farmers, and those in the southern hill country areas of Populist strength, owned their own land. Many aspired to own more. Large numbers speculated and increased their mortgaged indebtedness in good times, and believed in the possibility of individual advancement. American farmers aimed for property owning independence, not communal control of work. They wanted, and believed they could get, the new consumption goods, railroads, and telephones offered by homogenizing industrial capitalism. For the upper and most conscious strata of farmers and workers, individual mobility within capitalism seemed more possible than it did in Europe; this attenuated permanent and deep social divisions.

There is another side to this story. Sharing the American dream, most Populists spoke for a tradition they believed had once been dominant in America. They saw themselves not as reviving an ancient opposition, but as reasserting a claim to rule as once they had. This perspective gave them temporary confidence, but was not one from which an enduring opposition could be built. The European socialists and anarchists, not imagining themselves as dispossessed rulers, built more slowly and permanently. The American agrarian radical perspective could not stand adversity.

Populism lacked staying power as an independent alternative to industrial capitalism. It needed—as Populist visions of apocalypse and urgency suggested—to win immediately or not at all.

This very sense of crisis sent Populism in a moderate, single-issue direction. Although the Populist vote rose dramatically from 1890 through 1894, this success did not satisfy. In their search for immediate victory, writes John Hicks, Populists moderated their radical economic program, and emphasized the silver issue. This implied a return to the pre-Populist alliance of local businessmen and farmers, and the end of organizationally independent radical Populism. Support for Bryan, with his focus on the single issue of silver, was the logical outcome of these developments. Bryan emphasized the religious, panaceaic side of agrarianism, rather than its economic program.[16] He drove eastern workers and Catholics into the GOP, and ended the Populist Party's independent existence.

Populism did make a contribution to the future Socialist Party. Some areas of Populist strength later voted Socialist, and some Populist trade unionists and other activists joined the party. At the same time western farmers continued to sustain local agrarian radical movements, often attracting local working-class support as well.[17] But Populism had failed, either to reassert farm community control over the forces transforming American society, or to remain as a permanent opposition to those forces.

This is not to say that Populist leaders could have preserved the party by running their own candidates in 1896. The decision for fusion reflected longings in the Populist base as well as in its leadership, and Bryan would surely have swept Populist constituencies whether the party supported him or not. America did not provide Populism with the resources either to sustain itself as a community-based opposition to industrial capitalism or to evolve into socialism. As John Laslett writes, "the intense strains created by the process of rapid industrial change, which in Europe served to accentuate profound divisions which already existed in preindustrial society, in America found no such permanent roots in which to grow."[18] In Louis Hartz's language, the American liberal tradition, rooted in the absence of feudal class loyalties, defeated from within all potentially cohesive cultural alternatives to bureaucratic capitalism. Populism offers American radicals, once again, only nostalgia for a community lost.

NOTES

1. Norman Pollack, *The Populist Response to Industrial America* (Cambridge, Mass.: Harvard, 1962), pp. 68–84; Staughton Lynd, *Intellectual Origins of American Radicalism* (N.Y.: Random House, 1968); Michael Paul Rogin, *The Intellectuals and McCarthy: The Radical Specter* (Cambridge, Mass.: MIT, 1967), pp. 168–91; Michael N. Shute, "Populism and the Pragmatic Mystique" (unpublished ms., Berkeley, 1965).

2. Robert Wiebe, *The Search for Order, 1877–1920* (N.Y.: Hill & Wang, 1967), pp. 11–110.

3. The interpretation here follows John R. Hicks, *The Populist Revolt* (Lincoln, Neb.: University of Nebraska Press, 1961), pp. 128–300. Voting data is on pp. 263, 337. For further evidence of Populism's appeal to farmers cf. Rogin, op. cit., pp. 109–15, 138–43, 175–80, and sources there cited.

4. U. S. Bureau of the Census, *Historical Statistics of the United States; Colonial Times to 1957* (Washington, D.C., 1960), p. 688.

5. H. G. Gutman, "Black Coal Miners and the Greenback-Labor Party in Redeemer Alabama: 1878–79," *Labor History*, X (Summer 1969), p. 510.

6. Wiebe, op. cit., pp. 67–68. Cf. Norman J. Ware, *The Labor Movement in the United States, 1860–1895* (N.Y.: Appleton, 1929).

7. Pollack, op. cit., pp. 25–61; Norman Pollack (ed.), *The Populist Mind* (Indianapolis: Bobbs-Merrill, 1967), pp. 403–66; George Brown Tindall (ed.), *A Populist Reader* (N.Y.: Harper & Row, 1966), pp. 165–68; Leon W. Fuller, "Colorado's Revolt Against Capitalism," *Mississippi Valley Historical Review*, XI (Dec. 1934), pp. 355–57; Hicks, op. cit., p. 444; Wiebe, op. cit., p. 91; "A Bundle of Western Letters," *Review of Reviews*, X (July 1, 1894), pp. 43, 46. The Cincinnati meeting of third-party reformers, stressed by Saloutos but barely mentioned by Pollack, has little bearing on the widespread evidence of Populist support for labor.

8. John H. M. Laslett, *Labor and the Left* (N.Y.: Basic Books, 1970), pp. 59–63, 144–45, 148–54, 193, 200–1, 244–45, 278, 299; Fuller, loc. cit.; Gutman, op. cit., pp. 507–20; Michael Paul Rogin and John L. Shover, *Political Change in California: Critical Elections and Social Movements, 1890–1966* (Westport, Conn.: Greenwood, 1971), pp. 17–18; Chester McArthur Destler, *American Radicalism 1865–1901* (N.Y.: Octagon Books, 1965), pp. 175, 202, 208.

9. Michael Rogin, "Nonpartisanship and the Group Interest," in Philip Green and Sanford Levinson (eds.), *Power and Community* (N.Y.: Random House, 1970), pp. 120–36; Michael Rogin, "Voluntarism: The Political Functions of an Anti-Political Doctrine," *Industrial and Labor Relations Review*, XV (July 1962), pp. 521–35; Lewis L. Lorwin, *The American Federation of Labor* (Washington, D.C.:

Brookings, 1933), pp. 301–5, 447–52 *passim;* Wiebe, op. cit., pp. 124–25; Laslett, op. cit., pp. 81–88, 110–14.

10. Laslett, op. cit., pp. 150–51; Destler, op. cit., pp. 171–72, 181–88, 201–9; Rogin, *Power and Community,* pp. 126–29.

11. Laslett, op. cit., pp. 29, 77, 180; Destler, op. cit., p. 190; Marc Karson, *American Labor Unions and Politics 1900–1918* (Carbondale, Ill.: Southern Illinois University, 1958), pp. 212–84; David J. Saposs, "The Catholic Church and the Labor Movement," *Modern Monthly,* VII (May 1933), pp. 225–30 (June 1933), pp. 294–98.

12. Louis L. Levine, *The Labor Movement in France* (N.Y.: Columbia, 1912), pp. 21–68; Val R. Lorwin, *The French Labor Movement* (Cambridge, Mass.: Harvard, 1954), p. 41.

13. Destler, op. cit., pp. 250–51; Rogin and Shover, op. cit., pp. 17–18. German Socialist workers also voted Populist in Milwaukee. (Rogin, *Intellectuals and McCarthy,* p. 66; Destler, op. cit., p. 202.)

14. Adam Ulam, *The Unfinished Revolution* (N.Y.: Random House, 1960), pp. 28–57.

15. Levine, op. cit., pp. 164–95; V. R. Lorwin, op. cit., pp. 36–43; Gerald Brenan, *The Spanish Labyrinth* (Cambridge, Eng.: University Press, 1943), pp. 134–202.

16. Rogin and Shover, op. cit., pp. 22–24.

17. Laslett, op. cit., pp. 298–99; Rogin, *Intellectuals and McCarthy,* pp. 64–80, 116–31, 187–91.

18. Laslett, op. cit., p. 304.

REPLY

Theodore Saloutos

There is much in what Rogin says that I agree with and much that I disagree with. On the whole I agree with his conclusions on Marxism and Populism; his observations that Populists supported the strikes of the workers against the common enemy, the large corporations; that Populism had its greatest strength in the South and West; that some Populists became Socialists; that the American Federation of Labor had little to offer in the way of a radical past; and that the Populists disliked being ruled from a distance.

Rogin claims that I present a narrow group interest interpretation of Populism. I, of course, disagree. This is largely a matter of research, definition, and interpretation. Rogin, I fear, writes about the agrarians from the vantage point of the present when the farmers constitute but a fraction of the total population and their limited numbers make them appear self-centered, instead of from the early 1890s when the farmers and their families represented a very large part of the total population, and when the distances between rural and urban were not drawn as hard and fast as they are at the present. Nowhere does he allude to the over-all acceptance by the farmers of the principles of agricultural fundamentalism which governed so much of their thinking and so many of their actions. They, and many non-farmers as well, were convinced that the fortunes of America weighed heavily on the fortunes of the farmers. As the farmers went so did the rest of the country. If the farmers prospered the nation prospered; if the farmers were depressed the nation was depressed. This was a compelling argument in an age when the bulk of the population and the wealth of the nation were tied up in agriculture.[1]

Rogin, in my opinion, has not presented substantial evidence in support of his claim that the industrial working-class complexion of Populism was as great as he suggests. Personally I feel that he

158 / THEODORE SALOUTOS

has overworked this point. True, the working-class population of the industrial East consisted of many immigrants; but this immigrant background is more of an explanation of why they, the immigrants, failed to join or be accepted by the trade unions which were biased against them than of why they did not embrace Populism. The bulk of these former European peasants established themselves in the urban-industrial centers and not in rural America; hence the union and its affiliates, political and non-political, and not the agrarian-oriented Populist movement, are what they would have most likely joined—if they joined anything.

The cooperation between labor and the agrarian Populists was more rhetorical than real. The suspicions of the farmers ran strong. If the working-class influence was as formidable as has been suggested why was not a representative of the working classes put up by the Populists as a presidential or vice-presidential candidate to prove that the farmers and wage earners had reached a genuine and comprehensive agreement on political cooperation? My argument is that the labor leaders of the Knights of Labor variety, representatives of a decadent labor organization at the time the Populists reached their peak, sought the cooperation of the politically oriented farmers; and the Knights who were on the decline wanted this affiliation with the hope of pumping new life into their lingering organization; and that they, as a consequence, were more or less tied to the skirts of the agrarians. The overwhelming agrarian basis of Populism is attested to by the geography of the Populist vote, the South and the West, the two preponderantly agricultural sections of the country.

That the Populists sympathized with labor that was victimized by organized capital—that is, the corporations—as the farmers believed they also had been, is beyond doubt. The farmers and laborers had a common foe in "monopoly," and when the circumstances permitted they combined to resist the encroachments of the so-called "monopolists." The evidence that Rogin has mustered of farmers sympathizing and coming to the assistance of the striking workers is but an elaboration of this argument. What evidence of cooperation does he present when their interests collided?

The assertion has been made that the "emerging craft unions" represented a new direction in American labor. Certainly the idea of the craft union was not new. The first unions, according to labor historians, were ushered into existence by members of the crafts—the skilled workers, the shoemakers, the carpenters, the printers, and other artisan groups. Hence it would be closer to the truth to argue that the American Federation of Labor, seen in historical perspective, was in part a reaction against the ineffectiveness of the kind of industrial unionism preached by the Knights of Labor and a reassertion of old craft union principles.[2]

Rogin also speaks of working-class opposition to Populism and the wisdom of deemphasizing this argument. I think it more accurate to say that it was not so much working-class opposition to Populism as much as it was the lack of appeal that Populism had for the wage earners of the East and their tendency to associate the free silver arguments and other Populist demands with an increase in the prices and services of the things they bought. Contrary to what Rogin claims this was a real and genuine argument. These were years of hard times, a fact that does not come out very clearly in his statement, as well as a matter of self-interest. The wage earners, as American Federation of Labor leaders knew, were more concerned about their jobs, the size of their earnings, and the working conditions than in building an ideal world.

Rogin, I further believe, grievously errs in not making better use of agrarian sources and particularly the writings of southern scholars whose works have appeared since *The Populist Revolt* was first published in 1931; and in relying on resolutions, convention platforms, and other surface bits of information instead of going behind the scenes and digging up the hard facts of what actually happened. Years ago my own research in southern sources and the writings of southern scholars convinced me that the reformers were unwelcomed by the rank-and-file farmers, because they were suspicious of them and they wanted to incorporate their own pet schemes into an already long and unwieldy platform that would tend to confuse the voters and defeat their purpose.[3]

Rogin is right in stating that the religious impulse was manifest among the agrarians. My own research into the subject led me to conclude that this influence was felt especially at the local level, among organizations such as the Agricultural Wheel, which was absorbed by the Farmers' Alliance, rather than among the Populists. However, there is little proof that religious leaders or ministers of the gospel assumed a dominant role in organizing the Populist Party or in heading it. Ministers, often without churches, and broken-down preachers were attracted to Populism as lecturers and organizers of locals; and the Populists, as was brought out, won the support of preachers such as Washington Gladden and probably other preachers of the social gospel.

A state by state study of Populism in the southern states is likely to reveal something less encouraging than what Rogin suggests in the form of black and white cooperation; in fact, the picture is somewhat uglier than is implied. The resistance to Populism was great; apprehension and fear over what black and white cooperation would bring was formidable; and the force and violence considerable. Furthermore the reactions of the blacks themselves to a black and white alliance were mixed. This phase of the story has to be told along with the more favorable, if we want a better-balanced picture of what happened. The white backlash was substantial.

The resistance to black and white cooperation was greatest in the areas in which the Populists sought to operate. Once "the back of Populism was broken," "the black belt whites"—the most vigorous foes of the third party—solidified their position and recruited "enough upcountry support to adopt poll taxes, literacy tests, and other instruments to disfranchise the Negro. . . ." In fact, this began with the Mississippi Constitutional Convention of 1890, before Populism reached its peak, and continued until new constitutions were adopted by seven states from 1895 to 1910. ". . . 'understanding clauses' and the white primary provisions of constitutions and laws were of major importance in reducing the number of votes. . . ." Populism, by threatening white supremacy, backfired and strengthened the one-party system.[4]

Although I agree that Populism had some little influence on the growth of socialist thought and the American Socialist Party, especially in the Great Plains states rather than in the urban-industrial centers of the nation, the influence on the Progressive movement was greater. Socialists made some headway in Oklahoma, Kansas, and North Dakota before the rise of the Nonpartisan League in 1915, but their numbers were small compared with those of the Progressives in the Middle West, the East, and the South. By this one is not inferring that Populism alone accounted for the growth of Progressivism. Certainly the lily-white platforms of the Progressives in the South attracted larger numbers than their Populist forebears and the socialists. Rightfully or wrongfully, the bulk of the farmers believed that under socialism their lands would come under government control, and that the most hopeful among the tenants would be unable to achieve proprietorships. The ambitions of many, probably most, farmers who expected to climb the agricultural ladder to farm ownership would be quashed. Actually relatively small numbers achieved this, but the expectations were still there.

Populism in an ideological sense survived long after the formal party structure collapsed, and many, if not most, of its ideas were incorporated into Progressive platforms at the state and federal levels. By 1912 when Woodrow Wilson was elected President, much of what the Populists had proposed had gained a wide following. Of special concern to the farmers was the income tax, designed at least in part to lift some of the tax burden from the land which was the base for most of the taxes they paid, and later the Federal Reserve Act which was the most important piece of financial legislation to be passed since the Civil War. Still later, the Federal Farm Loan Act and the Federal Warehouse Act, both of which to a degree were of Populist vintage, were calculated to overcome the defects of the Federal Reserve Act and bring to the farmers more of the kind of assistance they sought.[5]

Populism by and large was grass roots in character, folkish in its ways of thinking and behavior, and certainly not an intellectual movement, as is sometimes imagined. The reactions of the agrarians stemmed from a feeling of insecurity brought on by the relegation of agriculture to a subordinate position in society, the upgrading of the money-maker and the downgrading of the farmer, the end of the era of cheap lands, the growing importance of the cities, the drift of farm children from the countryside to urban communities, the belief that youth was turning its back on the virtuous life of the farmer, the breakup of the farm family, and the gradual disappearance from the scene of the America the farmers idolized and wanted to preserve.

I find Rogin's argument that businessmen, merchants, and bankers who joined the Farmers' Alliance did not follow them into the Populist Party a bit difficult to accept. In most, if not all, instances the Farmers' Alliance aroused fear among the town merchants, the businessmen, and the bankers; and as a rule, the official business of the Alliance was conducted in secret as a means of preventing outsiders from knowing what they were doing. The Farmers' Alliance had an anti-business attitude directed against the large and more traditional business agencies, which its members suspected of defrauding or working against the interests of the farmers. Many of the local Alliances harbored a deep distrust of the business community, and as a consequence set up their own business arrangements as a means of obtaining better prices for what they sold and cheaper prices for what they bought. To say that town merchants, businessmen, and bankers who joined the Alliance were drawn away from third-party participation is misleading, because there were few, if any, to draw away.[6]

On the whole I believe that Rogin is stretching his argument too much in trying to build a broad popular base for Populism. The great majority of Populists were farmers and their allies. That the Populists attracted some reformers, some wage earners, some preachers, and some members of the professional classes is beyond question, but by no means as many as is inferred or suggested. Some Populists were attracted to the socialist movement after the Populist Party declined, but many more either were attracted to the Progressives or abandoned politics as a way of reform. In general the political and psychological ties between Populism and Progressivism were greater than between Progressivism and socialism.

NOTES

1. In 1890 almost 65 per cent of the total population of the United States lived in rural districts. *Abstract of the Fourteenth Census of the United States, 1920* (Washington, 1923), p. 77. The farm population of the United States in 1966, for instance, was only 5.9 per cent of the total. *Statistical Abstract of the United States, 1967* (Washington, 1967), p. 605.

2. George R. Taylor writes: ". . . unions of such skilled craftsmen as printers, carpenters, shoemakers, and tailors were common immediately following the War of 1812 in the larger cities such as Philadelphia, Pittsburgh, Baltimore, New York and Boston. . . ." George R. Taylor, *The Transportation Revolution, 1815–1860* (New York, 1951), pp. 251–52.

3. *Western Rural and American Stockman,* XXX (April 16, 1892), p. 243; St. Louis *Post-Dispatch,* February 19–23, 25, 1892; John D. Hicks, *The Populist Revolt* (Minneapolis, 1931), pp. 226–27; Theodore Saloutos, *Farmer Movements in the South, 1865–1933* (Berkeley, 1960), pp. 123–24; Mary Earhart, *Francis Willard* (Chicago, 1944), p. 234; James Reddick, "The Negro and the Populist Movement in Georgia" (M.A. Thesis, University of Atlanta, 1937), pp. 34–35; Helen M. Blackburn, "The Populist Party in the South, 1890–1898" (M.A. Thesis, Howard University, 1941), pp. 22–23.

4. V. O. Key, Jr., *Southern Politics* (New York, 1951), pp. 7–8, 117–18; Gunnar Myrdal, *An American Dilemma* (New York, 1944), p. 453; Albert D. Kirwan, *Revolt of the Rednecks* (Lexington, 1951), pp. 58–84; Cortez M. Ewing, *Presidential Elections* (Norman, 1940), p. 68; Joseph H. Taylor, "Populism and Disfranchisement in Alabama," *Journal of Negro History,* XXXIV (October 1949), pp. 410–27; A. A. Arnett, *The Populist Movement in Georgia* (New York, 1922); John B. Clark, *Populism in Alabama* (Auburn, 1927); Robert L. Hunt, *Farmer Movements in the Southwest, 1873–1925* (College Station, Texas, 1935); Roscoe Martin, *The People's Party in Texas* (Austin, 1933); W. Du Bose Sheldon, *The People's Party in Virginia* (Princeton, 1935); Robert F. Durden, *The Climax of Populism* (Lexington, 1965); William W. Rogers, *The One-Gallused Rebellion: Agrarianism in Alabama, 1865–1896* (Baton Rouge, 1970).

5. Theodore Saloutos, "The Professors and the Populists," *Agricultural History,* XL (October 1966), pp. 235–54.

6. Theodore Saloutos, *Farmer Movements in the South, 1865–1933,* pp. 88–101.

Chapter 5

CATHOLIC ANTI-SOCIALISM*

Marc Karson

A number of years ago Dr. David J. Saposs declared in an informal essay that the "significant and predominant role of the Catholic Church in shaping the thought and aspirations of labor is a neglected chapter in the history of the American labor movement. Its influence explains, in part at least, why the labor movement in the United States differs from others. . . ."[1] On the basis of the material which the author has accumulated, it appears that this generalization has considerable merit.

Papal Encyclicals

One of the first papal encyclicals which suggested that the Roman Catholic Church intended to modify its opposition to certain aspects of nineteenth-century social change was seen in Leo XIII's pronouncement regarding labor, *Rerum novarum* of May 1891. In essence the encyclical called for strong support of the doctrine of private property, unqualified rejection of and opposition to socialism, and acceptance of trade unions indoctrinated with Catholic social principles.[2] Devout Catholics were accordingly influenced by this important encyclical, which made it clear that impartiality for Catholics in the labor-capital conflict was an impossibility and that henceforth their intervention in modern social disturbances was mandatory.

Pope Pius X reiterated the Church's opposition to socialism in his first encyclical letter of 1903, *E supremi*. In 1912, he again warned, in the encyclical *Singulari quadam caritate,* that "unions, in order to be such that Catholics may join them, should abstain

* Marc Karson, "The Catholic Church and the Political Development of American Trade Unionism (1900–1918)," *Industrial and Labor Relations Review,* 4 (July 1951), pp. 527–42.

from all principles and acts which are not in accord with the teachings and regulations of the Church or the legitimate ecclesiastical authority." As a result of such papal pronouncements, Vincent McQuade declared that "opposition to socialism was acknowledged by devout Catholics to be the fundamental issue" within trade unions.[3] . . .

Catholic Strength in the AFL, 1900–1918

In interviews with persons who had firsthand contact with the trade union movement during the years 1900 to 1918, the present writer found opinion unanimous that Catholics were the largest religious group within the AFL. This was primarily because of the Irish Catholic membership, although other nationalities, particularly the Germans, also helped to account for this fact. As late as 1928, Professor Selig Perlman wrote that it was "the Catholics who are perhaps in the majority in the American Federation of Labor."[4] Seven years later Norman J. Ware stated that the AFL was composed of "predominantly Irish leadership of the national unions."[5] Of the eight vice-presidential offices on the AFL Executive Board from 1900 to 1918, Catholics numbered at least four during any one year. Additional research by the author concerning the number of Catholics who were presidents of the AFL international unions in the years 1900 to 1918 reveals an incomplete list of more than fifty Irish Catholics.[6]

The Position of the Cardinals

The highest American dignitaries of the Catholic Church in the first two decades of the twentieth century were three cardinals—William O'Connell, James Gibbons, and John Farley. Each of them, in their sermons and writings, vigorously espoused the doctrines set forth in *Rerum novarum*.

Cardinal Gibbons' biographer declared that the Cardinal felt that "the Church must be aroused to resist the threatened danger of socialism, [and] prepared to throw the whole force of the Church against the further progress of the [socialist] movement. . . ." Preaching in the Cathedral of Baltimore on February 4, 1916, Gibbons said that inequality of rank, station, and wealth was inevitable and "must result from a law of life established by

an overruling Providence."[7] In his reminiscences, the cardinal reiterated Leo XIII's view that social organizations must be based
on Catholic ethics. He wrote:

All social schemes based on the assumption that man's good lies
in the natural order alone, must fail. The brotherhood of man is a
dream unless it be founded in the Fatherhood of God. The Catholic
Church is the authorized representative and exponent of the supernatu-
ral order. True, it is not her official duty to devise special social schemes
for special social disorder; but it is her duty to see to it that all schemes
devised are founded on Christian principles and do not antagonize the
law of nature and the law of God.[8]

Gibbons' views on trade unions followed the principles of
Rerum novarum. The employers' Anti-Boycott Association reprinted in pamphlet form, with his permission, the text of one of
his addresses. In it he declared that trade unions needed leaders
who would not infringe "on the rights of their employers." He advised the unions to select conservative leaders and to be on guard
against socialists who would make the organization "subservient
to their own selfish ends, or convert it into a political engine."[9]

Cardinal O'Connell was equally definite and outspoken in making known his views on trade unions. In a pastoral letter read in
all the churches of the Archdiocese of Boston on Sunday, December 1, 1912, he announced that Catholic principles must dominate
trade unions and that employer-employee problems could only be
adjusted through the media of Catholic ideals. He denounced socialism and socialists at some length and emphasized that, as Leo
XIII had shown in *Rerum novarum,* "there cannot be a Catholic
socialist." The Holy Name Societies and workmen were exhorted
to study the social pronouncements of the Church and "those
having care of souls" were told to instruct the workmen "in the
true doctrine of the Church concerning their duties in the realm of
labor."[10]

Cardinal Farley of New York also closely followed the authoritative intention of *Rerum novarum.* At the annual convention of
the Confraternity of Christian Doctrine, in 1909, he referred to
socialism as "the heresy of the hour—a rampant heresy" which
was a serious obstacle to the success of Catholic teachers in keeping Catholic workers true to the faith. He concluded by suggesting
methods for Catholics to "combat the common enemy."[11]

Teachings of Bishops and Priests

In order that the papal pronouncements be understood and acted upon by Catholic workers, it was necessary for the bishops and priests to give time and effort to interpreting these encyclicals for the workmen. The devotion of these officials to Church authority accounted for the extensive number of addresses and writings that were directed toward the American Catholic workers. This duty was well stated by Father Kerby of Catholic University, in 1907, when he wrote:

The Church has entered the conflict as the avowed enemy of Socialism. Our colleges teach against it; we lecture and write, preach and publish against it. We have abundant official pronouncements against it, and an anxious capitalistic world looks to the Church, nervous with gratitude for the anticipated setback that Catholicism is to give to Socialism.[12]

Bishop James McFaul by 1908 had established a Labor Day Sunday in the Diocese of Trenton, and he directed "the priests of each parish on this day to speak to their people on the relations between Capital and Labor."[13] Likewise Bishop James Quigley of Buffalo in 1902 had issued a pastoral letter in his diocese in which he asked the priests to "warn their people against the theories advocated by the socialists through the means of labor unions." He also had requested that there be organized "circles in every parish in the diocese, to which both workingmen and employers shall belong."[14] In Kansas City, in 1912, Bishop Thomas Lillis reminded 110 priests who were meeting in a diocesan synod of the "inviolability of private property" and the Catholic conflict with socialism.[15] Archbishop Ireland told the trade unionists of St. Paul in a Labor Day sermon in 1903 that the "most sacred right of man is his right to private property" and, therefore, the Church was "opposed to the state socialism that is now and then preached as the panacea of labor grievances."[16]

At times Catholic clergymen spoke to AFL conventions or to the Catholic unionists attending AFL conventions. For example, Bishop John Carroll of Helena told the AFL delegates in 1913 that the Church had been a powerful body for over 2,000 years and would be more desirable as an ally than as an enemy of union-ism. Therefore, he cautioned that "it would be very impolitic for labor to favor any theory of economics . . . that must incur the enmity of the Church." There were millions of Catholics who were trade unionists, and these men, Carroll declared, because they "love their religion as their very lives," would be obliged to depart from a trade union whose doctrines threatened their Church.[17]

Father Charles Bruehl, Professor of Sociology in St. Charles Seminary, Philadelphia, also made this point in 1914 when he ad-dressed the Catholic delegates who had gathered for the AFL con-vention in his city. He warned them that if the principles of the AFL came into conflict with Catholic teachings, the Church would be unable to continue its endorsement of the organization. And this meant, Bruehl added, that "what the Church cannot approve, God will not bless and prosper." A conservative union, he said, was "in harmony with the Church" because she, too, "loves order and prefers to preserve rather than to destroy." He felt that those listening to him were not "dreamers of dreams" and "seers of visions" but instead were "conservative, pillars of order, and a bul-wark against revolution" who wisely accepted the existing eco-nomic system and merely desired "a fair share of remuneration." Therefore, he said, he wished to "hail labor organizations as one of the conservative forces of the community." The AFL properly recognized that there was no basic conflict between labor and capi-tal but that socialism was the enemy of both. The "Catholic ele-ment" in the unions, however, Bruehl asserted, would "overcome the contagion of socialism."[18]

The reception of Pope Pius X's encyclical *Singulari quadam caritate* brought forth two editorials from the German Roman Catholic Central Verein, an organization of German-American Catholics, vividly explaining the Catholic position on trade unions. . . . The second editorial specifically interpreted *Singulari quadam caritate* as a guide to the position that Catholic workers could take toward trade unions. It said that the Pope's words[19]

would exclude from the ranks of unions to which Catholics might belong all organizations influenced by and fostering socialism. . . . In short, in socialistic organizations we must behold a danger to society, morality and faith, Catholics therefore cannot be members of organizations founded and directed by Socialists or for Socialistic purposes as e.g., The Industrial Workers of the World, The American Railway Union, The Western Federation of Miners, the Socialistic Trades and Labor Unions, the Knights of Labor, etc., if they are what they are said to be.

Similarly, to give briefly an example of another kind, the Farmers Educational and Co-operative Union of America is not in conformity with the above teaching. From the *America* of November 26, 1912, we learn that this union is interdenominational; advocates—these are the objectionable points—religious interdenominationalism and puts aside the true standards of morality by declaring its aim and purpose to be "to secure equity, establish justice and apply the Golden Rule." These objectionable features make it fall under the unions censured by the Pope.

As for the AFL, the Central Verein editor wrote that it "has not adopted these pernicious and morally unsound principles. It intends to be a purely economic organization." He warned, however, that should the minority who were advocating such dangerous views as revolutionary strikes, free public school textbooks, and women suffrage gain in influence in the AFL, the Catholics would have no alternative but to depart. If this radical element "ever as some fear, comes into power, then the movement will be near the danger line at which all Catholics will have to halt and at which they would have to leave the Federation." Catholics could only remain in interdenominational unions "provided the latter are not opposed to the moral laws as regards membership and action. But, we repeat, this makes the adoption of safeguard, yea, of special assistance peremptory."[20]

Doubtless the writings and addresses of bishops and priests, such as those mentioned above, were partly responsible for Aaron Abell's conclusion that "to the very end of the pre-war era, despite efforts to strike a positive and constructive note, warring upon socialism seemed to most people perhaps the main interest of the American Catholic."[21]

The Role of Father Peter E. Dietz

In the period under consideration one priest, more than any other member of the American Catholic clergy, deserved credit for devoting himself unceasingly to the practical organizational

tasks that would carry the principles of *Rerum novarum* into daily
practice by devout Catholics. He was the Reverend Peter E.
Dietz, who has been largely ignored by labor historians, but who is finally
beginning to gain from Catholic historians the recognition long
overdue him.[22]

In 1940 Father Dietz answered a letter from Sister Joan de
Lourdes Leonard concerning his activity in the American trade
union movement.[23] In this letter he told that he had led a defeated minority of AFL delegates out of the Ohio Federation of
Labor convention in Toledo in October 1909 because "the socialists carried the convention." For several years, Dietz declared,
he fought the socialist-controlled Ohio Federation and finally
helped to bring about its defeat. From 1909 to 1917 he attended
the AFL national conventions as fraternal delegate of the American Federation of Catholic Societies and in 1921, at the request of
the AFL executive board, gave the opening prayer at the AFL
convention in Cincinnati, Ohio.

His letter to Sister Joan stated that it was "impossible to recall
the innumerable occasions" over a period of fifteen years when he
was able to champion "Leo XIII's famous Encyclical" within the
AFL. Nor could he estimate, as a result of his espousal of Catholic
social principles within trade unionism, the many "friendships
made, the enemies disarmed, the reconciliations effected, the policies considered and reconsidered, conflicts avoided or tempered."
Dietz even admitted that Samuel Gompers had once informed him
that he held "the unique distinction of having secured a reversal
of decisions by the Executive Board of the AFL." . . .

The Militia of Christ for Social Service

Probably Dietz's most significant accomplishment for translating
Rerum novarum into effective daily action occurred at the time of
the AFL 1910 convention. In an address before the assembled
delegates at St. Louis, he assured them of the Church's support
of conservative trade unions.[24] What wins for him a place in the
labor history of America, however, is the organizing work he did
outside the convention hall itself. At this St. Louis convention he
met privately with outstanding Catholic trade union leaders and
discussed with them the value of creating an organization that
would defend and advance Catholic principles in the labor move-

ment. Out of these discussions during the AFL convention there evolved a constitution and program for an organization envisaged by Father Dietz. A committee consisting of Dietz and visiting trade union executives was formed, and they called on the Archbishop of St. Louis, John J. Glennon, for his official blessing. Once this was received on November 22, 1910, the Militia of Christ for Social Service had become an actuality.[25] Father Dietz was named executive secretary, and other officers and the directorate included an imposing array of prominent Catholic trade union leaders in America at that time. The stationery of the Militia listed the following trade union leaders as the directorate: Denis A. Hayes, President, International Association of Glass Bottle Blowers (and AFL Vice-President); James O'Connell, President International Association of Machinists (and AFL Vice-President); John R. Alpine, President, International Association of Plumbers and Steam Fitters (and AFL Vice-President); John Moffat, President, International Association of Hatters of North America; John Mitchell, Chairman, Trades Agreement Department, National Civic Federation (and AFL Vice-President and former President, United Mine Workers); T. V. O'Connor, International President of the Longshoremen; John Golden, International President of the Textile Workers.

The general officers of the Militia of Christ were listed as follows: President, Peter J. McArdle (President, Amalgamated Association of Iron, Steel and Tin Workers); Vice-President, John S. Whalen (Ex-Secretary of the State of New York); Second Vice-President, Peter Collins (Secretary, International Brotherhood of Electrical Workers); Third Vice-President, John Mangan (Editor, *The Steamfitters Journal*); Recording Secretary, Thomas Duffy (President, National Brotherhood of Operative Potters, and Ohio State Deputy, Knights of Columbus); Executive Secretary, Reverend Peter E. Dietz.

As its "Motto," the Militia of Christ for Social Service adopted the precept, "Thy Will be Done." Its "Object," according to its Constitution, was "The defense of the Christian order of society and its progressive development." The Militia's "Platform" read: "The economic, ethical, sociological and political doctrines of Christian philosophy as developed in the course of history—the legacy of tradition, interpreted to modern times in the letters of Leo XIII and Pius X."

To implement this platform, a twofold method was to be followed: first, "The Promotion of Social Education," and second, "The Compelling of Social Action."

"Social Education" was to be furthered by:

(1) syndicate letters to the Catholic and Labor Press;

(2) social lectures and conferences;

(3) student apostolates in the colleges and universities;

(4) lyceum co-operation with diocesan apostolates, mission bands, K. of C. lectureships, societies, and parishes;

(5) social emphasis upon Confirmation sponsorship;

(6) a social reference bureau, social science libraries, social centers;

(7) the publication of leaflets, pamphlets, monograms, and a Journal of Social Service.

"Social Action" was to be spurred by:

(1) personal propagandist service and volunteer distribution of literature;

(2) the advocacy of Christian principles in trade unions;

(3) intelligent and active interest in the problems of labor legislation; municipal reform, civil service and general administration, industrial education, prevention of industrial accidents and diseases, workmen's compensation, workshop, factory and mine inspection, and uniform state legislation;

(4) the cultivation of fraternal relations with all Catholic societies and conservative social movements;

(5) yearly programmatic convention conjointly with the convention of the American Federation of Labor;

(6) a Catholic celebration of Labor Day;

(7) a policy of conciliation, trade agreements, arbitration of industrial difficulties.

Dr. David Saposs has been one of the very few labor historians to pay more than a passing word to the Militia. In his opinion[26] it was:

a secret organization of Catholic labor leaders designed to combat radicalism. It counted among its members the leading Catholic labor leaders, and had the approval of Gompers and the handful of other Catholic conservative labor leaders. The Militia of Christ was an auxiliary of the Church. It had large funds at its disposal. It was manned

by an able staff. It immediately became a formidable factor in the
fight against radicalism. It issued literature and retained a corps of
propagandists and lecturers. In addition it routed outstanding labor
leaders, and priests who had distinguished themselves in labor affairs,
on tours where they spoke to working class audiences against radicalism and for the conservative brand of laborism.[27]

The recent opinion of Professor Abell on the purpose and influence of the Militia is quite similar to that of Dr. Saposs. He has
written: "Members of the society, mostly Catholics in key positions
in labor unions, helped conservative trade unionists, 'the pure and
simplers' to thwart the continuous endeavors of the Socialists to
capture the AFL. . . ."[28]

At the end of one year's work with the Militia, Father Dietz
announced that "the earliest hopes of the Militia of Christ are not
fulfilled, yet I am equally sure that the movement has justified
itself." He acknowledged that the Militia had several hundred subscriptions, but he was not yet satisfied. He hoped to establish a
school of social service which would turn out a trained corps of
priests who could devote themselves entirely to Social Service as
defined in the pronouncements of Church authority. Since he estimated it would take ten or fifteen thousand dollars "for the foundation of the School" he suggested to Mitchell that "if we could talk
the matter over with some men of means, who are glad of your
acquaintance and friendship, matters would soon be arranged."[29]

Faced with financial difficulties and a huge amount of work
which was impossible for him to do without some assistance, Father Dietz gradually turned more and more to the Social Service
Commission of the American Federation of Catholic Societies,
which had been established to promote "the further amelioration
of conditions among the working people for the propagation and
preservation of the faith."[30]

This was not a defeat for Father Dietz, but, as he admitted,
a victory. "You are aware that for years I have been trying to influence Catholic Federation into this field. The Militia of Christ was
organized largely as a lever for that body. . . . I am satisfied to
relinquish the title of Militia of Christ."[31] The first published
Catholic paper on Father Dietz holds that "the continuance of
Dietz's work of conducting lectures, attending conventions, and is-
suing a weekly syndicated letter to the Catholic Press, seems to

indicate that the Commission became a kind of enlargement of the Militia."[82]

By 1917 Dietz reported that the Commission was sending out about 10,000 press letters and about an additional 4,000 other letters annually.[33] In the early 1920's, "the AFL gave him a gift of $2,500 in token of their friendship and esteem for a priest who had attended their annual conventions since 1909 and whom they had 'known, admired and heeded.' "[34] In the opinion of Father Henry Browne the work of Peter E. Dietz had helped to "make the word of Leo XIII's *Rerum novarum* come alive."[35]

American Federation of Catholic Societies

As noted, the Militia of Christ after a few years was absorbed by the Social Service Commission of the American Federation of Catholic Societies. The latter organization represented a movement, between 1901 and 1917, to unite existing Catholic organizations into a federation for the main purpose of defending the Church's interests and "to promote social reform along the lines of Leo's Encyclical."[36] The AFCS's constitution stated that the organization intended to spread Catholic principles in "social and public life, in the State, in business, in all financial and industrial relations."[37] By 1917 over forty Catholic societies representing three million Catholics were affiliated with the AFCS. Resolutions at the organization's annual convention regularly urged "Catholic trade unionists' faithful attendance to trade union duties, active participation in the affairs of their unions, and unceasing opposition to the abuse of their organizations by the destructive propaganda of Socialism."[38]

The German Roman Catholic Central Verein

Probably the most socially conscious of all the Catholic societies affiliated with the AFCS was the German Roman Catholic Central Verein, an association of Catholic men of German extraction, founded in 1855. The Verein in 1908 established a Central Bureau so that Catholic ethics could be more widely and effectively interpreted to the United States. The bureau sponsored study courses and discussion clubs for considering the Church's principles as applied to social reconstruction and for training Catholics for social leadership. It also issued *Central Blatt and Social Justice,* a widely circulated monthly published in German and English for the benefit of the clergy and devoted to the discussion of social problems. In addition, it issued weekly press bulletins in both German and English to one hundred Catholic newspapers.[39]

The fear of socialism and the call to social action given by Leo XIII's *Rerum novarum* led the Central Verein and the local vereins "to take an active interest in the labor movement."[40] Mr. Gonner, the president of the GRCCV, in an address to the delegates at the annual convention in 1909, explained that the Verein could have a strong influence on Catholic workmen and on trade unions through utilizing a Catholic social reform program, an effective organization, and zealous Catholic leaders. The Verein president explained that the Catholic social reform program "becomes clear when we say that for us the words 'To Restore All Things in Christ' mean the promotion and defense of Christian Order in society, especially against the dangers of Socialism and Anarchy in any form."[41] He asserted that the duty of Verein members was to contact Catholic unionists in the AFL, to arouse them against socialist penetration, and to teach them Catholic social principles. In addition, he proposed the establishment of Catholic workers' associations when he said:

. . . The Central Society is urging its more influential members in the various cities of the U.S. to gather around themselves in groups and circles, Catholic laboring men, members of the American Federation of Labor to instruct them on their duties and the Christian principles in the Labor Question, to enable these to counteract the baneful activity displayed by Socialistic agitators among the laboring men of the United States and thus while leaving intact American organized labor yet safeguarding Catholic religious and civic rights. . . . As a permanent solution of the problem of safeguarding Catholic laboring men, the Central Society advocates the formation of Catholic laboring-men's organizations, of course, without detriment to the American Federation of Labor.[42]

As the close of this address suggests, the AFL was well regarded by the Central Verein. That fact was confirmed by a letter in 1911 from F. P. Kenkel, the Central Bureau's director, to Samuel Gompers. Mr. Kenkel wrote that the Verein was interested in the AFL and was seeking to mold the opinion of Catholic unionists "in a manner favorable to the real interests of labor." The AFL President was informed that the Verein's 1910 Newark convention had adopted a resolution urging "Catholic workingmen to join the Trade Unions wherever possible [and] to combat the propaganda of Socialism in the Unions." Mr. Kenkel added that the Verein was pleased with Gompers' ideological leadership of the AFL because it was in consonance with the social teachings expounded by the Catholic Church. Gompers was extended the Verein's "best wishes for the success of organized labor along the lines most conducive to its real welfare, and to the real good of the working classes, to the good of society, of which you are so important a factor in conformity with Christian principles."[43]

An article in the Verein's official journal by a Catholic spokesman made even plainer that the attitude of the Catholic Central Verein toward trade union political thought and practice was one and the same as that of the Gompers administration. The workers were told to prize what their union had gained for them through their economic methods and to avoid any political policies that would be a departure from the slogan, "reward your friends, punish your enemies."

There is no graver danger lurking about than when trade unionists themselves fail to appreciate what their unions have done for them. It is then that the devils of disruption get in their underhanded, their hellish work. There is one other grave danger threatening us as trade unionists. Its onward march should meet with determined resistance. "No politics in trade unions" may be trite but it is a true guide to safe conduct. The attempt to commit our unions to a specific political party should not be tolerated in our midst, neither by resolution, by financial aid, by giving politicians special privileges to carry on a campaign in our unions or in our official journals. . . . Our business is not politics but economics. The friends of labor are the men for unionists to support and the policy of unionists is well expressed in the shibboleth that "we should reward our friends and punish our enemies."[44]

Another crusader for the Catholic social cause, Peter W. Collins, former secretary of the Electrical Brotherhood, was also provided with space in the Verein's journal. Collins reminded his readers that Catholic trade unionists represented "almost one half of the men of organized labor." Since they had the numerical strength to defeat socialism in the trade unions, he considered the moral guilt would be theirs if socialism triumphed. His positive proposal for a Catholic victory was put in these words:

We advocate Catholic workingmen's societies to be founded in each parish, whose members shall be instructed as to their special duties to church and society according to precepts laid down by Leo XIII . . . only when so instructed and fortified will Catholic laboringmen be able to do their full share in preventing the insidious enemy from capturing the Trade Union Movement and turning it into a recruiting ground for Socialism, into an appendix of the Socialist Party of the United States.[45]

The Central Verein, however, did more than propagate theory in its desire to educate Catholics on the proper application of the Church's doctrines to trade unions. It actually entered the sphere of social action by forming "Catholic workingmen's societies in several cities."[46] Director F. P. Kenkel mentions that two of these societies were the St. Anne's Arbeiterverein, formed in Buffalo in 1909 by Father Meckel (S.J.), and the Arbeiterwohl, organized in St. Louis by a number of German American priests, led by the Reverend Albert Mayer.[47] The St. Louis association's birth was in part due to the priests' fear of the influence of socialists in the brewing industry. The Arbeiterwohl's paper, *Amerika,* edited by Kenkel, "was read by every German speaking priest in St. Louis and could be found in most of the taverns frequented by German speaking workingmen."[48]

The social diligence of the Central Verein in translating the Church's doctrines to the American people earned the praise of Father John A. Ryan. He commended the Verein for recommending, as he said, "that Catholic workingmen take an active part in the regular trade union instead of forming separate organizations. In this way the Catholic workers will be able to oppose most effectively Socialism, unwise radicalism, and every other tendency or method that is hostile to genuine reform."[49]

The Catholic Press

A survey of the Catholic journals and newspapers from 1900 to 1918 reveals that the Catholic press was in accord with the principles laid down in *Rerum novarum,* and quite consistently advanced them. Leo XIII himself reminded the hierarchy of the importance of the press when he said: "All your work will be destroyed, all your efforts will prove fruitless if you are not able to wield the defensive and offensive weapon of a loyal and sincere Catholic press."[50] The wisdom of these words was not lost on the American hierarchy and in the "plenary councils, the bishops of the country have time and again pronounced on its importance, furthered it by every means within their power, urged and commanded and pleaded with the Catholic laity for its support."[51] A pastoral letter of Bishop McFaul of Trenton early in the twentieth century urged:

> Every Catholic family should subscribe for a Catholic newspaper and a Catholic magazine. . . . Catholics should ask their newsdealers for such newspapers as *The Freemen's Journal* of New York, *The Pilot* of Boston, *The Pittsburgh Observer,* and other religious newspapers published in their respective localities. They should also seek the inestimable Catholic periodicals like *The Messenger* and *The Catholic World* of New York, *Donahue's Magazine* of Boston and a host of others. . . . No better example of the power and influence of the press can be given than the results achieved in Germany. It was due to public opinion created by the Catholic press that the Center Party remained undivided and steadfast, triumphed over Kulturkampf, sent Bismarck to Canossa, and organized the Catholics of Germany so that they presented an unbroken front to their enemies.
>
> We will never attain the position due to us in the civil and religious life of America, unless we employ this powerful lever in the creation of public opinion.[52]

Besides drawing attention to Catholic publications, Church leaders also pointed out improper reading material. Husslein cautioned the Catholic trade unionists that, if they were to remain "men of clear insight and strong Catholic principles," they would not "endorse the socialist publications which were recommended to them." To accept socialist publications, he declared, meant bringing "into the house of the laborer a weekly apostle of radicalism in almost every shape condemned by the Church."[53]

The period 1900–1918 saw the birth of about fifty Catholic weekly publications, of the Catholic Press Association, and of several publications specifically dedicated to combating socialism.[54]

The Catholic Press Association was established in August 1911 at Columbus, Ohio, by Catholic editors convening in that city.

In New York City two anti-socialist publications were founded shortly before World War I by devoted Catholic sources. One was a newspaper, *The Live Issue,* the other a journal, *The Common Cause. The Live Issue*'s "Declaration of Principles," featured above its editorial page, stated that the paper "utterly repudiates and fearlessly combats Socialism." In consideration of the spirit and purposes of *Rerum novarum,* the editor saw his duty was to teach the workers the values of the Catholic social movement. *"The Live Issue*'s mission," he announced, "was to make our workingmen conscious factors in the moulding process which society is now undergoing. And it is to achieve this result that true social enlightenment is an imperative necessity no less than to expose the dangers and fallacies of Socialism."[55]

The Common Cause likewise proclaimed itself a journal which "comes to the defence of right-reason in things economic as against the theories of Socialism."[56] Its issues regularly contained indictments against socialism, and it periodically republished antisocialist articles originating elsewhere. The appearance of *The Common Cause* not only elicited an enthusiastic reception from a number of Catholic publications, but its editors also received a letter from Samuel Gompers complimenting its purpose.[57]

Conclusions

The weakness of socialism in the American Federation of Labor at the close of World War I was, in part, a testimonial to the success of the Catholic Church's opposition to this doctrine. The Church could credit itself with having waged an effective campaign in checking socialism within the trade union movement. Many other factors which labor historians have carefully brought out have accounted for the weakness of socialism within American trade unions, but certainly the definite opposition of the Catholic Church should be added to the reasons usually advanced. Professor Selig Perlman was evidently aware of this when he wrote in 1928 that for the American labor movement "to make socialism or communism the official 'ism' of the movement, would mean, even if the other conditions permitted it, deliberately driving the Catholics, who are perhaps in the majority in the American Federation of Labor, out of the labor movement, since with them an irreconcilable opposition to socialism is a matter of religious principle."[58] As can be readily understood, a labor party in an industrialized country derives its main strength from the support of the trade union movement. Where a trade union movement has neither socialist leadership nor a socialist political consciousness among its rank and file, it will not possess the ideology that would find its political expression in a labor party. The important generalization which Perlman has suggested, and which the research for this present study has confirmed, is that the failure of socialism and a political labor party to evolve in America were in some measure due to the hostility of the Catholic Church. Catholicism created a "bridge between the Church in America and the labor movement" enabling it to "take hold of the labor movement."[59]

It is also of importance to note that Catholicism engaged in this task during a period when American trade unionism, still in its infancy, was developing its institutional traditions. Like all traditions, these would prevail during future generations and tend to become almost conditioned responses. Furthermore, this period also began as one in which the socialist movement seemed on the threshold of becoming a major American political force. The awareness of these two facts on the part of the Catholic Church was evident in the extent of its exertions against socialist penetration of the trade unions. The victory achieved by Catholicism at the close of this period was shown by the weakness of the socialists in the AFL and the dominance of an antisocialist administration. At the conclusion of World War I, the similarity between the *AFL's Reconstruction Program* and the *Bishops' Program of Social Reconstruction* was more than a coincidence.[60] It was to some degree the result of the intensive efforts made by the Catholic Church to permeate the AFL with social principles. Aided by the predominantly Catholic officers of the international unions and by the large Catholic rank and file in the AFL responsive to their Church's views on socialism, Catholicism could take partial credit for the political philosophy and policies of the federation, for socialism's weakness in the trade union movement, and the absence of a labor party in the United States.

NOTES

1. David J. Saposs, "The Catholic Church and the Labor Movement," *Modern Monthly*, 7 (May–June 1933), p. 225.

2. Pope Leo XIII, *Rerum novarum*, May 15, 1891 (New York: Paulist Press, 1939).

3. Vincent A. McQuade, *American Catholic Attitude on Child Labor Since 1891* (Ph.D. Dissertation, Catholic University of America, 1938).

4. Selig Perlman, *A Theory of the Labor Movement* (New York: Macmillan, 1928), p. 168.

5. Norman Ware, *Labor in Modern Industrial Society* (New York: Heath, 1935), p. 35.

6. This list was prepared after consultation with Frank Morrison, AFL Sec. 1896–1929, and Dr. David J. Saposs. It does not include any Socialists.

7. Allen S. Will, "Checking the Tide of Socialism," in *Life of Cardinal Gibbons, Archbishop of Baltimore* (New York: Dutton, 1922), II, ch. 37.

8. Cardinal James Gibbons, *A Retrospect of Fifty Years* (Baltimore: Murphy, 1916), pp. 258–59.

9. Cardinal James Gibbons, *Organized Labor*, reprinted by Anti-Boycott Association as part of a pamphlet, *The Morals and Law Involved in Labor Conflicts*, in the New York Public Library.

10. Cardinal William O'Connell, "Pastoral Letter on the Laborer's Rights," *The Church and Labor* (New York: Macmillan, 1920), pp. 177–86.

11. *America*, vol. II, no. 13, January 8, 1910.

12. William Kerby, "Aims in Socialism," *The Catholic World*, 85 (July 1907), p. 511. Father Kerby was a good friend of Samuel Gompers. Occasionally he took his Catholic University Social Economy students to AFL headquarters for a lecture by Gompers on trade unionism.

13. Rev. James Powers (ed.), *Addresses of Bishop McFaul* (Trenton: American, 1908), p. 375.

14. *Messenger*, 38 (September 1902), p. 246, quoting Buffalo *Catholic Evening News*, July 5, 1902.

15. Kansas City *Journal*, April 10, 1912.

16. Archbishop John Ireland, *Labor and Capital*, p. 343 (in the New York Public Library).

17. *AFL Proceedings*, 1913, pp. 207–10.

18. Rev. Charles Bruehl, "The Conditions of Labor," in *Addresses at Patriotic and Civic Occasions by Catholic Orators* (New York: Wagner, 1915), I, pp. 63–82.

19. *Central Blatt and Social Justice*, 5 (February 1913), pp. 243–45.

20. Ibid. For a discussion of Catholic trade union leaders in Belgium and Germany who "separated themselves from unions that had fallen under socialist domination" and established Catholic unions see Henry Sommerville, *Studies in the Catholic Social Movement* (London: Burns, etc., 1933), pp. 5–6.

21. Aaron Abell, "The Reception of Leo XIII's Labor Encyclical in America 1891–1919," *The Review of Politics*, 7 (October 1945), p. 493.

22. Professor Abell in an essay, "Monsignor Ryan: An Historical Interpretation," *The Review of Politics*, 8 (January 1946), says that Ryan "left to others, notably the Rev. Peter E. Dietz, the organizational task involved in the [Leo's] Encyclical's official reception." Cf. Harrita Fox, "Peter E. Dietz, Pioneer in the Catholic Social Movement" (Ph.D. Dissertation, University of Notre Dame, 1950). In a letter to the author (March 14, 1948) she writes: "The influence of Father Dietz in the AFL was great since he numbered Samuel Gompers, John P. Frey and Matthew Woll among his friends. The fact, too, that he contributed to the *American Federationist* would indicate an appreciation of his opinions."

23. Sister Joan de Lourdes, now teaching at St. Joseph's College for Women, Brooklyn, kindly made this letter available to the writer. (Dietz to Leonard, Milwaukee, July 19, 1940.)

24. *AFL Proceedings*, 1910, pp. 202–3. At the 1911 Atlanta, Ga., convention Dietz preached the sermon at the Immaculate Conception Church on "The Relation of the Catholic Church to the Labor Movement" (*AFL Proceedings*, 1911, p. 184). At the 1912 convention he again spoke before all the delegates (*AFL Proceedings*, 1912, p. 223). He warned that even if the workers were able to carry out the slogan "workers of the world unite . . . you have a world to win," it would not "profit a man even if he does win the world but suffer the loss of his soul."

25. A copy of the Militia's constitution and platform and endorsement of Archbishop Glennon was seen by the author among the John Mitchell papers at Catholic University of America. A photostat of this document is now in the author's possession. The Reverend Henry J. Browne, while working on his Ph.D., realized the significance of the Mitchell papers and kindly introduced the author to them.

26. *The Catholic Church and the Labor Movement.*

27. The Militia, apparently, was no secret to the Socialist press. A news story in the Schenectady *Daily Union*, January 9, 1911, relating that "the work of getting Schenectady Catholic union men into the Militia will begin at once by the men in charge here," brought forth a vituperative editorial by De Leon in his *Daily People*, January 14, 1911. The *International Socialist Review* declared: "Every American Unionist knows how bitterly the Catholic Church has fought Socialism in the labor unions through its servile tools, such as the Militia of Christ and similar secret alliances" (Richard Perrin, "The German Catholic Unions," *International Socialist Review*, January 1914, p.

398). *The Masses*, in an editorial on AFL and Catholic Church opposition to Socialism, wrote: "The AFL is getting more and more into the hands of the Militia of Christ" (*The Masses*, July 1912, p. 3).

28. "The Reception of Leo XIII's Labor Encyclical," *The Review of Politics*, 7 (October 1945).

29. Dietz to Mitchell, December 30, 1911. In regard to raising funds, Mitchell proposed instead a circular letter of appeal for "small subscriptions from a large number of men" (Mitchell to Dietz, January 3, 1912).

30. Quoted by Aaron Abell, "The Reception . . . ," op. cit., p. 490, from *Catholic News*, September 2, 1911.

31. Dietz to Mitchell, Milwaukee, August 3, 1912.

32. Henry J. Browne, "Peter E. Dietz, Pioneer Planner of Catholic Social Action," *The Catholic Historical Review*, XXXIII (January 1948), p. 454.

33. *Bulletin* of AFCS, 12, nos. 8–10 (August–September 1917), p. 11.

34. Browne, op. cit., p. 456.

35. Ibid., p. 449.

36. Abell, op. cit., p. 479.

37. Matre, op. cit., IX, pp. 247–59. The present-day descendant of this organization is now known as the National Catholic Welfare Conference.

38. *Bulletin* of AFCS, 12, nos. 8–10 (August–October 1917), p. 11.

39. *The Central Verein: History, Aims and Scope*, Leaflet no. 82, published by the GRCCV's Central Bureau. This leaflet was kindly loaned to the author by Sister Joan de Lourdes.

40. Sister Mary Brophy, *The Social Thought of the German Roman Catholic Verein* (Ph.D. Dissertation, Catholic University of America, 1941), pp. 72–83.

41. Ibid.

42. Ibid.

43. *Central Blatt and Social Justice*, 4 (December 1911), p. 204.

44. David Goldstein, "Trade Unions: Their Foundation, Achievements, Dangers and Prospects," *Central Blatt and Social Justice*, 3 (December 1910), p. 189.

45. Peter W. Collins, "Catholic Workingmen's Association," *Central Blatt and Social Justice*, 5 (May 1912), pp. 35–36. Goldstein and Collins were two especially colorful lecturers routed on tours by the Militia of Christ and the AFC's Social Service Commission. Goldstein had been a member of the Socialist Labor Party before accepting the Catholic faith. Cf. David Goldstein, *Socialism: The Nation of Fatherless Children* (Boston: Union News League, 1902). Professor Abell rates Collins as second only to Father Dietz in extending Catholic principles within the trade unions at this time (Abell, op. cit., p. 489).

46. Abell, op. cit., p. 487.

47. F. P. Kenkel to Sister Joan de Lourdes, June 24, 1940. This letter was kindly loaned to the author by Sister Joan.

48. F. P. Kenkel to Norman McKenna, April 29, 1940, quoted by Sister Joan de Lourdes Leonard in "Catholic Attitude Towards American Labor 1884–1919" (unpublished M.A. Thesis, Columbia University, 1940).

49. John A. Ryan, "The Central Verein," *Catholic Fortnightly Review*, 16 (first March issue, 1909), p. 132. The devotion of Father Ryan to major social reform is well known. His support of AFL, its economic demands and strikes, endeared him to many. Space, however, prevents a consideration of Ryan's contributions (cf. Richard J. Purcell, "John A. Ryan—Prophet of Social Justice," *Studies,* June 1946).

50. Quoted by John Burke, "Convention of Catholic Editors," *The Catholic World,* October 1911, p. 9.

51. Burke, op. cit., p. 81.

52. James A. McFaul, "Some Modern Problems," *Pastoral Letter* (Trenton: American Publishing Co., 1908).

53. Joseph Husslein (S.J.), *The Catholic's Work in the World* (New York: Benziger Bros., 1917), pp. 112–16.

54. Cf. Apollinaris W. Baumgartner, *Catholic Journalism in the United States* (New York: Columbia University Press, 1931).

55. *The Live Issue* (New York City), April 11, 1914, p. 2.

56. *Socialism: The Nation of Fatherless Children.*

57. Gompers to *The Common Cause,* Washington, D.C., December 14, 1911, in *Gompers Correspondence,* AFL headquarters, Washington, D.C.

58. Perlman, op. cit., p. 169.

59. Dietz to Cardinal O'Connell, March 15, 1913, quoted by Sister Harrita Fox, op. cit., p. 105.

60. *Bishops' Program of Social Reconstruction* (Washington, D.C.: National Catholic Welfare Conference, n.d.).

COMMENT

Henry J. Browne

Religion traditionally gets blamed and credited for many things. In the history of the United States Catholicism has come in for more than its fair share of blame for being superstitious, priest-ridden, and out of step with prevailing American ways—if not actually politically subversive. Shortly before some of its devotees would credit it for producing John—or at least mother Rose—Kennedy, Marc Karson, a budding young scholar under Professor Harold Laski at the London School of Economics, blamed it for stopping the advance of socialism in the American labor movement, and hence for lessening the impact of socialism in the United States.

Karson's approach has always appeared to this writer to be essentially naïve and simplistic in a way almost mirroring the devotional believer's overclaim that when the Pope coughed all Catholics at least sneezed. Even the gently apologetic second statement of his thesis, which emphasized the unconscious brainwashing impact of a tradition of anti-socialism on Catholic trade unionists, only added to its gratuitous character. The argument's ideological milieu is more precisely that of the 1950s when the Kremlin-Vatican parallel was being made into an American secular dogma by Paul Blanshard.[1]

That there was a deviously organized and Church-directed Catholic bloc in the labor movement continued as part of the lore of the Left well into contemporary labor history. Catholic trade union enthusiasts did not always help to allay that suspicion. Father Peter Dietz, with what seems a kind of embarrassed encouragement from Catholic John Mitchell of the miners' union, did in 1912 organize the Militia of Christ for Social Service to encourage support of the American Federation of Labor. Though such a pious label telegraphed an image of religious proselytizing, the

Militia's work was mostly a one-man paper show in the form of press releases, prospectuses, and polemics.[2] Dietz, fortunately for Church and labor, soon moved into the more harmless field of educating Catholic social workers.

Some of Dietz's Militia activity indicated further the paradox of American Catholic trade unionists: at the very time they were supposedly infiltrating to keep the labor movement at least safe from socialism, if not Church-dominated, they were seeking clarification from Rome about their right to belong to a union that was not Catholic or at least interconfessionally Christian in character. Actually it was not until 1931 in *Quadragesimo anno* that such an explicit endorsement of Catholic membership in a so-called neutral or non-religious union was forthcoming from suspect Vatican headquarters.

In the Progressive era the most organized and people-connected Catholic voice of social reform was the German Catholics' Central-Verein. A recent sober and insightful account of that organization's conservative venture into the social question in 1908 leaves no doubt of its anti-socialist stand, its primary reason in fact for adding its program of social reform to those concerned with religion and ethnic identity. The real question of its real impact remains more mysterious, however. An intellectual director with a medieval orientation, editing a dull magazine in German, to be read mostly by priests and farmers, arranging lectures and pamphlet publication, and drawing inspiration from a very German and philosophic pattern of total social reorganization called "solidarism" hardly presents a picture of powerful influence. Outside the organization's own public statements, and the socialists' reciprocal claims about the power of the opposition, it is hard to find more than a rhetorical reality in that particular version of the mythic Catholic slaying of the red dragon among workers.[8]

On the other side is the evidence that some ethnic influence seems to have been at work in cases of Catholic flirtation with American socialism. In the mid-eighties New York Irish with more the auld sod than their own city tenements on their mind, in great numbers, and against the authority of the Church and their regular political party, backed Henry George's unsuccessful bid for mayor. His Single Tax platform denying private ownership in land had the endorsement of Dr. Edward McGlynn, who led largely by charisma instead of logic. Though the standard account of Catholic social action in the first two decades of the twentieth century is given to detailing the intellectual opposition to socialism, one can dig out Poles in Milwaukee, Italians in Colorado, Germans and Irish in Cleveland, and an organization of Christian Socialists in Chicago whose balloting proves that municipal socialism appealed to some Catholic laborers despite direct Church opposition. Clearly the intellectual's argument that made socialism intrinsically anti-religious did not have the impact claimed for it.[4]

Within the ranks of labor the Catholic-socialist debate was, in the final analysis, a conflict of power rather than of theory. American Catholics did not in any real conscious and effective way bring their ethical values to bear within the movement until 1937 with the Association of Catholic Trade Unionists. At least that was its manifest function. History might question its latent one, considering the success of many of its former members in positions with government, organized labor, and even as management consultants. The case in point may illustrate how long-abiding was the myth of the Catholic monolith sending tremors on every social and political doctrine from the Pope to the humblest parishioner. The ACTU was based on a paragraph in Pius XI's labor encyclical which advocated the creation of organizations, paralleling the unions, to inculcate Catholic ethical and religious principles. The training of unionist leaders and the education of rank and file for more active participation were pursued through labor schools and a lively newspaper, *The Labor Leader*. One of the chief focuses of organizational strength was the New York metropolitan area where the group had begun. Academic discussions sometimes led to action groups for reform within individual unions. The "bad guys" were usually racketeers or communists. Such specific union "conferences" were never restricted to Catholics nor were they clerically controlled, but of course they risked being labeled a religious caucus.

So it was that the issue of organized Catholic factionalism and anti-radicalism in unions did not get its real testing until the late 1940s. The question fought out was communist control of the United Electrical, Radio and Machine Workers of America. The ACTU concern began in their labor school conducted at New Rochelle College. For our purpose it may suffice to recall Michael Harrington's study of the case. He may be considered impartial since he is readily described as a Christian Socialist who was turned on by the Catholic Worker movement. Never were American Catholics so ready for such action against radicalism. There was a network of organizations across the country with competent unionist laymen working from a body of literature based on the social encyclicals. There was even a tie-in with the organizational power of the Church through the chaplains. Nonetheless, Harrington's detailed and detached study found that not only was the ACTU leadership opposed to a sectarian approach and religious factionalism but also that as a national force in the struggle it was not "cohesive and identifiable." A potpourri of organizations and personalities, clerical and lay, including the classic stimulant of anti-Catholic bile, Jesuits (in this case conducting labor schools), involved themselves in the fight. The conclusion, however surprising, is that the struggle which resulted in a victory for the newly established IUE was not a religious one but based on their convincing workers of their better delivery of union benefits. Indeed, the one priest who from the pulpit declared it sinful to vote for the communist leadership, was repudiated by the electrical workers of his community.[5]

This well-documented case seems to be the only available study of a confrontation between organized radicalism and organized Catholicism within the labor movement in the United States. Much research, it is suggested, remains to be done on the influence of the Church's teaching, particularly the role of its leadership, often both an ethnic and intellectual as well as a religious one, on the success or failure of trade unions in a specific locality. From the Molly Maguire pastors of the Pennsylvania coal fields to the as yet unsung priest members of mediation and arbitration boards who emerged in the 1930s, some interesting clerical examples of the interplay of religion and labor are being discovered. In general they indicate that no simple picture is to be drawn either depicting a Catholic rejection of Left extremism as evil or identifying the workers' efforts with radical and anti-social philosophy.

My own earlier research also points to the prevalence of a very pragmatic approach on the part of priest confessors and their bishop superiors on the question of American Catholics joining unions. They worried more about the secret character of the organizations than any other single factor in their programs. If a generalization might be risked it would be: the closer the spiritual leader or adviser was to the workingman's situation, the more he favored the union and the less concerned he was with its real or imagined radicalism. For example, it is impressive that confessional policy on union membership at the Baltimore cathedral, even before the mid-nineteenth century, was tolerant, and as early as the II Plenary Council in 1866, the American hierarchy in solemn panoply assembled approved of Catholics joining a bona fide organization for economic self-help.[6]

Several examples might illustrate this class-identity influence on churchmen. In the 1870s Bishop James Wood of Philadelphia allied himself with the powers that crushed the militant Mollies; many of their pastors were torn between knowledge of their miserable plight in the mines and rejection of their violence. Much more explicitly pro-worker was Father Cornelius O'Leary's defense of the Missouri railroad strikers in 1886. Before a congressional committee he blamed corporations for breeding radicalism and later, while in exile imposed by his archbishop, avowed he was a "socialist and rebel at heart as was every Irishman."[7] The passage of time brought class changes. In Lawrence, Massachusetts, in 1912 two Catholic working-class-community pastors of later ethnic arrivals (Italians and Syrians) were found endorsing the radical IWW textile workers strike in the face of the respectable clergy of the city led by the Irish Catholic pastor. At that same period Catholic clergy influence was alleged by the Socialist Party in New York City for the failure of its program to make any headway among Irish and Italian workers. Yet a recent scholar studying the case puts the religious factor secondary to political, economic, and social ones. These workers were getting their security and power elsewhere, including from the Church, Tammany Hall, and AF of L unionism, and did not need to turn to the despair of radical politics.[8]

It might be submitted that not only distance from the problems of the workers but also other class considerations such as educational and social background and connections had more influence than theological considerations or the hostile attitude of some American bishops toward the supposedly radical efforts of American workers. The late-nineteenth-century bishops outstanding for their fear of the menace of socialism working through unions were James Roosevelt Bayley of Baltimore, most certainly a social snob, and such European-connected types as Francis S. M. Chatard of Vincennes, John Dwenger of Fort Wayne, and John Baptist Salpointe of Santa Fe. The last of these, right after leaving his city torn

190 / HENRY J. BROWNE

by the strife of the rail strike in 1886, joined Archbishop Peter
Richard Kenrick of St. Louis to make the two votes out of the
twelve archbishops of the country against the Knights of Labor.
Kenrick was reported to be close to railroad interests, as was
Bishop Nicholas Matz of Denver said to have been friendly with
mining powers during the troubles in that area in 1903. Matz
denounced the socialist threat of the Federation of Miners and
clubbed them with the anti-socialist defense of private property
found in *Rerum novarum.* However, a recent study of Matz begs
the question of his influence on the workers. For example, out of
the approximately two hundred listed as deported by the occupying
military out of the mining district almost 50 per cent seem to have
Catholic ethnic names and so may be considered to have cordially
ignored the bishop's pro-Establishment threats.[9] For further enlightenment it might be useful to trace the growth of the fear of
socialism among American bishops, even such liberals as John Ireland of St. Paul, as they grew closer in friendship to such men
as James Hill, the railroad magnate.[10]

The major trouble with the Saposs-Karson thesis is that it takes
the word for the deed. The attitude of the organization and its
official spokesmen is presumed unquestionably to motivate members to accept the body of approved doctrine. The Catholic fears
of the danger of socialism expressed so vividly in *Quod apostolici
muneris,* the encyclical of 1878, hardly call one today to holy warfare against its programs in the light of *Mater et magistra* and
Progressio populorum. The question is whether the bugle sound
was ever heard or acted upon that well by the ranks even a hundred years ago. It has been established, to the satisfaction of social
science at least, that religion makes a difference in social and political attitudes. At the same time there is doubt about the authentic
relationship between attitudes expressed and actual positions
taken.[11] Philip Taft, for example, who was the first really to exploit in a scholarly way the archives of the American Federation
of Labor, could not find any such distinctive reaction to questions
relating to socialism in the votes of the Catholic members of the
executive council of that organization. The conclusion of this
study of the matter is worth quoting:

The theory that Catholic influence prevented American labor from
endorsing socialism and independent political action never gained a
following outside of radical and anti-Catholic circles. The opposition

to socialism in the early years was led by men such as Gompers, and McGuire, who was not a practicing Catholic although he was of a Catholic family and died in the church. Lennon, Duncan, Kidd and McCraith, who carried the attack against the Socialists, were of Protestant origin, McCraith being a philosophical anarchist without much religion of any kind. Moreover, the A.F. of L.'s defense of revolutionaries and anarchists refutes the implication of domination by the Church.[12]

It should also be pointed out that Catholic spiritual leaders in the United States were not as often on the spot as their counterparts in Europe, since control of the American economy was not in Catholic hands, and hence the Church not as beholden to such anti-labor power. The esoteric social doctrine of the Church was far removed from the masses of its members. That is not to say that the American Catholic blue-collar worker did not in time of crisis seek and even have volunteered for him the aid of the intellectuals and pastors of his faith. This was certainly true of the organizing days of the CIO in the 1930s when clerics and organizers worked hand in hand.

Yet John Brophy, who was one of the great forces in that movement and who, owing to his fostering the industrial councils' plan, was considered the rare self-made Catholic intellectual in the labor movement, testified to the absence of ideological formation. His memoirs credit his rejection of Marxist materialism to what he calls vaguely his Christian humanism. He registered his agreement with most socialistic reforms and stressed the pro-labor rather than the pro-private property aspects of the papal encyclical of 1891. He then went on to recall:

Had I known of the papal social encyclicals I could have saved much distress of mind. American churchmen were very slow about heeding the papal counsel on these important issues. I never read *Rerum Novarum* until a generation after it was issued. I heard of it only vaguely as an anti-Socialist tract, or even as an apology for capitalism. American churchmen seem not to have grasped the meaning of that great document for a long time; certainly I, like many others, was long left in ignorance of its criticism of capitalism and of its constructive counsel.[13]

American Catholic enthusiasm for such movements as New Deal reformism, industrial unionism, and even the Christian anarchy expounded in the *Catholic Worker,* not to mention the many other eddies of social change that flowed out of that movement of the thirties, may have abated during the last generation's flight to suburbia. Yet even if the "socializing," "cultural conformist," and "society sustaining" aspects of American Catholicism continue strong, it retains nonetheless room for even the revolutionary who may have caught some glimpse of the socialist dream. Peter McGuire, Terence Powderly, Fathers Thomas Haggerty and Thomas McGrady, the McNamara brothers, Tom Mooney, Elizabeth Gurley Flynn, and others like them gave up the Church as the defender of an unjust industrial status quo, and settled mostly for more radical doctrines of society. Today they might find themselves more at home in a loosened if not chastened Church on whose doctrine some of its members are now building programs of radical social change.[14]

The evidence at any rate leaves room to suspect that other factors—including the whole spirit of the country—were more potent than the religious in keeping organized labor from coming under the ideological dominion of socialism.[15] The claims even I made for the religious influence some twenty years ago have been tempered by a decade's efforts at moving people in social action and finding religion to be more a personal justification than a motivation to most men, whose concerns continue to be overwhelmingly bread-and-butter ones.

NOTES

1. Marc Karson, *American Labor Unions and Politics, 1900–1918* (Carbondale, 1958), pp. xi–xv.
2. Philip Taft, *The A.F. of L. in the Time of Gompers* (New York, 1957), p. 336, so characterized Dietz's efforts. This writer's agreement is found in "Roman Catholicism," *The Shaping of American Religion* (Princeton, 1961), p. 101. The opposite view is found in Mary Harrita Fox, *Peter E. Dietz, Labor Priest* (Notre Dame, 1953).
3. Philip Gleason, *The Conservative Reformers: German-American Catholics and the Social Order* (Notre Dame, 1968), pp. 69–143.
4. Robert Cross, *The Emergence of Liberal Catholicism in America* (Cambridge, 1958), pp. 119–24, gives a brief but balanced account of the New York scene, while the review of the 1900–17 developments is found in Aaron Abell, *American Catholicism and Social Action: A Search for Social Justice, 1865–1950* (Garden City, 1960), pp. 136–53.
5. Michael Harrington, "Catholics in the Labor Movement: A Case History," *Labor History*, I (Fall 1960), pp. 231–63.
6. Abell, op. cit., p. 47, in an ancient disagreement with this writer predicated hostility against unions on the part of bishops and priests up to the mid-1880s. Perhaps as a layman he was not as aware of how much pastoral counterforce it must have taken to get even a minimal statement of friendliness to unions in 1866. Henry J. Browne, *The Catholic Church and the Knights of Labor* (Washington, D.C., 1949), p. 16.
7. William B. Faherty, "The Clergy and Labor Progress: Cornelius O'Leary and the Knights of Labor," *Labor History*, XI (Spring 1970), p. 188. Cf. Wayne G. Broehl, *The Molly Maguires* (Cambridge, 1964), *passim.*
8. Philip S. Foner, *History of the Labor Movement in the United States*, IV (New York, 1965), pp. 333–34; Melvyn Dubofsky, "Success and Failure of Socialism in New York City, 1900–1918; a Case Study," *Labor History*, IX (Fall 1968), pp. 372–73.
9. George G. Suggs, "Religion and Labor in the Rocky Mountain West: Bishop Nicholas C. Matz and the Western Federation of Miners," *Labor History*, XI (Spring 1970), pp. 190–206; cf. "The List of Deported," in Emma F. Langdon, *The Cripple Creek Strike: A History of Industrial Wars in Colorado, 1903–4–5* (Denver, 1905), pp. 456–57.
10. It may be instructive that Liston Pope in his pioneer study of religious and economic factors in society found only two clergymen in Gaston County friendly to the labor organizer, two detached and non-influential Catholic monks. *Millhands and Preachers* (New Haven, 1942), p. 202.

11. Cf. Gerhard Lenski, *The Religious Factor: A Sociological Study of Religion's Impact on Politics, Economics and Family Life* (Garden City, 1961) and Irwin Deutscher, "Words and Deeds: Social Science and Social Policy," *Social Problems,* XIII (Winter 1966).

12. Taft, op. cit., p. 336.

13. John Brophy, *A Miner's Life* (Madison, 1964), p. 100. It may be interesting for comparative purposes to note that in 1969 a study in the diocese of Worcester, Massachusetts, indicated that 60 per cent of the Catholic laity were for all practical purposes unacquainted with the Second Vatican Council. Richard P. McBrien, *Church: the Continuing Quest* (New York, 1970), pp. 26–27.

14. Cf. Francine Gray, *Divine Disobedience: Profiles in Catholic Radicalism* (New York, 1970).

15. Sidney Hook, "The Philosophical Basis of Marxian Socialism in the United States," *Socialism and American Life,* I (Princeton, 1952), pp. 450–51.

REPLY

Marc Karson

Father Browne does not accept my analysis of his Church's role in the early-twentieth-century political development of American labor unions. I am criticized for being "essentially naïve and simplistic," and in the "ideological milieu" of anti-Catholic intellectuals like Paul Blanshard. I can understand that Father Browne is probably tired of the never-ending bigotry his Church encounters and has responded with an honest reaction to an article that has overtones of a stereotyped reaction to Catholicism. Priests have feelings, too. However, my article should be judged on the data it contains, not on my own particular views, and this data, which is repeated in a chapter of my book *American Labor Unions and Politics, 1900–1918,* received favorable reviews in such Catholic periodicals as *America* and *Social Order,* as well as being declared "admirably fair and objective" in a testimonial from Monsignor George Higgins printed on the jacket of the book.[1] I welcome Father Browne's criticism, however, because like that I received many years ago from Catholic clergy, it helps me examine my own motivation and increase my knowledge of Catholicism and priests, as well as of myself.[2]

It is tragically true that anti-Catholicism has been America's "most persistent non-racial phobia," a phobia not limited to Southern Baptists and Midwestern Republicans but which includes liberals, Unitarians, intellectuals, and socialists also. Paul Blanshard's *American Freedom and Catholic Power* well illustrates that anti-Catholicism can be the intellectual anti-Semitism of the Left. Father Browne is also correct in saying that there has been a "lore of the Left" which has seen "a deviously organized and Church-directed block in the labor movement." This view cuts across the Left from the *Miners' Magazine* of the militant Western Federation of Miners, the *International Socialist Review,* and Daniel De Leon's *The People* to the contemporary labor history volumes of Philip Foner.

It is also true that any implied criticism my article makes of the conservative influence of the Catholic Church as an institutional force in the early twentieth century certainly does not apply to today's Church. As Father Browne well puts it, today there is "a loosened if not chastened Church on whose doctrine some of its members are now building programs of radical social change." This remarkable reversal of a Church undergoing internal democratic transformation and crusading against war, racism, and poverty is one of the most hopeful and heartening political developments in my lifetime. Pope John's superb encyclicals, *Pacem in Terris* and *Mater et Magistra,* are a far cry from the war-on-socialism encyclicals that established political principles for Catholics during the period of my study.

From the hindsight of middle age, I can acquiesce in Father Browne's statement that "the major trouble with the Saposs-Karson thesis is that it takes the word for the deed." This is an unfortunate error that human beings are prone to make, "budding scholars" included. It is apparent to me now that in the late 1940s, when I was researching labor's early-twentieth-century political history, my motivation in pursuing leads on the role of the Catholic Church was not that of a disinterested academician, but rather of a left-wing partisan seeking material to document an a priori emotional conviction. In my political orbit, a class conflict existed and the Catholic Church was an ally of privilege far more concerned with the salvation of souls than with man's material suffering on earth. It was all very simple. Socialism declared it was for equality, human happiness, and the liberation of man; Catholicism was for obedience to authority, the acceptance of inequality, and preparation for the future life. Hence, socialism was right and Catholicism was wrong.

While I may have been guilty of overexaggerating the influence that the institutionalized anti-socialism of the Catholic Church had on Catholic workers, however, I never saw the Church as possessing the power unilaterally to account for the failure of socialism in the labor movement. Father Browne misinterprets the message in my article when he writes that I "blamed it [Catholicism] for stopping the advance of socialism in the American labor movement." I was blaming it for its compulsive anti-socialist role, which I saw as a negative kind of social action. At no point in my article did I assert that Catholicism was "more potent" than other factors in accounting for the weakness of socialism in the American labor movement. The contribution I hoped to make, as I stated in the "Conclusions" to my article, was that "the definite opposition of the Catholic Church should be added to the reasons usually advanced" for the failure of socialism to become the political creed of early-twentieth-century American unionism. My statements on the success of the anti-socialist role of Catholicism were always qualified ones which declared that the weakness of socialism in the union movement was "in part" and "in some measure" due to the Catholic Church and that "Catholicism could take partial credit" for this development.[3] As Father Browne has come around to recognize, I, too, see religion as a secondary, not primary, influence on men's motivation. As communist revolutions and socialist ballot box victories tell, bread-and-butter concerns and emotional needs move men more than encyclicals and priests' efforts.

There are a few areas in which I still would not share Father Browne's outlook. Father Dietz is downgraded as a "one-man paper show." I prefer to take the judgment of Sister Mary Harrita Fox, who did her Ph.D. dissertation and later a book on the life of Dietz. She writes that an evaluation of Dietz's Militia of Christ should go beyond its surface records of a four-year life, a peak membership of seven hundred, and a handful of functioning chapters and not "ignore the intangibles that are hard to evaluate." The Militia provided "Catholic solidarity" for its "individual members scattered throughout the various labor organizations" and gave them the conviction of its "founder, that Socialism, the insidious enemy of trade unionism, must be defeated at all costs."[4]

Most of Father Browne's comments on my paper do not focus exclusively on the period 1900–18. In touching on the influence of Catholicism on Catholic workers in the formative years of the labor movement, he cites the opinion of Philip Taft, who rejects the theory of Catholic influence within the early AF of L. While Taft is seen as the elder statesman among labor historians by the pragmatic school of labor philosophers and leadership, he is held in contempt by the Left as an apologist for the "Establishment" in the trade union world. Taft is so uncritical of the official line of labor that he can perpetuate the myth that the AF of L has acted in "defense of revolutionaries and anarchists."[5]

The difference, I think, between Father Browne and me is one of degree and not of kind with regard to the impact that the Church

had on the political behavior of Catholic workers in the early twentieth century. Father Browne maintains that this impact cannot
be determined objectively without utilizing the methodology of today's behavioral scientists. Some people, myself included, might
not feel it necessary to give such weight to behavioral research.
It does not take such empirical techniques, however, to recognize
a lesser but vital fact which my article communicated—that no
Catholic worker in early-twentieth-century America could be unaware that his Church was an adversary, not an ally, of socialism.

NOTES

1. Marc Karson, *American Labor Unions and Politics, 1900–1918* (Carbondale, Ill.: Southern Illinois University Press, 1958), 358 pp. (paperback: Beacon Press, Boston, 1965).

2. My review of Father Theodore Purcell's book *The Worker Speaks His Mind on Company and Union* in the *New Republic*, April 12, 1954, caused Monsignor George Higgins to voice his objections in his syndicated column, "The Yardstick." Father Purcell reacted with two letters in the *New Republic*, May 4 and August 2, 1954. I replied in the *New Republic*, June 21, 1954.

3. In the last chapter in my book I list the following characteristics of twentieth-century America as an explanation for the weakness of socialism within organized labor: (1) the vitality of American capitalism; (2) the middle-class psychology of American workers; (3) the American faith in individual rights; (4) the conservative features of the American political system; (5) the anti-socialist position of the Catholic Church; and (6) the anti-socialist leadership of Samuel Gompers.

4. Sister Mary Harrita Fox, "Peter E. Dietz: Pioneer in the Catholic Social Action Movement" (Ph.D. Dissertation, University of Notre Dame, 1950), p. 114.

5. There were instances when the AF of L supported efforts to free Leftists such as Tom Mooney and Joe Hill. Pressure from Leftist affiliates, however, was mostly responsible for such action. At other times the AF of L gave no major aid to imprisoned Charles Moyer and Bill Haywood or to imprisoned IWW leaders during and after World War I. Other myths relating to AF of L political ideas and policies that Taft repeats in his writings are that the Federation's political policy was non-partisan, that its support of Asiatic immigration exclusion contained no traces of racism, that it was opposed to discrimination against American blacks, and that it was a foe of American imperialism.

Chapter 6

SOCIALISM AND AMERICAN TRADE UNIONISM*

John H. M. Laslett

What were the reasons for the growth of socialist sentiment among a minority of American trade unionists during the crucial formative years of the American labor movement, between 1886 and 1917? Even more important, why did that sentiment remain a minority influence, instead of becoming a majority one as it did in the labor movements of several European countries during these years? Was it the case, as a number of historians have argued, that the hostility displayed by Samuel Gompers and other conservative leaders of the American Federation of Labor was primarily responsible for preventing the emergence of a widespread, grass roots radical movement which would, had it been allowed to develop, have transformed American labor into a revolutionary force? Or were other factors more important in precluding such a development?

In attempting to answer these questions, attention must also be paid to the tactics of the socialists themselves. It has been argued, by Philip Foner for example, that in the decade of the 1890s, when in relative terms the socialists were probably stronger in the American labor movement than they were at any other time, the dual unionist tactics of Daniel De Leon's Socialist Trades and Labor Alliance, followed in 1905 by the alleged impossibilism of the IWW, had a crucial effect in alienating moderate radicals who favored some form of independent radical coalition, but who stopped short of supporting the Socialist Party of America in part because of the divisive tactics of a minority of socialists. In particular, one might ask whether it would have made any difference during this period—when, for example, Thomas J. Morgan's 1894 Political Program, which included as Plank Ten "the collective

* Revised version of a paper delivered before the Organization of American Historians in Dallas, Texas, on April 19, 1968.

ownership by the people of all the means of production and distribution," came near to being adopted by the AFL—if the socialists, instead of dividing bitterly over tactics, had united in a common effort to secure the allegiance of the labor movement.[1] Or were external factors, deriving not so much from the character of the labor leadership or from the ideological positions adopted by the socialists, but from the more general characteristics of American political and industrial development during this period, primarily responsible both for the rise of socialist influence and for its limited appeal? Evidence drawn from six labor organizations, which included a large proportion of the radicals then active in the labor movement, suggests strongly that the second set of factors was more important than the first.[2]

I

It has long been established that Gompers personally, as well as several other national leaders of the labor movement, moved from a position of tolerance and even of limited support for certain socialist doctrines in the 1870s and 1880s to one of profound mistrust in subsequent years.[3] Inside the American Federation of Labor, this was evident in the failure to elect socialists to the Executive Council after 1889, despite their considerable strength in the organization;[4] in the dubious parliamentary tactics and the bitter speeches which Gompers and other AFL leaders employed against the socialists in the annual conventions of the Federation;[5] in the treatment meted out to Thomas J. Morgan's Political Program of 1894;[6] and in numerous other ways. Among the affiliates, it was apparent from such incidents as the Executive Council's offer of a charter to the racist International Association of Machinists, in preference to its already chartered (and both socialist and non-racist) affiliate, the International Machinists Union, in 1894–95.[7] It was clear from the AFL's post-1900 support for the conservative faction in the formerly socialist Boot and Shoe Workers Union;[8] and from Gompers' welcoming response to the increasing moderation of the Western Federation of Miners and other previously radical organizations in the period after 1912.[9] Where the socialists were strong, the AFL would sometimes make exceptions to this policy, as in Gompers' unwillingness to expel the socialist Brewery Workers Union from the federation in 1907, despite the fact that it had violated the Executive Council's jurisdictional rulings; in the general support which the AFL gave to the ILGWU and other socialist garment unions in the early 1900s; or in Gompers' indirect endorsement of Socialist Party candidate Meyer London and other socialists in the congressional elections of 1912.[10] But these exceptions were made for tactical reasons, or for the sake of the unity of the labor movement in general. They were not made out of sympathy with socialism on ideological grounds. In general, Gompers' opposition to the socialists within the AFL, reinforced by the self-perpetuating and bureaucratic character of the Executive Council, as well as by Gompers' own personal prestige, almost certainly prevented them from being more successful in this period than they might otherwise have been. For instance, in terms of delegate support the socialists enjoyed their largest influence in the AFL in the 1890s, before the Gompers' regime had been thoroughly established; whereas their peak was not reached in the labor movement generally until the period immediately preceding and following the presidential election of 1912.

It is also true that the dual unionist tactics of the impossibilists to some extent diminished the appeal of moderate socialism within the labor movement, and were used by the conservatives as a means of deterring other trade unionists from supporting the socialist cause. De Leon and the SLP turned against the AFL in the 1890s just at the point when the socialists were gathering strength, and when they might conceivably have been able to turn the labor movement, if only temporarily, into more radical paths.[11] Similarly, the dual unionist tactics of the American Labor Union, the IWW, and the communists after the First World War undoubtedly did some harm to the cause of socialist influence in the labor movement in later years. Among the affiliates, the mid-1890s attacks of the dual unionist, a De Leonite Socialist Trades and Labor Alliance against the locals of such AFL affiliates as the Boot and Shoe Workers Union in Rochester, Buffalo, New York, Chicago, and St. Louis, as well as in Massachusetts, were bitterly resented. Moreover, in this case, they helped to turn the boot and shoe workers away from their former socialist position, and toward conformity with the conservative job-conscience philosophy of the craft unions as a whole.[12] In the Western Federation of Miners, the unremitting hostility of the IWW toward the union after it had broken with the Wobblies in 1906-8 helped to weaken it to such an extent that it had little choice but to fall back upon the AFL.[13] After the Bolshevik revolution of 1917, fear of communism was also used as a weapon against the more moderate socialists in the United Mine Workers, the International Association of Machinists, and elsewhere.

But despite the attention which has been given to it by labor historians, the impact of impossibilism upon the bulk of trade unions in the American labor movement during these years was in fact quite small. In the sample analyzed here it was only in the Boot and Shoe Workers Union and the Western Federation of Miners that it had more than a marginal effect in weakening the position of the socialists as a whole. In the United Mine Workers of America, fear of communism and the efforts of extremists to exploit the discontents of the coal miners were not enough to prevent the reemergence of a strong labor party movement in that industry after the First World War. Over fifty miners' delegates attended the National Labor Party convention held in Chicago in November 1919—more than from any other trade union—and resolutions favoring an independent labor party and mine nationalization were passed by several post-war UMW conventions.[14] Similarly, in the International Association of Machinists and the ILGWU, moderate socialist influences remained powerful despite the criticisms of the impossibilists on the extreme Left and the wholesale denunciation of radicals from the Right during the period of the Red Scare. In the ILGWU, the bitter struggle which took place between the socialists and communists after 1919 did not prevent many garment workers from remaining socialists until the 1930s and beyond. In the immediate post-World War One period, President William Johnston of the IAM became chairman, as well as a leading initial advocate of third-party action, in the Conference for Progressive Political Action in 1922-24.[15]

The periods of influence of dual unionists in the American socialist and labor movements were also quite short. De Leon only maintained effective control of the SLP between 1891 and 1896, after which the moderates revolted against his policy of opposition to the AFL. The American Labor Union and the IWW had little influence over most craft unions, and it was not until the 1920s that the communists took up dual unionism once more. In 1901 the Socialist Party of America, while remaining critical (albeit insufficiently so) of the AFL for its failure to organize unskilled and semi-skilled workers and its hostility toward industrial union- ism, adopted a policy of cooperation toward the existing trade union movement which has maintained in effect, save for a minority on the extreme left of the party, throughout the whole of the twentieth century.[16] But this policy in itself appears to have had little to do with the reasons for either the growth or the decline of radical influences throughout the labor movement as a whole. For example the socialists received no spectacular increase in working-class votes because of the change in their trade union po- sition. Nor were they able to prevent a rapid loss of influence in the labor movement in the period after 1912.

Hence the preoccupation of various scholars with changes in the ideological position of the labor and socialist leadership, al- though valuable up to a point, does not in my judgment provide an adequate causal explanation for the failure of socialism to take root in the American labor movement, unless one assumes the views of these leaders to be wholly representative of the rank and file. But without discounting the influence of Gompers and the AFL Executive Council, or of the National Executive Committee of the SLP or the Socialist Party of America, this is clearly to carry the manipulative abilities of both the socialist and the trade union leadership much too far. In practice, for example, although in its in- ternal structure the AFL developed the characteristics of a bureau- cratic and machine-led organization quite early in its career, in its relations to the affiliates in this early period it had little in the way of formal power. On matters of trade autonomy, jurisdictional disputes, and strike action—which at this time were its central con- cerns—the AFL was primarily a collection of sovereign, independ- ent trade organizations, with Gompers and his colleagues serving mainly as a broker between them.[17] It is extremely unlikely, in other words, that the national leadership alone could have pre- vented the growth of a mass revolutionary movement, had the prevailing social and economic conditions been favorable for such a development.

II

To turn first to the reasons for the rise of socialist influence in the labor movement, a wide variety of factors determines the reasons for voting socialist, many of which of course are influenced by matters other than union membership and the experiences of work. Insofar as these are important considerations, however, I would argue that two sets of factors, one internal to the labor movement and one external, predominated over the particular tactics employed by the labor leadership in helping such revolutionary influence as did develop in the pre-World War American labor movement to grow. Within the labor movement, radical and in some cases socialist influence may be traced to the impact of an earlier tradition of Knights of Labor idealism, radicalized Populism, and strong dissatisfaction with the narrow craft unionism of the AFL. External or societal factors such as technological developments, a high degree of competition in several industries in the post-Civil War period followed by a period of rapid economic concentration, and the social and economic dislocation occasioned by the destruction of traditional crafts appear also to have played an extremely important role.

Taking the internal factors first, dissatisfaction with the AFL because of its political conservatism, its preference for craft unionism, its narrow view of the functions of trade unionism, and its voluntaristic attitude toward the state cannot be treated, except in an indirect way, as a cause of socialist sentiments as such. But taken together, these dissatisfactions undoubtedly served as a catalyst for more serious ideological conflicts which the socialists exploited to their advantage within the unions. It is no coincidence, for example, that several of the unions considered in our sample were industrial rather than craft organizations in their structure, and that at least two of them, the United Mine Workers of America and the Brewery Workers, were involved in severe jurisdictional conflicts with the dominant craft union majority in the AFL.

Industrial unionism as such is not necessarily a sign of socialist activism or militancy. But in the AFL in the 1890s, as in the English Trades Union Congress at a similar period, disappointment and irritation at the failure of the craft unionists to recognize the broader social philosophy which lay behind the demands of the industrial unionists certainly helped to create sympathy for socialism and the Socialist Party. For example, the withdrawal of the Western Federation of Miners from the AFL in 1897, and its decision to endorse the Socialist Party in 1902, in part resulted from frustration and anger at the refusal of the AFL to adopt a more radical course. Similarly, it was no coincidence that the International Association of Machinists coupled its 1903 questionnaire to union members concerning Gompers' continued leadership of the AFL with a request for the membership's views on political endorsement of the Socialist Party. The continued presence of conservative ex-president James O'Connell on the council of the AFL from 1912 to 1918, even though he was no longer president of the IAM, also created considerable bitterness among the machinists, and served to strengthen the hand of the union's socialist administration in the period after 1912.[18]

As to Knights of Labor idealism, it has, of course, long been established that this organization was considerably more radical than the AFL in its attitude toward industry-wide organization, third-party activity, and cooperation as a labor ideal. Less well remembered, however, is the fact that a significant proportion of the unions in the AFL had earlier been connected with the Knights of Labor, and that they retained considerable sympathy for that organization and what it stood for even after they had transferred their formal allegiance to the AFL.

At least four out of the six unions considered in the sample had strong ties with the Knights of Labor and its radical traditions, which persisted for years after the Knights had passed its peak. The Brewery Workers Union, for example, retained a joint affiliation with both the Knights of Labor and the AFL until 1896. In that year the AFL convention refused to endorse the union's label as long as it remained affiliated to the Knights, a matter which caused widespread bitterness within the union, especially in view of the important role which the label played in strengthening the brewery workmen through the selling of union beer. A similar dual affiliation also characterized the United Mine Workers of America for a time. The Boot and Shoe Workers Union developed originally out of the Knights of St. Crispin, a radical shoe workers' organization consisting largely of native-born workers which had much in common with the Knights of Labor, and which in 1869 helped to elect twenty-one independent labor representatives to the Massachusetts state legislature. In addition, the International Association of Machinists also had intimate connections with the Knights of Labor in the South. For some years it retained the secret ritual and fraternalistic nomenclature of the Knights, and even before it formally espoused socialism the *Machinists Monthly Journal* was imbued with the Knights' traditional commitment to moral improvement, third-party political action, and the hope for a regeneration of society along utopian and cooperative lines.[19]

Care must be exercised in dealing with the third source of radical influence listed under this head: namely, radical Populism. For it is still uncertain, pending the detailed study of voting returns, just how many urban workers voted Populist in the critical elections of the early 1890s.[20] And it is also unclear, save in the case of a few prominent men such as Debs, how many ex-Populists were dissatisfied with the petit bourgeois ideology of the Peoples Party and after the fusion of 1896 moved across into the socialist movement. Nevertheless, evidence from the International Association of Machinists, the United Mine Workers, and the Western Federation of Miners suggests strongly that those unions which had the strongest commitment to the ideals of Populism were also those in which socialist influence turned out to be considerable.

In the case of the UMW, Chester M. Destler demonstrated some years ago that a significant, albeit unsuccessful, labor-Populist-socialist alliance, which included a number of coal miners from the northern and southwestern portions of the state, was attempted in Illinois in the fall elections of 1894. My own research suggests that the Populists in Kansas and in West Virginia, because of their support for government ownership of the mines in those states, were also able to secure a number of coal miners' votes. An ambitious labor-Populist coalition, similar to that in Illinois, was also attempted in Ohio under the leadership of the president of the United Mine Workers, John McBride.[21]

A similar development occurred among the metal miners of the mountain West. In Colorado, Montana, Idaho, and elsewhere, partly because of the silver issue, Populism was a working-class rather than an agrarian movement, and after its collapse the metal miners in several of these states helped to develop the revolutionary, semi-syndicalist form of socialism which was later taken up by the WFM. Many of the radicals in the International Association of Machinists also moved into socialism via Populism, partly because the People's Party was strong in a number of the southern railroad towns in which the machinists were employed, and partly because of the antipathy and fear which many machinists, like many coal miners, felt toward the railroad corporations because of their dependence upon them for employment. For example,

Douglas Wilson, editor of the *Machinists Monthly Journal* from 1895 until 1915, ran unsuccessfully as a Populist for the Alabama legislature in 1894. Soon thereafter he became a socialist, developing a close personal friendship with Debs. Peter J. Conlon, a socialist member of the IAM's executive board, began his career as a Populist in Sioux City, Iowa. And the Machinists' conventions, which in the 1890s adopted numerous Populist resolutions in favor of the initiative and referendum and the democratization of the political process, as well as on other matters, in the early 1900s began to pass socialist ones which included much of the same kind of Populist rhetoric which had gone before.[22]

As to the external or second and more important set of factors which I have listed as causes of socialist influence in the labor movement, in the decades after the Civil War technological changes, changes in the nature of the market—both in the labor market and in the market for goods and services—and changes also in the relationship between employers and employees were proceeding rapidly throughout American industry as a whole. Nevertheless, they had a particularly severe impact upon several of the trades considered in our sample.

The shoe industry was one of the first American industries to suffer the effects of industrialization. Before 1850, the expansion of the market and the displacement of custom shops (in which a father and son worked together, with perhaps one apprentice or journeyman) by larger, competing retail or wholesale-order shops, had already begun to alter the traditional pattern of economic relationships in the industry, and had undermined, to some extent, the independence of the individual artisan. The possibility of a single journeyman attaining ownership and control of one of these larger shops still existed, and the handcraft of the shoemaker had not yet been undermined. But the pegging machine, introduced in 1857, the McKay sole-sewing machine, first used in 1862, and the Goodyear welt machine, introduced in 1875, quite rapidly destroyed the traditional craft skill of the journeyman shoemaker, and turned him into little more than a factory hand. By 1880 the factory system had already assumed much of its modern form in the shoe industry, and the journeyman or small master who had traditionally operated his own independent shop was increasingly forced to abandon his business and find employment in one of the new factories in Lynn, Haverhill, Brockton, or one of the other small shoe towns which grew up around the city of Boston.

In addition, the expanding post-Civil War shoe industry was going through an intensely competitive stage, so that in several cadres of employment the shoe worker's factory wages were for some years appreciably lower than the earnings of the labor force in the industry had previously been. In 1881, for example, in ten out of the fourteen major occupations associated with the industry in Massachusetts, average weekly wages had fallen to a level appreciably below what they had been in 1872, some by as much as 25 per cent. Those employed on the new machines suffered most: average weekly wages among the McKay sole operators, for example, which had been $22.22 in 1872, fell to $15.29 in 1897 (they had been even lower in the 1893–96 depression). It was not until 1903 that they returned to a level significantly higher than they had been thirty years before.[23]

There is quite a lot of evidence to suggest that it was these changes, with the loss of skill, of status, and of earning power which they (temporarily) entailed, which were primarily reponsible for the growth of socialist sentiment among the shoe workers. Frank Sieverman, a young shoe worker who became prominent in both the SLP and the Socialist Party, ascribed his socialist beliefs to the "disappointed aspirations and shattered ideals" which, he said, he experienced upon entering a shoe factory at the age of seventeen. President John F. Tobin of the Boot and Shoe Workers Union had undergone a similar experience as a young man. Thomas Philips, a leading advocate of producers' cooperation as the only effective means of restoring independent self-employment to the trade, declared in 1889 that he was continually "putting in more work than ever for less wage." And J. W. Sherman, the unsuccessful socialist candidate for mayor of Boston in 1899, attributed a significant proportion of the increased socialist vote in Massachusetts—which was the center of the shoemaking trade—to the discontented shoe worker, who today, "in a great shoe factory, . . . produces fully 20 times what he could do 40 years ago. Nobody thinks for an instant that he is getting 20 times as much in comfort from his labor as he did then. Looked at fairly it is at once seen that his present condition . . . grows from the fact that he is producing for somebody else, who takes for the service of furnishing him a machine to work with and a 'job', the slight toil of four-fifths of the product."

But it was Horace M. Eaton, the socialist general secretary of the Boot and Shoe Workers Union, who summed up perhaps best these economic discontents of the shoe workers in his report on behalf of the union membership to the BSWU convention of 1897. "So long as we allow the employer to traffic in human flesh," he said, "and to reduce wages simply on the ground that he must meet competition, so long as we submit to these brutal conditions without declaring and working for the abolition of such a brutal system of industry, so long have we, in greater or less degree, to endure the evils of which we now complain."[24]

A similar development took place in the machinists' trade. Until about 1870, the machinist resembled a carpenter who worked in metal instead of in wood. He worked at a bench, usually in quite a small shop, and used numerous small hand tools and lathes, which required great skill to operate. In the early years the capital outlay involved in such an enterprise was not so great as to prevent the individual journeyman from establishing a workshop of his own. For example, Grand Master Machinist Thomas W. Talbot, the first president of the International Association of Machinists, was one of many machinists who owned his own small machine shop in the period just after the Civil War. By the middle of the 1880s, however, this type of self-employment was increasingly difficult to achieve. John Morrison, for example, a New York machinist who gave evidence on behalf of his trade before a Senate committee in 1883, had this to say: "I understand that at this present day you could not start in the machinists' business to compete successfully with any of these large firms with a capital of less than $20,000 or $30,000. That is my own judgment. There have been cases known where men started ten or fifteen years ago on what they had earned themselves, and they had grown up gradually into a good business. . . . But since that time it appears that the larger ones are squeezing out the smaller, and forcing more of them into the ranks of labor, thus causing more competition among the workers."

In addition, the machinist's craft was revolutionized by the introduction of large and costly steam- or, later, electrically driven machinery, most of it automatic, which was set up in large machine shops very different from the workshops in which he had been traditionally employed. As in the shoe industry, these developments undoubtedly stimulated the development of radical discontent. In May 1898, for example, a correspondent in the *Machinists Monthly Journal* reported this about the condition of his fellow shopmates in Chicago: "The old feeling of mutual dependence between employers and men has disappeared under its blighting influences which have driven thousands of men into the streets of the cities and highways of the land as tramps and paupers without occupation for the present or hope and ambition for the future." The time had come, he said, for members of the union to face up to this problem if they hoped to live better than Chinese coolies.

Another rank-and-file member asserted in December 1898 that technological changes in the craft had destroyed the independence of the machinist and severely limited his opportunities for upward mobility. "The division and subdivision of work done by both man and machine," he wrote, "eliminates the skilled machinist, . . . and drives all skilled mechanics downwards to the level of all labor." The apprenticeship system, he went on, was out of date, and the machinist's job would soon be within the competence of any unskilled worker who chose to undertake it. Numerous other instances of this phenomenon could be cited also. The lesson was plain: the machinist could never hope to improve his condition so long as the machine, the great leveler, remained in private hands.[25]

In the coal mining industry the problem was not so much the development of the factory system or the destruction of a traditional craft, as it was depressed wage levels and chronic instability in employment resulting from the sudden incursion of cheap immigrant labor from eastern Europe and from a period of fierce competition followed by rapid trustification in the period following the Civil War. Before the Civil War, and for a brief period after it, coal mining was confined to a number of separate coal fields, such as those in Pennsylvania, Ohio, and Illinois, each of which served largely separate markets and each of which had a wage and price structure of its own. But the development of a sophisticated railroad system rapidly created a national market where earlier there had been a series of local ones, bringing fierce competition between individual coal operators, overinvestment, and strong pressure to reduce wages in the trade.

This was a tendency, it should again be noted, which was not simply dependent upon the severe depressions of the mid-1870s and mid-1890s, although it was accentuated by them. Coupled with this, there were the special hazards of the miner's task, almost total dependence on the company store, as well as, the brutal repression of both coal and metal miners' strikes by the militia and other agents of the civil state. The cumulative effect of these developments, as cheap immigrant labor flooded into the eastern mines, was to force the English-speaking miners in various parts of Pennsylvania, who had been accustomed to a relatively stable level of employment, westward into Indiana and Illinois. Partially as a result of this, there occurred the rapid growth of socialist sentiment among the coal miners of District 12 of the United Mine Workers in the southwestern counties of Illinois which has already been remarked upon.[26] Similar economic developments took place in the Rocky Mountain states, where the western metal mining industry was located.[27]

Even in the ILGWU and the Brewery Workers Union, which were dominated by foreign-born radicals, there is evidence to suggest that European socialist ideology was far from being the only source of revolutionary zeal. Among the brewery workers long hours, frequent beatings, the abuses of the boarding system (under which the workers were required to live with their masters), and the heavy drinking of beer—which was often given to the workers as a substitute for wages or as an inducement to work longer hours—were in themselves an independent source of radicalism. One group of immigrant brewery workers, for example, reminiscing in 1901, complained that "in the social life, the American brewery was just as much, if not more, depressed and disregarded as in South Germany." In the ILGWU, sweatshop conditions in themselves, in addition to the socialist influences brought over by Russian-born revolutionary intellectuals, have long been recognized as a contributing factor in the garment workers' socialism. However, it must also be remembered that in the crucial formative period of the New York Jewish labor movement, which lasted from approximately 1880 to 1910, there was a considerable initial gap between the philosophy and outlook of the atheistic, Russian-speaking socialists, who later rose to positions of leadership in the garment trades, and the orthodox, Yiddish-speaking, and often socially conservative small-town Jewish tailors and cloakmakers who made up part of the rank and file. It may be, therefore, that even more weight should be given to sweatshop conditions as a formative influence in the development of radicalism in the garment industry than has hitherto been allowed.[28]

English-speaking workers and northern Europeans generally, save to some extent the Irish, provided the main source of leadership and skill throughout American industry at this time. As such they usually rose fairly rapidly in the social and economic scale. It may be suggested from the preceding analysis, however, that in the four industries discussed in which these workers were extensively employed—coal mining, shoemaking, metal mining, and the machinist's trade—their progress was at least temporarily impeded by the processes of rapid industrial change. In each of them, the relative position of the English-speaking workers appears to have been undermined by technological changes, by rapid expansion and economic instability, by relatively static or falling wage levels, and by the threat posed (in imagination if not always in practice) by the incursion of cheap immigrant labor from eastern and southern Europe, and in some cases from the Orient. In these industries, it was ex-artisans and skilled or semi-skilled workers, not the recent immigrants or the poor, who tended to become radicals. In part this helps to confirm the hypothesis, which has been accepted by a number of labor historians, that it is from those with rising expectations, not the *Lumpenproletariat,* that we should expect radical tendencies. Even more interesting, however, is the future hypothesis that in an achievement-oriented society such as the United States the motivation for political radicalism may also have resulted partially from the frustrated aspirations of those bodies of workers whose expectations are traditionally supposed to have been high.[29]

III

Turning, lastly, to the decline of socialist influences in the pre-1930s American labor movement (which is of course to be kept separate from the period of the New Deal and the CIO, when radical influences revived under the quite different auspices of the Communist Party), the evidence from the six trade unions analyzed indicates less disagreement with previously held views. To the extent to which immigrant influences from continental Europe were responsible for the rise of socialism—and, of course, the main thrust of my argument has been to suggest that these influences were less influential than has hitherto been supposed—it is clearly important to reemphasize the consequences of the assimilation and Americanization of these groups, and their acceptance of the American political system and of American political values. The speed with which this assimilation took place depended in part upon the nature of the immigrant group involved, in part upon the strength of the immigrant culture, and in part upon the degree of ethnic concentration in particular cities. In Milwaukee, for example, where the Brewery Workers were powerful and the German socialist community quite large, the process of assimilation took longer than it did in smaller German communities. Equally, the size of the Jewish socialist community in New York City, and its initial concentration in the urban ghetto, undoubtedly helped to prolong its commitment to socialist ideals.

Nevertheless, over the long run this process of ethnic assimilation was one of the elements which were responsible for the decline of socialist loyalties. This is perhaps clearest in the case of the Brewery Workers Union, whose socialism may in large part be ascribed to the influence of socialists who came to this country after the abortive German revolution of 1848, and in greater numbers after Bismarck's anti-socialist legislation of 1878. The radicalism of the union noticeably declined as these older groups either died off, moved upward into the entrepreneurial or professional middle class, or were replaced by ethnic groups whose commitment to socialism was less intense.[30] A similar process occurred in the garment industry and in the ILGWU, although the tenacity with which the Jewish labor movement retained its socialist idealism even after several immigrant generations had been assimilated indicates that a high level of economic and status mobility is not in itself enough to put an end to political radicalism, once it has acquired the force of a tradition.[31]

But assimilation and Americanization also had an important meaning for those workingmen who were not immigrants. Pressure toward conformity was generated not so much by overt coercion from the AFL as by its acceptance in the eyes of public opinion generally as the proper model for an American labor movement. This made it harder for radical opponents of AFL political and economic policies to persist with their endeavors. In a society in which a high value was placed upon conformity, especially at a time when the labor movement was weak and under considerable pressure from outside, this was a matter of great importance. The response of the Irish in the Boot and Shoe Workers Union to organizing success or the results of the re-entry of the Western Federation of Miners into the AFL in 1911 illustrate this point very well.

More specifically, adaptation to prevailing American values had both an industrial and a political aspect. From the industrial point of view, there was an increasingly evident conflict between the logic of collective bargaining (which even the most radical trade unionists came in the end to accept) and the demands of the socialists for separate, revolutionary action on the part of a united working class. The most dramatic example of this was in the Boot and Shoe Workers Union, where acceptance by Massachusetts employers of the Union Stamp Contract (based upon the union label) in the period after 1898 helped to bring about a dramatic improvement in the union's membership which was reflected to some extent, also, in wage levels. As a result in 1904 President John F. Tobin, who in 1896 had been an orthodox De Leonite, went so far as to urge his fellow union members to take the profit margins of the shoe manufacturers into account before pressing for wage increases. "The employer gains an opportunity to adjust to a gradual change in wages," he argued, to the astonishment and anger of the remaining socialists in the union, "while propositions for a general advance . . . [have] resulted in failure."[32]

This change of heart might perhaps be attributed to the class-collaborationist tendencies of one particular union leader. But there are plenty of other examples of the same consequences occurring after similar developments in other formerly radical trade unions. For example, the adoption of time contracts by the Western Federation of Miners (which had earlier been bitterly resisted by most members of the union), the negotiation of the Protocol of Peace in 1910 in the ladies' garment industry by the ILGWU, and the increasing cooperation between management and labor in the brewing industry, over Prohibition, and over pension schemes for union members—all had similar effects. In the United Mine Workers the situation was more ambiguous, since acceptance of the principle of joint interstate agreements with the coal operators took place in 1898, *before* the most radical phase in the history of the union. But there too the checkoff system of paying dues, the need to abide by nationally negotiated contracts, and growing cooperation between the union and the coal operators in imposing order upon an anarchic coal market rapidly limited the union's potential for revolutionary change.[33]

In societies with more traditional class barriers, such as Great Britain or Germany, there was no necessary conflict between collective bargaining and the revolutionary assumptions of socialism, at least in the short run. But in the United States, where class lines were traditionally fluid and the pressure toward assimilation was strong, the adoption of collective bargaining techniques had profound and far-reaching implications for the relations between labor and management, especially where such cooperation (as in the garment and shoemaking industries) made a great difference to the worker's security of employment. As Paul Jacobs has pointed out, in a society dominated by the Lockeian tradition, the process of bargaining *within* the system inexorably endowed the contractual relationship with primary importance.[34]

In addition, the notion of time contracts implies a recognition by the union of its responsibilities for enforcement of a collective bargaining agreement, which sometimes placed radical union leadership in the seemingly anomalous position of having to act against the interests of its own membership when contracts were violated by members of the rank and file. Thus the price which the union had to pay for the benefits it received was to become part of the productive system itself, able to modify but not to change in any basic way the nature of that system. The most dramatic effects of this development, again, may be seen in the case of the Boot and Shoe Workers Union, where the Tobin administration felt itself obliged to break unofficial strikes by its own union members which were held in violation of the Union Stamp Contract.[35] But similar consequences occurred before 1914 in the coal industry, the garment industry, and in the western metal mines.

From the point of view of third-party politics, most historians of the Socialist Party are in agreement that it reached its peak either at or not long after the election of 1912, and that a series of subsequent events, most notably the Wilsonian reforms of 1913–16, the refusal of the Socialist Party to support American entry into the First World War, the socialist-communist split of 1919, the collapse of Wilsonian idealism, and the return to prosperity of the 1920s, were important factors in that decline. But there is considerable disagreement as to just which of these factors was the most important, and as to just when, in time, the main movement toward decline began. James Weinstein, in his book *The Decline of Socialism in America, 1912–1925*, takes the view that there was "no serious decline after 1912; the Party grew in strength and popularity during the war." "Socialist trade unionists," he argues, "played an increasingly prominent role in the Party during these years, and the Party seems to have developed greater solidarity with the labor movement. If one is to find a substantial decline of socialism in the trade unions, it must be after the United States entered the war, in April 1917."[36]

Weinstein bases this view upon limited and rather fragmented evidence. When one examines carefully the change of heart which took place between 1912 and 1916 in virtually all of the socialist trade unions examined in the sample under review, Weinstein's position is not borne out. Once President Wilson had been elected, and had begun to enact the series of social reforms for which his first administration became famous (the Clayton Act, the La Follette Seamen's Act, the establishment of a Department of Labor, and so on), virtually all of the unions considered in this sample began immediately to turn away from their earlier political support of the Socialist Party, and to align themselves with the Democrats. It is true that in some of the state federations of labor, notably those in Illinois and Pennsylvania under the direction of John H. Walker and James M. Maurer respectively, the socialists maintained, and in some cases increased, their influence for a time after America entered the First World War. But in this period the state federations of labor had very little influence within the trade union movement generally, either in terms of voting power at AFL conventions, or in terms of over-all labor policy. And in the case of the Illinois State Federation of Labor, at least, Walker from the first used his influence on behalf of the traditional "reward your friends, punish your enemies" philosophy of the AFL, not on behalf of socialist or labor party candidates.[37] For the socialist element in the trade union movement, in other words, American entry into the First World War simply served to confirm a trend toward the two major parties—and in particular, toward the Democratic Party—which had begun several years before.

Three examples of this development may be cited, although there were others also. The International Association of Machinists, which benefited particularly from President Woodrow Wilson's reforming legislation (notably from the Adamson Act of 1916, establishing an eight-hour day on the railroads), moved from open support for Debs in 1912 to almost equally open support for Woodrow Wilson in the election of 1916. "The time may come in this country when organized labor will have a party of its own," the *Machinists Monthly Journal* wrote in October 1916, "but until then labor will lend its sympathy to those in sympathy with its aims and objects." The Illinois miners, who had been strong supporters of the socialists up until 1912, began to move across into the Democratic camp very soon after that time; and the *United Mine Workers Journal* expressed open pleasure at President Wilson's narrow victory over the Republican candidate, Charles Evans Hughes.

A similar shift in allegiance can be seen even in the case of the Brewery Workers Union, which had hitherto been the most obviously Marxist of the radical trade unions. At the 1914 convention of this union, the national secretary asserted that there was no reason for the organization to change its support of the Socialist Party simply because of the progressive legislation which had been enacted in the past two years. But in 1916, when faced with the actual record of the first Wilson administration, an editorial in the *Brauer-Zeitung* admitted that the Democrats had done much for the organized labor movement; and it indirectly recommended the union membership to vote for Wilson.[38]

On this general point it seems clear as far as the socialists in the trade union movement were concerned that it was indeed the reforms enacted by the Democratic Party under Woodrow Wilson that were the decisive factors in undermining trade union support for the Socialist Party. Of course, the party included intellectuals, Negroes, middle-class reformers, and other elements in addition to trade unionists, and it does not follow, simply because of this, that the party went into an immediate decline. Nor is it suggested that the loss of support from the unions which the Socialist Party suffered brought to an end all radical political sentiment in the labor movement for the remainder of the period under review. Several of the unions described above played an important role in the Conference for Progressive Political Action, which nominated Senator Robert M. La Follette for the presidency on an independent party ticket in 1924, as well as in the labor party movement which emerged briefly in several states in the period immediately following the First World War. But as far as the Socialist

Party itself was concerned, with the single (and important) exception of the ILGWU, all of the unions in our sample had withdrawn at least their official support from the party by 1916. Although many other factors were involved in this changeabout—among them the fact that Allan Benson, the party's presidential candidate in that year, was virtually unknown compared to Debs, and he made a tactical error by concentrating on opposition to war preparedness in his campaign—this probably helped to account for the more than one-third drop which took place in the party's vote compared to 1912.

This disaffection of radical unionists was important, for if one accepts that strong trade union support is essential for a viable and successful independent political party of labor, then the loss of trade union support in the years after 1912 was in many ways an irremediable blow. On this point, I find myself in disagreement with Weinstein and in general agreement with earlier historians, such as Ira Kipnis, David Shannon, and, on this matter, also Daniel Bell.

Lastly, the effect of increasing economic affluence in undermining support for revolutionary behavior must be reemphasized. This has been remarked upon in general terms by a number of social scientists and historians,[39] but not in relation to specific industries and trade unions. The years between 1873–76 and 1893–97 were, with some exceptions, a period of depression in American industry, resulting in severe difficulties for the trade union movement. This helped to lay the foundations for a corresponding increase in third-party political activity.[40] As already indicated, in this period also money wages in several of the industries examined in this sample, notably in the garment industry, in the coal mining industry, and in shoemaking, were either static, or actively in decline. This was not necessarily the case with real wages, representing the purchasing power of the dollar, which in some cases rose rather than declined. But it is problematical whether a cut in money wages, which was overt and immediate in its impact, did not have a more important effect in inducing radical sentiments than a long-term, and often concealed, rise in purchasing power did in diminishing them.

At all events it seems clear that the return to prosperity in the years after 1900, coupled with the increasing economic success of trade unions, had an important long-term effect in undermining the militancy and radicalism of those who had formerly held socialist opinions. It is important to point out that the issue here was not only (perhaps not even primarily) one of rising wages.[41] It was also the fairly rapid, and in some cases quite sudden, increase in union membership which (although not nearly so large as that which occurred in the 1930s) brought collective bargaining and the other benefits of union membership to a significant proportion of the labor force in these industries for the first time. This appears to have had a particularly important impact in the case of the Boot and Shoe Workers Union, where the period of socialist influence coincided with a time of struggle and failure for the organization in the 1880s and 1890s, and the period of conservatism followed in subsequent prosperous years.[42]

Moreover, once trade unions had become successfully established as bargaining agents in these industries in the period after 1899, they were able to provide for their members not only a relatively high degree of economic security, but also—at least through the 1920s—the prospect of a continuing rise in their standard of living. The economic activities of the American trade union movement, the editor of the *Shoe Workers Journal* wrote in January 1919, citing numerous examples in support of his case, had helped to give American workers the highest standard of living in the world. "In our country not a few shoemakers working at the bench own automobiles, and this condition exists in other trades. Where else on earth can this be said of shopmen? It is not [a] labor party that we want, but more labor unionism."[43] In the 1930s, American industry went through a new crisis which was more severe than anything which had affected it in the 1870s or the 1890s, and which brought a new wave of labor radicalism, this time largely under the aegis of the Communist Party. But without passing judgment in detail upon the reasons for the failure of independent labor politics in that period, it is likely that the bonds between labor and the Democratic Party, which were finally cemented in 1936, were now so strong as to make it virtually impossible for a separate socialist party (whatever its label) to recover even the limited degree of strength which it had enjoyed before 1914.

In those unions in which the impetus for third-party activism was partially motivated by non-economic factors, socialist sentiment outlasted the improvements in labor's standards of living by a considerable number of years. The ILGWU obviously provides the best example of this kind of phenomenon. But even here, by the end of the period the effect of increasing complacency had begun to show its effect. "It should never be forgotten," Morris Hillquit reminded the delegates to the 1924 union convention, "that the labor movement and your movement are not based solely on material struggles and material conditions. Of course, we want better material conditions; but this is not the end. The labor movement is ever struggling for better and higher conditions of life, . . . for universal prosperity, and universal brotherhood, and for peace."[44] The ILGWU remained faithful to this vision of society longer than any of the other old socialist trade unions.

IV

This essay has attempted to argue that although many of the traditional arguments put forward to explain the weakness of socialism in the American labor movement may be valid, indigenous factors deriving from the effects of industrialization upon American society were more important than have hitherto been supposed. It has also suggested that both the rise and fall of socialist influence in the trade union movement were intimately affected by a wide variety of other factors, some of them internal to the labor movement at the time but some of them not, such as Populism, an earlier tradition of Knights of Labor idealism, the frustrated aspirations of northern European artisans, and the ideological flexibility of the American two-party system.

This suggests, further, that explanations based upon the particular policies pursued by the national leaders of the labor movement, whether in the trade unions or in the Socialist Party, are no longer adequate (if they ever were) to provide a general explanation for the relative weakness of socialism in the labor movement, even though they have often been used to do so. Throughout his work Philip Taft, for example, continuing to rely upon the conservative interpretation of the American labor movement initially put forward by Selig Perlman in his *Theory of the Labor Movement* in 1928 (which was in turn based upon the examination of a limited number of official trade union documents),[45] assumes the essential correctness of the AFL's position on industrial unionism, third-party politics, and other issues, without examining the relevance of job-conscious unionism to the affiliated membership in the already existing trade unions, still less to the great mass of un-organized unskilled and semi-skilled workers who remained out-side.

At the other end of the ideological spectrum Philip Foner, from the Left, argues that the failure of socialism in the American labor movement was largely due, on the trade union side, to the bourgeois and "class collaborationist" character of the labor lead-ership. On the side of the socialists he argues that it was due, in the case of the SLP, to the "incorrect policies" of dual unionism; and in the case of the Socialist Party of America to the domination of "Center-Right" elements which Foner erroneously suggests "abandoned altogether the battle against the Federation's narrow, craft, pure and simple trade unionism."[46]

Without denying the importance of these factors, I would chal-lenge the adequacy of both Marxist and (in the case of Taft) anti-Marxist interpretations of the American labor movement when they are based upon evidence drawn from the behavior of the national leadership of the labor movement alone, and suggest the impor-tance of more general economic, political, and structural factors as well. I acknowledge that any analysis based primarily upon the internal activities of the radical trade unions, as this has largely been, cannot in itself fully answer the more general social and economic questions which have been raised, even though in my view they provide a broader basis for judgment than the limited type of evidence made use of by the Perlman school. But I hope that enough has been said to demonstrate the need for a much more sophisticated and comprehensive type of explanation, if we are to answer the questions raised by this essay satisfactorily, or in full.

NOTES

1. Philip S. Foner, *History of the Labor Movement in the United States* (New York: International Publishers, 1947–65), II, ch. 19, IV, ch. 3. See also Anthony Bimba, *The History of the American Working Class* (New York: International Publishers, 1927), pp. 199–208; David Herreshoff, *American Disciples of Marx: From the Age of Jackson to the Progressive Era* (Detroit: Wayne State University Press, 1967), p. 180.

2. These are the Brewery Workers Union, a Marxist industrial union consisting largely of German immigrants in the East and the Midwest; the Boot and Shoe Workers Union, a New England craft organization composed of Yankee and Irish artisans; the ILGWU, the most famous of the New York Jewish garment workers' unions; the International Association of Machinists, originating among native-born railroad machinists in the South; and the Western Federation of Miners and the United Mine Workers of America, which between them incorporated most of the militant, direct-action industrial workers then organized into trade unions. For a more detailed analysis of the rise and decline of socialist influence in these unions, see my book *Labor and the Left: A Study of Socialist and Radical Influences in the American Labor Movement, 1881–1924* (New York: Basic Books, 1970).

3. For Gompers, among other works see Bernard Mandel, *Samuel Gompers: A Biography* (Yellow Springs, Ohio: Antioch Press, 1963); Louis S. Reed, *The Labor Philosophy of Samuel Gompers* (New York: Columbia University Press, 1930); and *Samuel Gompers, Seventy Years of Life and Labor* (New York: E. P. Dutton & Co., 1925), I, pp. 69–105, 188–204, 381–427. It tends to be assumed that Gompers himself was largely responsible for the anti-socialist bias of the AFL. In fact, his views were shared by most other members of the Executive Council, including First Vice-President James Duncan, Second Vice-President John Mitchell, Treasurer John Lennon, and Secretary Frank Morrison. See *Proceedings, Twenty-Fourth Annual Convention of the A.F. of L.* (San Francisco, 1904), pp. 193–202; *Proceedings, Thirty-First Annual Convention of the A.F. of L.* (Atlanta, 1911), pp. 177–230, 255–57. See also Philip Taft, "Differences in the Executive Council of the American Federation of Labor," *Labor History*, V (Winter 1964), pp. 40–56; and H. M. Gitelman, "Adolph Strasser and the Origins of Pure and Simple Unionism," *Labor History*, VI (Winter 1965), pp. 71–83.

4. The 1885 convention elected two acknowledged socialists, Henry Emrich of the Furniture Workers and Hugo Miller of the German-American Typographia, to the Executive Council. But no socialist sat on the council after Emrich relinquished the treasurership in 1890, despite the fact that the socialists continued to poll more than one

third of the vote in convention debates for a number of years. See *Proceedings, Fifth Annual Convention of the Federation of Organized Trades and Labor Unions* (Washington, 1885), p. 19; Taft, op. cit.

5. In 1895 the AFL inserted into its constitution a provision that party politics of whatever kind "should have no place in the conventions of the A.F. of L." At later conventions Gompers frequently invoked this as a means of declaring even non-political socialist resolutions out of order. See, for example, *Proceedings, Twenty-Fifth Annual Convention of the A.F. of L.* (Pittsburgh, 1905), p. 230; *Proceedings, Twenty-Seventh Annual Convention of the A.F. of L.* (Norfolk, 1907), p. 219.

6. Probably a majority of unions endorsed this program calling for the establishment of an independent labor party either by referendum or by convention vote in the period between January and December 1894, and had all the delegates from those unions which had previously supported it voted in favor at the December 1894 AFL convention, it might well have passed. But Gompers openly campaigned against the program in the *American Federationist* and in his report to the convention; P. J. McGuire led a behind-the-scenes attempt to persuade the delegates to vote against it; and Adolph Strasser reduced Plank Ten to ridicule by suggesting that collective ownership be achieved by "confiscation without compensation." See Foner, op. cit., II, pp. 289–92; *American Federationist*, I (October 1894), p. 172; *Proceedings, Fourteenth Annual Convention of the A.F. of L.* (Denver, 1894), pp. 14, 36–40; Gerald N. Grob, *Workers and Utopia: A Study of Ideological Conflict in the American Labor Movement, 1865–1900* (Evanston: Northwestern University Press, 1961), pp. 176–79.

7. In 1891 the AFL issued a charter to the socialist International Machinists Union, refusing one to the then largely conservative International Association of Machinists because, as a southern organization, it refused to admit Negroes. However, in the summer of 1895 the Executive Council reversed its position, admitting the IAM into the AFL even though its local unions still refused to admit Negroes; and in December 1895 it withdrew its charter from the IMU. This incident is rightly taken by labor historians to be the first important case in which the AFL chartered a national union which pursued an openly racist policy. But it also indicates the growing anti-socialist bias of the organization, since the Executive Council chartered the IAM irrespective of the fact that the IMU was already an affiliate, and that its policy was to charter only one union in a given trade. Although negotiations for a merger between the two organizations were begun before the chartering of the IAM took place, they were never completed, as stated in the accounts given by Foner, and by Spero and Harris. The locals of the IMU either joined the IAM one by one or lost their separate identity. See Foner, op. cit., II, p. 348; Mark Perlman, *The Machinists: A New Study in American Trade Unionism* (Cambridge: Harvard University Press, 1961), pp. 7, 16–17; Sterling D. Spero and Abram L. Harris, *The Black Worker: The Negro and*

the Labor Movement (New York: Columbia University Press, 1931), p. 88; *Monthly Journal of the International Association of Machinists,* V (January 1894), pp. 525–27, VII (July 1895), p. 236, VII (January 1896), p. 528; John McBride to T. J. Morgan, May 16, 1895 (Letterbooks of Samuel Gompers, Library of Congress).

8. In 1907 the radical elements in the Boot and Shoe Workers Union broke away from the parent body to form their own organization, claiming that the contracts negotiated by the Boot and Shoe Workers Union gave too much away to the manufacturers. However, the AFL gave its full support to the Boot and Shoe Workers leadership, and commended the union administration for taking a strong line against the radicals. Augusta E. Galster, *The Labor Movement in the Shoe Industry, with Special Reference to Philadelphia* (New York: The Ronald Press Co., 1924), pp. 138–39; Brockton *Times,* IV (October 5, 1907), p. 1, VI (March 21, 1909), p. 1, VII (March 4, 1910), p. 2; Brockton *Searchlight,* VI (August 5, 1910), p. 1; Michael J. Tracey to Frank Morrison, October 11, 1909, Morrison to Tracey, October 14, 1909 (Gompers Correspondence with Affiliates, A.F.L.–C.I.O. Collection).

9. In July 1916 President Charles Moyer of the WFM, reflecting on the difficulties which his union had encountered because of employer hostility and the radical image which the organization had projected among the public at large, urged it to abandon its socialist policies and become "a business institution, directing its efforts to the object for which it was organized, namely to unite the various persons working in the mines . . . into a central body, to increase their wages and improve their conditions of employment." Gompers considered this statement so striking a reversal of the WFM's former radical policies that he sent a copy of it to President John P. White (a conservative) of the United Mine Workers of America. *Proceedings, Twenty-Second Consecutive and Second Biennial Convention of the W.F.M.* (Great Falls, 1916), pp. 40–41; Samuel Gompers to John P. White, March 7, 1917 (Gompers Correspondence with Affiliates, A.F.L.–C.I.O. Collection).

10. The Brewery Workers were in fact expelled from the AFL for a brief period between May 1907 and early 1908 for refusing to relinquish their firemen and brewery engineer members to the appropriate craft unions, but this was despite Gompers' personal opposition. Benjamin C. Roberts, "Jurisdiction Disputes Between the Brewery Workers and other A.F. of L. Affiliates" (Unpublished M.A. Thesis, University of Chicago, 1936); *Brauer-Zeitung,* XXII (November 1907), p. 1. For the support given to the ILGWU, and the endorsement of Meyer London, see Louis Levine, *The Women Garment Workers: A History of the International Ladies' Garment Workers Union* (New York: B. W. Huebsch, Inc., 1924), pp. 115–17, 136–39, 272, 292; M. Shamroth to Gompers, October 10, 1912, Gompers to M. Shamroth, October 25, 1912 (A.F.L. Collection, Wisconsin State Historical Society).

11. On August 13, 1893, De Leon's *The People* urged all socialists to leave the AFL, causing concern among moderate socialists, and leading Gompers to write H. D. Lloyd: "Until the advent of Prof. De Leon in the Socialist movement we managed matters so that we could at least work together. . . . He has simply widened the chasm between the different wings of the labor movement." On the other hand it must be remembered that the high vote which the Morgan Program received and the defeat of Gompers for the AFL presidency in 1894–95 were probably due as much to the prevailing depression, to the loss of the Pullman strike, to the inability of the larger unions to send a full complement of delegates to the 1894 convention, and to general dissatisfaction with Gompers' leadership, as they were to an increase in socialist sentiments as such. Grob, op. cit., pp. 176–82; Foner, op. cit., II, pp. 286–94; Gompers, op. cit., I, pp. 356–60, 391–94; clipping from Boston *Labor Leader*, December 22, 1894 (A.F.L. Collection, Wisconsin State Historical Society); Gompers to H. D. Lloyd, July 2, 1894 (Letterbooks of Samuel Gompers, Library of Congress).

12. "For years," President John F. Tobin of the Boot and Shoe Workers Union wrote in May 1898, he had considered De Leon "an able exponent of the doctrine of Socialism." But the deliberate efforts which the ST&LA had made to undermine the locals of his own union had destroyed that faith. De Leon had become nothing but an "unscrupulous falsifier." *Monthly Report* of the Boot and Shoe Workers Union (May 1898), pp. 20–21; "Transcript of debate between Tobin, De Leon, and others April 24, 1898," pp. 2, 4–5, 7, 9, 11, 15, 22 (Archives of the Boot and Shoe Workers Union).

13. For relations between the IWW and the Western Federation of Miners, see Vernon H. Jensen, *Heritage of Conflict, Labor Relations in the Non-ferrous Metals Industry up to 1930* (Ithaca: Cornell University Press, 1950), pp. 244–46, 272, 298–353ff.

14. *Proceedings, First Convention of the Labor Party of the United States* (Chicago, 1919), pp. 126–31; *Proceedings, Twenty-Seventh Consecutive and Fourth Biennial Convention of the U.M.W. of A.* (Cleveland, 1919), pp. 392–97, 631–32, 841–49, 867–70; *Proceedings, Twenty-Eighth Consecutive and Fifth Biennial Convention of U.M.W. of A.* (Indianapolis, 1921), p. 1137.

15. For a description of the socialist-communist conflict in the ILGWU, see David Schneider, *The Workers (Communist) Party and the American Trade Unions* (Baltimore: The Johns Hopkins Press, 1928), pp. 87–104. For Johnston's role in the CPPA see Kenneth C. McKay, *The Progressive Movement of 1924* (New York: Columbia University Press, 1947), pp. 60–70; *Machinists Monthly Journal*, XXXIII (March 1921), pp. 197–98, XXXIII (April 1921), pp. 293–95, XXXIV (April 1922), pp. 269–73.

16. The founding convention of the party, held in July 1901, specifically repudiated the tactics of the De Leonites, and urged all socialists to "join the unions of their respective trades." "We recognize," the party declared, "that trades unions are by historical necessity organized on

neutral ground, as far as political affiliation is concerned." See *Proceedings, Socialist Unity Convention* (Indianapolis, 1901), pp. 529–30. Similar resolutions were passed at the party conventions of 1904, 1908, and 1912.

17. Philip Taft, *The A.F. of L. in the Time of Gompers* (New York: Harper, 1957), pp. xii–xiv, 163–82ff.; Louis Lorwin, *The American Federation of Labor, History, Policies and Prospects* (Washington: The Brookings Institution, 1933), pp. 48–50.

18. For the WFM, see Jensen, op. cit., pp. 59–71. For the IAM, see *The Worker*, XII (June 7, 1903), p. 4; *International Socialist Review*, IV (January 1904), pp. 435–36; *Machinists Monthly Journal*, XXIV (September 1912), p. 851, XXVII (January 1915), pp. 82–83, XXVIII (May 1916), pp. 530–35; Taft, "Differences in the Executive Council," pp. 55–56.

19. Marion D. Savage, *Industrial Unionism in America* (New York: The Ronald Press Co., 1922), pp. 62–64, 82; Perlman, op. cit., p. 3; Commons, *History of Labour in the United States* (New York: Macmillan, 1936), II, pp. 138–44; Norman J. Ware, *The Labor Movement in the United States, 1860–1895* (New York: D. Appleton and Co., 1929), pp. 209–27. For the Knights of St. Crispin, see Don Lescohier, *The Knights of St. Crispin, 1867–1874; A Study in the Industrial Causes of Unionism* (Madison: University of Wisconsin Press, 1910).

20. For recent suggestive accounts of how rural (and some urban) workers may have voted in the South and the Southwest, however, see James R. Green, "Industrial Workers and Agrarian Socialism in the American Southwest, 1895–1915" (Unpublished Paper, American Historical Association, December 1971) and J. M. Kausser, "The Disenfranchisement Movement in the South, 1890–1910" (Unpublished Ph.D. Dissertation, Yale University, 1971).

21. Chester M. Destler, *American Radicalism, 1865–1901: Essays and Documents* (New London: Connecticut College, 1946), pp. 166–71, 175, 179, 207–8; *United Mine Workers Journal*, III (June 8, 1893), p. 1, III (March 22, 1894), p. 5, IV (August 9, 1894), pp. 4–5, IV (August 23, 1894), p. 4.

22. Melvyn Dubofsky, "The Origins of Western Working Class Radicalism, 1890–1905," *Labor History* (Spring 1966), pp. 140–41; *Machinists Monthly Journal*, VI (September 1894), p. 315, X (October 1898), pp. 594–95; Perlman, op. cit., pp. 8, 36; *Proceedings, Tenth Convention of the International Association of Machinists* (Milwaukee, 1903), p. 522. On the general issue of Populism and socialism, it may be suggested that it was not so much the case, as Norman Pollack argues, that the Populists were more radical in their ideology than agrarian historians have supposed. It was rather that in certain limited areas and on a certain limited range of issues (leaving aside ethnic and economic-interest differences between the two groups), such as control over the railroads, mine nationalization, and the threat which the growing power of the trusts presented to the bargaining position

228 / JOHN H. M. LASLETT

of the trade unions, there was, temporarily, sufficient common ground
between urban workers and farmers to make possible a political coalition between the two. See Norman Pollack, *The Populist Response
to Industrial America, Midwestern Populist Thought* (Cambridge: Harvard University Press, 1962), pp. 1–24, 103–43ff.

23. Lescohier, op. cit., pp. 12–24; Galster, op. cit., pp. 3–8, 16–21,
30–37; John R. Commons, *Labor and Administration* (New York:
Macmillan, 1913), pp. 255–66; *Twenty-Eighth Annual Report of
the Massachusetts Bureau of Statistics of Labor* (Boston, 1898), pp.
12–13; *Labor Bulletin of the Commonwealth of Massachusetts*, Nos.
39–44 (Cincinnati, 1904), pp. 16–17.

24. *The Comrade*, III (November 1903), pp. 32–33; Haverhill *Social Democrat*, I (December 23, 1899), p. 1; *Proceedings, Third Convention of the Boot and Shoe Workers Union* (June 1897), pp. 34,
42; Thomas Philips to John C. Mulryan, March 30, 1890 (Thomas
Philips Papers, Wisconsin State Historical Society). See also the testimony of Horace Eaton, George McNeill, Edward Cole, J. E. Tilt,
I. B. Myers, and others before the Congressional Industrial Commission in 1899–1900. *Report of the Industrial Commission on the
Relations and Conditions of Capital and Labor Employed in Manu-
factures and General Business*, 56th Cong., 2nd sess., House Doc. 495
(Washington, 1901), VII, pp. 119, 359–73, 684, 728–30ff.

25. Perlman, op. cit., p. 5; *Monthly Journal of the International
Association of Machinists*, VII (April 1896), pp. 90–91, X (May
1898), p. 278, X (December 1898), pp. 722–24; Harold M. Groves,
"The Machinist in Industry: A study of the History and Economics
of His Craft" (Unpublished Ph.D. Dissertation, University of Wisconsin, 1927), pp. 75–85; William H. Buckler, "The Minimum Wage in
the Machinists' Union," in J. H. Hollander and G. E. Barnett (eds.),
Studies in American Trade Unionism (New York: H. Holt & Co.,
1912), pp. 114–16, 136; U. S. Cong. Sen., *Report of the Committee
of the Senate upon the Relations Between Labor and Capital* (Washington, 1885), I, pp. 755–59.

26. William A. McConagha, "The History and Progress of the
United Mine Workers of America" (Unpublished Ph.D. Dissertation,
University of Illinois, 1925), pp. 37, 40–48, 50–57; McAlister Coleman, *Men and Coal* (New York: Farrar and Rinehart, Inc., 1943),
pp. 41–44; John Brophy, *A Miner's Life* (Madison: University of Wisconsin Press, 1964), pp. 38–46; Andrew Roy, *A History of the
Coal Miners of the United States from the Development of the Mines
to the Close of the Anthracite Strike of 1902* (Columbus: Trauger
Printing Press, 1907), pp. 81–85, 186–214, 267–72, 281–89,
370–79, 427–40; Frank J. Warne, *The Slav Invasion and the Mine
Workers: A Study in Immigration* (Philadelphia: J. B. Lippincott,
1904), pp. 65–83, 88–90. For a more detailed study of the impact of
Slav immigration, see Peter Roberts, *Anthracite Coal Communities: A
Study of the Demography, the Social, Educational and Moral Life of
the Anthracite Regions* (New York: The Macmillan Co., 1904). For

the economic development of the industry, see Harold W. Aurand, *From the Molly Maguires to the United Mine Workers: The Social Ecology of an Industrial Union, 1869–1897* (Philadelphia: Temple University Press, 1971).

27. Dubofsky, op. cit., pp. 133–34; Jensen, op. cit., pp. 4–9; Rodman K. Paul, *The Mining Frontier of the Far West, 1848–1880* (New York: Holt, Rinehart & Winston, 1963), pp. 136–38, 143–44; *Report of the Industrial Commission on the Relations of Labor and Capital Employed in the Mining Industry* (Washington: G.P.O., 1901), pp. lxi–lxiv, lxxvii–lxxx, 191–618 *passim;* Edward Lord, *Comstock Mining and the Mines* (Washington: U. S. Government, 1883), p. 319, 397–99, 403.

28. *Brauer-Zeitung,* XVI (March 30, 1901), p. 4, XVIII (February 28, 1903), p. 1, XXV (January 29, 1910), p. 1; *Proceedings, Tenth Convention of the Brewery Workers Union* (Boston, 1897), pp. 5–6; Hermann Schlüter, *The Brewing Industry and the Brewery Workers' Movement in America* (Cincinnati: International Union of United Brewery Workmen of America, 1910), pp. 92–94, 123; Joel Seidman, *The Needle Trades* (New York: Farrar & Rinehart, Inc., 1942), pp. 55–56, 60–61ff.; Benjamin Stolberg, *Tailors Progress: The Story of a Famous Union and the Men Who Made It* (New York: Doubleday, Doran and Co., Inc., 1944), pp. 4–12; Aaron Antonovsky, *The Early Jewish Labor Movement in the United States* (New York: 1961), pp. 246–71.

29. Both of these hypotheses, however, must remain nothing more than that until detailed statistics have been undertaken into both occupational and geographical mobility rates among properly constructed local samples of the workers in these trades. In their researches into both volatility and occupational mobility in the American labor force Stephan Thernstrom, Clyde Griffen, and others have rightly pointed to the need to examine available sources of employment in alternative industries, as well as the opportunities for upward mobility among the sons of threatened artisans, before drawing any firm conclusions about the supposed consequences of "blocked mobility" resulting from the mechanization of the skilled trades. Pending the results of such detailed analysis, however, the economic history, at least of the shoemakers' and machinists' groups considered in this study, suggests that mechanization and the growth of large-scale production may have taken place so rapidly that they occurred within the working life of a single generation. The effect of this seems to have been that in the absence of alternative sources of employment (which were less likely to be available in depression years such as 1873–79, 1883–86, and 1893–97), technological developments may indeed have had a severe impact upon the established cadre of workers in a trade (who were those most likely to join a union), irrespective of the opportunities which were available to their sons. Secondly, it should be pointed out that we are dealing here not simply with the results of mechanization, but with the combined effect of a variety of complex and sometimes conflicting developments, including unstable industrial conditions resulting from

rapid economic expansion, the influx of unskilled and semi-skilled immigrant labor—which made unionization difficult and created a temporary oversupply of labor in certain trades, such as textiles and coal —and the effects of several prolonged periods of depression. None of this invalidates the need for detailed analysis of mobility rates among both organized and unorganized elements of the labor force. It does, however, suggest that the problem is more complicated than may at first be supposed. For Thernstrom's views, see his *Poverty and Progress: Social Mobility in a Nineteenth Century City* (Cambridge: Harvard University Press, 1964), especially Chapter 8; "Urbanization, Migration, and Social Mobility in Late Nineteenth Century America," in Barton J. Bernstein (ed.), *Towards a New Past, Dissenting Essays in American History* (New York: Pantheon Books, 1969, Vintage ed.), pp. 171–72; and Thernstrom and Knights, "Men in Motion: Some Data and Speculations about Urban Population Mobility in Nineteenth Century America," *Journal of Interdisciplinary History*, I (Autumn 1970), pp. 7–35. For those of Griffen, see his "Making It in America: Social Mobility in Mid-Nineteenth Century Poughkeepsie," in *New York History*, LI (October 1970), pp. 479–99; "Workers Divided: The Effect of Craft and Ethnic Differences in Poughkeepsie, New York, 1850–1880," in Stephan Thernstrom and Richard Sennett (eds.), *Nineteenth Century Cities* (New Haven: Yale University Press, 1969), pp. 49–93; and his very suggestive "Problems in the Study of Social Mobility" (Unpublished Paper).

30. Louis Kemper, the German-born national secretary of the Brewery Workers Union, died in 1914; Gustav Mostler, the editor of the *Brauer-Zeitung,* died in 1917. Julius Zorn, another German-born editor of the union journal who succeeded Mostler until his death in 1926, found that his socialist editorials became increasingly unpopular among the newer members of the union, who consisted largely of native-born yeast, vinegar, alcohol, wine, and cider workers with political backgrounds quite different from the initial core of German radicals. Savage, op. cit., p. 75; *Proceedings, Twenty-First Convention of the Brewery Workers Union* (Houston, 1917), pp. 13, 40–51, 60; *Brauer-Zeitung,* XXXVII (March 18, 1922), p. 1.

31. For an interesting discussion of the evolution of the political outlook of the urban Jewish community, see Nathan Glazer and Daniel P. Moynihan, *Beyond the Melting Pot: The Negroes, Puerto Ricans, Jews, Italians, and Irish of New York City* (Cambridge: M.I.T. Press, 1963), pp. 137–80.

32. *Proceedings, Sixth Convention of the Boot and Shoe Workers Union* (Cincinnati, 1904), pp. 16–17.

33. *Miners' Magazine,* XII (November 1912), pp. 4–6, XIII (January 1913), pp. 4–5; *Solidarity,* III (September 28, 1912), p. 3; *Proceedings, Twentieth Annual Convention of the W.F.M.* (Victor, 1912), pp. 191–213, 221–22; Levine, op. cit., pp. 249–72 *passim;* Hyman Berman, "Era of Protocol: A Chapter in the History of the International Ladies Garment Workers Union, 1910–1916" (Unpublished Ph.D.

Thesis, Columbia University, 1956), pp. 2–3; Savage, op. cit., p. 73; *Brewers Journal*, XXXIX (December 1914), pp. 71–74; *Proceedings, Twentieth Convention of the Brewery Workers Union* (Baltimore, 1914), pp. 131–34; McConagha, op. cit., pp. 79–380; *United Mine Workers Journal*, IX (November 3, 1898), p. 4.

34. Paul Jacobs, "What Can We Expect from the Unions?", in Irving Howe (ed.), *The Radical Papers* (New York: Doubleday, 1966), pp. 262–64.

35. Galster, op. cit., pp. 91, 106–10, 114; *Shoe Workers Journal*, XI (September 1910), p. 8; *Proceedings, Sixth Convention of the Boot and Shoe Workers Union* (Cincinnati, 1904), pp. 10–11.

36. James Weinstein, *The Decline of Socialism in America, 1912–1925* (New York: Monthly Review Press, 1967), pp. x, 45.

37. For this, see John H. M. Laslett, "End of an Alliance; Selected Correspondence Between Socialist Party Secretary Adolph Germer, and U.M.W. of A. Leaders in World War One," *Labor History*, XII, 4 (Fall 1971), pp. 567–77ff.

38. *Machinists Monthly Journal*, XXIV (October 1912), pp. 925–27, 942, 944, 950, XXV (November 1913), pp. 1203–5, XXVII (April 1915), pp. 296–300, XXVIII (October 1916), pp. 1026–29; *United Mine Workers Journal*, XXIII (October 24, 1912), p. 4, XXVII (November 16, 1916), p. 4; William Green, *Labor and Democracy* (Princeton: Princeton University Press, 1939), pp. 26–27; Roger W. Babson, *W. B. Wilson and the Department of Labor* (New York: Brentano's, 1919), pp. 122–26; *Proceedings, Twentieth Convention of the Brewery Workers Union* (Baltimore, 1914), p. 140; *Brauer-Zeitung*, XXXI (October 14, 1916), p. 2.

39. See, for example, David M. Potter, *People of Plenty, Economic Abundance and the American Character* (Chicago: University of Chicago Press, 1954), pp. 91–127; Charles A. Gulick and Melvin K. Bers, "Insight and Illusion in Perlman's Theory of the Labor Movement," *Industrial and Labor Relations Review*, VI (July 1953), pp. 528ff.

40. For graphs illustrating the relationship between third-party voting and changes in the business cycle, see Murray S. and Susan W. Stedman, *Discontent at the Polls: A Study of Farmer and Labor Parties, 1827–1948* (New York: Columbia University Press, 1950), pp. 79, 81, 84, 90.

41. The extent to which collective bargaining is able to raise wage levels above those prevailing throughout industry in general is still somewhat unclear. The consensus seems to be by some 10 to 15 per cent. See Albert Rees, *The Economics of Trade Unions* (Chicago: University of Chicago Press, 1962), pp. 75–80; Arthur M. Ross, "The Influence of Unionism upon Earnings," *Quarterly Journal of Economics*, XXXVIII (February 1948), pp. 241–59.

42. The membership of the Boot and Shoe Workers Union rose from 8966 in 1898 to 69,290 in 1904; that of the ILGWU from under 9000 in 1908 to over 90,000 in 1913; that of the IAM from 18,000

in 1899 to 75,000 in 1915; and that of the UMW of A from just over 8000 members in 1894 to over 30,000 in 1905.

43. *Shoe Workers Journal,* XXI (January 1919), p. 17.

44. *Proceedings, Seventeenth Convention of the International Ladies' Garment Workers Union* (Boston, 1924), pp. 115–16.

45. Selig Perlman, *A Theory of the Labor Movement* (New York: Macmillan, 1928), pp. 262–79.

46. Philip Taft, *A.F. of L. in the Time of Gompers,* pp. xii–xiv, 163–82ff.; Foner, op. cit., II, p. 280, III, p. 391.

COMMENT

Philip S. Foner

Dr. Laslett asserts that I have attributed "the failure of socialism in the American labor movement," so far as the trade unions are concerned, "to the bourgeois and 'class collaborationist' character of the labor leadership." So far as the socialists are concerned, he quotes me as having asserted that it was due, in the case of the SLP, to the "incorrect policies" of dual unionism; and, in the case of the Socialist Party, to the domination of the "Center-Right" elements which I have "erroneously" suggested "abandoned altogether the battle against the Federation's narrow, craft, pure and simple trade unionism." Laslett repeats this sweeping declaration in his book *Labor and the Left: A Study of Socialist and Radical Influences in the American Labor Movement, 1881–1924.*[1] In both cases, he cites as a source for this conclusion one page from the second and one from the third volume of my *History of the Labor Movement in the United States.*

A reading of these pages should convince any objective student that I certainly did not attempt to explain in such simplistic terms so complicated a problem as the "failure of socialism in the American labor movement." For one thing, though I have been criticized for using the words "correct" and "incorrect" in evaluating the policies of the AF of L leaders and the socialists—as though a labor historian, after an examination of the sources, has no right to pass judgment on the policies pursued in the past—I believe one should be careful in discussing "success" or "failure" in generalities. One must first clearly establish a criterion as to what constitutes "success" or "failure." I believe this to be one of the major weaknesses of Dr. Laslett's own writings on the subject. Neither in his article "Reflections on the Failure of Socialism in the American Federation of Labor," published in the *Mississippi Valley Historical Review,*[2] nor in his present paper or his recent book does

Dr. Laslett establish any criteria by which to measure success or failure. To be sure, there is little doubt as to which was the winning side between "pure and simple unionists" and the socialist-minded in the American labor movement. But is success to be measured by the number of socialist leaders in unions or by the adoption of resolutions at conventions favoring socialist candidates for office?

The fact that some unions had socialist leaders is no indication of the influence of socialism in these organizations. In his account of the Illinois Central and Harriman Lines strike of 1911, Carl E. Person describes a meeting with the leaders of the International Association of Machinists arising out of his charge that they had collaborated with the railroad companies to break the strike. Person describes how these union leaders set out to convince him that they could not possibly be guilty of his accusation:

"Yes, I've been a comrade now for eighteen years," said Mr. Johnston [President William H. Johnston of the IA of M], and as he passed a small book over to Buckalew he added, "and I was the party's choice as candidate for governor of Massachusetts at one time."

"I am proud of my red ticket," said Wharton [Arthur O. Wharton, General Executive Board member of the IA of M], as he started to pass his duesbook around for inspection.

"We have a fine little movement in Topeka," said Buckalew as he started his book out for the once-over by the comrades.

As I sat there perfectly injured over the cheapness of the situation, smiling Hugh Molly was introducing his ticket, after which a conversation was carried on for my benefit. They had, of course, agreed among themselves to put on this preliminary show for the purpose of persuading me to "come along," being fully aware of the fact that I had read Bellamy's *Looking Backward* with delight and considered Karl Marx one of the family.[3]

Other socialist trade union leaders, including those in the garment unions, proudly displayed their red cards and delivered lengthy speeches about the evils of capitalism. But in practice they often turned their membership against socialism by proving to be corrupt and despotic as many of the "pure and simple" trade union leaders.[4] For all his faults, De Leon had a point when he argued that many socialists changed their faces as soon as they became officeholders in a trade union and immediately began to pursue a policy of appeasing the conservatives. He warned that such conduct only brought inestimable harm to the prestige of socialism among workers.[5] He might have added that socialists did not lift the prestige of socialism among workers when, as mayors of cities, they discharged municipal workers seeking to organize and called in the police to break their strikes.[6] In short, one must certainly consider what was socialism and who were the socialists when one passes judgment on the "success" or "failure" of socialism. *The Independent* raised this point in 1912 in an editorial entitled "The Mystery of Socialism," and indicated that an answer to the question of "What is socialism?" was "confusing" because of the conduct of many who called themselves socialists.[7]

Dr. Laslett tends to dismiss my criticism of the dual unionist policies of De Leon and the SLP as an important factor in the waning influence of socialism in the AF of L. It is true that after 1900 Gompers became increasingly paranoid on the subject of socialism and insisted that there was a dichotomy between socialism and trade unionism which could not be resolved.[8] But Laslett concedes that the "socialists enjoyed their largest influence in the A.F.L. in the 1890's, before the Gompers regime had been thoroughly established. . . ." Yet it was precisely at this point that the dual unionist policies of De Leon and the SLP resulted in an exodus of the elements who should have influenced the course of the labor movement. It is significant that Gompers sought to obtain Frederick Engels' backing for his stand against the SLP and that Engels, while no admirer of Gompers, criticized the De Leonites for precipitating a conflict with the AF of L leadership which ended with their isolation from the main body of the American labor movement.[9] It is also significant that Lenin, whose *What Is to Be Done?* Dr. Laslett cites though without making the connection clear, repeatedly criticized the SLP and other dual unionists in this country for having weakened the struggle for socialism by refusing to work in the reactionary trade unions. As Lenin noted, this policy made it easier for the Gompers regime to become thoroughly established.[10]

As for the socialists who worked within the AF of L, it is becoming clearer, as new studies emerge, that the American Socialist Party never really defined a socialist policy for the American labor movement and had no well-developed trade union program. The trade union position of the Socialist Party emphasized the analogy of the two-armed labor movement—but with the two arms completely independent.[11] In practical terms, this meant a pro-AF of L policy regardless of the position the Gompers leadership took on fundamental issues. Algernon Lee maintained as early as 1904 that this pro-AF of L policy had shown such good results that the proposition to abandon it could be put aside as academic.[12] But then socialist unionists in the AF of L were easily satisfied. Resolutions favoring independent political action or even what Lewis Lorwin calls a "vague promise" to favor such action convinced them that they were making headway for socialism. Max S. Hayes, the chief socialist spokesman in the AF of L, regularly welcomed any departure from "pure and simple" trade unionism by the AF of L as bound to lead to the formation of a Labor Party like Great Britain's, or to the "endorsement" of the Socialist Party as the one party which would give unqualified support to labor's demands. The socialists, of course, were doomed to disappointment, but the fact remains that they concentrated most of their energies in this direction as the means of "making the socialist movement" felt inside the AF of L.[13]

As has been pointed out by a number of scholars, the factionalism between right and left wings which constantly plagued the Socialist Party during the first two decades of its existence revolved mainly around the question of trade unionism. The Left became increasingly alienated by the uncritical attitude of the socialist leadership toward the AF of L and complained repeatedly of the party's reluctance to offend influential leaders of the craft unions.[14] Even when the party's convention in 1912 conceded to the Left that more could be done to organize the unorganized, it claimed no desire to interfere in any union disputes. On the contrary, it declared the party duty was to support the unions morally and materially regardless of their policies.[15] Hence it is not surprising that when the AF of L was unwilling to move in the direction of organizing the unorganized, the socialists, fearing that relations with the Federation would deteriorate, did nothing on the issue. In his autobiography, socialist James H. Maurer, long-time president of the Pennsylvania State Federation of Labor, emphasized that organization of the unskilled was a key to the rise in socialist influence in this country, and that the failure of the socialists to press for this policy more actively in the AF of L was a serious weakness of the movement.[16]

This, of course, is linked to the whole issue of industrial unionism. It is true that in *Syndicalism, Industrial Unionism and Socialism,* published in 1913, John Spargo discussed the severe drawbacks of craft unionism. But the socialists did little to advance the cause of industrial unionism. With the IWW pressing from the Left, the socialists in the AF of L had until 1912 made a concerted attempt to push the issue of industrial unionism. But after the "cleansing" of the party in 1912 of the pro-IWW elements and the withdrawal of Haywood and his followers, the fight for industrial unionism diminished. At the AF of L conference in 1913 the motion for industrial unionism was defeated without a roll call vote and with no one speaking in favor of it. In 1914 the issue was taken up by the non-socialist Illinois Federation of Labor and again defeated. Militant socialists who were still in the party criticized the leadership for failing to conduct a campaign in behalf of "a thorough working knowledge of that powerful weapon— industrial unionism."[17] Probably the party was so weakened by the split that it could not have done much in this direction. In 1915, Hillquit admitted to Berger that the Socialist Party organization was "in an awful mess."[18]

Whatever the reason, the fact remains that the socialists in the AF of L had all but abandoned any real opposition to the Gompers policies. Like the Commons-Wisconsin school, many socialists in the Federation had reached the conclusion that the AF of L was the only labor organization which could have established a permanent foothold in the American environment and its continued existence was proof of the correctness of its policies and of its leadership. Saul Yanovsky, editor of *Justice,* official organ of the ILGWU and a leading socialist theoretician in the labor movement, revealed that the socialists had abandoned any pretense of combating the "pure and simple" craft unionism of the AF of L when he wrote in 1919:

An organized labor body, millions strong, can surely not be spoken of as the labor aristocracy, we will go even further and say that in our opinion, these three and one quarter million workers represent not the cream, but indeed the body of American labor—whether they be conservative or radical. Its voice will be the voice of American labor and not that of a particular radical or conservative group or clique. . . .

Gompers has been at the head of the labor movement for these many years because he knows best how to voice the true sentiments, views, and aspirations of the workers of America. It is beside the question whether the aspirations of American labor are radical and wise enough . . . the fact is that the views of American workers are what they are, and that only the man who will truly reflect their views and give them voice will be acknowledged as their leader, even though it may seem to some that he rules them with an iron hand.

An Iron Hand! How ill-suited this phrase is to Samuel Gompers. . . .[19]

In his book, Laslett concedes that "the opposition of the Catholic leaders toward socialism did later help to prevent its further growth," but insists that Karson oversimplifies in asserting that the "opposition of the Catholic church precluded virtually all socialist influence among Irish workingmen." But this avoids the real issue. Certainly an increasing number of studies have demonstrated how important a force was the Catholic Church in offsetting socialist influence in the American labor movement. Mark Hanna may have exaggerated when he boasted that the Catholic Church was America's greatest bulwark against socialism in the opening decade of the twentieth century. But according to statistics drawn up by a competent labor commission and quoted in *The Nation* in 1909, "about one-half of those in trade unions are Roman Catholics, the rest Protestants or without religious differences." Peter Collins, Catholic trade union official and publicist in these years, estimated that 50 per cent of all delegates to AF of L conventions were Roman Catholics.[20] Equally important, Catholics occupied a proportionate number of seats in the Executive Council. The Church not only served a warning to the AF of L to avoid socialist tendencies, but as Edward G. Roddy points out: "By open and subtle warnings, the Church hierarchy threatened to forbid Catholic participation in any union that opted for socialism."[21] Certainly the socialists did not underestimate the importance of this influence; at the 1912 AF of L convention and again in 1913, socialist resolutions to "exclude fraternal delegates of church organizations from all future conventions of the A.F. of L." were introduced, but tabled.[22]

But while trade unionists were bombarded with anti-socialist propaganda from the Catholic Church and by groups like the Presbyterian Department of Church and Labor, headed by Charles Stelzle,[23] the party did little to try to impress the workers with its message. Morris Hillquit conceded, "We have often tried to coax, cajole and browbeat the trade unions into socialism, but we have made but little systematic effort to educate their members in the socialist philosophy." While organizing for the Socialist Party, White of the Molders Union was "surprised at times at the density of the ignorance as to the meaning of socialism, but found that they were willing to come and listen." He and other socialists noted that the party had never taken any efforts to introduce the rank-and-file members to socialist principles, and this despite the fact that "when they heard the position of socialism they stated they were glad to buy books and pamphlets, and learn more of the movement." In 1909 the Socialist Party did make a halfhearted effort to get a number of socialist trade unionists to conduct a general educational campaign among the local unions, but the attempt was soon abandoned. There remained, therefore, in the American labor movement a body of untapped support which the socialists failed to reach.[24]

In addition to paying little attention to the conversion of the already organized, the Socialist Party did precious little to reach the mass of the unorganized workers who, even the socialists admitted, were more apt to be influenced by a socialist message. For one thing, most of the unorganized workers were unskilled and their organization would have necessitated an all-out policy of industrial unionism, but this meant combating the policies of the AF of L. Moreover, to bring the message of socialism to the unorganized in many industrial centers where the companies completely dominated the economic, political, and social life required more courage than most socialist leaders possessed. Since the Socialist Party's approach to the Negro workers was similar in many respects to that of the AF of L, despite its nod to the principle of working-class solidarity, it could not accomplish much in influencing black workers in socialist principles.[25]

In his book Dr. Laslett also points out, as does David Shannon, that the Socialist Party "at its height contained more native-born Americans than it did immigrants," and that the "evidence from the trade union movement" sustains this conclusion. But he fails to see that this was precisely a reflection of the indifference of the Socialist Party to the unskilled workers in the mass production industries. Socialist trade unionists conceded that the IWW was able to succeed temporarily in organizing these workers, for they could "easily be got to participate in a strike." But these workers were actually of little value for a socialist movement since their ideas "of maintaining a permanent organization are very hazy and confused."[26] Yet these were the workers who made up the bulk of the American working class and it was among them that the socialist message could have received the greatest response. Given this approach, it is not surprising that, as one student of socialism and the American labor movement has pointed out, "socialism remained weakest where it probably had most to offer in the long run."[27]

To conclude: while Dr. Laslett has added new and interesting information about socialism and American labor, he has not, in my judgment, altered the fact that a decisive reason for the weakness of socialism in the American labor movement arose from the sectarian, dual unionism of De Leon and the SLP and others who followed this policy as well as the nature of the trade union program pursued by the Socialist Party of America.

NOTES

1. (New York, 1970), p. 290.
2. L (March 1964), pp. 634–51.
3. Carl E. Person, *The Lizard's Trail* (Chicago, 1918), p. 100.
4. Philip S. Foner, *The Fur and Leather Workers Union* (Newark, N.J., 1950), pp. 78–81. One writer in the *Bakers Journal* saw a correlation between a decline in socialist feeling in the union and an unwillingness of the socialist leadership to conduct a truly socialist policy and their tendency to "make disparaging remarks about the mob"—i.e., the rank and file. (*Bakers Journal*, March 13, 1909.)
5. *Proceedings*, Socialist Labor Party Convention, 1900, pp. 211–17.
6. Kenneth E. Hendrickson, Jr., "George R. Lunn and the Socialist Era in Schenectady, New York, 1909–1916," *New York History* (January 1936), pp. 23–40; Webb Waldron, "Jasper Goes to Town," *American Magazine*, April 1938.
7. *The Independent*, October 10, 1912, p. 850.
8. *American Federationist*, XXII (August 1915), p. 675, XIX (November 1912), p. 923, XVII (March 1910), p. 211. In his article "Reflections on the Failure of Socialism in the A.F. of L.," in op. cit., Laslett accepts Gompers' view that there was a basic incompatibility between trade unionism and socialism.
9. Philip S. Foner, "Samuel Gompers to Frederick Engels: A Letter," *Labor History* (Spring 1970), pp. 207–11; Frederick Engels to Hermann Schluter, January 29, 1891, and to F. A. Sorge, January 6, 1892, Alexander Trachtenberg (ed.), *Karl Marx and Frederick Engels: Letters to Americans, 1848–1895* (New York, 1953), pp. 233–34, 240. Gompers' high opinion of Engels at this time is evidenced by his concern over the fact that the co-father of scientific socialism believed that the Knights of Labor was the organization of the proletariat of America. (Gompers to Florence Kelley Wischnewetsky, October 17, 1888, Samuel Gompers Letterbooks, Library of Congress.)
10. V. I. Lenin, *Left-Wing Communism: An Infantile Disorder* (New York, 1934), pp. 36–38; Philip S. Foner, "Lenin and the American Working-Class Movement," in Daniel Mason and Jessica Smith (eds.), *Lenin's Impact on the United States* (New York, 1970), pp. 121–31. Even Carl Reeve, in his effort to refute the charge that De Leon's dual-unionist policies disastrously affected socialist influence in the AF of L, ends up his discussion of "Dual Unionism-Splits and Expulsions" by proving that "De Leon's entire program of dual unionism" had precisely this result. (*The Life and Times of Daniel De Leon*, New York, 1972, pp. 57–67.)
11. *Proceedings*, Socialist Party Convention, 1908, pp. 94–102.
12. *Proceedings*, Socialist Party Convention, 1904, pp. 123–24.
13. *International Socialist Review*, VII (August 1906), p. 112, VIII (March 1908), pp. 566–69; Lewis L. Lorwin, *The American Federa-*

tion of Labor: History, Policies, and Prospects (Washington, D.C., 1933), p. 416; *Proceedings*, AF of L Convention, 1913, pp. 314–15.

14. *International Socialist Review*, XIV (July 1913), p. 22.

15. *Proceedings*, Socialist Party Convention, 1912, p. 195.

16. James Hudson Maurer, *It Can Be Done* (New York, 1938), p. 244.

17. *International Socialist Review*, XIV (July 1913), p. 17; W. H. Kinger to Frans Bostrom, January 13, 1913, Socialist Party Collection, Duke University Library; Michael E. R. Bassett, "The Socialist Party of America, 1912–1919: Years of Decline" (Unpublished Ph.D. Thesis, Duke University, 1963), pp. 52–53.

18. Morris Hillquit to Victor Berger, September 25, 1915, Socialist Party Collection, County Historical Society, Milwaukee, Wisconsin. Weinstein concedes that the Socialist Party lost influence in the AF of L after 1912, but argues that it did increase its influence in certain specific unions as well as in the Pennsylvania State Federation of Labor. (James Weinstein, "The Socialist Party: Its Roots and Strength, 1912–1919," *Studies on the Left*, I [Winter 1960], pp. 15–18.) This is a subject that would require more space than is available to discuss in full, but it should be noted that for all his criticism of the tendency of labor historians to rivet their attention on the national federations of labor, Dr. Laslett ignores in his analysis the radicalization that took place in the local city central bodies and the state federations of labor. Under the AF of L constitution, to be sure, the role of city centrals and state federations was very much circumscribed, and efforts to change this in the interests of permitting them to play a more active part in the labor movement proved fruitless. Undoubtedly this was due to a fear of the traditional radicalism of the local federations. (See Lorwin, op. cit., pp. 348–49.)

19. *Justice*, I (June 14, 1919), p. 4. Norman H. Ware, historian of the Knights of Labor, saw nothing inevitable in the success of the American Federation of Labor, and James H. Maurer pointed out that the AF of L had still not accomplished in the 1930s what the Knights of Labor had attempted—organization of the unskilled. (Norman J. Ware, *The Labor Movement in the United States, 1860–1895* [New York, 1929], p. xiv; Maurer, op. cit., p. 244.) As for Gompers' "iron hand," Yanovsky could have profited from reading socialist Duncan McDonald's report on his experiences at the AF of L convention during which he noted: "If anybody can get a progressive idea through the A.F. of L., he deserves a monument bigger than that built to George Washington. . . ." (*Proceedings*, United Mine Workers Convention, 1912, pp. 310–12; 1914, pp. 353–61.)

20. *The Nation*, August 12, 1909; *Central-Blatt and Social Justice*, II (February 1910), p. 10.

21. Edward G. Roddy, "The Catholic Church and the A.F. of L., 1910–1920; A Study in Ambivalence" (Unpublished paper before the joint meeting of the Labor Historians and the American Catholic

Historical Association at the fifty-eighth annual meeting of the Mississippi Valley Historical Association, April 22, 1965), p. 13.

22. New York *Call,* November 19, 1912; November 20, 1913.

23. See William John Villaume, "The Federal Council of the Churches of Christ in America and Labor Problems in the United States" (Unpublished Ph.D. Thesis, Hartford Seminary Foundation, Hartford, Conn., May 1951); George H. Nash, III, "Charles Stelzle: Apostle to Labor," *Labor History* (Spring 1970), pp. 151–74.

24. New York *Call,* December 12, 1909; Socialist Party, Minutes of National Executive Committee Session, December 11–13, 1909 (Socialist Party Collection, Duke University Library); Socialist Party Press Release, May 28, July 2, 1913 (Socialist Party Collection, Duke University Library).

25. A recent study points out: "During the years under consideration the [Socialist] party failed to raise any significant protest against trade union discrimination unless one counts the labor organization resolution adopted at the 1912 convention. . . ." (R. Laurence Moore, "Flawed Fraternity—American Socialist Response to the Negro, 1901–1912," *Historian,* November 1969, pp. 13–14.) It is rather interesting that Dr. Laslett in discussing a number of unions in which socialists had influence, such as the Machinists, says nothing about the attitude toward black workers. The *Machinists Monthly Journal* may have been "imbued" with ideas stemming from the Knights of Labor, but organization of workers regardless of race and color was not one of them.

26. A. Rosebury in *Ladies' Garment Worker,* April 1914, pp. 12–14.

27. William Milnor Dick, "Labor and Socialism in America: The Gompers Era" (Unpublished Ph.D. Thesis, University of Toronto), p. 304. In his Memoir, at the Columbia University Oral History Project, John Brophy concedes that the Socialist Party was always rather remote from the mass of the working class. (Columbia University Oral History Project, John Brophy Memoir, p. 315.)

REPLY

John H. M. Laslett

Despite protestations to the contrary, in his Comment on my essay Philip Foner has chosen to confine himself, as he has in his books on the subject, almost entirely to defects in the policies pursued by the leaders of the SLP and the Socialist Party of America as the major reasons for the weakness of socialism in the American labor movement, largely ignoring my efforts to demonstrate the limited value of this limited kind of explanation, and to draw attention to the relevance of other kinds of factors as well. In particular, he accuses me of oversimplifying the analysis of the problem which he presents in his own previous writings, of neglecting to define what is meant by "success" or "failure," in relation to the record of the socialists in the labor movement, and of failing to recognize that it was the indifference of the Socialist Party toward the mass of unorganized, unskilled, and immigrant workers that was a crucial reason for their inability to build up a strong third-party movement.

The question of how one measures socialist success or failure in the labor movement is certainly an important one, and I would agree that it is not resolved simply by pointing to the number of socialists elected to union office or the type of resolutions adopted by union conventions—although I believe Foner goes much too far in arguing that evidence of this kind "is no indication of the influence of socialism in these organizations." Although labor historians are now quite properly making use of a wide variety of new types of material to determine the potential for radical consciousness among various segments of the American working class, given the paucity of source material available it is sometimes the only major index that we have.

Even if one adopts a more sophisticated criterion of success or failure, however, such as the level of "socialist" rather than trade union consciousness achieved as the result of a strike or some other particular act—which is what Lenin took as his standard in the *What Is to Be Done?* essay to which Foner refers[1]—the record of the American labor movement in this period does not, unfortunately, appear to be a great deal more encouraging. The alleged sellout of the Illinois Central and Harriman Lines strike by the socialist leadership which Foner takes as his example (which did not take place until June 1915, incidentally, after the union's treasury had become exhausted with supporting the strike for more than four years[2]) is an example of the kind of tactical compromises which were—and still are—carried out by all types of labor unions, whether socialist or not; and the question which it raises is not whether President William H. Johnston of the IA of M or Saul Yanovsky of the ILGWU were not socialists for most of their union careers, which by a wide variety of measures they undoubtedly were. Rather, it is whether there was something peculiar about the American environment which made labor leaders succumb to this kind of behavior to an unusual degree.

The point is an important one, but it is not in the nature of things capable of solution simply by looking at the nature of socialist and trade union tactics, as Foner does, instead of at the reasons which lie behind them. As early as the 1850s both Marx and Engels noticed the particular difficulty which American working-class leaders seemed to experience in remaining faithful to their original beliefs once they had secured positions of power in the society.[3] I attempted to discuss the same problem (in connection with time contracts, relations with non-socialist union officials, and the rewards of union office) at various points in my own book.[4] What lies behind this problem, however, is the more general question—which Foner ignores—of whether the behavior of American labor leaders in this matter was simply a response to the corrupting and bureaucratizing effect which union office often has upon labor leaders of proletarian origin, or whether it is also attributable to something peculiar about the American environment and American business values, as Robert Michels argued in his *Political Parties* as long ago as 1911.[5]

On this matter, as in so many other areas of labor history, we need a thoroughgoing comparative analysis to settle the issue. But David Brody's 1968 essay on careerism in the American labor movement represents a most useful start. The higher ratio of full-time officials to union members in the United States compared to a number of European countries, he argues, suggests that American labor leaders may have placed a greater value than their European counterparts on advancing their own individual careers, rather than upon preserving their sense of solidarity with members of the rank and file.[6] This, in turn, takes us back to the need to examine problems of American individualism, assimilation, and business values, which point to characteristics of the society generally, not to problems of the labor movement as such.

More generally, we cannot know whether the particular policies pursued by the trade union and socialist leadership were the crucial determinant of success or failure until we examine much more carefully the political and economic environment in which they operated, as well as the particular characteristics of the labor force with which they had to deal. This does not mean that leadership is unimportant. It may well be that the quality of socialist and trade union leadership in America was lower than it was in a number of other countries due, perhaps, to higher rates of geographical and occupational mobility which siphoned off potential leaders from the radical movement, or to the availability of free public educational facilities for advancement into other fields. But just as not even a Lenin or a Rosa Luxemburg could have made a revolution in Russia or in Germany without the prior development of a revolutionary mentality among crucial sections of the working class, so we cannot know whether a mass working-class party could have grown up in this country simply by examining the policies of the party and trade union leadership alone.

The same remark can be made concerning Foner's argument, which given the assumptions of his analysis is well taken up to a point, that despite its initial efforts to secure the support of the existing trade unions, the Socialist Party of America made few really serious attempts to educate the workers generally into socialism, or to reach the mass of immigrant, unskilled, or black elements in the labor force. It may well be that this policy (or lack of a policy) helped contribute to the alienation of the left wing within the Socialist Party, to its lack of any really extensive ties with the proletariat, and hence to its excessively bourgeois character. The trouble is, however, that this kind of analysis only looks at one side of the coin. How do we know that it was among the immigrants, the unskilled, and the black elements "that the Socialist message could have received the greatest response"? (Foner, incidentally, misunderstands my remark that evidence from the trade union movement confirms Shannon's finding that the socialist movement at its height was more native-born than immigrant. The point there was simply to rebut the popular misconception that the pre-1914 Socialist Party was foreign-dominated, not to commend it for so being.)

On this general point, it is obvious that little can be done in the way of organizing a mass working-class party without securing a mass base within the labor movement from which to operate—as, for example, the British Labour Party had in the 1890s within the "new union" wing of the TUC, which may have been one of the crucial reasons for the difference in political outlook between the labor movements in the two countries. But even if we leave aside the thorny question—which a more extended analysis could not afford to do—of whether political radicalism is more likely to arise among the labor aristocracy, i.e., from among skilled craftsmen and artisans, rather than from among the poorer segments of the working class (an issue which I discussed indirectly in my book, and which has recently been the subject of an interesting academic debate among labor historians in England[7]), Foner's approach to the problem assumes that we know a great deal more about the political outlook—and hence about the potential for radicalization—among black, unskilled, and immigrant workers in this country in the early part of this century when the Socialist Party should have taken root than we in fact do.

So far, such research as has been carried out on blacks and socialism, for example, has been largely confined to criticizing the Socialist Party because of the racism of some of its spokesmen, and because it tolerated segregated locals in the South for fear of offending its white supporters in the South and elsewhere.[8] What is needed now is to look at the other half of the problem by seeking answers to a number of basic questions concerning black political attitudes to which we still do not have satisfactory replies. Among northern black workingmen who actually registered to vote, for example, how many were tied by reasons of tradition and political mythology to the Republican Party? Did disenfranchisement and the relatively small number of blacks in industrial jobs in the South mean that the Socialist Party made a realistic (if ideologically retrograde) choice in preferring to pursue the white voter rather than the black, if, indeed, such a conscious choice was made at all? Still more important, was the Socialist Party (and later the Communist Party too) hampered in its appeal to this section of the "absentee proletariat" by persistently treating the problem primarily as one not of race, but of class?

The same kind of basic research into the political orientation of the urban immigrant worker, who made up most of the unskilled element in the labor force in the late nineteenth century, is also needed before we can venture any kind of definitive judgment as to their potential for radicalism. It is now twenty years since Oscar Handlin (followed by Richard Hofstadter) offered the broad but largely unsubstantiated judgment that "the failure of the socialists and anarchists to win an important position in the associational life of the immigrants" was due largely to the "peasant's inherited distrust of radicalism," or to his supposed lack of the "faculty of abstraction"—as if all immigrants to the United States after the late 1880s were ex-peasants, and differences in generation or in place of origin were of no account.[9] And yet, although the Handlin-Hofstadter thesis has been effectively challenged concerning the ability of the Progressive movement to secure political support among immigrant workers, very little work has been done on the attitudes of the immigrants toward socialism. One of the few exceptions, Melvyn Dubofsky's article on the political appeal of the Socialist Party among ethnic voters in New York City between 1900 and 1918, tends to confirm the view that only the Jewish voters were drawn to the Socialist Party in any numbers: Irish and Italian workers remained largely indifferent. What is needed now is a detailed state-by-state analysis of the orientation of immigrant workingmen toward both reform and socialist politics (they may have been quite different), on the order of Joseph Huthmacher's studies of immigrant attitudes toward the Progressives in Massachusetts and New York.

It may turn out, as Victor Greene implies in his interesting study of strike solidarity among Slav coal miners in the anthracite district of Pennsylvania in the 1890s, that the relative indifference of the socialists toward unskilled and immigrant workers was indeed one reason for the weakness of the party—if, that is, the kind of evidence which Greene presents about class solidarity in strike situations can be shown to carry over into the realm of politics, which is in itself a large question.[10] But in order to demonstrate this it will be necessary to examine the whole complex of influences which helped to shape the political orientation of those workers themselves, instead of simply looking at the policies of the socialist and trade union leadership alone. The Marxist tendency to assume inherent, or at least latent, class consciousness among rank-and-file elements in the labor force, to which Foner subscribes, is at bottom just as deterministic and ahistorical as the earlier tendency of Perlman and the Wisconsin school of labor economists to assume American labor's inherently conservative or job-conscious orientation.

In saying this, I do not wish to suggest that I have myself escaped the historian's tendency to overgeneralize. As I acknowledged at the end of my initial essay—and as at least one reviewer of *Labor and the Left* has quite rightly pointed out[11]—evidence drawn even from a broad spectrum of opinion within the labor movement cannot, in itself, supply complete answers to the questions which I attempted to raise. I remain convinced, however, that only by examining the full range of influences which affected the American workingman's political behavior in this period, preferably in a comparative context, will we be able to judge whether sectarianism on the part of the socialist leadership or class collaboration on the part of the trade unions was more important than structural factors in contributing to the failure of socialism to secure the support of the American worker. At present, I do not believe they were.

NOTES

1. V. I. Lenin, *What Is to Be Done? Burning Questions of Our Movement* (New York: International Publishers Co., 1969), pp. 30–34ff.

2. John H. M. Laslett, *Labor and the Left: A Study of Socialist and Radical Influences in the American Labor Movement, 1881–1924* (New York: Basic Books, 1970), pp. 165–66.

3. R. Laurence Moore, *European Socialists and the American Promised Land* (New York: Oxford University Press, 1970), p. 5.

4. Laslett, op. cit., pp. 90, 135, 179–80ff.

5. "Whilst in Europe such corruption gives rise to censure and anger," Michels wrote, "in America it is treated with indifference or arouses no more than an indulgent smile. . . . We cannot wonder, then, that North America should be pre-eminently the country in which the aristocratic tendencies of the labour leaders, fostered by an environment often permeated . . . by a gross and unrefined materialism, should have developed freely and upon a gigantic scale." Robert Michels, *Political Parties* (New York: Dover, 1959), pp. 310–11.

6. David Brody, "Career Leadership and American Trade Unionism," in Frederick C. Jaher (ed.), *The Age of Industrialism in America: Essays in Social Structure and Cultural Values* (New York: Free Press, 1968).

7. See Eric Hobsbawm, *Labouring Men: Studies in the History of Labour* (New York, 1964), ch. 15, and Hobsbawm's review of Henry Pelling, *Popular Politics and Society in Late Victorian Britain* (London, 1968), in *Bulletin* No. 18 of the Society for the Study of Labour History (Spring 1969), pp. 49–54. The only two methodologically rigorous studies of the occupational background of sample elements within the American socialist movement which to my knowledge have so far been completed tend to confirm the view, which I put forward on the basis of very limited evidence in *Labor and the Left*, that it was from the more skilled elements in the American labor force, rather than from the unskilled and the more recent immigrants, that support for the Socialist Party came. One study, based upon a detailed statistical analysis of two nationally conducted samples of Socialist Party membership in 1908 and 1914, shows that socialists tended to be "more heavily concentrated among craftsmen, professionals, proprietors (in descending order)." The other, contained in an excellent recently completed statewide study of socialism in West Virginia, suggests that radical sentiments developed more readily among skilled iron molders, glass blowers, machinists, and painters than it did among unskilled miners and other "non labor aristocracy" workers in that state. See Shannon Ferguson, "American Social Reform; 1896–1912: The Grass-Roots of Socialism and Populism" (Unpublished Research Paper, Yale University, 1963), pp. 22–23; Frederick A. Barkey, "The Socialist

Party in West Virginia from 1898 to 1920: A Study in Working Class Radicalism" (Unpublished Ph.D. Thesis, University of Pittsburgh, 1971), pp. 89–93.

8. See, for example, Ira Kipnis, *The American Socialist Movement, 1897–1912* (New York: Columbia University Press, 1952), pp. 134ff.; James Weinstein, *The Decline of Socialism in America, 1912–1925* (New York: Monthly Review Press, 1967), pp. 63–74. Somewhat more illuminating is Sally Miller's article "The Socialist Party and the Negro, 1901–1920," in *Journal of Negro History*, LVI (July 1971), pp. 220–29, although her analysis is still almost wholly confined to the Socialist Party's own attitudes.

9. Oscar Handlin, *The Uprooted* (Boston: Little, Brown, 1951), pp. 217ff. See also Richard Hofstadter, *The Age of Reform* (New York: Knopf, 1955), pp. 180–84.

10. Melvyn Dubofsky, "Success and Failure of Socialism in New York City, 1900–1918: A Case Study," *Labor History* (Fall 1968), IX, pp. 361–75; Joseph Huthmacher, *Massachusetts People and Politics, 1919–1933* (Cambridge: Harvard University Press, 1959); Huthmacher, "Urban Liberalism and the Age of Reform," *Mississippi Valley Historical Review*, XLIX (September 1962), pp. 231–41; Victor R. Greene, *The Slavic Community on Strike: Immigrant Labor in Pennsylvania Anthracite* (Notre Dame: University of Notre Dame Press, 1968), *passim*.

11. See, for example, that by Frederick Olson in the *American Historical Review*, 76 (December 1971), pp. 1613–14.

Chapter 7

SOCIALISM AND SYNDICALISM*

Melvyn Dubofsky

From 1909 to 1919 a legend enveloped the IWW. Many Americans, especially during World War One and the postwar Red Scare, became convinced that the Wobblies were "cut-throat, pro-German, or . . . bolshevik, desperadoes who burn harvest-fields, drive iron spikes into fine timber and ruin sawmills, devise bomb plots, who obstruct the war and sabotage the manufacture of munitions—veritable supermen, with a superhuman power for evil, omnipresent and almost omnipotent."[1] The hobo Wobbly had replaced the bearded, bomb-carrying anarchist as a bogeyman in the middle-class American's fevered imagination. This version of the Wobblies died hard.

It died hard because violence and bloodshed *did* follow Wobblies wherever they fought for free speech or higher wages. It died hard because IWW rhetoric and songs fed the myth of the Wobbly as a wild and woolly warrior, a man who contemptuously scorned the conventional morality of what he characterized as a "bushwa" society. While organizers like James P. Thompson were boasting that only *"red-blooded"* revolutionaries belonged to the IWW, Wobbly bards like Joe Hill were deriding voting machines and suggesting that workers "may find out that the only 'machine' worth while is the one which the capitalists use on us when we ask for more bread for ourselves and our families. *The one that works with a trigger.*"[2]

With the IWW, as with other radical organizations that have been romanticized and mythologized, the legend is several removes from reality. Wobblies did not carry bombs, nor burn harvest fields,

---

* Taken from Chapters 7 and 19 of Melvyn Dubofsky, *We Shall Be All: A History of the Industrial Workers of the World* (Chicago: Quadrangle Books, 1969), pp. 146–70, 480–84. In the original the chapters are entitled "Ideology and Utopia: The Syndicalism of the IWW," and "Remembrance of Things Past: The IWW Legacy."

nor destroy timber, nor depend upon the machine that works with a trigger. Instead they tried in their own ways to comprehend the nature and dynamics of capitalist society, and through increased knowledge, as well as through revolutionary activism, to develop a better system for the organization and functioning of the American economy.

The IWW, it is true, produced no intellectual giants. It did not spawn a Karl Marx or a Georges Sorel, a Lenin or a Jean Jaurès, or even an Edward Bellamy or a Henry George. It offered no genuinely original ideas, no sweeping explanations of social change, no fundamental theories of revolution. Wobblies instead took their basic concepts from others: from Marx the concepts of labor value, commodity value, surplus value, and class struggle; from Darwin the idea of organic evolution and the struggle for survival as a paradigm for social evolution and the survival of the fittest class; from Bakunin and the anarchists the "propaganda of the deed" and the idea of "direct action"; and from Sorel the notion of the "militant minority." Hence, IWW beliefs became a peculiar amalgam of Marxism and Darwinism, anarchism and syndicalism— all overlaid with a singularly American patina.

True, they did read books—IWW libraries included works by Marx, Engels, Kautsky, Sorel, Jaurès, Bellamy, George, and others; IWW publications advertised complete bibliographies of socialist literature—but they read to understand better what they already knew from life. For above all else, Wobblies derived their beliefs from their own experiences in America. The Coeur d'Alenes, Leadville, and Cripple Creek taught them that society was divided into contending classes; that American business had evolved from small-scale endeavors to giant corporations; that labor was divided, not united; and that a "militant minority" could surmount the resistance of a complacent majority. In other words, European theoreticians explained in coherent, analytical, and learned terms what most Wobblies grasped instinctively.

As early as 1912 William E. Bohn, an astute journalist and observer of the American scene, could declare that the IWW "did not come into being as the result of any foreign influence. It is distinctly an American product." Ben Williams agreed. For seven years, as editor of *Solidarity,* he vigorously criticized those who associated the IWW with foreign ideologies. "Whatever it may have in common with European labor movements," he insisted, the IWW

is a distinct product of America and American conditions. . . . Neither "in aim and methods" is the I.W.W. European. . . . Whatever terms or phrases we may borrow from the French or other language to denote our methods cut no figure: the methods conform to American conditions. . . . The form of structure of the I.W.W. is also distinctly American, and differs materially from the less developed forms of European labor organization . . .[3]

IWW beliefs must be understood in terms of those whom the organization tried to organize. After the defection of the Western Federation of Miners in 1907, Wobblies concentrated upon those workers neglected by the mainstream of the labor movement: timber beasts, hobo harvesters, itinerant construction workers, exploited eastern and southern European immigrants, racially excluded Negroes, Mexicans, and Asian Americans.

Contemporaries frequently remarked the IWW's unique following. Rexford Tugwell poignantly described the timber beast attracted to the IWW: "His eyes are dull and reddened; his joints are stiff with the rheumatism almost universal in the wettest climate in the world; his teeth are rotting; he is wracked with strange diseases and tortured by unrealized dreams that haunt his soul. . . . The blanket-stiff is a man without a home. . . . The void of his atrophied affections is filled with a resentful despair and a bitterness against the society that self-righteously cast him out." The same could be said of the IWW harvest worker and construction hand. After a careful study based upon personal interviews with West Coast Wobblies, Carleton Parker concluded that they were floaters, men without homes, wives, women, or "normal" sex; the men who appear in his case studies shared lives of brutality, degradation, and violence, "starting with the long hours and dreary winters of the farms they ran away from, or the sour-smelling bunkhouse in a coal village, through their character-debasing experience with the drifting 'hire and fire' life in the industries, on to the vicious social and economic life of the winter unemployed . . ."[4]

Wobbly recruits thus shared aspects of what cultural anthropologist Oscar Lewis has only recently labeled the "culture of poverty." Like Lewis' more recent case-study families in Mexico, Puerto Rico, and New York City, America's Wobblies had life histories revealing "family disruption, violence, brutality, cheapness of life, lack of love, lack of education, lack of medical facilities . . ."[5]

Lewis also contends that the "culture of poverty" emerges within a society that possesses the following dominant characteristics: (1) a cash economy, wage labor, and production for profit; (2) a persistently high rate of unemployment and underemployment for unskilled labor; (3) low wages; (4) a paucity of social, political, and economic organization, whether on a voluntary basis or by government imposition, for the low-income population; and (5) a pervasive set of values, imposed by the dominant class, which stresses the accumulation of wealth and property and the possibility of upward mobility through thrift, and explains low economic status as the result of personal inadequacy or inferiority.[6]

Although Lewis' loosely drawn characteristics might apply to almost any society in the process of industrialization, they are particularly relevant to the America of 1877–1917. Unencumbered by a feudal-aristocratic tradition and the paternalistic anticapitalism associated with it, America's dominant business class could impose its values on society with relative ease. This was singularly true in the American West, where, in less than a generation, industrialization and urbanization tamed a wilderness. There, where social structure was fluid and government relatively weak, the spirit of rugged individualism reigned supreme and the strong prevailed. Those who failed to rise were pushed into society's backwaters to endure, as best they could, the stigmata associated with failure in a competitive industrial society.

Wobbly members, like Marx's proletariat and Lewis' poverty-stricken, were "people . . . from the lower strata of a rapidly changing society and . . . already partially alienated from it." The men who associated with the IWW in its heyday were largely first-generation citizens of an industrial society. As is frequently noted, immigrants from the south and east of Europe often first experienced urban-industrial life upon their arrival in the new world. But dispossessed native Americans were equally newcomers to industrial society; like E. J. Hobsbawm's first-generation English industrial workers, such native Americans may be considered internal immigrants who also made the frightening journey from a preindustrial to an industrial society.[7] Caught between two systems and two modes of existence, these immigrants—internal and external—were indeed uprooted. Torn from an old, ordered, and comprehensible way of life, they found themselves unable to replace it with an integrated and meaningful mode of existence, and soon became the human flotsam and jetsam of early industrial capitalism's frequent shipwrecks.

Feeling impotent and alienated, these men harbored deep grievances against the essential institutions of the ruling classes: police, government, and church. Hence, Wobblies, like Lewis' Latin Americans living in a "culture of poverty," exhibited a high susceptibility to unrest and to radical movements aimed at destroying the established social order.[8]

This is what IWW leaders sensed, though they themselves did not come out of the "culture of poverty." The leadership consisted largely of two types: skilled workers and formerly successful trade-union officials such as Haywood, St. John, Ettor, and Little; and restless intellectuals such as Williams, Ebert, and the Swedish immigrant syndicalist John Sandgren. These men shared a common desire to effect a nonpolitical revolution in America and a common alienation from the AFL and from reformist American socialists. Eager to make a revolution which would destroy the existing system root and branch, they naturally turned to those most alienated from the American dream—and located them in the lower strata of a rapidly changing society.

The IWW clearly shaped its doctrines and its tactics to attract such recruits. That is why it maintained low initiation fees and still lower dues, why it allowed universal transfer of union cards, why it belittled union leaders as the labor lieutenants of capitalism, and why, finally, it derogated business unionism as pork-chop unionism and trade-union welfare systems as "coffin benefits." IWW members simply could not afford the initiation fees and dues required to sustain business unionism; partly because of their feelings of impotence and partly because they moved from industry to industry, Wobblies also needed self-leadership and self-discipline more than the counsel of professional, bureaucratic union officials. Thus, only by implementing policies sure to keep its treasury bare and its bureaucracy immobilized could the IWW attract the followers it sought. Accordingly, the IWW's formal defense of its non-benefit system should be understood more as a rationalization of what existed than as a hard-core belief in what should exist. The same kind of rationalization, or ambivalence, as we shall see, permeated many other Wobbly beliefs and practices.

Basically, the IWW did what other American unions refused to do. It opened its doors to all: Negro and Asian, Jew and Catholic, immigrant and native. Wobbly locals had no closed membership rolls, no apprenticeship regulations. As West Coast organizer George Speed put it: ". . . One man is as good as another to me; I don't care whether he is black, blue, green, or yellow, as long as he acts the man and acts true to his economic interests as a worker."[9]

The disinherited joined the IWW by the thousands because it offered them "a ready made dream of a new world where there is a new touch with sweetness and light and where for a while they can escape the torture of forever being indecently kicked about." Or, as Carleton Parker discovered of his wandering rank and file, the IWW offered "the only social break in the harsh search for work that they have ever had; its headquarters the only competitor of the saloon in which they are welcome. They listen stolidly to their frequent lecturers with an obvious and sustained interest . . . the concrete details of industrial renovation find eager interest."[10]

Most important of all, the IWW promised its members a way out of their respective "cultures of poverty." "When the poor become class-conscious or active members of trade-union organizations," Lewis notes, "they are no longer part of the culture of poverty." He adds: "Any movement . . . which organizes and gives hope to the poor and effectively promotes solidarity and a sense of identification with larger groups, destroys the psychological and social core of the culture of poverty." That is just what the IWW attempted to do, as it sought to improve the self-image and self-respect of its members. Wobblies instilled among their alienated following what Lewis found Castro offering the Cuban peasants: ". . . a new sense of power and importance. They were armed and were given a doctrine which glorified the lower class as the hope of humanity."[11]

But, as Rexford Tugwell perceptively noted in 1920, the revolutionary potential of the poor in America is limited. "No world regenerating philosophy comes out of them and they are not going to inherit the earth. When we are a bit more orderly they will disappear."[12] When Tugwell wrote those lines, the IWW had been fatally weakened by federal and state repression. Yet for a time, from 1909 to 1917, the IWW seemed well on the way to organizing the revolutionary potential of the poor.

The IWW's ideologues, as suggested earlier, had few original thoughts about the nature of society, the place of workers within it, or the manner by which society changes. For social theory and its economic foundations they turned, as we have seen, to the writings of others, particularly Marx and Darwin. Yet they also drew upon an older American tradition, dating back to the era of Jefferson and Jackson, which divided society into producers and nonproducers, productive classes and parasites.

Wobblies never questioned the labor theory of value, or the other basic tenets of Marxian economics. Indeed, since labor created all value, the worker was robbed when (as under capitalism) he did not receive the money equivalent of his full product. Capitalism and thievery were thus synonymous: profits represented the capitalist's seizure of his worker's surplus value. This robbery could end only with the abolition of capitalism.[13]

Like Marx, the Wobblies also believed that the working class, or proletariat, would rise up in wrath and destroy the capitalists. Like Marx, they asserted that capitalism carried the seeds of its own destruction, and that workers would create "the new society within the shell of the old." Like Marx, again, they saw in the class struggle "the relentless logic of history," which would roll on until, as the IWW proclaimed in its preamble, ". . . the workers of the world organize as a class, take possession of the earth and the machinery of production and abolish the wage system."

The IWW was never precise in its definition of class. Sometimes Wobblies divided society into two classes: capitalists and workers; sometimes they perceived distinct and separate sub-classes within the two major categories; and sometimes they followed Haywood's example of dividing "all the world into three parts: the capitalists, who are the employing class that makes money out of money; the skilled laborers; and the masses."[14] The IWW, of course, represented the masses who would act as the agents of the new and better social order.

Wobblies also reversed common American assumptions about the applicability of Darwinian evolution to social change. Carrying the theory of biological evolution over into social analysis enabled many Americans to conclude that the wealthy had risen to the top of the economic heap solely as a result of their fitness in the struggle for business survival; conversely, failure, poverty, and dependence were signs of unfitness. Eric Goldman has called this ideology conservative Darwinism, in contradistinction to reform Darwinism, the ideology which used the theory of biological evolution to promote reform and attack the status quo.[15] If Goldman's concept of conservative versus reform Darwinism has any validity, then Wobblies may properly be termed radical, or revolutionary, Darwinists. For IWW ideology began with the belief that "social evolution differs in no essential respect from organic evolution." "The central fact or principle which we cannot ignore except at our own peril," wrote Ben Williams, "is the fact of social evolution, which is not always a direct or simple process, but often a slow, painful, and tortuous course of human development with the wrecks of social experiments scattered along the way." Whatever the perils along the way, the IWW sought to ride the evolutionary wave of the future. In the IWW's amalgam of Marxism and Darwinism, capitalism was the stage preceding the establishment of the workers' paradise. As Ben Williams expressed it: "Trustified American Capital leads the world. The I.W.W. aims to trustify American labor." In the IWW's view, since the working class was most fit, its mode of organization would be superior to that of the capitalists, and thus would enable the IWW to build its new order within the shell of the old.[16] Thus was social Darwinism stood on its head; thus would the beaten become the fit; thus would the slaves become the masters.

Wobblies glorified themselves as the saviors of society. The IWW perceived in America's disinherited the raw material for the transformation of a basically sick society. Writing to the *Industrial Worker* from a Louisiana jail, the organizer E. F. Doree was moved to poetry: "Arise like lions after slumber / In unvanquishable number. / Shake your chains to earth like dew / Which in sleep have falled on you. / Ye are many, they are few." John Sandgren added: "The world is gone mad. We are the only sane people on earth. The future belongs to us."[17] IWW ideology, in essence, saw America's downtrodden masses, no longer satisfied with mere crumbs from their masters' abundant tables, emerging from the abyss of society to seize for themselves the world of industry. "We are many," proclaimed *Solidarity*. "We are resourceful; we are animated by the most glorious vision of the ages; we cannot be

conquered, and *we shall conquer the world for the working class.*"
Listen to our song, urged the paper, printing the IWW's own version of the "Internationale":

> Arise, ye prisoners of starvation!
> Arise, ye wretched of the earth!
> For Justice thunders condemnation.
> A better world's in birth.
> No more tradition's chains shall bind us;
> Arise, ye slaves! No more in thrall!
> The earth shall stand on new foundations;
> We have been *naught*—We shall be *All!*
> 'Tis the final conflict!
> Let each stand in his place.
> The Industrial Union
> Shall be the Human Race.[18]

The song epitomizes the IWW's ultimate objectives: a combination of primitive millennarianism and modern revolutionary goals.
"The essence of millennarianism," Eric Hobsbawm writes, "is the
hope of a complete and radical change in the world which will be
reflected in the millennium, a world shorn of all its present deficiencies . . ."[19] It seems clear that the IWW shared with primitive
millennarians an instinctive distaste for the world as it was, as
well as hope for the creation of a completely new world. But the
Wobblies had rejected the apocalyptic Judeo-Christian vision of
the way in which the millennial society would be established. In its
place they substituted more earth-bound ideas about how to topple
the old order and create the new one. Modern revolutionary movements—Marxism and syndicalism especially—would be the means
to achieve what Hobsbawm calls "the transfer of power." Yet
Wobblies always remained more vague about the processes of revolution than the Marxists, and never abandoned primitive millennar-
ian dreams of a final conflict, a Judgment Day when the exploiters
would be turned out and the banner of Industrial Freedom raised
over the workshops of the world "in a free society of men and
women . . ."[20]

Notwithstanding this belief in ultimate revolution, the IWW
constantly sought opportunities to improve the immediate circumstances of its members. Speakers and publications emphasized a

twofold purpose: "First, to improve conditions for the working class day by day. Second, to build up an organization that can take possession of the industries and run them for the benefit of the workers when capitalism shall have been overthrown." Or as William D. Haywood phrased it in testimony before the Commission on Industrial Relations: "I don't think that I presented any Utopian ideas. I talked for the necessities of life, food, clothing, shelter, and amusement. We can talk of Utopia afterwards."[21] For, as St. John insisted, before it could have utopia the IWW must necessarily handle the workers' everyday problems: shorter hours, better wages, and improved shop conditions. A Wobbly organizer said simply: "The final aim . . . is revolution. But for the present *let's see if we can get a bed to sleep in, water enough to take a bath and decent food to eat . . .*"[22]

But utopia and revolution always lurked just beneath the surface. To the convinced Wobbly, each battle, whether for higher wages or shorter hours, better food or better bedding, prepared the participant for the final struggle with the master class. Only by daily fights with the employer could a strong revolutionary organization be formed. ". . . The very fights themselves, like the drill of an army, prepare the workers for ever greater tasks and victories."[23]

IWW leaders made no bones about their quarrel with other labor leaders who contented themselves with wringing short-term concessions from employers. Joe Ettor proudly proclaimed the IWW's unwillingness to subvert its ideas, make peace with employers, or sign protocols and contracts. Like Marx, he said, "we disdain to conceal our views, we openly declare that our ends can be attained only by the forcible overthrow of all existing conditions." "Big Jim" Larkin, émigré Irish labor leader and in 1914 a new recruit to the IWW, gloried in the IWW's refusal to endorse the palliatives and outworn nostrums (arbitration, time agreements, and protocols) proposed by the "sycophants masquerading as labor leaders, whose sole purpose in life seems to be apologizing for and defending the capitalist system of exploitation." The IWW, Larkin averred, "true to its mission as the pioneer movement of the newer time . . . advocates perpetual war, and the total abolition of wage slavery that blights humanity." Organizer James Thompson reminded government investigators that "the I.W.W. is aiming not only to better our condition now but to prepare for the revolution." He warned businessmen: "You are doomed. The best thing you can do is to look for a soft place to fall."[24]

Only the revolution could produce the dream which inspired Haywood:

> . . . I have had a dream that I have in the morning and at night and during the day, that is that there will be a new society sometime in which there will be no battle between capitalist and wage earner . . . there will be no political government . . . but . . . experts will come together for the purpose of discussing the welfare of all the people and discussing the means by which the machinery can be made the slave of the people instead of a part of the people being made the slave of machinery . . .

Haywood's dream also included a day when no child would labor, when all men would work—either with brain or with muscle—when women would be fully emancipated from bondage to men, and when every aged man and woman would have at least the assurance of dying in peace.[25]

Unlike primitive millennarians, Wobblies did not expect their revolution to come about through "a divine revelation . . . an announcement from on high [or] . . . a miracle." Furthermore, they expected neither the inevitable Marxist class struggle nor the ineluctible Darwinian evolution of society alone to make their revolution. Inevitable it was, but they could assist the course of history. "Our organization is not content with merely making the prophecy," asserted *Solidarity*, "but acts upon industrial and social conditions with a view to shaping them in accord with the general tendency."[26]

To make history, as Marx advised all good radicals to do, the Wobblies followed the pattern of modern revolutionaries: they proposed a program, developed a doctrine concerning the transfer of power, and elaborated a system of organization. But unlike most other modern revolutionaries, with the exception of the anarcho-syndicalists whom they resembled, Wobblies excluded politics from any role in their struggle for utopia.

The Wobblies believed they could best make history by seizing power. He who held power ruled society. The IWW proposed to transfer power from the capitalists, who used it for anti-social purposes, to the proletariat, who, they fondly believed, would exercise it for the benefit of humanity.

In *The Iron Heel,* a novel well known to Wobblies, Jack London expressed better than any IWW pamphlet the organization's notions about power. Ernest Everhardt, London's fictional Haywood, responds to a capitalist adversary who has just given him a lesson in *realpolitik:* "Power. It is what we of the working class preach. We know and well we know by bitter experience, that no appeal for the right, for justice, can ever touch you. . . . So we have preached power." "Power will be the arbiter," Everhardt proceeds, "as it has always been the arbiter. . . . We of the labor hosts have conned that word over till our minds are all a-tingle with it. Power. It is a kingly word."[27]

The IWW's gospelers with their doctrine of power made a great deal of sense to men in the social jungle who saw naked force—by employers, police, and courts—constantly used against them. When an IWW pamphlet proclaimed, "It is the law of nature that the strong rule and the weak are enslaved," Wobblies simply recognized the reality of their own lives writ large. George Speed, an admired IWW organizer, expressed their emotions tersely. "Power," he said, "is the thing that determines everything today . . . it stands to reason that the fellow that has got the big club swings it over the balance. That is life as it exists today." When Speed asserted that neither socialism nor politics nor legislation could aid the Wobblies, and that they would suffer until they learned the uses of power, he made sense to those he represented.[28]

The IWW's antipathy toward political action also made sense to its members. Migratory workers moved too often to establish legal voting residences. Millions of immigrants lacked the franchise, as did the Negroes, the women, and the child workers to whom the IWW appealed. Even those immigrants and natives in the IWW ranks who had the right to vote nourished a deep suspicion of government. To them the policeman's club and the magistrate's edict symbolized the state's alliance with entrenched privilege. Who knew the injustices of the state better than a Wobbly imprisoned for exercising his right of free speech, or clubbed by bullying policemen while picketing peacefully for higher wages? Daily experience demonstrated the truth of Elizabeth Gurley Flynn's comment that the state was simply the slugging agency of the capitalists. Or, as *Solidarity* phrased it: all governments in history "have

264 / MELVYN DUBOFSKY

become cruel, corrupt, decayed and perished by reason of their own internal defects. To this rule the government of the United States is no exception."[29] Hence, Wobblies refused to believe that stuffing pieces of paper—even socialist ones—into a box would transform the basically repressive institution of the state into a humane one.

Even the wonderful list of reform legislation enacted during the Progressive years did not impress Wobblies. When IWW members were reminded of marvelous labor reforms newly placed on the statute books, their reply was: "How are they *enforced?*" To Wobblies, as to most other trade unionists, labor legislation was worthless without the organized power to enforce it on the job. Wobblies were as perceptive as AFL members in realizing that American workers were more concerned with what went on at the plant than with what transpired in the state capitol, that they cared more about a higher wage and a more secure job than about a Democratic or a Republican—or even a Socialist—victory.

By thus refusing to endorse political parties, the IWW did not, as Philip Foner asserts, divorce itself from the mainstream of the American labor movement. Quite the contrary. The IWW's political position brought the organization closer to the masses to whom it appealed and more in harmony with the attitude of AFL members—those to whom the political party and the state always remained a distant and fearful enemy.

Representing workers who could not conceive of political power as a means to alter the rules of the game, Wobblies had to offer an alternative. This they discovered in economic power. Naively believing themselves better Marxists than their socialist critics, Wobblies insisted that political power was but a reflex of economic power, and that without economic organization behind it, labor politics was "like a house without a foundation or a dream without substance."[30] IWW leaders concentrated on teaching their followers how to obtain economic power. To quote some of their favorite aphorisms: "Get it through industrial organization"; "Organize the workers to control the use of their labor power"; "The secret of power is organization"; "The only force that can break . . . tyrannical rule . . . is the one big union of all the workers."[31]

From the IWW point of view, direct action was the essential means for bringing its new society into existence. As defined by Wobblies, direct action included any step taken by workers at the point of production which improved wages, reduced hours, and bettered conditions. It encompassed conventional strikes, intermittent strikes, silent strikes, passive resistance, sabotage, and the ultimate direct-action measure: the general strike which would displace the capitalists from power and place the means of production in working-class hands.[32] "Shall I tell you what direct action really means?" an IWW manifesto asked. "The worker on the job shall tell the boss when and where he shall work, how long, and for what wages and under what conditions." Direct action, according to Haywood, would eventually reach the point at which workers would be strong enough to say: "Here, Mr. Stockholder, we won't work for you any longer. You have drawn dividends out of our hides long enough; we propose that you shall go to work now and under the same opportunities that we have had."[33]

The emphasis on direct action in preference to parliamentary politics or socialist dialectics represented a profound insight by IWW leaders into the minds of industrial workers and inhabitants of the "culture of poverty." Abstract doctrine meant nothing to the disinherited; specific grievances meant everything! Justus Ebert expressed this idea for the IWW:

Workingmen on the job don't care a whoop in hell for free love . . . they are not interested in why Bakunin was fired from the International by Marx . . . nor do they care about the co-operative commonwealth; they want practical organization first, all else after. They want to know how they can win out against the trusts and the bosses. . . . Give us specific shop methods. We plead for them.[34]

Richard Brazier on the West Coast echoed Ebert's plea. He asked fellow Wobblies to stop telling men to stay away from bum jobs; instead, Brazier urged workers to take such jobs and fight. The Philadelphia Longshoremen, an IWW affiliate which successfully used direct action and actually controlled job conditions, urged: "We have work to do. We function as a job organization and have no time to split hairs. Job control is the thing."[35] How much like the AFL!

But while the IWW's emphasis on direct action, job control, and economic power resembled the AFL's line, the Wobblies' rhetoric was of an entirely different order. Restrained in action, Wobblies were considerably less restrained in utterance. Where the

AFL spoke cautiously of law and order, the IWW exuberantly discussed the law of the jungle. Where the AFL pleaded for contracts and protocols, the IWW hymned clubs and brute force. Where the AFL sought industrial harmony, the IWW praised perpetual industrial war.

Consequently, it became easy for critics of the IWW, whether on the right or the left, to listen to Wobbly speakers, to read Wobbly propaganda, and to conclude that the IWW actually *preferred* bullets to ballots, dynamite to mediation. After all, Wobblies constantly announced that their organization respected neither the property rights of capitalists nor the laws they made. *"I despise the law,"* Haywood defiantly informed a Socialist party audience, "and I am not a law-abiding citizen. And more than that, no Socialist *can* be a law-abiding citizen." Equally defiant, he told the Commission on Industrial Relations: ". . . I have been plastered up with injunctions until I do not need a suit of clothes, and I have treated them with contempt." He warned Socialist party members fearful of breaking the law and going to prison: "Those of us who are in jail—those of us who have been in jail—all of us who are willing to go to jail care not what you say or what you do! We despise your hypocrisy. . . . We are the Revolution!"[36]

Wobblies even enjoyed comparing themselves to antebellum abolitionists, who also had defied laws which sanctioned human bondage, and who had publicly burned the Constitution. As James Thompson boasted: "We are the modern abolitionists fighting against wage slavery."[37] Some Wobblies may indeed have considered unsheathing the Lord's terrible swift sword. St. John, for one, admitted under questioning that he would counsel destruction of property and violence against persons if it accomplished improvement for the workers and brought the revolution closer. Other IWW leaders conceded they would be willing to dynamite factories and mills in order to win a strike. All of them hurled their defiance at "bushwa" law.[38]

Such talk led most Americans to conclude, as did Harris Weinstock of the Federal Commission on Industrial Relations, that "it is the organized and deliberate purpose of the I.W.W. to teach and preach and to burn into the hearts and minds of its followers that they are justified in lying; that they are justified in stealing and in trampling under foot their own agreements and in confiscating the property of others . . . that it would make a Nation of thieves and liars and scoundrels."³⁹

Having created this image of itself, the IWW simultaneously tried to dispel it. To the convinced Wobbly, Weinstock's words better described the practices and attitudes of the American capitalist. Although the IWW employed the vocabulary of violence, more often than not it practiced passive resistance, and was itself the victim of violence instigated by law-enforcement officials and condoned by the law-abiding. In fact, even the Wobblies' vocabulary was ambivalent, the language of nonviolence being employed at least as frequently as that of violence. Big Bill Haywood, for example, whose career with the WFM had been associated with labor violence, told a reporter during the 1912 Lawrence textile strike: "I should never think of conducting a strike in the old way. . . . I, for one, have turned my back on violence. It wins nothing. When we strike now, we strike with our hands in our pockets. We have a new kind of violence—the havoc we raise with money by laying down our tools. Pure strength lies in the overwhelming power of numbers."⁴⁰

Any careful investigator of the IWW soon becomes aware that the organization regularly proclaimed the superiority of passive resistance over the use of dynamite or guns. Vincent St. John, while conceding the possible usefulness of violence under certain circumstances, nevertheless insisted: "We do not . . . want to be understood as saying that we expect to achieve our aims through violence and through the destruction of human life, because in my judgment, that is impossible." Joe Ettor similarly commented: ". . . We are organized against violence and our war cry is 'War against war.' " Haywood remarked in 1912 that he regarded hunger strikes as "action more violent than the discharge of bombs in St. Patrick's Cathedral."⁴¹ Big Bill now looked forward to a "bloodless revolution."

Solidarity, the *Industrial Worker,* and IWW pamphlets all preached the same nonviolent message. The *Industrial Worker* cautioned members against being misled by *agents provocateurs* into resorting to violent means of economic action. *Solidarity* noted: "The revolutionary industrial union promises the only possible safeguard against violence in industrial warfare." Sometimes it puts its position another way: "Our dynamite is mental and our force is in organization at the point of production." Again and again IWW publications advised members: *"We do not advocate violence;* it is to be discouraged."[42]

In actuality, Wobblies looked to *non*violent tactics in order to throw into sharper relief the brutality of their enemy, and to win sympathy for their sufferings. Passive resistance, *Solidarity* editorialized, "has a tremendous moral effect; it puts the enemy on record; it exposes the police and city authorities as a bunch of law breakers; it drives the masters to the last ditch of resistance. 'Passive resistance' by the workers results in laying bare the inner workings and purposes of the capitalist mind. It also reveals the self-control, the fortitude, the courage, the inherent sense of order, of the workers' mind. As such, 'passive resistance' is of immense educational value."[43]

But IWW passive resistance should not be confused with pacifism. Nonviolence was only a means, never an end. If passive resistance resulted only in beatings and deaths, then the IWW threatened to respond in kind. Arturo Giovannitti, sometime poet and Wobbly, put the IWW's position bluntly: "The generally accepted notion seems to be that to kill is a great crime, but to be killed is the greatest." Haywood cited Abraham Lincoln's alleged advice to citizens suffering from hunger as a result of wartime food speculation: "Take your pickaxes and crowbars and go to the granaries and warehouses and help yourselves . . ." That, said Haywood, "is good I.W.W. doctrine."[44]

In most cases the IWW hoped to gain its ends through nonviolent measures, through what it described as "Force of education, force of organization, force of a growing class-consciousness and force of working class aspirations for freedom."[45] One forceful method explicitly advocated by the Wobblies—indeed, the tactic with which they are most indelibly associated—was sabotage. To most Americans, sabotage implied the needless destruction of property, the senseless adulteration of products, and, possibly, the inexcusable injuring of persons. Wobblies did not always dispel such images. The *Industrial Worker* suggested to harvest hands in 1910: "Grain sacks come loose and rip, nuts come off wagon wheels and loads are dumped on the way to the barn, machinery breaks down, nobody to blame, everybody innocent . . . boss decides to furnish a little inspiration in the shape of more money and shorter hours . . . just try a little sabotage on the kind hearted, benevolent boss . . . and see how it works." For the next three years the paper continued to urge this method upon its readers, telling them: "Sabotage is an awakening of labor. It is the spirit of revolt." This campaign culminated in 1913 with a series of twelve editorials fully explaining the methods of sabotage and when they should be utilized.[46]

Eastern Wobblies proved no less restrained in their emphasis on sabotage. Haywood informed the same Socialist party audience mentioned above, which he had encouraged to break the law: "I don't know of anything that can be applied that will bring as much anguish to the boss as a little sabotage in the right place at the proper time. Find out what it means. It won't hurt you, and it will cripple the boss." To help Wobblies find out what sabotage meant, Elizabeth Gurley Flynn prepared a new translation of Emile Pouget's classic, *Sabotage,* which the IWW published and distributed in 1915. Even Ben Williams, generally unenthusiastic about the effectiveness of sabotage, felt constrained to recommend its use. "Sabotage has great possibilities as a means of defense and aggression," he explained. "It is useless to try to argue it out of existence. We need not 'advocate it,' we need only explain it. The organized workers will do the acting."[47]

What was actually meant by all this talk? Some Wobblies might have agreed with James Thompson, who said, ". . . I not only believe in destruction of property, but I believe in the destruction of human life if it will save human life." But most stressed sabotage's nonviolent characteristics. Repeatedly, IWW speakers asserted that sabotage simply implied soldiering on the job, playing dumb, tampering with machines without destroying them—in short, simply harassing the employer to the point of granting his workers' demands. Sometimes, it was claimed, the workers could even effect sabotage through exceptional obedience: Williams and Haywood were fond of noting that Italian and French workers had on occasion tied up the national railroads simply by observing every operating rule in their work regulations. They suggested that laborers refuse to cooperate in the adulteration of products, and that labor unions warn consumers against purchasing inferior goods. That, the Wobblies argued, was benevolent sabotage: *"sabotage not aimed at the consumer but at the heart and soul of the employing class—the pocketbook."*[48]

One might scarcely expect the typical Wobbly to comprehend the subtleties of nonviolent as compared to violent sabotage. Sabotage, after all, is a weapon of the disorganized, the defeated, the dejected, and, as such, it must have had great appeal to workers drawn from the "culture of poverty." What better way to strike back against one's enemy than to destroy what he most worships —in this case, private property! Yet, hard as they tried, state and federal authorities could never establish legal proof of IWW-instigated sabotage. Rudolph Katz, a De Leonite who had followed his leader out of the St. John IWW in 1908, was perhaps close to the truth when he informed federal investigators: ". . . The American Federation of Labor does not preach sabotage, but it practices sabotage; and the . . . I.W.W. preaches sabotage, but does not practice it."[49]

Wobbly ideology and tactics explained why Katz was right. In revealing testimony before the Commission on Industrial Relations, Jim Thompson declared: "The greatest weapon in the hands of the working class is economic power. . . . All we have to do is fold our arms and industry is paralyzed. . . . I would much prefer as a lesson to . . . other workers . . . instead of destroying the street car in times of a street car strike that they should stop that car by shutting off the juice at the power house. That would be a lesson." Ben Williams phrased this attitude simply: "Organized a little we control a little; organized more we control more; organized as a class we control everything."[50]

Until the IWW succeeded in organizing all workers into industrial unions which combined to form the celebrated "One Big Union" which would eventually seize control of industry, it had to employ practices and tactics much like those of any labor union. Accordingly, the IWW encouraged strikes to win immediate improvements in working conditions, for such strikes served a dual purpose: they offered the men involved valuable experience in the class struggle and developed their sense of *power,* and they weakened the capitalist's power. When conventional strikes failed, the IWW recommended the on-the-job strike—essentially a form of nonviolent sabotage—and the intermittent or short strike begun when the boss least expected it and ended before the strikers could be starved or beaten.[51]

The IWW never lost its vision of the ultimate revolution. Thus, many demands associated with AFL industrial conflicts were absent from those of the IWW. With improvements in working conditions, the AFL unions demanded recognition and ironclad contracts. The IWW spurned both. It would achieve its closed shop "by having an 'open union' for everybody who toils." In other words, collective action and voluntary cooperation by the exploited, not capitalist concessions, would bring the true closed shop. Wobblies were convinced that employer benevolence only lessened working-class solidarity. For somewhat similar reasons, the IWW refused to sign contracts which restricted the right to strike for stated periods of time. All workers had to retain the right to strike simultaneously, the IWW reasoned, or employers could play one group of workers off against another, as had happened time and again in the AFL's history. No agreement could be allowed to impinge upon the IWW's governing principle: "An injury to one is the concern of all." Workers, moreover, had to be free to strike when employers were weakest, but time contracts provided employers with the option to choose the moment of conflict and to prepare for it in advance. Finally, without the unreserved right to strike, the IWW could not wage the class war, and without the ongoing class struggle there could be no revolution and no cooperative commonwealth.[52]

But even on the issue of time contracts the IWW could be ambivalent, conceding the possibility that it might sign agreements which concerned only wages, hours, and conditions of work. Nevertheless, it regularly reiterated its belief that employers had no rights that workers were obliged to respect. "The contract between an employer and a workman is no more binding than the title deed to a negro slave is just."[53]

The organization's refusal to sign contracts raised problems that the IWW never resolved. American employers were never particularly happy dealing with labor unions, and certainly under no circumstances would they negotiate with a labor organization that refused to sign contracts and insisted that capitalists had no rights worthy of respect. Hence, employers constantly used the IWW's no-contract principle to rationalize their own resistance to any form of collective bargaining. If the IWW could not negotiate with employers, how could it raise wages or improve working conditions? If it could offer its members nothing but perpetual industrial warfare, how could it maintain its membership, let alone increase its ranks? On the other hand, if the IWW did sanction contracts, win recognition, and improve its members' lives, what would keep them from forsaking revolutionary goals and adhering to the well-established AFL pattern? If the IWW began to declare truces in the class war, how could it bring about the ultimate revolution? In the end, IWW leaders usually subordinated reform opportunities to revolutionary necessities, while the rank and file, when it could, took the reforms and neglected the revolution.

Even for those Wobblies who cherished the hope of revolution, the means of achieving their dream remained vague. Politics or working-class violence would not accomplish it. What, then, remained? "In a word," wrote Haywood and Ettor, "the general strike is the measure by which the capitalistic system will be overthrown."[54]

Neither Haywood nor any other Wobbly ever precisely defined the general strike. Haywood described it as the stoppage of all work and the destruction of the capitalists through a peaceful paralysis of industry. Ben Williams insisted that it was not a strike at all, simply "a 'general lockout of the employing class' leaving the workers in possession of the machinery of distribution and production." Whatever the exact definition of the general strike, Haywood wrote, when its day comes ". . . control of industry will pass from the capitalists to the masses and capitalists will vanish from the face of the earth."[55] That utopian day would come peaceably if workers had their way, violently if capitalists attempted to postpone it with "roar of shell and whine of machine-guns."

The precise date of the general strike which would usher in the arrival of the IWW's utopia remained as vague for Wobblies as the millennium, or Judgment Day, does for Christians. But the *prospect* of such a Judgment Day was intended to stir among the toiling masses the same ecstatic belief and fanaticism that anticipation of the Second Coming arouses among evangelical Christians. Only with such true believers could the IWW build its One Big Union which would, when fully organized, ring the death knell for American capitalism. In other words, in IWW ideology workers represented a chosen people who, through faith and works— faith in the One Big Union and such works as peaceful sabotage —would attain salvation and enter the Kingdom of Heaven here on earth.

In a jail cell in Aberdeen, Washington, John Pancner dreamed the pleasures of an IWW utopia, where there would be no poverty, jails, police, army, or marines; no Christians, no churches, no heaven or hell. The cities would be clean and beautiful, filled with wide streets, parks, flowers, and fine homes; the workers would be "no longer stoop shouldered and consumptive looking . . ." Prudery would have vanished, and naked children would frisk on the grass and bask in the sun. Economic freedom, plus an abundance of food, shelter, clothing, leisure, and education, would lead "all hearts and minds . . . [to] turn . . . towards solving the mysteries of the Universe."[56]

Wobblies never quite explained how their terrestrial paradise would be governed. They did agree that the state, as most Americans knew it, would be nonexistent. "There will be no such thing as the State or States," Haywood said. "The industries will take the place of what are now existing States." "Whenever the workers are organized in the industry, whenever they have a sufficient organization in the industry," added St. John, "they will have all the government they need right there." Somehow each industrial union would possess and manage its own industry. Union members would elect superintendents, foremen, secretaries, and all the managers of modern industry. The separate industrial unions would also meet jointly to plan for the welfare of the entire society. This system, "in which each worker will have a share in the ownership and a voice in the control of industry, and in which each shall receive the full product of his labor," was variously called the "Cooperative Commonwealth," the "Workers' Commonwealth," the "Industrial Commonwealth," "Industrial Democracy," and "Industrial Communism."[57] Unsure of what their system was, the Wobblies could not label it.

Perhaps Ben Williams came closest to describing how the IWW commonwealth would function. Writing primarily about city government, Williams suggested that every aspect of urban life would be managed by different groups of municipal workers, "their efforts being correlated by whatever central body they may find necessary. The members of that central body will not be 'placemen' or 'politicians,' but *technical experts,* trained for that special service" [italics added]. Haywood also foresaw a future society molded and managed by experts in the different branches of industry, "brain workers" who directed the activities of scientifically organized laborers.[58]

A future society based upon "brain workers," technical experts, and scientific controls resembled St. Simon's ideal state or Bellamy's society of the year 2000 more than it did the Marxian "dictatorship of the proletariat," or the revisionist socialist's equalitarian parliamentary society. It was this aspect of the IWW, combined with its abiding distrust of political parties and the state, which made the American Industrial Workers so much like the continental European syndicalists of the same era.

It was in their views about the general strike and the governance of utopia that Wobblies diverged farthest from the modern revolutionary spirit, for these two vital matters were indeed left as vague as the primitive millennarians' eschatology. How the IWW expected to displace capitalism from power peaceably, when the masters of "The Iron Heel" couched their answer in "roar of shell and whine of machine-guns," advocates of the general strike failed to explain. How the IWW would defend its utopia from counter-revolutionary terror, supporters of its syndicalist commonwealth never clarified. Like primitive millennarians, but unlike modern revolutionaries, Wobblies almost expected their revolution to make itself, if not by divine revelation, at least by a miracle (secular, of course). Some Wobblies even saw the roots of their doctrine in the works of the "Hobo Carpenter from Nazareth," whose call, "stripped of the mystical and mythical veil of Constantine and his successors, and clothed in the original garb of communism and brotherhood, continues to sound intermittently across the ages."[59]

While IWW ideology derived much of its spirit from Socialist party doctrine, the two maintained only an uneasy harmony. Both Wobblies and Socialists drew their inspiration from similar ideological sources, both opposed the capitalist order, and both demanded the establishment of a just and equalitarian new order. Beyond that, they conflicted more often than they agreed.

Industrial unionism, Haywood once said, was socialism with its working clothes on. But after 1913, when Haywood was recalled from the Socialist party's National Executive Committee, IWW industrial unionists and American Socialists had little in common. When Socialists talked of capturing control of existing government through the ballot box and transforming the capitalist state into the Cooperative Commonwealth, the IWW responded with a proverb: "A wise tailor does not put stitches into rotten cloth."

To American Socialists who prided themselves on their intellectual abilities, Haywood asserted: "Socialism is so plain, so clear, so simple that when a person becomes an intellectual he doesn't understand socialism."[60]

In short, American Socialists, optimistic about their future prospects and eager to widen the popular base of their party, subordinated revolutionary fervor to the cause of immediate reform and popular acceptance. Wobblies, more pessimistic about the future and more respectful of capitalism's staying power, tried to instill revolutionary fervor in their adherents. The Socialist party, unlike the IWW, had no room for men who counseled defiance of the law, neglect of the ballot box, and "real" revolution. Hence Haywood's recall from the National Executive Committee in 1913. After that date, though some "left-wing" Socialists still looked to the IWW as the hope of the working class and the vanguard of revolution, most Socialists and Wobblies went their own separate ways—ideologically as well as organizationally.[61]

Actually, as Will Herberg perceptively pointed out more than fifteen years ago, the IWW was much more the left wing of the American labor movement than of the socialist movement. Herberg emphasized that the AFL's early approach, "with its stress on proletarian direct action and its marked distrust of government and politics, shows definite affinity to basic syndicalism. It differs from the more familiar radical variety of syndicalism in very much the same way as the gradualistic socialism of Eduard Bernstein differed from the revolutionary socialism of his orthodox opponents."[62] What Bernstein and evolutionary socialism were to Marx and revolutionary socialism, Gompers and the AFL were to St. John, Haywood, and radical syndicalism.

Indeed, the IWW *was* the American variety of the syndicalism which at that time was sweeping across the Italian, French, and Scandinavian labor movements. There is no escaping the similarities. Even when the IWW denied its syndicalist nature, it would simultaneously counsel syndicalist principles. One editorialist, for example, while maintaining that the IWW was not a syndicalist organization but an industrial union, went on to assert: "Industrial unionism accepts all of the syndicalist tactics that experience has shown to be available for present purposes." Despite the fuzzy-mindedness of some Wobbly thinkers, there was absolutely no incompatibility between industrial unionism and syndicalism. The

IWW even took over George Sorel's syndicalist concept of the militant minority, claiming in the words of the *Industrial Worker:* "Our task is to develop the conscious, intelligent minority to the point where they will be capable of carrying out the imperfectly expressed desires of the toiling millions," who were still "hopelessly stupid and stupidly hopeless."[63] Whenever some Wobblies attempted to dispute their organization's syndicalist tendencies, other more perceptive members stressed the IWW's basic similarity to European syndicalism. John Sandgren, a Swedish immigrant and IWW theorist who maintained close contact with the labor movement of his native land, tried to impress upon Wobblies their obvious likeness to Scandinavian syndicalists. The Socialist Robert Rives LaMonte, while acknowledging that "because Revolutionary Unionism is the child of economic and political conditions, it differs in different countries," nevertheless firmly asserted: "In spite of superficial differences this living spirit of revolutionary purpose unifies French and British syndicalism and American Industrial Unionism. To forget or even make light of this underlying identity can but substitute muddle-headed confusion for clear thinking."[64] Finally, John Spargo's 1913 definition of syndicalism clearly encompasses the IWW's mode of operation. Syndicalism, he wrote,

is a form of labor unionism which aims at the abolition of the capitalist system. . . . Its distinctive principle as a practical movement is that these ends are to be attained by the direct action of the unions, without parliamentary action or the intervention of the State. The distinctive feature of its ideal is that in the new social order the political state will not exist, the only form of government being the administration of industry directly by the workers themselves.[65]

Certainly nobody should expect American syndicalism to be precisely like that of France or Italy; also, nobody should seek to explain the emergence of syndicalism in America, as does Philip Foner, by tracing its roots to Europe and then treating it as a foreign import transplanted to fertile native soil.

In the final analysis, ideological disputation remained a form of academic nitpicking to most Wobblies, for the organization always appealed to the activist rather than the intellectual. It sought to motivate the disinherited, not to satisfy the ideologue. As an

IWW member, reviewing John Graham Brooks's *American Syndicalism,* noted: "It is not the Sorels . . . the Wallings, LaMontes and such figures who count the most—it is the obscure Bill Jones on the firing line, with stink in his clothes, rebellion in his brain, hope in his heart, determination in his eye and direct action in his gnarled fist."[66] To such as "Bill Jones" the IWW carried its gospel from 1909 to 1917.

In their analyses of the IWW's eventful history, several scholars have concluded that had it not been for America's entry into World War I and the repression of the organization that ensued, the IWW might well have usurped the CIO's subsequent role in organizing mass-production workers. These scholars believe that the base established by the IWW among harvesters, loggers, and copper miners would have become sufficiently stable, had war not intervened, for the Wobblies later to have penetrated other unorganized sectors of the economy.[67] This rendering of history leads one to conclude that the IWW's ultimate failure was more a result of external repression than of internal inadequacies.

Nothing, of course, need be inevitable. Yet given the internal deficiencies of the IWW, the aspirations of most of its members during the organization's heyday, and the dynamics of American capitalism—what might better be called the "American system"—the Wobblies' attempt to transform American workers into a revolutionary vanguard was doomed to failure. Wobbly doctrine taught workers how to gain short-range goals indistinguishable from those sought by ordinary, non-revolutionary trade unions. Able to rally exploited workers behind crusades to abolish specific grievances, the IWW failed to transform its followers' concrete grievances into a higher consciousness of class, ultimate purpose, and necessary revolution; to create, in short, a revolutionary working class in the Marxist sense. This was so because the IWW never explained precisely how it would achieve its new society—apart from vague allusions to the social general strike and to "building the new society within the shell of the old"—or how, once established, it would be governed. Wobblies simply suggested that the state, at least as most Americans knew it, would disappear. Hence, at their best IWW ideologues offered only warmed-over versions of St. Simon's technocratic society, with gleanings from Edward Bellamy's *Looking Backward*—scarcely a workable prescription for revolution in the modern world. In their imprecise ideology and vague doctrine, the Wobblies too often substituted romantic anarcho-utopianism for hard analysis of social and economic realities.

Even had the IWW had a more palatable prescription for revolution, it is far from likely that its followers would have taken it. In fact, IWW members had limited revolutionary potential. At the IWW's founding convention Haywood had alluded to lifting impoverished Americans up from the gutter. But those lying in Haywood's metaphorical gutters thought only of rising to the sidewalk, and once there of entering the house. Individuals locked in the subculture of poverty share narrow perspectives on life and society; as Oscar Lewis has observed, the main blight of the "culture of poverty is the poverty of its culture."[68] Struggling just to maintain body, such men lacked the time or comfort to worry much about their souls; they could think only of the moment, not the future, only of a better job or more food, not of a distant utopian society.

This placed the IWW in an impossible dilemma. On the one hand, it was committed to ultimate revolution; on the other, it sought immediate improvements for its members. Like all men who truly care about humanity, the Wobblies always accepted betterment for their members today at the expense of achieving utopia tomorrow. This had been true at Lawrence, McKees Rocks, and Paterson, among other places, where the IWW allowed workers to fight for immediate improvements, a result which, if achieved, inevitably diminished their discontent and hence their revolutionary potential. Even at Paterson, where IWW-led strikers failed to win concessions, some Wobblies discerned the dilemma of their position —the leaders' desire for revolution coming up against their members' desire for palpable gains.

Internally, the Wobblies never made up their minds about precisely what kind of structure their organization should adopt. By far the most capable IWW leaders favored an industrial union structure under which largely independent, though not entirely autonomous, affiliates organized by specific industry would cooperate closely with each other under the supervision of an active general executive board. But many lesser leaders, and more among the rank and file, were captivated with the concept of the One Big Union (the mythical OBU) in which workers, regardless of skill, industry, nationality, or color, would be amalgamated into a single unit. Incapable of negotiating union-management agreements owing to its protean character, the OBU would be solely the vessel of revolution. Considering the inherent difficulties involved in organizing unskilled workers on a stable basis, organizational form and structure was an issue of the utmost importance. Yet it remained a problem that the Wobblies never resolved satisfactorily.

This was not the only issue the IWW failed to resolve. Operating in industries traditionally hostile to unionism, Wobblies aggravated hard-core employer prejudices. To employers who rejected negotiations with AFL affiliates that offered to sign and to respect binding legal contracts, the IWW offered unremitting industrial war, for it refused to sign time agreements reached through collective bargaining, and declined to respect labor-management contracts. Hesitant to recognize unions on any basis, management thus had less reason to acknowledge the IWW. If the IWW had had the raw economic power to win concessions without time agreements and written contracts, its policies might have made some sense. But time and again it challenged powerful employers from behind union fortifications erected on sand.

Its mythology concerning rank-and-file democracy—comprising what today is known as "participatory democracy"—further compounded the IWW's internal deficiencies. The IWW had been most successful when led by strong individuals like Haywood, who centralized general headquarters in 1916, or Walter Nef, who constructed a tightly knit and carefully administered Agricultural Workers' Organization. Too often, however, jealous and frustrated Wobblies, lacking the abilities of a Haywood or a Nef, but desiring their power and positions, used the concept of "participatory democracy" to snipe at the IWW's leaders on behalf of an idealized rank and file. And without firm leadership the organization drifted aimlessly.

Even had the IWW combined the necessary structure, the proper tactics, and experienced, capable leaders, as it did for a time from 1915 to 1917, its difficulties might still have proved insurmountable. There is no reason to believe that before the 1930's any of America's basic mass-production industries could have been organized. Not until World War II was the CIO, an organization with immense financial resources, millions of members, and federal encouragement, able to solidify its hold on the nation's mass-production industries. And even then the CIO made no headway among migratory workers or Southern mill hands.[69] What reason, then, is there to think that the IWW could have succeeded in the 1920's or earlier, when it lacked funds, counted its members by the thousands, not the millions, and could scarcely expect government assistance? To ask the question is to answer it.

Yet had the IWW done everything its academic critics ask of it—established true industrial unions, accepted long-term officials and a permanent union bureaucracy, signed collective agreements with employers and agreed to respect them—done, in other words, what the CIO did, what would have remained of its original purpose?[70] Had the founders of the IWW been interested in simply constructing industrial unions on the model of the CIO, the advice of their scholarly critics would be well taken. But the IWW was created by radicals eager to revolutionize American society, and to have asked them to deny their primary values and goals would have been to ask too much.

Whatever the IWW's internal dilemmas, the dynamics of American history unquestionably compounded them. Unlike radicals in other societies who contended with established orders unresponsive to lower-class discontent and impervious to change from within, the Wobblies struggled against flexible and sophisticated adversaries. The years of IWW growth and success coincided with the era when welfare capitalism spread among American businesses, when all levels of government began to exhibit solicitude for the workingman, and when the catalyst of reform altered all aspects of national society. This process became even more pronounced during World War I, when the federal government used its vast power and influence to hasten the growth of welfare capitalism and conservative unionism. Whatever success the Wobblies achieved only stimulated the reform process, for employers who were threatened by the IWW paid greater attention to labor relations, and government agencies, initially called upon to repress labor strife, encouraged employers to improve working conditions. While IWW leaders felt federal repression during World War I, their followers enjoyed eight-hour days, grievance boards, and company unions. Put more simply, reform finally proved a better method than repression for weakening the IWW's appeal to workers.

Although the IWW ultimately failed to achieve its major objectives, it nevertheless bequeathed Americans an invaluable legacy. Those young Americans who practice direct action, passive resistance, and civil disobedience, and who seek an authentic "radical tradition," should find much to ponder in the Wobblies' past. Those who distrust establishment politics, deride bureaucracies, favor community action, and preach "participatory democracy" would also do well to remember the history of the IWW. Indeed, all who prefer a society based upon community to one founded on coercion cannot afford to neglect the tragic history of the IWW.

In this history, two lessons stand out. The first underscores the harsh truth of Antonio Gramsci's comment, quoted earlier, that in advanced industrial nations revolutionaries should take as their slogan: "Pessimism of the Intelligence; Optimism of the Will." The second lesson emphasizes the irony of the radical experience in America, and elsewhere in the Western industrial world. As a result of their commitment to ultimate revolution as well as to immediate improvements in the existence of the working class, radicals the world over quickened the emergence of strong labor unions and acted as midwives at the birth of the "welfare state." But success, instead of breeding more success, only produced a new working class enthralled with a consumer society and only too willing, even eager, to trade working-class consciousness for a middle-class style of life. The ultimate tragedy, then, for all radicals, the American Wobblies included, has been that the brighter they have helped make life for the masses, the dimmer has grown the prospect for revolution in the advanced societies.

Yet no better epitaph could be written for the American Wobbly than A. S. Embree's comment from his prison cell in 1917: "The end in view is well worth striving for, but in the struggle itself lies the happiness of the fighter."

NOTES

1. Lewis S. Gannett, "The I.W.W.," *Nation,* CXI (October 20, 1920), p. 448.

2. Joe Hill to Editor, *Industrial Worker,* May 25, 1911, p. 3; *Final Report and Testimony of the United States Commission on Industrial Relations* (Washington, D.C., 1915), V, pp. 4234–35 (hereafter cited as CIR).

3. B. H. Williams in *Solidarity,* September 14, 1912, p. 2; William E. Bohn, "The I.W.W.," *Survey,* XXVIII (May 4, 1912), p. 221.

4. Rexford G. Tugwell, "The Casual of the Woods," *Survey,* XLIV (July 3, 1920), p. 472; Carleton Parker, "The I.W.W.," *Atlantic Monthly,* CXX (November 1917), pp. 651–62.

5. Oscar Lewis, *La Vida* (New York, 1966), p. xlv.

6. Ibid., p. xliii.

7. E. J. Hobsbawm, *Primitive Rebels and Social Bandits* (New York, 1963), p. 108.

8. Lewis, op. cit., pp. xiv, xlv–xlvi.

9. CIR, V, p. 4947; W. D. Haywood, "To Colored Working Men and Women," *Solidarity,* March 10, 1917, p. 2; *Industrial Worker,* April 29, 1909, p. 4, June 17, 1909, p. 2.

10. R. G. Tugwell to Editor, *Survey,* XLIV (August 16, 1920), pp. 641–42; Parker, op. cit., p. 656.

11. Lewis, op. cit., pp. xlviii–xlix.

12. Tugwell to Editor, *Survey,* XLIV (August 16, 1920), pp. 641–42.

13. *Solidarity,* July 1, 1911, p. 2.

14. Quoted in Arno Dosch, "What the IWW Is," *World's Work,* XXVI (August 1913), p. 417.

15. Eric Goldman, *Rendezvous with Destiny* (New York, 1952), pp. 90–97.

16. Ben H. Williams, "Trends Toward Industrial Freedom," *American Journal of Sociology,* XX (March 1915), p. 627; Williams also in *Solidarity,* April 15, 1911, p. 2, and September 14, 1912, p. 2; John Sandgren, "Industrial Communism," ibid., July 31, 1915, p. 12.

17. E. F. Doree to Fellow Workers, *Industrial Worker,* November 7, 1912, p. 4; Sandgren, op. cit., p. 12.

18. *Solidarity,* March 22, 1913, p. 2.

19. Hobsbawm, op. cit., p. 57.

20. Ibid., p. 60.

21. *Solidarity,* February 19, 1910, p. 2; CIR, II, pp. 1446, 1449, XI, p. 10,598.

22. *Industrial Worker,* July 1, 1909, p. 3.

23. Ibid., June 3, 1909, p. 2; Ben Williams to Editor, August 20, 1907, *Industrial Union Bulletin,* September 7, 1907, p. 2.

24. J. J. Ettor, "A Retrospect on Ten Years of the IWW," *Solidarity*, August 14, 1915, p. 2; James Larkin in *International Socialist Review*, XVI (December 1915), pp. 330–31; CIR, V, pp. 4234–35, 4239.
25. CIR, XI, pp. 10,574, 10,579.
26. Ibid., V, p. 4239; *Solidarity*, March 14, 1914, p. 2; cf. Hobsbawm, op. cit., pp. 58–59.
27. Jack London, *The Iron Heel* (New York, 1924), pp. 96–99.
28. CIR, V, pp. 4940, 4946–47; *The Lumber Industry and Its Workers* (Chicago, n.d.), p. 59.
29. *Solidarity*, April 2, 1910, p. 2; CIR, XI, p. 10,574.
30. CIR, V, p. 4942; *Solidarity*, July 9, 1910, p. 3.
31. V. St. John, "Political Parties Not Endorsed by Us," *Industrial Worker*, August 12, 1909, p. 3; Vincent St. John, *The I.W.W.: Its History, Structure, and Methods* (Chicago, 1919 ed.), pp. 40–45; CIR, II, p. 1449, XI, p. 10,575; *Lumber Industry and Its Workers*, p. 59.
32. *Industrial Worker*, June 6, 1912, p. 2.
33. *Lumber Industry and Its Workers*, p. 73; CIR, XI, p. 10,575.
34. J. Ebert, "Suppressing the IWW in New York," *Solidarity*, February 14, 1914, p. 20.
35. R. Brazier to Editor, *Industrial Worker*, February 2, 1911, p. 3; *Solidarity*, May 30, 1914, p. 2.
36. *International Socialist Review*, XII (February 1912), p. 467, XIII (September 1912), pp. 246–47; CIR, XI, p. 15,580.
37. CIR, V, p. 4237.
38. Ibid., II, pp. 1451, 1555, V, pp. 4947–48; Frank Bohn and W. D. Haywood, *Industrial Socialism* (Chicago, 1911), p. 57.
39. CIR, XI, p. 10,581.
40. Quoted in Dosch, op. cit., p. 417.
41. CIR, II, pp. 1452, 1456, XI, p. 10,592.
42. *Industrial Worker*, I (June 1906), p. 8; *Industrial Union Bulletin*, June 29, 1907, p. 2, April 4, 1908, p. 2; *Industrial Worker*, May 8, 1913, p. 2, August 12, 1909, p. 2; *Solidarity*, June 8, 1912, p. 2.
43. *Solidarity*, December 24, 1910, p. 2.
44. *Industrial Worker*, October 8, 1910, p. 2; Arturo Giovannitti, "Syndicalism: The Creed of Force," *The Independent*, LXXVI (October 30, 1913), p. 210; CIR, XI, p. 10,578.
45. *Industrial Union Bulletin*, April 6, 1907, p. 2.
46. *Industrial Worker*, May 28, 1910, p. 1, February 23, 1911, p. 2, July 1912–January 1913.
47. *International Socialist Review*, XIII (February 1912), p. 469; *Solidarity*, February 25, 1911, p. 4.
48. J. Thompson quote from CIR, V, pp. 4240–41; Haywood in ibid., XI, pp. 10,578–79; *Solidarity*, February 25, 1911, p. 4; *Industrial Worker*, March 13, 1913, p. 2.
49. CIR, III, p. 2482.

50. Ibid., V, pp. 4240–41; B. H. Williams, *American Labor in the Jungle: The Saga of the One Big Union* (microfilm copy, Wayne State University Labor Archives), p. 45.

51. *Industrial Worker*, May 23, 1912, p. 2; *Industrial Union Bulletin*, September 7, 1907, p. 2.

52. *Industrial Worker*, I (May 1906), p. 1; W. E. Trautmann, *Industrial Unionism* (Chicago, 1908), pp. 16–18; *Industrial Worker*, May 6, 1909, p. 2; *Solidarity*, June 4, 1910, p. 2; CIR, II, pp. 1450–51, III, p. 2598.

53. *Industrial Worker*, May 6, 1909, p. 2; *Solidarity*, June 4, 1910, p. 2.

54. Haywood and Ettor, "What the IWW Intends to Do to the USA," reprinted from the New York *World* in *Solidarity*, June 27, 1914, p. 3.

55. Haywood quoted in Dosch, op. cit., p. 417; Williams, *One Big Union*, p. 45.

56. *Solidarity*, August 24, 1912, p. 2.

57. CIR, II, pp. 1449, 1455, 1459, XI, pp. 10,574, 10,588; *Industrial Worker*, October 3, 1912, p. 2, October 13, 1910, p. 3; *Lumber Industry and Its Workers*, p. 73.

58. CIR, XI, p. 10,584; *Solidarity*, November 1, 1913, p. 2.

59. *Solidarity*, December 28, 1912, p. 3.

60. For the working-class definition of socialism, see WFM, *Proceedings of 1905 Convention* (Denver, 1905), p. 304; CIR, XI, p. 10,583; W. D. Haywood, "Socialism: The Hope of the Working Class," *International Socialist Review*, XII (February 1912), pp. 461–71.

61. See Philip S. Foner, *History of the Labor Movement in the United States*, Vol. 4: *Industrial Workers of the World, 1905–1917* (New York, 1965), ch. 17.

62. Will Herberg, "American Marxist Political Theory," in Donald D. Egbert and Stow Persons (eds.), *Socialism and American Life* (Princeton, 1952), I, pp. 491–92.

63. *Industrial Worker*, November 2, 1910, p. 2, October 3, 1912, p. 2, January 9, 1913, p. 2; CIR, XI, p. 10,587.

64. John Sandgren, "The Syndicalist Movement in Norway," *Solidarity*, February 14, 1914, p. 3; Robert R. LaMonte, "Industrial Unionism and Syndicalism," *New Review*, I (May 1913), p. 527.

65. John Spargo, *Syndicalism, Industrial Unionism and Socialism* (New York, 1913), pp. 13–15.

66. *Industrial Worker*, May 8, 1913, p. 3.

67. Philip Taft, "The I.W.W. in the Grain Belt," *Labor History*, I (Winter 1960), p. 67; Michael L. Johnson, "The I.W.W. and Wilsonian Democracy," *Science and Society*, XXVIII (Summer 1964), p. 274; William Preston, Jr., *Aliens and Dissenters* (Cambridge, Mass., 1963), pp. 150–51.

68. Oscar Lewis, op. cit., p. 1. Cf. Seymour Martin Lipset, *Political Man: The Social Bases of Politics* (New York, 1960), pp. 115–22.

69. For employer resistance to the IWW, see Selig Perlman and Philip Taft, *A History of Trade Unionism in the United States, 1896–1932* (New York, 1935), pp. 280–81. Cf. Walter Galenson, *The C.I.O. Challenge to the A.F.L.* (Cambridge, Mass., 1960); and David Brody, "The Emergence of Mass Production Unionism," in John Braeman et al., *Change and Continuity in Twentieth Century America* (Columbus, Ohio, 1966), pp. 221–62.

70. Ray Ginger, *The Bending Cross* (New Brunswick, N.J., 1949), p. 257; Bert Cochran, "Debs," in Harvey Goldberg (ed.), *American Radicals* (New York, 1957), p. 173; Robert F. Tyler, "Rebels of the Woods and Fields: A Study of the I.W.W. in the Pacific Northwest" (Unpublished Ph.D. Dissertation, University of Oregon, 1953), pp. 2, 21, 204–6; Paul F. Brissenden, *The I.W.W.* (New York, 1919 ed.), pp. xx–xxi, among numerous other works.

COMMENT
Robert L. Tyler

However American cultural "exceptionalism" has operated in the past to soften the class struggle and to frustrate hopes of socialist revolutionaries, the same forces, whatever they are precisely, must also account for the failure of the Industrial Workers of the World. At the outset one might quibble at such an assessment of failure, finding evidences all around one today that the IWW, like "Bird" Parker or the late James Dean, still "lives." Joan Baez sings "I Dreamed I Saw Joe Hill Last Night" at Woodstock and on a recent phonograph record for a younger generation of dissidents; East Village boutiques sell Joe Hill buttons advising that same younger generation not to mourn but to organize; Joseph Robert Conlin in a recent book describes an IWW commune of a hippie character in Chicago's Bohemian Near North Side, which somewhat disconcerts the Wobblies of an older generation still surviving at their moth-eaten headquarters on Halsted Street;[1] and Melvyn Dubofsky, as well as this writer, adds to the new flood of books and monographs on the IWW. But, of course, it would be only a quibble. The IWW did indubitably die. It did not bring off the apocalyptic "general strike" it preached. It did not bring in the age of "Industrial Democracy" or of the "Cooperative Commonwealth" it also preached. It did not even succeed, at least for very long, in organizing industrial workers into viable labor unions to work practically for such less ultimate objectives as higher wages or better working conditions.

The IWW arrived on the American scene in 1905, not even on center stage, and by 1920 it was in disarray and retiring to the wings. Its *floruit* thus coincides with that of the Socialist Party, and it is probably safe to assume that the same social forces explain the waxing and waning of both movements. The Socialist Party reached its greatest strength in the presidential election of 1912.

The peak of the IWW, in the Lawrence, Massachusetts, strike, came early in the same year.

This symposium as a whole is addressed to that larger question of why socialism found America inhospitable. Any answers to the question would cover the IWW because the IWW was rather like the fundamentalist wing of the socialist church, or like that purist proletarianism which Lenin was in a few years to castigate as "left-wing communism," or an "infantile disorder." In 1912 and 1913 the Socialist Party purged the IWW and its leaders from the party, ridding itself of a public liability in those days of its rapid growth. The IWW had a decidedly bad press, rather like that of the Black Panthers or the Weatherman faction of the Students for a Democratic Society. After attracting almost a million votes for Eugene V. Debs in the 1912 election, the Socialist Party "politicos" —as the IWW came to call them disparagingly—had reasons to want to be "practical." The IWW, in or out of the Socialist Party, preached and acted out a reductivist version of Marxist doctrine, urging the primacy of the "class war," the futility of bourgeois politics, the state as an ultimately otiose institution. As one IWW spokesman put it: "Revolutions do not come through politics or politicians. . . . To think that by electing a Socialist President we can hasten the dawn of the Cooperative Commonwealth is to imagine that we can veer the wind around by sheering the weather vane."[2] The young Walter Lippmann, in his socialist phase, complained that the IWW mistook a means or a tactic for the end.[3]

The first historians and journalistic analysts of the IWW—Paul F. Brissenden,[4] John Graham Brooks,[5] Andre Tridon,[6] Louis Levine[7]—seem to have agreed, if on nothing else, that the IWW was the American reflection of the international syndicalist movement. Indeed, Robert Hunter, in an early study of violence and the labor movement, dismissed the IWW in a footnote as a rather disorganized and ineffectual appendage to the labor movement whose only significance was as a peddler of "French ideas."[8] Syndicalism—in large part a "French idea"—was that modish revolutionary ism of the early twentieth century, influential in the French labor movement and attaching itself to the Bakunin anarchist tradition in Spain and elsewhere. Syndicalists, like the IWW we have characterized, plucked the leading idea of class warfare from the Marxist socialists, distilled it to high-proof purity, and used it as a heady apolitical, or even anti-political, revolutionary tactic. The working-class revolution would be accomplished through the agency of the labor movement, through the tactic of the general strike. All that history required of the class-conscious and revolutionary proletariat was that it stop work, "fold its hands," and watch capitalism crumble. Workers' organizations would then pick up the pieces, administer things rather than people, and thus establish the post-revolutionary socialist society of equality and justice. Intellectuals and activists from both the labor movement and the socialist movement came to advance such an ideology out of disillusion with the political "game" of bourgeois democracy which was seen as a preemptive trick being played on the workers. The very rules of that "game" were, of course, laid down by the bourgeois enemy.

However accurately this thumbnail sketch may fit the Sorels and Pougets of the French syndicalist movement, newer American scholars and historians have tended to question any easy association of the IWW with the European counterpart. Dubofsky and others have found few transatlantic ties between the IWW and, let us say, Georges Sorel. They prefer to locate the sources of the IWW in the American grass roots. But they then finally agree—as does Dubofsky[9]—that the IWW can be considered America's syndicalism, as if there is no great harm in the linguistic usage.

In a way it is curious that Dubofsky, and this writer, and Conlin, and others have felt obliged to go through this somewhat elaborate examination of the "syndicalism" of the IWW. It is probably an idle effort, an argument at bottom over definitions. The method seems to be to try to find whether certain IWW pamphlets were written under the influence of some Frenchman, whether the author could have read Pouget on sabotage, or whether he knew of Sorel. The solution to such a question proposed by John Spargo back in 1913—and requoted by Dubofsky[10]—settles the matter quite sensibly by merely proposing an adequate definition of syndicalism to cover both the French and the American phenomena. Thus, by agreeing on a definition, the IWW becomes America's syndicalism. Dubofsky, for example, finds no way "to escape," as he puts it, the similarities between the IWW and its European contemporaries.[11]

Such a question of social taxonomy, of "influence" in almost the literary historian's sense, is the kind of question to which historians are given professionally. They are not necessarily idle questions. Such a question as the "syndicalism" of the IWW does relate, in its way, to the more substantial question under examination in this symposium: why did socialism fail in America? The indigenousness of the IWW—or its foreignness—is obviously pertinent to any examination of the reasons for its failure. The missing premise in this enthymematic explanation would be: cultures tend to reject any too exotic influences, rather like organ rejection in transplant surgery. If the IWW did indeed lack roots in American culture, if it were only a curiosity imported from France by bemused intellectuals and radical dreamers, then its failure is rather simply explained. But rather too simply.

Dubofsky argues, as has this writer in his own proffered explanations of the failure of the IWW, that it was a peculiar and paradoxical conflict of practice and purpose *within* the IWW which accounts, at least in part, for its demise.[12] This debilitating conflict at the core of the IWW was suddenly exposed when the organization was attacked and checked violently during the First World War. The enthusiasm and *élan* of the IWW before the war, and its sometimes successful but temporary representation of the grievances of unskilled immigrant workers in the East and of migratory workers in the West, bore it along with an illusion of success until it ran into the cruel brick wall of reality during the war. What was the integral confusion or contradiction within the IWW? It was a failure to realize that its two simultaneous goals, effective bread-and-butter unionism and revolution, were in reality contradictory.

Most of the well-known, half-legendary exploits of the IWW, upon close examination, reveal this confusion of purpose, this masking of reality temporarily with a splendid activism and a wonderful revolutionary style. The twice- or thrice-told tale of the Lawrence, Massachusetts, strike of 1912, for example, reveals the problem. But two much lesser-known IWW episodes might better show the typicalness of the problem.

In December 1912 IWW railroad workers on a grade outside Eugene, Oregon, walked off the job in a spontaneous protest against low wages and abusive foremen. They marched into town singing revolutionary songs. The following day they apparently decided that their protest was a strike, and from the local IWW hall they issued a series of demands including the nine-hour day, reinstatement on the job, and an end to bullying by the foremen. The strikers and hangers-on at the hall then tried to induce all other workers on the project to join the strike. They met the railroad work car as it left the town in the morning and as it returned to town in the evening, and, amid scenes of near riot, tried to persuade the workers to stop scabbing. Every evening of the strike, forty or fifty Wobblies paraded down Willamette Street, the main street of Eugene, carrying placards, singing irreverent songs, shouting their grievances. They also picketed the Quick Lunch restaurant on lower Willamette Street because the restaurant catered to scabs and because it supplied free eggs to spectators who wished to pelt Wobblies during the evening parades. The leader of the strike, James Morgan, was thrown in jail for assaulting one of the non-strikers at the nightly proselytizing at the work train. The Wobblies began to drift away to other casual laboring jobs in the region. From his jail cell, Morgan promised a resumption of the "strike" in the spring, and he evinced no remorse for having beaten up the non-striker, an ignoramus who was just walking around "to save funeral expenses" in any case.[13]

A local strike of loggers in the Coos Bay region of Oregon in May 1913 set off another medley of troubles. The strike began, as usual, in a spontaneous protest over a particular grievance, the laying-off of a number of IWW agitators. The following day, for good measure, the IWW designated their protest a strike and listed a number of demands such as higher wages and better living conditions in the logging camps. By June the strike had died out, but the local burghers had been roused by it to take radical action of their own. A group of Marshfield citizens—six hundred in all—deported W. J. Edgworth of the local IWW hall. They marched the IWW leader out of town and gave him a boat ride eight miles down the coast. The vigilantes, however, let two Wobblies slip through their net, and while they deported Edgworth, the two Wobblies, with splendid effrontery, mounted soapboxes in Marshfield to harangue the few lethargic citizens remaining in town. The returning vigilantes discovered them and deported them on a second boat, first marching them through the streets and forcing them periodically to kneel and kiss an American flag.[14]

From such episodes as these—which could be multiplied almost indefinitely—it is obvious that the IWW was often more sinned against than sinning. But apportioning justice was not the lesson intended in these brief illustrations of IWW methods and style. In the harsh circumstances of their lives Wobblies could not decide

—or even distinguish—between the demands of labor unionism and a kind of quixotic revolutionary vanguardism. As Dubofsky describes this conflict of purpose, the IWW failed to transform its occasional and local organizational successes into any effective "higher consciousness," i.e., revolutionary consciousness and discipline.[15] Or, we might add, into effective labor unions.

In this respect Dubofsky assumes with most historians of the IWW, early or late, the peculiar lack of hospitality of American culture to class-conscious movements. Americans have viewed their society as idyllically classless. But the IWW stubbornly acted out its dilemma, insisting on simultaneous unionism and revolution. Of course, it failed to achieve either objective. But analyzing these peculiarities of the IWW as it struggled with its own problem in the matrix of American culture only partly explains its failure. It is really the hostility of American culture that is the basic cause of the failure. And that is assumed, not explained, in emphasizing the idiosyncrasies of the IWW.

It is clear that any explanation of failure and decline specific to the IWW must be but a variant or special case of the explanation for the failure of socialism in general. Any hypothesis seeking causes in the peculiarities of the IWW only seems to beg the larger question. Therefore, Dubofsky—as well as this writer and most other historians of the IWW—has not really shed much light on this underlying question, however admirable and definitive is his new narrative history.

It seems to this critic—however against the grain of the newest revisionism it may seem—that such "consensus" historians as Louis Hartz may have proposed the most persuasive explanations of this indubitable hostility of America toward socialism and all its class-conscious relatives, including the early labor movement itself. Even radicals themselves, late or soon, come to be overpowered by the reality of this bourgeois consensus at the heart of the American culture. Dubofsky has cited—in the quotation from Ben Williams, for example[16]—a recurring IWW protestation of its essential "Americanism," a protestation appearing even more unabashedly in the IWW's rejection of the Comintern in 1919 and after. Perhaps Earl Browder's equation of communism with "twentieth-century Americanism" during the Popular Front era of the mid-1930s is an even more obvious, if not embarrassing, instance. The New Left, of more contemporary experience, can be observed doing the same thing, as in Staughton Lynd's recent quest for a usable American past, accommodating Tom Paines, abolitionists, and Vietniks into his party and earning the charge of unhistorical behavior from Eugene D. Genovese in a hostile review of the book.[17] I do not imply that such efforts—by Wobblies, Earl Browder, or Staughton Lynd—to "Americanize" their radicalisms are capitulations or disingenuous. But the phenomenon is interesting. The radical assumes the role of suppliant, a petitioning outsider, knocking on historical doors to be let in. To plead and argue one's essential Americanism is a tactic, of course, in practical politics, but it also is an obvious admission of both alienation and of the ubiquity of the consensus which triggers the supplication. The radical is proffering a wistful code word which seems to say, "Look, I am a real American too. And, moreover, I am not *really* dangerous because my people are your people." That such a state of affairs holds in the history of American radicalism only confirms that already recognized hostility of American culture to socialism, the problem to which this book addresses itself. It again reveals the cogency of the question, but does not answer it.

If the methods of historical research and narrative can answer the question—certainly an arguable proposition—the answer may not lie in more and better histories of the radical movements themselves, such as Dubofsky's generally excellent history of the IWW, but rather in putting different and more clever questions to the surrounding culture, perhaps in the directions established in Louis Hartz's study. The answer to the question of the failure of socialism in America may lie not in histories of the Socialist Party and its satellites but in better historical anatomies of American culture.

Also, Dubofsky's history of the IWW illuminates another more general problem in the uses of history, and points to a radical skepticism that is a possible response to the central question of this symposium. Dubofsky makes a heroic effort, for which he is to be commended, to connect his story of the IWW to contemporary social problems and thus, hopefully, to improve our understanding of both the past and the present, to make his work "relevant" in the newest cant meaning of the term. By trying to relate the story of the IWW to the "culture of poverty," discussed by Oscar Lewis and other contemporary social critics and observers, and to the situation of the dispossessed, exploited, or economically redundant, then or now, he only brings into sharp focus those debated problems of the very uses of history.[18] This critic, for one, thinks he has not improved our understanding of either the IWW or the contemporary poor in the "culture of poverty." But he has done a service nonetheless by trying. All historical investigation designed, as Dubofsky apparently designed this part of his work, to improve our understanding of the present rests on a logic of analogy, loose and amateurish as in the case of, say, Harry Truman in some of his historical justifications, or tight and professional as in the case of a research historian seeking the "roots" of some present situation. The "lessons" of history, if there be any, are necessarily analogies. Because social change has been so precipitate, radical, and dizzying over the last several generations we can reasonably ask whether such a logic of analogy has become unworkable, whether there is sufficient continuity to justify comparisons. If we are really sailing in new seas, then old navigational experience may be useless, and we may be in regions of dreadful freedom indeed. It may be useless to study the Socialist Party, the IWW, or whatever, except for their own sakes, as exercises in literary re-creation. History as explanation may be in greater logical difficulties than it has been before. Perhaps socialism as a lost option in America is simply unexplainable, or open only to speculative answers. Or, in a world of radical discontinuity, it may be coming tomorrow, a possible scenario that can be extrapolated from a pastless present.

NOTES

1. Joseph Robert Conlin, *Bread and Roses Too: Studies of the Wobblies*, Greenwood Contributions in American History (Westport, Conn.: Greenwood Publishing Corp., 1969), pp. 136–40.

2. Robin Ernest Dunbar, "A Conflict Among Leaders," *International Socialist Review*, X (August 1909), p. 151.

3. Walter Lippmann, "The IWW—Insurrection or Revolution?" *New Review*, I (August 1913), p. 705.

4. Paul F. Brissenden, *The IWW: A Study of American Syndicalism* (New York: Columbia University Press, 1919).

5. John Graham Brooks, *American Syndicalism: The IWW* (New York: Macmillan, 1913).

6. Andre Tridon, *The New Unionism* (New York: B. W. Huebsch, 1913).

7. Louis Levine, "Development of Syndicalism in America," *Political Science Quarterly*, XXXVIII (September 1913), pp. 451–79.

8. Robert Hunter, *Violence and the Labor Movement* (New York: Macmillan, 1914), p. 247.

9. Melvyn Dubofsky, *We Shall Be All: A History of the IWW* (Chicago: Quadrangle Books, 1969), p. 169.

10. *Ibid.*, p. 170.

11. *Ibid.*, p. 169.

12. *Ibid.*, p. 449. Dubofsky refers to this problem as "internal inadequacies." Robert L. Tyler, *Rebels of the Woods: The IWW in the Pacific Northwest* (Eugene, Ore.: University of Oregon Books, 1967), ch. 1.

13. This episode can be traced in issues of the Eugene, Oregon, *Guard*, between December 2, 1912, and December 13, 1912.

14. This episode can be traced in the Coos Bay, Oregon, *News* for May 13, 1913, and in the Portland *Oregonian* for June 26, 1913.

15. Dubofsky, *op. cit.*, pp. 480–81.

16. *Ibid.*, p. 148.

17. Staughton Lynd, *Intellectual Origins of American Radicalism* (New York: Pantheon, 1968). Eugene D. Genovese's review appeared in *The New York Review of Books*, XI (September 26, 1968), p. 69.

18. Dubofsky, *op. cit.*, pp. 149–51.

REPLY

Melvyn Dubofsky

Robert L. Tyler's Comment raises two points fundamental to any sound interpretation of the role of radicalism and socialism in American society. One question involves the essential dilemma, or dichotomy, between reform and revolution confronting *all* radicals, and the second concerns the alleged "exceptionalism" of American history. According to Tyler's formulation—which might be considered the conventional academic wisdom—a combination of piecemeal reforms and American uniqueness rendered ineffectual political socialism and IWW-style syndicalism. In my book I dissented from the conventional wisdom in several basic particulars, and at great length. Here, however, I can only present a bare-bones outline of my disagreement with Tyler's version of the quandary of the radical in American history, and trust that the reader will tolerate some of my bald assertions, necessitated as they are by the brief compass of this response.

With Tyler's assertion that the Wobblies (also the socialists) faced a problem in the intrinsic contradiction between bread-and-butter unionism (political reforms) and ultimate revolution, I take no exception. That, after all, is the predicament of all revolutionaries in periods of non-crisis. Certainly, today, we realize that societies simply do not exist in a state of permanent crisis, and that a revolutionary situation is a rare moment indeed in history. In the absence of what for want of a better term might be labeled a "revolutionary situation," radicals, no matter how dedicated to their cause, make no revolutions. Moreover, most radical political and social movements, particularly those with a mass base, are led by a vanguard which maintains its influence and power by winning immediate demands for its constituents. It was the French Communist Party, functioning in a society with a living revolutionary tradition, which chose during the May days of 1968 to spurn the possibility of immediate revolution in preference to tangible economic and political gains. The history of Western European radical movements suggests that Tyler's dilemma is common to all revolutionaries, *not* unique to American socialists or Wobblies.

But to go further and to allege that "Wobblies could not decide —or even distinguish—between the demands of labor unionism and a kind of quixotic revolutionary vanguardism" is to engage in self-delusion and, perhaps, falsification of historical reality. From the first, as I thought my book made clear, IWW leaders perceived the distinction between the "demands of labor unionism" and the imperatives of revolution, which was why they broke with the AF of L. The IWW's difficulty was not to distinguish between reform and revolution; rather it was to bring the two into harmony. Wobblies fought to improve conditions today, while struggling consistently toward revolutionary goals. Awareness of the distinction between reform and revolution and of the gap in consciousness between vanguard and mass was made evident in Elizabeth Gurley Flynn's analysis of the strike defeat in Paterson (1913), in which she acknowledged: "We are dealing with human beings and not with chemicals. People are not material, you can't lay them down on the table and cut them according to pattern. You may have the best principles, but you can't always fit the people to the best principles."[1] That Miss Flynn and other Wobblies failed ultimately to permeate the masses with a higher, or Marxian, consciousness of class was unique neither to the IWW nor to American society. A similar failure has vitiated the endeavors of socialists and labor radicals in Western Europe. Which brings us now to the notion of American exceptionalism.

Both in my book on the IWW and elsewhere I have argued that to view American society as unique is to mystify history. Still, I would be among the first to concede that no two societies are precisely alike. That point conceded, it must be added, however, that much of our perception of contemporary and historical reality is relative, or as a sociologist might say, *situational.* An individual from one society is usually most aware of differences in another society; hence contrasts become magnified and similarities fade from view. Frenchmen remark on the bourgeois, shopkeeper mentality of Englishmen; Englishmen on the open, middle-class nature of American society; and Americans on the more closed, class-bound structure of British society. Yet, as a colleague of mine

in Asian history has observed: as the Chinese came increasingly
into contact with the Western world in the nineteenth and twentieth
centuries, they were impressed more by resemblances among Westerners of diverse nationalities than by disparities. And who is to
say that the Chinese perception is not more accurate than various
Westerners' self-images?

Tyler's references to Louis Hartz and to the concept of a "bourgeois consensus" throughout American history as the principal explanation for the failure of American socialism also rest more on
faith than on evidence.[2] The consensus that Tyler, Hartz, and
others maintain was at the heart of American life was an import
from England, the society, after all, which produced John Locke,
Hartz's putative creator of the "bourgeois consensus." Asa Briggs
in a remarkably insightful essay on "The Language of 'Class' in
Early Nineteenth-Century England" describes an ideology that in
its particulars resembles Hartz's and also Seymour Martin Lipset's
model of an American ideal-type, middle-class consensus.[3] In
Great Britain this consensus prevailed as long as the ruling class
remained confident, united, and able to satisfy the ruled with minimal reforms. This was particularly true of English history from
the end of the Chartist era to the last decade of the nineteenth
century, c. 1850–90. From 1890 on, and especially after the blows
inflicted by World Wars One and Two, the English ruling class
lost part of its confidence and some of its ability to retain the
acquiescence of the ruled. As a result, the consensus version of
society weakened.

In the United States over the same period of time, that is since
1890, the ruling class grew more confident, more united, and much
more able to pay off the lower classes with political reforms and
material gains.[4] Recently, however, under the strains of the war
in Southeast Asia and challenges from long-oppressed minority
groups at home, the American ruling class has met its own crisis
of confidence. Today the Hartz-Lipset version of the basic American consensus seems less convincing and resembles more in fact
what it always was: an attempt to mystify the reality of class
relationships in American society by lumping all citizens together
in an amorphous, middle-class mass. This was something Robert
and Helen Lynd realized back in the 1920s when they wrote their
classic sociological analysis of industrial society, *Middletown,* and
consciously refused to use the rubric "middle class," because the

term cloaked more about society than it revealed.[5] What I am suggesting is this: the Wobblies and socialists failed not because American society was exceptional, but because they reached their respective peaks when the nation's rulers were most confident, united, and propagated an illusion with a basis in reality.

Finally, Tyler's claim that American radicals have been singular in seeking to "Americanize" their movements also collapses under close scrutiny. What Tyler considers the Wobblies' attempt to Americanize their organization is a phenomenon common to radicals in other societies who ordinarily seek to sanction their programs on the basis of a real or an imagined national past. Such was the case of E. P. Thompson's radical English workers of the late eighteenth and early nineteenth centuries who strove to reassert the rights of freeborn Englishmen; of generations of French radicals who have revived the tradition of the "revolution of '89"; of E. J. Hobsbawm's "primitive rebels" who used the past as their constant bench mark; and even of a Communist Party-endorsed biography of the radical English labor leader Tom Mann, which devotes nearly half its pages to reviving the hallowed English tradition of liberty and freedom.[6] In other words, American radicals, searching for indigenous roots, have behaved in much the same manner as revolutionaries in other societies and other times.

Rather than end by discussing the IWW's relevance—need it be said that relevance is an illusive quality in the mind of the reader— I would like to suggest that the time has passed for further analyses of the failure of American socialism. To me it appears evident that the uniqueness of American society lies not in its exceptional middle-class bourgeois structure and mentality, but rather in the enormous success of the owners and managers of our industrial capitalist society. It is high time we scholars discovered why and how, since the decline of what Herb Gutman has called the era of American Chartism (1873–97),[7] corporate leaders and their political allies have successfully extended their hegemony into the values, attitudes, and actions of the working-class masses—that is, why American culture has been, as remarked by Thomas Cochran, a preeminently business culture.[8]

NOTES

1. Melvyn Dubofsky, *We Shall Be All* (Chicago, 1969), p. 284.

2. Louis Hartz, *The Liberal Tradition in America* (New York, 1955), and *The Founding of New Societies* (New York, 1964), pp. 69–122. Cf. Seymour Martin Lipset, *The First New Nation: The United States in Historical and Comparative Perspective* (New York, 1963), *passim* and esp. p. 175. For other examples of this same thesis see David Shannon, "Socialism and Labor," in C. Vann Woodward, *The Comparative Approach to American History* (New York, 1968), p. 249; Kent and Gretchen Kreuter, *An American Dissenter: The Life of Algie Martin Simons* (Lexington, Ky., 1969), p. 220; John H. M. Laslett, *Labor and the Left* (New York, 1970), p. 304.

3. Asa Briggs, "The Language of 'Class' in Early Nineteenth-Century England," in Asa Briggs and John Saville, *Essays in Labour History* (London, 1967 ed.), pp. 43–73, esp. pp. 70–71.

4. The most complete, though tendentious, analyses of this development can be found in Gabriel Kolko, *The Triumph of Conservatism* (Glencoe, Ill., 1963) and James Weinstein, *The Corporate Ideal in the Liberal State, 1900–1918* (Boston, 1968). A more subtle and believable version of this period in American history is offered in Robert H. Wiebe, *The Search for Order, 1877–1920* (New York, 1967), esp. chs. 5, 7–8, 11.

5. Robert S. and Helen M. Lynd, *Middletown* (New York, 1929), pp. 22–24.

6. E. P. Thompson, *The Making of the English Working Class* (London, 1965), chs. 4–5, 12, 16; E. J. Hobsbawm, *Primitive Rebels* (New York, 1965 ed.), and also the same author's *Labouring Men* (London, 1964), chs. 17–18; Dona Torr, *Tom Mann and His Times: Volume One: 1856–1890* (London, 1956). For a similar analysis of the sources of violence in society see Charles Tilly's essay "Collective Violence in European Perspective," in Hugh D. Graham and Ted R. Gurr (eds.), *Violence in America* (New York, 1969), pp. 4–42.

7. Herbert Gutman, "Culture, Conflict, and Discontinuity in American Labor History: Some Comments and Some Evidence" (Unpublished Paper, 1968).

8. Thomas C. Cochran, "The History of a Business Society," *Journal of American History*, LIV (June 1967), pp. 5–18.

Chapter 8

THE PROBLEMS OF THE SOCIALIST PARTY
A. BEFORE WORLD WAR ONE

James Weinstein*

During the decade ending with 1912, the Socialist Party of America enjoyed continuous growth and exerted a wide impact upon the political life of the nation. Starting with 10,000 members in 1901, the Party had grown to 120,000 by 1912, had elected some 1,200 public officials throughout the United States, and was publishing over 300 periodicals of all kinds. In the labor movement and in many of the reform movements of the period, Socialists were prominent and the Party had substantial followings. The Party's growth filled many of its members with untroubled optimism. Convinced that the expansion would continue indefinitely, these Socialists looked forward confidently to the emergence of their Party as the dominant force in American politics. In the next decade, however, the Party not only ceased to grow, but by 1922 had all but ceased to exist.

In the spring of 1912, Morris Hillquit and others envisioned a party of 200,000 or more members in the near future.[1] Instead, membership actually declined by about 22,000 in 1913, and although it rose slightly before war broke out in Europe in 1914, it then dropped again to 79,000 for 1915.[2] This drop, along with Debs's high presidential vote in 1912, and the departure of a few thousand syndicalists after the recall of William D. Haywood from the Party's National Executive Committee in 1913, sustain a widely held misconception that 1912 was the watershed of American so-

* This essay represents a summary and reevaluation of the views on the reasons for the decline of the Socialist Party of America during the World War One period which are given in my book *The Decline of Socialism in America, 1912–1925,* and in my articles "Anti-War Sentiment and the Socialist Party, 1917–1918," *Political Science Quarterly,* 74 (June 1959), pp. 215–39; and "The Socialist Party: Its Roots and Strengths, 1912–1919" and "Socialism's Hidden Heritage: Scholarship Reinforces Political Mythology," in *Studies on the Left,* 1 (Winter 1960), pp. 5–27, and 3 (Fall 1963), pp. 88–108.

cialist history. The misconception, however, is ideological. It flows from the need of both liberal and Communist to obscure the extent of popular socialist consciousness and Party strength in the period from 1912 to 1919.

The liberal need emerges from the assumption that the advent of Wilsonian liberalism in 1913 rendered socialism irrelevant in American political life. The Communist need emerges from an inability to explain the disintegration of the socialist movement after the split of the Party and the formation of the various Communist parties in 1919. Thus, Ira Kipnis (expressing the Communist view) asserts that overcome by opportunism, racism, and the lack of inner Party democracy, the socialist movement started on an irreversible decline in 1912. And Daniel Bell (expressing the liberal view) argues that "the eclipse of American Socialism took place in 1912," and that "the rest of the years were a trailing penumbra," because the Party "could not relate itself to the specific problems of social action in the here-and-now, give-and-take political world."[3]

It is true that if any one year can be considered the high point of Socialist strength it is 1912. But that year was no great divide. Neither in its impact on American society nor in its internal development did the movement change fundamentally in 1912. Contrary to Kipnis' thesis, Left activity and influence increased in the Party after 1912, despite Haywood's departure. All the other leading left-wingers remained in the Party; Socialists became less racist in their public attitudes and Negroes were recruited in both the North and the South; the Party continued to be active in support of the suffrage and women played an increasingly important role in the Party; Socialists remained a major force in the trade unions until the United States entered the war. By the time of the Emergency Convention in 1917, the various Left tendencies were in the ascendancy. And contrary to Bell's thesis, Party strength did not decline substantially from 1912 to 1916, and during the war (which Bell views as an unmitigated disaster for the Party) it greatly increased its popular following despite continual attacks on its organization and individual members. A leveling-off did occur after 1912. But factionalism was somewhat reduced. On balance the years from 1912 to 1917 were more nearly a period of consolidation than of disintegration.

While the Socialists never succeeded in winning a majority

within the American Federation of Labor, their strength had become considerable by 1912. In that year Max Hayes received almost one third of the vote running against Gompers for the presidency of the Federation, and William H. Johnston, a Socialist Machinist, received almost two fifths in his contest for a vice-presidency. A majority of the delegates from the Machinists, the Brewery Workers, Bakers, United Mine Workers, Western Federation of Miners, Painters, Quarry Workers, and Tailors voted for the Socialist candidates.[4] The strength of the Socialists in the AFL at this time constituted a potential, if not immediate, challenge to Gompers' leadership and was greater than the standard generalizations about the ideology of American labor would lead one to expect. The general reasons advanced to explain the failure of socialism in the American labor movement may be valid, but they do not explain the fluctuations of Socialist strength within the AFL in pre-war years.

One Socialist historian concludes that the alleged sharp decline after 1912 followed from a policy of non-militance adopted by the right wing when it gained control of the Party. He sees the adoption of the anti-sabotage clause as part of the Party constitution in 1912, and the subsequent recall of Haywood in 1913, as evidence that the Party was corrupted with opportunism. The fruits of the policy are said to be a failure to oppose Gompers for the presidency of the AFL after 1912, a virtual cessation of agitation for industrial unionism, and a decrease in the financial support of strikes from $21,000 in 1912 to $400 in 1913, and to zero in 1914.[5]

The argument has several weaknesses. First is the equation of the IWW with industrial unionism and the apparent assumption that the rejection of syndicalism in 1912 also involved a renunciation of industrial organization. There is no evidence that this was so. Most Socialists shared the view expressed by the Party's Information Department in 1915 that "all Socialists believe in the industrial form of labor organization," but disagree with the IWW as to "the best method for bringing [it] about."[6] This had been the meaning of the return of the Brewery Workers and the Western Federation of Miners, both Socialist-led and industrially organized, to the AFL in 1908 and 1911. Nor were the Right and Center groups opposed to industrialism. In New York, Hillquit's main strength after 1914 came from the Amalgamated Clothing Workers, while in Milwaukee, Berger's basic support came from the Brewers. Both the Clothing Workers and the Brewers were industrial unions.

Second, after the election of Woodrow Wilson, the passage of the Clayton Act, and the appointment of a former UMW official, William B. Wilson, as the first Secretary of Labor, Gompers' position of leadership was greatly strengthened. In addition, by 1912, Catholic strength in the AFL had been mobilized solidly against the Socialists by the increasingly active Militia of Christ, organized by Father Dietz in 1909.[7] It does not necessarily follow that the Socialists ceased attempting to influence AFL unions, however, but merely that their tactics changed. Marc Karson writes that after 1912 the number of "progressive resolutions" passed at AFL conventions increased greatly, and that this reflected increased Socialist influence in the Federation.[8]

It is true that reform legislation during Wilson's first administration adversely affected Socialists in the trade unions, as did the Adamson Act and Wilson's campaign for reelection in 1916 as the "man who kept us out of war." In 1916, for example, the Machinists supported Wilson for reelection and failed to comment either on the campaign of Allan Benson, the Socialist presidential candidate, or, later, on the election of the Socialist Machinist leader Thomas Van Lear, as mayor of Minneapolis.[9]

Likewise, by 1916 the Western Federation of Miners, though still friendly to the Socialists, had begun to draw back from its close affiliation with the Party. President Charles Moyer explained politics in the union had proved a detriment in organizing the miners.[10] After Wilson's victory, the *Miners' Magazine* expressed pleasure that the "candidate of peace" had won. At the same time, however, it commented that there was another party "that blazes the paths of progress, that sows the seed of human betterment, whose harvest is reaped by others." This party "teaches the voiceless to speak and stirs the hopeless to action." It is "the Socialist."[11]

In two major industrial state federations of labor Socialists made substantial gains after 1912. Previously, no major state federation had been controlled by Socialists, but in that year James H. Maurer began his long tenure as president of the Pennsylvania Federation of Labor. Maurer led the Party in central Pennsylvania and was elected to the Pennsylvania state assembly in 1910, 1914, and

1916. Under his leadership the state federation endorsed industrial unionism and woman suffrage and aided the IWW-led strike at Paterson, New Jersey, in 1913.[12]

The year following Maurer's election to the presidency of the Pennsylvania Federation, the Illinois Federation elected the Miners leader John H. Walker as its president. Walker was a resident of Danville, where he ran for mayor on the Socialist ticket in 1915.[18] Walker remained president of the Illinois Federation until 1919; under his leadership Illinois delegates to the AFL conventions in 1914 and 1915 introduced resolutions in support of industrial unionism.[14]

Just as Socialists were active in the unions after 1912, so were trade unionists prominent in the Party. Many Party trade unionists participated in local and state politics. Probably their most important victory was the election in 1916 of Thomas Van Lear as mayor of Minneapolis. Van Lear, a business agent of the International Association of Machinists, received full support from both his Party and the organized labor movement in Minneapolis and in a two-way race gained a clear majority of the votes.[15] In hundreds of smaller municipalities as well, Socialist trade unionists often led their Party tickets, frequently to victory. John Schieldknecht, a switchman on the Santa Fe Railroad and a member of the Brotherhood of Railway Trainmen, for example, was elected mayor of Frontenac, Kansas, in April 1917.[16]

Thus, in the years from 1912 to 1917, Socialist activity and strength in the trade unions seem to have remained at their earlier level or to have increased. The losses in the Western Federation of Miners and in the Machinists union were more than offset by the gains in other internationals, and in state and local labor bodies. Socialist trade unionists played an increasingly prominent role in the Party in these years, and the Party seems to have developed a greater solidarity with the labor movement. If one is to find a substantial decline of socialism in the trade unions, it must be after the United States entered the war, in April 1917.[17]

In his history of Marxian socialism in the United States, Daniel Bell comments that by opposing the First World War the Socialist Party "cut itself off from the labor movement and created widespread distrust of itself among the American people."[18] Certainly the Party's opposition to preparedness and later to participation in the war brought it into conflict with the policy of the American

Federation of Labor. Gompers, who had previously played an ambiguous role on preparedness, became an ardent advocate in late 1916 after Herbert Hoover, Woodrow Wilson, and Ralph M. Easley convinced him that if it wanted better treatment from the government, the trade union movement must support the national preparedness program.[19] Just before war was declared, most AFL affiliates agreed to a Gompers-sponsored pledge of loyalty to the government in the event of war. Only about a dozen Internationals did not.

Yet, even on the upper levels of the trade union movement, support for the war was not universal. The Quarry Workers pledged "wholehearted" support to the war effort but the union journal continued to give as much space to the anti-war Socialists as to the pro-war ones.[20] Other union publications, notably Max Hayes's Cleveland *Citizen, The Tailor,* and the *Railway Carmen's Journal,* followed the pattern of the *Quarry Workers Journal.* Hayes supported the pro-war Socialists and pushed the Liberty Loan in his paper, but the news columns of the *Citizen* carried full reports of Party activity and Hayes exulted in Party gains and lamented its losses throughout the war.[21]

The Brewery Workers took a somewhat ambiguous position on the war. The International acquiesced in the AFL programs, but the president of the union was dispassionate. At the union's convention in December 1918, he commented that the main effect of the war was that the workers had less money to spend on luxuries; as a result fewer people were buying beer. The wage earner, he said, had no trouble keeping within the "appeal of Food Dictator Hoover" for the conservation of food, since earning power had not kept pace with "the ever-increasing cost of all the necessities of life."[22]

Among the international unions only those in the clothing industry gave open support to the Party during the war. The Amalgamated Clothing Workers commented that the St. Louis Manifesto "vindicated" American socialism. Two of the seven Socialists elected to office in Rochester, New York, in 1917 were leaders of the union.[23] Similarly, the International Ladies' Garment Workers' Union gave strong support to the Socialist anti-war campaign in the fall of 1917. Elmer Rosenberg, first International vice-president, was one of the ten Socialists elected to the New York assembly.[24]

In the state federations Socialists were also divided. James H. Maurer took an active part in the anti-war campaign of the Reading, Pennsylvania, Socialists in November 1917, and played a leading role in the anti-war People's Council.[25] As a result, Maurer faced the personal opposition of Gompers in his attempt at reelection as president of the Pennsylvania Federation in 1918. However, Maurer was reelected by a vote of more than three to one.[26] In Illinois John H. Walker, state federation president, supported the war, declaring in 1918 that there were no more pacifists, "only patriots and traitors."[27] But the Socialists retained their following in the state. In early 1919, Walker was succeeded as president by Duncan MacDonald, also a Miners leader, who had remained a loyal Socialist throughout the war.[28] In his first presidential address, MacDonald commented that labor had been "assured on every hand that the war was for Democracy and that we were required to make sacrifices to carry it on." Now that the war was over, however, and "the workers seek to usher in the new Democracy," they found that wartime ideals were "only a myth," and that business leaders had set up an oligarchy in industry "more arrogant than that enjoyed by the crowned heads of European monarchists."[29]

* * *

Turning now to a second (and hitherto disenfranchised) potential source of support for the Socialist Party during the war years, "it is noteworthy," wrote Vida D. Scudder in 1914, "that the Socialist party was first among political parties to give women an equal vote with men in public affairs and an equal share in managing the movement."[30] This recognition of women was consistent with international socialist tradition,[31] and was bolstered by the large number of active women Socialists. Well before the formation of the Party, such outstanding women reformers as Frances Willard and Florence Kelley had been outspoken socialists. At the 1897 convention of the Women's Christian Temperance Union, for example, President Willard addressed the delegates as follows:

I believe that competition is doomed. The trusts . . . have proved that we are better without . . . it. . . . What the socialist desires is that the corporation of humanity should control all production. Beloved comrades, this is . . . the higher way; it enacts into everyday living the ethics of Christ's gospel. Nothing else will do it.[32]

Florence Kelley, in addition to her leadership in the National Consumers' League, the NAACP, and many other reform movements, was a lifelong socialist. She helped put the Intercollegiate Socialist Society on its feet in 1911, and later served as president. In 1912 she joined the Socialist Party and retained membership for many years. Like Kelley, Margaret Sanger was a socialist for many years. Sanger was a close friend of William Haywood, and a frequent contributor to the New York *Call,* where in 1912 she published the first articles on birth control to appear in the United States.[33]

Socialist writers also played a leading role in the fight for women's rights. Rheta Childe Dorr, for example, was a frequent contributor to *Hampton's Magazine* on such subjects as prostitution, women in industry, and child labor. One series of her articles, published as a book entitled *What Eight Million Women Want,* sold half a million copies and placed Miss Dorr in the forefront of the fight for women's rights. Other contributors to the campaign were Reginald Wright Kauffman and the ubiquitous Upton Sinclair, who contributed two novels, *Sylvia* and *Sylvia's Marriage.*

Within the Party after 1910 women played an increasingly prominent role in general activity. In 1910 Lena Morrow Lewis (who in 1917 became the founding editor of the Seattle *Daily Call*) was elected to the National Executive Committee. In 1912 Kate Richards O'Hare, co-publisher of the *National Rip Saw,* was elected to the NEC, as was Anna Maley in 1916 (when she was serving as campaign manager to Thomas Van Lear in Minneapolis).[34] During these years "Mother" Jones and Ella Reeve Bloor frequently worked as Party organizers, and several women ran for public office on the Socialist ticket. Kate O'Hare ran for Congress from Kansas in 1910 and was the unsuccessful candidate for the vice-presidential nomination of the Party in 1916. In 1912 Anna Maley was Socialist candidate for governor of Washington, while in 1915 Estelle Lindsay was elected to the Los Angeles City Council. In New York, in the first election after the suffrage victory of 1917, Ella Reeve Bloor was the Socialist candidate for lieutenant governor and Jesse Wallace Hughan for state treasurer. In Illinois, where women were not then eligible to run for statewide office, three Socialist women ran for local office in Quincy in 1914. And in Daly City, California, the Socialist mayor in 1912 appointed the first woman police judge in the state's history.

Woman suffrage was the main concern of the women's commit-

tees in the Party, and, after 1912, of major importance to the Party
as a whole. In many states Socialists played a key role in winning
the suffrage. In 1914 in Nevada, for example, suffrage was won
by a 1,500-vote majority. Credit was claimed by Socialists, who
"campaigned steadily" for the reform. The claim seems reasonable
since the Party polled 5,451 votes out of a total of 21,567.³⁵ A
climax in the movement was reached in 1917, when New York
adopted the suffrage. During the campaign Morris Hillquit, Socialist candidate for mayor of New York City, urged all the candidates to join him in a declaration that would assure a suffrage
victory. When this request was turned down, the Socialists re-
doubled their efforts. Every night, suffrage meetings were held
in every part of the city, separate from the Socialist meetings.³⁶
The two major Socialist unions, the Amalgamated Clothing Workers and the International Ladies' Garment Workers, both campaigned actively for suffrage. In every part of the state the Party
threw itself into the campaign.

After the election, many gave the Socialists credit for the victory.
The Rochester *Herald* lamented that in the campaign, "The forces
of Socialism and its ally, antagonism to . . . the war, are more
numerous and formidable than ever before, and their strength was
enlisted solidly for woman suffrage. Wherever the Socialist . . .
propaganda made headway . . . the suffrage vote was automatically increased."³⁷

Thirdly, let us examine the Socialist Party's relationship with
another potential source of support during this period: Negroes,
who were moving into northern cities in increasing numbers during this period. By present-day standards the Socialist Party's
relative lack of interest in the Negro in the early years of its
history is surprising. Although the Party considered that women
required special attention and a special program, this was not so
with respect to the Negro. Kipnis and Shannon both point out the
extent of racism in the Party, especially, but not exclusively, among
the right-wingers who tended to support the AFL position on immigration and the colored races.³⁸ Victor Berger and Ernest Unter-
man were perhaps the most outspoken. Berger even appealed to
the defense of white womanhood against the invasion of "yellow
men."³⁹

Nevertheless, on the question of Negro rights the Socialist Party was more advanced than any other contemporary organization, with the exception of the IWW.[40] Debs, especially, opposed discrimination. He toured the South speaking in defense of Negro rights and calling on Negroes to reject the false doctrines of "meekness and humility."[41] Charles Edward Russell and William English Walling, both leading Socialists, were among the founders of the NAACP in 1909; Walling, more than any other white man, was responsible for the formation of that organization.[42] Furthermore, W. E. B. Du Bois, although he resigned from the Party to support Wilson in 1912, and criticized the Party in 1913 for "failure to face fairly the Negro problem,"[43] was not unfriendly toward socialism. In 1914 *Crisis,* the organ of the NAACP edited by Du Bois, commented, in a review of Walling's *Progressivism and After,* that "slowly but surely colored folk are beginning to realize the possible meaning of socialism for them." And in 1916 Du Bois wrote that the Socialist candidates were "excellent leaders of an excellent party," although a vote for them would be "thrown away."[44]

Kipnis writes that, as of 1905, there were no Negroes in southern Socialist locals.[45] But by 1915, except in Florida and Mississippi, Socialist locals were not segregated in the South; nor was the Party inactive in southern states. Oklahoma, until late 1917, was the leading Socialist state and the Party there fought consistently for the full enfranchisement of the Negro.[46] At one time or another Socialists made strong showings in Texas, Florida, Louisiana, and Arkansas.[47] Kipnis also claims that by 1912 the Socialist Party "not only refused to fight for equal rights for Negroes . . . but displayed a chauvinism seldom equaled by the most conservative A.F. of L. officials." Yet the *Socialist Congressional Campaign Book of 1914* states that the "capitalists exploit all of us in common, regardless of whether we are . . . black or white . . . [and] we therefore ought to stand solidly together as a United working class. . . . The person who seeks to divide the working class by appealing to race . . . prejudice is an enemy of the working people."

Until 1917 there was no Socialist Negro periodical, but in that year, A. Phillip Randolph began publishing *The Messenger,* billed as "The only Magazine of Scientific Radicalism in the World Published by Negroes." In 1917 Randolph urged Negroes to vote for Hillquit as mayor of New York because he represented "the working people and 99 percent of Negroes are working people"; because "the Socialist Party, which Hillquit represents, does not even hold race prejudice in the South"; and because "Hillquit believes that the war is over the exploitation of the darker peoples—the stealing of their land and labor—and is the only candidate who dares to say so." After the election Randolph estimated that 25 per cent of the Negro vote had gone to Hillquit.[48] In 1920, Randolph was the Socialist candidate for comptroller of the state of New York, the first Negro candidate for statewide office in the twentieth century.

Turning now to the Socialist Party's relationship with intellectuals and middle-class reformers, few active intellectuals could avoid the challenge of socialism in the early twentieth century. Whether accepted or rejected, the questions raised and the solutions prescribed by Marx were an integral part of the debates of the day. Walter Lippmann, for example, began his career in 1911 as secretary to the Socialist mayor of Schenectady. By 1914, in *Drift and Mastery,* he finally rejected Marxism because, contrary to Marx's predictions, the middle class had not disappeared but was in his view "the dominant power expressing itself through the Progressives and through the Wilson Administration."[49] Also in 1911, Walter Weyl started writing his never-finished book "The Class War" as a counterattack on the socialist challenge to middle-class progressivism. By the time of his death in 1919, he had abandoned "bourgeois reform movements," and, according to his widow, had been ready to join the Socialist Party.[50] As Charles Beard noted in 1913, the early twentieth century was an age when socialism was "admittedly shaking the old foundations of politics the world over and penetrating our science, art and literature."

Beard's comment answered a query of the *Intercollegiate Socialist,* a sometimes quarterly of the Intercollegiate Socialist Society (ISS).[51] The society maintained its strength at about seventy chapters until after the United States entered the war in April 1917.[52] Then, because of disagreements among its leaders and restrictions on many campuses, the number of chapters declined to forty-two by late 1918.[53]

Despite this, students and intellectuals of all socialist tendencies and many non-Socialists participated in the activities of the ISS, which served as a forum for a wide range of views.[54] The *Inter-*

collegiate Socialist carried discussions of the "possible methods of socializing industry," the proper attitude of Socialists toward the Wilson administration, the activities of Victor Berger in Congress, and other tactical matters. However, there were few, if any, serious attempts to analyze the changes taking place in the class structure of the United States, or even of the theories of middle-class progressivism as expounded by Herbert Croly, Lippmann, and Weyl. Though many leading intellectuals participated in the activities of the society, surprisingly little of substance appears to have been produced by it. Indeed, the *Intercollegiate Socialist* served primarily as a house organ for the Socialist student movement. If academic intellectuals were influenced by the writings of Marx and Engels, as in varying degrees they were, American Socialist theoreticians offered them little. Possibly for this reason, few academicians developed more than a flirting interest in the political movement in the United States. Many campus intellectuals participated in the activities of the ISS, but few played a role in the Party. It was the non-academic intellectuals, muckrakers, and writers who were drawn into practical political action.

As a group, muckrakers showed little interest in political theory, preferring, instead, simply to concentrate upon being "good reporters." William Hard was an exception among the muckrakers when he called for "intervention of the public authorities" to supervise industrial establishments, as had been done "in many of the countries of Europe."[55] For although some muckrakers, notably Lincoln Steffens, were aware of the German efforts at government intervention in behalf of social welfare, most of them were essentially unconcerned with the prescription of solutions. Or, if they were concerned, their usual appeal was to the good old days, to honest men (by which they typically meant businessmen) in office. Their analysis rarely went beyond moral indignation.[56]

Some, like Lincoln Steffens and Frederick C. Howe, concerned themselves with social theory. But Steffens, and even Howe, while they supported particular men or movements, were primarily uncommitted observers. Among the muckrakers, only the Socialists consistently attempted an explanation of social problems in terms of the structure of American society; only they offered more than particular solutions to particular problems. While most of the muckrakers looked longingly backward, the Socialists looked to the future. To young intellectuals, aroused by the literature of exposure, socialist ideas were stimulating and gave hope. As Louis Filler has pointed out, Socialists became the "outstanding educational force," to be found "in every field where reform was in progress."[57]

The relationship between the politics and journalism of these writers varied. Some developed deepened social consciousness as a result of their literary explorations. Others, animated by their socialist conviction, aimed at converting their readers. Thus Charles Edward Russell and Rheta Childe Dorr were converted to socialism by the experience of muckraking. In *Why I Am a Socialist,* Russell describes his conversion after discovering that low wages, brutal treatment, and neglect of even the elements of safety were forced on capitalists by competition. A kind capitalist, Russell concluded, would soon be an ex-capitalist. Russell came to believe that capitalism, though still possibly a viable system, had ceased to be a civilizing force. Only a reorganization of society along socialist lines could bring morality back into public life.[58]

Other writers, such as London, Sinclair, and Gustavus Myers, wrote primarily to expose the inhumanity of the system. These men almost inadvertently became leaders in the art of popular disclosure. Thus Upton Sinclair wrote *The Jungle* as an impassioned plea for socialism. Intending "to frighten the country by a picture of what its industrial masters were doing to their victims," he had aimed at the public's heart. But, he lamented, "by accident I hit it in the stomach." Sinclair succeeded in sickening hundreds of thousands of Americans and in giving impetus to the movement for regulation and inspection of the meat-packing industry, but he made few converts to socialism. Like Sinclair, Gustavus Myers wrote his *History of the Great American Fortunes* as a lesson in the nature of capitalism. Myers attacked muckrakers who gave "no explanation of the fundamental laws and movements of the present system, which have resulted in these vast fortunes."[59]

Of the meeting grounds between Socialists and intellectuals described here, only the Intercollegiate Socialist Society survived American participation in the World War, and it declined after 1917. Muckraking declined rapidly after 1912, largely, but not entirely, because of the pressure on the muckraking magazines organized by the National Civic Federation and groups of creditors.[60] Socialists continued to write exposures of the evils of capitalism, but more and more they were restricted to publishing in the Party press. Few of the informal clubs and salons continued for long. Mabel Dodge's, for example, lasted about two years, ending in 1914. Those, like the "X" club, that were still in existence in 1917 divided hopelessly and with hostility over the question of American participation in the war.

Despite all this, however, throughout the years from 1912 to 1917 socialism remained a central concern of intellectuals, and their organized connections with the movement did not change drastically during this period. When America entered the war, the ISS was considerably stronger than it had been in 1912, although this was balanced by the increasing interest and participation by journalists and intellectual reformers in the concerns of Wilsonian liberalism. Even so, it was the war that disrupted the relationship of the Party and its intellectuals.

Another index of the relative degree of influence enjoyed by the Socialists in these years is the Socialist press, which reached its high point in 1912, when the Party claimed a total of 8 foreign-language and 5 English dailies, 262 English and 36 foreign-language weeklies, and numerous monthlies. The total circulation of these papers was in the neighborhood of 2 million, although an exact estimate cannot be made. Among the leaders in circulation in 1913 were the *Appeal to Reason,* with a weekly average of 761,747; the *National Rip Saw,* with 150,000; the *Jewish Daily Forward,* with 142,000; the Philadelphia *Socialist,* with 46,444; the *International Socialist Review,* with 42,000; the *National Socialist,* with 35,000; the Milwaukee *Leader,* with 35,000; and the Hallettsville, Texas, *Rebel,* with 26,145.[61] Among these Socialist publications were weekly and monthly periodicals with national circulation, such as the *Appeal* and the *International Socialist Review;* daily and weekly local newspapers, such as the Milwaukee *Leader* and numerous small-town weeklies; union papers, such as the Cleveland *Citizen;* and various cultural, theoretical, and special group publications. Of these, only the *American Socialist* was under the direct control of the national Party organization, and, naturally, the various publications represented many views and tendencies. The most striking feature of the Socialist press of this period, however, is the emphasis, in the words of the *Appeal,* on the common goal of "tearing down the walls of capitalism."

After 1912 the number of Socialist periodicals declined, but not nearly as precipitously as Daniel Bell states and Ira Kipnis implies.[62] Among the more popular Socialist publications, circulation did not decline sharply from 1913 to 1917. The *Appeal* showed the greatest drop, from 761,747 to 529,132. The *National Rip Saw* maintained a steady 150,000 in these years, while the Milwaukee *Leader,* the New York *Call,* and the *American Socialist* gained circulation. (See Table 1.) Some important Socialist papers appeared as late as 1917. For example, the Seattle *Daily Call,* which was the first new English-language daily to appear since 1911; *The Messenger,* edited by A. Phillip Randolph, which claimed to be the first Negro Socialist publication in the world, and which attained a circulation of 33,000 by 1920; and *Advance,* the militantly socialist weekly organ of the newly organized Amalgamated Clothing Workers' Union.

Not faltering support, but the war and wartime suppression were the major cause of the disruption of the Socialist press. Within five months after war had been declared, every leading Socialist paper had been suspended from the mails at least once; some were barred for weeks on end, others permanently. Always on the brink financially, many Socialist papers succumbed to this government pressure.[63] In the small towns and cities, local bankers and businessmen, the most zealous "patriots," added to the difficulties of Socialist publications.[64] Since in these areas Socialist papers were particularly dependent on the mails, the combination of hostile forces was too great, and the vast majority of these papers collapsed in late 1917 or early 1918. Probably the greatest single loss to the anti-war Socialists occurred in December of 1917, when, following President Wilson's espousal of the Socialist demands, "no annexations, no indemnities," the *Appeal* came out in support of the Administration.[65] By the middle of 1918, the Socialist press consisted almost entirely of periodicals published in the larger cities and not dependent on the mails for their circulation. Nevertheless, papers like the New York *Call,* the Milwaukee *Leader,* and the Miami *Valley Socialist* had held their own or increased their circulation in these years, despite all the harassment they had to endure.

If 1912 represented the high point of the Socialist movement in any area, it was in electoral strength; for in that year Debs polled 6 per cent of the total presidential vote, a figure never again equaled by a Socialist candidate. In 1912, also, Socialists held their greatest number of offices—some 1,200 in 340 municipalities from coast to coast, among them 79 mayors in 24 states. (See Table 2.) A contemporary commented that these Socialist successes represented, on the whole, "a liberal and progressive type of socialism" which was "one phase of the progressive movement" then sweeping the country.[66]

It is also true that many local Socialist successes were the result of the need for reform. Indeed, on a municipal level, Socialist administrations could attempt little more. They could certainly not bring socialism to Red Cloud, Nebraska, while the rest of the country remained capitalist. And yet the reform programs caused much questioning of the socialist integrity of these administrations.[67] In part this criticism was valid, for many Socialists in office were indistinguishable from Left progressives.[68] But in the election campaigns, Left Socialists were indistinguishable from Right; both advocated reform.[69]

The prominence of municipal reform issues in these local Socialist victories explains in part the decline that followed. For in the next few years, reformers were especially active in municipal politics, primarily in the commission and city manager movements which swept the country after the adoption of the commission by Des Moines in 1907 and the manager plan by Dayton, Ohio, in 1912. Designed to rationalize city government and to enable municipalities to meet some of their more pressing social needs, these plans were the adaptation, under the guiding hand of local chambers of commerce, of corporate methods to city government. For the first time, in hundreds of cities throughout the United States, organized business threw its support behind civic reformers, adopted programs that differed little from those of the Socialists, and carried the day for reform.[70]

However, although in the face of Wilsonian progressivism Socialist electoral strength declined generally after 1912, the drop was not nearly so sharp as the decline in the presidential vote from 1912 to 1916 would indicate. The drop in 1916 was the result of many things. Wilson's campaign as the man who "kept us out of war" presented the classic problem to minority-party supporters: whether to support the Party in whose principles they believed or to use their votes to achieve an immediate practical goal. Many chose the latter alternative. Of equal importance was the fact that for the first time Debs was not the Socialist candidate. Instead a

316 / JAMES WEINSTEIN

relative unknown, Allan Benson, led the Party ticket; and he waged
a very weak campaign, running from 10 to 20 per cent behind the
ticket in many states.[71] Of less importance was the disillusionment
among Socialists over the support given the war by European Socialists.

In the cities, the upsurge of the commission and manager movements, the use of fusion against successful Socialists, and the frequent inability of the Socialists to deliver all they had promised—
usually because of charter limitations—led to a sharp decline in
the number of Socialist officials elected after 1912. In many places,
however, the Socialist vote increased while the number of officials
elected went down. In Dayton, Ohio, for example, the Socialists
received 25 per cent of the vote in 1911 and elected two councilmen and three assessors. In 1913, after the adoption of the manager plan, the Socialists received 35 per cent and elected no one.
In 1917 they received 44 per cent, again electing no candidates.[72]
In Hamilton, Ohio, the Socialists elected a mayor in 1913 in a
three-way race, but lost to fusion in 1915 and 1917 despite an
increase in their vote in each of these years.[73]

In the face of the general decline, in fact, there were some significant electoral gains in the years from 1912 to 1917. The number
of Socialist state legislators increased from twenty-two in 1912 to
thirty in 1918. (See Table 3.) In 1914 the second Socialist congressman, Meyer London, was elected from New York's East Side.
In 1916 the Socialists captured the mayoralty of Minneapolis,
second largest city ever to elect a Socialist mayor.

After the low Socialist vote in 1916, *The Nation,* in recognition
of the specific factors involved, commented that "the future of the
Socialist party should not be predicated from its showing in
the last election."[74] Only a few months later, America entered the
war, and soon after, the world entered a new era of revolution.
Caught up in this stormy course, the Socialist Party was in the end
to emerge shattered and torn, but at least during the first year of
war the Party made the comeback at the polls that *The Nation*
had prophesied.

Three days after the United States declared war on Germany,
the Socialist Emergency Convention in St. Louis overwhelmingly
condemned the declaration as "a crime against the people of the
United States." The St. Louis Resolution called on the "workers

of all countries to refuse to support their governments" in the war, and promised "continuous, active and public opposition to the war" and to conscription. Written jointly by C. E. Ruthenberg, Algernon Lee, and Morris Hillquit, the resolution symbolized a new unity of Left and Right. The sharply class-conscious tone of the resolution reflected the increased strength of the new left wing which had grown up since 1913, as did the almost unanimous vote to repeal the anti-sabotage clause which had been adopted in 1912.[75]

During the spring and summer of 1917, Party members distributed a million copies of the St. Louis Resolution, and in many states Socialists were "in evidence almost everywhere," speaking against the war and against conscription.[76] A few months later, during the fall of 1917, this activity reached a climax.

In the municipal election campaigns that fall, Socialists demanded the calling for immediate peace negotiations and announced that they would not buy Liberty bonds. On this program, the Party greatly increased its vote over 1916, and, in many places, over its previous high.[77] (See Table 2.) Paul H. Douglas estimated that the Socialist vote in 1917, if projected on a national scale, would have totaled four million.[78] The most striking aspect of these elections was the great increase in the Socialist vote in the larger cities where Socialists had previously had little strength: New York, Chicago, Cleveland, and Cincinnati, for example. In the smaller cities and towns, where the percentage of foreign-born was negligible, Socialists ran equally well. Each of the five municipalities to elect Socialist mayors that fall had fewer than fifteen thousand inhabitants.[79] Again in 1918, in those places where Socialists could still conduct campaigns, they continued to run unusually well. In April Victor Berger received 110,487 votes (26 per cent) for senator from Wisconsin, better than four times the 1916 Socialist vote in that state. In November Berger finally won reelection to Congress, while the number of Socialist state legislators increased from thirteen to twenty-three.[80] (See Table 3.) In Minnesota the formation of the Farmer-Labor Party cut heavily into the Socialists' gubernatorial vote in 1918, but four Socialists were elected to the legislature, more than ever before. In Minneapolis, Thomas Van Lear was narrowly defeated for reelection in a campaign of unprecedented slander, but the Party increased its number of aldermen from four to seven.[81] And in Davenport, Iowa, the Socialists almost elected a mayor.[82]

The Socialist vote in 1917 and 1918 indicates that the Party's position on the war did not isolate it from the American people, and that the Party was capable of effective action even in the face of unprecedented attack and intimidation. This was so at least in the cities, where Socialists were not isolated or dependent on the mails. After 1918 the Party was rent from within over the question of whether or not to adopt Soviet tactics in the United States. At the same time, harassment continued unabated. And yet in 1920, with little organization remaining, Debs polled 923,000 votes. This, in the year of reaction, is usually considered purely a personal triumph for Debs.[83] But it is also possible that war-weary and disillusioned Americans remembered that the Socialist Party had been the only party to oppose war.

By the end of the war, it is true, American socialism was beset with many problems. Yet, at the same time, the movement had survived the severe wartime buffeting and faced a situation not without opportunity. Before the war, Wilsonian progressivism had made some inroads on the fringes of socialism, particularly among intellectuals and among labor leaders. Despite Wilson's espousal of the Fourteen Points, however, the war and the peace that followed stripped the mask of liberalism from his administration. The wartime attacks on the Party greatly weakened its press; but Socialist opposition to the war received substantial popular support in the cities, and in the rural areas of such states as Minnesota, Oklahoma, and Nevada,[84] during the war, Party membership increased considerably.[85] Throughout the period from 1912 to 1918, the Socialists had probably gained strength among women and among Negroes. In the labor movement, despite losses to Wilsonian progressivism and wartime patriotism, the trend was mixed. The Party made significant gains among workers in these years in the garment trades, in the Pennsylvania Federation of Labor, and in the labor movements in Minneapolis and Milwaukee; and the post-war militancy of labor, which reached a high point in the AFL-sponsored steel strike of 1919, would have presented many opportunities to a united socialist movement. A revival, given unity, was not an unreasonable dream.

The trouble was, of course, that there was no unity. In September of 1919, the socialist movement split into three major parts, with many splinters falling aside. In the early part of 1919 there were 108,000 Socialist Party members; by the next year the combined membership of the three parties was 36,000.[86] The details of the split and the manner in which it influenced the course of socialist development in America cannot fully be discussed here. But it is important to point out that the breakup was not a result of long-standing tendencies inherent in the Socialist Party. Kipnis clearly implies that after 1912 the division was merely a matter of time, and that the final result was foreshadowed in 1915, with the formation of the Socialist Propaganda League.[87] Theodore Draper, however, writes that in the early years of the war the "new Left Wing" was so amorphous that it is best to think of it as a "haphazard collection of individuals, rather than as anything resembling an organized group."[88] Daniel Bell makes the further point that the left of 1918 "was completely unlike the left of 1912," and that the emergence of the New Left owed much to the presence in the United States of tens of thousands of Russian *émigrés,* among them Trotsky, Bukharin, and Madame Kollontay, in 1917.[89] In 1920 Morris Hillquit made a similar claim. He stated that the specific left wing which sprang up in 1918 "was entirely different in origin and character" from the pre-1917 Left. "It was not a legitimate reaction against undue conservatism in the party," but a "peculiar echo of the Russian Revolution, a quixotic attempt to duplicate it in the United States, to copy its methods, repeat its phrases, and imitate its leaders and heroes."[90]

Those who remained Socialists believed that the United States had emerged from the war "the strongest capitalist country in the world," and that prospects for revolution were dim because "the power of capitalism" had been "less shaken in the United States than in any of the advanced countries of Europe."[91] It was not over support of the Russian Revolution that the split had occurred, Hillquit wrote. For the Socialists always supported the Soviet government of Russia: "It is the government of the working class of Russia . . . a government which strives to abolish every remnant of capitalism and for that reason is being persecuted by every imperialistic and reactionary power on the face of the globe. The reasons that impel our government in Washington . . . to make war upon Russia, are exactly the same reasons that impel us, as Socialists, as working class representatives to support Soviet Russia in all of its struggles. But that does not mean, Comrades," Hillquit went on, "that we abdicate our own reason, forget the circumstances surrounding us, and blindly accept every formula, every dogma coming from Russia as holy, as a Papal decree. It also does not mean that . . . we accept for this country . . . the special institutions and forms into which struggles have been moulded by the historical conditions of Russia."[92]

That Hillquit had correctly stated the issue was confirmed by the Third International itself. In its reply, in 1921, to the request for affiliation, which the Socialist Party had made in 1920, the new International stated that it was "not a hotel" but an army in wartime; "volunteers who join the Army of Revolution . . . must adopt as their program the program of the Communist International—open and revolutionary mass-struggle for Communism through Dictatorship of the Proletariat, by means of the Worker's Soviets. . . . They must create a strongly centralized form of organization, a military discipline; all party members . . . must be absolutely subject to the full-powered Central Committee of the Party. . . . They must sever all connections with the petty bourgeoisie, and prepare for revolutionary action, for merciless civil war."[93]

At issue was the prospect of immediate revolution in the United States, and, consequently, the form which the movement should assume in post-war America. A similar issue had once before been important in the life of the Party: in 1912, when the anti-sabotage clause was adopted. The syndicalists believed that with the organization of the general strike the Cooperative Commonwealth would be at hand; while the Socialists believed that the revolution was not in the foreseeable future. Even after the syndicalists left the Party, differences in the estimate of the imminence of socialism remained; but these differences never crystallized, and would not have split the movement.

The Socialist Party had been a vital force in many areas of American life; it remained strong—although it fluctuated in its electoral strength—from 1912 to 1917. The weakening of the movement after 1918 resulted neither from conditions in the United States, nor simply from weaknesses inherent in the American movement, though there were many. The excitement and glamour of the Russian Revolution, combined with the Third International's policy of insisting on Russian-style Bolshevik parties, was the main ingredient in the split. At issue was whether or not the Americans would find their own road and their own timetable to socialism. Although the question was complicated by many other currents, it was on this rock that American socialism foundered.

TABLE 1

Socialist Periodicals 1912–1918[94]

y=publishing at the time
x=known to be out of business
d=daily; w=weekly; m=monthly; s=semi

State	City	Name	Founded	1913	1916	1917–18	Frequency
Alaska	Fairbanks	Alaska Socialist	1913	y	y	y	s-m
Ala.	Girard	Ala. Soc. Dem.	1914	–	y	x	w
Ariz.	Phoenix	Ariz. Soc. Bul.	?	?	y	y	w
Ark.	Clarendon	Monroe Co. Soc.	?	y	?	?	w
	Hot Springs	H. Springs Clarion	?	y	?	?	w
	Huntington	So. Worker	1901	y	y	800	m
	Jonesboro	Revolutionist	?	y	?	?	?
	Judsonia	White Co. Worker	?	y	?	?	w
	Little Rock	Pulaski Co. Soc.	?	y	?	?	?
	Pine Bluff	Jeff. Co. Agitator	?	y	?	?	w
	Rogers	People's Friend	1909	y	y	x	w
	Van Buren	Crawford Co. Star	?	y	?	?	w
Calif.	Fresno	Abarez (Armenian)	1908	y	y	1250	w
	Llano	Colonist	1916	–	y	y	w
	Los Angeles	Cal. Soc. Dem.	1911	11,600	y	4900	w
		Western Comrade	1913	y	5200	5200	w

State	City	Name	Founded	1913	1916	1917–18	Frequency
	Oakland	World	1905	4300	y	2500	w
Colo.	San Francisco	Vorwarts (German)	1910	y	y	y	w
	Denver	Colorado Worker	?	y	?	?	m
		World for the Workers	?	y	?	?	w
Conn.		Miners Magazine	1900	2750	2750	2750	w&m
	New Haven	Criterion	1917	–	–	y	w
	Waterbury	Weekly Worker	1915	–	y	x	w
Idaho	Moscow	The Palouser	?	y	?	?	?
Ill.	Canton	Socialist	1913	y	x	x	w
	Chicago	Amer. Socialist	1914	–	y	60,000	w
		Arbeiter (German)	1876	15,000	y	15,000	d
		Christian Soc.	1904	19,000	y	18,000	w&m
		Eritassard Hayastan (Armen.)	1904	y	y	5000	bi-w
		Eye Opener	1912	y	y	y	m
		Int. Soc. Review	1900	42,000	26,000	25,000	m
		Parola Proletaria (Italian)	1906	3000	y	4500	w
		Proletarec (Sloven)	1904	4250	y	3100	w
		Radnicka Straza (Cr)	1908	2700	y	y	w
		Revyen (Scand)	1894	5000	y	4500	w
		Rovhost Ludu (Slovak)	1907	5500	y	9500	w
		Spraredelust (Bohem)	1905	12,000	y	11,000	w
	Granite City	Svenska Soc. (Sw)	1905	3900	y	7000	w
	Moline	Tri-City Leader	1911	900	y	x	w
	Quincy	Rock Is. Co. Soc.	?	y	?	?	w

State	City	Newspaper	Year				
	Waukegan	*Quincy Socialist*	?	y	?	?	w
Ind.	Marion	*Free Press*	1910	y	y	x	w
	Valparaiso	*Econ. Intelligencer*	1913	y	x	x	w
Iowa	Albia	*Social Educator*	?	y	?	?	m
		Monroe Co. Leader	?	y	?	?	w
	Boone	*Boone Co. Searchlight*	?	y	?	?	w
	Cedar Rapids	*Linn Co. Searchlight*	?	y	?	?	w
	Centerville	*Voice of the Tailers*	?	y	?	?	w
	Charles City	*Floyd Co. Soc.*	?	y	?	?	w
	Clinton	*Clinton Co. Soc.*	?	y	y	y	w
		Merry War	1914(?)	-	y	(Rep.)	w
	Council Bluffs	*Council Bluffs Soc.*	?	y	y	y	w
	Davenport	*Scott Co. Soc.*	?	y	?	-	w
		Tribune	1918	-	-	y	w
	Grinnell	*Searchlight*	?	y	?	y	w
	Lyons	*Clinton Co. Soc.*	?	y	?	?	w
	Marshalltown	*Marshall Co. Tocsin*	?	y	?	?	w
	Mason City	*Cerro Gordo Leader*	1912	y	-	?	w
	Muscatine	*Muscatine Co. Soc.*	1913	y	y	-	w
	Ottumwa	*Ottumwa Referendum*	1912	y	-	?	w
	Perry	*Dallas Co. Worker*	?	y	?	-	w
	Waterloo	*Vanguard*	?	y	?	?	w
Kansas	Chanute	*Chanute Leader*	?	y	y	900	w
	Dexter	*Dispatch*	1905	850	y	y	w
	Girard	*Appeal to Reason*	1895	761,747	y	529,132	w
		Natl. Socialist	1912	35,000	-	-	m

State	City	Name	Founded	1913	1916	1917–18	Frequency
	Iola	Iola Co-operator	1912	200	–	–	w
	Lawrence	Prog. Herald	1911	y	–	–	w
	Leavenworth	Leavenworth Soc.	?	y	?	?	w
	Newton	Harvey Co. Searchlight	?	y	?	?	w
	Pittsburg	Workers' Chronicle	1911	y	y	y	w
	Pleasanton	Linn Co. Searchlight	?	y	?	?	w
	Salina	Salina Co. Soc.	?	y	?	?	w
	Sedan	News and Views	?	y	?	?	w
	Topeka	Shawnee Co. Soc.	1913	y	–	–	w
	Wichita	Socialist	1910	y	–	–	w
La.	New Orleans	Rebellion	1915(?)	–	y	?	?
	Shreveport	Southern Light	1912	y	–	–	w
Maine	Portland	The Issue	1911	2100	2000	2000	m
Mass.	Boston	Hairenik (Armen.)	1889	y	y	5000	w
		New International	1917	–	–	y	w&m
		Laisve (Lith.)	1911	5000	y	y	w
	Fitchburg	Leader	1912	y	y	11,000	w
		Raiveaja (Finn.)	1905	6500	y	10,000	bi-w
		Strahdneeks (Lett.)	1905	6500	y	13,000	
Mich.	Ann Arbor	Call	?	y	y	–	w
	Detroit	Michigan Socialist	?	?	y	y	?
	Flint	Flashes	?	y	(Ind.)	(Ind.)	w
	Grand Rapids	The Commonwealth	1918	–	–	y	m
	Hancock	Call	?	y	–	–	w
		Tyomes (Finnish)	1903	y	y	y	d

State	City	Paper	Year				Freq.
	Holland	*Prog. Worker*	1911	y	y	y	w
	Kalamazoo	*Billy Goat*	?	y	y	–	m
Minn.		*People's Paper*	1911	y	–	–	w
		People	1915	–	y	y	w
	Manistee	*Workers Advocate*	?	y	y	y	w
	Saginaw	*Socialist*	?	y	y	–	w
	Badger	*Herald Rustler*	1896	700	y	480	w
	Bemidji	*Examiner*	1911	1102	–	–	w
	Crookstown	*Eye Opener*	1911	y	–	–	w
	Duluth	*Socialisti* (Finn.)	1910	y	5243	y	d
		Labor Leader	1917			y	w
	Faribault	*Referendum*	1899	1400	y	y	w
	Minneapolis	*Forskaren* (Sw.)	1893	2500	y	y	m
		Gaa Paa (Nor.)	1904	4500	4000	4000	w
		Minn. Socialist	1910	y	–	–	w
		New Times	1910	y	y	y	w
		Rights of Man	1897	y	–	–	w
	Two Harbors	*Socialist*	1913	y	752	900	w
Mo.	Benton	*Scott Co. Kicker*	1902	1200	1200	1200	w
	Hyati	*Critic*	1912	4000	–	–	w
	Independence	*Soc. Democrat*	?	y	?	?	w
	Joplin	*Socialist*	1912	y	y	–	m
		The Question	?	?	?	?	w
	Kansas City	*Socialist*	?	y	?	y	w
	Kennett	*Justice*	?	y	–	?	w
	St. Joseph	*People's Appeal*	?	y	y	?	w

State	City	Name	Founded	1913	1916	1917–18	Frequency
	St. Louis	Natl. Rip Saw	1904	150,000	150,000	150,000	m
		Melting Pot	1913	y	y	y	m
		St. Louis Labor	1900	6000	6000	6000	w
		Arbeiter Zeitung	1898	3000	3000	3000	w
Mont.	Butte	Montana Soc.	?	y	y	?	w
	Helena	Montana News	1902	4000	–	–	w
	Sheridan	Forum	1911	y	y	y	w
Neb.	Byron	Advocate	1912	y	–	–	w
	Lincoln	Neb. Worker	1910	7000	y	11,391	m
Nev.	Ely	White Pine Worker	?	y	?	?	?
	Fallon	Ballot Box	1911	y	–	–	w
N. J.	Camden	Camden Co. Soc.	?	y	?	?	?
		Voice of Labor	1916(?)	–	y	y	w
	Dover	Morris Co. Educator	?	y	?	?	?
	Elizabeth	Issue	1911	y	2800	2800	w
	Gloucester	Gloucester Soc.	?	y	?	?	?
	Orange	Socialist	1911	300	–	–	w
	Paterson	Issue	1911	y	y	y	w
	W. Hoboken	Soc. Review	?	y	–	–	w
N. Y.	Brooklyn	Laisve (Lith.)	1911	y	14,850	14,850	w
	Buffalo	Arbeiter Zeitung	1886	7750	7500	7500	w
	Jamestown	New Age	1912	y	y	y	w
	New York	Free Press	1915	–	y	y	w
		Advance	1917	–	–	60,000	w
		Call	1909	22,200	y	23,003	d

State	City	Publication	Year				Freq.
		Elore (Hung.)	1900	9250	y	19,000	w
		Intercol. Socialist	1913	y	4000	4500	quart.
		Masses	1911	10,000	y	17,000	m
		New Review	1913	y	y	–	w, m, bi-m
		Messenger	1917	–	–	y	m
		Novy Mir	1910	y	14,000	14,415	d
		Obrana (Bohem)	1910	y	y	y	w
		The Class Struggle	1917	–	–	y	bi-m, quart.
		The Hotel Worker	1917	–	–	y	m
		The Fur Worker	1916	–	y	y	w
		Jewish Daily Forward	1897	142,000	130,000	198,000	d
		Pilot	1911	y	y	–	w
		Young Soc. Mag.	1908	y	y	y	m
		Zukunft	1892	69,000	69,000	69,000	m
	Schenectady	*Citizen*	1910	5000	5000	5000	w
	Utica	*Centr. N.Y. Soc.*	1911	925	–	–	w
N. D.	Devils Lake	*N.D. Call*	1911	y	–	–	w
	Milnor	*Sargent Co. Teller*	1883	750	750	(Rep.)	w
	Minot	*Iconoclast*	1912	y	y	–	w
Ohio	Akron	*Summit Co. Soc.*	1911	y	y	–	w
	Cleveland	*Citizen*	1891	y	12,000	13,000	w
		Socialist News	1911	y	1500	3000	w
	Columbus	*Socialist*	1910	y	y	–	w
	Conneaut	*Ashtabula Co. Advance*	1913	y	(Dem.)	–	w
	Dayton	*Miami Valley Soc.*	1912	y	2500	2400	w
	Hamilton	*Searchlight* (Soc.)	1910	y	y	y	w

State	City	Name	Founded	1913	1916	1917–18	Frequency
	Lorain	Lor. Co. Pol. Outlook	1912	y	–	–	w
	St. Marys	Socialist	1910	y	–	–	w
	Zanesville	Socialist	1911	y	–	–	w
Okla.	Alva	Constructive Soc.	1910	y	–	–	w
	Boswell	Submarine	1912	y	–	–	w
	Carter	Beckman Co. Advoc.	1913	y	y	y	w
	Goltry	News (Eagle)	1901	700	y	(Ind.)	w
	Hobart	Woodrow's Monthly	1915	–	y	–	m
	LaVerne	Beacon Light	1912	y	y	y	w
	May	Record	1911	(Prog.)	1400	y	w
	McAlester	Pitts. Co. Hornet	1911	y	–	y	w
	Okemah	Sledge Hammer	1912	y	y	–	w
	Okla. City	Social Democrat	1912	y	y	–	w
	Rosston	Review	1915	–	–	(Ind.)	w
	Shattuck	Ellis Co. Socialist	1914	–	y	y	w
	Snyder	Otter Valley Soc.	1914	–	y	y	w
	Strong City	Herald	1912	(Loc.)	y	600	w
	Sugden	Clarion	1911	y	–	–	w
	Sulphur	New Century	1911	2727	–	–	w
	Taloga	Times	1915	–	y	–	w
	Tishomingo	News	1913	y	y	y	w
	Okla. City	Oklahoma Leader	1914	–	y	y	w
Oreg.	Astoria	Oregon Ballet	1912	y	–	–	w
	Astoria	Toveri (Finnish)	1907	4548	4000	4000	d
	Milwaukee	Alliance	1912	2000	–	–	s-m

State	City	Publication	Year				
Penna.	Portland	*Voice of the People*	?	y	y	y	w
	Charleroi	*Union de Travailleurs*	1901	1500	1500	–	w
	Erie	*Truth*	1911	y	y	y	w
	Lancaster	*Lanc. Co. Socialist*	1911	y	–	–	w
	New Castle	*Free Press*	1908	y	–	–	w
	Oil City	*Venango Co. Soc.*	1910	y	y	y	w
	Philadelphia	*People's Press*	1915	–	2000	2000	w
		Socialist	1912	46,444	2000	2000	m
	Pittsburgh	*Gornik Polski*	1912	y	y	–	w
		Justice	1911	y	y	y	w
	Pottstown	*Social Educator*	1911	y	y	y	w
	Reading	*Labor Advocate*	1900	1500	1500	1500	w
	Rochester	*Saturday Journal*	1911	y	y	y	w
	Smitmill	*Pick and Plow*	1917(?)	–	–	y	w?
S. D.	Mitchell	*Co-Op Commonwealth*	1914	–	y	–	m
	Sisseton	*Co-Op Commonwealth*	1914	–	350	500	m
	Sturgis	*Call to Action*	1913	(Prog.)	y	y	s-m
Tenn.	Memphis	*Social Democrat*	1910	y	y	y	w
Texas	Anson	*Frying Pan*	1914	–	y	–	w
	Corpus Christi	*Socialist*	?	y	y	?	w
	Corsicana	*Plain Dealer*	?	y	?	?	w
	Dallas	*The Laborer*	1904	515	1350	1350	w
	Halletsville	*Rebel*	1911	26,145	25,000	25,000	w
	Hillsboro	*Hill Co. Worker*	?	y	y	–	w
	Longview	*Gregg Co. Red Ball*	?	y	?	?	w
	Marshall	*Harrison Co. Soc.*	?	y	?	?	w

State	City	Name	Founded	1913	1916	1917–18	Frequency
	Mt. Pleasant	Eye Opener	?	y	?	?	w
	San Antonio	Amigo del Pueblo	1908	y	y	–	w
	Taylor	Searchlight	?	y	?	?	w
	Teague	Freestone Co. Truth	?	y	?	?	w
	Temple	Bell Co. Socialist	?	y	?	?	w
	Terrell	Kaufman Co. Soc.	?	y	?	?	w
	Texarkana	Texarkana Soc.	?	y	?	?	m
	Thornton	Limestone Co. News	?	y	?	?	w
	Tyler	Common Sense	?	y	?	?	w
Utah	Myton	Dawn	1912	y	5000	5000	m
	Salt Lake City	Inter. Mt. Worker	1912	y	y	y	w
Vt.	Barre	Quarry Workers Journ.	1904	4500	4500	4500	m
Va.	Brookneal	Union Star	1906	y	3000	3147	w
Wash.	Aberdeen	New Era	?	y	?	?	?
	Centralia	Lewis Co. Clarion	1912	y	?	?	?
	Everett	No. West Worker	1911	4500	2400	2400	w
	Kelso	Socialist News	1911	y	y	y	w
	N. Yakima	No. West Forum	1905	y	–	–	w
	Seattle	Call	1917	–	–	y	d
		Herald	1912	y	5600	y	w
		Internatl. Weekly	1918	?	?	6000	w
		World	1916	–	y	y	w
	Tacoma	Truth	1912	y	?	?	?
W. Va.	Charleston	Labor Argus	1905	y	–	–	w
	Clarksburg	W. Va. Leader	?	y	?	?	?

Huntington	Soc. & Labor Star	?	y	?	?	?
Parkersburg	Socialist	1912	y	–	–	w
Wheeling	Majority	1907	7000	7000	7000	w
Milwaukee	Leader	1911	35,000	37,201	y	d
	Wisc. Comrade	1914	–	y	y	w&m
Superior	Tyomies (Finnish)	1903	y	12,131	y	d
Two Rivers	Reporter	1905	y	y	y	s-w

Wisc.

TABLE 2

Cities and Towns Electing Socialist Mayors or Other Major Municipal Officers, 1911–1920

State	City	State	City
	1911 (74)	New Jersey	Rockaway
Arkansas	Winslow	New York	Schenectady
California	Berkeley	North Dakota	Deslacs
	Watts	Ohio	Amsterdam
Colorado	Nederland		Ashtabula
	Victor		Barnhill
Idaho	Coeur d'Alene		Conneaut
Illinois	Davis		Fostoria
	Dorrisville		Lima
	Grafton		Linden Heights
	Granite City		Lorain
	O'Fallon		Martin's Ferry
	Thayer		Mineral City
Iowa	Madrid		Mineral Ridge
Kansas	Arma		Mount Vernon
	Curransville		Osnaburg
	Girard		St. Marys
Michigan	Flint		Salem
	Greenville		Sugar Grove
	Kalamazoo		Toronto
	South Frankfort	Oklahoma	Antlers
Minnesota	Wilson	Oregon	Coquille
	Crookstown	Pennsylvania	Broad Top
	LaPorte		Township
	Pillager		Hazeldell
	St. Hillaire		New Castle
	Ten Strike		North Versailles
Missouri	Two Harbors		Roulette
	Buffalo		Wheaton
	Cardwell	Utah	Cedar City
	Gibson		Eureka
Montana	Minden Mines		Mammoth
	Butte		Murray
	Beatrice		Stockton
Nebraska	Red Cloud	Washington	Edmonds
	Wymore		Tukwila

State	City	State	City
West Virginia	Star City		Hilyard
Wisconsin	Manitowoc	West Virginia	Hendricks
	Milwaukee (1910)		Star City
	West Salem	Wisconsin	Manitowoc

1912 (8)

1914 (5)

State	City	State	City
California	Daly City	Florida	Lakeworth
Florida	Gulfport	Montana	Missoula (2
Louisiana	Winnfield		Commissioners)
New Jersey	Haledon	New Jersey	Haledon
West Virginia	Adamston	West Virginia	Star City
	Miami	Wisconsin	Manitowoc
	Star City		

		State	City
Wisconsin	Manitowoc		

1913 (32)

1915 (22)

State	City	State	City
		Alabama	Birmingham
Arkansas	Chant		(Commissioner)
	Hartford	California	Eureka
Colorado	Buena Vista	Illinois	Canton
	Edgewater		Eagle River
	Grand Junction		Jerseyville
	Lafayette		Lincoln
	Longmont		Phelps
Connecticut	Naugatuck		Riverton
Illinois	Canton		Torrino
	Granite City	Indiana	Hymeria
Michigan	Harbor Springs		Clinton
Missouri	Liberal	Michigan	Gustin
Minnesota	Brainerd	Minnesota	Cloquet
	Crookstown	New York	Schenectady
	Eagle Bend	Ohio	Conneaut
Montana	Butte		Krebs
New Jersey	Haledon		Cleveland
North Dakota	Minot (1	Pennsylvania	Pitcairn
	Commissioner)		Williamsport
	Rugby		(Commissioner)
Ohio	Canal Dover	Virginia	Brookneal
	Conneaut	West Virginia	Star City
	Coshocton	Wisconsin	Manitowoc

1916 (6)

State	City	State	City
	Hamilton	Michigan	Traverse City
	Martins Ferry	Minnesota	Minneapolis
	Shelby	New Jersey	Haledon
	Talent	Vermont	Barre
South Dakota	Sisseton	Wisconsin	Milwaukee
Washington	Burlington		West Allis

State	City	State	City
	1917 (18)		Union City
Illinois	Buckner	Utah	Eureka
	Granite City	Washington	Camas
	Sylvis		**1918 (2)**
Indiana	Elwood	Illinois	Mascoutah
	Gas City	Wisconsin	Milwaukee
Kansas	Frontenac		**1919 (5)**
	Hillsboro	New York	Buffalo (High vote for Councilman-at-Large)
Minnesota	Duluth (Commissioner)		
	Dawson		Lackawanna
Ohio	Byesville	Ohio	Byesville
	Jenera		Massillon
	Piqua	Wisconsin	Sheboygan (assessor, municipal judge)
Pennsylvania	Garrett		**1920 (2)**
	McKeesport (Controller)	Iowa	Davenport
	Pitcairn	Wisconsin	Milwaukee

TABLE 3

Socialist State Legislators, 1910–1920

State	1910/11	1912/13	1914/15	1916/17	1918/19	1920/21
California	1	1	2			
Idaho			1			
Illinois		3	2			
Kansas		3	1	2		
Massachusetts		1	1	1	1	
Minnesota	1	1	3	2	4	2
Montana		1	3			
Nevada		2	2			
New Mexico			1			
New York	0/1		0/1	2/10	3/5	5
North Dakota	1					
Oklahoma			6	1		
Pennsylvania	1		1	1		
Rhode Island	0/1					
Utah			1	1		
Vermont				1		
Washington		1				
Wisconsin	13	7	9	10	22	10
TOTALS	19	20	34	29	32	17

NOTES

1. *Proceedings of the National Convention of the Socialist Party of America* (1912), p. 302.

2. Membership records of the Socialist Party, 1912 through 1915, (Socialist Party Collection, Duke University).

3. Ira Kipnis, *The American Socialist Movement: 1897–1912* (New York, 1952); Daniel Bell, "The Background and Development of Marxian Socialism in the United States," in Donald D. Egbert and Stow Persons (eds.), *Socialism and American Life* (Princeton, 1952), pp. 216–17.

4. American Federation of Labor, *Report of the Proceedings of the National Convention*, XXXII (1912), p. 374.

5. Kipnis, op. cit., pp. 418–19.

6. "The I.W.W. and the Socialist Party," Information Department, The Socialist Party, January 13, 1915; see also *Christian Socialist*, May 16, 1911, for the Christian Socialist Fellowship endorsement of industrialism, and *Rebel*, May 16, 1914, for the endorsement of the Texas party of industrialism.

7. Marc Karson, *American Labor Unions and Politics, 1900–1918* (Carbondale, 1958), p. 243. See Chapter 9 for a revealing discussion of the role of the Catholic Church in combating socialism in the AFL.

8. Ibid., p. 131. As for Kipnis' contention about Socialist Party contributions to strikes, it can only be said that he is mistaken. In 1912 the Party did contribute about $21,000 to various strikes, including $18,630.97 to the IWW strikers at Lawrence, and $307.25 to the IWW Timber Workers in Louisiana. However, in 1913 and 1914 the Information Department of the Party reported contributions of approximately $40,000, including $30,912.45 to the Western Federation of Miners copper strikers at Calumet, Michigan, and $8,515.96 to the United Mine Workers strikers in Colorado. Reported by Conrad F. Nystrom, "Socialist Corner," Galesburg (Ill.) *Labor News*, June 25, 1915. I have found no other records of contributions. See also *The Appeal Almanac and Arsenal of Facts for 1915* (Girard, Kan., 1915), p. 62, which gives a figure of $33,500 for 1913–14.

9. *Machinists Monthly Journal*, XXVIII (November 1916), p. 1124, XXVIII (December 1916).

10. Report of President Charles H. Moyer, *Official Proceedings of the Twenty-Second Consecutive and Second Biennial Convention of the Western Federation of Miners* (Great Falls, Mont., July 17–29, 1916), p. 39.

11. *Miners' Magazine*, December 1916.

12. *International Socialist Review*, XIV, 1 (July 1913), p. 40.

13. *Quincy Labor News*, October 25, 1913, July 23, 1915.

14. Kipnis, op. cit., p. 419; *Report of Proceedings of the Thirty-*

Fifth Annual Convention of the American Federation of Labor (1915), p. 299.

15. Duluth *Labor World,* November 11, 1916.

16. *Appeal to Reason,* April 28, 1917; *Rebel,* April 4, 1917. Schieldknecht won a majority of the votes, receiving 460 votes to 422 for his opponent. Although the Santa Fe allowed Schieldknecht to campaign, he was fired for winning the election.

17. For a contrary view, that the crucial period in the decline of socialist influence in the trade union movement took place *before* the war, see the six case studies of socialist trade unionism analyzed by John H. M. Laslett in his *Labor and the Left: A Study of Socialist and Radical Influences in the American Labor Movement, 1881–1924* (New York: Basic Books, 1970), *passim.*

18. Bell, op. cit., p. 328.

19. Karson, op. cit., pp. 92–94.

20. *Quarry Workers Journal,* April 1917–December 1918.

21. Cleveland *Citizen,* April 1917–December 1918.

22. *Proceedings of the Twenty-First Convention of the International Union of United Brewery and Soft Drink Workers of America* (Houston, Tex., December 3–13, 1917), pp. 59–60.

23. *Advance,* April 20, May 18, November 2, November 9, 1917. On April 20 the paper reprinted the entire St. Louis Manifesto.

24. *Ladies' Garment Worker,* November, December 1917.

25. Reading *News-Times,* November 5, 1917.

26. Maurer, op. cit., pp. 228–30.

27. Quoted in Galesburg *Labor News,* June 7, 1918.

28. *Ohio Socialist,* January 22, 1919. The *Ohio Socialist* at this time was the organ of the left-winger Charles E. Ruthenberg. The reference to MacDonald as a loyal Socialist indicates that he not only remained in the Party but also supported its anti-war stand.

29. Illinois Federation of Labor, *Proceedings: Thirty-Seventh Annual Convention,* October 20–25, 1919 (Peoria, Ill., n.d.), pp. 29–30.

30. "Woman and Socialism," *Yale Review* (April 1914), p. 459.

31. R. C. Dorr, *What Eight Million Women Want* (Boston: Small, Maynard and Co., 1910), pp. 70ff.; Walling, *Socialism,* ch. XIX, pt. II.

32. Quoted in *The Socialist Woman,* December 1908.

33. Dorothy Rose Blumberg, "Florence Kelley: Revolutionary Reformer," *Monthly Review* (November 1959), pp. 234–42; *Crisis* (October 1914), p. 292; Margaret Sanger, *An Autobiography,* pp. 75–78, 265.

34. Kipnis, op. cit., p. 378; *Socialist Party Monthly Bulletin,* January 1912; *American Socialist,* May 27, 1916.

35. Miami *Valley Socialist,* November 13, 1914; *Annual Report of Secretary of State of Nevada* (1913–14), p. 48.

36. New York *Call,* September, October 1917, *passim.*

37. Rochester *Herald,* November 7, 1917.

38. Kipnis, op. cit., pp. 130ff.; David A. Shannon, *The Socialist Party of America: A History* (New York, 1955), p. 52.

39. Kipnis, op. cit., pp. 278, 286.
40. Kipnis, op. cit., p. 134; *The Weekly Industrial Worker,* September 19, 1919; *The Messenger,* September, November 1919. Haywood was a consistent foe of racism and anti-alienism.
41. Quoted in Kipnis, op. cit., p. 133.
42. Shannon, op. cit., p. 53; *Crisis* (August 1914), pp. 184–88; Walling, Russell, and Florence Kelley were members of the Board of Directors of the NAACP in 1915. *Crisis* (April 1915), p. 308.
43. Shannon, op. cit., p. 53; *New Review,* February 1, 1913.
44. *Crisis* (August 1914), p. 195, (October 1916), p. 268.
45. Kipnis, op. cit., pp. 132–33.
46. Walling, op. cit., p. 505.
47. In terms of Socialist votes, Florida ranked third in 1916, ninth in 1912. Texas ranked ninth in 1916. Several towns in Arkansas and Louisiana elected Socialist mayors in 1911 and 1912.
48. Kipnis, op. cit., pp. 211–12; *Socialist Congressional Campaign Book* (1914), p. 15; *The Messenger,* I (December 1917), pp. 18–19.
49. Charles Forcey, *The Crossroads of Liberalism* (New York, 1961), p. 169.
50. Ibid., p. 286; Charles Forcey, "Intellectuals in Crisis: Croly, Weyl, Lippmann and the New Republic" (Unpublished Ph.D. Dissertation, University of Wisconsin, 1954), pp. 308, 586. Mrs. Weyl joined the Socialist Party in 1920, shortly after her husband's death.
51. Letter from Beard to the *Intercollegiate Socialist,* I, 2 (Spring–Summer 1913), p. 3.
52. Kipnis, op. cit., pp. 259–60; Shannon, op. cit., pp. 55–56; *Intercollegiate Socialist,* I, 1 (February–March 1913), p. 2, III (April–May 1915), pp. 3–4; ISS letterheads, various dates, 1915–18 (J. G. Phelps Stokes Papers, Columbia University). In April 1917 there were seventy college chapters.
53. Harry W. Laidler to Stokes, New York, November 28, 1917 (Stokes Papers). In August 1917 ISS chapters had been reduced to sixty. By December 1917 there were thirty-eight; by August 1918, forty-two.
54. A survey of 580 members of the ISS, made in 1918, showed that 209 were Socialists, 210 non-Socialists, and 35 "anti-Socialist." *Intercollegiate Socialist,* VI, 3 (February–March 1918), p. 21.
55. William Hard, "Making Steel and Killing Men," *Everybody's Magazine,* XVII (November 1907), pp. 579–96. Reprinted in Arthur and Lila Weinberg (eds.), *The Muckrakers, 1902–12* (New York, 1961), p. 353.
56. See, for example, Lincoln Steffens' comments in his autobiography (New York, 1931), p. 434; Ray S. Baker, *American Chronicle* (New York, 1945), pp. 185, 434; Ida M. Tarbell, *The History of the Standard Oil Company* (New York, 1904), II, pp. 288ff.; Frederick C. Howe, *Confessions of a Reformer* (New York, 1925), pp. 176–81; Fremont Older, *My Own Story* (New York, 1926), pp. 339–40.

57. Louis Filler, *Crusaders for American Liberalism* (Yellow Springs, Ohio, 1939), p. 124.

58. Charles Edward Russell, *Why I Am a Socialist* (New York, 1910), pp. 298–301 and *passim*.

59. Upton Sinclair, "What Life Means to Me," *Cosmopolitan*, XLI (October 1906), pp. 591–601.

60. See letters from F. G. R. Gordon, an ex-Socialist and self-styled "industrial expert," to Harry Payne Whitney, Theodore Roosevelt, and a number of the larger companies, such as Hudson Motor Company, Campbell Soup Company, that advertised in the *Metropolitan Magazine*. Gordon tells these manufacturers of the alleged support given socialism by *Metropolitan Magazine*, and urges them to review their policy of advertising therein, since an application of these policies would lead to confiscation of the companies' property (Box 82, NCF papers, March, April 1915). In reply, the president of the Beech-Nut Packing Company promised to "study much more carefully the editorial policy of the *Metropolitan Magazine* in the future," and blamed his past advertising on the advertising agency (Bartlett Arkell to F. G. R. Gordon, Canajoharie, New York, April 29, 1915, loc. cit.).

61. N. W. Ayer, *Directory*, 1914.

62. Bell, op. cit., p. 309; Kipnis, op. cit., ch. XIX.

63. H. C. Peterson and Gilbert Fite, *Opponents of War* (Madison, University of Wisconsin Press, 1957), ch. IX; Lindsay Rogers, "Freedom of the Press in the United States," *Living Age* (September 28, 1918), p. 770; *Current Opinion* (November 1917), p. 293.

64. Peterson and Fite, op. cit., p. 45.

65. *Appeal to Reason*, December 14, 1917.

66. *National Municipal Review*, I (1912), pp. 492ff.; Grady McWhiney, "The Socialist Vote in Louisiana, 1912" (Unpublished M.A. Thesis, Louisiana State University, 1951), p. 6; *International Socialist Review* (June 1913), p. 854; quote from R. F. Hoxie, in NMR, I (1912), p. 500.

67. See, for example, W. E. Walling, *Socialism As It Is* (New York: Macmillan, 1916), pp. 181–85; Kipnis, op. cit., p. 363, describes how Walter Lippmann attacked the Socialist administration in Schenectady for being merely reformist.

68. See Ira B. Cross, "Socialism in California Municipalities," *National Municipal Review*, I (1912).

69. In 1912 Charles E. Ruthenberg, Ohio left-wing leader, acknowledged that "It was upon municipal reform issues that most of the Ohio victories were won" (New York *Call*, July 30, 1912, quoted in Theodore Draper, *The Roots of American Communism* [New York: Viking, 1957], p. 44). Draper makes the point, which was particularly true in this period, that the left wing was mainly a factor in the inner life of the Party; as soon as the Left went outside the Party to ask for broad popular support, it became almost indistinguishable from the Right.

70. This material is taken from a paper on the commission and city manager governments in preparation by the author.

71. See Shannon, op. cit., p. 91. Benson ran 50 per cent behind the congressional vote in Oregon; 40 per cent behind the senatorial vote in North Dakota; 35 per cent behind in Massachusetts; 33 per cent behind in New York; 25 per cent behind in New Jersey; 5 per cent in Pennsylvania. He ran 30 per cent behind the candidate for governor in Minnesota and 10 per cent behind in Wisconsin. In Tennessee he ran 50 per cent behind the Socialist candidate for railroad commissioner, and in Nevada he ran 200 per cent behind the candidate for senator, who received 30 per cent of the total. Illinois was the major exception to this trend. There Benson ran ahead by 9,000 votes (15 per cent).

72. William C. Seyler, "The Rise and Decline of the Socialist Party in the United States" (Unpublished Ph.D. Dissertation, Duke University, 1952), p. 237, quotes a letter from Joseph Sharts, editor of the Miami *Valley Socialist*, dated November 14, 1913. For 1917 see Dayton *News*, November 7, 1917.

73. Miami *Valley Socialist*, November 12, 1915; Hamilton *Evening Journal*, November 8, 1917.

74. *The Nation*, January 18, 1917, pp. 65–66.

75. *International Socialist Review* (May 1917), pp. 670ff.; Leslie Marcy, "The Emergency National Convention," ibid., p. 669.

76. *Revolutionary Radicalism*, pt. I, vol. I, pp. 545–46; Dayton *News*, August 18, 1917.

77. James Weinstein, "Anti-War Sentiment and the Socialist Party," *Political Science Quarterly*, 74 (June 1959), pp. 227, 231, 232–34.

78. "The Socialist Vote in the 1917 Municipal Elections," *National Municipal Review* (March 1918), p. 138.

79. Weinstein, op. cit.

80. Ibid., pp. 236–37; Milwaukee *Journal*, April 10, 1918; Milwaukee *Leader*, November 6, 1918.

81. Weinstein, op. cit., pp. 237–38; Peterson and Fite, op. cit., pp. 189–91, gives a picture of the 1918 campaign in Minnesota, although it deals with Charles A. Lindbergh, rather than Van Lear; Minneapolis *Journal*, June 15, 1918, June 19, 23, 1918, November 7, 8, 9, 13, 1918.

82. Milwaukee *Leader*, April 12, 1918. In Davenport the Socialist vote jumped from 423 to over 3,300. Two Socialist aldermen, of six, were elected. The Socialists' mayoral candidate lost by 28 votes. In Muscatine, Iowa, the Socialists lost by 215 votes. In Kalamazoo, Michigan, they elected three of seven commissioners, and in Grand Rapids they elected two councilmen, for the first time. *New Age* (Buffalo), May 4, 18, 1918.

83. Kipnis, op. cit., p. 429; Bell, op. cit., pp. 320, 429.

84. Weinstein, op. cit., pp. 218–21. In Nevada, in 1916, the Socialist candidate for governor received almost 30 per cent of the vote; during

the war a Socialist came within a few votes of election as county clerk. Peterson and Fite, op. cit., p. 161.

85. Bell, op. cit., p. 314.

86. Theodore Draper, *The Roots of American Communism* (New York, 1957), p. 207; Shannon, op. cit., p. 158.

87. Kipnis, op. cit., p. 420.

88. Draper, op. cit., p. 57.

89. Bell, op. cit., p. 320.

90. "Radicalism in America," *Socialist World*, October 15, 1920.

91. Letter from Hillquit to New York *Call*, May 21, 1919, quoted in *Revolutionary Radicalism*, I, p. 529.

92. Morris Hillquit, "Dictatorship and the International," *Socialist World*, August 1920.

93. Quoted in *Socialist World*, May 15, 1921, p. 8.

94. It would be almost impossible to annotate each periodical listed here, since there were many sources, and some publications had to be traced and verified through several, each of which produced a part of the information included in a particular listing. The major source was *N. W. Ayer's American Newspaper Annual and Directory* for the years 1914, 1917, and 1918. *Ayer's Annual* lists a very large proportion of all the newspapers and magazines published in the United States and gives information which includes the year of original publication, frequency of publication, circulation (where available), political affiliation, and names of editor and publisher.

COMMENT

Gerald Friedberg*

During World War I the Socialist Party of America reached a decisive turning point, yet this period of party history has received only superficial attention from students of the movement. The one scholar who has studied the SP during these years systematically

* Ten years ago when I wrote this piece, which originally appeared in *Studies on the Left*, IV, 3 (Summer 1964), pp. 79–98, I felt 1) that James Weinstein was wrong and I was right, and 2) that it was important to argue the point. Now I believe neither of those things.

James Weinstein and I were both right. He was intent upon showing how foreign-dominated Bolshevism undermined the more indigenous elements in the Socialist Party—an important and sad point. So he focused upon the extent to which the Socialist Party maintained its character and strength before 1919, and changed only with the Communist-Socialist split. I was intent upon showing how and why the Socialist movement always had been relatively weak in the United States, foreign to and rejected by this country's classical liberal politics—another important and sad point. So I focused upon the extent to which the Socialist Party gained strength as it became more moderate and more "American" before 1914, then lost headway as it became increasingly foreign and radical during World War I. Both of us were right, just getting at and focusing on different aspects of socialism's relative weakness and decline in this country. Each of us was wrong, of course, in attempting to make his point as *the* right one, and thereby exaggerating it.

More important, the *incredible* amount of time, energy, and ink spent trying to prove this argument right and the other wrong seems to me to have been, in good part, a sad waste. I was chiefly concerned with radical personal and social change, and became caught up in arguing about the past, as if historical perspective can define a stance for today. But conditions have changed, historical wisdom for the present never gets proved, and most important, I've not seen such historical argument have half the effect upon anyone's life as the more difficult exercise of paying full attention to the present. For me, it is more and more important to refocus those great amounts of time and energy upon radically reshaping my own life and upon connecting social and personal change in the now. And this personal/ social revolution includes moving away from rather than more deeply into the argue-prove-put-down syndrome, itself a rotten part of our classical liberal heritage.

Since some may be genuinely interested, I'm consenting to have my original piece republished here, unrevised. I only ask that the reader, as he explores the debate, ask of himself, in relation to his present experience, "So what?"

and in depth, James Weinstein, has unfortunately obscured, where he has not denied, the most striking and most important developments of this period.[1]

Weinstein argues that "there were no issues dividing the Socialist party that arose from the American experience," that right-left divisions within the party were minimal, that the war position emerging from the SP convention of 1917 reflected "genuine consensus of party opinion" and that, "In general, in the years from 1912 to 1917, Socialist strength and organization seem to have remained fairly stable." Weinstein's point: "Ironically, it was only after the first successful Socialist revolution [November 1917] . . . that the American movement changed decisively and disintegrated from its previous position as a significant indigenous movement."[2]

This position is both misleading and mistaken. As the evidence which follows indicates, 1) there were deep and continuous right-left divisions before, during, and after the war, 2) the SP lost strength markedly during the war, 3) the party—most important and almost completely omitted by Weinstein—changed both in position and composition, 1914–18, and 4) the change and disintegration following the Bolshevik revolution did not derive suddenly from that event, but were the culmination of a steady and striking development beginning in 1914. My concluding remarks will suggest briefly how the fortunes of the SP during these years are related to the more general reasons for the failure of Socialism in America.

I. *Right Versus Left*

The issues most prominent prior to World War I in dividing right from left within the SP were emphasis upon immediate reform versus emphasis upon ultimate revolutionary goals, noninterference in intra-labor movement struggle versus official SP support of the newer industrial unionism against the AFL majority, flexibility versus doctrinal purity, and peaceful parliamentary and economic tactics versus sabotage, the general strike, lawlessness, and violence.[3] A two-thirds majority of "opportunists" on the right and center successfully repelled left wing "impossibilist" attempts to secure exclusion of immediate (reform) demands from the party platform and to commit the party to industrial unionism.

In 1912–13, the "yellow" majority pushed through an amendment to the party constitution, Section 6, providing for expulsion of any SP member opposing political action or advocating violence or sabotage. The most prominent "red" leader, William D. Haywood, was then recalled from the party Executive for violation of that amendment, and a left wing exodus from the party followed. By 1914, the "reds," one-third of the party before that year, were less than one-fourth of total SP membership.

The sudden chaos of World War I brought new intensity to old divisions. With the union issue temporarily in the background, left and right battled again over reform versus revolution, peaceful versus direct action, and doctrinal and organizational purity versus flexibility. The left brought forth once more the general strike (now to prevent war), insisted that capitalist national struggles must give way to worldwide revolution, developed a pseudo-Marxian creed of indifference to capitalist national conflicts, and demanded party discipline to force adherence to the dogma. The right and center at first managed only to continue their former position, asserting only the usual democratic-socialist reforms along with "no annexations, no indemnities" peace terms. The sudden nationalism of the European Socialists was rationalized or ignored, while the outraged left uttered bitter condemnation. As the radical left in Europe gained strength and asserted itself, the left in America responded swiftly and enthusiastically, while the right and center dragged their heels. When the party finally held an Emergency Convention at St. Louis in April 1917 it was faced with the one day old fact of war, and was permeated by frustration, bitterness, and intolerance.

Ohio, which had led the left in 1912, led it once more in 1917, followed closely by Illinois, Washington, and Michigan, also states of the 1912 left. They were joined by the eastern European language federations, which represented the most striking development on the left during the war: the decline in indigenous elements and rise in foreign radicalism. The right, as before the war, was led by California, Connecticut, New Jersey, and Wisconsin.[4] The left declared that the worker had no country and opposed all war efforts; the center admitted the possibility of Socialist interest in the outcome of capitalist wars, but agreed with the left on indifference to the present war; and the right agreed with the center on the possibility of Socialist interest, and found such interest in the outcome of the European conflict.

The compromise proclamation which emerged after four days and nights of bitter wrangling condemned the war virulently, and called for "all mass movements in opposition to conscription" and for "continuous, active, and public opposition to the war through . . . all other means within our power." The more extreme phrases of the report closely approached, if they did not arrive at, a worker-has-no-country theoretical position, a rejection of defensive as well as offensive wars, and a call for the general strike. The net result of the convention was a victory for the left which alienated the right and saw the center ill-satisfied with the proclamation's extremism. Hillquit was displeased and upset, but determined to live with the center-left differences and the left's gains for the sake of unity on some anti-war position.

The shaky left-center alliance was sustained in 1917 in mutual anti-war spirit, and in 1918 in mutual desire to protect the Russian revolution. But the "reds," rallying more enthusiastically to the Leninist concept of elite-led and violent dictatorship of the proletariat, became increasingly restive in viewing the center's extremes of new-found patriotism and its violations of the letter and spirit of the St. Louis proclamation. The end of the war marked the end of whatever unanimity had existed.

Again, the continuity of issues into 1919 was clear. The left viewed with disgust the center's emphasis upon reform in the 1918 campaign and opposed to it a revolution to parallel European upheaval. The left fiercely reasserted its pre-war insistence that immediate demands be dropped completely from the party platform. If the center was squeamish about violence and about dictatorship (the single new issue) and was still attached wistfully to democratic parliamentary methods, the "reds" were not so constrained. Militancy and doctrinal purity once again became fetishes of the left while the center sought a more flexible approach to social revolution. In addition to continuity of issues, and, more important than continuity of individuals and publications,[5] areas of left and right strength were continuous with those of 1912 and 1917. Ohio, Michigan, Illinois, Washington, and the eastern European language federations once again led the "reds," this time into the Communist party. The major development of the left continued to be loss of strength in areas of indigenous radicalism, such as Texas and Minnesota, and growth of foreign radicalism, particularly in New York, Michigan, Illinois, Massachusetts, and Ohio.

In leaders and publications and, far more important, in fundamental issues and areas of strength, right-left divisions were deep and continuous before, during, and after World War I.

II. *SP Strength, 1914–18*

The SP's decline during the war was swift and dramatic.[6] From over 100,000 average monthly membership during the first eight months of 1914, party rolls fell to 93,589 for the full year, then to 79,374 for 1915. The presidential campaign of 1916 brought membership to 83,539 for that year, still 29% below the 1912 average. Voting statistics told the same story. The SP presidential vote fell in 1916 to over 33% below the 1912 total, and from nearly 6% of the popular vote to 3.2%. It took no oracular vision for party leader Victor Berger to see, as early as October 1915, that, "The National party is in a bad way and is sliding down rapidly."[7]

1917 brought some encouragement. In 15 major cities the SP vote increased to four times its previous strength. With the country at war, the party suddenly became the only vehicle for electoral expression of anti-war sentiment and other protest. The 1917 campaigns correspondingly lacked all the usual Marxian analysis and propaganda, emphasized peace and school lunches instead, and converted few to Socialism.[8] The *Appeal to Reason,* which reported over 3,000 Socialists holding public office at the end of 1912, down to 475 in 1915, now reported victories "in only a few of the more important cities."[9] Meanwhile, party membership continued to decline to 80,379 in 1917 and then to 74,519 in 1918. Membership had fallen over 25% during the war, and was down 40% from the 1912 total.

Socialist strength in the labor movement also declined during the war. Before 1914, Socialist influence was considerable and growing among some of the largest and most powerful unions, but few of these followed the SP on its leftward course during the war. (For this leftward movement, see below Section III.) SP in-

346 / GERALD FRIEDBERG

volvement in mass strikes declined. Gompers and most of the AFL rallied to Wilson's preparedness program as early as 1916, and after St. Louis even the Miners, Machinists, and ILGWU swung behind the pro-war labor groupings. Before the end of the war Socialist influence in such pre-war strongholds as the Mine Workers and Machinists was vanishing, and the Amalgamated Clothing Workers, the last Socialist stronghold, had declared full support of Wilson and repudiated the SP's war stand. The Socialists never again threatened to dominate the AFL or approached their pre-war strength in the labor movement.

Finally, turning to the Socialist press, there were 40 publications in 1904, 70 in 1910, and 323 in 1912. But between 1912 and 1916, the Socialist press declined at a rate over 50% greater than the rate of general press decline.[10] In membership, vote, influence in the labor movement, and the press, the SP, *previously increasing rapidly in strength on all fronts,* lost strength during the war.

III. *Changes in Nature, 1914–18*

As the war went on, the party moved leftward in position, and became foreign in composition.[11]

The pre-war coalition of right and center at first retained its dominance, refusing to condemn the European Socialists for their sudden nationalism when not excusing it, avoiding any mention of the general strike or other revolutionary tactic to turn national war to class war, and proposing only the usual reforms and peace terms. The left, however, was energized by the war issue, and the membership was rapidly frustrated by the unworkability of the party's initial program, disgusted by the breakdown of the Second International in Europe, and inspired by the appearance of a European left wing anti-war minority in 1915.[12] In mid-1915 the party membership overwhelmingly ratified both a Peace Manifesto and Program of "aggressive . . . uncompromising opposition to the whole capitalist system, and to every form of its most deadly fruits —militarism and war," and a constitutional amendment providing for expulsion of any Socialist office-holder voting funds for *any* military purpose.

When the European left wing minority gathered at Zimmerwald, Switzerland, in late 1915, the American left, attacking the right for its continued vacillation and compromise, hailed "the new

International that is even now taking definite form."[13] The rest of the party more slowly and less enthusiastically praised the European minority left and, finally, condemned the majority. A 3-2 majority of the SP Executive assured the Zimmerwald left of approval and cooperation.

Although some Socialists questioned whether Marxism could justify any national defense and whether such defense could be justified in the present conflict, the questions were lost in the rancor, dogmatic bitterness, and frustrated militancy that grew with the war. When "reds" moved to recall Berger from the Executive for his insistence on national defense and a citizen army, they polled a surprising portion, over 40% in the party referendum. Finally, the general strike to prevent war was incorporated into the party's 1916 platform. The party had come a long way since the last International Socialist Congress, in 1910, when it voted overwhelmingly against a far more limited general strike proposal than it placed before the American public in 1916.

The striking decline in party fortunes, abundantly clear by the end of 1916, only hastened the movement leftward. The SP had experienced, for the first time, a major drop in its percentage of total popular vote, a 47% decline since 1912, while membership was down some 30% from the 1912 total. The major factors behind the decline were two: Wilson and the war. Wilsonian liberalism and the progressive legislation of 1912–16 attracted many on the party's right who had labored for a more just economic and political arrangement of society, yet saw little connection between that goal and the party's refusal to distinguish between belligerents and to prepare for defense or support of the side whose victory was more desirable. As the party shifted leftward, the right was increasingly alienated and attracted to Wilson; and, as the right was siphoned off and political action yielded losses, left wing ascendancy and direct action militancy increased. Soon after the 1916 election, the "reds" of Boston, mostly Slavic, formed the Socialist Propaganda League, which issued a manifesto declaring that the worker had no country, disparaging political activity, calling for mass action and industrial unionism, and pledging support for the Third (Communist) International forming in Europe.[14]

By the St. Louis convention of April 1917, the left had become so threatening that the right joined with the center in accepting an anti-war position in order to oppose the most extreme left on theory and tactics. The final victory of the left and alienation of the right was clear not only in the war proclamation, described above, but in other important actions of the convention. The anti-sabotage amendment of 1912, Section 6, was now repealed, a proposal to permit SP membership for Non-Partisan League members was defeated as a threat to party discipline, and a resolution on the League strongly disparaged political action and stressed revolutionary propaganda as the party's proper sphere.

The vast majority of the remaining SP right, including the party's most prominent writers, lecturers, and organizers, withdrew from the party after St. Louis, leaving the center and left in a temporary coalition based first upon hostility to the war and later upon desire to defend the Russian revolution. With the end of the war that coalition could not be maintained, and the party split into Communist and Socialist fragments. The degree to which the entire SP spectrum had moved leftward during the war was, however, manifest in the actions of the center even after the withdrawal of the left: the party membership voted over two to one for immediate adherence to the Comintern, agreed that no party cooperating with bourgeois government should be allowed to attend any international Socialist Congress, and endorsed industrial unionism unqualifiedly.

Beginning in 1914 the SP had reversed its pre-war movement rightward toward a less dogmatic democratic-socialism, and had moved steadily leftward. At the same time the party had changed in other ways closely related to the movement leftward. The percentage of English publications in the Socialist press was almost nil in 1901, 50% in 1910, and 85% by 1912. But during the war years the trend was reversed, and the percentage fell to 79% in 1915 and then to 70% in 1916. The Socialist press not only declined, it also changed in character from increasingly English before the war to increasingly foreign language during the war.

The change is also clear in party membership. In 1908 the foreign-born percentage of SP membership was 29%, and by 1912 it was below 15%. During the war years the trend was reversed. By the end of 1915 the party was 32.5% foreign-born, in 1916 foreign language federations comprised 34.7% of SP membership, in St. Louis this percentage was 40%, and in 1918 it was 45%.

While total membership had declined, foreign language membership doubled and English speaking membership was halved.[15]

Radicalism in the party centered increasingly in the foreign language federations, inspired increasingly by European rather than American conditions. The German, Scotch, Welsh, and Irish elements which dominated the early years of Socialism in America were assimilated into the American mainstream fairly rapidly; but the new influx from eastern Europe was kept from leaving the ghetto by educational and occupational limitations. And it was precisely these groups which grew rapidly during the war. Just before the Russian revolution, the language federations of eastern Europe comprised more than three times their pre-war percentage of total party membership.

The change in the nature of the party is reflected, too, in its electoral fortunes. By 1918 the party had lost much of its widespread grassroots strength of pre-war times and had centralized its strength in a few states and larger cities, mostly in the northeast.[16] While the party had benefited somewhat from its position as haven for anti-war and protest expression, it had changed dramatically in position and composition, moving rapidly leftward, and losing its support in the labor movement and areas of indigenous radicalism while becoming increasingly foreign in areas of strength,[17] press, and membership.

IV. *Reaping the Harvest, 1919*

The rapid consolidation of left wing forces in America after the war, bitter antagonisms of early 1919, and splintering of the party into Socialist and Communist factions were developments continuous with and deriving from fundamental changes in the SP dating back to 1914.[18] The party's decline in strength, movement leftward, alienation of its right wing, loss of its roots in the union and indigenous radical movements, and increasingly foreign nature completely estranged it from the broader American milieu by the end of the war. The spiral of movement to the left and alienation of everything to the right continued. Suicidal factionalism and romance with the Comintern were the results.

This development was evident at least as early as 1915, when the left hailed the Zimmerwald left, and the center and right less happily went along. There were no illusions about the position of the emerging Third International; it represented a new left wing militancy not only on the war issue, but on the entire range of issues separating left from right before, during, and after the war. The Socialist Propaganda League of early 1917 and the left wing press before and during the war were direct forebears of the Communist Propaganda League of 1919 and left wing publications after the war.[19] The break with the Second International was definitive in 1919, but was clearly in view and being moved toward steadily since 1914. To the extent that there was a great divide in SP history, that divide was crossed beginning in 1914.

It was the eastern European language federations which formed the bulk and backbone of the Communist split from the SP in 1919. The federations, 45% of SP membership in 1918, were 53% just before the split, and, for the first time, English speaking Socialists were a minority in the party. But the following facts may be more significant: of the seven federations suspended for left wing activity, only three existed before the war, constituting 4.4% of party membership; but by October 1917, *before* the Russian revolution, all seven existed, constituting 14% of SP membership. In December 1918 they composed 20% of the party, and, of those suspended, 28%. In short, the Russian revolution did not bring forth the radical left of 1919 out of the whole cloth; the event was rather the final, great impulse in a long series of developments which had moved the SP leftward during the war, made it increasingly foreign, and added to the power and militancy of its "reds." The SP in 1919 was reaping the harvest sown during the war.[20]

V. *Conclusion*

The founding of the SP in 1901 marked an attempt to change the movement from an imported sect to an American party appealing to and rooted in the values and concerns of the American working class. From 1901 to 1912 the movement successfully repulsed attempts to "revolutionize" the party, and grew as a significant and buoyant political force. The war years saw the reversal of the party's development, and it became again, in both theoretical and tactical position, in membership and press, and in source of strength and inspiration, increasingly foreign. The result of these developments was the party's complete alienation from the American political spectrum after the war.

This analysis, if correct, suggests an understanding of the failure of Socialism in America.[21] Finding the cause of failure in the war, the Russian revolution, or Wilsonian liberalism is little help in explaining why the SP never approached the strength of the Populists in 1892 or the Farmer-Labor Party in 1924; not to mention the larger fact that the SP never was comparable in vitality and strength to its European counterparts. The comparative analysis of the American and European movements and their contexts which is required lies outside the scope of this paper,[22] but some brief concluding suggestions may be worthwhile.

Despite the violence accompanying the more intense labor struggles in the early 1900's, and partially through that violence, the great majority of the American working class had a greater experience of social mobility, economic plenty, and political democracy than did the European working class. Socialists occasionally recognized the paradox of a comparatively minor Socialist movement in the most advanced capitalist country in the world. Morris Hillquit observed,

Paradoxical as it may sound, our very democracy has militated against the immediate success of Socialism. The American workingmen have never had to struggle for the attainment of their political emancipation, as their disfranchised (sic) brothers in most other countries have.[23]

The American worker faced a reality different from that faced by his European counterpart, and also felt the force of a different ideological context. Berger noted that

the feeling of class-distinction in America, at least among native workingmen, has not the same historic foundation that it has in Germany, France, or England. There the people were accustomed for over a thousand years to have distinct classes and castes fixed by law.[24]

These observations contain the essential causes of the failure of Socialism in America: the experience and ideology of the American working class, each deriving from and reinforcing the other, were far more resistant to Socialism than were the experience and ideology dominant among the European working class. As Berger noted, these differences had to do, ultimately, with differing historic foundations. The nature of the initial migrations to America, the subsequent absence of feudal antagonisms to either side of those settlements, and the plenty of the land in which they grew, permitted those communities to thrive and maintain their liberal ideological development.

The relative and continuing success of democracy, plenty, and reform in America spelled the failure of revolutionary movements. Socialism in America, beginning as a foreign import, was evolving toward a more flexible democratic-socialism and showed sufficient vitality before World War I that there must remain tantalizing doubts as to what its fate as a less doctrinaire movement might have been. The tragedy of Socialism in America is that in its confrontation with Wilsonian liberalism, the war, and European events of 1914–19, the party's development up to that point was reversed, so that it became again foreign and removed from the American milieu.

NOTES

1. See James Weinstein, "Anti-War Sentiment and the Socialist Party, 1917–1918," *Political Science Quarterly,* vol. 74, no. 2 (June 1959), pp. 215–39; "The Socialist Party: Its Roots and Strengths, 1912–1919," *Studies on the Left,* vol. 1, no. 2 (Winter 1960), pp. 5–27; and "Socialism's Hidden Heritage: Scholarship Reinforces Political Mythology," *Studies on the Left,* vol. 3, no. 4 (Fall 1963), pp. 88–108. Limits of space require confinement of this response to the most important issues. If only because it would be tedious, continual citation and response will be avoided. Instead, the reader is urged to the more reliable and exciting business of full comparison. Where cited, the articles mentioned will be designated as Weinstein I, II, and III respectively.

2. Quotations are from Weinstein I, 104, 101, 97; and II, 7.

3. Lines between right and left were crossed from time to time on issues peculiar to the American context and calling to geographical divisions, such as immigration and the farm problem. The exceptions, however, only emphasized the rule. Left and right strengths were consistently found in certain states and population elements. See pages 343f. and note 4.

4. The leading state of pre-war indigenous radicalism, Texas, was so reduced during the war that it had but one delegate at St. Louis. New York, previously a leader of the right, now was split, its foreign element voting on the left. The same thing was happening in Massachusetts, where the SP was almost completely foreign in membership. For the rise in foreign radicalism and decline of indigenous strength, see also below, sections III and IV. The Ohio SP state convention of 1912 adopted a resolution urging industrial unionism on the workers; Ohio, Washington, and Michigan provided substantial left wing strength at the 1912 convention (along with Kansas, Minnesota, Montana, Oregon, Pennsylvania, and Texas); Ohio and Washington led an unsuccessful fight in May, 1913, to repeal Section 6; Ohio was the only state to give over 1,000 votes and 30% of the total vote cast against Haywood's recall; Washington and Texas were the only states giving Haywood over 500 votes and a majority of those cast; Illinois gave 962 votes to Haywood, over 40% of those cast in the state; Michigan's Finnish language federation was torn as early as 1915 by "red" agitation for sabotage, violence and the general strike; and in the same year the Michigan party declared absolute refusal to fight in any capitalist war. See note 3 above.

5. Main protagonists on the left in 1919 were Ruthenberg, Nicholas I. Hourwich, Louis Fraina, Wagenknecht, Katterfeld, and Ludwig Lore among others. All had been on the SP left well before 1919 and before the Bolshevik revolution. Principal figures on the center were Berger, Hillquit, Germer, Oneal, Nearing, Stedman, Lee and Feigenbaum, *all*

of whom had always been on the right or center. Caught between these groups were figures like Debs and O'Hare, outstanding figures of indigenous radicalism refusing to follow the left into the Communist movement.

Fraina, Hourwich, and Lore had been among leaders of the developing left since the outbreak of war. Their publications, *The New Review* and *Internationalist,* succeeded after St. Louis by *The Class Struggle* and *Revolutionary Age,* heralded and chronicled the Communist Party's formation in America. (The *International Socialist Review,* hereafter the *ISR,* was the only other major left wing publication; it published from 1900 to February 1918.) The New York *Call,* Milwaukee *Leader, American Socialist,* and *Appeal to Reason* remained principal right-center publications throughout.

6. Weinstein contends that "during the war, party membership increased considerably" (II, 22), that SP strength in the labor movement did not fall off but gained (III, 92), that performance of the Socialist press was "only slightly worse" than that of commercial papers (III, 96), and that the SP vote showed notable strength during the war. At one point, perhaps inadvertently, Weinstein does speak of "general decline" from 1912 to 1917 (II, 20).

7. Berger to Morris Hillquit, October 29, 1915. Berger Papers, Milwaukee County Historical Society. After the 1916 elections, the *American Socialist,* official party organ, noted, "We hoped that the workers would show increased solidarity born of a growing intelligence. Instead they were divided more than ever along racial lines and swayed as never before by the politicians' empty pre-election promises."—November 25, 1916.

8. The most notable gains, those in New York City, accompanied Hillquit's mayoralty campaign, but were hardly Socialist victories. Hillquit proposed a straightforward peace and reform program; violated principal canons of SP campaigning by urging ticket splitting by non-Socialists and by accepting endorsement from such non-Socialists as Amos Pinchot, Dudley Field Malone and J. A. H. Hopkins, with whom he spoke from the same platform; dropped all Marxian propaganda and asked, in his acceptance speech, for votes of "protest against the war"; and used a campaign leaflet headed "Bread, Peace, and Liberty! If you want these you want Hillquit for Mayor *even if you are not a Socialist!*" (italics added). Hillquit's campaign was dubbed the Peace and Milk campaign. See also *New Republic,* November 10, 1917; New York *Post,* November 9, 1917; and *The Nation,* December 27, 1917. Both Debs and Berger acknowledged that persecution of the party and press during 1917 worked strongly to the SP's benefit, further emphasizing its role as victimized articulator of protest.

The 1918 elections were disappointing. The sprinkling of states having Socialist legislators decreased from 9 to 4, the number of SP assemblymen at Albany was reduced from 10 to 2, Meyer London lost his Congressional seat and the vote in New York was 25% below Hillquit's 1917 tally. Wisconsin, where Socialists swept the field, was the only bright spot in a generally dark picture. With the total popular vote increasing, the SP barely held its own against its 1916 low.

9. See issues of November 30, 1912, and November 17, 1917. The number of mayoralty elections won by the SP declined from 81 for 1911–12 and 37 in 1913–14 to 26 for 1915–16 and to 19 for 1917–18. Weinstein II, 26–27, and III, 97n.22. The shift from widespread support to big city gains reflected profound changes in the party. (See below, Sections III and IV.) In 1911, eleven Midwest states accounted for 70% of Socialists in public office, and over ⅔ of all Socialist public officials were in cities of less than 10,000.

10. Weinstein estimates a decline of 18% for the Socialist press from 1912 to 1916 (omitting the less stable cooperative Socialist press) and compares this with the decline of American weeklies from 1914 to 1920, about 12% (III, 96–97). But 1) the decline in the Socialist press was much greater after 1916 than before, and 2) the comparison made is between all Socialist publications and American weeklies, and between 1912–16 and 1914–20, so that all points of the comparison are questionable. Even setting these facts aside, the decline of non-Socialist publications was less than 12%, since American press includes Socialist press, and so the decline of the Socialist press was not slightly worse, not 6% worse, but over 50% greater than non-Socialist press decline.

11. Weinstein maintains that the great change came after 1917 and "was not a result of long-standing tendencies inherent in the Socialist party" (II, 22).

12. The SP program included mediation by neutrals, embargo on shipments to belligerents, convening of the International, and a conference of American labor and Socialist organizations to determine common war policy. Distance from the conflict, absence of deep immersion in the labor movement, and a multitude of other factors also influenced the leftward movement.

13. *ISR*, vol. 16, no. 12 (June 1916), p. 728.

14. In Ohio, a Lettish branch declared preparations for the revolution, while the *ISR* proclaimed "rather insurrection than war!"—vol. 17, no. 10 (April 1917), p. 595.

15. One Socialist attempt to penetrate America's middle-class milieu was the Intercollegiate Socialist Society, an organization designed to bring Socialism to the campus. The ISS had 13 chapters by the beginning of 1910, 18 by the beginning of 1911, 42 by the beginning of 1912, 52 by the 1912 convention, and 73 in 1913 (including 13 alumni chapters). With the war, growth stopped. Through mid-1917 ISS strength hovered around 72 chapters, and then declined to under 40 chapters in 1918. (Weinstein gives figures for 1911 and 1915 only, suggesting growth between those years. II, 9.)

16. The number of Socialist state legislators, having grown from 0 to 31 from 1904 to 1914, remained fairly static during the war, but two states alone, New York and Wisconsin, accounted for the following percentages of the totals: 1910–11, 76.5%; 1912–13, 35%;

1914–15, 30%; 1916–17, 68.9%; 1918–19, 84.3%; and 1920–21, 88.2%. New York and Wisconsin, of course, were centers of immigrant, pro-German, anti-Russian, and anti-war strength. There were Socialist legislators in 9 states in 1912–13, 14 in 1914–15, 9 in 1916–17, 4 in 1918–19, and 3 in 1920–21. Socialist mayors were elected in 25 states in 1911–12, 16 in 1913–14, 14 in 1915–16, and 9 in 1917–18.

17. Between 1912 and 1918, Pennsylvania, New York, Ohio, Illinois, Wisconsin, and Massachusetts increased their combined percentage of party membership from 38.5% to 58.3%, while Texas, Washington, Minnesota, and Oklahoma, states of native radicalism, decreased from 18% to 8.65%. Before the war, growth had been more rapid in areas of indigenous radicalism.

18. Weinstein: The Communist parties "were in fact an appendage of the Russian revolution. . . . [They] originated, at Russian urging . . ." (III, 105).

19. See footnote 5 above.

20. In 1920 despite public sympathy for the imprisoned Debs, widespread disillusionment with Wilson and the Democratic Party, and strong protest against wartime and post-war violations of civil liberties, Debs polled only 3.4% of the popular vote, compared to nearly 6% in 1912 and 3.2% in 1916. (The absolute figure was slightly higher than the 1912 tally, but the total all-party vote had risen considerably.) Party membership was down to 26,766, less than one fourth the 1912 total and lower than it had ever been since 1906, and was declining steadily (13,484 in 1921 and 11,277 in 1922). The Socialist Party was never again a vital political force on the American scene.

21. Weinstein raises this question (I, 89) but never answers it. To Bell's answer, that Socialism was irrelevant in a society dominated by Wilsonian liberalism, Weinstein responds that the SP was viable and deep-rooted prior to WWI. But why was it minuscule compared to the main European Socialist parties?

22. One of the few such analyses available is Werner Sombart's *Warum gibt es in den Vereinigten Staaten keinen Sozialismus?* (Tübingen: J. C. B. Mohr, 1906).

23. Hillquit, "Problems and Prospects of American Socialism," New York *Call,* December 5, 1909.

24. Berger, *Appeal to Reason,* July 18, 1903.

REPLY

James Weinstein

I agree in part with the note that Gerald Friedberg adds to the beginning of his Comment, that the debate we had over the old Socialist Party ten years ago generated many arguments that now have little meaning. But lurking beneath the surface of what appears to have been a narrowly empirical dispute there were (and are) important questions for socialists: what set the limits on the growth of a mass socialist movement in the early 1900s, and what was responsible for the breakup and decline of that movement and its transition to the sectarian politics of the old socialist (including communist) Left of the following decades?

First, we should define what is in dispute. My concern was not about the failure of the Socialist Party of America to become a major party. When I began my research on the old Socialist Party I believed the myths advanced alike by liberals and communists: that the old Socialist Party had never amounted to much, that its leadership was "middle class," that it did not seriously oppose the war, and that it was constantly split by factional disputes. But I discovered that the party had much more of an impact on American society than the mythology granted, that it was relatively stable (as compared, for example, to the major parties), that it opposed the war consistently, and that it remained strong and essentially unchanged until 1919. I then became concerned about what went wrong. Why did a substantial popular movement for socialism disappear, to be replaced by the sectarian party politics of the 1920s and thereafter?

The issue for me was not why the party was not as large as its European counterparts, but why it did not continue as the minority popular movement that it had been—why no popular socialist tradition and organized movement remained through which socialist politics could have continued to develop.

Having defined the issue as I was attempting to understand it, it is still necessary briefly to consider the inability of socialism to have become a majority movement in the United States during the Progressive era. Friedberg's point about the absence of feudal class distinctions and of a hereditary, relatively homogenous working class is valid, but it does not get us very far. True, the differences in the makeup of the working class, the tradition of parliamentary democracy, the rapid expansion and development of industrial capitalism after the Civil War all militated against the sustained growth of a major anti-capitalist party. But that does not make socialism a foreign idea or an illegitimate need.

What Friedberg likes about the old Socialist Party (its reformist tendencies) he considers American. What he dislikes (its class-conscious internationalism) he considers foreign. By that token, capitalism, or certainly industrial capitalism, could also be considered foreign—since, like socialism, it originated in Europe. In fact, industrial capitalism grew out of mercantile capitalism in the United States just as it did in Europe, and socialism emerged as a response to industrial capitalism just as it did in Europe. But the Socialist Party came together in 1900 as a coalition of several groups that were distinctly American. These included the remnants of Eugene Debs's American Railway Union, the Christian Socialists (who were the political descendants of Bellamy nationalism), one strand of Populism, the Rochester faction of the Socialist Labor Party, and the Milwaukee Social Democrats (mostly 1848 Germans). Within this coalition, it was the native Midwestern and Southern members of the party who sought to "revolutionize" it from 1900 to 1917. The Hillquits, Bergers, and Spargos (all immigrants) were relatively reformist, while Debs, Kate Richards O'Hare, Tom Hickey, and William D. Haywood (all native-born with "old American" constituencies) were the allegedly "foreign" radicals.

In short, the argument that American socialism failed because it became foreign obscures the common fate of American and European socialism during the twentieth century. Granted that socialism has fared better in the industrial nations of Europe in the sense that nominally socialist parties have lasted longer and gained more followers than did the American party. Yet with the development of large-scale corporate capitalism in Europe and in the United States, the socialist movements there and here began to stagnate and lose their potential (as constituted) as revolutionary forces. Socialist movements continued to exist in Europe (although the party was wiped out in Italy in the 1920s and in Germany in the 1930s), but after 1920 these parties no longer took themselves seriously as revolutionary organizations.

The Socialist Party was frustrated by the development of modern American liberalism (what I call corporate liberalism[1]). But the Socialists were not done in by diverging too far from liberalism, as Friedberg implies. On the contrary, they lost the initiative because the new liberalism took over more and more of their immediate demands, and because the party was unable to understand the changes in capitalism that accompanied the growth of the large corporations or to develop responses appropriate to monopoly capitalism. Increasingly, the large corporations required the intervention of the state to help rationalize and stabilize the system in the interest of undermining the growing threat of socialist consciousness among workers and tenant farmers, and also to combat the anti-trust activities of the neo-Populists. Because Socialists did not understand that the meaning of trade unionism was changing as competition ended, and because they did not understand how the large corporations could utilize the state for social reforms, the party continued to function as if the experience of trade union struggles and parliamentary struggles for reform would "naturally" create socialist consciousness among workers and tenant farmers.

Yet this was no longer so even to the limited extent that it had been in the past. Increasingly the more sophisticated business leaders, along with progressive politicians such as Theodore Roosevelt and Woodrow Wilson, understood that neither trade unionism nor social reform was inherently disadvantageous to the large corporations. The key question was who was to control the union or define and administer the reform. Taking their cue from Bismarck, and to a lesser extent from English social reform (and unperturbed at the foreign source of these policies), the corporate liberals pushed for accommodation with the conservative leaders of the AFL, and for social reforms like workmen's compensation, conservation, the Federal Trade Commission, or the Pure Food and Drug Act. Within this new context of progressivism, many people concluded that socialism was unnecessary, or was merely the left wing of liberalism. In short, the problem for the Socialists after 1912 was how to increase the distinction between themselves and the liberals, not how to get closer to them.

Socialist opposition to the war, as it turned out, provided the party a way clearly to reject liberal policies and to do so within a framework of socialist analysis. The party not only opposed the war and American participation in it, but its view of the war as one of imperial rivalries was sharply at odds with those of both pro-war liberals and liberal pacifists. Furthermore, once the party made it clear that it would not follow the European socialist movement in supporting the war, the party gained strength rapidly at the polls and regained many of the members it had lost after the war had started in Europe in mid-1914.[2] Friedberg attempts to dismiss the large increase in the Socialist vote in 1917 as a reflection of anti-war sentiment and not truly socialist by claiming that the campaigns "lacked all the usual Marxian analysis and propaganda." He neglects to note that party gains were greater in the allegedly dogmatic left-wing areas of Ohio and Illinois than in the right-wing state of New York.[3] Further, Friedberg's argument is that the manner in which the party opposed the war was sectarian and that its increasing dogmatism isolated it from its indigenous supporters. He cannot have it both ways. If the party's method of opposing the war was dogmatic and sectarian, then support for it cannot be dismissed as not truly socialist.

In any case, the more popular Socialist analysis of the war and its active opposition became, the fiercer was the wartime repression. This consisted of removing almost all Socialist publications from the mails, prosecution of over two thousand people under the wartime Espionage and Sedition Acts, and government-inspired vigilante attacks on anti-war mass meetings, party locals, etc. The end result was a serious weakening of party organization, especially in the agrarian states. Thus the war produced contradictory results for the party—mass popular support for its position, but also disruption and in many places destruction of its organization. What happened after the war is complex and not easily summarized.[4] But it is clear that the post-war debates and issues revolved around the meaning of the Russian Revolution and the policies of the Third International. It was in this new political context that the party, already greatly weakened organizationally, broke up and re-formed as a number of warring sects.

NOTES

1. See James Weinstein, *The Corporate Ideal in the Liberal State, 1900–1918* (Boston: Beacon, 1968, 1969).
2. During the first six months of 1914 party membership averaged 103,000—only 15,000 below the all-time high of 1912. Disillusionment over the failure of European socialists to oppose the war led to a drop of 24,000 during the first six months of 1915. From then until April 1917 membership continued to decline slowly. Then it rose by some 12,000 in the first three months after war was declared and by 1919 was up to 109,000. (See membership records, Socialist Party papers, Duke University.)
3. See ch. III of James Weinstein, *The Decline of Socialism in America, 1912–1925* (New York: Vintage, 1969).
4. For a full discussion of the process of breakup and decline after the war see Ibid., chs. IV through VIII.

Chapter 8

THE PROBLEMS OF THE SOCIALIST PARTY
B. AFTER WORLD WAR ONE

Martin Diamond*

During the nineteen twenties the Socialist Party of America declined disastrously from its robust beginnings in the first two decades of the century. Party membership fell from more than 100,000 in 1919 to a figure below 7,000 by the end of the decade. In 1920, while still in prison under an Espionage Act conviction, Eugene V. Debs polled over 900,000 votes; this was the highest vote total the party ever received.[1] From this high point, the party's electoral strength dwindled rapidly until the Depression years. In 1924, the party ran no candidate of its own and supported the La Follette campaign in the hope that a permanent farmer-labor party might result. The La Follette unionists and progressives, disappointed by what they considered a poor showing, abandoned all further efforts in this direction and left the Socialists stranded, more isolated and weaker than before. In 1928, Norman Thomas, running for the first time, received only 267,835 votes, a presidential vote smaller than the party had polled at any time since its first campaign in 1900. At the end of the twenties, then, still not fully recovered from the bitter struggle with the communists at the beginning of the decade, withering in the prosperity, the opinions, and the mood of the twenties, with a plummeting electoral vote and a tiny membership, the Socialist Party seemed on the verge of extinction.

The Great Depression changed all that almost at a stroke. The collapse of American capitalism that Socialists had so long awaited seemed at last to have arrived. (The great European crises of those same years seemed also heartening proof that the apocalyptic moment for socialism was finally at hand.) National income sank

* Revised version of Chapter 6 from Martin Diamond, "Socialism and the Decline of the American Socialist Party" (Unpublished Ph.D. Dissertation, University of Chicago, 1956), originally entitled "The Socialists and the New Deal."

astonishingly; unemployment averaged more than ten million workers; there were "breadlines standing knee-deep in wheat"; banks and great financial concerns were failing and the business community had become panicky; and the policies of the Hoover administration failed utterly to persuade the great majority of people. Almost overnight the Socialist situation was changed. "No longer would Socialists have to begin their proselytizing work by making their audiences dissatisfied with the economic *status quo*."[2] Great numbers of people were ready to hear and respond sympathetically to the Socialist message. The party began to grow rapidly and its sense of mission was restored even more rapidly.

Socialists made a greatly improved showing in the 1930 elections, and in the presidential election of 1932, in a campaign marked by a vastly increased public response, Norman Thomas polled 881,951 votes, more than three times the 1928 vote, although still disappointingly small compared with what Socialists had hoped for.[3] Organizationally, the results were also heartening. Hundreds of new party locals were formed; many old members returned to activity; membership more than doubled (to fifteen thousand); many liberals turned to the party and, in particular, to Norman Thomas; even a number of trade unionists responded; and campus youth organizations became numerous, active, and even romantically revolutionary. The party activity and literature reveal an enthusiastic renewal of confidence. It seemed that the American march to socialism had commenced.[4]

By 1937, the Socialist revival that had commenced dramatically with the Depression as dramatically had ended. The New Deal completely undermined the Socialist efforts. As Norman Thomas put it, and as anyone understands who in those days tried to plead the Socialist cause, "it was Roosevelt in a word."[5] But precisely how and why the New Deal undermined the Socialist Party and what is thereby revealed about socialism requires careful consideration. The pre-history of socialism as a teaching or set of doctrines must especially be taken into account. That is, the New Deal was rather like a knockout blow the effects of which can only be understood in the light of the series of blows that preceded it. In short, the party and its doctrines had become ripe for undermining.

Socialism had initially come to the world messianically, proclaiming its unlikeness to all other parties and doctrines and promising the advent of the "truly human" society. A kind of millennium, socialism claimed, was the promise of history, which inexorably would cause the collapse of the capitalist economy, the revolutionary emergence of the working class, and its final triumph in the class struggle. Capitalism overthrown, the millennium would then be ushered in by force of collectivism; the socialist economic arrangements of themselves would transform the human condition and generate the new human order.[6] The fullness of the utopian intention must be kept firmly in mind. Socialists did not intend merely to mitigate the evils of capitalism or merely to introduce some regulation and control of the economy. They intended its wholesale replacement. Socialists did not intend merely to improve international relations or to moderate the scale or frequency of war. They intended to create the universal family of mankind and to end war forever. They did not intend merely an extension of democracy and equality, but rather the transcendence of democracy and the creation of a new human order of profoundly equal and elevated mankind. These were the beliefs that gave to socialism its meaning and identity. Socialism was an ideological phenomenon through and through; these beliefs *were* the socialist movement.

But, beginning with the First World War, life delivered a series of hammer blows to the socialist beliefs. New events and ideas combined to break in upon the old socialist certainties; there occurred a slow but deepening process of disillusionment and a hollowing of the socialist principles. The profundity and duration of the World War rendered dubious the socialist faith in progressive history. The failure of the working classes to resist the war shocked the socialist faith in the historic role of the proletariat. The triumph of Bolshevism, the consequent splitting of the international movement and the internecine warfare waged from then on, and the mounting evidence that socialist collectivism might eventuate not in socialism but in some new kind of tyranny all further undermined socialist conviction in the principles upon which the movement was based. And, finally, the appalling triumphs of fascism and, especially, of Nazism demonstrated once again the easy vincibility of the proletariat and offered a rival quasi-collectivism that threatened to displace socialism as the "wave of the future."

At the end of the nineteen twenties, the only intact tenet in the socialist scheme was the conviction that capitalism was fatally flawed and doomed to the "dustbin of history." The disasters of the World War, the Bolshevik fragmentation of the movement, and the rise of fascism and Nazism were at least not incompatible with the view that capitalism was doomed. The Depression had seemed further heartening confirmation of that socialist belief. Now the New Deal proceeded to invalidate that one last unimpaired tenet. Roosevelt began the long process of applying sufficient regulatory and redistributive measures to the capitalist economy to prevent its collapse and render it reasonably durable. And, crucially, in the process he readily rallied the working class, fickle once again, away from any possible movement toward socialism.

It was the latter development, the success of the New Deal with American labor, that had the direct and immediate impact upon the Socialist Party. Two New Deal measures, the National Industrial Recovery Act and especially the National Labor Relations Act, actively encouraged trade union organization. President Roosevelt sympathized with labor's aspirations and his statements contributed much to the success of the great organizing campaigns of the Committee for Industrial Organization (CIO). The surge of labor organization, and not least the militant aspect of the new "sit-down" strikes, was enormously attractive to the Socialists. It was the development of working-class consciousness so long awaited; but it came with a crippling price for the Socialist Party. The union leaderships became committed to Roosevelt and their organizing campaigns were waged, as it were, in the name of the New Deal. Thus, although the unions often wanted and welcomed the able and devoted Socialist organizers, and although the Socialists desperately wanted a share in the new mobilization of labor,[7] the price was usually silence about their party membership, abstaining from the party's electoral campaigns or actually working for the Democratic Party, and even public resignation from the party. Walter Reuther and Leo Krzycki were the two outstanding cases. In Reuther's case, his support of Michigan's Democratic governor, Frank Murphy, was the price of the organizational assistance Reuther and the automobile workers had to have from John L. Lewis.[8] Krzycki was the party's national chairman and also a vice-president of the Amalgamated Clothing Workers; the union president, Sidney Hillman, obliged him to resign from the party so as not to embarrass the union's political activities on behalf of President Roosevelt.[9]

Many of the men who left the party for work in the unions were, ironically, among the party's most militant members. But this is easily understood. Their militancy consisted in a Marxism that often bordered on Leninism, in which the prime revolutionary duty is to forward the class consciousness and development of the workers. Given the character of full-fledged Leninism, there was little danger that the ultimate party loyalty of the Communist Party cadres would be weakened by publicly functioning as New Deal unionists. But the Socialist Party revolutionaries had not the necessary hardness, discipline, party organization, and fully Leninist principles; they did not capture and transform the unions, but rather they themselves became not decisively distinguishable from the other unionists and the New Dealers. This was inevitable given the essential character of the socialist movement.

Reformist Socialists were also vulnerable to the appeal of the New Deal via labor. They had remained sufficiently orthodox Marxists to find it intolerable that the party be separated from the main direction of working-class development. Many of them also had close personal associations with some of the established union leaderships. Thus, when labor was drawn into the New Deal camp, the moderate Socialists were drawn along in the wake. Moreover, unlike the militants, the right-wing Socialists, and especially their constituencies, came increasingly to see in the New Deal not only a valuable development of the labor movement, but also a more general step forward politically. The famous Old Guard split from the party (1934–36) partly involved this sympathetic response to the New Deal.[10] The party, thus, suffered losses through organized labor to the New Deal of some of its ablest members, from both the left and right wings of the party.

The regulatory and social reform program of the New Deal, however, and the heady prospect it opened of further and greater reform possibilities, had the deeper and more permanent effects upon the party. Thousands of Socialists and their supporters turned to Democratic Party politics as a new and effective way to advance their beliefs. For example, Upton Sinclair, then a party member, entered the Democratic primary in California in 1934 and won the nomination for governor. The party opposed his strategy and ultimately expelled him; but many of its members and most of its supporters joined Sinclair's exciting campaign, and in consequence the California party organization was shattered. An able young

California Socialist, Jerry Voorhis, left the party and later was elected to Congress for several terms as a Democrat. (He was defeated, it is interesting to note, by Richard Nixon in 1946.) Andrew Biemiller, one of the most ardent Militants against the Old Guard, soon after became a Wisconsin Democratic state legislator and was later elected to Congress. Paul Blanshard and some other New York Socialists supported Mayor Fiorello La Guardia and later held important offices in his administration. Many other less well-known examples could be cited. The point is that many of the party's ablest members joined the New Deal "bandwagon." Their reasoning ran as follows. Inadequate though it may be, the New Deal is a great step forward in educating and preparing the American people for a socialist society. Moreover, it is the progressive direction toward which the masses are moving, and to oppose it is to isolate Socialists from the very people whom socialism must win. The correct tactic is for Socialists to join the New Deal forces and steer them in a truly socialist direction.

Whether this argument was sound or not is the central question for understanding the impact of the New Deal upon both the party and socialism. It was the underlying question that racked that socialist generation. And, not unnaturally, much subsequent scholarship likewise turns on it; right-wing scholars chide the party for failing to take the shrewd and flexible course, and left-wing scholars chide it for not having been revolutionary enough. If the argument sketched above was sound, then the party's collapse before the New Deal must be explained as due to an egregious strategic blunder. If the argument was unsound, then the party's collapse was due, as shall be argued, to a profound dilemma from which no socialist party could ultimately escape. We consider this matter below.

In any event, the party's opposition to President Roosevelt and the New Deal terminated the sympathetic hearing that had been so encouraging during the first years of the Depression. Liberals and independents who in 1932 supported or were moving toward Norman Thomas were, by 1936, almost wholly on the side of Roosevelt and the New Deal. Even the Communists, following the Popular Front policy of the Comintern, supported the New Deal and were gaining influence in many labor and liberal organizations. The few Socialist-dominated unions, and others where Socialists had been influential, became ardent Roosevelt supporters and quarreled bitterly with the Socialist Party's stand. The presidential election of 1936 revealed how completely the party's hopes had been disappointed. Thomas polled only 187,720 votes, a worse result than even the poor showing in 1928; indeed, as a percentage of the national vote, it was an even poorer result than the party had achieved in its very first campaign in 1900. The party was once again in the wilderness. And from this disaster it was all downhill thereafter until the party finally, out of sheer weakness, abandoned electoral campaigning entirely after 1956.

The story of the decade for the Socialists, then, was indeed "Roosevelt in a word." The full meaning of this can be seen by examining the party's changing response to the New Deal as it became more and more aware of how profoundly the New Deal was blighting the party's hopes. During the 1932 campaign, the party was cheerfully contemptuous and rather disregardful of Roosevelt, seeing in him no principle or program that threatened seriously to rival socialism. (It must be remembered that in 1932 the New Deal was perhaps not yet fully contemplated by Roosevelt and certainly was not yet fully presented to the country.) But by 1934, the New Deal had worked major changes in the country's practice and thinking and had achieved a dramatic presence. The party was increasingly dominated by the need to deal with the new challenge. The party's literature reveals that in 1934 the major thrust was to deny that the New Deal was as liberal as prevailing opinion claimed. Norman Thomas argued that the "Roosevelt Revolution, in so far as it was a revolution at all, was a revolution from *laissez-faire* to state capitalism."[11] All that the New Deal had done, he claimed, was to adopt some of the "immediate demands" of the Socialist platform. Militant Socialists had always regarded these demands only in a strategic light; they were means by which the workers could be drawn into struggles for limited gains but which over time would bring them to a socialist consciousness. "The essential thing about the Socialist platform," Thomas rightly emphasized, "has always been its purposes and its goal rather than its immediate demands."[12] The party's posture in 1934, then, was to depreciate the particular reforms that had been adopted and to disparage in general the liberalism of the New Deal.

However, by 1936, because he was speaking to deserting Socialists and not just to unheeding voters, it was no longer enough for Thomas to deny the liberalism of the New Deal. It had become so formidable a challenge that by then he had to deny that it was socialistic.

> President Roosevelt . . . is not a Socialist, and he is rather proud that he has saved the capitalist system by reforming it a little. . . . [W]hat he has given us is a more or less liberal capitalism.[13]
>
> Not only is it not socialism. . . . What Roosevelt has given us . . . is a state capitalism which the Fascist demagogues of Europe have used when they came to power.[14]

More moderately, Thomas also wrote that the New Deal was "as much of an achievement along its own line and within capitalist limits as we could reasonably expect in a country where labor unions and other forces desiring change were so weak."[15] And in the same book, Thomas also ungrudgingly credits Roosevelt with the massive achievement of having restored popular faith in democratic and constitutional government.

As the decade wore on, the Socialists tried hard to maintain their belief that the New Deal was only a temporary makeshift and to denigrate the depth and permanence of the changes it was making in American life. Thus the Socialists often spoke of the New Deal in the past tense, always ready prematurely to report its death. When Roosevelt made his famous remark that Dr. New Deal was replaced by Dr. Win-the-War, the Socialists seized upon it as confirming their repeated prediction that capitalism would revert to type. Yet the war, of course, saw an extension of the principles and techniques of governmental controls and planning that went far beyond the New Deal. And after the war, President Truman further extended the principle of the welfare state. The Socialists had initially seen in Truman a reaction from the New Deal; they expected that with Roosevelt's death the "true" character of the Democratic Party would reassert itself. President Truman's energetically liberal campaign in 1948 took them quite by surprise.[16] But by 1951 Norman Thomas was writing of the welfare state policies of the Democrats (and, for that matter, of the Republicans as well) as a major and durable fact. The New Deal, he now acknowledged, had done more than just adopt the Socialist "immediate demands"; indeed, he said, "Roosevelt advanced his country to a pragmatic socialism." But the adjective "pragmatic" greatly modifies the noun "socialism"; "pragmatic socialism" simply meant, deprecatingly, the welfare state.

Some sort of welfare state we are bound to have and any welfare state, however far short of the socialist ideal, requires such a degree of governmental intervention in economics as to constitute proof of the decline of private capitalism and a massive qualification on free enterprise.[17]

The Socialist Party's view of the New Deal, then, changed from one which saw it as an aberrant last-ditch capitalistic palliative to one which recognized in the New Deal a profound qualification of the American conception of government and society; in short, the welfare state. But one view the Socialists did not change: whether palliative or profound qualification of American life, the welfare state was not socialism, not what they had meant and dreamt of; it was not—and it would not become—socialism.

This vital point is brought out vividly in the *New Fabian Essays,* published in 1952, in which leading English socialists had to confront from a position of power essentially the same problem that Thomas had to face from a position of weakness and defeat. The central theme of the essays is the relationship of the welfare state to socialism. The main conclusion is:

The post-war Labor Government marked the end of a century of social reform and not, as its socialist supporters had hoped, the beginning of a new epoch. . . . Capitalism has been civilized, and to a large extent, reconciled with the principles of democracy.[18]

None of this would have surprised John Maynard Keynes, who much earlier had made all this clear in explaining the relation of his views, and roughly thus of the welfare state, to socialism.

There is nothing [in my proposals] . . . which is seriously incompatible with what seems to me to be the essential characteristic of Capitalism, namely the dependence upon an intense appeal to the money-making and money-loving instincts of individuals as the main motive force of the economic machine.[19]

It was precisely the truth of this statement that long made socialists skeptical and even fearful of Keynesianism, and unable to take socialist satisfaction in the welfare state.

Thus, in the early fifties, after a generation of the New Deal and the welfare state, both the English and American socialists, from their very different political situations, agreed that the welfare state, however useful its reforms, fell far short of the socialist aspiration. Further, and of the utmost importance, they also agreed in effect that they did not know how to proceed beyond the welfare state. The whole tone and spirit of socialist proposals here and abroad revealed a barrenness and uncertainty. For the first time in its history, the socialist movement was without a radical critique of the existing society and without a confident program for its replacement. The Frankfurt Declaration of the newly reconstituted Socialist International, for example, accurately reflected the pathetic state of socialist thought at the time. Of that Declaration, Crosland rightly concluded that the "name may still be Socialism, but the features look uncommonly like those of the Welfare State."[20]

In a bitter and despairing passage, G. D. H. Cole accurately summarized the full effect of the welfare state upon socialism.

> Socialism is dissolving even as an ideal related to current practice, and is being replaced by a striving towards the Welfare State, in a form which leaves open the indefinite continuance of a "mixed economy," still largely capitalist, but involving a growing amount of centralized state regulation designed to secure full employment and an improved distribution of spendable incomes. . . . Obviously, in the relatively advanced countries . . . the majority of the electors do not want the upsets involved in overthrowing capitalism and installing a complete Socialist system *if* they can have full employment, good living conditions, and expanding social services *without* these upsets. Obviously, most Trade Union and party leaders share this attitude. If the welfare state can be lastingly sustained and developed *without* Socialism, Socialism is not coming in the West—*and not even the Socialist leaders will try to make it come.*[21]

Cole's despairing conclusion supplies, as it were, a rejoinder to a famous American socialist boast of the thirties. It is attributed to Heywood Hale Broun, then a well-known columnist, and is supposed to have been made at the Socialist Party's 1936 convention. "They can steal our thunder, but they can't touch our lightning." That puts the whole matter of the New Deal and socialism in a nutshell. Everyone knows that the thunder—the immediate demands—was stolen. But the question is why didn't anyone still want the lightning—the socialist purpose, the leap forward to the truly human society? Not the workers, nor the great popular mass, "not even the Socialist leaders" any longer truly tried "to make it come."

Why this time did the theft of its thunder so completely undo the party? After all, socialism had had many similar experiences over a century. In Germany, Bismarck launched a substantial program of social legislation. Despite this, the German socialists held reasonably fast (Bernstein's revisionism was only a portent of things to come) to the essence of socialism despite the blandishments. In England, from 1905 to 1911, the Liberal Government introduced a program of social legislation and granted many of Labour's demands (e.g., regarding the Taff-Vale Judgment); yet during precisely these years the Labour Party grew and deepened its socialist commitment. The Populist and Progressive movements in America did not devastate the Socialists when they proposed substantial reforms; again, it was precisely during these years that the Socialists and their doctrines flourished. Every earlier attempt to steal the socialist thunder was taken by Socialists as a confirmation of their own wisdom, of the merit of socialism, and of the certainty of ultimate triumph.

The most obvious explanation of why socialism succumbed to the New Deal and not to the earlier challenges is the massive difference between the New Deal and the earlier reforming efforts. The New Deal more profoundly modified the nature of capitalist society than anything done by Bismarck, the British Liberals, or by American Populism or Progressivism. The welfare state is more than some particular reforms; it is more nearly a new kind of society, although not what Socialists wanted. The New Deal therefore represented a more comprehensive and attractive alternative to socialism. And, understandably, it therefore satisfied those—the labor movement, intellectuals, Socialist sympathizers—whose dissatisfaction was indispensable to socialism.

Consequently, unlike the earlier experiences, the New Deal and the welfare state "brought vast ideological confusion" to the Socialists. It undermined the idea that any capitalist government was necessarily inimical to workers and necessarily doomed to overthrow.

No more shattering blow to socialist morale—based as it was on the *mystique* of intransigeant class struggle—could be imagined. It left socialist principles in a state of utter chaos. . . .[22]

The New Deal gave the lie to the essential principles of socialism, which is to say, to the beliefs upon which the socialist faith rested.

It took history and the proletariat away from socialism, it defused the class struggle, and it employed quasi-collectivist means for non-socialist ends. And all this in an undeniably decent and reasonably democratic way. Thus, the unbridgeable gulf that socialists had always believed to exist between capitalism, evil and doomed, and socialism, virtuous and certain of victory, was spanned by the New Deal. Henceforward, virtue was no longer the exclusive preserve of socialism, but was instead a matter of degree, of this or that extent of planning, regulation, and redistribution. The New Deal marked a comfortable path of compromise between socialism and capitalism. Socialists beset by doubts and yearning to work with labor could now move toward the center without trauma or tears; in short, it was a lot easier to become a Keynesian or a New Dealer than it had formerly been to become a "class collaborationist," to use the old Socialist term of ultimate opprobrium.

Moreover, as powerful as the pull of the New Deal on the Socialists and their potential following would have been in any case, its effect was magnified by the ideological vulnerability of the Socialists. When the New Deal struck, their ideology was already in tatters or at least coming apart at the seams. As indicated earlier, the Socialist sense of mission, of a distinctive and worthwhile sense of identity, had been undermined by a generation of consternating events. Socialism had always been a rational faith; it was always based on what socialists thought was a realistic analysis of how the world was, what it was becoming, and why the historic outcome would be good. The Socialist capacity to withstand the New Deal, therefore, depended largely upon their ability to believe the socialist teaching still to be true and that their plans when effectuated would indeed radically transform mankind. But the integument of Socialist belief had burst asunder; they could no longer heartily believe. As reasonably rational men, they had begun to admit—or were being prepared to admit—the inadequacy of their principles in the face of mounting adverse evidence.

The socialist encounter with the New Deal, then, cannot be considered in isolation. A generation of experiences subversive of socialist convictions had preceded the encounter and, during the thirties, each day seemed to bring a new budget of events that further belied the socialist beliefs and expectations. Norman Thomas, always the most reflective of American socialists, poignantly conveys what it felt like in those days.

Looking back on the years, I find it hard to put into words the strain upon the thinking and emotional feeling of western socialists as they contemplated in succession the failure of German social democracy, the seeming success of Bolshevism, the rise of fascism to power in Italy and Germany, the proof which the purges brought of communist degradation, and, finally the temporary alliance of the two forms of dictatorship.[23]

These events had a cumulative and mutually reinforcing effect. Few socialists concluded at a given moment that some single event or development contradicted their previous entire way of thinking and obliged its abandonment. That is not how most men hold, revise, or abandon their important political convictions. The contradicting evidence sinks in and is mediated by time and personal attachments and habits. Slowly but finally men yield. Such was the case with the Socialists. Battered on every ideological front, but still too socialist in their marrow to slide down into mere New Dealism, too liberal and democratic to take the Bolshevik way, and too intelligent to harden into a latter-day De Leonism, the Socialist Party in the fifties simply withered away into a decent impotence.

Many quite sympathetic and perceptive critics of the party do not appreciate how profound the Socialist dilemma was. Their analysis convinces them that a better understanding of the American political system and a shrewder strategy would somehow have saved the party and better advanced the socialist cause. All these critics presuppose that the party erred in its opposition to the New Deal. The party, they argue one way or another, should have abandoned the electoral field and should have tried instead to influence the development of the New Deal.

The grandest version of this view is to be found in Professor Daniel Bell's brilliant work on American socialism. The simple gravamen of his criticism of the American Socialist Party is that it was consistently stupid politically. For example, it did not see, as Upton Sinclair or the Nonpartisan League did, how "socialists could utilize the primary system to great political advantage."[24] Bell's simple charge is wrapped, however, in a complicating application of Max Weber's famous distinction between the "ethics of responsibility" and the "ethics of conscience."[25] Holding to the "ethics of conscience," the American Socialists had an absolute end; they lived "in" but were not "of" the world, and they persisted in their end without responsible regard to strategic consequences in the world which they were not "of." But the problem is really much plainer than the Weberian approach causes Bell to make it. Socialism was not at all an "ethics of conscience." It was a political "ethics of responsibility," but a mistaken one. The Socialists were entirely regardful of the world in which they lived; they just didn't understand it aright. They believed that history *was* bringing their plans to fruition, that man *could* be transformed by the means they proposed, that their message *would* in time be responded to by the proletariat, etc. They were not conscientiously for socialism regardless of consequences, which is what Weber's "conscience" ethics means; they believed in socialism as practicable, that is, in terms of the "ethics of responsibility." They were wrong, that is all; and, when they came to see the error, they moderated or abandoned their views.

At bottom, that is what Bell is saying too, that the Socialists were wrong. But he trivializes their error by making it, finally, only strategic. They would have done better to be more flexible, adaptive to American institutions, etc. But surely now, after the last two generations of social democratic experience in the Western world, it is clear that no change in strategy would have altered the bankruptcy of historic socialism. Had the party moved sooner within the orbit of the New Deal, the sooner would its socialist principles have been displaced by those of the welfare state. The sooner it would have found its failure by a different path.

The Socialists simply had nowhere to turn. They could grasp neither horn of their dilemma. The fatality of their difficulties can be understood by contemplating the perennial struggle between the left- and right-wing tendencies of democratic socialism. Everywhere socialism had to choose between these two grand alternative strategies for its achievement. Whatever the specific issue or circumstances, the fundamental left-wing case was always this: you right-wingers (usually in the leadership) are diluting and betraying socialism with your "opportunism" and your compromises. The right-wing case always was: you left-wingers are insane fanatics, "impossibilists," you alienate the masses and keep socialism from gaining power. The tragedy of socialism is that both arguments were right. Right-wing successes did not advance *socialism;* left-wing policies *were* incapable of bringing socialism to pass (one good proof being that the left-wingers but rarely could even win the party over, let alone the masses). Cleverness of strategy was purchasable only at cost to the essential nature of socialism, intransigent purity only at cost to effectiveness.

The untenability of socialism was such that it could not be achieved by either of the means available to it. Criticisms of the Socialist Party, which imply that socialism would have been better served by a more reformist, or more revolutionary, strategy, all miss the central point: an untenable goal cannot be served well by any means. This untenability of socialist thought is the starting point for any investigation of the fate of socialism and its parties. That is what is taught by the encounter of socialism with the New Deal.

NOTES

1. Since the woman's suffrage amendment had been passed in the interim, the 1920 vote actually represented a lesser percentage of the national vote than the party obtained in 1912, which was the true high point of the party's electoral career. Debs received 6 per cent of the vote in 1912 and 3.4 per cent in 1920.

2. David Shannon, *The Socialist Party of America: A History* (New York: Macmillan, 1955), p. 218.

3. Norman Thomas frequently referred to the number of people who at the time told him that they thought he was the best candidate, but that above all they wanted to "get" Hoover. Thomas often argued that the American presidential two-party system strongly disposes voters to vote for the "lesser evil"; Socialist strength, he thought, would have been significantly, but not decisively, greater under some other structural arrangement.

4. Speaking of the socialist movement and of intellectuals and radicals more generally, Daniel Bell writes: "There was in the excitement of the early thirties, a frosty, tingling sense, almost with cobblestones in hand and Phrygian cap on head, of history being 'made.'" "The Background and Development of Marxian Socialism in the United States," in D. D. Egbert and S. Persons, *Socialism and American Life*, 2 vols. (Princeton, N.J.: Princeton University Press, 1952), I, p. 349.

5. Quoted in Shannon, op. cit., p. 248.

6. "Collectivism is, of course, the keynote of the new social order . . . as not merely a new form of economic organization but as the veritable ethos of the society of the future . . .—a kind of higher existence as compared with the 'selfishness' of 'individualism.'" Will Herberg, "American Marxist Political Theory," in *Socialism and American Life*, I, p. 507.

7. In addition to the obvious reasons for being attracted to labor, the Socialists had the further motivation to limit the success of the Communists who were actively infiltrating the CIO.

8. See Daniel Bell, op. cit., pp. 390–91.

9. See Shannon, op. cit., p. 246. The problem posed by the cases of Reuther and Krzycki came up at national committee meetings for years afterward.

10. The Old Guard split is an important party episode but can be relegated here to a footnote because its details do not affect the main argument of this essay. The Old Guard was drawn largely from veteran New York Jewish Socialists and veteran members of successful local organizations like those of Milwaukee, Wisconsin, Reading, Pennsylvania, and Bridgeport, Connecticut. An age gulf of more than a generation tended to exacerbate the theoretical differences between the Old Guard and most of the newer members attracted by Norman

378 / MARTIN DIAMOND

Thomas' leadership during the early Depression years. An embarrassing conflict arose when an attempt was made in 1932 to remove Old Guard Morris Hillquit from the party chairmanship. Some who sought his ouster wanted a native American to represent the party and their language sometimes seemed to verge on anti-Semitism. But at bottom, the party split reflected the perennial conflict between the left- and right-wing tendencies of socialism.

11. *The Choice Before Us* (New York: Macmillan, 1934), p. 92.

12. Ibid., p. 93.

13. *Radio Speech by Norman Thomas . . . Over Station WCFL, Chicago, 7:30 P.M., October 16, 1936,* mimeographed copy, University of Chicago Library.

14. *Is the New Deal Socialism? An Answer to Al Smith and the American Liberty League* (Chicago: Socialist Party [1936]), pamphlet reprinting a radio speech of February 2, 1936. Especially after the passage of the NRA, the Socialists frequently attacked the New Deal as a forerunner of fascism. Thomas always took pains, however, to make clear that he did not consider President Roosevelt in any sense an actual or even potential fascist. The term reflected the Socialist view that the New Deal *could not* be a stable development of democratic capitalism. Since that was impossible according to socialist theory, it *had* to be the forerunner of something else.

15. *After the New Deal, What?* (New York: Macmillan, 1936), pp. 24–25.

16. Thomas' quip, at a public meeting at the University of Chicago near the end of the 1948 campaign, conveys the then characteristic view: "How low have the waters of liberalism sunk that the heads of Truman and Barkley are able to stand out from the muddy stream!" Shortly afterward, Thomas came to admire President Truman and spoke and wrote in praise of much of his program.

17. *A Socialist's Faith* (New York: W. W. Norton Co., 1951), pp. 101 and 170.

18. R. H. S. Crossman, "Towards a Philosophy of Socialism," in Crossman (ed.), *New Fabian Essays* (London: Turnstile Press, 1952), pp. 5–6. See also John Strachey, "Tasks and Achievements of British Labour," in ibid., p. 188: "British capitalism has been compelled, by the sheer pressure of the British people, acting through our effective democratic political institutions, to do what we used to say it could never, by definition, do."

19. *Laissez-faire and Communism* (New York: New Republic Inc., 1926), p. 73.

20. Op. cit., p. 60.

21. *The Development of Socialism During the Past Fifty Years* (London: The Athlone Press, 1952), p. 29. Italics are supplied to the last clause. Change the rhetoric from somber to frenetic and the resemblance to Marcuse and the contemporary Left is evident. The democratic welfare state in the West is *the* enemy of socialism, the impassable barrier.

22. Will Herberg, op. cit., p. 504. Herberg's instructive essay rightly emphasizes the ideological problems that tormented American socialism during this period.

23. *A Socialist's Faith*, p. 55.

24. Bell, op. cit., p. 374.

25. See Laslett, *supra*, for a somewhat different and more extended consideration of this issue.

COMMENT

Bernard Johnpoll

The role of the New Deal in the demise of the Socialist Party of America was admittedly significant; but it would be an oversimplification to blame the party's disintegration solely on that economic and social revolution of the 1930s. The Socialist Party died of many causes—of which the New Deal was one major component. Chief among the other causes was the internal struggle between the older, less rhetorically revolutionary, trade union-oriented, working-class Old Guard, and the younger, more rhetorically revolutionary middle class of professionals—primarily ministers, professors, and publicists. Whether the Socialist Party could have survived the New Deal is an academic question. There are indications that it could. But that it could not survive its own suicidal internal feuding is a matter of record.

The Socialist Party's rendezvous with death had its origins long before the New Deal. Its demise was almost a direct result of its sudden, unexpected growth from 1929 until 1932. During this period the party admitted many young men mainly from the universities and theological seminaries. These young men were imbued with the idea that they could bring into being during their lifetimes the kingdom of God on earth in the form of socialism. They were not all of one mind: some were pacifist Christian, others were violent revolutionists, and some were intellectuals in search of a cause. They all came from middle-class backgrounds and had degrees in liberal arts and/or theology, and were able to agree on only two things: they despised the "Slowcialists" who controlled the party, particularly in New York, and they wanted the party to dissociate itself from the stodgy, often corrupt leadership of the trade union movement. Moreover, they soon found an ally in the nominal leader of the Socialist Party, Norman Thomas, who was himself a Presbyterian minister, an intellectual, and who had great disdain for party and trade union functionaries.

The New Deal's role in the collapse of American socialism has been exaggerated primarily because Thomas, in rationalizing his role in the party's demise almost twenty years after the fact, blamed it all on the New Deal and minimized the internal party struggles, which, "unfortunate as they were, were never the major cause of our decline. . . ."[1] The first signs of the latter-day Socialist decline began to appear before the New Deal and even after the New Deal was well under way the Socialist Party scored major electoral victories. It was only after the party splintered that it evaporated. In the 1932 election, Thomas had expected a minimum of 2 million votes for President; instead, he polled fewer than 900,000. Moreover, the Socialists fared exceedingly poorly in their long-time stronghold, Wisconsin, where "we have lost every seat but two in the [State] Assembly. . . . And our Congressional candidates did poorly indeed."[2] Norman Thomas, upset by the meager vote he had polled, blamed it on a "blind, anti-Hoover stampede to the Democratic Party."[3] But Thomas was being less than candid. It is probable that there was a mass stampede to the Democratic Party, but there was also a feud raging in the Socialist Party during the 1932 campaign, a feud which had made electioneering exceedingly difficult. Behind that feud were Norman Thomas' efforts to "Americanize" the party—that is, depose the largely foreign-born and second-generation Old Guard from their positions of prominence in the party—and the effort by the young militants to capture control of the Socialist Party. Thomas' move against the Old Guard came at the national convention, where Thomas and his followers —with the cooperation of anti-New York and incidentally anti-Semitic Midwesterners and the small but growing militant wing of the party—attempted unsuccessfully to depose Morris Hillquit as a party chairman and replace him with Milwaukee's mayor, Daniel W. Hoan.[4]

During the campaign, the party feuds reached fever pitch. The hiring of two minor militants to help direct the national campaign brought vehement outcries from Old Guard stalwarts, who refused to cooperate with the national office. An inane suggestion by Paul H. Douglas on how independent voters might support Thomas by use of a complicated and unworkable formula brought further outcries from among the old-line party faithful. The naming of an independent committee for Thomas—a normal campaign tactic—led to a near-open rift between the Old Guard leaders in New York and the national party office, which was headed by pro-Thomas national secretary Clarence Senior. The Old Guard leadership sabotaged his vote in New York City to such an extent that Thomas, the most popular figure in the party, ran considerably behind the rest of the ticket.[5]

After the election the feuding grew in intensity. At times the fighting was over minor matters. On election day, an Old Guard stalwart urged Hillquit to force Senior from his post because the national organization had given some modicum of recognition to the populist socialist weekly in Oklahoma, *The American Guardian*. Hillquit could, of course, do nothing. A leader of the California Old Guard inferred that Thomas was building a personal machine and urged a concerted effort to smash the attempt. Socialist congressman Victor Berger's widow, Meta, feared that Thomas and his followers were trying "to transform the Socialist movement into a youth movement." And James Oneal, editor of the *New Leader*, was "on the warpath against the [pro-Thomas] League for Industrial Democracy domination of the party." The LID was the center of intellectualism in the party.[6] Oneal complained of friction between the working-class Socialists and the "collegiates" (by which he meant the pro-Thomas intellectuals) and warned that the intellectuals, centered in the LID, were planning to take over the party in 1934. James H. Maurer, Thomas' running mate and former president of the Pennsylvania State Federation of Labor, complained that there were too many preachers prominent in the party.[7] Even militant Paul Blanshard, himself an intellectual and a friend and colleague of Thomas, resigned from the party in 1933 because its intellectuals were leading it to destruction. "The brilliant professors, journalists, and preachers who write analyses of Socialist Party and liberal policy in American journals stress the things which we ought to do rather than the things which are practically possible in the United States in 1933."[8]

Although the Socialist municipal vote of 1933 was less than cheering in New York, the Socialists were swept into power in Bridgeport, Connecticut, and they did exceedingly well in Reading, Pennsylvania, Toledo, Ohio, and a number of other cities. There was thus in late 1933 no sign that the New Deal was cutting sharply into the Socialist vote. Actually, there were indications that the New Deal period might have boded well for the Socialists had not internal strife intervened. In November 1934, fully eighteen months after the origin of the New Deal and in the face of a great Democratic victory, the Socialists made remarkable advances. In Connecticut, the Socialists elected three members to the state senate; in Pennsylvania, Darlington Hoopes and Lilith Wilson polled majority votes for the first time in their re-election to the state legislature; Norman Thomas polled almost 200,000 votes, a record for any statewide Socialist candidate, in his race for senator from New York; and Charles Solomon polled a record off-year Socialist vote of 126,580 against the popular Jewish governor of New York, Herbert Lehman. And this at a time when the over-all vote in New York State was down by almost a million. In California, where Upton Sinclair running for governor as a Democrat on a Socialist platform was cutting the Socialist vote for governor to less than 3,000, George Kirkpatrick, the Socialist candidate for senator, was polling a record Socialist vote of 108,748. And these votes were attained at a time when the party was unable to raise campaign funds from usually sympathetic labor leaders who now shifted their support to the Democrats.[9] In 1936 the Wisconsin Socialists showed remarkable resiliency: Daniel Hoan was re-elected mayor of Milwaukee with a record vote, Glenn Turner polled more than 250,000 votes statewide in a judicial race, and the Socialists joined the Farm-Labor Progressive Federation and carried eleven seats in the state assembly, showing remarkable strength in Kenosha, Racine, and Sheboygan—cities where Socialists had rarely threatened the old parties.[10]

If the New Deal did not cut the Socialist vote, neither did the differences of opinion on the New Deal affect the party. The Old Guard was, if anything, less enamored of the New Deal than were its party opponents. Norman Thomas called the New Deal "a real revolution"; admittedly it was inadequate for the needs of 1933, but Thomas conceded in August 1933 that it had accomplished much for the working class. Old Guard leaders such as Hillquit and Oneal, on the contrary, were less than enthusiastic about the Roosevelt reforms. Hillquit called the New Deal "a dangerous deal as far as the working people are concerned," and warned that it "is not possible to remove the poisonous fangs of capitalism without hurting the monster." Hillquit feared that the New Deal was a prelude to a war against strikes and the union shop; moreover, he was apprehensive about the immense power Roosevelt appeared to have accumulated.[11] Oneal warned that the New Deal "has enormously expanded . . . booty politics."[12]

It should thus be apparent that the New Deal—alone—could not have been responsible for the demise of the Socialist Party. The Socialist vote, except for President, held up well during the period of the New Deal's greatest popularity. Moreover, the Socialist analyses of the New Deal were hardly divided on a right-left basis. Opposition to the New Deal was as strong—or stronger—in the right wing, which finally supported Roosevelt in 1936, than it was in the so-called militant or left wing, which campaigned against him in Thomas' quixotic campaign of 1936. The Old Guard supported Roosevelt for internal party reasons in 1936. The militants campaigned against him for the same reasons. Behind the internal feuds were innumerable issues of policy. One of the key problems was the relationship between Socialists and labor unions. The Old Guard wanted to support existing unions, no matter what their social outlook. James D. Graham, president of the Montana Federation of Labor, and an Old Guard Socialist, was incensed that an intellectual such as Thomas dared tell the working-class trade unionists how to run their unions. Thomas had, after all, never worked at manual labor a day in his life—nor had most of his followers. Thomas and the militants, on the contrary, invariably supported trade union rebels against the established labor leadership. Thomas had an uncanny knack for alienating the working-class leadership of most unions. He supported the Communist-led fur workers against the AF of L fur union in their bloody battles. And in Illinois he supported the Progressive Miners in their war with John L. Lewis. "The fight in Illinois is a fight for progressive, militant organization of miners and their families, instead of for an intrenched [sic] officialdom," he wrote.[13] The Progressive Miners soon became an anti-Semitic organization with pro-Nazi overtones.

Another cause of the party fissure was the issue of pacifism. Many of the so-called militants were, in fact, absolutist pacifists. Even in the face of the rise of fascism after 1933, they continued to oppose the use of any force to stop fascist aggression. The section on war of the Detroit Declaration of Principles, enacted at the 1934 party national convention, was a product of such pacifism. Its author, Devere Allen, was a devoted pacifist and a Christian Social Gospel publicist. The Declaration called for absolute opposition to all wars—at the same time that it spoke of a militant (albeit apparently non-military) seizure of power. It was this contradictory Declaration, which mixed revolutionary phrasemongering with pacifist declarations against war, that became the center of the party controversy from 1934 to 1936 while the party was literally tearing itself apart. To the Old Guard the Declaration's section on war meant "Super-pacifism," the refusal of Socialists effectively to oppose the fascists. And to the Old Guard, "Super-pacifism, facing a deadly conflict between the fascist and democratic nations, is really the accomplice of fascism." To Norman Thomas, who was more a pacifist than a Socialist, the revolutionary-pacifist Declaration was a warning to the capitalist class that "we will not fight, you lords and rulers of men."[14] Within three years the pacifists who remained within the Socialist Party were to leave in bitter disgust when their erstwhile comrade, Norman Thomas, supported the sending of a military contingent of American Socialists to aid in the fighting against the fascist rebels in Spain. And four years later the few remaining militant Socialists were again split into virtual non-existence when most of them left the party in disgust after Thomas reverted to his pacifist isolationism during the first two years of World War II.[15]

Besides pacifism and revolutionary phrasemongering, no issue rent the party with such ferocity as did the question of uniting all pro-Socialist radicals. This was an old problem among Socialists, dating at least to the 1870s, but which reached its peak from 1919 to 1933. In 1928–32 the Socialists considered merging with progressive, semi-Socialist intellectuals in the League for Independent Political Action, headed by John Dewey and Paul H. Douglas. But after five years of ineffective effort the LIPA virtually disappeared. Then the Socialists tried to work with the Conference for Progressive Labor Action headed by A. J. Muste, a Christian-Marxian pacifist. But the CPLA soon moved too far to the left and Muste turned it into his own sect, The Workers Party, which lasted only a few months before being swallowed up by the Trotskyites.[16] There were a few later efforts, notably the Continental Congress of Workers and Farmers of 1933, but little came of any of them.

The Communist issue was of a different nature. Socialists had learned through hard experience not to trust the Communists. The most serious Communist assault on a Socialist meeting came in February 1934 during a memorial meeting at New York's Madison Square Garden for Socialists slain during the uprising in Vienna. After this meeting Socialists generally agreed that there could be no united front, that the Communists aimed to destroy the Socialist Party. Yet within seven months after the Madison Square Garden affair, Norman Thomas argued that "recent events . . . have given hope that the time has arrived when negotiations [between the Socialist and Communist parties] in America might not be in vain. . . ." The Old Guard would have none of it. "We drive Communism out of the front door in 1919; it enters through the window in 1934," Oneal complained. Very little came of the united front efforts; the Communists and Socialists could not agree on key issues for long enough to unite on them; the Communist line kept shifting with the sands of Soviet foreign policy.[17]

Incorporating the worst elements of both the inclusive party doctrine, which dominated the militants' organizational design, and the problem of the united front with the Communists was the admission into the party of splinter group Communists, Trotskyists, Lovestoneites, and Gitlowites. These men were experts at Talmudic interpretations of Marxian minutiae and past masters at internal party politics, but they offered little political know-how or organizational stability to the floundering Socialist Party. Thomas had dreamed since 1919 of creating a party composed of all "socialist" elements from the Nonpartisan League to the Industrial Workers of the World. In 1935, having assumed the mantle of party leadership, Thomas decided to make his dream a reality. He had the National Executive Committee invite all radicals into the party. The result was disastrous. First Ben Gitlow, Herbert Zam, and a collection of ex-Communist Party members now affiliated with one or another Communist sect of minor proportions joined the party. Except for organization of short-lived factions, their effect was minimal because they were so few. But at the same time Albert Goldman, a Chicago Trotskyite, joined the party as a scout for the Trotskyite leadership. He did not hide his aims; he explained in a pamphlet that "I still adhere to the principles of revolutionary Marxism as generally interpreted by Lenin and Trotsky. . . . Of course, I expect to see struggles in the Socialist Party between reformists and militants. I even expect to see splits. . . ." Despite the obvious warning of the Trotskyites' intentions, the Socialists under Thomas admitted them. The Trotskyites found the Socialist Party fertile soil for their hairsplitting theorizing about revolution. Meetings went on interminably as minor points of revolutionary precision were debated endlessly; new journals appeared in endless procession as Trotskyites and non-Trotskyite quasi-revolutionists vied with each other for the apex in revolutionary incomprehensibility. In the end, the Thomas dream of an all-inclusive party had to be abandoned within eighteen months after it had begun—the Trotskyites were ousted; the semi-vital party they had entered was little more than a shell-shocked wreck when they left.[18]

It is obvious that the internal feuding made it impossible for the Socialist Party to remain viable. In New York the Socialists spent most of their efforts in 1936 struggling over a primary election contest for control of the party. In Reading, where Socialists held power, all militants lost their jobs in the city administration while Socialists fought in court and primary election for party control. In Bridgeport, Devere Allen and Mayor Jasper McLevy fought a pitched battle for the party organization. In the end the Socialist Party was paralyzed; the two Socialist legislators were soundly defeated in Reading, and the three Socialist state senators lost their seats in Bridgeport. Where there was no internal feuding, as in Wisconsin, the Socialists remained viable.[19]

Admittedly, the New Deal signified a major revolution in American social and economic life. Admittedly, it took much of the wind out of the Socialists' sails. Admittedly, despite brave talk of socialism, most Socialists had in fact been proposing New Deal reforms. Yet, it is fair to assume that the Socialist Party could have survived the New Deal. Election returns from 1933 and 1934 make it appear that a left-wing alternative to the New Deal—perhaps not entering the presidential elections—could still garner sufficient following to have some influence, possibly within some Labor League for Political Action. But no organization could exist which spent its time debating minor points of revolutionary holy writ.

James Oneal said in 1936 that "no party of the working people can afford to permit itself to come under the control of intellectuals of middle class and capitalist origins. . . . All of their training and associations render them unfit to understand working-class life and psychology."[20] In this statement is the root of the Socialist Party's destruction. It was far less the New Deal than the inability of the middle-class Socialist intellectuals to comprehend the aims and aspirations of the working class which led to the demise of American socialism. It was far less the New Deal than the intellectuals' proclivity for incessant, incoherent, and divisive debates over dogma, invariably leading to schisms, which led to the death of American socialism between 1930 and 1942.

NOTES

1. Norman Thomas, "The Split of 1936," 1957, p. 3 (Typescript in Socialist Party of America Papers, Duke University).

2. Meta Berger to Morris Hillquit, November 10, 1932; Morris Hillquit to Meta Berger, November 16, 1932 (in Morris Hillquit Papers, State Historical Society of Wisconsin, Madison).

3. Norman Thomas to Morris Hillquit (telegram), November 9, 1932 (Hillquit Papers).

4. See, for example, *Jewish Daily Forward*, May 24, 1932; Anna Bercowitz, "The Milwaukee Convention," in *American Socialist Quarterly*, I (Summer 1932), pp. 49–53.

5. William H. Feigenbaum to Meta Berger, Daniel W. Hoan, Leo Krzycki, William A. Cuneo, July 23, 1932; Herbert Merrill to National Campaign Committee, August 1, 1932; Julius Gerber to Daniel W. Hoan, September 2, 1932; Julius Gerber to Daniel W. Hoan, November 12, 1932 (all in Hoan collection, Milwaukee County Historical Society). Paul H. Douglas, "Pairing Votes for Thomas," in *The Nation*, CXXV (November 2, 1932), p. 430; Daniel W. Hoan, "Pairing Votes," *The Nation*, CXXV (December 7, 1932), p. 560.

6. William H. Feigenbaum to "Dear Morris," November 18, 1932; Morris Hillquit to William H. Feigenbaum, November 23, 1932; Julius Gerber to Morris Hillquit, December 9, 1932; John C. Packard to Morris Hillquit, March 14, 1933; Meta Berger to Morris Hillquit, November 10, 1932; Algernon Lee to Morris Hillquit, May 9, 1933 (all in Hillquit Papers).

7. James Oneal to Morris Hillquit, May 30, 1933 (in Hillquit Papers).

8. "A Confidential Statement by Paul Blanshard Regarding His Resignation from the Socialist Party" [August? 1933] (in Hillquit Papers).

9. *New Leader*, November 10, December 15, 1934; February 14, 1935.

10. *Socialist Call*, April 18, 1936, November 14, 1936; *New Leader*, June 27, 1936.

11. Morris Hillquit to City Executive Committee of Socialist Party [September 17, 1933] (Hillquit Papers).

12. *New Leader*, July 14, 1934.

13. See, for example, Clarence Senior to National Executive Committee, January 5, 1933; Morris Hillquit to Clarence Senior, January 5, 1933; James D. Graham to Clarence Senior, January 10, 1933 (at Duke University). See also James Oneal to Morris Hillquit, March 16, 1933 (in Hillquit Papers).

14. Bernard K. Johnpoll, *Pacifist's Progress* (Chicago: Quadrangle Books, 1970), pp. 120–26; "Stenographic Report of the Debate on the Declaration of Principles," in *American Socialist Quarterly*, III (Special Supplement, July 1934); *New Leader*, February 29, 1936.

COMMENT / *389*

15. John Haynes Holmes to Norman Thomas, December 23, 1937 (in Norman Thomas Papers, New York Public Library). See also Johnpoll, op. cit., pp. 220–26.

16. Karl Denis Bicha, "Liberalism Frustrated: The League for Independent Political Action, 1928–1933," in *Mid-America,* XLVIII (January 1966), pp. 19–28; Nat Hentoff, *Peace Agitator: The Story of A. J. Muste* (New York: Macmillan, 1963), pp. 76–77.

17. *New Leader,* September 8, September 15, 1934; May 11, May 18, 1936.

18. Johnpoll, op. cit., pp. 155–58; *New Leader,* January 19, February 2, 1935.

19. *New Leader,* May 9, August 29, September 19, November 7, November 14, 1936; *Socialist Call,* April 18, 1936.

20. *New Leader,* January 18, 1936.

REPLY

Martin Diamond

Professor Johnpoll begins unexceptionably by cautioning against "oversimplification"; the New Deal must be seen, he therefore admonishes us, as only "one major component" among the causes of the party's demise. He wants attention paid also to what was "chief among the other causes," namely, the militant-Old Guard internal struggle. Fair enough. But as he proceeds, the New Deal somehow keeps becoming less and less important while the internal struggles keep becoming more and more important. Thus, he tells us, scholars were misled into exaggerating the importance of the New Deal, in the first place, by Norman Thomas, who, wanting to rationalize his own role, turned attention away from the internal struggles and to the New Deal. By the end of Johnpoll's remarks, the cause of the party's demise "was far less the New Deal than the intellectuals' proclivity for . . . divisive debates . . . leading to schisms." I am strongly inclined to think that the "far less" goes too far. Yet, at one point, Johnpoll goes ever further; "there were indications that the New Deal might have boded well for the Socialists had not internal strife intervened." That I *know* goes too far. Perhaps, however, at the end of my response I can propose to Professor Johnpoll a way to accommodate our differences. But first let us develop them.

Johnpoll's view that the internal struggles rather than the New Deal primarily destroyed the party depends, in large part, on his interpretation of a handful of election results. He emphasizes the "remarkable advances" the party made in some local elections in 1933–34. They prove that the "Socialist vote, except for President, held up well during the period of the New Deal's greatest popularity"; and therefore indicate that "the New Deal might have boded well for the Socialists had not internal strife intervened." But Johnpoll's own sketch of the party during these years supplies the basis for the refutation of his argument. The party did less well than it expected in 1932, remarkably well in 1933–34, and disastrously in 1936. Now, by his own account, while these electoral results were varying widely, the party's internal struggles were a constant factor. Thomas' presidential vote in 1932, Johnpoll tells us, was relatively poor because of the "feud raging" in the party. But he neglects to remember that the same feud was raging even more when the "remarkable advances" were being made in 1933–34; indeed, the internal struggles were about at their worst in New York when Thomas polled the record vote that Johnpoll mentions. And, of course, the disastrous presidential vote of 1936 likewise occurred while the party feud was raging. Now how can the constant factor of the party feud account for these widely varying electoral results? The answer is that it cannot, and something else does—the New Deal. It really was "Roosevelt in a word" as far as the elections were concerned. Against Roosevelt, Thomas ran relatively poorly in 1932[1] and miserably in 1936. In between, in a handful of places, when FDR and the New Deal were not at issue, but while the Depression was still radicalizing part of the electorate, where local circumstances prevailed as they can in nonpresidential elections, and where the local organization was strong, the Socialists did extremely well. That is all that that handful of election results of 1933–34 means. Those results do not at all sustain the weight Johnpoll places on them.

Moreover, Professor Johnpoll's account of the nature of the party's internal struggles, while instructive in many respects, is also not free of difficulties. Chiefly, he oversimplifies the problem by blaming the internal struggles wholly on one side. They were caused by the "ministers, professors, and publicists" (have a care, Professor Johnpoll; we are all professors now), all middle-class intellectuals, whom Norman Thomas, the villain of the piece, led into the party in 1929–32. It was the "intellectuals' proclivity for . . . devisive debates" that caused the internal struggles and thus ruined the party. These intellectuals drained the party's energies by causing it to spend "its time debating minor points of revolutionary holy writ."

Now, as Johnpoll's own account makes perfectly clear, the party was not primarily disputing about "minor points." The two wings of the party were differing over classic Left-Right issues that no socialist party could avoid resolving: what posture to take regarding organized labor, how to deal with pacifism and at the same time with the rising menace of fascism, how to deal with the other elements of the Left, and, in general, how revolutionary a party should be. Johnpoll does not really think that these were minor matters. He thinks they were terribly important and that Thomas and his followers were in the wrong regarding them.

They were wrong because, as middle-class Socialist intellectuals, they were unable "to comprehend the aims and aspirations of the working class." (To which one can only respond that, if Socialists had from the first really comprehended the nature of the working class, they would have given up the ghost at the outset! But let us pursue the argument soberly.) Instead of following their fatally un-working-class policies, the party should have become a "left-wing alternative to the New Deal"; perhaps by having continued local but not presidential campaigning, perhaps by supporting "existing unions, no matter what their social outlook," by having been able "to have some influence, possibly within some Labor League for Political Action," etc. In short, Johnpoll's remarks are a brief for the Old Guard. Had their views prevailed in a united party, the demise of the Socialist Party could have been avoided. Its demise was, therefore, the product of its own folly.

Now most of Johnpoll's policy observations sound quite commonsensible. (And, very likely, if I had it to do all over again, I too would find myself with the Old Guard on most policies.) Johnpoll is perfectly correct in seeing that its left-wing path led the party to oblivion. But, as my essay argued, the party was equally correct in understanding that the right-wing path now retrospectively recommended by Johnpoll would simply have led to a different kind of failure and oblivion. Can anyone believe that Johnpoll's suggestions add up to a remotely viable strategy for a socialist party? There was no path that led to socialism.

This is not the place for an extended consideration of Johnpoll's brief against Norman Thomas. One or two observations must suffice. One very small point first. Johnpoll says that the Old Guard was if anything cooler to the New Deal than Norman Thomas; indeed, he seems almost to make Thomas out an enthusiast of the New Deal. I note only that the Old Guard "*finally* supported Roosevelt in 1936," that is, after a lapse of only two or three years, while Thomas never did. The record, I think, supports the view presented in my essay. Another point. Johnpoll blames Thomas for bringing into the party in 1929–32 the influx of intellectuals who later ruined it. Now whether that is what ruined the party or not can be debated. But what is indisputable is that, if Norman Thomas had not produced that influx in 1929–32, there would have been no party to ruin later; it would have expired then and there. And this, in general, is what Johnpoll neglects. Whatever may have been his faults and weaknesses, Thomas became the life and soul of the party; without him the party would simply have been lost in the shuffle of the decade. The tens, perhaps hundreds of thousands drawn under the influence of socialism by Norman Thomas, and by him only, testify to his singular and immense value to the party. It is my judgment that neither Thomas nor any leader, no matter how wise and attractive, could have saved socialism's untenable cause. But Thomas kept it as alive and for as long as seems to have been possible in the circumstances. Moreover, he was, finally, movingly open, thoughtful, and decent in confronting the dilemmas of socialism. And, in the process, he managed to make some valuable contributions to his country.

At the outset of this response to Professor Johnpoll's remarks, I suggested that there might be a way to accommodate our differences. Since we are both studying the demise of the Socialist Party, it will not be inappropriate to think of the matter in medical terms. Grave diseases make the victim vulnerable to all sorts of ailments, any trivial one of which can carry him off. Professor Johnpoll has concentrated on those minor ailments which I believe were themselves, or at least in their fatality, the product of the underlying grave disease. As one pathologist to another, if he will allow me the diagnosis of the underlying disease, I will cheerfully grant him jurisdiction of the final throes.

NOTE

1. Johnpoll blames the party feud and Old Guard sabotage for the fact that "Thomas, the most popular figure in the party, ran considerably behind the rest of the ticket" in New York in 1932. Perhaps the reason is that the rest of the ticket was not running for the presidency against Roosevelt.

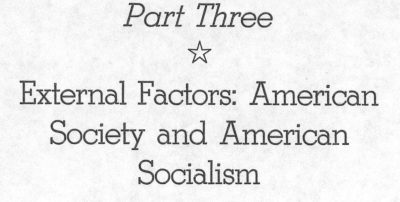

Part Three

☆

External Factors: American
Society and American
Socialism

Chapter 9

THE LIBERAL TRADITION*

Louis Hartz

1. *Liberal Reform in America*

One can use the term "Liberal Reform" to describe the Western movement which emerged toward the end of the nineteenth century to adapt classical liberalism to the purposes of small propertied interests and the laboring class and at the same time which rejected socialism. Nor is this movement without its ties to the earlier era. If there is a link between Progressivism and the Jacksonian movement, there is a link also between the Jacobinism of 1848 and that of the French Radicals. The socially conscious English Liberals at the turn of the nineteenth century had their progenitors even during the age of the First Reform Act. But the American movement, now as during that age itself, was in a unique position. For swallowing up both peasantry and proletariat into the "petit-bourgeois" scheme, America created two unusual effects. It prevented socialism from challenging its Liberal Reform in any effective way, and at the same time it enslaved its Liberal Reform to the Alger dream of democratic capitalism.

The fate of America's socialism was thus deeply interconnected with the fate of its Liberal Reform, as both were involved in the triumph of its reconstructed Whiggery: we are dealing with an equation of interdependent terms. Because the Progressives confronted no serious challenge on the left, they were saved from a defensive appearance, were able to emerge as pure crusaders. And yet this very release from the tension of the European Liberal reformers was reflected in a peculiar weakness on the part of the Progressives themselves, which was their psychic susceptibility to the charm and terror of the new Whiggery. America's "petit-

* Chapter 9 from *The Liberal Tradition in America: An Interpretation of American Political Thought Since the Revolution* (New York: Harcourt, Brace, 1955), originally entitled "Progressives and Socialists."

bourgeois" giant, in other words, if he would not flirt with Marx, was in constant danger of falling into the hands of Elbert Hubbard. And who can deny that the Progressive movement has a spottier history than anything to be found in the Liberal Reform of Europe? During the dizzy decade of the 'twenties, when Alger and the American Legion locked hands against the background of Bolshevism, Republican Presidents were not only elected but even the Democratic party reshaped itself in their image. If the Catholic Church was a refuge for Brownson after 1840, the left bank of Paris provided a refuge for many of his successors during the age of the stockmarket boom. Flight from the American liberal world itself, the technique of the "frustrated aristocrat," became the technique as well of the "frustrated radical."

But moments of utter collapse are not all that we have to consider. What sort of program did the American Progressive advance even during the vivid days of the New Freedom and the Bull Moose? The answer in general is obvious enough. He advanced a version of the national Alger theme itself, based on trust-busting and boss-busting, which sounded as if he were smashing the national idols but which actually meant that he was bowing before them on a different plane. Wilson, crusading Wilson, reveals even more vividly than Al Smith the pathetic enslavement of the Progressive tradition to the "Americanism" that Whiggery had uncovered. To be sure, there is a quaint academic touch in Wilson's Algerism, which inspired him to depict "what it means to rise" by reference to Princeton freshmen and priests in the Catholic Church during the middle ages, but in essence he is as sound as a Chamber of Commerce orator. So is Teddy Roosevelt, although here we find, if not the atypical atmosphere of the classroom, the rather unusual bombast of a frustrated Nietzschean in the American setting. Certainly the contention of Croly that there was a great and "fundamental difference" between the New Freedom and the New Nationalism can hardly be defended, when we consider their common allegiance to democratic capitalism, and William Allen White had one of his keenest insights when he described the chasm between them as the chasm between Tweedledum and Tweedledee. One need not deny, of course, that both movements called for social measures such as hours legislation and workmen's compensation which were not entirely within the ambit of "Americanism" and which in their own small way offered a hint of the European Liberal reformers. But these were loose marginalia, lacking a definite rationalization other than that which the Alger scheme afforded, and certainly without the concept of a permanent "working class" or a permanent "social debt" such as the English Liberals and the French Radicals hurled against reactionary capitalism and Toryism.†

Which brings us again to the crucial significance of ideology: the Algerism of the Progressives was no more due in the last analysis to the boom of the time than was the Algerism of Whiggery. Boom sustained it, as it did the other, but after the crash of 1929 it would not disappear but would go underground to serve as the secret moral cosmos on the basis of which New Deal pragmatism moved. It was an expression of the dogmatic Lockianism of the nation, which is why it has a very peculiar pathos. Essentially, though of course in modified form, the American Progressive confronted the same realities as confronted the European Liberal reformers: the irreversible rise of a proletariat, the irreversible inequity of the capitalist race. But in the irrational grip of "Americanism," and not yet having learned through the agony of the crash the New Deal technique of burying ethics and "solving problems," he could not look these frightening facts in the face. He could not speak of "proletarians" or "capitalists" or even "classes." He could not see what every Western Liberal reformer saw with ease. Come what may, he had to insist that the Alger formula would work if only given a chance.

Here we have the clue to the whole trust obsession of the time. We think of the trust as an economic creation of American history, and we fail to see that it was just as much a psychological creation of the American Progressive mind. Granted that America now superseded England as the home of the "great industry," to use the words of Ashley,[1] it is still a fact that the relative concentration

---

† European Liberal Reform was not, of course, all of a doctrinal piece, and one can refer to it as a whole only in the sense that it sought generally to transcend the earlier individualism. There is a world of difference between Mazzini's nationalist idealism, influenced by the utopian socialists, and Bourgeois' theory of solidarity, influenced by French sociology. And there is a lot of difference between both and the collective idealism of T. H. Green and his liberal followers. What is involved in all cases of the "New Liberalism" is a frank recognition of the need for collective action to solve the class problem (though in fact this action was not always taken on a comprehensive scale). The image of Horatio Alger, for all of the effort of the movement to retain the core of individualism, was alien to it.

of economic power was greater in almost any part of Europe than it was in America. And yet the European Liberal reformers, though they blasted "monopoly"—the English in the case of the tariff and land, the French in the case of large business in general—did not make the same fetish of the symbol that the American Progressives did. They spoke of other things, the large alignment of classes. The truth is, the trust in America was in significant part an intellectual technique for defining economic problems in terms of a Locke no one dared to transcend. If the trust were at the heart of all evil, then Locke could be kept intact simply by smashing it. It was a technique by which a compulsive "Americanism" was projected upon the real economic world.

But this technique, simple as it seems, was not without its problems. As time went on more and more of economic fact had to be obscured in order to make it work. Representative minds like Lloyd and Brandeis were fairly good at this, which is why the surface of their thought does not show the problem clearly. It is in figures apparently more complicated, men like Croly and Ward, where the tension between reality and projection suddenly explodes to the surface, that we see the agony it involved. These were the courageous minds of the Progressive era, Comtians indeed, men who dared to think of "planning." But put their Comtism alongside Comte himself, and what do you find? A pathetic clinging to "Americanism" which in the case of Croly led to practically unintelligible rhetoric when the crucial questions were posed, and in the case of Ward led to a queer "sociocracy" half based on the very Lockian animism that Comte so vigorously assailed. Granted that the European Liberal reformers, even in France, did not advance the Comtian state, still they were a good deal closer to it than anything we find in these American iconoclasts. Is it any wonder then, if these intellectual heroes suffered so, that the common man should flee in his leisure hours to the fantasy Bellamy offered? It is only a superficial paradox that a utopia based on perfect planning should sell so widely in an age that struggled for perfect individualism. The dream is the subconscious wish: utopias are mechanisms of escape. Could there be any sweeter release for the tormented trustbuster than to dream of a perfect trust, a trust so big that it absorbed all other trusts, so big that the single act of its nationalization collectivized all America? Moreover notice this: there was nothing "un-American," "socialistic," or "alien" about

THE LIBERAL TRADITION / 401

this vision. "On the precise contrary," as the good Dr. Leete himself said, "it was an assertion and vindication of the right of property on a scale never before dreamed of."[2]

Surely it is not accidental in the light of this that American socialism was isolated. Actually, though the whole of the national liberal community sent the Marxists into the wilderness, the final step in the process which did so was the nature of American Liberal Reform. For what is the hidden meaning of all this compulsive "Americanism," with its rejection of the class and social language of the European Liberal reformers, if not precisely the burning of every conceivable bridge between Progressivism and the socialist movement? A man could move from Lloyd George's defense of the working class to socialism, as many Englishmen in fact did. A man could move from Bourgeois's theory of solidarity to socialism, as many Frenchmen did. But how could a man move to Marx from a Progressivism which even in its midnight dreams ruled out the concepts of socialism? Here we see why the American socialist movement could not cut into the Progressive vote appreciably, save in areas like the German-populated Wisconsin, for it was the drift of disenchanted Liberal reformers into the socialist camp which accomplished this process in Europe. It was the discovery by labor that Liberal Reform did not go far enough which produced the Labor party in England and the rise of Socialism in France. To be sure, there was in one sense less objective ground for such a drift in America, since it cannot be said that Progressivism permitted vestiges of the feudal order and feudal ethos to survive as European Liberal Reform did, since such vestiges were not here to begin with. Everywhere in Europe, in MacDonald's England hardly less than in Kautsky's Germany, socialism was inspired considerably by the class spirit that hung over not from capitalism but from the feudal system itself. On the other hand, since we are dealing with mythological assets and liabilities, we can also note that Progressivism paid for this advantage by an inability to dominate the socialists in a campaign against the old feudal institutions, a technique which European Liberal Reform took over from European Whiggery. The real issue remains, however, that the vital point at which the American world isolated socialism was the point at which Progressivism compulsively embraced the Alger ethos.

And yet we must not dismiss this irrelevant European analysis too easily, since it was soberly reflected in the American socialist literature, which suggests that if the socialists were isolated by the mechanism of the national life they did little enough to sweeten their lot. Of course, their persistent use of the European concepts of Marxism when the nation was frantically ruling them out of its mind displays their behavior in the broadest way. But when we consider their own internal struggles, the battles over which they expended the colossal energies dammed up by political failure, we see how completely they were dominated by the European patterns of thought. For if the whole issue of collaboration with the "bourgeois reformers" took a unique shape in America, this did not prevent them from fighting, line by line and issue by issue, the European battle over the question. Even before the formation of the Socialist party in 1900 the struggle between Guesde and Jaurès arising out of a Dreyfus affair America never saw was dutifully fought out by the American Marxists, with De Leon, the eccentric half-genius of the movement, emerging as the leading "impossibiliste" of the New World. And, of course, when around 1910 the Socialist party split into two wings over the reform question, Victor Berger and the Milwaukee socialists, followers of Bernstein in a world Bernstein never knew, emerged as the leading "bourgeois collaborators." If the American socialists were determined not merely to advance the basic "un-Americanism" of the socialist scheme but also its secondary, interstitial, and post-Marxian "un-Americanism," is it surprising that their fate was even worse than that of the Southern "feudalists"? . . .

The attitude toward socialism remains, therefore, the final test of Progressive "Americanism." Here we need not expect an inner tension, since it is the indomitable drive to stick to a nationalistic Locke which inspires the peculiar pathos of the Progressive mind. What we ought to expect, and what indeed we find, is a rejection of the Marxian creed no less fanatical than the one in Whiggery itself. When W. D. Howells said that socialism "smells to the average American of petroleum, suggests the red flag, and all manner of sexual novelties, and an abusive tone about God and religion,"[3] he had in mind, with good reason as we have seen, even his fellow Bellamy enthusiasts. The issue, of course, is this matter of the "petroleum" odor, for the European Liberals opposed socialism as well, only with much the same concepts that socialism itself used, which meant that, instead of being horrified by the atmosphere of Marx, they could easily drift into it. We are brought directly to the isolation of socialism.

2. *Socialism in the Wilderness*

It is good for the analyst of the American liberal world, if not for the socialists themselves, that they were men of such fine European courage. Of course, they compromised a bit: they would be inhuman if this were not the case. When for a moment some of them dissolved and joined the "nationalist" movement of Bellamy, were they not compromising pathetically, as if the American fantasy, which as we know was American enough, could ever be the same as the European theory of Marx? Even within the context of socialism, moreover, and even in De Leon the revolutionary, we occasionally find a curious twisting of Marxian doctrine in order to satisfy the Alger ethos. But by and large the sins were remarkably few, and Spargo noticed the charge against even reform socialism that it sought "to apply to American life judgments based on European facts and conditions."[4] All in all the movement went doggedly ahead, even without feudal remnants, even without the power to make a serious impact on Liberal Reform. So that one might say it has the same relationship to the general pattern of Western Marxism that a postage stamp has to a life-size portrait: all the lines are there, all the features, but the size is very small.

It is not surprising that when the American socialists did begin to twist their Marxism a bit they did it with reference to the great American fetishes of the trust and direct democracy. Needless to say, Marxism, even of the Kautsky-Bernstein variety, which stressed the educational impact of the democratic process on the proletariat, did not yearn for anything like the long ballot, and yet the Socialist party again and again made it a crucial part of the Marxian scheme. One might call this, if he were in a satirical mood, "Jacksonian socialism," and ask how direct democracy would work under socialism when it could hardly work under capitalism where the business of government was comparatively small. But it was the trust issue which really played havoc with the American socialists, not because socialism did not blast monopoly but because its approach to it was radically different from anything the Progressives advanced. First of all, it did not blast monopoly in order to establish individualism, but rather to establish collectivism, so that when Atkinson spoke of creating "opportunities" by smashing trusts he was really being the worst thing in the socialist book: "petit-bourgeois." Even Jaurès, when he modified French socialism to satisfy the peasant, did not go as far as this. Ironically enough, moreover, it was the "impossibiliste" De Leon who integrated Atkinson's trustism into the Marxian historical theory. He said that he agreed with Bryan and Roosevelt that America had once been a land of freedom and that trusts had changed it when of course Marxism held that no capitalist society at any time, even in its early fluid stages, was ever really free.

But these sell-outs to "Americanism," considering its devastating impact upon the socialists, can easily be excused. Certainly they did not—by means of borrowing from Liberal Reform rather than challenging it, a kind of inversion of the European process—lead to any serious socialist inroad into the Progressive vote. To be sure, they helped the socialists in 1912, but this triumph could not last and even then it was minor compared to the Progressive enthusiasm on which it so obviously fed. The idea that Wilson could have been driven out of New Jersey by Debs as Clemenceau was driven out of Paris by Guesde and Lafargue is of course fantastic. Even the pressure that the Independent Labor party in England put on the liberals before the World War was out of the question. Even after Bellamy wrote his American introduction to the *Fabian Essays,* the average American still, as he said there, "conceived of a socialist, when he considered him at all, as a mysterious type of desperado, reputed to infest the dark places of continental Europe and engaged with his fellows in a conspiracy as monstrous as it was futile, against civilization and all that it implied."[5] Nor was this the sort of hatred of "the continental agitators" that the English Marxist Hyndman used to entertain. That was a natural British distaste, as with Mill, for the Blanquist, putschist nature of radicalism across the channel, not a dislike of the socialist scheme itself. The American view involved the very foundations of socialist thought.

The fact that Progressivism could not be accused of compromising with an original feudal ethos, of failing to complete the original liberal campaign, was of course critical in the socialist fiasco. If Helen Lynd can list as one of the sources of the incipient English socialism of the eighties the "leaders and followers" pattern of British life, and if Adam Ulam can list it as one of the sources of

THE LIBERAL TRADITION / 405

the rise of the Labor Party itself, pointing out that labor could have bargained with the Liberals for specific policy measures,[6] is not the lesson for America clear? Could Debs argue that socialism was essential to abolish the class spirit emanating from Henry Adams? If the socialists were not lured in the direction of Progressivism by the desire for a united front against Adams, and thus avoided one of the significant European sources of internal factionalism, this was small consolation. In the long run Jaurès and Briand, as well as Guesde and Sembat, gained more than they lost from the Millerand question at the time of the Dreyfus affair. Without the *ancien régime,* the issue of collaborating with the Radicals against it would not to be sure have split French Marxism, but French Marxism would not have existed either.

In any case, the question of collaborating with the Radicals, so to speak, was fought out by the American socialists as well, thus sending them even farther into the wilderness they occupied in a liberal society. Of course the matter of "bourgeois collaboration" extended much beyond the issue of a united front against reaction. There were aspects of it, indeed, which were given a peculiar vividness by the nature of American liberal society. In a land where labor was truly bourgeois, the issue of what Lenin called "trade union consciousness" was indeed interesting: witness De Leon's battle against Gompers. In a land where democracy had been established early, the issue of what Bernstein called the "partnership" of liberalism was also vivid: witness Berger's plea for peaceful change. But these interesting intellectual twists were purchased at the price of isolation, so that if "parliamentary idiocy" was fascinating in a very parliamentary country, the term was also meaningless there.

There is this parallel between the problem of Progressivism and the problem of socialism: both were in the grip of fetishes, "Americanism" on the one hand, Marxism, or "Europeanism" if such a term exists, on the other. But if these are in some sense similar psychological experiences, "word-worship," to use a term of Henry Carey's, they were antagonistic in a profound way. The word of Alger excluded the word of Marx, so that in a community of the blind and half-blind a significant logic was in play. Word-worship is peculiarly bad for scholarship, which is why the social science both of Progressivism and American socialism failed in its analysis of America. And that is our next problem. . . .

3. *The Problem of Historical Analysis*

There can be no doubt that there were other reasons, apart from activism, which prevented American Marxists from exploring the implications for America of the absence of the feudal factor in the Marxian scheme. Concentrating on labor and capital within the bourgeois order, for one thing, meant that the Marxist necessarily viewed feudalism as an antique phenomenon. This orientation was even true of Marx and Engels themselves who predicted socialism in America and yet explicitly noted the fact that America had skipped the feudal stage of Western development. Moreover the instinctive tendency of all Marxists to discredit ideological factors as such blinded them to many of the consequences, purely psychological in nature, flowing from the nonfeudal issue. Was not the whole complex of "Americanism" an ideological question? But after all of this has been said, the simple refusal to face unpleasant facts stands out as crucial. Let us recall again that a law of combined development did appear in Russia when the facts it seemed to produce were pleasant.

To be sure, however blind he was about history, it was not always easy for the American socialist to whistle in the American dark. Usually he conceded that he was in the poorest position of any Western socialist, holding that this was due to transient material prosperity, in line with the Marxian materialist emphasis. Noting that "until quite recently" it was easy for the worker to become a capitalist in America, and that land had been abundant, Spargo traced the whole of the socialist isolation to passing economic circumstances. The fact that a thousand strikes a year were taking place showed that the circumstances were passing.[7] De Leon, possibly because being more revolutionary he was more impatient, could not always tolerate even this analysis. Pointing out that capitalism was "full-orbed" in America, he argued that the revolution would come most quickly here, avoiding the unpleasant fact that where capitalism is "full-orbed" even the people who are supposed to make the revolution are inveterate capitalists. "Plutocracy," another point made by practically all socialists, did not prove anything. So long as the American millionaire stood at the apex of the Alger scheme he did not symbolize the fulfillment of the Marxian hope.

The historical insight lost by this frenzied optimism is clearly revealed in the familiar socialist effort to root socialism in the American past. When De Leon cites Jefferson as the "great confiscator,"[8] how can he grasp the nonrevolutionary nature of American life? Even Veblen, outside the strategic compulsion of Marxism, was forever making the same mistake. Though an acute observer of the capitalist spirit in America, he lumped the "American Declaration of Independence, the French Declaration of the Rights of Man, and the American Constitution" in the same liberal category.[9] But the eighteenth century was of course not the only thing at stake. Given this orientation, which obscured the relevance of the nonfeudal issue, how could American socialism understand anything about its fate? How could it understand the crucial importance of the absence of surviving feudal elements? How could it understand the nature of its failure to make an impact on Progressivism? How could it understand its odd link with the fate of the Southern "feudalists"? In the end Marxist theory paved the way for socialist disappointments as Progressive theory paved the way for Progressive disappointments, which is another way that the two "radicalisms," one nativistic and the other alien, seemed to blend together. A valuable historical analysis, which might have laid bare much concerning the American liberal world, went unused.‡

‡ The question is bound to be raised: In terms of the whole concept of a liberal society, what is the general estimate of Marxism? On the one hand there is a negative view of Marxism stemming from the fact that socialism is traced ultimately to the *ancien régime* as well as to capitalist growth. On the other there is an affirmative view of Marxism stemming from the breadth of its categories as compared with those of the Progressives. These two views are not incompatible, even if the first has implications for economics and ideology which, when carried to their logical conclusion, are damaging to the basic metaphysics of the Marxian scheme. Categories can still be useful even if they are misapplied. However one may legitimately ask, after all of this watering down has taken place, whether there is much more of Marx left than the Western concepts of class which one can find practically everywhere in the Western literature. I would not deny this. The only reason for insisting on the peculiar utility of Marxism here is that it happened to be the one manifestation of the European viewpoint which had followers in America.

NOTES

1. W. Ashley, *Surveys Historic and Economic* (New York, 1900), p. 385.

2. E. Bellamy, *Equality* (New York, 1913), p. 12.

3. Quoted, J. Dorfman, *The Economic Mind in American Civilization* (New York, 1949), vol. iii, p. 152.

4. J. Spargo, *Socialism* (New York, 1906), p. 139.

5. G. Shaw et al., *Socialism; the Fabian Essays*, with introduction by E. Bellamy (Boston, c. 1894), p. ix.

6. H. Lynd, *England in the Eighteen Eighties* (New York, 1945), p. 110; A. Ulam, *Philosophical Foundations of British Socialism* (Cambridge, Mass., 1951).

7. Spargo, op. cit., pp. 143, 144.

8. Quoted, Olive M. Johnson, *Daniel De Leon* (New York, 1935), p. 24.

9. T. Veblen, *The Vested Interests* (New York, 1920), p. 20.

COMMENT

Kenneth McNaught

Now that we are all beyond consensus we can see that consensus history has been, like Progressive history before it, markedly influenced by the political climate of the years in which it flourished. In this light we may find it ironical that Louis Hartz chose the term "liberal" to define the theme of a book which became at once central to an essentially conservative passage in American historiography. Professor David Donald has pointed out that the exponents of consensus have been, by and large, the historical Establishment—an Establishment which now finds itself under surprisingly fierce and un-consensual attack by younger historians of both the Old and New Left.[1] It further strikes a non-American historian that a principal feature of consensus history is one inherited, not surprisingly, from mainstream American historical writing. That is a trait which Hartz recognizes implicitly and which he exhibits explicitly. It is a proclivity, far more pronounced than in the historiographical traditions of other nations, to employ the causal notion of inevitability. But Hartz reinforces this inevitabilism with the insights of intellectual history and the goals of sociological history to produce a basically conservative account of how-it-had-to-be.

The brilliance of Hartz's argumentation and his frequently startling perceptions—reminiscent of those of a Veblen or a McLuhan—guaranteed *The Liberal Tradition in America* immediate and widespread acclaim. The need, now that the Hartzian analysis has been so broadly incorporated in consensus explanations of American history, is not to identify its points of strength. Rather, as the consensus shows signs of weakening both in the field of historical interpretation and on the battlegrounds of contemporary society, it is reasonable to speculate about the weaknesses in Hartz's Locke/Alger Law. And since it is the Left that is tugging most fiercely at the rents in the consensual fabric the Hartzian explanation of how such criticism cannot produce serious results may most properly be examined.

I should like to look at three aspects of *The Liberal Tradition:* the nature of Hartzian comparative history, the problem of definitions, and Hartz's application of his absence-of-feudalism law to the history of American socialism.

Throughout *The Liberal Tradition* Hartz employs a heady mixture of comparison, analogy, and allusion. While the allusions and the analogies raise specific problems of definition for other historians the comparisons lie at the very heart of the method and the thesis. The only way, Hartz argues, to grasp fully the uniqueness of American history, is by comparison with other national histories. The uniqueness which such comparison will reveal lies in the definitive role played by liberalism. Belief in the tenets of John Locke, later popularized in the mythology of Horatio Alger, has dictated the course followed by American political, economic, and social growth. The reason for the strength of this liberal tradition in America is that Americans have enjoyed the Tocquevillian condition of being "born equal." They broke cleanly from their European parent stem, leaving behind the feudal tradition and retaining only the Lockian premises of a contractual, market-oriented society.[2] The validity of this conception depends, of course, not only upon its self-evident truth, but also upon the accuracy of Hartz's historical comparisons and analogies.

A historian who is at all skeptical of "inevitability" is particularly apt to take exception to the specific points of comparison in the Hartzian edifice. Such a historian is likely to conclude that the parts do not add up to the whole and even that many of the parts are not historically valid at all. He will be very tempted to say that, having decided to prove American liberal uniqueness, Professor Hartz has gone abroad in search only of differences and has thus blinded himself to similarities. In effect, it might be argued, Hartz seeks the lawmaking results of the quantitative method without actually using that method. This line of criticism leads quickly to the problem of definitions and thus to a selective examination of the Hartzian method.

When Hartz asserts that socialism could never have succeeded (or even have taken firm root) in America because America lacks a feudal tradition, a critic can only argue with him on the basis of his definitions and imprecisions. Hartz himself tries to disarm in advance such a critic by observing that his use of the word "feudal" is not only imprecise but that "its technical meaning is stretched when one applies it in the modern era."[3] Having entered this apology, however, he goes on throughout his book to use "feudal" just as if its "stretched meaning" were clearly understood. Well, the meaning to a historian is not clearly understood. Moreover, if Hartz means by "feudal tradition" and "feudal institutions" what one might reasonably expect (a tendency toward legal enforcement of class privilege, various forms of latter-day latifundia, corporate concepts of society, landholding in return for payment in kind, etc.), the historian is bound to say either that Hartz misunderstands his own "stretched meaning" or else that he does not prove his case.

Whatever feudalism as a legacy or tradition may mean, it is clear that as a set of institutions and laws England and Europe were free of it at least as soon as was the United States (or the American colonies). If it means huge landed estates, established churches, class privilege legally enforced, and an organic view of society, then all of these things have been present to the American experience. No American colony was without its land question, most had some experience with established churches, in some the concept of entailed inheritance had to be beaten down, and the "habit of authority" was scarcely unknown throughout one of Hartz's great "exceptions," the American South. Again, if America was born equal because it accepted John Locke, then we must presume that England was born equal somewhat sooner.[4] One might well follow up this logic by recalling that the illiberal institutions of imprisonment for debt and slavery were both abolished in England before they were ended in the United States—and with somewhat less difficulty.

These preliminary remarks about Hartzian comparisons and definitions suggest that there is a basic flaw in his schema. That flaw may now be identified more precisely. It is Hartz's requirement of his readers that they accept, first, his use of terms which are either not defined or whose meanings appear to change in the course of the argument and, second, that they accept comparisons and analogies based upon this impressionistic device. Some further specific illustrations must stand for many that could be given. At the outset Hartz argues that American history *is* the escape from Europe—feudalism and all—and that not until recently has America had to confront Europe. Here, of course, the historian simply cannot agree. How, he must ask, can one explain the origins of American party divisions without taking account of America's reaction to French revolutionary doctrines and Napoleonic (let alone British) policies?[5] What Hartz says of twentieth-century communism is, in fact, just as true of earlier French and English influences on America, namely that they "redefined . . . the issue of our internal freedom in terms of our external life." Again, when Hartz employs Tocqueville's aphorism that Americans are "born equal" he ignores the need to deal with what is plainly another big exception to his format. Tocqueville, after all, was describing Jackson's America rather than the political battles by which Jacksonian "equality" had been achieved—battles which *had* conjoined the forces of liberalism and radicalism in the very manner which Hartz argues cannot happen in non-feudal America. To admit this, of course, would be to concede either a) that such political combination does not require a "conservative" target or b) that there was a conservative target.

Part of the confusion lies in Hartz's equating of liberalism and democracy, and part lies in his cavalier attitude to the sequences of American history. At one point Locke seems to stand for liberty against the tyranny of the majority; at another we hear of the "hidden conformitarian germ" in Lockianism which "transforms eccentricity into a sin."[6] The point which Hartz misses here seems to be that Jacksonian democracy is not implicit in Locke, let alone in Alger; and that liberalism is more usually antipathetic to democracy than otherwise. Perhaps the signal of warning for this misconception was the erratum slip in the first edition of *The Liberal Tradition* which corrected the Tocquevillian misquotation about Americans being "born free." Which is different from being "born equal." The confusion in definitions is the symptom of Hartz's necessity to skirt the obvious conclusion from much of his own evidence that the real spirit of Locke *is* conservative—and thus that the ubiquitous Whigs in the Hartzian system are in fact conservatives. Recent writing by Gabriel Kolko, James Weinstein, Martin Sklar, and others seriously undermines Hartz's argument that Lockians (or Whigs) cannot be conservatives. Theodore Roosevelt and Woodrow Wilson were as thoroughgoing conservatives, by any other standard than that of livery and maintenance, as one can well imagine. Thus the historian is not likely to be much impressed by the Hartzian implication that to be a real conservative in, say, the period 1876–1920, you had to have a title or perhaps what H. G. Wells called Disraeli's "oriental imagination." Indeed, when Hartz chooses Disraeli as a principal example of the kind of Tory democrat that America could never produce he gives the whole game away—for Disraeli himself was an outstanding example (a kind of British Alexander Hamilton) of how an aristocratic cast of mind can be voluntarily adopted without benefit of birth or determining historical laws.

What thus emerges as Hartz's crucial obfuscation is his recurrent assumption that because America had no hereditary titles it had no real class system and therefore no defenders of that system against whom liberals, democrats, and socialists could ally themselves. Thus he declares, for example, that the southern "feudalists" failed inevitably and, like "the modern socialists," made no "dent in the American liberal intelligence." Well, the historian can only reflect that the southern "failure" was made "inevitable" only by means of horrendous civil warfare (which itself is an interesting comment on being "born equal") and that the present condition of American political life strongly suggests that socialism left something more than a dent. Moreover, if Lockianism means, as Hartz says, a curious combination of equality, classlessness, liberty, and democracy, how does one adjust this conception of Americanism to the consistently neo-mercantilist (and triumphant) drive of the Whigs, the political capitalists, and the "national class" discerned so effectively by William A. Williams, Gabriel Kolko, et al.? And, to pursue further this problem of categories or definition, one must ask (ignoring the internal contradictions): is Alger really a symbol of Lockian, egalitarian, liberal democracy? The fact is that the Alger whom Hartz selects as symbol is redolent of class feeling. His theme is always how to get to the top, which is scarcely a classless concept. Indeed, Alger's tiresomely repeated accounts of how one gets to the top are a compound of good fortune, loyalty, and acceptance of what Veblen called the business discipline of the High Command. The fact that Veblen's instinct of emulation led most Americans to hope for a summer palace at Newport, unquestioned credit at Delmonico's, and a gingerbread monstrosity on any town's highest elevation does not suggest that Americans believed America was classless—especially if they read Alger. Rather, it is to say that American commoners (how did Bryan cut so much ice with such a phrase?) have envied the class above them just as much and just as consciously as have the commoners of "feudal" states. They have believed in Alger, Daddy Warbucks, and any other agent of an illiberal fate just as others have believed in the "guv'nor" or the football pools. One might plausibly argue that Alger's great contribution was to Americanize the classic "feudal" fairy tale of the suitor, the princess, and the king.

At one point Hartz suggests that no effort has been made to pursue the comparative analysis suggested by the fact that Hamiltonianism has been called by the English term "Whiggery." It is particularly unfortunate, surely, that he himself did not pursue such an analysis. For it would then be made clear that the elitism of Hamilton did not die in America and was, in fact, the dominant intellectual component of Progressivism—which in turn found so much inspiration (from Lippmann and Croly to Wilson) in English thought. It is this failure to keep an eye out for similarities that leads Hartz into a whole series of misconceptions. Only by using evidence selectively and by looking exclusively for differences can he argue that socialism in America could not find allies among liberals for an attack on anti-democratic "feudal remnants." There were, he argues, no such remnants (and by remnants Hartz means conservative ideology and interest as well as institutions—such as the ideas of the "Southern Filmerians") and this robbed socialism of "a normal ground for growth." But this crucially important point is "proven" by allusion and a rhetorical question: "Could De Leon take over the liberal goal of extended suffrage as Lassalle did in Germany or the crusade against the House of Lords as the Labor Party did in England?"[7] Well, De Leon did not stand in the United States for "American socialism"—certainly not for the socialism of Debs, of Berger, or of Hillquit.

But there is a still more insidious error in the Hartzian rhetoric. That is the assumption that Americans believed that democracy had been won (or received as a gift). This assumption, if we take Populist-Progressive platforms, speeches, and tactics at all seriously, does not flow from the facts. The fact is that most Americans of the Progressive era felt they were engaged in a battle *for* democracy. That battle required and received the full cooperation of socialists and liberals. The point here, surely, is that the British Lib-Lab assault on the House of Lords was for exactly the same purposes and employed the same arguments as the American battle for direct democracy (especially for direct election of the Senate). That the Lords had "feudal" titles should not be allowed to obscure the fact (well known to liberal-socialists on both sides of the Atlantic) that they were defending the same capitalism that was defended by American senators. The undemocratic Lords were leashed in the same democratic interest that required the senators to submit to the elective process—and with much the same result.

It is because of this basic confusion in definitions and comparisons that Hartz's chapter on Progressives and Socialists is so unconvincing among its illuminations. This chapter brings to a focus the inevitabilist argument that runs through the whole of *The Liberal Tradition:* socialism failed because America was non-feudal in origin and experience and thus had no feudal-conservative targets which would compel liberals to cooperate with (and thus eventually be absorbed by) socialism. Ambiguity of definition, frailty of allusion, and disregard of similarities here reach a crescendo. Yet the key to this interlocking fallacy Hartz himself provides when he earlier writes that "socialism arises not *only* to fight capitalism but remnants of feudalism itself. . . ."[8] For this reveals that he will take surface differences (e.g., between a House of Lords and an undemocratic Senate) and treat them as absolutes. Thus he rejects the obvious similarities between the Hobhouse-Green-Mill liberals (who could slide into socialism) and the Lippmann-Croly-Weyl-Dewey liberals for whom the socialist option is denied by Hartz and yet who could and did slide into various kinds of socialism. Moreover, avoidance of such obvious similarities leads Hartz to miss other, more subtle similarities altogether. The most important of these is that the liberal-socialists of American Progressivism faced the same basic problem of "socializing" the labor unions as was faced by their British counterparts with whom they often corresponded on the subject.

These similarities which emerge in any comprehensive comparison lead again to the principal criticism of the Hartz schema: socialism is demonstrably not a *natural* working-class growth in "feudal" societies but is, rather, a response to the particular power structure and inequities fostered by capitalism. Feudal or aristocratic traditions, in other words (and quite apart from Hartz's shaky analysis of the non-feudal background of America), are largely irrelevant to the reasons for socialist growth. With one exception. In a society which enters the age of democracy with a strong anti-aristocratic bias liberals are more likely to find it dangerous to offer basic criticisms and alternatives, let alone effective reform leadership. Thus the American Progressives on the Left, just at the point when American social democracy was becoming respectable, abandoned the leadership role which they had vociferously prescribed, and which their British Fabian counterparts were bringing to a fruitful outcome in the Labour Party—abandoned it in the face of patriotic preparedness and a carefully conducted campaign of calumny. Their socialism had proved *too* ready to accommodate itself to the American context, to cooperate with Progressives, and to undermine the goals of the National Civic Federation—goals which were, incidentally, neo-mercantilistic and therefore un-Lockian in all respects (at least as Hartz uses "Lockian"). Socialism was, in fact, proclaimed un-American because it had become too American.

To prove his point Hartz has further to ignore the fact that the voluminous Progressive and muckraking literature (indeed the entire American press) was alive with the terminology of class—from workingmen to bosses, magnates, and barons. He has further to overlook the plain evidence that socialists in a "feudal" or deferential society such as England had their own special difficulties in converting the trade unionists to socialism and, in fact, never did succeed entirely. In short, Hartz fails to prove that socialism was in a fundamentally different position in the United States and therefore that it never did (and never could have) become a legitimate or indigenous part of American political life. The failure results from the transparency of the veil he draws across the face of reality. Not only is this made clear by the work of Kolko and Weinstein, and by numerous unpublished theses, it is crashingly evident to any historian who has measured the concern expressed by Theodore Roosevelt, Woodrow Wilson, S. S. McClure, Ralph Easley, et al. in the face of socialist growth. Indeed, the debates within the SPA itself show that the "Marxist" minority were as uneasy about the roots being struck by democratic socialism as was the High Command of American capitalism. Conversely the practical and intensely American socialist leaders such as Debs, Hillquit, and Berger regularly displayed the power of class analysis and the strength to be gained by working, like Fabians, at the grass roots and on particular issues of general progressive concern. One American of the kind that Hartz does not much like to quote put this whole matter very well in 1916. Commenting on a labor union-

socialist municipal victory in Minneapolis, the socialist lawyer
G. B. Leonard wrote:

Is it not possible that we have been too much carried away with
the deductive methods of thought of the German Socialists? After all,
the German mind, as indicated by its history and literature, proceeds
from the general to the specific, while we have not developed that
train of mind. We are rather an empirical people. . . . We proceed
from the practical to the theoretical. Even the general propositions
laid down in the Declaration of Independence have lost their significance. Maybe we are on the wrong track [in Minneapolis]. But in
this campaign the reason for our success lies in the fact that we dealt
with concrete things and fought shy of general theories. We chose
our battle cry and battle ground for the purpose of this campaign—
qualifications of the respective candidates and the stand they respectively took on what we call the main issue in this campaign, the streetcar franchise. The opposition tried to force upon us everything else.
We refused, and they were beaten. This is political tactics, but if it
accomplishes the result of solidifying the elements that ought to be
with us, it must be the proper procedure. . . .[9]

Well, one can debate forever the relative merits of doctrinaire
purity vs. pragmatic adjustment, of programmatic politics vs. single-
issue politics. What is now really beyond debate is that socialism,
particularly in its progressive-intellectual and local-machine aspects, did strike roots in America—and that its ideas and methods,
while clearly subject to international cross-fertilization, were no
more derivative than were those of Lockianism, social Darwinism,
sea power, or a lot of other pretty central currents of American
thought. Socialist fortunes in America were decided not by abstract
and congealed ideological determinants but by policies selected by
both socialists and anti-socialists in an American and worldwide
context. The line dividing liberal progressives from socialists was
frequently just as fine as the similar line in England and elsewhere.
Insofar as a feudal-aristocratic tradition existed in England and
Europe, but not in America, this fact seems to have strengthened
conservatism (Whiggery in Hartzian terminology) in America and
liberalism in Europe and England. What Hartzian analysis most in-
hibits is recognition of the fact that democracy is not a synonym
for liberalism—a Tocquevillian point that surely should not have
been missed. Conversely, and equally from Tocqueville, democracy

can be the most conservative of all political systems. Hartz's juggling of the definitions only obscures the fact that American democracy ("born equal"), when manipulated by genuine conservatives, is an anti-liberal force which is neither Lockian nor socialist—but nationalist and conservative. It is a force which could, perfectly conceivably, *become* socialist just as it has been persuaded to become mercantilist and imperialist. If one policy does not seem to work Americans will choose another policy—and their choice will not be predetermined either by John Locke or Horatio Alger, although it would undoubtedly be explained in terms of the Declaration of Independence as modified by the *Federalist Papers*.

The Hartzian tradition, then, seems open to some pretty basic questions. While such questions often apply equally to the whole conception of consensus history they apply with particular force to Hartz's comparative method and to his erratic use of terms such as "liberalism," "democracy," "Lockian," and "Algerism." Pursuit of such questions is unlikely to lead us to identify liberalism with Americanism, socialism with conservatism, or American history with inevitability.

NOTES

1. New York *Times Book Review*, July 19, 1970.
2. I here anticipate Hartz's later book, *The Founding of New Societies*, in which he and others develop the "congealment" thesis and extend the comparative method to countries such as Canada, Australia, and South Africa. Contributors to *The Founding* underline and elaborate Hartz's assumption that new nations cast off from European societies find their political-economic beliefs congealed in the mold of their founding years—except when they are directly confronted by the impact of external ideologies-cum-power. As applied to Canada this thesis is spectacularly unimpressive. Indeed its weakness is made manifest in the work of a protégé of Professor Hartz's: *Canadian Labour and Politics* by Gad Horowitz (Toronto, 1968). In an introductory chapter Horowitz compares the history and fates of socialism in the United States and socialism in Canada. In the course of his review he confesses the impossibility of determining any point at which political ideology in Canada may be said to have congealed. While the Horowitz chapter does not necessarily affect the argument about American exceptionalism it directly refutes the case put in *The Founding* and certainly raises some nagging questions about the congealment of ideology in the United States.
3. Louis Hartz, *The Liberal Tradition in America* (New York, 1955), p. 4.
4. For a persuasive argument that in England capitalism had replaced feudalism by the time that either Hobbes or Locke wrote, see C. B. Macpherson, *The Political Theory of Possessive Individualism* (Oxford, 1962).
5. Post-Hartzian analysis of the extent to which American expansionism shared many features in common with "feudal" European nations suggests that "confrontation" and its resulting influences have been coterminous with American history. Mahan does not appear in *The Liberal Tradition* nor does Hartz discuss Woodrow Wilson's debt to Burke and Bagehot.
6. *The Liberal Tradition*, pp. 11–12.
7. *The Liberal Tradition*, p. 9. Throughout the book Hartz hangs his argument on the De Leon peg. Like Daniel Bell he would have us believe that only "Marxian Socialism" is at issue, and thus both analysts stack the deck in their own favor; e.g., p. 205: Because "the language of De Leon was just about as different from the language of Wilson as it was from the language of McKinley" therefore "while it was possible for a European liberal reformer to drift into socialism . . . it was extremely difficult for a Wilsonian Progressive to do the same thing." Or again, at p. 237, impossibilism is directly imputed to Victor Berger (!) by referring to his "messianic world." One could,

by such means, construct a Hartzian analysis of England, identifying English socialism only with Hyndman and calling Ramsay MacDonald "messianic."

8. *The Liberal Tradition*, p. 9. Italics added.

9. G. B. Leonard to Algernon Lee, November 14, 1916 (Lee Papers, Tamiment Institute, New York). As a postscript to this reasoning (and a tangential reflection on inevitability) one might also refer to Karl Kautsky's letter to Lee (September 18, 1932): "I am very happy to hear from you on the new spirit in the A.F. of L . . . we may be sure that this is no passing whim, but a permanent current in the ranks of American trade unions for state intervention. . . . The only way in the Anglosaxon world to create a powerful Socialist party is to interest the trade unions for interference of the state for the working class to such a degree that only a separate working class party can satisfy them. That [party] may not be a Socialist one in the beginning, but the logic of events will propel them inevitably in the direction of Socialism. That was the way in England and will be the way in America."

REPLY

Louis Hartz

Professor McNaught maintains a logical position in his criticism of my work: having asserted the presence in the United States of the elements yielding a powerful socialist movement, he goes on to imply that such a movement in fact existed. However, I am afraid that I must disagree with him on both counts.

At various points I have isolated three factors stemming from the European feudal inheritance the absence of which in the United States precluded the possibility of a major socialist experience. One is a sense of class which an aristocratic culture communicates to the bourgeoisie and which both communicate to the proletariat. Another is the experience of social revolution implemented by the middle class which the proletariat also inherits, as when Babeuf arises out of the French upheaval of the eighteenth century. Finally, I have cited the memory of the medieval corporate spirit which, after liberal assault, the socialist movement seeks to re-create in the form of modern collectivism. It has been my contention that when the great migration which created American history left these factors behind in the Old World, it left behind also the seeds of European socialism.

Professor McNaught seeks to undermine my first point in two ways. He argues that American colonial culture and southern slave culture were truly aristocratic and that the liberal culture of Hamilton and Alger were at any rate aristocratic enough. However, it is stretching the empirical data much too far to hold that colonial elitism, which fell so rapidly in the Revolution, amounted to the elitism of Europe and it is also torturing the facts to make out of the southern slaveholder, the heir of Jefferson and in many ways a classic capitalist, a symbol of Western feudal culture. Certainly it is to obscure the issue almost completely to stress the "class" component in Whiggery or Alger. In earliest times the elitism of the

American Whig did not match that of the English Whigs and the French Liberals, themselves apostles of capitalism, and the very absence of the class passion induced by the aristocratic encounter is what stands out even in the case of a man like Hamilton when we compare him with Brougham. Professor McNaught says that I have not followed up the comparative analysis involved in this transatlantic correlation but I believe I have done precisely that. And what the analysis suggests is not merely the looser elitism of the Americans but the much more crucial fact that in a liberal society even that elitism could not survive long and had to redefine itself, under the Jacksonian impact, into the democratic capitalist ideology of Alger. As for the effort to extract from Alger himself the class spirit of socialism, I must say that I find it to be an unusually dramatic misconception of the data. I would not deny that there was in the Alger cosmos a very exclusive position for millionaires, the significance of which may in fact have been overlooked in terms of the national discipline required for industrialization. But that position was associated precisely with the idea that access to it was universally available, down to the personage of Ragged Dick, an idea which notoriously undermined the crystallization of class feeling in America.

My second point, that the basic experience of social revolution is missing in America, Professor McNaught scarcely deals with at all. If he intends to do so by his remark that America reacted to French revolutionary doctrines and that this was reflected in American party divisions, surely we have here slight evidence of an authentic domestic experience of social upheaval. Of course the inheritance of the experience of social revolution involves to some extent also the carrying forward of anti-aristocratic goals by the working class itself, and Professor McNaught's identification of Senate reform with the Lib-Lab assault on the House of Lords is relevant in this connection. But he is right to say that what relates the two movements is an attack on financial power. The passionate revolt against sheer snobbishness which motivates British Labour is not part of the American movement of political reform. The truth is, Professor McNaught adduces practically nothing to demonstrate that the American worker had historic contact with one of the factors which Marx himself recognized as crucial to the making of the socialist movement: the precedent of the middle class in assailing an aristocratic order arising out of the Middle Ages.

Even less is said by Professor McNaught concerning my third
argument: that there could not in the United States be a working-
class movement motivated by the desire to reconstitute medieval
collectivism. The reference to an "organic view of society" in the
colonial era or, again, to the Southerners has precious little to do
with the affirmative ambitions of the American labor movement or
the central drift of Progressivism. The whole meaning of the Alger
syndrome, and the reason why it flourished in the United States as
it did not in Europe, is to be found in the compulsiveness of an
individualist ethic coeval with the national culture. There was some
organicism in Puritanism, to be sure, some persistence of the
medieval world, but its great contribution to Western culture was
individualism, and by the time Alger appeared on the scene that
contribution had in America, Puritan from the outset, reached a
blazing national climax. The "memory" of the American laborer
went back to the *Mayflower* but not to the medieval corporation.

When in line with his historical analysis Professor McNaught
seeks to prove that there was a socialist movement in America
comparable to the European, he becomes very vague indeed. His
central point seems to be that socialism "was, in fact, proclaimed
un-American because it had become too American." But it is hard
to know what this means. The fact that "the American Progressives
on the Left" did not behave like "their British Fabian counterparts"
cannot really be explained by the fact that socialism had become
overwhelmingly accepted in the United States. What Professor Mc-
Naught calls their compromise with the "Progressives," presumably
the normal Alger Left, suggests this clearly enough. So in fact the
failure of Fabianism in the United States is proof of the power of
the liberal tradition. Indeed, toward the close of his paper Professor McNaught makes some rather startling concessions to my general position. After saying that feudal traditions are irrelevant to
socialism, he mentions "one exception." This is that "(i)n a society
which enters the age of democracy with a strong anti-aristocratic
bias liberals are more likely to find it dangerous to offer basic criticisms and alternatives, let alone effective reform leadership." But
why does a society enter the democratic age with such a bias? It
can only be because it has somewhere along the line left the feudal
world behind. And why should such a bias militate against "basic
criticisms and alternatives?" It can only be because the society is
not split apart in terms of class and because, lacking contact with

the experience of social revolution, liberalism has become a moral absolute. I am afraid that Professor McNaught comes close to restating my own argument here but in terms rather vaguer than the ones I have employed.

Let me say a final word concerning my use of the comparative method to which Professor McNaught often alludes. I have tried to vindicate my interpretation of socialism in terms of a number of other "fragment" cultures derived from Europe like the American: Professor McNaught refers to this work but curiously in connection with the technical issue of the congealment of the fragment rather than the evidence which concerns socialism itself. Yet that evidence everywhere, whether in Canada, South Africa, or Australia, not only demonstrates a sufficient amount of congealment to produce an American "liberal tradition" but also emphasizes the significance of the very factors affiliated with socialism that I have been discussing here. The volume published by Professor Horowitz[1] further confirms the importance of these factors, even though Professor Horowitz and I might not be in complete agreement on the precise characterization of Canadian history in comparative terms. Professor McNaught says that I do not stress "similarities" with Europe. There are indeed critical similarities between America and Europe derived from a common heritage of Western culture, and when world history has come into its own we will understand them much better than we do now. But these are not the similarities of a common socialist experience within the Western framework. Here the United States is distinctive as against Europe, and its distinctiveness derives from the fact that the *Mayflower* left behind in Europe the experiences of class, revolution, and collectivism out of which the European socialist movement arose.

NOTE

1. Gad Horowitz, *Canadian Labour in Politics* (Toronto, 1968).

Chapter 10

AMERICANISM AS SURROGATE SOCIALISM*

Leon Samson

I

When we examine the meaning of Americanism, we discover that Americanism is to the American not a tradition or a territory, not what France is to a Frenchman or England to an Englishman, but a doctrine—what socialism is to a socialist. Like socialism, Americanism is looked upon not patriotically, as a personal attachment, but rather as a highly attenuated, conceptualized, platonic, impersonal attraction toward a system of ideas, a solemn assent to a handful of final notions—democracy, liberty, opportunity, to all of which the American adheres rationalistically much as a socialist adheres to his socialism—because it does him good, because it gives him work, because, so he thinks, it guarantees him happiness. Americanism has thus served as a substitute for socialism. Every concept in socialism has its substitutive counter-concept in Americanism, and that is why the socialist argument falls so fruitlessly on the American ear.

America is, for all intents and ambitions, a capitalist civilization. It has all the earmarks of capitalism: a strong political state—a profit-wages system of imperial dimensions—a religion—a navy—all the features in fact of a capitalist community. And yet, in the mind of its inhabitants, in their manner, their rhythm, their style of life, this American civilization appears to be in no sense capitalistic, appears, on the contrary, socialistic, proletarian, "human," at any rate far from imperialistic. It is this socialistic fantasy in the mind of the American that acts as an anticlimax to the socialist agitation. The American does not want to listen to socialism, since he thinks he already has it.

*Taken from Chapter One of Leon Samson, *Toward a United Front* (New York: Farrar and Rinehart, 1935), pp. 16–32, 40–53, originally entitled "Substitutive Socialism."

Socialism is, to begin with, brought to him as a new world, as a new social universe displacing the old. Well, America is for him also a new world. And so indeed it is. "America is . . . the land of the future, where in the ages that lie before us the burden of World's History shall reveal itself. . . . It is a land of desire for all those *who are weary of the historical lumber-room of old Europe.* Napoleon is reported to have said, 'Cette vieille Europe m'ennuie.' *It is for America to abandon the ground on which hitherto the History of the World has developed itself.*"[1] The American feels himself to be of another social planet. Aloofness from world affairs, a sense of isolation—so clearly expressed in his diplomacy—that this new-world man experiences with respect to the old world, a holier-than-thou distance from the old world, in a word, a planetary posture toward world events. America is indeed a new social planet that has torn itself off and away from the old-world system and that, therefore, induces among its inhabitants, much as does socialism, the feeling of having made a clean break with the past. Particularly does it do so among the proletarians of the world. "I always consider the settlement of America with reverence and wonder," said John Adams once, "as the opening of a grand scene and design in providence, for the illumination and emancipation of the slavish part of mankind over all the earth."[2]

"Workers of the World, Unite,—you have nothing to lose but your chains." So far as the disinherited of the earth are concerned, there have been up to now but two ways open to them out of their misery: to go to socialism or to go to America. America as a substitute for socialism—the one new world which proletarians do not have to rise to, but run to. But a new world nevertheless.

Now, in this new world new ideals were hatched, or rather old ideals were given a new dress. The American ideals are in their origin and essence like the system in America—capitalistic, imperialistic, bourgeois. "Liberty, Equality, Democracy." But, refracted in the prism of Americanism, they take on an anti-capitalistic, a pseudo-socialistic form. How, for instance, does the American look at the ideal of Liberty? Not like the European, as mere laissez-faire. To the American, liberty is more than that. It is human self-emancipation—Individualism. The American, be it said, is a rugged individualist, and yet he is no individualist in the bourgeois sense of that term. To be an individualist in that sense of the term is, in the first place, to have put away all softness and sentimentality with regard to everything that is in the way of one's capitalist competence and careerism, to be a brazen, imperial buccaneer and competitor. And who can say that the American has achieved any such Napoleonic release of the ego impulses? The American is an individualist for the same reason and in the same way that his neighbor is an individualist. Individualism is in America a social style. It is a collective individualism.[3] Bourgeois individualism is a bird of a different color. It is confined to the bourgeoisie. In America everybody is an individualist, but the ideal of universal individualism is a socialist conception of individualism. "And behold the result. Look down at that crowd on the Avenue. Nothing but straw hats—and all exactly alike. Not a shadow of variety. They even fix a day to change to straw hats in the spring, and everyone must comply with the custom. Clothes are all the same, too, as if they had come from the hand of the same tailor. Get down among them and you will find that their faces are all the same. I tell you, the American people are the most docile, the most easily led, the least individualistic people in the world."[4]

Now as to the ruggedness. The ruggedness of American individualism derives from the fact that pioneering, buccaneering, in a word "frontiering," has here been an attribute, not necessarily of the business man risking his capital but of the man in the street—off the street would be more correct—risking his hide. Thus it was that the gambling attitude toward life[5]—the idea that life itself is a gamble—and the rough and tumble temper that that induces and which elsewhere is confined to the class of capitalist entrepreneurs was here not so confined. Every American was by the phenomenon of the frontier transformed into an entrepreneur and so became rugged. But the aim of this rugged individualist is not empire—which is capitalism, but security—which is socialism, a state of affairs "Where every man is a Freeholder, has a vote in publick Affairs, lives in a tidy warm House, has plenty of good Food and Fewel, with whole clothes from Head to Foot. . . ."[6] This is as true today as it ever was. For every American who strikes out to make a million there are thousands who simply want a home.

Opportunity is a key word in the dictionary of American idealism. But opportunity is not, strictly speaking, a capitalist concept. It is, strictly speaking, a socialist or rather a "socialistic" concept. Opportunity is the bourgeois concept of competition as it is refracted by Americanism, that is to say, as it is brought down from its bourgeois base to the broadest layers of the population—and so is made to take on a social-democratic meaning. The idea that everybody can become a capitalist is an American conception of capitalism. It is a socialist conception of capitalism. Socialism is of all systems the only one in which everybody is in it. Capitalism is, in theory, and in Europe, for the capitalists—just as feudalism is for the feudal lords.

Competitive opportunity is one of the cornerstones of the American system. So also is it of the socialist system. It is not true that socialism wants to abolish competition. It wants to abolish only the brutal aspects of competition. From the utopian Fourier to the most unutopian Lenin, socialist philosophers have advanced the view that far from doing away with competition, socialism would in certain spheres of life and labor give a keener edge to competition than does capitalism. It is the emulative aspects of competition that go under the concept opportunity—that socialism would heighten and intensify, and that in its own utopian way America similarly emphasizes. It is important to bear in mind this emulative aspect of American competitive opportunity for it is not, strictly speaking, capitalist competition but a sort of pseudo-socialistic competitivism. "Everybody has a chance to be president." The presidential plum is typical of all the other plums and prizes that American capitalism holds out to the hard-winning rivals that have done their capitalist homework well. . . .

There is democracy in America—who will deny it? But it is a democracy that does not have its roots in reality. In a class society—and ours is a class society—democracy is only for the ruling class. And yet in the American mind democracy is for all. Here democracy has a way of overriding the reality of class, of concealing it, of substituting for it an amorphous and intangible all-around democratism—a general, good-natured camaraderie of the spirit that here goes hand in hand with a most dis-spirited, oligarchic, unprincipled violation of the democratic ideal in the actual relations of life.

This mask is as old as America. As early as 1776 it has been observed. "How many poor men, common men and mechanics, have been made happy within this fortnight by a shake of the hand, a pleasing smile and a little familiar chat. . . . Blessed is the state which brings all nearly on a level."[7] Such an indelicate unrealism that the class structure of our society weaves into the texture of our democracy has been noted later by Lincoln. "I am not a Know Nothing, that is certain. . . . How can anyone who abhors the oppression of negroes be in favor of degrading classes of white people? Our progress in degeneracy appears to me pretty rapid. As a nation we began by declaring that 'all men are created equal.' We now practically read, 'all men are created equal, except negroes.' When the Know Nothings get control, it will read, 'all men are created equal except negroes, and foreigners, and Catholics.' When it comes to this, I shall prefer emigrating to some country where they make no pretense of loving liberty—to Russia for instance where despotism can be taken pure and without the base alloy of hypocrisy. . . ."8

What adds to the unrealism of democracy in America, and at the same time serves to conceal it, is the democratic make-believe that introduces itself in the very dress of the American, which despite the underlying real differences in quality that correspond very strictly to the class distinction nevertheless manages to achieve a surface similarity. The clerk wears the same straw hat as his employer. That it is not really the same straw hat does not matter so long as he wears a straw hat just the same. The generic similarity hides the real dissimilarity, the abstract category takes the place of the concrete, and the American moves in a world of abstract straw hats that all but obliterates the class relation. Yet it must not be assumed that the equal and undistinguishable Americans do not know the difference between a hat and a hat. Class in the American mind is a synonym for elegance, for style: "some class"— a "classy" hat—a "classy" figure. Thus instead of dividing his society into classes, instead of recognizing the real class divisions, he recognizes only the results of these divisions. In America the products are divided into classes instead of the producers. In this way there is achieved a dressing or rather an undressing of the social categories. As when a shop girl is said to be wearing a classy gown, that is to say, a gown that does not really belong to her class. The shop girl through her gown escapes from her class. The misconception is consummated, and everybody is happy. So far as the American mind is concerned, "social" (?) democracy acts as a substitute for democratic socialism.

Individualism then for mere laissez-faire, equalitarianism for simple democracy, competitive opportunity for plain competition— there is not a single bourgeois concept that is not as it passes through the prism of Americanism broken up into substitutive pseudo-socialistic forms.

II

Not only are the bourgeois ideas here given a socialistic turn, but the socialist ideas are here given a bourgeois interpretation, are, so to speak, decomposed and personalized. Private socialism is an American manifestation. Let us take a few examples in point. It is a fact that "rising" is a favorite idiom with the American ("rising to the top"—"sitting on top of the world"). But the whole ideology of "rising" is a socialist, a revolutionary ideology ("arise, ye prisoners of starvation") proper to proletarians who feel themselves enslaved. Every American feels himself enslaved, and that is why he is forever rising. The emancipation of the proletariat here breaks up into so many emancipations from the proletariat, the Dictatorship of the Proletariat into so many breath-taking success stories. The class struggle is with the American a private affair. He fights it out with himself. There is no more representative an American than Emerson. Here is how Emerson tortures the social struggle, and translates it into psychic terms: "The battle of patrician and plebeian, of parent state and colony, of old usage and accommodation to new facts, of the rich and the poor, reappears in all countries and times. This war not only rages in battlefields, in national councils, and ecclesiastical synods, *but agitates every man's bosom with opposing advantage every hour.*"[9]

It is among other things his Puritan heritage that has trained the American to decompose the social into the personal.[10] If his Christianity is with the American a matter of individual conscience, his socialism too gets to be a matter of individual conscience. The spurious and, it goes without saying, pathetic attempt on the part of Americans to "practice" socialism, to "live" socialism, is in no small measure to be traced to just such puritanic displacement of concept. Now, while it may be possible for one's conscience to become one's pope, it is hardly possible for a pope to become a conscience. And if a church cannot dissolve into a state of mind, all the more idiotic is it to assume that a mode of production—and that is what socialism is—can be a state of mind. An individual can no more practice socialism than a society can, let us say, take a drink.

Such decomposition of socialist theory goes on here on every hand. Class consciousness is a socialist concept, but class consciousness seems hardly possible in the presence of so many other kinds of consciousness—"bath conscious"—"cigarette conscious"—"beauty conscious." How can one expect class consciousness to crystallize in the face of such a distraction and dissipation of the general social consciousness, its focusing on so many fixed points.

Or take the conspiratory side in socialism—what in other countries is an underground movement here works itself off in a private, whispering, sort of speakeasy socialism.[11] "Between you and me," the American is, in his after-dinner off moments, apt to confide, "I am really a socialist. But I can't afford to come out with it just now. My position, my friends, my future—wait till I make a million then I will be a bolshevik. . . ." Who has not heard such sentiments in most unexpected places?

Superstitious social gossip, then, in place of undergroundism.

And dissent as a substitute for sectarianism. It is a practice for whole neighborhoods in America to dissent and depart. And in the measure as the American community is nonconformist, radical, does it, much in the manner of a revolutionary sect, exact strict conformity from members.[12]

Talk about private socialism, all the theories concerning the post-capitalist society—syndicalism, communism, anarchism, the American appropriates as his own personal philosophy. That is why a revolutionary theoretician meets with such resistance at the hands of the American. Ask an American to be an anarchist, and he will tell you he is a better anarchist than you are, and point with pride to his unbridled rugged individualism; a syndicalist, and he will shrug his shoulders and remind you of lobbies, checks and balances, and all the apolitical mores and machinery here set up against the political state; a socialist, and he is bound to bring up American sociability. In a crude, raw, ahistoric way, the American harbors in his own mind all the post-capitalistic modes of social thought. . . .

But of all the symptoms of private socialism its manifestation in the political sphere is most to be marveled at. The politics of socialism is the abolition of politics. The "withering away of the State" is a concept of historic socialism. The American proceeds to do away with the state all by himself. "Hello, Cal"—"Hello, Al." The American abolishes the state by shaking hands with the statesman. The American hates great men.[13] He prefers big men. The big man is the genius of the small man, the idol that serves the small man as his own substitutive counterstroke to the statesman.

People make sermons on graft and the growing disrespect for the law, and see in it a sign of social reaction. Rather is it a sign of social revolution. The American has an instinct against government, a truly revolutionary passion to dispense with government. He would like to see the state "wither away"; he is apolitical, but not post-political. He is a private socialist in this respect; instead of predicting the disappearance of the state, he practices the disappearance of the state—in terms of a personal dash and disrespect for the state—and for the statesman. He lets the state disgrace itself through graft, and he feels all the more familiar with it, and the less fearful in its presence. In America, democracy and graft go together, and both are substitutes for socialism.

Socialism means that the people are the government. Americanism would have it that the government is the people. Of course, it makes all the difference in the world whether the people are absorbed in the state, according to Karl Marx, or whether the state is dissolved among the people, à la Jackson. The American, however, is slow to see this difference. All he knows is that here the government and the people are one, so that the state as such, the state as an independent political category, achieves a marvelous disappearance from the American mind. With the result that the American regards those who actually govern him in the state with an arrogance, a familiarity, a well-nigh anarcho-syndicalist cynicism and suspiciousness that is, in the face of the real power these governors have over him, fantastic to say the least.

III

Let us, now, look a little further into this superstition so chronic with the American that here in America classes are abolished. The abolition of classes—the ultimate aim of socialism, and one that involves class war and revolution, painful political overturns and economic transitions—is here taken for granted as an already established fact. "There are no classes in America," so says the American, as if he were already living in the final stages of socialism. What is the reason for such vulgur and obvious as-if-ism? First the fact that, in America, capitalism as a system overshadows the capitalists as a class . . . and so it comes about that Americans think themselves victims of a system rather than slaves of a class. Thus they relate themselves to capitalism socialistically. Only under socialism does system take precedence over class. Socialism is a system minus a class. This minus the American assumes. But why does he assume it?

Because the classlessness of the American is the origin of his Americanism. The very act of coming to America is an act of escaping classes. It was those elements in European society that have refused to participate in the class struggle that have, and during periods of the sharpest class struggles, fled hot-haste away from it all in order to enter, and without struggle, into the classless state. Americans from the very beginning have thus been the "lumps" of the world, the declassed mass, those who have stood on the border line between the classes, in that twilight zone of social transition where nothing is sociologically fixed and final and so nothing is ideologically fixed and final, wherein everything hangs in a state of socio-neurotic doubt and indetermination. *Lumpen* proletarians, *lumpen* bourgeois, *lumpen* intellectuals, landlords, revolutionaries—lumpism that elsewhere is an exceptional phenomenon, appearing on the border lines between the classes and in the interludes between events, is here the dominant social manifestation.

There is a deep-seated reason for this. The act of becoming an American is an act of baptismal import. It is an act of sudden shedding of ideas and habits of life that are proper to the civilized, i.e., to the class relation. Theoretically such a shedding is a result of history. When a society is through with the class ideology it is also through with the class division. It is ready for a socialist, i.e. a classless frame of mind only when it is rid of the class relation. America, however, is still under classes, but its mind has leaped forward toward classlessness.[14] Too far forward and therefore too far backward—back to classlessness in a primitive sense, to the barbaric classlessness of rugged equalitarianism and "human"-ism. The American is "human" for the same reason that he is rugged—his classless as-if-ism, his lumpism. The American lives in nature, not in history. He escapes the disciplines and limits that history imposes on a society and becomes human—just human. Thus has the American mind overreached itself. Activated by the fallacy of its great ahistoric As-If, it generates within itself attitudes and modes of belief fit only for a society that has emerged triumphant from class history and tragedy, and so has become human. The American is "human" in the presence of a civilization that is, strictly speaking, still political.[15]

Mass, as against class, this is an American preference—and one that has done much to discourage class theory and struggle in America. It may in fact be said that by far the most virulent of the substitutes that Americanism holds out against socialism, the one that more than any other has dulled the sharp edge of proletarian thought and struggle, has been precisely this concept mass. This concept is an ideological staple with Americans. Even their poets find inspiration in it. "The mass I sing." It is not a proletarian concept but an amorphous anarchic populist[16] counter concept to class serving to conceal this concept from the American mind. Mass, which in the socialist theory is placed next to class (in Leninism, the toiling mass is led by the working class), here takes the place of class. Mass as a substitute for class, as the abstract, attenuated, conceptualized, spiritualized, in a word, orientalized version—or rather inversion—of the Marxian by the Whitmanesque has served to lend to American life and thought a distinctive proletarian flavor, and at the very same time and by the very same token to dry up the bloodstream of proletarian thought and struggle at its very source.

What havoc this concept has worked with revolutionary theory. And how eagerly the American ruling class makes use of it. "It is," says Hoover, "by the maintenance of equality of opportunity and therefore of a society absolutely fluid in the movement of its human particles that our individualism departs from the individualism of Europe. We resent class distinction because there can be no rise for the individual through the frozen strata of classes, *and no stratification of classes can take place in a mass livened by the free rise of its particles.*[17] The displacing of class by mass is the displacing of history by nature. In mass social form gives way to, dissolves into social substance. This is what is meant by the spontaneity of mass both as concept and as phenomenon. The spontaneity of the American mass is made possible by the fact that the American is trained to naturistic rather than to historic modes of response. The natural is the spontaneous, and the American reacts upon his environment in accordance with the general

laws of (human) nature. The American mass is neither a mob
in the European sense nor an assembly of minds in, let us say,
a soviet sense. It is neither passional nor intellectual, but is a product purely of social physics. What keeps it up in equilibrium is
its ordered instability. This is the root of the spontaneous self-
activity of the American, and incidentally of his rugged individualism. The American is propelled, on the one hand, by the primitive
"passions of the human soul," and so falls into ritualistic styles
of life (primitivism is ritualism), and, on the other hand, by the
release of his ego impulses through the refining influences of civilized individualism. Whitman is the literary reflex of this great
American fact—the formation of the American mass—that concealment and substitute for the real individual and the real class. Whitman is real but only in so far as mass is real, and mass is, when
compared to class, very unreal. The spontaneous and self-acting
American mass—free at once from the ritualism of the primitive
and the individualism of the civilized—how can one explain this
strange form of freedom—this individualism in America in the presence of the monotonous mass-uniformity—how otherwise than that
the individual here is not the ego differentiating itself, separating
itself off from the mass, but the atom, undifferentiated from and
yet distinct from the social mass, the atomic bearer and embodiment of the social energy—at one and the same time himself and
his society, distinguished from the social mass by the same token
by which he is undistinguished from the social mass.

This phenomenon of mass accounts also for the amazing uni-
formity of American thought. Ideas in America spread very fast
because Americans are of one mind, and they are of one mind
because they are, in their consciousness at least, of one class. It
is this feeling of classlessness, ahistoric though it be, that brings
about the marvelous homogeneity of the American mind. And of
the American emotion. The American feels—just "human." He has
arrived, in his mind, at a state of classlessness, i.e., of humanity,
and so is touched off by those sentiments only that are universal,
uniform, "human."

With the class line blurred and blotted out from his mind, the
American is blind to the real meaning of the state. The state is
in the American mind not the dominion of class over class, but
the (perfectly human) administration of the perfectly classless
mass. Such shift of concept from the political to the administrative

has its deepest roots in the American mind. It is noteworthy that what in other countries is known as "The Government" ("The French Government was defeated today") is here called "The Administration." Our political scribes may not be aware of it, but when they thus speak of the "administration" instead of the "government" they are reciting socialist phraseology straight from Engels. It will, of course, at this point be objected that the American uses the term "administration" without any reference to Engels or socialism, that the choice of the word is purely accidental. But no such distinctive tribal idiom can so easily be explained away. The idiom of a people, like the lapsus linguæ of an individual, is, when considered socio-analytically, expressive of its deepest unconscious wishes and longings. To the American socialism is an unconscious wish.

IV

It is usually assumed that the American is the born bourgeois, and that socialism is, therefore, at variance with American human nature. And, if the American is defined in terms of his objective relationships, there is much to be said for this assumption. Nowhere in the world is the bourgeois relation so developed as here. Nowhere is capitalism so well advanced. But one must be careful to distinguish between the development of American capitalism and the development of the American as capitalist. For, if one were to examine the underlying aspirations of the American, his real sentiments and moods, it would not be difficult to discover in him trends of the soul that, far from being the traditionally capitalistic trends, are on the contrary tinged with every variety of socialism. Thus, for example, so unmistakable an American as Hoover from time to time unburdens himself of the belief that it is the destiny of the American system to abolish poverty. Now, Hoover may not know it but when he talks this way he is simply talking socialism. To "abolish poverty" is a time-honored socialist aim. Who has ever heard a responsible spokesman of European capitalism announce that it is the aim of, let us say, the French or the English "system" to "abolish poverty"? Normally, phrases such as this are uttered by spokesmen of the working class. Socialism is, normally, the philosophy of the working class. And when a Hoover, or any of the accredited representatives of the American capitalist class, thus articulates in the idiom of socialism, the socialism at once begins to sound spurious, irresponsible, unconscious. This is precisely the point I want to make: the American is an unconscious socialist. And that is why, though he acts capitalistically, he speaks and thinks pseudo-socialistically. "Standardization of commodities," said Schwab once, "is the aim of the machine age in America," without perhaps having read that Trotsky similarly speaks of the standardization of commodities as one of the objectives of socialism. Henry Ford's strictures against the money motive in industry are uttered with the socialistic passion of a Robert Blatchford. And who but a Hoover could have uttered such a classically Marxian boast as "There are more men in my Cabinet who have worked with their hands than there are in the Labor Cabinet of Ramsay MacDonald"! Talk about being socialists without knowing it—in America reputable Republicans vie with clergymen in proclaiming as "sacred" the right to work, a phrase first used by the revolutionary proletariat of Europe and which the bourgeois regiments of Paris had to fight down on the barricades. There is not a word in bourgeois philosophy and law that even hints at guaranteeing this right. The right to work is socialism. And when, as happens every day now, American statesmen advocate "the right to work" one is tempted to forgive them for they know not what they are saying.

It is a fact, observed by every visitor from abroad, that the American is very frightened in the midst of misfortune. Though far less hit by the crisis than any of the Europeans, the Americans have been far worse upset by it, and have shown their anxiety in no uncertain manner, crying and screaming in a most infantile fashion. And yet it has also been observed of Americans that "the jobless, the near-jobless, the countless victims of the market and bank failures are bearing their personal change of fortune with a gallantry and good humor. . . ."[18] This contradiction in the social behavior of the American is simply his unconscious socialism at work. Consciously, the American is a lone-wolf individualist, rugged, egotistical, but in an infantile sense; and so when he is up against it, he screams. Unconsciously, he is a "comrade," facing life's battles in barricade style, and bearing up under misfortune with the heroism and sense of fatality of a fighting revolutionist. It is this unconscious revolutionism that leads him into moods of social stoicism and self-renunciation.

How unconscious Americans can be of their socialism often comes out in their political campaigning. An Al Smith, a Roosevelt runs for office, and the Republicans, for reasons of their own, simply charge them with socialism. And the Democrats just as simply deny the charge. They will not, even while advocating their socialistic measures, admit their socialism. They are underground socialists, not, however, in the conspiratorial sense, but in the sense of harboring their socialism in the dark haunts of their Unconscious.

Anyone who has tried to talk socialism to Americans must have had this strange experience. The American will follow the argument of class and class struggle, get it, and agree with it. Logically, the argument is as clear to him as to anyone else. But not psychologically. For the moment he is through admitting the correctness of the Marxian thesis is the very moment he will burst forth with a sudden and upsetting "but there are no classes in America," a sentiment he utters with the decisiveness of a sudden revelation. This phrase, "there are no classes in America," is not an idea— as an idea it has no legs to stand on—but an idiom. As such it must express, as to idioms, an unconscious wish. It is as if the American really wished there were no classes and class struggles, so that he as well as everyone else might be liberated from the capitalist class competition and be placed on the happy hunting ground of socialist competitivism.

The American, then, is a socialist, but unconsciously so. Unconscious socialism is something to be reckoned with in understanding the resistance the American offers to the socialist agitation. His socialism is unconscious for the reason that the socialistic instincts in him, coming into conflict with the capitalistic institutions and ideas that surround him, are repressed.

NOTES

1. Hegel, *Philosophy of History* (1857 edition), p. 90.
2. Works, vol. I, pp. 66–1765.
3. "The frontier social life may be said to have its beginning at the log raising that attended the construction of the cabin. The single axman could cut his trees, and notch them, but he lacked appliances or strength to lay the logs in place. When the timbers were ready the neighbors of the countryside would ride in on horseback, from thirty or forty miles away. With wives on pillion and infants in arms they came; for where one went it was easier for all to go. They made a picnic of the occasion, and the able-bodied men in a few hours, too few to spoil the play, piled up the logs and laid the roof. The frontier welcomed the legitimate excuse for such a gathering. Weddings became boisterous and rude, with home-stilled whiskey in an open tub, a drinking gourd at its side. Funerals lost something of their solemnity when relatives and friends so manifestly welcomed the opportunity to get together. The occasions came unfrequently, but when they came there were stores of pent up loneliness to be relieved. In politics and in religion, *there was a formative condition in this fact that every gathering was a neighborhood festivity and that teaching and argument must be phrased in the language of excitement to meet the need of loneliness.*" Frederic L. Paxson, *History of the American Frontier, 1763–1893*, p. 115.
4. Lord Northcliffe's remark to a friend, as he stood one day at the window of his New York hotel. Quoted by Van Wyck Brooks, in *Sketches in Criticism*, p. 175.
5. "Speculators went to bed at night hugging themselves with delight over the prospect that the succeeding morning would double their wealth. . . . Fortunes hung on every bush, were buried in every corner lot, and were lying scattered promiscuously over all the real estate in the vicinity." (Gregory, *History of Milwaukee*, vol. I, p. 72.)
6. *The Writings of Benjamin Franklin*, edited by A. H. Smyth, vol. V, p. 362.
7. Pa. *Evening Post*, April 27, 1776.
8. Lincoln letter to Speed, 1865. Quoted by K. Young in *Baiting the Alien: An Old Habit*.
9. Emerson Lecture, "The Conservative," Boston, 1841. (Italics mine.)
10. "But all the Protestant Revolutions differed in character from the great French Revolution; they did not need to make a complete breach of continuity, nor to dethrone religion because Protestant civilization, by the religious transformation it produced, had already accomplished the revolution on the inward side." Ernst Troeltsch, *Protestantism and Progress*, p. 172.

11. Even the regular revolutionary organizations cannot escape this keyhole misinterpretation of the socialist conspiracy. The Knights of Labor were "hedged about with the impenetrable veil of signal, sign, grip and pass-word, so no spy of the boss can find his way into the lodge room to betray his fellows." The Knights even added a Russian touch to their speakeasy socialism. They were called "Teapot Society" because at their Thursday evening meetings the Knights drank nothing but tea.

12. "The partisan attitude and the particular party affiliation passed down from father to son. A man got his politics as he got his table manners and sectarian beliefs. And just as a person who was drawn away from his own church by an attraction in another was despised, so was the voter who was 'always shopping around' and voting for one party one year and another the next. The independent voter was laughed at. What did his independent ideas amount to! The only way to count in politics was to be a member of a party.

"Partisanship meant loyalty to party. Any enthusiastic loyalty involves a relation to persons. So sectarian loyalty involved loyalty to the local clergyman and to the great historical leaders of the sect; and partisan loyalty involved loyalty to the local leaders and to the great leaders of the party." J. Williams, *Our Rural Heritage*, pp. 186, 187.

13. "A curious instance of this is the following: a conversation in London during the Battle of Waterloo between Henry Clay and Lord Liverpool.

Lord Liverpool—'If he (Napoleon) goes there (to America), will he not give you much trouble?'

Clay—'None whatever. We shall be glad to receive such a distinguished though unfortunate exile, and we shall soon make a good Democrat of him.' "

E. L. Magoon, *Living Orators in America*, p. 140.

14. This feat is accomplished by way of pragmatism. Pragmatism is the lever whereby the American by an act of criticism reads himself out of the institutions and ideas that annoy him, but he does not really do away with them. He does away with the emphasis and apotheosis of them. He does away with them, in other words, in his mind. Here is where the pragmatist turns up a utopian face. The pragmatist substitutes for the political process a purely psychologic As-If.

15. The liberal, the real liberal, is possible only in worlds wherein the political problem being already resolved, both the revolutionary and the reactionary—those wielders or potential wielders of war and state power—vanish from the scene. To act the liberal in a world wherein the state, war, etc., is still on the order of the day is once more to be laboring under the happy illusion of an ahistoric As-If. This is precisely what the American is found to do who goes about Peter-Pannishly sweeping off one problem of statecraft after another with his liberal broom.

16. The use of the term labor instead of labor-power in the pseudo-socialistic jargon of the American is also a substituting of a proletarian

with a populist concept. Labor is to labor-power what mass is to class. Labor is the unmeasured substance behind labor-power, just as mass is the undefined, undifferentiated social stuff out of which the classes emerge. The American likes the term labor. Even before Marx elaborated a labor theory of value, Franklin had already done so, and Lincoln later added a sentimental touch to the misconception.

17. Madison Square Garden Speech, November 1, 1932. (Italics mine.)

18. A. R. Wylie, *Sunday Times,* April 26, 1931.

COMMENT 1

Warren I. Susman

The problem of revolutionary politics might well be illuminated by a brief reference to the injunction repeatedly put upon the solid middle-class Puritans who came to American shores in the seventeenth century, not merely to found their own "City on a Hill" but to undertake the even more breathtaking task of reforming the Reformation itself—and thus the whole world. They must remain, they were constantly reminded, *in* the world but they must never become *of* the world. The enormous difficulty in obeying that injunction informs the whole history of the Puritan experience. It is also, in effect, the same challenge that faces any group determined to alter radically the world in which it finds itself, the very world in which the group must continue to live while laboring to transform it.

Those who wish to see a socialist America might well learn from the history of those who strove to create a Christian America. As H. Richard Niebuhr brilliantly demonstrated in *Christ and Culture,* Christianity could and has served as a compelling counterculture, providing an often devastating judgment against the ongoing patterns of a culture. But at the same time conversion to the Christian creed might very well serve a far different function of mitigating feelings of oppression and even thus becoming an ideology sustaining the very culture to which it originally offered critical opposition. Thus in 1921, Frank Tannenbaum (a Socialist attracted both to the IWW and to John Dewey to whom he dedicated his book) warned in *The Labor Movement* against political movements, suggesting that they functioned much like "a Billy Sunday meeting . . . dime novels, drink, baseball scores, moving pictures" as rationales or "a means of emotional dissipation in things."

The Socialist Party differs from other political organizations in that it concerns itself consciously about those things which *seem* to be most vital to the worker's life and labor. By its agitation it helps to crystallize discontent, gives it meaning and sets for it a definite goal. It must, however, be noted that the Socialist Party concerns itself *about* those problems *rather than with them*. It tends to postpone immediate activity by centering interest in things outside the sphere of daily contact and function in which the worker operates, and *thus in a measurable degree unconsciously participates in the work performed by all other agencies that go to distract the worker's attention from his immediate problems.*[1]

Tannenbaum saw the revolutionary transformation as coming primarily as an inevitable end of the process of unionization; yet in his own work he realized that the labor movement itself could and would have "conservative consequences," stabilizing and ordering the social system, eliminating friction and discord and creating harmony and true community. And as early as the turn of the century the leaders of American industry realized, in the formation of the National Civic Federation, the desirable role organized labor might play in rationalizing the new industrial order. By 1948 when C. Wright Mills published his *The New Men of Power* few Americans on the Left retained any illusion about the significant role organized labor had in fact played in sustaining the existing American system.

The problem of how to function *in* the world and yet not become *of* that world is thus the crucial question of strategy and tactics; that problem has been immeasurably complicated by a set of special conditions in the American experience. There was from the outset the problem of the relationship of theory to that experience itself. Both American and European socialists have repeatedly raised the question of American uniqueness, the "special" nature of American history and development.[2] Some have seen the problem in terms of the relationship between (or the failure to establish such a relationship) a theoretical or ideological viewpoint and some form of political action. Others have insisted that the key question rested in the definition of the potential "mass base" of any such movement, some praising ventures (like the almost legendary IWW) dedicated to and centering around those "marginal" to the ongoing system: unskilled and unorganized labor, immigrants, blacks, women; others calling for a movement that could draw the widest possible support including the resources of the intellectuals, the established trade unions, sympathetic members of the middle class. And while political activity of some sort has been central to many who sought a socialist America, some would insist the initial struggle must take place in the community, within local institutions, while others believed an attempt at national power was paramount. Others, in effect, renounced all political activity and proposed in its place activity in the cultural area, often in a vision of a special kind of literary or cultural radicalism.

But in almost all of these cases there was the persistent and very special question: how does or can socialism relate to the specifically American experience? And often the question was put even more crudely: was socialism a "foreign" ideology or was it actually a "native" movement that belonged within the American Way? One of the many paradoxes of American history is how a nation of immigrants could be at the same time a nation which could so often be roused to fear and even hysteria over ideas, movements, and people labeled "foreign"—or how often other ideas, movements, and people could be defended and even enthusiastically supported if they could be thought of as "native"— or accepted if they could be proven to have been effectively "Americanized."

It is vital to the history of socialism in America to realize that the very years that witnessed the growth of considerable interest in and support for socialist ideas and the Socialist Party itself were the years that saw as well the development of "Americanism" as an ideology, especially the first few decades of the twentieth century. Certainly by the 1920s, as Elwin H. Powell contends, the whole new order created in the United States under the reign of Progressivism and tightened by the experience of the war itself "was 'sacralized' or sanctified by the mystique of Americanism, which replaced the older Protestant ethic as an ideological foundation of corporate capitalism."[3] And it is further true that the experience of the Depression and still another World War extended the sway and power of the vision of an American way of life.[4]

Even the most superficial reading of history suggests there was a greater appeal in a socialism under the leadership of a man like Eugene V. Debs, for example, who for all of his references to Marx and class struggle gave the appearance of "native" American radicalism in his person, rhetoric, and even conduct than in the growing power of foreign-language federations on the left of the American socialist movement or in the IWW, with its methods ("anarchism," "violence," uncharacteristic unionism) and membership (with its appeal to "bums" and marginal men). Historians, too, have argued that the growing power of foreign-language federations and the emergence of the new Communist Party in the 1920s tended to reflect European events, especially the experience of the Russian Revolution and its consequences. In his superb essay on "The Collapse of Socialism," Christopher Lasch sums up the characteristics of American radicalism from the 1920s until the present: "sectarianism, marginality, and alienation from American life."[5]

Precisely. In this great century of "Americanism" socialists worried the problem of their "alienation from American life," but they made every effort (consciously or unconsciously) to overcome that sense. "Perhaps the most important symptom of the progress of Socialism in America," wrote Upton Sinclair jubilantly in 1911, "is the flood of Socialist books which are pouring from the presses nowadays, books written by native-born Americans and dealing with American questions from American points of view."[6] The literary radicals of the period who also felt themselves aliens regarded themselves most often as socialists while they eschewed any political path to the revolution they sought. Rather, with one of their leaders, Van Wyck Brooks, they struggled to create an American cultural renaissance. One of their most important magazines, *Seven Arts,* stated in its opening editorial: "It is our faith and the faith of many, that we are living in the first days of a renascent period, a time which means for America the coming of that national self-consciousness which is the beginning of greatness." And even those who sought in part to make their revolution in terms of a life-style that would challenge the American middle class with departures in dress, in experimentation in a wide variety of life experiences, new attitudes toward sex and traditional institutions and values (culminating perhaps in the Greenwich Village "Bohemian") often chose as a model or culture hero a figure like Jack London or John Reed or the tramp, vagabond, social outcast. As James B. Gilbert shrewdly observes, "a characteristic American social type was now depicted as a social revolutionary, but he could now be seen as the creator of a new sort of culture contained in songbooks and IWW newspapers and as a prophet in his own life, a man on the fringe of society, yet capable of seeing clearly to its center." Yet it is significant that such a figure has American roots in Walt Whitman, in Mark Twain's Huck Finn, in a long American tradition that was in fact slowly being pieced together and brought to stand in the service of a counterculture dedicated to overturn (as George Santayana observed) the sterile Genteel Tradition that no longer stood for life and experience in America but only in support of the established order. Thus socialists adopted a wide range of techniques but they did so in reference to putting themselves in some kind of proper relationship with the Americanism of the era.

It is clearly possible to propose that the socialism of the era—in whatever form—had an impact on American developments. Indeed, the newly defined Americanism of the period was increasingly broad in its definition to encompass many things Americans might once have rejected as "socialistic." The new liberal social thinkers in their revolt against formalism had also been in revolt against the more ruthless forms of individualism that had generated the robber barons and the chaos in corporate capitalism that made for inefficiency. The whole Progressive effort to rationalize the new industrial order had led as well to a renewal or continuation of the search for community, a search as old at least as John Winthrop's famous "Model of Christian Charity" written aboard the *Arbella* in 1630. The trend toward "socializing the services and goods of the community and placing them at the disposal of the individual" was an outstanding characteristic of the American Way by the 1920s, as Frank Tannenbaum wrote in his *The Labor Movement,* published in 1921:

> We have socialized things as water, public highways, education, lighted streets, bridges, medical service for the sick through public hospitals, dental services for children in public schools, parks, museums, books through libraries, and information services of various kinds. . . . To this must be added sickness insurance, unemployment insurance, care for the old through old age pensions and for the young through maternity pensions, factory and mine inspections, and legal enforcement of protection against dangerous machinery.[7]

To this list Tannenbaum might well have added the income tax among other transformations of governmental roles previously held to be socialistic attacks on private property and even the gradual but grudging respect to the workers' rights to organizing and bargaining collectively. It might very well be in fact that all of these "socialized things" were part of an effort to rationalize the industrial order; it might very well be that they were designed primarily to aid the middle class and the organized and that millions of Americans did not benefit significantly or directly from them. But the fact remains that such transformations could lead a Buffalo newspaper to declare editorially in 1917: "We are all more or less socialists nowadays. Some of us call our socialism by the name State Regulation or Municipal Ownership or Organized Benevolence. But it is socialism pure and simple as distinguished from the individualism of Herbert Spencer."[8]

Even that radical new life-style which presented such a deliberate affront to middle-class Americans and especially to those middle-class values so long associated with the Puritan work-save ethic proved in the end (although it clearly did as well play a role in significantly altering American life and manners and morals generally) supportive of the new Americanism. As Malcolm Cowley has shown, the very things valued by the new ethic of Greenwich Village provided a necessary new ethic of *consumption,* encouraging people to spend and buy, changing the nature of American habits and helping to create the consumer aspect of Americanism so necessary if the new industrial system was to survive. Cultural radicalism could be accepted (in part at least); Americanism could encompass this variant of socialism.[9]

On the Fourth of July, 1935, the *Daily Worker* announced in a bold headline: TOWARD A SOVIET AMERICA. The goal was by no means new; the means appeared to be. No longer would a major thrust in American socialism be "alienated" from the American world (as it appeared to many to be in the 1920s). On page 2 the reader of the *Worker* would find, side by side, pictures of the two great revolutionaries, Lenin and George Washington. A reprint of the Declaration of Independence completed the obvious message. American socialism had joined Americanism with a vengeance. Communism became twentieth-century Americanism. "We," Earl Browder would say of his comrades, "are the only true Americans." No matter what the formal policy considerations—and of course the idea of the Popular Front was by no means singular nor an American development conditioned by unique American circumstances—it was but another step in the whole history of the special relationship between Americanism and socialism, an almost predictable part of the shift and countershift that marks the whole history of the interplay between socialism and the American experience in our century. Leon Samson has argued that Americans, unconscious socialists all along, had used Americanism as a substitute for conscious socialism. The Popular Front would now try to capture that Americanism as a device for turning Americans into conscious socialists.

This is not the place to assess the consequences of the Popular Front in America. In the 1940s and after much attention was paid to the supposedly pernicious role the communists were able to play under the cover of the Front by insinuating themselves into government and a wide variety of American institutions. Too little attention has been paid to the harm done to American socialism itself: out of it came an absurd vision of the American past, a peculiar notion of American society in the present, a ludicrous attitude toward American culture in general. At a most critical juncture in our history American socialists helped us little in understanding ourselves or the world. The effort to partake of Americanism led to gross comedy in which ideas—to say nothing of ideology—took a back seat. A university communist group could even announce:

Some people have the idea that a YCLer is politically minded, that nothing outside of politics means anything. Gosh no. They have a few simple problems. There is the problem of getting good men on the baseball team this spring, of opposition from ping pong teams, of dating girls, etc. We go to shows, parties, dances and all that. In short, the YCL and its members are no different from other people except that we believe in dialectical materialism as a solution to all problems.[10]

Irving Howe and Lewis Coser have shown how the Popular Front in fact became a kind of culture. While they may concentrate, perhaps, too much attention on the absurd aspects of that culture (with its social-minded nightclubs, for example) they also brilliantly highlight the contributions it made to the style of mass culture in the United States, a style which they rightly suggest continued long after the Second World War. The Popular Front (like previous socialist confrontations with Americanism) helped shape that Americanism, but few would be willing to suggest that the kind of society and kind of culture that resulted could in any legitimate sense be designated as socialist.

As early as 1936 many Marxist intellectuals had begun to wonder whether indeed Marxism was compatible with the American Tradition, and by 1937 William Phillips and Philip Rahv, editors of the distinguished *Partisan Review,* had concluded that "an essential contradiction existed between Marxism and domestic intellectual traditions that could only be resolved through the 'Europeanization of American Literature.' "[11] (One is immediately reminded of Van Wyck Brooks's early sense of frustration at his inability to find a meaningful basis in the literary life in America for the base of a new socialist culture. For a bibliography in connection with his essay on the subject in Harold Stearns's *Civilization in the United States* (1922) Brooks wrote: "For a sense of everything American literary life is *not,* one might read, for instance, the Letters of Ibsen, Dostoievsky, Chekhov, Flaubert, Taine, and Leopardi. . . .)"[12] But by 1952—after years of war, hot and cold, and McCarthyism, in a symposium on "Our Country and Our Culture" many *Partisan Review* authors could again speak of the end of alienation, of the return to America and her traditions, the end of exile and rebellion. Americanism will out.

Yet there is another sense in which Americanism itself must be taken: it stands for industrialism itself. "Industrialism," a group of critics of the entire system argued in 1930,

is the economic organization of the collective American society. It means the decision of society to invest its economic resources in the applied sciences. . . . The capitalization of the applied sciences has now become extravagant and uncritical; it has enslaved our human energies to a degree now clearly felt to be burdensome. The apologists of industrialism do not like to meet this charge directly; so they often take refuge in saying they are devoted simply to science. They are really devoted to the applied sciences and to practical production. . . . It is an Americanism, which looks innocent and disinterested, but really is not either.[13]

Above all, perhaps, as many Europeans already knew in the 1920s, Americanism meant *Fordismus.* Add to our gallery of pictures another pair: it was not at all unusual during the 1920s to find in factories in the USSR, hanging side by side as portraits of the two men who had "revolutionized" the twentieth century, pictures of Lenin and Henry Ford. Without worrying about ideological consequences or the danger of foreign ideas, the Soviets could admire the genius of Ford and his contribution to the technological developments which transformed the industrial order. American engineers reciprocated: many returning from visits to Soviet factories during the 1920s and 1930s were enthusiastic about Soviet industrialization and industrial organization and progress, again without ideological or political concern but with professional admiration at achievement and production. And in the United States itself Ford's action of January 1, 1914, establishing the five-dollar, eight-hour day for all Ford workers who could pass his Sociological Department's examination "on the clean and wholesome life" (the department also provided services that would enable workers to pass the examination, adjust themselves to proper conditions of home and community living, sound work habits, and the good citizenship required of them), was frequently hailed as a major contribution of a new vision—not merely of man as a producer but man as a member of the American community. Ford himself realized that part of what he was doing created customers for his automobiles but even here his vision of a car for every man would provide workers a share, not in essential decision-making power in the shop, industry, the community, or the nation, perhaps, but in a kind of fundamental social equality through the ownership and use of energy and mobility resources of a society usually reserved in past orders for the very few. And Tocqueville had said so long ago that Americans preferred equality to liberty anyway. Some writers have gone so far as to insist (not socialist writers, to be sure) that Ford's over-all revolution *was* as significant as Lenin's.[14] But whatever one's interpretation of *Fordismus* it was undeniably part of what came to be called Americanism.

And socialism was from the outset significantly related to industrialism. No matter what criticism it might find in the kind of industrial order that existed under capitalism it was committed to that basic order itself. It thus shared from the start many assumptions and many basic values. If Samson can find in Americanism substitutes for socialist values or socialist concepts turned on their head, it is possible to see as well in socialism those values and beliefs associated with industrialism easily acceptable in Americanism: a belief in order, rationality, and science; a respect for production, efficiency, power, discipline, and above all work; the need for planning, organization, and even bureaucracy and the state (at least at a certain stage of development); an intense interest in mass culture or the culture of the masses; stress on cooperation, participation, the importance of the well-being of the community; a vision of Progress, especially under science. Both accepted trade unionism and both paid special homage to the role of the worker: socialists argued the worker deserved "full value of his product" and even Henry Ford spoke of profit sharing (even before profits) in which workers would receive their "just share." Americanism ordered a Labor Day while the Popular Front proposed an Americanism Day. Both claim to seek a stability and order to end insecurity, anomie, and alienation. Both value the concept of social equality. The list could be extended with ease: the point is that both are the products of industrialism.

Thus there *is* a real challenge in the criticism of the Twelve Southerners quoted previously. These critics called themselves "Agrarians" and put themselves in opposition to all forms of industrialism. They found that even some critics of the industrial order find remediation in only more industrialism.

Sometimes they rely on the benevolence of capital, or the militancy of labor, to bring about a fairer division of the spoils: they are Cooperationists or Socialists. And sometimes they expect to find super-engineers, in the shape of Boards of Control, who will adapt production to consumption and regulate prices and guarantee business against fluctuations: they are Sovietists. With respect to these last it must be insisted that the true Sovietists or Communists . . . are Industrialists themselves. . . . We therefore look upon the Communist menace as menace indeed, but not as a Red one; because it is simply according to the blind drift of our industrial development to expect in America at last much the same economic system as that imposed by violence upon Russia in 1917.[15]

I do not accept this analysis but I do believe that socialists must accept the challenge it contains: how much have socialists accepted of the world in which they find themselves and how much of that often uncritical acceptance of Industrialism-Americanism has in fact hampered them from building toward a program with genuine consequences for the quality of human life and fundamental thought about human aspirations?

Socialism has contributed to the American experience in ways that have perhaps broadened the definition of Americanism without significantly altering its fundamental structure or proposing a genuine alternative culture. As it strove to operate in this century in its own strange game with Americanism, it often found itself not only in the world but of it, sometimes dramatically reinforcing the very order it proposed to alter radically. It is true that socialists in America have never been able to sustain a mass movement; but perhaps there is another question of as much significance related to it: why have we produced no Luxemburg, no Gramsci, no Lukács, no Gorz, no Althusser—no theoretical contributions to the great discussion Marx began well over a century ago? why have we produced no school of social analysis equal to the work of the Frankfurt School to help us come to an understanding of the nature of our industrial society? why no school of historical scholars in the tradition of the English *Past and Present* group, for example, to make it possible for us to understand our past and present?

Why have we allowed sentiment and rhetoric to replace the good hard work of analysis and deep thought? Why have we so often found ourselves playing the Americanism game ending up ironically reinforcing the order we propose to change, contributing more to the "socializing" of things than the socializing of America, supporting too often the liberal American substitute for socialism: the idea of the new middle class of professional as expert, the engineer, planner, designer, social scientist as savior; or the support of movements like trade unionism without seeing it in any larger social context? We have contributed to the making of mass culture without developing any position from which to evaluate it. Even our Bohemian Left has often, as we have seen, ended up reinforcing certain values necessary for the system. Have we really been wise in our pursuit of Americanism in an effort to capture it for socialism, or has that very Americanism ended up capturing us because we have not been sufficiently self-aware or self-critical?

Socialists *are* alienated by definition; the end of our alienation we believe will not come through private solutions; it certainly will not come through acceptance of Americanism-Industrialism. We are too often conscious only of our alienation and too little conscious of what that alienation means, too ready to accept for ourselves or our group some more immediate answer to that problem for us with too little attention to what it means in the totality of experience and social relations. Howe and Coser shrewdly point out in a parenthetical remark: "American radicalism has always functioned as a kind of prep school for the leaders of American capitalist society."[16] Is it not possible to find that place *in* but not *of* the world we have inherited? Must Americanism win?

NOTES

1. Frank Tannenbaum, *The Labor Movement* (New York, 1921), pp. 64–65.
2. On this whole subject see R. Laurence Moore, *European Socialists and the American Promised Land* (New York, 1970). The last chapter deals with American socialists.
3. Elwin H. Powell, *The Design of Discord* (New York, 1970), p. 104. A provocative study by a sociologist with some ideas worthy of considerable development. Chapter 7 on "Class Warfare in Buffalo" is of special interest to those concerned about the questions raised in this volume.
4. I have developed this notion as a significant aspect of the 1930s that contributed to the essential conservativism of the period in two essays: "The Thirties," in S. Coben and L. Ratner (eds.), *The Development of American Culture* (Englewood, N.J., 1970) and "Introduction," to my own *Culture and Commitment* (New York, 1972).
5. This is a most important essay. It appears in his volume *The Agony of the American Left* (New York, 1969). The sentence quoted is on page 40 but the whole essay must be read by anyone interested in social movements in America.
6. All of the quotes in this paragraph are taken from the first chapter of James B. Gilbert, *Writers and Partisans* (New York, 1968), pp. 12, 33, 14. Gilbert's book is the most valuable book we have on literary radicalism. But see also Daniel Aaron, *Writers on the Left* (New York, 1961).
7. Frank Tannenbaum, *The Labor Movement* (New York, 1921), p. 208.
8. Powell, op. cit., p. 93.
9. Malcolm Cowley, *Exile's Return* (New York, 1934), pp. 72–73.
10. Irving Howe and Lewis Coser, *The American Communist Party* (New York, 1962). The quotation appears on page 338. While many writers on the Left have been critical of this volume I find that Chapter VIII on the Popular Front is especially brilliant, and its conclusions are bolstered by my own research in the period.
11. Gilbert, op. cit., p. 147.
12. Harold Stearns (ed.), *Civilization in the United States* (New York, 1922), p. 541.
13. Twelve Southerners, *I'll Take My Stand* (Harper Torchbooks reprint, New York, 1962), pp. xxi–xxii. The original edition was 1930.
14. I am thinking in particular of R. L. Bruckberger, *Image of America* (New York, 1959), pp. 195–97 especially. There is a whole

section comparing Ford to Marx and Lenin in this book and it is very suggestive.

15. Twelve Southerners, op. cit., p. xxiii.
16. Howe and Coser, op. cit., p. 358.

COMMENT 2

AMERICANISM AS SUBSTITUTIVE SOCIALISM

Irving Louis Horowitz

We have to understand Leon Samson as someone who believes in the ideals of socialism, rather than an analyst of the actual practices of socialism. We learn very little about Soviet practice here, although the book was written about fifteen years after the "Soviet experiment" had gotten under way. Socialism, for Samson, is a series of objectives and ideals: specifically, the ideals of universal democracy and universal prosperity. Similarly, Samson is not terribly bothered by the actualities of the American Revolution, or for that matter, the 150 years that transpired between the event and this book. For it is the *aims* of capitalism and Americanism which are important to Samson—and they, of course, turn out to be also democracy and prosperity. Within this dialectic of prosperity and democracy Americans are said to be compelled to make a choice: to choose democracy ultimately will be to favor socialism, and to choose prosperity will be to make capitalism work better. This idealism provides the framework within which Samson evolves his theories of the dialectic of American society, or what he calls "substitutive socialism," and later on, in Chapter 4 of his book, "substitutive revolution." For the utopianism of American thought frustrates socialist development, by perceiving Americanism as satisfying the basic needs of man; and at the same time, the theatricality of American behavior prevents the evolution and development of political realism—or that kind of political party structure that would provide the machinery for bringing about socialism.

When reading the book today, one is impressed by the fact that Samson could just as well be commenting on the Abbie Hoffmans and Jerry Rubins of the recent period as on heroes of his own times. He notes that "Life in America tends to become art, just as art in America is life. There are no distances here between art and life, but tangents of intersection" (p. 193). And here, Samson understands that all political events in America provide the foundations for melodrama rather than the foundations for social change; that even violence is harnessed to theatricalism, and that such show business frustrates rather than enhances the possibility of political organization. Indeed, one would have to say that Samson's writing on substitutive revolution is at least as important as the chapter on substitutive socialism. Because if the American dream displaces socialism at the level of economic realities, American show business displaces socialism at the level of political realities.

Samson is far more concerned with the absence of socialist politics than with the absence of a socialist economy. He dedicates an entire chapter to American theatricalism; and here too, Samson articulates the American drive toward leisure, love, romance, and toward the conversion of the crudities of violence into the driveling of sentimentalism. He writes: "The very structure, then, of America as a business civilization is enough to make an actor of the American. And so, out on the American scene crowd actors of every shade and sort, in the courthouse, in the market place, in the assemblies of salesmen and literary men, and above all, in the American mob, that self-conscious, and stage-struck American mob, parading under the arcs and floods of American advertising and super-publicity. Living on the spot and on the spur of the moment, the Americans are caught up in a veritable harlequinade of happiness, through the doors of which the masks troop in from every field of American life. The field of politics, for instance" (p. 147).

The second chapter, on "American Utopianism," is really a peculiar attempt to show that Americans juxtapose the ideal to the real and the utopian to the social; and that this utopianism has its origins in a firm belief that American liberty and American politics ultimately derive from God and not from the social order. He argues that American utopianism is, in effect, American individualism —the juxtaposition of the free and unfettered personality over and against the collective will of the society or the state. All men are born equal, but the sanctification of egalitarianism is supposedly divinely inspired. The texture of the American social mind is rooted in a religious faith and therefore links Americanism to utopianism and idealism rather than socialism and materialism.

In a sense, Samson is saying that America is the land of psychology rather than sociology. Its faith is in the individual will rather than in the collective will, and its belief is in individuals and not institutions. Of course, the difficulty here is that Samson extrapolates the "American mind" from American realities. Curiously, very much like Seymour Lipset in his writings on American society, he makes hardly a reference to militarism in American society, overseas expansion, the Civil War, or any of the events which, in fact, turned Americans into much more "socialistic" directions than their individualistic origins would indicate.

The change in pragmatism from William James to John Dewey, from the Gay Nineties to the proletarian thirties, was precisely a shift from the individual as a repository of all goodness and wisdom to society as the repository of goodness and wisdom. If Dewey was compelled to devise strange formulas to slot the individual into the social whole, this nonetheless was done. I am not entirely sure, however, that Samson did not appreciate this; he was certainly aware that the constant tension between social and individual behavior in America does not itself reflect the real movement toward bureaucratization and fascism in American society.

We have discussed the middle chapters in Samson's book, those on American utopianism, American theatricalism, and substitutive revolution. Before we turn to his analysis of political realism, which in effect is Samson's theory of developing a third-party system based on power and Marxian premises, let us return to that famous first chapter which is excerpted here and which contains the core of his argument.

First, Samson's main point is that American society reveals a dichotomy between the class nature of society and the universal egalitarian nature of the American mind; that in effect, the entire dialectic of American life can be described precisely in terms of this bifurcation of what is real and what is ideal.

Second, Americanism is the mask of socialism: the socialism of fools, American-style. That concept and that ideology disguise the class character of American society, and disguise too the need for anything beyond the present moment.

Third, socialism in America becomes privatized; it decomposes the social into the personal. This peculiar privatization was part of the Protestant Puritan inheritance.

Fourth, the deception of American democracy comes in the assumption of every man being as good as every other man, by the use of first names, informality of dress, inconspicuous rather than conspicuous consumption, laughing at the rich; but all of these devices are, in fact, devices intended to provide political substitutes for social change.

Fifth, the American ideology underwrites this bifurcation of mind and society by divesting the American of any sense of history. Being a young country, the world always begins anew; there is no sense of continuity with the European past. The past is futile and it is alien. Therefore, everything is a sense of the present moment, and there are no laws of society or nature governing the American wilderness. To the American individual, socialism is not a historic inevitability, but an unconscious Freudian wish.

Sixth, one would have to say that the American does not believe in science so much as he believes in instinct. He does not have consciousness; he has unconsciousness. Socialistic manners and habits weave into the texture of capitalist relations, and therefore, capitalism itself seems better than in fact it is.

Seventh, the capitalists themselves are very different from their European ancestors; sharing this sense of the new and the dynamic, they behave in terms of philanthropic moods rather than selfish modes, and they begin to develop a social sense or rather a community sense of helping one's neighbor and preserving the dignity of the community. The model of the evil capitalist, while real, is nonetheless tempered by huge foundations and agencies, created by capitalists and for capitalism, which at the same time enshrine the dignity of American individualism.

There is a final point, which somehow has to be considered separately, since it occurs beyond the excerpts included here; and that is Samson's critique of the American as a dialectical madman, who does not want straight capitalism, nor straight socialism, nor straight government, nor straight union organizations. Samson sees the American as a "socioneurotic"; he sees him as infantile, viewing a social world not on the reality principle, but on the pleasure principle. And here, of course, one feels that Samson, in his own rage at the American, abandons Marxist analysis in favor of Freudian analysis. He speaks of reality and illusion, not in terms of class, but in terms of instinct. Perhaps there is no other way for him to move, given his position, cut off from the analysis of reality and limited by a dialectic which already takes perhaps too seriously the socialism of fools it sets out to condemn.

That brings us to the final chapter of the work, entitled "Toward

Political Realism." Again, one senses a frenzied search for answers outside the mainstream of the dialectic Samson helps us to understand. For example, he says that the American mind is more Oriental than European, and that therefore, working-class politics in the United States must "Europeanize the American mind, to make it more realistic, less mystic." (As if European politics is either more successful or somehow more socialistic than American politics!) He then goes on to deal with "the very first Marxist party of America"—the Socialist Labor Party, from De Leon to Eastman. However, he criticizes even the Socialist Laborites for allowing themselves to be overcome by the "American weakness"; that is, the weakness of becoming ineffectual. Utopian fantasies and fallacies filled the heads of American socialists, not because what they find in the Soviet Union is good, but because they are Americans and eternal optimists. All of the banalities of the communists are in fact attributed to this American dilemma of an idealistic model and a harsh reality that cannot be accepted for what it is. All is American, and all socialism is corrupted by Americanism, "Everything is rent, everything is a racket. Everything is selling. Everything is propaganda. Everything is everything" (p. 240).

The book ends not so much with a plea for realism (although it does make the usual obeisance to working and agitating for a united front of labor against capital) as with sheer frustration, a frustration with an American society that simply will not obey the rules of the game. Class history is turned into agrarianism. The struggle between workers and capitalists dissolves into a struggle between farmers and bankers. Samson argues that the first step is to convince the working class of their own weight and importance. They must constitute themselves as the vanguard of the American working class (p. 271). However, the entire book is a polemic against such a possibility, and the entire book inveighs against the Europeanization of American politics that Mr. Samson says must happen, if socialism is to be brought about. And yet, even with his frustrations and temptations to dialecticize all reality, in a sense Samson understood and predicted the American course of events. He pointed out that "war or revolution, this will be the real alternative before the American people, and not capitalism or socialism." And this certainly is far truer than I suspect Mr. Samson himself ever realized.

What is to be said about these arguments concerning Americanism as substitutive socialism? Kierkegaard once remarked that those who ignore history are doomed to repeat its errors. Perhaps the converse is equally true; those who pay too much attention to history, especially intellectual history, are similarly doomed to repeat its errors. What calls this to mind is the incapacity of so many critics of revolutionary and radical approaches to social and political affairs to think outside of their own preconceptions.

Writings on socialism, whether of Leon Samson or the followers and devotees of such "symbolic" interpreters of politics, share the tenacious belief that American society is not susceptible to collapse. What links Samson to Lipset's writings on the question of socialism, or those of other commentators who agree with his general position, far more than any ideological commonalities, is precisely this unspoken component concerning the self-regulatory capacities of the American social system. The metaphysical pathos that one finds in so much "social democratic" and "functionalist" writing is not so much a celebration of the cooptational features of American society, but a belief that such cooptation is really omnipotent.

It seems to me that this omnipotence has thunderously broken down on a wide variety of fronts: black people, for the most part, have not participated in this idea of socialism as Americanism. Other minorities have even less claims to assert such a presumed isomorphism. The federalist system has not produced a situation of consensus, in which egalitarianism would be the outcome of every man counting as one. Quite the contrary, federalism has now been strained to the limits by mass society, and in its place has emerged a series of interest groups and interest group politics that makes one wonder whether Americanism is not much more nearly like a surrogate fascism than a surrogate socialism. Then there is the war system itself. Writing before the Second World War, Samson could not possibly envision a social order which had bread-and-butter interests (proletarian bread as well as bourgeois butter) in the maintenance of a World War Three system for more than thirty years. Indeed, whether this system be defined in Millsian terms of a "military-industrial complex" or Galbraithian terms of a "technostructure," it is clear that new combinations and permutations of class behavior, rather than any implicit acceptance of nonclass behavior, is at the core of the American system.

Then there is the problem that any work based on a huge argument by analogy entails. One might just as easily write a book on Bolshevism as surrogate capitalism, and perhaps with equally telling effects. This calls attention to a prevailing superficial tendency among ideologically adroit social scientists to judge social systems on the shabbiest grounds of abstract thinking, rather than on real information or even hard data. This, to be sure, is not a peculiar monopoly of the social democratic wing. But there is a strong tendency of the present-day Samsonites (if I may be permitted such a weird notion), of Bell, Kristol, Schlesinger, Lerner, and yes, painful as it is to say, of Lipset, to prove or disprove tendencies by similar arguments by analogues. One might argue that Lipset's notion of America as a first new nation, for example, is derived largely if not exclusively from modernizing literature on the Third World. In fact, it represents old wine in a new bottle—the old wine being Americanism, the new bottle being surrogate developmentalism in place of surrogate socialism.

The "problem of socialism" in America is simply that it never came. But quite frankly, this is only a problem if such expectancies are held on tenacious ideological grounds. For the rest of the human race, the fact that socialism failed to materialize, and became a prime instance of where prophecy fails, was not so much a problem for America, but rather the problem for socialism. It is the great merit of the Lipset school of sociology that it finally recognizes this. It is nonetheless their great demerit that it took them so much time and energy to reach that understanding—time and energy that might better have been spent on addressing themselves to the "problem of society" in America.

Chapter 11

THE RELEVANCE OF MARXISM*

Clinton Rossiter

1. Marxist and American Views of Human Nature, and of Liberty and Equality

When I wrote [earlier on] . . . . of the essential pluralism of the American tradition, I had our view of the behavior and capacities of man uppermost in mind. To say the very best we can about it, this view is pleasantly clouded. Few American political thinkers have moved more than a step or two into the trackless field of psychology, and among these men there have always been serious disagreements. Thanks to the stern Calvinists among us, we have never been able to laugh off entirely the Augustinian warning that all men are miserable sinners; thanks to our happy liberals, we are still tempted by the Pelagian (if not Marxist) dream that all men can be made perfect. We are distinctly more sanguine about the nature of man in explicit words with which we exhort one another than in the implicit assumptions that account for our laws and institutions.

Yet having taken note of both the inadequacies and the contradictions in the view of man professed in the American tradition, I am prepared to draw at least the outlines of a consensus. We seem to have operated through most of our history in response to a mixed view of man's nature and capacities; yet, except for a deep suspicion we entertain of man in power, the mixture is still made up largely of the ingredients of hope. If the American tradition is not perfectibilist, it is certainly meliorist. It makes more of man's benevolence than of his wickedness, more of his educability than of

* Taken from Chapters 3, 4, 6, and 8 of Clinton Rossiter, *Marxism: The View from America* (New York: Harcourt, Brace, 1960), pp. 74–78, 81–82, 85–92, 110–14, 184–92, 237–43. In the original the chapters are entitled "Marxist Man," "Marxist Society: The Classes," "The Marxist State," and "America and Marx."

his perversity, more of his urge to be free than of his need to submit, more of his sense of justice than of his capacity for injustice; and it plainly lacks any secular counterpart to the doctrine of Original Sin. It assumes that the forces of good, if nurtured carefully by education and supported by a favorable environment, can generally hold the upper hand; at the same time, it insists that the forces of evil may be checked but never completely driven from the field, neither from the conduct of any one man nor from the behavior-patterns of the race. If we have been entertained but not impressed by the old line of revivalists, we have been excited but not convinced by the new breed of psychologists. The man of the American tradition is a rational man, one who, when given half a chance, will make political decisions calmly and thoughtfully with the aid of Aristotelian reason—reason tempered by experience. What we mean by "half a chance" is a decent environment and a system of constitutional restraints that can hold his ineradicable love of power in fairly close check. No matter, then, how we look at man, we see him as a jumble of cross-cutting tensions between good and evil; and no matter how far we look ahead, we see no final resolution of any of the tensions, especially of the tension between his sense of justice and capacity for injustice. The nature of man is changeable only slowly and within limits ordained by God and nature.

To men who stand on this ground the Marxist psychology presents a mixed picture of appealing insight and distressing prescription. We may be happy to find support for our own long-standing confidence in the power of human reason, but we are obviously not as prepared as Marx—certainly not in our political and social calculations—to give it first place among the forces that direct men's minds. We may rouse to his proclamation of human perfectibility, but in this instance, too, the sober side of our tradition forbids us to act too impetuously on such an assumption. The new man of Marxism, we are bound to say, is a dream in which a line of tough-minded thinkers from John Adams to Reinhold Niebuhr has forbidden us steadily to indulge at all purposefully.

Where we begin to part company decidedly is with Marx's view of man as "the *ensemble* of the social relations,"[1] as the exclusive creation of labor, class, and the system of production; for this, we think, is to see man as a collectivized and abstracted image of his unique and robust self. We give much credit to social and economic environment, but certainly not half so much as does Marx. We are far more skeptical than he in our evaluation of its role in the development of the species in history and its influence on the behavior of each individual in his own time. As to history, the American tradition teaches that forces deeply implanted in human nature had a great deal to do with the making of modern man; as to the individual, it assumes that he can rise above or fall below his alleged destiny, and that his class and occupation may often have little to do with his behavior. Our tradition asks us to believe that there is such a thing as a good man, and not just a good member of an economic class. The notion of proletarian man and bourgeois man as two different species is one that we cannot accept on proof or principle. The American tradition insists that there are some things common to all men, at all times, and in all classes, and that men can transcend society, as they have transcended nature, by virtue of their spirit, self-reliance, and desire for freedom. Many things have made each man what he is, and one of these has been the man himself.

We are not totally deaf to the argument for the plasticity of human nature, yet we are bound to say that Marx carries it much too far for our tastes with his call for "the alteration of men on a mass scale."[2] Man's nature is malleable, yes, but even continuously favorable circumstances existing over a long period of time can do little to erase or even recast those traits in his make-up which have set him eternally far below the angels. What Marx calls "vicious tendencies" are not wholly a product of present environment or a relic of past environment; rather they are a burden that man is destined to carry with him on his pilgrimage as far as the eye of sober imagination can see. The doctrine of plasticity, to tell the truth, is doubly unacceptable from the American point of view, for it appears politically dangerous as well as psychologically unsound. If we were to concede the point that a new race of men can be created by conscious manipulation of the social environment, what power could we then properly withhold from those in whose hands have been placed the levers of political control? The assumption of the infinite plasticity of human nature is a major intellectual support of the total state, and for this reason, if for no other, we cannot admit its validity.

The concept of alienation touches upon matters about which we have begun to think seriously only recently, and Marx deserves much credit for having made us think about them. Americans, I trust, cry out as loudly as do the Marxists at the sight of fragmented, depersonalized, dehumanized men, but we deny that such men exist in very large numbers, and deny further that capitalism or any other merely economic arrangement is the sole cause of their estrangement. We are not ignorant of the particular dangers to a healthy mind and spirit that flow from overspecialization and "fetishism," but we consider these the price of industrialism rather than of capitalism (a price, incidentally, which the whole world seems willing to pay). To the extent that men in Western society are alienated, the fault lies with them as much as it does with their surroundings. Life without anxiety, which appears to be the essence of the Marxist promise, is a will-o'-the-wisp, a Utopian dream that can never be made reality. Life without anxiety, I am tempted to add, would not be life at all, and it might well be argued that the elimination of all the tensions and frustrations that we label collectively as "alienation" would be undesirable as well as unattainable. The perfectly integrated mass-society would very likely be a sink of boredom and mediocrity in which creativity would be lost without a trace. Man, in any case, will always be alienated, troubled within and estranged without, simply because he is trapped in the paradox of human existence that we see fuzzily and the Marxists simply ignore: that he is always one alone and yet one among many.[3] The American tradition assumes that man has his best chance of self-fulfillment in a system that cuts him loose from the state and puts a large part of the responsibility for his conduct on his own will and capacities. If there is perhaps a little too much naiveté in this assumption, surely we can correct that without going outside the bounds of the tradition. This is one of those points at which we can learn from Marx's insights without embracing his prescriptions. . . .

The liberty of any man, Marx insisted, was determined by his membership in a class, just as were his nature, conduct, and morality. Each man was free to the extent that his class was free, and no man, therefore, was free at all. Even the vaunted liberty of the English and Americans was a weak, stunted, imperfect abstraction. Marx surveyed with arrogance what he liked to call "the narrow horizon of bourgeois right."[4] He had withering contempt both for the philosophical foundation on which Western man has grounded his claims to personal liberty, the concept of natural and inalienable rights, and for the practical machinery through which he has exercised his claims, the "pompous catalogue" of laws and customs that guarantee the freedoms of speech, press, worship, suffrage, assembly, petition, association, and fair trial.[5] The foundation of Western liberty was the rankest sort of idealism, the machinery was a legal cloak for the exploitation of the working class. As for constitutions and bills of rights, Engels had this to say of the most famous one:

> It is significant of the specifically bourgeois character of these human rights that the American constitution, the first to recognize the rights of man, in the same breath confirms the slavery of the colored races existing in America: class privileges are proscribed, race privileges sanctioned.[6]

In this context Marx made his famous distinction between "formal" and "effective" freedom.[7] Formal freedom is the kind that exists under capitalism and bourgeois democracy. In theory, it is the freedom to pursue one's ends in the absence of legal restraints; in fact, it is the harsh mixture of privilege and bondage that is guaranteed—privilege to the few, bondage to the many—by the complicated legal structure of "bourgeois right." Effective freedom is the kind that Marx promised in the future. In theory, it is the power to realize the ends one has chosen to pursue; in fact, it will be the happy condition of life for the proletariat under socialism and for all men under Communism. Formal freedom, Marx warned, will never become effective until private property in the means of production is rooted out and destroyed. The unequal distribution of control of property leaves most men in a state of subjection—as commodities to be bought and sold—and no amount of "prattle" about freedom of speech or the right to vote can mask this cruel fact from the honest eye. Marx was never more certain of the truth of his analysis of contemporary society than when he looked upon its painfully wrought structure of political rights and judicial safeguards, and pronounced it an extravagant fraud from top to bottom. And the most fraudulent part of the whole formal structure, in his opinion, was the boasted "freedom of contract." No one who studied the history of this "right" so precious to the bourgeoi-

468 / CLINTON ROSSITER

sie could fail to grasp the essential connection between freedom and exploitation in even the most "democratic" bourgeois societies. The "free" labor market, he wrote with savage irony in *Capital,* "is in fact a very Eden of the innate rights of man. . . ."[8]

It hardly seems necessary to make an elaborate statement of the meaning of liberty in the American tradition. There are a dozen ways of making such a statement, and no one who reads these pages will fail to have his own version of American liberty in mind. It will be enough, I think, to move directly into a critique of the Marxist theory of liberty, in the course of which the essentials of the American tradition should emerge into sufficiently clear view. In making this critique I will refrain from beating Marx over the head with the fact of the Soviet Union. Let us once again concentrate on Marx himself.

The first thing to be noted is that any meaningful debate with Marx and the Marxists on liberty is quite impossible to conduct.[9] This is not so much because our approach to liberty, which concerns itself largely with the relation of man to authority and is therefore concrete, contrasts so sharply with that of Marx, which concerns itself largely with the relation of man to history and is therefore metaphysical—although this difference in approaches does raise at least one insoluble problem. It is, rather, because our definitions and assumptions are so radically at odds with those of all the Marxists who have ever lived. We and they seem truly to live in two different worlds. What they call freedom, we call either airy fancy or real bondage; what they scorn as "formal," we cherish as real. They, too, as we know to our despair, define our freedom as bondage, and they do it so confidently that we cannot deny their sincerity.[10] Yet even if we were to accept their definitions, how could we then take the next step, which is to agree that the minimum price of genuine freedom is the root-and-branch destruction of our entire social, economic, and political system? And even if we were to agree to that—for the sake of the argument, I hasten to add—what concrete things can they tell us about freedom in the Communist society of the future, a society about which Marx and Engels were never more vague than when they spun their fine words about the "kingdom of freedom"? At no point is the gulf between Marxism and the American tradition so impossible to bridge, even for the sake of a verbal duel.

There are a few adverse comments, however, that we can make about Marx's view of liberty in language that Marxists can understand. No matter how his words are twisted and turned, he cannot escape these criticisms:

1) that he never came to grips with the paradox of freedom, the pattern of unceasing tension between liberty and authority, which he may have thought he had resolved by prophesying the "withering away of the state," but which, as the Soviets have proved,[11] he had not resolved at all;

2) that, as a result, he had nothing to say about political power, at once a mighty threat to, and stout guardian of, personal liberty;

3) that he failed to understand the importance of the instruments of "mere formal freedom," of laws and charters and elections, in protecting men against the abuses of public authority and the exploitations of private power;[12]

4) that in grounding the case for human rights exclusively on the fact of human needs, he did a serious disservice to the concept —so necessary to liberty as either fact or aspiration—of human dignity;

5) that in denouncing the distinction between public and private man he passed a sentence of death upon privacy, one of the most cherished of our legacies from the past and one of the saving refuges of our present;

6) that in this, as in all matters of importance to mankind, he put too much stress on economics, and thus refused to tell us how men might move beyond the negative if essential freedom from exploitation to the positive and creative practice of liberty;

7) that in this, as in all matters, he put too much stress on class, and thus failed to place the chief responsibility for the day-to-day practice of liberty, now or in the future, where it surely belongs: on man himself;

8) that in concentrating his attention on the element of effective power in personal freedom, he ignored the central question of who was to hold control of this power—the individual or some authority outside him? Few Americans will now deny a place to power in the formula of liberty, but not at the expense of independence and privacy.

Marx and Engels were most remiss, I think, in making so absolute a connection between liberty and necessity, and in making it

—how else can we put it?—in so offhand a manner. Since the time of the Flood we have told ourselves, and have been told, that liberty is obedience to necessity, that (to state this principle in the Scholastic version) it is the freedom to do that which is right and good. Now most of us have no quarrel with the argument, in either its metaphysical or practical form, that the freedom to do wrong is less sacred than the freedom to do right, and that those who do wrong will suffer sooner or later for having ignored the dictates of necessity. But the question we go on to ask is: Who is to say in fact, in the real world of laws and penalties, what is right and what is wrong? Who is to judge what is necessary and therefore proper? John Winthrop's answer was the Word of God, to be spoken by the Puritan elect; Rousseau's was the General Will, to be interpreted by the people massed in the public square; Hegel's was the Absolute Idea, to be brought to earth by the rulers of Prussia; and Marx's was the Laws of History, to be proclaimed by those who understand them best, by "the most advanced and resolute" of the Communists. With none of these solutions, all of which put final authority in the hands of supposedly infallible men, can we have anything to do. Law, popular will, tradition, and custom must all have a hand in deciding what is right and what is wrong, and a way out must be left to men who cannot agree with the definitions operative at any particular time. . . .

The appeal of Communism to millions of . . . people all over the world lies chiefly in its promise of an end to unjust privilege and degrading discrimination. It is therefore essential for us to learn what Marx and his followers have had to say about equality. The first and most surprising thing to learn is that they have had very little to say, that no leading Marxist, from Marx himself to Mao, has given himself over to long or searching thoughts about the matter.[13] For a man who is celebrated for having made equality the essence of justice, Marx was amazingly reticent in dealing with its philosophical supports or practical applications. This, in any case, is the sum of his ideas about equality; if the sum be trifling, let the blame fall on Marx himself:

To begin with, as we have learned to expect of Marx, he branded all other affirmations of equality, even those of the radicals who had gone before him, as nothing more than "obsolete rubbishy phrases."[14] The "equality" for which men had struggled in the

French and American Revolutions was, in Engels' words, simply a "bourgeois demand for the abolition of class privileges."[15] The political and judicial "equality" guaranteed in the laws of the bourgeois democracies was, like the "liberty" they also proclaimed, "mere formal" equality that masked the most shocking of all inequalities: the division of men into exploiters and exploited.

Marx and Engels refused to be lured into any rhetoric about the brotherhood of man. They recognized that men are not created equal and cannot be made equal; they even went so far in the *Manifesto* as to charge the Utopian socialists with preaching "universal asceticism and social leveling in its crudest form."[16] The Marxists of the Soviet Union, who gave up on equality long ago in the face of human nature and in the interests of an advanced technology,[17] have even less patience with those who insist on being naive about social and economic equality. "It is time it was understood," Stalin told the Seventeenth Party Congress in 1934, "that Marxism is opposed to leveling."[18] It is opposed, moreover, during the long period of socialist transition to anything resembling equality of income—to what Vyshinsky castigated as "petty bourgeois wage-leveling."[19] Marx himself made the great and careful distinction in his *Critique of the Gotha Programme* between the lot of men under socialism, who would continue to be rewarded on the basis of their contributions to society, and of men under communism, who would be satisfied, like the members of a family, on the basis of their needs.[20] Thus the Communists are able to rest their present case against the "left-egalitarian" call for equality of income—"a petty bourgeois deviation"—directly on scripture.[21]

What, then, we may ask, is equality in Marxism? And the answer comes in two parts: first, in words of Engels that are held sacred by the orthodox:

The demand for equality in the mouth of the proletariat has . . . a double meaning. It is either . . . the spontaneous reaction against the crying social inequalities, against the contrast between rich and poor, the feudal lords and their serfs, the surfeiters and the starving; as such it is simply an expression of the revolutionary instinct, and finds its justification in that, and in that only. Or, on the other hand, this demand has arisen as a reaction against the bourgeois demand for equality, . . . and in this case it stands or falls with bourgeois equality itself. In both cases the real content of the proletarian demand for equality is the demand for the *abolition of classes*. Any demand for equality which goes beyond that, of necessity passes into absurdity.[22]

And second, in words of Marx that are even more sacred:

In a higher phase of communist society, after the enslaving subordination of individuals under division of labour, and therewith also the antithesis between mental and physical labour, has vanished, after labour has become not merely a means to live but has become itself the primary necessity of life, after the productive forces have also increased with the all-round development of the individual, and all the springs of co-operative wealth flow more abundantly—only then can the narrow horizon of bourgeois right be fully left behind and society inscribe on its banners: *from each according to his ability, to each according to his needs.*[23]

Abolition of classes in the socialist future, equal satisfaction of human needs in the communist future beyond: this is the Marxist promise of equality. This promise has obviously been of little value in preventing the resurgence in the Soviet Union of the sharpest disparities in rank, privilege, and income. Yet in fairness to Marx it should be said that his own impatience with easy egalitarianism never blinded him, as it has blinded the Communists, to this great hope and truth: that while society must take the differences among men into honest account, it must not exploit these differences to the illicit advantage of the naturally superior and unseemly degradation of the naturally inferior. Most important of all, it must be careful always not to confuse artificial with natural inequalities.

The American tradition of equality is also, in essence, a protest against the existence of unjust, unnecessary, unnatural privileges. But it looks beyond the limited horizon of class determinism to account for the origin and persistence of such privileges. As a result, it prescribes quite different methods for achieving meaningful equality among the American people. Instead of concentrating passionately on one kind of equality, it proclaims the excellence and necessity of many: moral equality, the right of each man to be treated as end and not means; judicial equality, the right of each man to justice on the same terms as other men; political equality, the right of each man to a vote that counts no more and no less than any other man's vote; legal equality, the right to be exempt from class legislation; and, at the heart of the tradition, equality of opportunity, the right of each man to exploit his own talents to their natural limits. No American with a conscience can deny the existence of a grim wall between the ideal and the reality of equality in our way of life. Every American with a conscience is anxious for the wall to be torn down stone by stone, especially to demolish the crazy-quilt structure of privilege and exploitation that sits upon the treacherous foundation of racial discrimination. But we are determined, thanks to our tradition, that the struggle for equality be carried on through constitutional and customary processes, that it be directed exclusively toward the reduction of illicit privilege, and that it not sacrifice genuine liberty to spurious equality.

I think it useful to close on this very last point, for it represents one of the most serious breaks between Marxism and the American tradition. There can be no doubt that in a showdown between liberty and equality, which must often take place in both theory and practice, the Marxist chooses for equality and the American for liberty. There are many reasons for the choice that each of them makes, but the most important, I think, is the two different views they have of man. Marxism, by its own admission, is interested primarily in the "toiling masses" and therefore treats any one man as an abstraction of millions of men. Whenever it may be necessary for revolutionary purposes, Marxists have not the slightest trouble voicing the slogans of equality. The American tradition is more concerned with "self-reliant individuals." It therefore treats any one man as just that—one man—and even when we talk of equality, as we do with feeling, we tend to emphasize equality of rights rather than of goods or position. . . .

2. *Marxist and American Views of Social Class*

America has spawned some notable sociologists—Lester Frank Ward, William Graham Sumner, E. A. Ross, Thorstein Veblen, Arthur F. Bentley, W. Lloyd Warner, C. Wright Mills, and David Riesman, to mention a few of the best known—but as yet they have had little success in shaping our ideas about society to their findings or insights. The American social tradition is a kaleidoscope of contradictions. We talk a great deal about the classless society, yet we must admit under close questioning that such a society has never existed in America. We still love to toss about the slogans of rugged individualism, yet we know that the practice of such individualism by more than a few well-placed persons is disruptive of social stability. And certainly we manage to keep an uncomfortable distance between the way we preach and the way we practice the principle of equality. More disturbing than that, the kaleidoscope is only half-assembled. Our thoughts about society have been few and casual, as befits a people that has made a fetish of individualism. There are many questions about America that we have not even asked, much less answered, and this is one of those points at which the man who seeks to describe the American tradition must draw on the implicit workings of our customs and institutions rather than on the explicit words with which we are fond of praising them. What I am trying to say is that the real American social tradition is a benign reflection of the real American social structure. Its essence, which is Madisonian rather than Marxist, is roughly this:

Society is the sum of all the social units, and nothing more. From one point of view, it appears as a loose heap of freewheeling individuals; from a second, as a pattern of natural and voluntary groups; from a third, as a rough pyramid of social classes. Although no one of these views is any more "real" than the others (and all must be taken in order to get a clear picture of society), let us, out of deference to Marx, take the third, and so come up with these further observations:

Classes are an inevitable fact of social life, and what is inevitable is probably also necessary, not only for maintaining social stability but also for insuring social progress.

Classes in America are stages rather than castes. Our class system is a ladder, with at least six or eight rungs, up and down which heavy traffic moves constantly. (Here we have always been more sanguine than the statistics entitle us to be.)

Not only is there a vast amount of vertical movement between the classes, but the whole society is moving steadily upward in the scale of human existence. In specific terms, this means the steady growth, relative to all other classes, of an ever more prosperous and secure middle class.

The chief criterion of class distinction is achievement, especially economic achievement, although birth, wealth, taste, manners, power, and awareness all play their part.

The natural relationship of classes is a mixture of dependence and antagonism. There is friction in the joints, but not nearly enough to force us to talk of a "class struggle."

The best of all classes—in many ways, the only class that counts —is the middle class. The performance of any institution is to be judged finally in terms of how well it serves to expand or strengthen or reward this class.

A few additional details will emerge in the critique of Marxism to follow, but these, I think, are the basic points in the American social tradition. It would be hard to imagine a sharper confrontation between Marxism and the American tradition than exists in this field. Not even in the clash of materialism and idealism are the lines of battle more clearly drawn. These would seem to be the most compelling reasons for our inability to accept the lessons and exhortations of Marxist sociology:

First, Marx places far too much stress on economics as the decisive force in shaping social groups and patterns. It is simply not true that the institutions and tastes and habits and taboos of the American people are what they are and could be no different because of our mode of production. It is simply an exercise in definition, and not a very clever one at that, to say that a social class is fundamentally an aggregate of persons who perform the same broad function in the economy. History, psychology, cultural anthropology, and sociology all unite to affirm that both the origin and persistence of social classes can be understood only in terms of a plurality of causes, many of which defy economic determinism. Long before Marx, at least as early as James Madison, Americans knew well that men divided socially and politically on economic grounds, and certainly we should be the last people on earth to deny the power of production to influence our lives. But once again Marx has made one of the great determinants of social behavior the only determinant, and common sense bids us demur.

Second, we must demur, too, from the analysis of the class structure in Western society upon which he bases his revolutionary call to arms and his confident promise of a new society. When he talks of several kinds of bourgeois, several kinds of workingman, and of peasants and landlords and "third persons," we listen with interest and respect. When he insists that all these groupings are resolving inexorably into two, those who own and those who labor, interest turns to amusement, and respect to exasperation. There is no place in our thinking for this dialectical mania for shuffling all the complexities of social existence into a pattern of polar contradictions.

Third, even if we were to assume that his diagnosis was essentially correct, we could not take seriously his description of either of the two great classes. As the land of the bourgeoisie, a fact that Marx and Engels both acknowledged, what are we to say of the contempt he heaps upon us, our institutions, and our ideals? As the land with no proletariat (or so we like to think), what can we do but gasp when we hear of the role assigned to it? The fact is, as a hundred learned critics of Marx have pointed out, that the proletariat as Marx described it is a colossal myth, one of the most absurd if compelling in the Marxist armory (or whatever place it is in which men store myths). The Marxists themselves have never acted as if the proletariat were more than a useful abstraction, for always and everywhere it has been a select few—before the revolution a handful of intellectuals, after it a handful of bureaucrats—who have acted for and as the proletariat. The proletariat described by Marx does not and cannot exist; even if it did we would hardly care to put our destiny in its keeping.

Fourth, our history and tradition protest in unison against Marx's assertion that the class struggle is the normal condition of society and the motive power of history.[24] To the contrary, the pattern of class relationships in this country, as in many countries that come to mind, has been one of collaboration as well as of conflict. The advances of one class have brought benefits as well as injuries to other classes. We have long since abandoned the happy view of perfect harmony among classes, but this does not mean that we must now rush to the other end of the spectrum and embrace the bitter view of total war. One may find evidence of class antagonisms at many points in our history, but rarely has there been an antagonism that was not dampened eventually by the democratic process of give and take, if not dampened sooner by the flow of men from class to class. There is a wide gulf between the tensions and envies that can be found in even the healthiest society and the kind of "war to the knife" in which Marx saw the promise of revolution.

3. *Marxist and American Views of the Role of Power and the State*

The structure of government is grounded on certain manifest truths about the mixed nature of men. The fact that men can be wise and just, that they can govern themselves and other men fairly, is reflected in provisions for popular elections and for popular participation in the decision-making process. The fact that they can be unwise and unjust, that they can be hurried into rash decisions and corrupted by the taste of power, is reflected in arrangements that divide and check the total authority of government. Of these the most important are: the *separation of powers,* the distribution of political authority horizontally among a series of independent offices and agencies; *federalism,* the distribution of authority vertically among two or three levels of government; *checks and balances,* the provisions that guarantee mutual restraint among all these centers of power; *constitutional restraints,* the written laws and unwritten customs that reduce the discretion of public servants to the lowest level consistent with the effective operation of the political machinery; and *representative government,* the system under which the laws are made at a level once removed from the people, that is, by representatives elected to serve a limited period and held directly responsible by their electors.

The great services of all these arrangements, which bear the generic label of *constitutionalism,* are that they force men to think, talk, and bargain before they act, and that they institutionalize the processes through which public policy is made, administered, and enforced. The rule of the majority is the essence of democracy, but the majority must be coolheaded, persistent, and overwhelming, and it must be forced to recognize those things it cannot do by right or might. Without limitations there can be no constitutionalism; without constitutionalism, no democracy.

Finally, democracy flourishes strongly only when social and spiritual conditions are favorable. Some of these conditions are a healthy political system, in which two or more parties contest seriously but not savagely for power, and thus provide both a spur (the majority party) and a check (the opposition) to the process of government; a network of associations not beholden to the state, through which the legitimate interests of society may express and defend themselves; a productive economy, which guarantees a broad distribution of property and gives most men a "stake in society"; a sound pattern of morality, under which men may put trust in other men; a sound system of education, which raises men who can live decent lives and make prudent decisions; and, most essential, a faith in the rightness and fairness and competence of democracy, a faith that spreads wide and deep among the people.

I have made this statement of our political tradition in a "characteristically American" vein, that is, in ideal terms. I am aware of the gap between ideal and reality in our application of many of these principles. I am aware, too, that our political history has been a long battle to suppress our own urges toward Jacobin democracy. And I suspect that several principles of our tradition may need extensive reshaping in response to the pressures of an advanced industrial civilization. Yet I consider this a fair statement of the principles of good government to which we will be giving our allegiance for a long time to come, one that presents the American tradition in a light neither brighter nor darker than it deserves. Viewed in this light, most of the points at which Marxism and the American political tradition are in opposition are so visible to the naked eye that it would be a waste of time, not to say an insult to intelligence, to tick them off one by one. If ever there was a system of political institutions designed to exasperate the Marxists of this world, it is the "smokescreen for the dictatorship of capital" that operates in Washington and all over America through "ideological fictions" like the separation of powers and "Babbitt ideals" like federalism.[25] If ever there was a set of political ideas calculated to quicken the Marxist talent for abusive ridicule, it is the "apology for decay and oppression" I have just done my best to present. Marxism has no respect at all for our constitutional democracy, and I feel sure that my readers can be counted on to understand the reasons why. For my own part, I should like to single out the fundamental reasons for the inability of any constitutional democrat to accept the teachings of Marxism about politics and government, to list the points at which Marx and Engels and all their followers left the path of political reality to go astray in the fields of error.

The first of these points I discussed at some length earlier, the flaw in the Marxist view of the realities and potentialities of human behavior. No orthodox Marxist, from Marx himself through the latest apologist for the Soviet state, has ever grasped the implications of the universality of man's desire for power, nor ever stopped to observe or imagine the changes that can come over even the noblest members of the race when power without restraint or responsibility is placed in their hands. Marx's prescription for the dictatorship of the proletariat, like the dictatorship that has actually emerged in one Communist country after another, is based on the assumption that some men can be trusted to wield absolute power over other men without succumbing to the corruptions of greed or ambition or pride or even spite. To us this assumption, whether it be made out of indifference or conviction, appears absurd and dangerous. We are not yet prepared to base our own prescriptions for good government on the notion that all men are perfectible and a few men, whether Communists or Republicans or professors of political science or graduates of West Point, already perfect.

The second point is a corollary of the first. In failing to make room in his system for the psychology of power, Marx also fails to grasp the essentials of what we may call its sociology, that is, the way in which political power is structured and manipulated in society. We have already noted how strangely blind he is to the realities and ambiguities and perils of economic power, at least under socialism; and he is, if anything, even less conscious of the play of forces in the political arena. The most unacceptable result of this indifference, certainly from our point of view, is the gaping absence in his thought of any appreciation of the uses and merits of constitutionalism, a gap that has been filled by the Bolsheviks with their autocratic doctrine of "democratic centralism."[26] What we think is the first prerequisite of a sound system of government —the diffusion and restraint of authority through the techniques of constitutionalism—Marx and the Marxists consider either counterfeit or irrelevant. We may shudder at what we hear from Hobbes or Machiavelli about the uses of power, but at least we hear something. We may squirm when we read Madison or John Adams on the abuses of power, but we know that they are grappling honestly with a universal problem of government. It would be hard to find a figure in the whole history of political thought who has less to say than Marx on either aspect of the problem of power, indeed who gives less appearance of knowing that the problem even exists. Our aim has always been to *institutionalize* the uses of political power, that of the Marxists to *personalize* it, and their aim is a direct legacy from Marx and Engels. Marx or no Marx, it continues to amaze us that the repeated purges of Soviet officials for "abuses of authority" has never led to even a whispered reconsideration of the necessity of constitutionalism.

It is no wonder, then, that we fall out with the Marxists irreconcilably over the importance to human liberty of the instruments of "mere formal freedom." As Karl Popper writes, "This 'mere formal freedom,' i.e., democracy, the right of the people to judge and to dismiss their government, is the only known device by which we can try to protect ourselves against the misuse of political power; it is the control of the rulers by the ruled."[27] And since it is admitted today, in both the Soviet Union and the United States, that political power can go far to control economic power, "political democracy is also the only means for the control of economic power by the ruled." In our opinion, the Marxists have grossly undervalued the efficacy of what Lenin called the "hackneyed forms of routine parliamentary democracy"[28] as the means of making the state the servant and guardian of the entire people. No small part of the world's present grief may be traced to the distressing truth that Marx never understood what institutions and rules were essential to the proper conduct of popular government. He was altogether right in pointing out that the trappings of democracy can be used to serve the selfish interests of a ruling class, altogether wrong to insist that they can never be used to serve the common interests of an entire society.

The truth is that Marxism has never been able to get the role of political authority in proper perspective. It has never really attempted to answer the question posed by Edmund Burke, whom Marx saluted as that "celebrated sophist and sycophant,"[29] of "what the state ought to take upon itself to direct by the public wisdom, and what it ought to leave, with as little interference as possible, to individual discretion."[30] This, needless to say, is a central question of politics, and we condemn the Marxists for their refusal even to think about it. Marx himself errs in the direction of granting the state too little competence; the latter-day Marxists, who share his sentiments on the futility of bourgeois politics, err in the direction of granting it too much. Marx was a peculiar sort of anarchist, the Marxists are straight-out statists; and for neither of these polar positions can we have respect. We can show sympathy for the old Marxism, since we, too, were once classical Liberals who suspected that the power of government was both evil and useless. We were, to be sure, far better Liberals in theory than we were in practice, yet it cannot be denied that we now give a larger assignment and thus a larger measure of respect to government than we did twenty-five or fifty or a hundred years ago, and that anarchy is no more than a fleeting thought in which Americans indulge once a year when they file their income tax returns. Marx himself, we feel, is never more mistaken than when he derides the capacity of government to serve the general welfare —to humanize industrialism, to reduce class and group tensions, and generally to improve the lot of all men. We think we have proved what he denies: that government can manage efficiently and direct equitably the pursuit of at least some of the common interests of society. . . .

4. *America and Marx*

"I hope," Marx once wrote in a mixed mood of jest and spite, "that the bourgeoisie as long as they live will have cause to remember my carbuncles." I expect that we will have cause, as long as we live; and we may give thanks that only rarely has he proved so keen a prophet. Marx is a giant who reigns in awe over the world—even over those parts that deny his sovereignty—as no man of ideas has reigned in all history. He is, in his own words, a "specter . . . haunting" every country, every party, every interest, indeed every thinking man in the world, and not just because he is the father of Communism. Marx the thinker may be a man to reckon with long after Communism has joined the other legendary tyrannies in "the dustbin of history." For all his trespasses against reason, science, history, and common sense, he owned one of the mighty minds of the human race, and we may be prisoners of his words and categories and eccentricities as long as we were of Aristotle's. The prospect is appalling, but it lies before us, and we had better learn to live with it bravely.

We in the West, especially in America, have most to learn, for upon us Marx unleashed the brunt of his attack, and upon us the attack continues in undiminished violence. Indeed, it almost seems as if he were as vibrantly and censoriously alive today as he was in 1848. We have no social arrangement—our welfare capitalism, the ascendancy of our middle class, the variety of our groups and interests—for which he can say one kind or even understanding word. We have no institution—church, family, property, school, corporation, trade union, and all the agencies of constitutional democracy—that he does not wish either to destroy or to transform beyond recognition. We have no ideals or ideas—from the Christian ethic through patriotism to individualism—that he does not condemn out of hand. The essence of Marx's message is a prediction of doom for the Western, liberal, democratic way of life. He announces that prediction not sadly but gladly, not timidly but furiously, not contingently but dogmatically; and so, of course, do his heirs. Lenin was once again a faithful child of Marx when he wrote, "In the end one or the other will triumph—a funeral requiem will be sung over the Soviet Republic or over world capitalism," and Khrushchev a faithful grandchild when he laid to rest all doubts about our future by promising happily, "We will bury you." He will bury us, he thinks, because we deserve to be buried, and because Marx promised that we will get what we deserve. Khrushchev harbored a quasi-religious conviction of the overpowering rightness of Communism and the overweening wrongness of Western democracy. He made the sharpest possible confrontation of his system and ours, and he makes it, let us not forget, apocalyptically—that is, by predicting the total victory of the one and the total defeat of the other, whether the game be played on the battlefield, in the laboratory, or in the heavens.

It is time that we, too, made this confrontation far more sharply than we have made it in the past generation. Whether we, too, must come to an apocalyptic conclusion I am not yet ready to say, but I am certain that we must not fear to look orthodox Marxism straight in the face. That is why I have attempted this small beginning by looking into the assumptions and motives which make that face so grim as it stares back at us and so hopeful as it scans the future. Let me collect and restate the many points of confrontation we have discovered, in the form of three deep-cutting, irreconcilable conflicts:

The first arises primarily in the realm of ideas: the head-on collision of monism and pluralism. Marxism is, as Engels said jokingly, "an all-comprising system" constructed by men of a "ter-

THE RELEVANCE OF MARXISM / 483

ribly ponderous *Gründlichkeit*"; it is, as Lenin said solemnly, a "solid block of steel," a "prolific, true, powerful, omnipotent, objective, and absolute human knowledge." Marxism is the latest and greatest (and easily the most presumptuous) of all those celebrated systems of thought with which learned men, moved by the doubts and fears of the unlearned, have sought to interpret the world in terms of a single principle. It has an explanation of everything, and to everything it grants one explanation. The whole range of man's behavior is explained in terms of the business of making a living, the whole configuration of society in terms of the class structure, the whole sweep of history in terms of the class struggle, the whole phenomenon of classes in terms of private property; and all these primary forces, most notably property, are hung upon a hook fashioned from the "solid block of steel": dialectical materialism. The dialectic of Hegel and the materialism of Hobbes and Holbach are clamped together, if never really consolidated, to account for all things from "the dance of the electrons" to "the conflicts in human society."[31] Marxism, at least as theory, is a closed system in which all new facts and ideas are made to conform to the original pattern, which is itself a thing of breathtaking simplicity.[32]

The American tradition, to the contrary, is consciously pluralistic. Its unity is the result of a process through which unnumbered diversities of faith and intellect seek to live together in accommodation, if not always in harmony. Man, history, society, politics, nature—all are explained, to the extent that they can be explained, in terms of multiple causation. Our system of ideas is open to new thoughts and fresh evidence. It has its bedrock beliefs in the dignity of man, the excellence of liberty, the limits of politics, and the presence of God; but on these beliefs, even in defiance of the last, men are free to build almost every conceivable type of intellectual and spiritual mansion. For this reason, we find it hard to grant much respect to Marxism, a system that presumes to relate all thoughts and all wonders to a single determining principle. More to the point, we find it increasingly hard to grant it license, for too much evidence is now before our eyes that monism in the world of ideas leads to absolutism in the world of events. In order to survive, a truly monistic system must put an end to the great debates that have gone on for thousands of years,[33] give dogmatic answers to questions that men can never answer finally, and de-

484 / CLINTON ROSSITER

stroy all other systems, closed or open, that seek to understand
something of the mysteries of life. The monism of Marxism makes
it the ideology of ideologies, and we can never make peace with
it. Those Americans who have themselves succumbed to monism
are in palpable violation of one of our most cherished principles,
and they could profit a great deal from the Communist example.

The second conflict arises primarily in the realm of institutions:
the head-on collision of collectivism and individualism. Marx, we
have learned, seems more concerned with abstract men in the real
mass rather than with real men in the abstract mass. He talks of
classes rather than of individuals, of systems rather than of persons; he seems to have no respect at all for private man. His prescriptions are based on an honest assumption that all conflicts
between the interests of any one man and the interests of all society, between what a man owes himself and what he owes his
fellows, can be eliminated by social reconstruction. On both "the
individual withdrawn into his private interests" and the family with
even a symbolic fence between itself and the community he pro-
nounces a sentence of doom; and he does it in the best of faith
because he cannot believe that any man or family will feel the
need to hold something of value aloof from the proletarian or classless community. His prescriptions are therefore, as we have seen,
thoroughly collectivistic. No man, no group, no interest, no center
of power is to defy the dictatorship of the proletariat in the period
of socialist transition or to remain outside the harmonious community in the endless age of Communism. That age would surely
be marked, as I wrote earlier, by a state of "togetherness"
that would obliterate every barrier between man and mankind. Collectivism is Marx's means, and it is also his end. It may be gentle,
comforting, and unforced—once the dictatorship has passed—but it
is still collectivism with a vengeance.

The American tradition is doggedly individualistic. It makes
room for the state, for society, and for natural and voluntary
groups; and only a few men on the fringes of the tradition have
ever denied the intensely social nature of man. Yet it leaves a
wide sphere to private man, the private family, and private groups
even in its most socially conscious moments, and it insists on a
meaningful, lasting contradiction between the interests of this
sphere and those of the common weal. Lacking the monistic urge
to have all things in order, it understands that freedom is an eternal

paradox. It is prepared to live indefinitely with the division of each person into an "individual" and a "citizen." If this leaves all thinking men in a state of ceaseless tension, the tension must nonetheless be borne as part of the human condition.[34] Marx tries to resolve it, and that is where he goes off the track, or rather down the wrong track. We try to live with it, and that is why we go bumping along on the right track. There have been times, to be sure, when we hurried down it much too blithely. We have lost sight of the free group in our anxiety to celebrate the free individual; we have made too much of competition and too little of co-operation as engines of social progress. But fundamentally our tradition is a challenge to collectivism at both levels; a challenge in behalf of the free individual, a challenge in behalf of the free group. The full measure of this giant confrontation should be understood as a collision of collectivism with both individualism and social pluralism.

The last confrontation is both ideological and institutional: the not quite head-on, yet resounding enough collision of radicalism with conservatism and liberalism. Marxism is, by almost any standard, the supreme radicalism of all time. It is radical in every sense of that sticky word: because it is revolutionary, because it is extremist, because it proposes to dig down to the roots of all things. It insists that the political and social institutions of the West are oppressive and diseased, the values that support them rotten and dishonest; it bids us supplant them with an infinitely more just and benign way of life. So complete is its commitment to the future, so unwilling is it to suffer delay, that it is prepared to force entry into this future by subversion and violence. Its attitude toward the social process is simple and savage: it means to disrupt it as thoroughly as possible in defiance of all rules of the game. The rules, in any case, are monstrous cheats, which may be ignored, manipulated, or turned against their makers—whatever course seems most likely to serve the cause of revolutionary radicalism. The Marxist is a man with a blueprint for rebuilding society, and the first three items on the sheet of instructions that goes with it read: smash the foundations of the old society into rubble; cart the rubble away; start to build a new foundation with new materials that have never been used before.

The American tradition, like most successful traditions with a broad appeal, is a casual blend of conservatism and liberalism. It is conservative in all the useful senses of that sticky word: because it is cautious and moderate, because it is disposed to preserve what it has inherited, because it puts a high value on tradition as a social force and prudence as an individual virtue. It does not encourage, to put it mildly, an attitude of bitter criticism among its children; it is committed to a discriminating but dogged defense of the American system against radical change. Yet it is liberal, too, in most senses of that stickiest word of all: because it is open-handed and open-minded, because it really expects the future to be better than the past, because it is interested first of all in the development of free men. Product of a history of ceaseless change and growth, it makes a large place for progress through conscious reform and prescriptive innovation. It breeds optimism rather than pessimism about the next hundred years, even in the teeth of the Marxist challenge. Some Americans interpret their tradition as a stamp of approval on things as they are, others interpret it as a summons to restless experiment; but all (or almost all, because the tradition also makes room for the men on the fringes) have little use for the kind of radicalism Marx proclaims. While there is still room for Utopia in the American dream, short cuts to it are looked upon as roads to ruin. The American mind has been sold some amazing prescriptions for specific ills; it has never been sold a panacea, and probably could not be.

NOTES

1. Sixth "Thesis on Feuerbach," Karl Marx, *Selected Works* (New York, n.d.), vol. I, p. 473.

2. Karl Marx, *German Ideology* (New York, 1947), p. 69.

3. On this point, see M. Watnick, "Georg Lukacs," *Soviet Survey*, January–March 1958, pp. 60, 65, and works there cited.

4. Karl Marx, *Critique of the Gotha Programme*, in *Selected Works*, vol. II, p. 566.

5. *Capital* (Chicago, 1906–9), vol. I, p. 330.

6. Friedrich Engels, *Anti-Dühring* (Moscow, 1954), pp. 147–48.

7. A. L. Harris, "Utopian Elements in Marx's Thought," *Ethics*, vol. LX (1949), pp. 79, 87–89.

8. *Capital*, vol. I, p. 195. See Engels' strictures on this "freedom" in his *Condition of the Working Class in England* (New York, 1887), pp. 51–52.

9. Even, I fear, with so reasonable a Marxist as John Lewis. See his contribution to the UNESCO symposium on human rights in his *Marxism and the Open Mind* (London, 1957), pp. 53–76, and also 77–93. And note Stalin's insistence, in his famous interview with Roy Howard in 1937, that "we have not built this society in order to cramp individual freedom." A. Vyshinsky, *The Law of the Soviet State* (New York, 1954), p. 539. For an excellent critique of Marxist ideas about freedom, see H. B. Parkes, *Marxism: An Autopsy* (New York, 1939), ch. 4.

10. I know of no book that gives a more completely orthodox statement of the Marxist concept of liberty than Roger Garaudy, *La liberté* (Paris, 1955), esp. pts. II, IV. Christopher Caudwell, *Studies in a Dying Culture* (London, 1938), ch. 8, is an eloquent Marxist statement of the irreconcilability of the two liberties, one a "bourgeois illusion," the other the "social consciousness of necessity."

11. Note Vyshinsky's comment, so much at odds with our way of thinking, that "any contrasting of civil rights with the state is alien to socialist public law." *Law of the Soviet State*, pp. 562–63.

12. This is why, as an English Marxist points out, a "higher synthesis" of the "earlier inherent individual rights" and communist "social and economic rights" is an impossible dream. Lewis, *Marxism and the Open Mind*, p. 58.

13. For a useful bibliography on this subject, see D. D. Egbert and Stow Persons, eds., *Socialism and American Life* (Princeton, 1952), vol. II, pp. 340–42. Werner Sombart, *Der proletarische Sozialismus* (Vena, 1924), vol. I, ch. 9, is an excellent introduction.

14. *Critique of the Gotha Programme*, in *Selected Works*, vol. II, p. 567.

15. *Anti-Dühring*, p. 148.

16. *Selected Works*, vol. I, p. 237.

17. John Strachey, *The Theory and Practice of Socialism* (New York, 1936), p. 117. Barrington Moore, Jr., *Soviet Politics—The Dilemma of Power* (Cambridge, 1956), pp. 405ff., puts the necessary connection between industrialism and a "system of organized social inequality" with particular conviction. So, in his own way, does Milovan Djilas, *The New Class* (New York, 1958), esp. pp. 37ff. Engels beat them both to the draw by pointing out in *Anti-Dühring*, p. 193, that "each new advance of civilization is at the same time a new advance of inequality."

18. Marguerite Fisher, *Communist Doctrine and the Free World* (Syracuse, 1952), p. 216. See R. N. Carew Hunt, *A Guide to Communist Jargon* (London, 1957), pp. 69–73; B. Moore, *Soviet Politics*, pp. 182–88, 236–46, 404.

19. *Law of the Soviet State*, p. 209. For the sad story of Lenin's doctrine of "maximum income," see E. H. Carr, *The Bolshevik Revolution* (New York, 1951–53), vol. II, pp. 112–15. See his orthodox comments on equality in *State and Revolution* (New York, 1932), pp. 76–82.

20. *Selected Works*, vol. II, pp. 560–68; Lenin, *State and Revolution*, pp. 75–85.

21. Joseph Stalin, *Leninism* (New York, n.d.), vol. II, pp. 373–77.

22. *Anti-Dühring*, pp. 148–49. The italics are Engels'.

23. *Critique of the Gotha Programme*, in *Selected Works*, vol. II, p. 566. The italics are mine.

24. On the difficulties inherent in this concept, see Alexander Gray, *Socialist Tradition* (London, 1946), pp. 499–504. G. H. Sabine, *Marxism* (Ithaca, N.Y., 1958), ch. 3, is a powerful indictment from the democratic point of view.

25. Vyshinsky, *Law of the Soviet State*, pp. 166, 220, 312ff. See Julian Towster, *Political Power in the U.S.S.R.* (New York, 1948), pp. 52, 61–62, 184–86, for typical Marxist statements on federalism and the separation of powers. On Soviet federalism, see John N. Hazard, *The Soviet System of Government* (Chicago, 1957), ch. 6; Richard Pipes, *The Formation of the Soviet Union: Communism and Nationalism, 1917–1922* (Cambridge, 1955). Lenin sealed the theoretical doom of federalism in *State and Revolution*, pp. 46, 60–62.

26. On this concept, see R. N. Carew Hunt, *A Guide to Communist Jargon* (London, 1957), pp. 53–56; B. Moore, *Soviet Politics*, pp. 64ff., 81, 139, 232; Towster, *Political Power in the U.S.S.R.*, pp. 186, 207–8; Merle Fainsod, *How Russia Is Ruled* (Cambridge, Mass., 1953), pp. 180–81. This is an essentially party concept now transferred in application to the whole state.

27. There are other known devices, but the hyperbole serves its purpose. K. R. Popper, *The Open Society and Its Enemies* (Princeton, 1950), p. 316.

28. Marguerite Fisher, *Communist Doctrine and the Free World* (Syracuse, 1952), p. 166.

29. *Capital*, vol. I, p. 354.

30. *Works* (9th ed.; Boston, 1889), vol. V, p. 166.

31. J. M. Cameron, *Scrutiny of Marxism* (London, 1948), p. 25.

32. On the intellectual dangers of working within such a system, see Arthur Koestler, *Arrow in the Blue* (New York, 1952), pp. 260–61, and for an intelligent Marxist's warning of the sorrowful consequences of intellectual monism, see Pierre Hervé, *La révolution et les fétiches* (Paris, 1956).

33. The course of events in Red China over the past few years is a fascinating case study in the inevitable results of monism. In February 1957, Mao Tse-tung made his famous appeal to the Supreme State Conference in Peiping: "Let a hundred flowers bloom, let a hundred schools of thought contend." No sooner had Mao's garden begun to grow, however, than most of the new flowers were identified as "poisonous weeds," and rooted out savagely. As the New York *Times* said editorially, any flower may grow in Chinese soil if it meets these conditions: "First, views expressed must serve to unite and not divide the people. Second, they must benefit socialist transformation and construction. Third, they must help to consolidate the 'people's democratic dictatorship.' Fourth, they must help to consolidate 'democratic centralism.' Fifth, they must strengthen the leadership of the Communist party. Sixth, they must benefit international Communist solidarity and that of 'peace-loving peoples.'" This hardly leaves much room in the garden for even slightly mutant blooms. The text of Mao's speech is printed in the New York *Times,* June 19, 1957. An interesting commentary is Michael Walzer, "When the Hundred Flowers Withered," *Dissent,* vol. V (1958), p. 360.

34. H. M. Roelofs, *The Tension of Citizenship* (New York, 1957).

COMMENT 1

Tom Bottomore

Clinton Rossiter's study of Marxism in an American context is disappointing in several respects. It deals with a rather simplified version of Marxism, which verges at times upon the crudities of the political doctrine once known as Marxism-Leninism-Stalinism. Represented in this fashion Marxism is then contrasted with an "American tradition," which is portrayed in a very abstract way and not subjected to any critical examination. Finally, Rossiter explains the lack of appeal which Marxism has had in America entirely in terms of a conflict of ideas, without reference to the institutions and conditions of American society which provided the framework and material of this conflict.

Let me comment first, very briefly, upon Rossiter's view of Marxism. He concentrates his attention on two themes: one, the question of individual liberty in relation to Marx's conceptions of human nature and of social classes; the other, Marx's idea of government, or political power, in present-day and future society. In a number of different contexts Rossiter argues that the tendency of Marxist thought is to deny or devalue the autonomy and freedom of the individual. Thus he writes: "we begin to part company decidedly . . . with Marx's view of man as 'the *ensemble* of the social relations'"; and in another passage: "The liberty of any man, Marx insisted, was determined by his membership in a class, just as were his nature, conduct, and morality." But this is to disregard the complexity of Marx's thought, and in particular the tension in it between the idea of the determining influences of the economy, property relations, and social classes on one side, and on the other side the idea of men's ability to grasp their situation rationally and to act in such a way as to change it. Rossiter himself, in other passages, attributes to Marx an excessive confidence in the power of human reason, but he does not see that this is an element which modifies profoundly Marx's "determinism."

The phrase which Rossiter quotes from the *Theses on Feuerbach* to the effect that man's "real nature" is the *"ensemble* of social relations" itself needs to be interpreted in the light of Marx's thought at that time; his argument is directed against Feuerbach's conception of man as an abstract, isolated, unhistorical individual, and asserts that what is needed is a critical examination of man's "real nature" as it is revealed in the historical development of societies. Only by looking at Marx's early writings, and especially his *Economic and Philosophical Manuscripts* (which were less well known when Rossiter published his study than they are today), can we see clearly his intention to lay the basis of a doctrine of human emancipation which would be historical and realistic, taking into account both men's ideal strivings, the product of their reason and imagination, and also (against the utopians) the actual social conditions in which men live, struggle, and form their ideals. This intention was less prominent in Marx's later writings, when he was preoccupied with the analysis of the economic structure of capitalism, but it was always present in some form, whether in his discussion in *Capital,* vol. III, of the "true realm of freedom" as the "development of human potentiality for its own sake," which requires as an essential precondition the shortening of the hours of work, or in his judgment of the Paris Commune as "the political form, at last discovered, under which to work out the emancipation of labour."

Marx's analysis of the experience of the Commune also helps to elucidate his ideas on political power and the manner in which it might be transformed in a future type of society. What Marx criticized in the bourgeois state was that it organized political power as a separate and limited sphere of activity, detached from civil society and claiming to be independent of it, although in fact it had its basis in the social structure inasmuch as it upheld and consolidated the interests of an economically dominant class. The bourgeois state is an alien force, beyond the control of the great majority of individuals; and the "general interest" of the whole community which it claims to represent is illusory so long as there is a real conflict of interests in civil society, between classes, and among individuals themselves as a consequence of the fact that civil society is organized on the principle of a war of all against all in the pursuit of particular interests. When Marx referred to the supersession *(Aufhebung)* of the state in a socialist society he meant that political power would become truly universal; all men would participate in its exercise (thus taking back the powers which they had alienated), and political power would be used to regulate all the conditions of men's collective existence, so that there would no longer be a contradiction between the state as representative of a general interest and civil society as the arena of antagonistic private interests. Marx saw in the Commune a first, tentative realization of this new political form, the principal features of which were that it was based upon universal suffrage, that its elected representatives were well known and trusted by the people, and were subject to recall, and that they were not separated from the rest of the population by differences in their wealth, income, or style of life. In Marx's words, the Commune would bring about "in place of the old centralized government the self-government of the producers." The Commune thus provided an occasion for Marx to elaborate, in terms of a practical experience, the political ideas formulated early in his life in his *Critique of Hegel's Philosophy of the State* (1842–43), which were directed against the centralized autocratic state. There is no justification, if Marx's political theory is systematically examined as a whole, for Rossiter's exclusive concentration upon the "dictatorship of the proletariat," or for his claim that Stalinism is a direct legacy from Marx's theory. On the contrary, it is all too evident that the theory and practice of the Bolsheviks diverged widely from Marx's own theoretical and practical aims: it was Lenin, not Marx, who formulated the doctrine of the leading role of the party, and thus prepared the way for a political dictatorship; it was Lenin who suppressed, after the Revolution, the workers' and soldiers' councils which embodied the same political principles that Marx had praised in the Commune.

To say this is not to deny in any way that the process in which Marx's theory was transformed into the Bolshevik ideology constitutes an important social and intellectual problem; or that this historical metamorphosis may provoke (as it has indeed done) new critical reflections upon Marx's own conception of the transition to socialism and of the institutional framework of a socialist society. But Rossiter has a curious way of proceeding. He expounds Marx's ideas in a form which makes them appear wholly consistent with Soviet reality, and then condemns them by reference to that reality; yet when he discusses the "American tradition" he presents it only in an ideal form, and does not confront it at all with the reality of American society. (At most he makes a formal acknowledgment, from time to time, that there is a gap between ideal and reality.) It is evident, in any case, that a "tradition" constitutes a body of ideas considerably less precise, articulated, and homogeneous than a systematic theory such as Marxism; it may include divergent or even contradictory elements, and what is referred to as *the* tradition (or in sociological language, the "central value system") is unlikely to be more than a dominant ideology, interpreted from a particular point of view. As an ideology it needs to be critically examined, in terms of the ideas which it chooses to emphasize, the interests which it sanctions, its relationship with opposing doctrines, and its degree of correspondence with the actual processes and development of social life.

Rossiter singles out, as vital elements in this American tradition, liberty and pluralism. The idea of liberty which he propounds may be summed up in his own phrase as that of the "self-reliant individual." Undoubtedly this notion has had great historical importance in America, but it corresponds much more with the conditions of early American society than with the state of affairs which has come to exist in the twentieth century. As Wright Mills observed in *White Collar* (1951): "Over the last hundred years, the United States has been transformed from a nation of small capitalists into a nation of hired employees, but the ideology suitable for the nation of small capitalists persists, as if that small-propertied world were still a going concern." Today this ideology, which Rossiter merely reasserts, is much less widely accepted; more and more people seem to feel trapped and powerless in a society dominated by large business corporations, large military establishments, and inaccessible party machines, and they are seeking changes in society which would allow them to restore and develop their freedom, not so much as "self-reliant," but as "self-directing" and "self-governing" individuals. This is the sense which is to be found in one of the most widespread radical conceptions of the 1960s—"participatory democracy"—and it leads necessarily to a reconsideration of Marx's fundamental ideas about the ending of class domination and the introduction of "self-government of the producers" as essential conditions for personal freedom.

The notion of "pluralism" which Rossiter outlines is equally open to criticism. American pluralism has always been confined within a limited sphere, in this century especially by the powerful ideology of "100 per cent Americanism" (and its counterpart, "un-American activities"). In practice, pluralism has meant on one side the acceptance of a laissez-faire market economy with minimum government interference (as Charles Beard put it in describing conditions at the end of the nineteenth century, political leaders believed in "the widest possible extension of the principle of private property, and the narrowest possible restriction of state interference, except to aid private property to increase its gains"), and on the other side diversity of political views and organizations so long as they did not challenge in any fundamental way the capitalist market economy. Those political movements which presented, or seemed to present, such a challenge—from Populism to the socialist movement of the first two decades of this century—were either absorbed by the existing parties or if necessary repressed. Thus American pluralism can be defined broadly as "right-wing pluralism." Even this kind of pluralism has tended to decline during the twentieth century, according to the critics of "mass society," with the disappearance or assimilation of those autonomous groups which could have an influence upon public policy in particular areas of social life. From this aspect the radical movements of the 1960s can be seen in part as attempts to re-create such autonomous groups, and to enhance their influence, in such diverse fields as civil rights, education, poverty programs, consumer protection, and women's rights. But in this case too Rossiter shows a lack of concern for the trends in practical social life, and confines his attention to the ideal of pluralism.

The radicalism of the 1960s is only the latest manifestation of a long-established alternative tradition in America which has many affinities, even where it does not have direct connections, with Marxism. From the 1880s onward the development of large-scale capitalism and the consolidation of the class structure in American society brought into existence opposing forces in the shape of new political and industrial organizations and a wave of social criticism. These diverse groups of intellectuals and activists engendered, in the first decade of the present century, a rapidly growing socialist movement through which, despite many differences of ideology and political practice, the essential ideas of Marxism about the conflict of class interests and the opposition between capitalism and socialism as forms of society began to be clearly expressed. At this time it seemed possible, and even likely, that the divisions in American society would result in the formation of a political labor movement on a scale similar to that which already existed in many of the European countries. This sense of a new direction in politics found its intellectual expression in various attempts to introduce Marxist methods and ideas in the study of American society, and to expound and assess the Marxist theory or defend it against its critics; for example, in the work of the historians, Beard and Robinson, in E. R. A. Seligman's *The Economic Interpretation of History* (1902, rev. ed. 1907), in Louis Boudin's *The Theoretical System of Karl Marx* (1907), in Veblen's *The Socialist Economics of Karl Marx and His Followers* (1906–7), and somewhat later in the writings of Randolph Bourne, who concluded that ". . . the three cardinal propositions of Marx—the economic interpretation of history, the class struggle, and the exploitation of the workers by the capitalistic private ownership of the means of production—if interpreted progressively are the *sine qua non* of Socialism."[1]

The development of Marxist and socialist thought was interrupted by the entry of America into the war, which provided an occasion for extreme repressive measures against radicalism; and after the war the socialist movement failed to regain its momentum. This failure has only recently begun to be systematically investigated,[2] but the studies so far undertaken already lead toward a reinterpretation of the history of ideas and political movements in America. It is clear that socialism became for a time a significant force in American life, and that large sections of the population were far from being as unresponsive to Marxism as the exponents of a unique "American tradition" have claimed. The decline of socialism in the 1920s needs to be explained in terms of specific features of American society and particular historical events; it cannot be taken simply as the continuation of a natural state of affairs, attributable to the overwhelming strength of an established tradition, when it is seen that this tradition was seriously and extensively questioned, or in some cases rejected, during the first decade of this century. One reason for the post-war decline may be found in the fact that the socialist movement, in spite of its successes, had not yet acquired the mass character which would have provided it with the strength to survive both the repressive actions of the government and internal dissension on the scale which followed the Russian Revolution, the organization of the Third International, and the creation of new doctrinaire parties, based upon the Bolshevik model, in the United States.[3] This relatively slow development in the pre-war period can itself be explained, in part, as a consequence of mass immigration, ethnic diversity, and the particular form which American trade unionism had assumed. These factors need to be considered just as much as the possible influence of an ideology which proclaimed, against the experiences of everyday life, the values of equality, mobility, and individual success.

From the mid-1920s, under Bolshevik influence, Marxism became the affair of small political sects, and it retained this character through the economic and social crisis of the following decade. In the 1930s Marxism attracted many literary intellectuals, who debated the "proletarian novel" and later on gave their support to the Republican government in the Spanish Civil War, but most of them were quickly disillusioned. By contrast, the influence of Marxism as a social theory was slight and its impact upon the American working class negligible; despite the extent of the economic crisis no broad socialist movement developed and popular discontent was channeled into the limited reforms of the New Deal. In this period Marxism actually took on the character of an alien doctrine which Rossiter implicitly attributes to it.

Only since the end of the 1950s has Marxism again found a large audience in America, its intellectual revival coinciding, here as elsewhere, with the decay of the Bolshevik ideology. Marxist ideas have reappeared in the social sciences, from which they had been largely absent for three or four decades, and Marx's writings are probably more widely known and more thoroughly studied than ever before. Thus at the very moment when Rossiter was asserting the incompatibility between Marxism and the "American tradition" there was in fact beginning a renewal of Marxist thought, marked by a more direct relevance to American society than at any time since the early years of this century.

It is, however, a different style of Marxism, not tied to any political orthodoxy, and diversely interpreted as one element in a tradition of socialist thought and practice. The variety of interpretations, and the numerous attempts to amend and supplement previously accepted versions of the Marxist theory, may of course signify that Marxism is beginning to lose its distinctive character and will eventually be absorbed into a new radical or socialist theory of society. I think this is a plausible view of what is now happening. But such a development would not involve any *rap-*

prochement with the ideas of the "liberal-pluralist" theory. Any radical theory which advanced beyond Marxism would still include among its major preoccupations the class inequalities in American society; the conflicts which arise, sometimes in curious forms, from these inequalities; the widespread sentiments of dissatisfaction and disenchantment with the present organization of society; and the possibility of creating a classless society in which individuals would experience a genuine liberation insofar as they ceased to be dominated by other men through the instrumentalities of wealth, political power, or social privilege.

These conceptions of conflict, liberation, and a radical transformation of society are quite foreign to "liberal-pluralist" theory, which is characterized above all by an acceptance (and sometimes idealization) of the present social order. It assumes, in Rossiter's notion of a single American "tradition," or in conceptions of American democracy as the final attainment of the "good society," the fundamental unchangeability of American institutions. Reforms and improvements are possible, economic growth is taken for granted, a decline in social antagonisms is assumed; but all this is regarded as no more than the unfolding of what has always been implicit, and partially realized, in the established framework of society. The possibility of any radical change to a new form of society—a change from the dominance of private corporations to industrial democracy within a system of public ownership, from competitive and acquisitive individualism to public service and cooperation, from the present organization of political parties and the state to a less centralized system without party bosses and political elites—is simply not conceived.

The intellectual predominance of this liberal theory is the result, certainly, of some particular features in the development of American society, and especially the failure of socialism to become established as a major political force. It does not correspond, however, with any factual existence of a single American "tradition," or "political culture," or "way of life," for there has often been, as I have indicated, widespread dissent and acceptance of alternative political ideas. There is very plainly a radical tradition in America, though it has never become predominant. Least of all can one speak of a single tradition at the present time, when dissatisfaction and opposition have grown rapidly, and there exists, throughout a large part of society, a profound sense of the need for fundamental social change.

NOTES

1. Randolph Bourne, "The Next Revolution," *Columbia Monthly* (May 1913).

2. Notably in James Weinstein, *The Decline of Socialism in America, 1912–1925* (New York, 1967).

3. See Weinstein, op. cit., ch. 4.

COMMENT 2
Ann J. Lane

The selections from the late Clinton Rossiter's *Marxism: The View from America* suggest the aura—I cannot say charm—of a period piece, the quality of another era, not so long gone but hopefully in our past permanently. The specter that was haunting Rossiter surely could not be as simple-minded as he would have it, else how explain the seriousness of its threat or the seduction of its appeal. To account for the tone and substance of the comments excerpted here, in the context of a life's work of otherwise impressive and significant stature, one must point to the heavy hand of the 1950s and sadly recognize the enormous price extracted, although voluntarily, from the intellectual community during those grim years.

The important body of Marxist thought does not end with Marx, in spite of Rossiter's implication to the contrary. In a general way Marx himself foresaw the limitations of his own analysis; he recognized in advance that social relations would undoubtedly alter in important ways that were not predictable. Since his day, and especially in the last generation, there have been sustained and valuable efforts to extend the essentials of his argument to contemporary experiences. Although the Marxist intellectual community is somewhat less developed in the United States than elsewhere, the increasing number of sophisticated and competent scholars in this country too, respectably established in universities, will make difficult a recurrence on that level of the charges directed at what purports to be Marxism. The list of contributors in the table of contents of this volume alone attests to the existence of an ongoing debate. To refuse to recognize, as Rossiter seems to, the extended body of Marxist thought as encompassing an entire intellectual community is to distort and deny the value of its total contribution and to reduce markedly the value of his criticisms.

What can one say in response to Rossiter's description of the American tradition as rooted "in the dignity of man, the excellence of liberty, the limits of politics and the presence of God"? (And note that it is soon followed by an assertion, made in the name of liberty, that Marxism is so inherently authoritarian that it is "hard to grant it license.") In a few pages Marx is ridiculed for giving "first place" to the power of human reason and then denounced for locking man permanently as a "good member of an economic class," which is the way Rossiter erroneously interprets Marx's view of man as the ensemble of social relations. At the same time Rossiter denies that man is as plastic as Marx suggests, or as Rossiter says Marx suggests. Rossiter too would like man to be capable of perfection, but he is burdened with "vicious tendencies" (Marx's phrase which Rossiter misuses) that are "deeply implanted in human nature." As if to compensate for this tragic failing, Rossiter asserts that man is also imbued with a "spirit of self-reliance and desire for freedom" that transcend any given society. We are then informed that Marx believed a new race of men will be derived by "conscious manipulation of the social environment." Marx's extraordinary and complex views of alienation are reduced to "anxiety," which, Rossiter tells us, is a permanent condition because humanity "is trapped by the paradox of human existence." Freedom becomes to Rossiter "an eternal paradox" that leaves all men in a state of tension "as part of the human condition."

Setting aside, for the moment, what Marx meant, or at least what I think Marx meant, the contradiction that spills out of Rossiter (and represents one element in American conservative thought in general) is what fascinates. On the one hand there is the "human condition" and "the paradox of human existence"—a secularized original sin. On the other hand, Rossiter is committed to the American myth. If radicals have failed to untangle their view of mankind from the American dream machine, conservatives such as Rossiter are no further along. (There are other conservatives who offer a more serious challenge to the traditional radical view, or views, of mankind, but it is not possible to confront their analysis here.)

Rossiter also presents the reader with a difficult methodological problem. His conclusion, that the Marxist critique, as he re-creates it, is invalid because the American experience disproves it, is built into the method. He presents a tautology that cannot be criticized but only accepted or rejected. He takes as given that which must be tested and then, not surprisingly, proudly proclaims he has proved his case.

In the process of redesigning Marx to fit a Cold War mold, Rossiter ignores several painful historical and contemporary social problems; the evolution of political theory from John Locke and John Stuart Mill to the present suggests some of the reasons for Rossiter's neglect.[1] Seventeenth- and eighteenth-century liberal democratic theory developed as a way of enlisting support from the whole of society against the common enemy; at the same time it wished to protect itself from increasingly radical pressures. Its definitions of liberty, equality, and fraternity as the formal protection of law, minimal state power, and economic struggle independent of others—all conformed to the needs of an emerging market economy. Liberal democratic theory, in an effort to generalize its appeal, went on to argue that these procedural protections ultimately led to substantive ones. Rossiter simply proclaims the truth of that proposition and offers no demonstration of its validity, despite overwhelming evidence in recent years to the contrary from liberals as well as radicals.

Locke and Mill, in an effort to defend their position, resorted to some ambivalent conceptions, of which they were at least dimly aware. Locke begins with the assumption of equality of men in a state of nature (even as a theoretical model Marx rejected the possibility of man outside of society, but saw society as a force for defining humanity) and ends up with a political and economic system that protects unequal property, without providing a satisfactory explanation of how the first led to the second and without being content with the inequities. C. B. MacPherson in his extended essay on Locke brilliantly locates the source of the contradiction in Locke's ambivalent views of human nature. While MacPherson emphasizes the logical evolution of Locke's thought, rather than a struggle between conflicting elements within it, he concludes by exposing those confusions, which he describes as the "result of honest deduction from a postulate of equal natural rights which contained its own contradiction."[2] John Stuart Mill too struggled, unsuccessfully but nobly, to explain how the human values he cherished could flourish in an inhuman society he defended. Forced to choose, because he forced himself to examine honestly, he chose the system over the values. In Mill's words:

In all human affairs, every person directly interested . . . has an admitted claim to a voice. . . . But though everyone ought to have a voice—that everyone should have an equal voice is a totally different proposition. When two persons who have a joint interest in any business differ in opinion, does justice require that both opinions should be held of exactly equal voice?[3]

It is, as one critic said, "the equal right of all to participate in an unequal . . . system,"[4] and while Locke and Mill were concerned with establishing a political structure in which different interests would be protected from each other, they recognized and did not challenge the desirability of those different interests. The very existence of a political system based upon checks and balances and the division of power, a system Rossiter endorses, suggests a social order built on inequality, a conception Rossiter denies but early political theorists reluctantly admitted. At least they, and many others, including Adam Smith, who struggled to understand the origin of profit, confronted the problems directly and maintained and endorsed commitments to democracy if they could not convincingly reconcile all disparate aspects of their thought. Most twentieth-century theorists deny the problem and reject the ideal, Rossiter placing himself in the first category but not having the consistency to recognize that he also belongs in the second. Contemporary spokesmen for the "American way of life" no longer are concerned with the roots of social inequality but rather accept it as given and speak instead to the existence of mass manipulation and "the human condition." If it is "realistic" in relation to current conditions, it also illustrates the degeneration of the democratic doctrine. The freedom for which Locke and Mill spoke denied dependence on others and repudiated social obligations. In the seventeenth and eighteenth centuries these weaknesses were balanced by the strength of the vision they endorsed, for if their notion of freedom inherently denied freedom to many it did provide it for many others. By the twentieth century the social good to be gleaned from their propositions has worn bare and we are left with only the inhuman and antisocial elements. It becomes less painful simply to proclaim an end to ideology than to confront its bankruptcy.

If Rossiter's answers are disappointing, the kinds of questions to which he addressed himself are provocative and important. Marx's work is not without error, limitation, or incompleteness. Capitalism has obviously proved more flexible than he anticipated. Indeed, much of the ambivalence with which later supporters have had to contend is inherent in the body of Marx's writings, though not in the way it is represented by Rossiter. Although the world has much changed, Marx's analysis remains in its essentials valid. Despite the many differences among Marxists, there is a large body of thought, from Marx and Engels to the present, whose fundamentals are shared. To paraphrase one contemporary analyst, if we must go beyond Marx to understand the present world we cannot go without him.[5] Advances made in socialist theory in years past can be dramatically compared to the increasing impoverishment of liberal democratic theory. One thinks immediately of André Gorz, George Lukács, Antonio Gramsci, and Louis Althusser, among many others, without easily discovering liberal counterparts.

Rossiter's critique challenges many of Marx's basic conceptions such as the source of state power, class structure, and class struggle but I would like to single out for brief comment Marx's and Marxist views of individualism, political democracy, and ideology.

Rossiter's claim that Marx was uninterested in individuals, a traditional complaint, misrepresents Marx, who saw the reality of the individual in the totality of his social relations. Man's individuality, to Marx, is a product of his relationships; it has no meaning beyond them. Marx believed with Rossiter that man has an "essence," but not one that is eternal and permanent. Not only is man always in the process of change but that change is the core of the process of development. Man, not raw economic fact, as Antonio Gramsci said, is the center of Marx's thought. Rossiter may insist that man can transcend his social relations, but Gramsci's observation that man "is a conformist to some conformity" is considerably more perceptive.[6]

The political rights that the individual in this society enjoys are to Marx the rights of persons in civil society, of the individual separated from his fellows and from his community. Under this social order political rights are the rights of self-interest. "As a result every man finds in other men not the realization but rather the limitation of his freedom," said Marx. By defining freedom as a private matter, freedom under capitalism is what one obtains by depriving others. While Marx paid great attention to the achievements of capitalist society, total human freedom, as Marx defined it, must come in the realm of social relations.

Marx's balance of choice and determinism is complicated and not entirely satisfactory. "Man makes his own history, but he does not make it out of whole cloth, he does not make it out of conditions chosen by himself but only of such as he finds at hand." The difficulties that are inherent in such a proposition, that indeed can be traced to Marx's work—where does choice end and determinism begin?—have been commented on by many, perhaps most brilliantly by André Gorz, who examines the idea of man as "half-victim, half accomplice," or as "involuntarily accomplice," who, "having produced an involuntary order [is] led to will that order."[7]

On the matter of political power as defined by the franchise, Marx, frequently impatient, probably was, as Rossiter said, "contemptuous"; his critique, nevertheless, goes beyond ill temper. The counting of votes, while undeniably an important ingredient in legitimate democratic process, is hardly by itself a measure of democracy. Voting itself is the last phase of a long process; that process, which includes all levels and qualities of a society's "ability to . . . persuade,"[8] demonstrates that voting may be a necessary part of a democratic society but it is not a sufficient one.

The "ability to . . . persuade"—the realm of ideology—leads to one of Marx's most significant contributions. Representing the way a given epoch looks at the world, any ideology distorts and imposes its distortions on reality, at the same time that it reflects a certain degree of reality, without which it could not adequately function. What is crucial, this total world view is accepted voluntarily by those living under it. It is easier to see the ideological force of societies other than one's own, but the capitalist vision is as subject to examination as any other, particularly for those, like Rossiter, to whom the world of ideas is familiar. Capitalism has created a world view in which the pursuit of material wealth is glorified, a view that maintains that material progress is an important ingredient of human happiness and one in which individual effort, multiplied many times, results in the general good. It is a world view that defends and claims to be based, as to an extent it is, upon reason, law, and efficiency. Marx saw his role as critic to remove the ideological façade and expose the social mechanisms that underlie it. Rossiter offers the façade as real.

COMMENT 2 / 505

The world being much more complicated than it was, revolutionary critiques will in the future have to confront the problems of two world views: capitalism and socialism. If Marxism is to be a critique of all existing societies we need "a relentless Marxist critique of Marxism"[9] and a careful examination of those societies that claim to operate under its principles.

Rossiter, after asserting that he does not fault Marx for the failures of the Soviet Union—a concession he ought not to have made in the first place—then faults Marx for the failures of the Soviet Union. Where he might have examined the development of that nation in its relationship to Marxism and thereby deepened our understanding of both, he instead relied on invective. "All history is but the continuous transformation of human nature," Marx wrote. In the course of the many centuries that capitalism struggled within the existing feudal order "bourgeois man" was born and matured slowly. By the time capitalism emerged as the victor, those qualities associated with bourgeois man—rationalism, competitiveness, individualism—had been long developed and refined. The "transformation of human nature" had already occurred in the process of the struggle between two competing social orders.[10] The transition to socialism did not and probably cannot occur as the result of that kind of slow process. "Socialist man"— one whose ideology should encompass a commitment to cooperation, equalitarianism, community—does not develop in the process of capitalist growth and decay. The establishment of socialism requires not simply a new set of social relations but a changed consciousness. Without engaging in dispute over the "real" nature of Soviet society it is now clear that the construction of socialism there is at best incomplete and unsatisfactory. The Russian experience provides "devastating proof of the impossibility of infusing seemingly socialist forms—such as nationalized means of production and comprehensive economic planning—with genuine socialist content unless the process goes hand-in-hand with the formation of social human beings." The limited information from China suggests that there for the first time the significance of this problem is recognized. Whatever failures occur in the coming years in China, much has apparently been learned from the Russian catastrophe.[11]

In addition to a Marxist critique of Marxism, the traditional Marxist critique of world capitalism requires extension, refinement, and revision. Socialism has failed in the United States because it has not convinced the American community that it is preferable. There are many and serious reasons in this century for the disinterest that Americans have shown to socialism, beyond the obvious one of affluence. Socialist doctrine has been too long burdened by its inability to offer a reasoned and reasonable analysis of Soviet, Chinese, and Cuban experiences. At the same time, and connected to that failure, has been the inability to examine judiciously and intelligently "bourgeois rights" in a way that recognizes their limitation and their historic role but also their immense value for human development. Marx's criticism of bourgeois rights, when seen as part of the specific political struggle in which he was actively engaged, and not as justification for denial of those rights in communist countries, has an entirely different significance from that attributed to it by Rossiter. If bourgeois rights are a fraud, they are also real. If they are limited they must be extended, not denounced for being limited and then denied. Marxism attempts to offer an explanation of the origin and function of liberal democratic social order but it does not follow that the gains made by it are insignificant or undesirable.

The struggle in the West is, in Gramsci's words, not in "pitched battles between classes: the class struggle becomes a 'war of position,' and the 'cultural front' the principal area of conflict."[12] The difficulties facing any socialist movement become enormous when one recognizes the overwhelming strength of the dominant ideology and the success with which the ruling class has been able to persuade the mass of the population that its interests represent those of the society at large. Thus it is the "totality of the bourgeois world view," as one contemporary Marxist said, "—the enormous complex of prejudices, assumptions, half-thought-out notions and so small number of profound ideas—that infects the victims of bourgeois rule, and it is the totality of an alternative world view that alone can challenge it for supremacy."[13]

The socialist movement in this country has traditionally tried to work within the trade union movement in an effort to demonstrate that capitalism has been unable to satisfy the needs it created and provide the kind of life it promised, not an easy or wise task to set for itself in the face of the material progress many Americans have enjoyed. Radical movements in our past have trapped themselves into accepting the definition of those needs and satisfactions as created by the capitalist vision: essentially more and better commodities. The very instrument for evaluating the "good life" in twentieth-century America—the statistic that can tell us how many people own automobiles—is itself an ideological tool and ideological concept that parades as an objective measure of an objective world. Only recently has the notion that well-being is identified with the accumulation of commodities been challenged. American society is torn by what seems to be disparate elements demanding entirely different satisfactions. There are, first, the poor, whose existence we can no longer explain away as a product of individual weakness or temporary social maladjustment but have come to recognize, reluctantly, as a permanent and organic part of the system. They see the wealth all around and most still maintain the hope that someday they will share in it. Then there are those, small in number but vocal, who, having grown with the affluence, reject it. They recognize, as earlier radicals did not, that this kind of abundance is insufficient and inhuman. Those who are poor and demand equity and those who have certain material comforts but reject them are largely unaware that their dissatisfactions derive from the same social process. Most Americans, who fall into neither of those categories, do share a sense of unease about the malfunctioning of their society: problems of air, water, food, the aged, the young, war, racism, crime, violence, drugs, but see these difficulties as part of the "human condition," or the process of industrialization, which to some extent they are, amenable to amelioration but not elimination. Industrialization, regardless of social system, generates great problems: the possibility of a solution to those problems resides in another realm.

We have yet to forge a critique that connects this social malaise with what is known as the "consumer society," with the phenomenon of men as owners of the machine, not the machines of production, but the machines of consumption, which give an unreal sense of power and provide the façade of control. The acquisition of things provides us as consumers, one analyst asserts, the power to make "technical choices in the service of inhuman needs, a passive 'freedom,' in which our choice is limited to which form of passivity we wish," increased physical comfort that leads to a "reduction of our *being* to the dimension of *having*."[14] Unfortunately, Rossiter's critique does not get us on our way.

NOTES

1. For a useful critique, upon which my remarks are based, see Richard Lichtman, "The Facade of Equality in Liberal Democratic Theory," *Socialist Revolution,* vol. I, no. 1 (January–February 1970), pp. 85–126.

2. *The Political Theory of Progressive Individualism: Hobbes to Locke* (London: Oxford University Press, 1962), p. 251.

3. *Considerations on Representative Government* (Indianapolis: Bobbs-Merrill, 1958), p. 24, as quoted in Lichtman, op. cit., p. 106.

4. Lichtman, op. cit., p. 106.

5. Svetozar Stokanovic, "Marxism and Socialism Now," *New York Review of Books,* July 1, 1971, p. 16.

6. *The Modern Prince and Other Writings* (New York: International Publishers, 1959), p. 58.

7. *The Traitor* (New York: Simon & Schuster, 1959), p. 46.

8. In discussing the importance of the franchise, Gramsci said: an "instrumental value, which offers a measure and a relationship and nothing more. . . . What is measured is precisely the effectiveness and ability to expand and persuade." Op. cit., p. 183.

9. Stokanovic, op. cit., p. 16.

10. See discussion by Paul Sweezy, *Monthly Review: An Independent Socialist Magazine,* vol. 23, no. 1 (May 1971), pp. 1–16.

11. Ibid., p. 12.

12. John Cammett, *Antonio Gramsci and the Origins of Italian Communism* (Stanford: Stanford University Press, 1967), p. 190.

13. Eugene D. Genovese, *In Red and Black: Marxian Explorations in Southern and Afro-American History* (New York: Pantheon, 1971), p. 408.

14. Richard Lichtman, "Capitalism and Consumption," *Socialist Revolution,* vol. 1, no. 3 (May–June 1970), p. 92.

Chapter 12

SOCIALISM AND SOCIAL MOBILITY*

Stephan Thernstrom

Few clichés are more venerable than that which holds that the more fluid the composition of the working class of a given society and the greater the opportunity to climb from lower to higher rungs of the class ladder, the less the likelihood of sharply class-conscious collective working-class protest. Marx, of course, assumed this in his well-known remark about mid-nineteenth-century America, where, "though classes, indeed, already exist, they have not yet become fixed, but continually change and interchange their elements in a constant state of flux," and American public figures from the Age of Jackson to the Age of Johnson have devoted much rhetoric to the same alleged phenomenon, though disagreeing with Marx, I need hardly say, about both its permanence and its desirability.[1]

It is the fate of clichés, however, to escape serious critical scrutiny. So at least in this instance. It is impossible to write about a social group—the working class, the bourgeoisie, or whatever—without making assumptions about the extent to which its composition is stable or in flux, without making assumptions about patterns of social recruitment and social mobility. And yet few students of working-class history have made systematic—in this case, I believe, systematic is synonymous with quantitative—attempts to measure the social mobility of ordinary working people in the past. Thus we have an excellent and generally well-documented survey of the American laboring man in the 1920's baldly asserting, without supporting evidence, that "the worker was seldom afforded the opportunity to rise in the social scale. He lacked the qualifications for the professions and the capital for business."[2] More surprising and amusing is a major historical study of the American

* Chapter 8 from Melvin Richter (ed.), *Essays in Theory and History* (Cambridge: Harvard University Press, 1970), originally entitled "Working-Class Social Mobility in Industrial America."

labor force by one of the "new" economic historians, who prefaces some ingenious new statistical estimates of unemployment rates in nineteenth-century depressions with the sound remark that the traditional historian's tendency to rely upon the impressions of contemporary observers yields a better measure of variations in the prose styles of those observers than of variations in actual unemployment; he then blithely proceeds to explain America's rapid economic development as the consequence of the country's exceptionally fluid social system, with nary a hard fact to support the claim that American society was less rigidly stratified than any other.[8] The need for careful empirical examination of propositions such as these should be self-evident.

This paper reports on some of the recent work which is beginning to provide something more than an impressionistic outline of working-class social mobility patterns in the United States in the past century or so, drawing heavily on my own work on Boston in the period 1880–1963. Research of this kind, I believe, can take us one small step toward a better understanding of the vast question of the relationship between social mobility and class solidarity, and the slightly less vast related question of the sources of American exceptionalism. Studies of American materials alone, of course, can take us but a limited distance, for these questions demand comparisons between nations. The absence of an American labor party cannot be explained in terms of the uniquely high level of mobility opportunities open to the American worker without demonstrating that the composition of the working class in the United States has been highly volatile not in some absolute sense, but volatile relative to other societies in which a strong labor or socialist party has emerged.

As yet there has been very little historical research on social mobility in other societies, though there has been a good deal of contemporary work by sociologists, so that for the present we must settle for the unsatisfactory tactic of evaluating the American findings largely in isolation. It should be noted, however, that the two major efforts at comparative analysis of national differences in mobility rates and patterns since World War II, those by Lipset and Bendix and S. M. Miller, pose a powerful challenge to the assumption that American society has been uniquely open and that its relatively classless politics may be attributed to that circumstance. Lipset and Bendix argue that "widespread social mobility has been a concomitant of industrialization and a basic characteristic of modern industrial society, and though Miller is somewhat more impressed with differences between nations, his analysis too has a basically revisionist thrust.[4] There are a good many technical objections which might be raised against these studies—most important, that their measure of mobility, the rate of intergeneration movement between blue-collar and white-collar occupations, is much too narrow, that major differences between national social structures cannot be captured in so crude a sieve. And there is the obvious objection that occurs to the historian: that whatever similarities there may be between mobility rates in various industrialized countries since World War II, it is by no means evident that we may safely extrapolate these findings backward to the time, probably somewhere in the nineteenth century, at which the political role of the working class was initially defined. The as-yet unpublished research of William H. Sewell, Jr. on the working class of nineteenth-century Marseille, coupled with my own work on Boston, suggests that such extrapolation may be quite unfounded. The two of us are presently collaborating on a paper which will argue that the sons of Marseille workers escaped into nonmanual occupations with far less frequency than was the case in Boston.

Nevertheless, we must be prepared for the possibility that further mobility research, which should some day permit elaborate and systematic comparative historical analysis, will yield the conclusion that variations in objective mobility opportunities, between nations or over time within a nation, do not in themselves explain very much, that mobility data are meaningless except within a context of well-defined attitudes and expectations about the class system, and that these attitudes and expectations may be most unstable and susceptible to change. Thus, as I have argued elsewhere, the current complaints of American Negroes about their constricted opportunities are the result not of any real deterioration of the position of blacks, but rather of the fact that blacks today are no longer comparing their achievements with those of blacks yesterday, but with those of previous white immigrants and indeed with a romanticized stereotype of the immigrant experience, a stereotype drawn more from the experience of the Jews than that of the Irish or Italians.[5] Similarly, in a fascinating recent paper on social mobility in France on the eve of the explosion of 1789, Philip Dawson and Gilbert Shapiro have shown paradoxically that in those areas where the institutional structure of the ancient regime "made it possible for a bourgeois to improve his social position in a most significant way—by becoming legally a noble—... disapproval of the existing system, particularly the details of class and status, was most vigorously manifested. And conversely, where the bourgeois was denied the right to improve his social position in this way ... demands for change in general and for reform of the system of rewards for achievement in particular were neither powerful nor widespread."[6] This too should remind us that there is no simple mechanical relationship among social mobility, class solidarity, and political radicalism that holds for all classes, societies, and historical epochs, and that the austerely objective facts uncovered by empirical social research influence the course of history only as they are mediated through the consciousness of obstinately subjective human beings. Though in the body of this paper I largely confine myself to some conveniently measurable aspects of the historical experience of the American working class, I would agree with Edward Thompson that the development of the working class "is a fact of political and cultural, as much as of economic, history."[7] The political and cultural dimensions get short shrift in what follows, not because I think them unimportant but because space is limited and I think it appropriate to concentrate on the least well-known aspects of American working-class history.

I

The first phenomenon which demands attention—geographical mobility, or population turnover—is not normally considered an aspect of social mobility, but I suggest that movement through space, movement into and out of communities, may retard the development of class consciousness in a manner somewhat analogous to movement into a higher social stratum. In his suggestive paper on interindustry differences in the propensity of workers to strike, Clark Kerr proposes that varying degrees of social integration or isolation of the labor force account for the tendency of workers in certain industries to be exceptionally strike-prone and in others to be exceptionally quiescent.[8] In some industrial environments—most notoriously the logging camp, the mining town, the ship, the docks—laboring men form what Kerr calls "an isolated mass." One element making for isolation in these cases is the absence of a complex occupational hierarchy—the absence of a labor aristocracy, really—and minimal opportunities for upward social mobility. This is the venerable assumption mentioned at the outset of this paper, and I will present some data pertaining to it at a later point. But Kerr also alludes to the related variable which is of immediate concern when he remarks that men in the "isolated mass" not only "have the same grievances, but they have them at the same time, at the same place, and against the same people." Conversely, it is well known that certain occupations are inordinately resistant to efforts at trade union organization because they have spectacularly high rates of job turnover. When only 5 percent of the men working at a particular job in a given city at the start of a year are still employed there twelve months later (as is the case in the United States today with short-order cooks and menial hospital employees, for instance), how do you build a stable disciplined organization? An adequate model of the conditions which promote working-class solidarity must presume not only relative permanence of membership in the class—that is, low levels of upward occupational mobility—but also some continuity of class membership *in one setting,* so that workers come to know one another and to develop bonds of solidarity and common opposition to the class above them. This might require a stable labor force in a given place of work; data on labor turnover at the plant level are important if this be the case. But I will give "continuity of class membership in one setting" a looser definition and use it to mean considerable stability of the working class at least within a given city, which would seem to be a minimal necessity if mere complaints are to be translated effectively into class grievances and to inspire collective protest.

Such is the model suggested by Kerr, but he regrettably did nothing to *test* his assumptions about rates of labor turnover, or for that matter rates of occupational mobility, in relatively strike-prone and relatively strike-free industries. Kerr's article provides a persuasive theoretical rationale for systematic scrutiny of labor turnover and occupational mobility; we will have to look elsewhere for solid evidence bearing on these two subjects.

As to the first—geographical mobility—it has long been assumed that the American population has been exceptionally volatile, that Americans have been a uniquely restless, wandering breed. Not until 1940, however, did the Census Bureau include a census question asking where respondents had lived five years previously. Before 1935, population mobility from place to place can be studied in only two ways. One can examine the Census Bureau's tabulations of state of birth data and discover in any census year what fraction of the American population was living in a state other than their state of birth, a useful but exceedingly crude index of internal migration patterns.[9] The other method is what I and a few others have begun to do—to take manuscript census schedules or some other lists of a city's inhabitants at two points in time, and to compute rates of persistence and turnover for the intervening period. This is slow, tedious, and expensive, but it gives a far more accurate sense of the degree to which past Americans—and in particular, working-class Americans—have characteristically remained long within the boundaries of a unit more meaningful than an entire state.

All of the work which has been done—and it is admittedly exceedingly fragmentary—tends to support the stereotype of American rootlessness and to suggest that an "isolated mass" whose members have grievances "at the same time, at the same place, and against the same people" has been a rare species in the United States. The first study of this kind was James C. Malin's classic article "The Turnover of the Farm Population in Kansas," written thirty-three years ago and little noticed.[10] Both Malin's article and the later inquiry which stimulated much of the current American interest in quantitative social history—Merle Curti's 1959 book on a Wisconsin frontier county in the 1850–1880 period—seemed for a time to be of doubtful relevance to the larger question, since the staggeringly fluid and shifting population they described was on the booming agricultural frontier.[11] It was entirely possible that Americans were more settled in more settled regions of the country, perhaps especially within the cities. And there was the further possibility that figures registering high turnover rates for the population as a whole concealed large deviations from the mean by particular groups—that, for example, there was a majority of ambitious, rising men incessantly on the move, but a substantial minority of low-skilled laborers trapped in urban ghettos.

Both of these possibilities may now be dismissed. Blake McKelvey's examination of Rochester, New York, in the middle of the nineteenth century, my Newburyport inquiry for the same period, and Doherty's research in progress on Northampton, Massachusetts, suggest that the urban population was highly volatile, with half or more of the adult population disappearing from the community in the course of only a decade.[12] Nor is it the case that men on the bottom were immobilized by their poverty, an isolated mass, unlike their restless superiors. To the contrary. In Newburyport and Northampton the working class was more volatile than the middle class, with the least skilled and least well-paid workers most volatile of all. Ray Ginger's analysis of the turnover of textile workers in Holyoke, Massachusetts, in the 1850's points to the same conclusion.[13]

When I began my Boston study, however, I was still a little uneasy about how far this argument could be pressed. Newburyport, after all, was a way station in the orbit of a major metropolis—many of the Irish laborers there had landed in Canada and were in fact slowly working their way down the coast to Boston. Rochester was similarly a stepping stone to the West. Thus these cities might have an unusually large transient population, and there was the more general consideration that relatively small cities might well differ from big cities in this respect. It seemed reasonable to assume that the laborers who drifted out of Newburyport so quickly after their arrival must eventually have settled down somewhere else and that a great metropolis would have offered a more inviting haven than a small community, where anonymity was impossible and institutions of social control pervasive, as contrasted with the classic big-city lower-class ghetto, in which the down-and-out might huddle together in an enduring, protective "culture of poverty." In a major metropolis like Boston, if anywhere in the United States, one might expect to find a stable lower-class population, an isolated mass, a permanent proletariat.

This expectation proved false. If Boston was at all typical, and I believe that it was, in no American city has there been a large lower-class element with continuity of membership. More or less continuously lower-class *areas* can be identified, but *the same individuals do not live in them very long.* As in Newburyport and other small nineteenth-century cities which have been studied, the chance that a worker appearing in a Boston census would be in the community to be counted at the next one a decade later was roughly fifty-fifty throughout the period from 1880 to the present. It is possible that these men in motion typically went to find better jobs, if not fame and fortune, elsewhere. American folklore has always held that migration and upward social mobility go hand in hand, but the point has never been demonstrated with historical evidence; given the sources, it is virtually impossible to explore the issue before the age of modern survey research. In any event it is clear that the bottom layer of the social order of the American city in the past century has included large numbers of permanent transients, unable to sink roots and to form organizations. So rapid was the turnover at this level that the seemingly innocuous residency requirements for voting—typically requiring a year's residence prior to the election—must have disenfranchised a sizable fraction of the working-class population. If the population turnover for Boston is computed on an annual rather than a decennial basis, as I have been able to do using the city directories for the period 1837–1921, it can be determined that roughly a quarter of the population at any one date had not been living in the community 365 days before! This figure is for the entire population, not simply the working class, and the volatility of the working class, especially the unskilled and semiskilled portion of the working class, was even greater. A great many workers, therefore, were legally barred from political participation because they were birds of passage; a great many more, though they remained in Boston long enough to meet the legal residency requirement, were doubtless sufficiently transient in psychology to be politically and socially inert.

These findings are very suggestive, even in the absence of comparable information about working-class-population turnover rates in other societies. The absolute figures themselves are so dramatic as to give considerable credence to the interpretation I put upon them. But it is, of course, important to know if the American experience is at all special in this respect, or if we are instead confronted with a phenomenon common to all industrial societies—or indeed all societies. We know pathetically little about this aspect of demographic history. There are some recently published fragments which raise questions about the assumption of American uniqueness—the remarkable volatility disclosed by the Laslett and Wrigley studies of two seventeenth-century English villages and Lawrence Wylie's demonstration that the population of the seemingly placid, sleepy rural commune of Rousillon today is strikingly unstable.[14] Some fascinating research in progress on late nineteenth-century France, however, squares nicely with the argument advanced here. Joan Scott's study of the glassblowers of Carmaux and Albi links the sharp rise in labor militancy that occurred in the 1890's to the sudden settling down of formerly itinerant artisans.[15] With the French glassblowers as well as Eric Hobsbawm's "tramping artisans" and the sheep shearers of Australia and the United States, of course, a high degree of solidarity and craft identification was possible even in the itinerant phase; the distinction between labor turnover of this type and what I have been describing in the American city should be obvious. But that the disappearance of the itinerant pattern should heighten solidarity and militancy as it did in Carmaux and Albi helps to confirm the general hypothesis I have drawn from Clark Kerr's paper. Clearly it will take a good deal of European work comparable to that now going on in the United States to further clarify the relationship between physical mobility and class identification, but pending that I think there is a prima facie case for the view that remarkable volatility of the American working class, past and present, has been an important influence retarding the development and expression of distinctive class loyalties.

II

Let me now turn to the question of occupational mobility. Sometimes it is mistakenly taken to be the only dimension of social mobility worthy of close study, but that it is an important one goes without saying.

Enormous gaps exist in our knowledge about occupational mobility patterns in nineteenth and early twentieth-century America. A good deal is known about patterns of recruitment into the national business and political elite, but this tells us very little indeed about the range of opportunity at the lower and middle levels.[16] There is Curti's study of Trempeaulau County in the 1850–1880 period, but it would obviously be perilous to generalize from the Wisconsin frontier to the urban frontier. There is my work on the unskilled laborers of Newburyport in the same years. But my attempt at the end of that book to argue that Newburyport was America in microcosm was more open to questions than I realized at the time. I had found little movement from working-class to middle-class occupations in my samples, though there was considerable upgrading within the manual category; the major achievement of the typical laborer in the community was to become a homeowner. At least four questions about the generalizability of this finding remained open:

1) Was it possible that the social structure of the large cities of this era was notably different—either more or less fluid?

2) Was Newburyport atypical even for small cities, in that its rate of population growth and economic expansion in the years I treated was unusually low?

3) I examined the career patterns of unskilled workmen and their children. Might not a study of the skilled craftsmen have yielded much greater evidence of interclass mobility?

4) A large majority of the unskilled laborers in Newburyport were recently arrived Irish immigrants. To what extent would mobility patterns have differed in a community in which the working class was less heavily immigrant, or immigrant but not Irish?

It was in hopes of clearing up some of these uncertainties that some years ago I began work on a large-scale statistical study of the career patterns of some 6,500 ordinary residents of Boston in the years 1880–1963. The analysis is not yet complete, but the main outlines of the argument are fairly clear.

It does appear either that Newburyport was an unusually sluggish place for aspiring laborers, or that small cities in general offer fewer opportunities; rates of movement from blue-collar to white-collar posts, both in the course of a career and between generations, were much higher in Boston throughout the entire period. If an individual's first job was in a blue-collar calling, the odds were that at the end of his career he would still be in the working class. But a substantial minority of men climbed to a middle-class post, usually in small business or in minor clerical and sales positions, and remained there—25 to 30 percent in the five cohorts I traced. There were, in addition, others who began in the blue-collar world, worked for a period in a nonmanual position, and fell back into a manual job later in life. Very little of this upward mobility involved penetration into the upper reaches of the middle class, to be sure; these men did not become professionals, corporation managers, or the heads of large business operations. But certainly here was evidence which challenged the socialist critic's assumption that the dream of individual mobility was illusory and that collective advance was the only realistic hope for the worker.

Even more impressive was the opportunity to escape the class into which one was born—the class of one's father. Fully 40 percent of the working-class sons in Boston held middle-class jobs of some kind by the end of their own careers. The comparable figure for mid-nineteenth-century Marseille, William H. Sewell, Jr., has found, was a mere 11 percent. And if there was any rationality in the system by which the 40 percent who climbed were selected from the entire pool of working-class sons, they must have included much of the leadership potential which would have accrued to the working-class cause in a more rigidly stratified society.

Both types of mobility—career and intergenerational—occurred at a relatively constant rate over this entire eighty-year period. There were some minor temporal fluctuations, with the Great Depression of the 1930's showing diminished opportunities, as we would expect, but the overall similarity of the figures is very striking. To lament the creeping arteriosclerosis of the class system has been a popular American pastime for many a year, but the facts do not sustain this diagnosis.[17] The economy, the political structure, and a good many other aspects of Boston changed dramatically over this long span of time, but whatever governs the rate of circulation between occupations seems to have been highly resistant to change.

It is also noteworthy, and not a little surprising, that the sons of the least advantaged members of the working class—the sons of the unskilled and semiskilled—fared just as well in the competition for middle-class jobs as did the children of the labor aristocracy. That my Newburyport study dealt only with unskilled laboring families was therefore not as limiting as I had feared. The average rate of penetration into the middle-class world by the sons of unskilled and semiskilled workmen in Boston was actually a little above the 40 percent figure for the entire working class, with the figure for the children of skilled craftsmen a little below 40 percent. Similarly with respect to intragenerational, or career mobility, the 25 to 30 percent rate of ascent into the middle class for men who began their careers in a working-class job held for all grades of manual jobs—the lowest as well as the highest.

This is striking in light of the observation of Eric Hobsbawm and Royden Harrison that in nineteenth-century Britain perhaps the greatest break in the class hierarchy was between the labor aristocrat and the less skilled men below him. "The boundaries of the labor aristocracy were fluid on one side of its territory," the upper side, where it "merged with" the lower middle class, but "they were precise on the other." This is in part, though only in part, a judgment about mobility opportunities; the English labor aristocrat's "prospects of future advancement and those of his children" were allegedly much better than the prospects of ordinary workingmen.[18] That does not seem to have been the case in Boston. Now it is possible that Hobsbawm and Harrison are mistaken in their claim; the most judicious observers can go astray when they attempt to gauge mobility rates on the basis of qualitative rather than quantitative evidence. It should also be noted that we are not talking about precisely the same group; my working-class elite is simply all men in recognized skilled trades, whereas Hobsbawm and Harrison have in mind a much more select group, at most the top 15 percent of wage earners. For a variety of reasons I was unable to isolate a small element within the skilled category that would be exactly comparable to what they mean by "the labor aristocracy." Nevertheless, it is quite possible that we are dealing here with a genuine historical difference between the social structures of the two societies, with the imperceptible blending of the British labor aristocracy into the lower middle class taking in the United States the form of a blending of the entire urban working class into the lower middle class. Sewell's work in Marseille suggests that there was indeed a labor aristocracy there; the sons of skilled craftsmen rose into middle-class callings at three times the rate of sons of unskilled workers.

The work of Hobsbawm and Harrison is also helpful in suggesting the desirability of examining occupational advance within the working class, as well as from the working class to the middle class. The mobility of a common laborer's son into the skilled category as I have defined it was less of an achievement than the presumably rare entry of a laborer's son into the labor aristocracy of nineteenth-century Britain, but it was surely a clear-cut advance with respect to wages, vulnerability to unemployment, and so forth. If we consider the total movement of sons of unskilled or semi-skilled workmen into skilled or white-collar occupations in Boston, we find that somewhat more than 60 percent of the sons of the semiskilled and slightly less than 60 percent of the sons of the unskilled were upwardly mobile. (The comparable figure for the sons of skilled craftsmen—the percentage who reached either skilled or nonmanual occupations—was 75 percent.) If this is at all valid as a measure of opportunity for working-class children—if entry into a skilled trade is a significant accomplishment, as I think it was—a distinct minority of the sons of Boston workers had grounds for doubting that the United States was the land of opportunity, where classes "have not yet become fixed, but continually change and interchange their elements in a constant state of flux."

I should hasten to say that these figures are, in one significant way, inflated. They sum up the mobility experiences not of all of the hundreds of thousands of workingmen who lived in Boston at some time in the 1800–1963 period, but rather of those who settled down in the community long enough to have careers which might be measured. I have already stressed the remarkable volatility of the American population, and here I should point out that this fact must be taken into account in interpreting findings based on the study of people who were sufficiently settled to remain under the investigator's microscope long enough to be examined. This would pose no great difficulty if it could be assumed that disappearance from the universe of the study was more or less random, but the problem is that migration and occupational mobility were intimately and intricately related, that those men most likely to leave the community and to go uncounted probably had different occupational mobility prospects than those who remained. Different types of people left the city for a host of different reasons, and I wouldn't dare attempt to generalize about them all. But I would suggest that though much of the movement of men with skills or capital was in response to new opportunities elsewhere, much of the movement of relatively unskilled and uneducated working-class people was of a very different kind—it was helpless drifting rather than rational pursuit of more favorable circumstances elsewhere. I strongly suspect, therefore, that if it were possible for me to track down all of the laboring men who appeared in one of my Boston samples but migrated elsewhere—most likely several elsewheres—and worked the rest of their lives outside of Boston, the net effect of including them would be to depress somewhat the mobility rates I have reported. Some of these working-class migrants were doubtless highly successful elsewhere, but my guess is that most were not and that indeed their departure from Boston was a symptom of failure and an omen of future failure.

This is speculative—necessarily speculative, I fear, in that there is no way of systematically tracing migrants from an American community in the past. But it does appear from my data that the American city—perhaps the European city too, but it remains to be seen—is a kind of Darwinian jungle into which vast numbers of low-status migrants pour. Most of them do not flourish, most of them do not stay very long; a process of selection, of unnatural selection if you like, takes place. Those who do manage to make a go of it economically are not as likely to depart physically, which is why any collection of individuals who simply survive ten years to be counted in the next census have an average occupational rank higher than a sample of newcomers in the intervening decade. . . .

If the Boston data on working-class occupational mobility is any guide, [therefore] most American workers in the past eighty years who were in a position to make themselves heard had good reason to think that they were edging their way up the social scale, that there was no impassable gulf which separated the exploited masses from the privileged class which lived on the fruits of their labor. Many workers did not make it in Boston, but they did not remain on the scene long enough to make their weight felt and were tossed helplessly about from city to city, alienated but invisible and impotent. . . .

III

The final question on which I wish to comment briefly involves another discrepancy between the Newburyport and Boston studies. Perhaps the most striking finding of the former inquiry was that despite wage levels hovering close to what middle-class observers thought bare subsistence, recurring unemployment, and slight opportunities for occupational advance, the laborers of Newburyport (especially the Irish) were remarkably successful in accumulating substantial property holdings, largely in the form of small homes and plots of land. I argued that such property mobility—movement not into the middle class but from the floating lower class into the stable working class—was of great significance in minimizing discontent and tying these men into the prevailing order.

Herbert Gutman has quite properly taken me to task for my somewhat vulgar assumption that homeownership is an inherently conservatizing influence, and I am happy to retreat from my ex-

posed position and concede that it all depends—upon the social
setting, the expectations of the group in question, and perhaps
other things as well.[19] What I would insist upon is only that possession of property is an important determinant of a man's social
position and social allegiances, and that students of working-class
history have been insufficiently diligent about investigating this aspect of their subject. Royden Harrison notes that at one point in
Order and Progress (1875) Frederic Harrison wrote that "there is
no greater break in our class hierarchy than that between the lowest of the propertied classes and the highest of the non-propertied
classes" and at another place that "throughout all English society
there is no break more marked than that which in cities divided the
skilled from the unskilled workmen" without detecting the inconsistency.[20] One appreciates Frederic Harrison's confusion, for it is
a neat question whether occupational rank or property position is
the more powerful influence. Not enough thought has been given to
this question, partly because we have too readily assumed that the
latter can safely be inferred from the former—that few workmen,
except for the highly skilled, were able to save significant amounts.
Doubtless this has been true of many societies, and it may well
explain Frederic Harrison's seeming inconsistency; the distinction
between the unskilled and the nonpropertied may have been a distinction without a difference in the England of the 1870's. It was,
however, an important distinction in the United States, if the Newburyport experience is any guide. The Newburyport evidence suggests that a substantial fraction of the American working class,
including many unskilled and semiskilled workers, stood on the
propertied rather than the nonpropertied side of the break in the
class hierarchy.

I had hoped to be able to illuminate this matter further with my
Boston materials, but that hope was disappointed. The only records
available for the period since 1880 disclose real-property but not
personal-property holdings, and it happens that Boston was a city
with very few single-family dwellings; the $1,000 which purchased
a small dwelling in Newburyport had to be increased several-fold
to buy a triple-decker tenement. The very inadequate measure I
have of working-class property holdings—a measure of real estate
holdings only—thus drastically underestimates total wealth of the
group. At the last date at which the sources include information
about personal as well as real property, 1870, real estate owners

were only 41 percent of the total group of Boston workers holding some property. I therefore can say with confidence that the true incidence of property ownership in the Boston working class since 1870 was much higher than the real estate tax records suggest, but since I don't know which individuals in my samples had large savings accounts and which didn't, I cannot analyze the characteristics of the propertied as opposed to the unpropertied worker. For a variety of reasons I was unable to fill this gap by consulting the savings bank depositor's records that I found so helpful in Newburyport.

Future investigators who are fortunate enough to have more adequate sources of information about personal savings, however, will still face difficult problems of interpretation, for it is evident that American working-class attitudes toward saving, investment, and consumption have shifted dramatically in this century. Whether today's automobiles and appliances, often purchased on the installment plan, are in any way equivalent to the nineteenth-century home—which is not to imply that working-class homeownership is a vanishing phenomenon, quite the contrary—is a knotty question I can't attempt to answer here, except to suggest that it seems important that becoming a homeowner in nineteenth-century Newburyport required prolonged disciplined behavior long before the goal could be attained, whereas today even the poor have become accustomed to flying now and paying later. This makes them highly vulnerable to economic vicissitudes, because many have made long-term financial commitments based on the most optimistic assumptions about future income and few have developed the remarkable penny-pinching facility of the laborers of Newburyport. They have more possessions, certainly, but perhaps less security comes with the possessions.

Systematic knowledge about working-class social mobility in industrial America, in sum, is scanty and spotty, but what little there is does seem to square with the age-old belief that social classes in the United States "continually change and interchange their elements in a constant state of flux." High rates of occupational and property mobility and selective patterns of urban migration which weeded out the unsuccessful and constantly reshuffled them together produced a social context in which a unified "isolated mass" of dispossessed, disaffected workmen could not develop. It would be valuable to be more certain that these generalizations do indeed apply throughout industrial America in the past century. It would be interesting to see if deviations from what I take to be the national pattern could help explain these instances in which groups of American workmen acted in a more militantly class-conscious manner than has generally been the case; studies of population turnover and social mobility in such settings as mining towns organized by the Western Federation of Miners and the I.W.W. could be very revealing. It would also be helpful to discover whether these forms of working-class mobility were equally available in societies in which class solidarity was a more conspicuous fact of national life—Britain, France, Germany, and so forth. The answers to these questions are by no means obvious. I am certain only that they are worth asking and exploring if the social history of the common people is to advance beyond mere impressionism.

NOTES

1. Karl Marx, *The Eighteenth Brumaire of Louis Bonaparte* (New York, n.d.), p. 22.
2. Irving Bernstein, *The Lean Years: A History of the American Worker, 1920–1933* (Boston, 1966), p. 58.
3. Stanley Lebergott, *Manpower in Economic Growth: The United States Record Since 1800* (New York, 1964), pp. 187, 227–28.
4. S. M. Lipset and Reinhard Bendix, *Social Mobility in Industrial Society* (Berkeley, Cal., 1959); S. M. Miller, "Comparative Social Mobility: A Trend Report and Bibliography," *Current Sociology,* IX (1960).
5. Stephan Thernstrom, "Poverty in Historical Perspective," in Daniel P. Moynihan (ed.), *On Understanding Poverty: Perspectives from the Social Sciences* (New York, 1959); Thernstrom, "On Black Power," *Partisan Review,* XXXV (1968), pp. 225–28. For a fascinating discussion of changing English attitudes toward social inequality since 1918 and their failure to correspond to changes in social reality, see W. G. Runciman, *Relative Deprivation and Social Injustice* (London, 1966).
6. Philip Dawson and Gilbert Shapiro, "Social Mobility and Political Radicalism: The Case of the French Revolution of 1789" (Unpublished paper delivered at the American Sociological Association meetings, August 1967).
7. E. P. Thompson, *The Making of the English Working Class* (London, 1964), p. 194.
8. Clark Kerr and A. J. Siegel, "The Interindustry Propensity to Strike—An International Comparison," in Kerr, *Labor and Management in Industrial Society* (Anchor paperback edition, Garden City, N.Y., 1964), pp. 105–47.
9. This material is exhaustively analyzed in Simon Kuznets, Dorothy S. Thomas, et al., *Population Redistribution and Economic Growth in the United States, 1870–1950,* 3 vols. (Philadelphia, 1957–64).
10. James C. Malin, "The Turnover of the Farm Population in Kansas," *Kansas Historical Quarterly,* IV (1935), pp. 339–71.
11. Merle Curti, et al., *The Making of an American Community: A Case Study of Democracy in a Frontier County* (Stanford, Cal., 1959). For comparable data on an Iowa farming county in the same period, see Mildred Throne, "A Population Study of an Iowa County in 1850," *Iowa Journal of History,* LVII (1959), pp. 306–30.
12. Blake McKelvey, *Rochester, The Flower City, 1855–1890* (Cambridge, Mass., 1949), p. 3; Stephan Thernstrom, *Poverty and Progress: Social Mobility in a Nineteenth Century City* (Cambridge, Mass., 1964), pp. 84–90, 167–68; Robert Doherty, "Social Change in Northampton, Massachusetts 1800–1850" (Unpublished paper for the Yale Conference on Nineteenth Century Cities, 1968).

13. Ray Ginger, "Labor in a Massachusetts Cotton Mill, 1853–1860," *The Business History Review*, XXVIII (1954), pp. 67–91.

14. E. A. Wrigley (ed.), *An Introduction to English Historical Demography* (London, 1966), pp. 165–66; Lawrence Wylie, "Demographic Change in Rousillon," in Julian Pitt-Rivers (ed.), *Mediterranean Countrymen* (Paris, 1963), pp. 215–36.

15. Joan W. Scott, "Les Verriers de Carmaux," in Thernstrom and Sennett, *Nineteenth Century Cities*. Cf. the observations on itinerant English workingmen of the same period in Eric Hobsbawm's "The Tramping Artisan," in *Labouring Men: Studies in the History of Labor* (London, 1964), pp. 34–63.

16. The literature on the American business elite is conveniently reviewed in Lipset and Bendix, op. cit., ch. iv.

17. For a lengthy critique of the view that the opportunity structure in the United States today is less favorable than in the past and that poverty is accordingly "a permanent way of life" for the so-called "new poor," see my "Poverty in Historical Perspective," in Moynihan, op. cit.

18. Hobsbawm, "The Labour Aristocracy in Nineteenth Century Britain," in *Labouring Men*, pp. 272–315; Royden Harrison, *Before the Socialists: Studies in Labour and Politics, 1861 to 1881* (London, 1965), pp. 26–33.

19. Herbert G. Gutman, "Labor in the Land of Lincoln: Coal Miners on the Prairie" (Unpublished manuscript, 1967), p. 39.

20. Harrison, op. cit., p. 30.

COMMENT

Seymour Martin Lipset

As Stephan Thernstrom notes, many of the efforts to account for the lower level of working-class political consciousness in America as compared with much of Europe have stressed the supposed effect of a high American rate of social mobility in defusing class resentments. The emergence of a class political culture is presumably related to generational class continuity, i.e., limited opportunity to move up the occupational ladder. And the argument went, and is still reiterated, socialist and other efforts at working-class politics have suffered from the fact that American workers could realistically hope and work to improve their circumstances, to get out of their class, while European workers living in societies which offered much less opportunity were more likely to support socialist efforts to change the distribution of reward and opportunity. Those socialists, from Marx on, who made these assumptions anticipated the emergence of working-class consciousness and radical political movements in a future period when changes in the economic system would sharply reduce upward mobility.

These interpretations have been subject to two kinds of empirical challenge. First, a number of students of social mobility in comparative perspective (Sorokin, Glass, Lipset and Bendix, Miller, Blau and Duncan, and Boudon) have concluded from an examination of mobility data collected in various countries that the American rate of mass social mobility is not uniquely high, that a number of European countries have had comparable rates; and second, that with increasing industrialization and urbanization, rates of social mobility have not declined.

These observations, if valid, cast some doubt as to the value of emphasizing differences in patterns of opportunity comparatively and historically as a major structural explanation for variations in the political response of social classes in different countries.

In attempting to report and evaluate the implications of this literature, it is important to acknowledge that, as Thernstrom indicates, most such efforts at comparability are inadequate since they are often dependent on quite forced comparisons; many restrict their definition to shifts between manual and non-manual categories of occupations.[1] It may be noted, however, that the earliest such effort at broad international comparisons, that of Sorokin in 1927, reported on literally hundreds of limited studies of social mobility in various countries, some dating back to the late nineteenth century. While these data did not permit any systematic statistical evaluation of variations in rates, they did suggest that none of the societies or structures reported on could be described as "closed" or "non-mobile" systems. That is, all studies located substantial minorities who rose or fell in occupational status as contrasted with that of their fathers or their first jobs.[2]

These findings detailed by Sorokin, as well as the many subsequent results from national surveys in many countries, do not imply identical rates of social mobility. There are a number of relatively minor differences among the various countries, with the United States having a "slightly higher" rate, according to Blau and Duncan, the authors of the most comprehensive extant survey in the United States. They conclude that "there is indeed little difference among various industrialized nations in the rates of occupational mobility between the blue-collar and the white-collar class."[3] A more recent effort at a systematic quantitative comparison of data from thirteen countries by Philips Cutright does suggest that countries with a higher industrial level (and lower proportion of the work force in agriculture) do have higher rates of social mobility for the population as a whole. The differences, however, are considerably reduced when comparisons are limited to the non-farm population.[4] In any case, the variations are not great, and still serve to confirm Joseph Schumpeter's insistence that "class barriers are always, without exception, surmountable, and are in fact surmounted. . . ."[5]

In recent years, the Sorokin thesis which suggests that forces making both for the hereditary transmission of advantages and for considerable mobility occur in varying types of social systems has received additional striking confirmation in the rapidly growing number of empirical surveys of social mobility in different Communist countries. This is apparent, for example, in the findings of highly comprehensive and sophisticated surveys of rates and patterns of social mobility in the United States and in the most industrialized Communist country, Czechoslovakia. Czech sociologists systematically compared their 1967 data with those gathered by Blau and Duncan in 1962. Zdaněk Šaféř, a Czech scholar, concludes that the "openness of both systems . . . is surprisingly great." He stresses this finding in the context of refuting "the hypotheses frequently presented in the Western sociological literature concerning the 'mobility blockade' of the socialist countries."[6] That is, Šaféř argues it is not true that socialism means a lower rate of social mobility, that in fact their rate is as high as that under capitalism.

It may be worth noting that, as far as I am aware, no Western sociologist has suggested the existence of a "mobility blockade" in Communist countries. It may be, however, that such a hypothesis is current among internal critics of the system. For example, the Soviet dissident author Andrei Amalrik, after discussing the sharp differences in the standard of living of ordinary people and the elites in the Soviet Union, argues that the country has an "upper class which is trying to avoid any change and to prevent society from having any mobility, and . . . make permanent the breakup of our society into tightly closed castes."[7] The report of a conference on the social structure of Communist countries held in Moscow in the mid-1960s indicates that scholars also point to restrictions on opportunity.

"Social mobility of young people in Poland is still very much dependent upon social origin" declared S. I. Wilderspil [a Polish sociologist]. . . . N. M. Blinov of the sociological laboratory at Moscow University supported him at the same conference, basing himself upon research made among employees of the First Ballbearing Factory in Moscow and at Moscow University itself. His conclusion was that "class differences still have a bright imprint (strong influence) upon social advancement of the individual. . . ."[8]

In reporting on the results of research in Hungary, Sandor Ferge notes the existence of a "vicious circle" inhibiting social mobility in her country and calls for "building security measures into the new economic mechanism as to prevent rigidity in the *already existing* or *newly developed social differences*. . . ."[9] Some statistical support for the thesis that Communist countries have lower rates of mobility than non-Communist ones is also suggested in the thirteen-nation comparison by Philips Cutright, which found that Hungary had the lowest rate of all, and that Yugoslavia was fourth lowest, following Finland and Italy.[10]

In spite of these analyses, however, the fairly comprehensive evidence from Communist countries, some like Šafář's report more recent than those used by Cutright, would seem to support the theoretical analysis of the prospects for mobility in Communist societies by the Polish sociologist Stanislaus Ossowski, who argued persuasively that the basic processes which affect rates of social mobility are structural, are linked to the pace of economic development rather than to political or economic systems, and should, therefore, be comparable in socialist and capitalist countries. Writing in the mid-1950s, he observed:

A socialist system needs economic development even more than a capitalist one . . . such development is a necessary condition of its success and even of its existence. Therefore one of the immediate aims of the leaders of the socialist states was to reach the level of more advanced capitalist countries in industrialization, urbanization, development of communications, and mass education. *All these processes imply an increase in social mobility in socialist countries as well as elsewhere,* and since they were induced by social revolutions we can therefore postulate a plain causal relation between social revolution and this increase of social mobility. *But it is the "social-economic expansion" and not the revolutionary introduction of a socialist order which can be considered a necessary condition of this increase.* Increased mobility of this type could have been accomplished also if the capitalist system had persisted; it could have been done, e.g., with the help of schemes like the Marshall plan.[11]

A recent Hungarian study of social mobility presented in a comparative context in an explicit effort to test Ossowski's thesis indicates that the results correspond to the expectations of the Polish scholar. In two separate sets of comparisons, first using the simple manual-non-manual dichotomy for five non-Communist countries and Hungary, and second measuring mobility among a much wider set of occupational class categories in Britain, the United States, and Hungary, Adorka found that when comparing outflow rates, i.e., the percentage shift from fathers' generation to sons, the Hungarian rates are more or less similar with those of other countries. When contrasting inflow rates, the proportion of sons in a given stratum who come from a parental class, a larger proportion of Hungarians in higher positions came from manual or peasant background than did those in the non-Communist countries. But he notes that as Ossowski had suggested this was *"a consequence of structural factors and ultimately of the rate of economic development."* That is, it reflected the fact that during the period of the comparison, Hungary's "occupational structure was at the lower level of development than that of the United States and England . . . the change of occupational structure was probably faster in Hungary than in the United States and England." Clearly, as Adorka states, the "doubling in one generation of the percentage of intellectuals [professionals] with university qualifications and of top executives implies an inflow of 50 per cent of persons originating from other social strata even in the case of the total occupational inheritance of the children of intellectuals."[12]

Hungarian research based on a sample of 15,000 looking at three-generational mobility illustrates Adorka's thesis. "In 71% of families where parents and grand-parents were in intellectual [requiring higher education] professions, all the employed children are in an intellectual [professional] career. Where the head of the family was an intellectual, but the grand-parents were still manual workers, the proportion falls to 57%, and drops to 41% if the grand-parents worked on the land." For those whose fathers and grandfathers were manual workers, over two thirds of the employed young were in manual employment.[13]

The comparability thesis is also strongly supported by an earlier comparison of mobility rates in seven countries, one Communist, Poland, and six non-Communist, by a Polish sociologist who found slightly lower rates of upward mobility in Poland than in the United States, West Germany, Sweden, Japan, France, and Switzerland. The author, however, drew no general conclusions concerning the mobility propensities of different systems. In any case, his estimates of the proportion of city populations of urban origin who were upwardly or downwardly mobile did not vary greatly among the seven countries, although Poland remained toward the lower end (24 per cent mobile as contrasted with 30 per cent in the United States).[14] Vojin Milić, the author of a Yugoslav study based on 1960 data which shows patterns similar to other countries, rejects making international comparisons of changes between manual and non-manual strata on the grounds that Yugoslav manual workers do not conceive of white-collar jobs as socially higher. He does, however, report that "the children of [white-collar] employees were relatively about ten times more heavily represented among [university] students than the children of workers, and even more [heavily] than the children of peasants." In a more comprehensive analysis of intergenerational mobility using multi-class (occupations) categories, Milić secured results similar to those found in studies in Sweden and Denmark.[15]

There is a growing body of literature in the field of social stratification and social mobility in the Soviet Union itself. Sociologists now begin to speak openly of "social differentiation" as involving different qualities of labor, related to "complexity and social significance."[16] Unfortunately, there are no published studies of mobility based on national samples. The available research, however, does point to pressures making for upward occupational mobility, inherent in the differential prestige, income, and skill associated with occupations which make Russian youth regard manual and peasant work as jobs to be avoided. Following the publication of a recent survey of the occupational preferences of a sample of Russian youth, the manager of an industrial plant wrote to a newspaper asking "where am I to find my turners and milling machine operators," occupations which placed seventy-fifth and seventy-sixth out of eighty occupations in one community. Two articles in *Pravda* by Georgi Kulagin, the manager of a Leningrad factory, complain that the emphasis on classes for "gifted children" and the rewards for higher education serve to denigrate manual occupations. As he notes:

Families and children fight for admittance to such courses, because otherwise they would feel "inferior." Naturally not all are of a high enough standard, and many who could be excellent workers become very bad technicians and functionaries, thus providing a loss to society twice over. "Enough of the classes for the elite," appeals Kulagin. "The school must ensure a more realistic preparation for a working life. And we must remember that we need engineers, but we need workers too."[17]

The phenomenon seems to be a general one in the Soviet Union (as it is in other countries). M. Dobrynin, the author of a sociological study based on a sample of 25 per cent of the high school graduates in Vilnius, the capital of Lithuania, states: "The graduates dream of becoming medical doctors, scientists and artists, geologists and jurists, fliers and sailors. . . . The question, however, arises: 'who, after all, will build houses?' "[18]

The assorted surveys of the relationship between family occupational position and educational attainments indicate, however, that the concern of these Soviet factory managers for a supply of workers is somewhat exaggerated, though they may be right that young workers and peasants feel unhappy in their jobs because these are deemed lowly. At the same time there are strong forces pressing for hereditary transmission of privileged position, inherent in the considerable advantage which the children of the educated and cultured members of the class of intelligentsia have in obtaining the kinds of education which are necessary to secure the more interesting and better-rewarded work.

Mobility in Historical Perspective

If the patterns and rates of social mobility are relatively comparable in industrialized societies, whether Communist or non-Communist, the logic which suggests that economic growth, industrialization, should result in higher rates of mobility (rural to urban migration apart) would imply an increase in mobility during periods of rapid expansion, and a decline whenever economic stagnation occurred. Even more surprising, therefore, than the comparative findings are the results of historical studies, a field in which Thernstrom has played an initiating and major role, which also emphasize similarity rather than differences over time.[19] As Thernstrom notes in this book and in various others of his writings, quantitative research by himself and other American historians suggests the continuation of a high rate of social mobility over an eighty-year period, from the 1880s on. The most comprehensive effort to measure change by a sociologist, that of Natalie Rogoff, which compared mobility rates in Indianapolis in 1910 and again in 1940, holding constant changes in the occupational structure, made the same case for a shorter span.[20] Seeking to locate trends, Blau and Duncan analyzed the mobility patterns of different generations of Americans by relating family occupational background to first job (thus permitting a comparison of the very young still on their first job with the experience of the very old when they were young). They report, congruent with the findings of Thernstrom and Rogoff, that ". . . the influence of social origins has remained constant since World War I. There is absolutely no evidence of 'rigidification.' "[21] In his essay here, Thernstrom suggests that the high rates of social mobility in the United States may help to explain the lower level of class consciousness in this country in the nineteenth century as compared to Europe, since the research of William H. Sewell, Jr., on the working class of Marseille in the nineteenth century indicates that "the sons of Marseille workers escaped into non-manual occupations with far less frequency than was the case in Boston." The generality of the Marseille findings for European cities, however, is thrown into doubt by a recent comprehensive analysis of social mobility in Copenhagen from 1850–1950. Tom Rishøj found to his surprise that mid-nineteenth-century Copenhagen had an extremely high rate of social mobility, one which corresponded to 80 per cent of the maximum possible in a totally egalitarian society, i.e., roughly equal to that found by Natalie Rogoff for Indianapolis in 1910 and 1940.[22] And Rishøj was forced to conclude that there had been no change in the rate of social mobility (using a nine-class scale, not simply two) over a hundred-year period, "that in a preindustrial or early industrial community of Copenhagen we find the same rate of mobility as in the modern industrialized Copenhagen. This finding is in contrast to most of the expectations held by researchers and theorists in the field."[23] It corresponds, however, to the assumptions posited by Sorokin in his classic early work that there is no trend in the rise or fall of rates of vertical social mobility, that at most there may be short-run cyclical changes.

Elsewhere, Thernstrom has written eloquently concerning the doubt which these historical findings raise for the often voiced beliefs that changes in American capitalism and industrial society have created a permanent and growing class of the "poor" or the poverty-stricken. As he notes, there simply is no evidence in support of this argument; all the available data point in the opposite direction.[24] It may be noted that studies of the social background of the business elite also do not sustain the image that this stratum has become more restrictive, particularly to those of poor background. The most recent survey of the backgrounds of big business executives (president and chairman or principal vice-presidents of

the six hundred largest U.S. non-financial corporations) found that
the bureaucratization of American corporate life, the growth of the
public corporation replacing the family-owned concern, had seemingly opened the business elite to entry from below in a way that
had never before been true in American history. Since this study
has never been widely disseminated, it may be worthwhile repro-
ducing some of its salient results here:

Only 10.5 percent of the current generation of big business executives . . . identify themselves as sons of wealthy families; as recently
as 1950 the corresponding figure was 36.1 percent, and at the turn
of the century, 45.6 percent. . . . The [subjective] finding is sustained
. . . by quite objective data on the occupations of the fathers of the
executives: two-thirds of the 1900 generation had fathers who were
heads of the same corporation or were independent businessmen; less
than half of the current generation had fathers so placed in American
society. On the other hand, less than 10 percent of the 1900 generation
had fathers who were employees; by 1964 this percentage had increased
to nearly 30 percent.[25]

Surprisingly both to scholars in the field and to those radicals
convinced that a mature capitalism would become increasingly im-
mobile, particularly with respect to sharp jumps into the elite, the
evidence indicates that the post-World War II period brought with
it the greatest increase in the proportion of those from economically "poor" backgrounds (from 12.1 per cent in 1950 to 23.3
per cent in 1964) who entered the top echelons of American business, and a corresponding great decline in the percentage from
wealthy families (from 36.1 per cent in 1950 to 10.5 per cent
in 1964).[26] The underlying structural trend which made these
figures possible is the fact that large corporations increasingly have
drawn their top management from the ranks of college graduates,
that men enter these firms in various junior managerial and professional capacities from the university, and that higher posts are secured through a competitive promotion process, much as in
government bureaucracy. Privileged family and class background
obviously continue to be an enormous advantage here as in the
Soviet Union, but training and talent can make up for them in
an increasing number of cases.

Although the increase in opportunity to move to the very top
clearly does not affect the life chances of most people, it reflects

the tail end of a process which is a mass phenomenon, namely the spreading out of higher education into the ranks of the working class. Studies of parental aspirations for children indicate that the vast majority of American workers desire higher education for their children, and today, in spite of the continued inequality noted earlier, close to half of them can see this aspiration become a reality. And seeing their children enter on this first step of the competitive ladder to bureaucratic success may serve to reinforce further the belief that opportunity exists even among those frustrated by their own minimal occupational achievements and work experiences.

The fact that the business elite include so many who have demonstrated the Horatio Alger story of the poor hard-working boy who becomes wealthy may also have political consequences in strengthening the conviction of the upper class that an important part of the ideology of the system, the idea of equality of opportunity, corresponds to reality. The more convinced a ruling elite is of the validity of its title to rule, of its social legitimacy, the better able it is to resist attacks on its power. One of the conditions for successful revolution is a "failure of nerve" of the elite, a loss in its confidence that it deserves to govern. Since the legitimating dogma of the American system has always included as a major component the notion that those at the top are there because they have won a race, the continued presence within the elite of large numbers of sharply upwardly mobile people is important for the system.

Two Mobility Systems

If differences in rates of mobility among countries and over time are not sufficient to account for the continued belief in opportunity, there is an aspect of American development which must be seen as part of the picture, the fact that class position has been differentially distributed among ethnic and racial groups.[27] For much of its history, the United States has been divided between "majority" and "minority" ethnic groups. The latter have, in effect, repeatedly provided new sets of recruits for the lowly paid, low-status positions, thus enabling others of less recent settlement to rise. An analysis of census data reported that in 1870 and 1880, "the foreign-born were most typically employed in the factories, in heavy industry, as manual laborers and domestic servants. Clerical, managerial and official positions remained largely inaccessible to them."[28] The census of 1890 gathered information for the first time on the occupations of the native-born children of immigrants, thus permitting a comparison of the two generations. They varied considerably. "Unlike the immigrant males who were in highest proportion among domestic and personal service workers, the second generation males were most numerous relatively among workers in trade and transportation and in manufacturing. It is also notable that those in the second generation were more successful in entering the professions, even though not as successful as members of the native stock (the native born of native parents). . . . Altogether, the second generation conformed more closely to the occupational distribution of the entire white labor force than did the foreign born."[29] This pattern in which the second generation, the children of immigrants, was as a group in much better positions than the immigrant generation continued for the duration of mass immigration. Thus, in 1900, "the data indicate that the foreign born were no more widely distributed by occupation . . . than in 1890, but that the second generation became more widely distributed and moved closer to the occupational distribution of the entire labor force in 1900."[30] The census was not as comprehensive in gathering comparable occupational data from 1910 on, but the evidence clearly indicates comparable patterns to those summarized above for the remaining period of mass immigration, i.e., prior to passage of restrictive legislation in 1924.

More recently, particularly since the economy began a prolonged period of relatively full employment in the 1940s, migrants from various parts of North America, blacks, Puerto Ricans, Mexicans, and to a small extent French Canadians, have furnished the bulk of the less skilled underprivileged labor force. As Reinhard Bendix and I wrote in our analysis of mobility processes in the late 1950s:

Now, as before, there is a close relationship between low income and membership in segregated groups. A large proportion of seasonal farm laborers and sharecroppers in the South and Southwest come from them. In the cities, Negroes, Mexicans and Puerto Ricans predominate in the unskilled, dirty, and badly paid occupations. These twenty million people earn a disproportionately low share of the national income; they have little political power and no social prestige; they live in ethnic ghettos, in rural and urban areas alike, and they have little social contact with white Americans. Indeed, today there are two working classes in America, a white one and a Negro, Mexican, and Puerto Rican one. A real social and economic cleavage is created by widespread discrimination against these minority groups, and this diminishes the chances for the development of solidarity along class lines. In effect, the overwhelming majority of whites, both in the working class and in the middle and upper classes, benefit economically and socially from the existence of these "lower classes" within their midst. This continued splintering of the working class is a major element in the preservation of the stability of the class structure.[31]

The assumptions made in that analysis concerning the relative difference between the situations of initially underprivileged whites and blacks have recently been given more elaborate statistical confirmation in the largest and methodologically most sophisticated study of American social mobility, that of Blau and Duncan. These authors found that lowly social origin *had little negative effect on the chances of whites, including the children of white immigrants, to advance economically.* The mobility picture for the whites is such that Blau and Duncan reject the idea that a "vicious cycle" perpetuating inequality exists "for the population at large." But if whites, including working-class whites, have experienced a fluid occupational class system, in which the able and ambitious can rise, the reverse is true for the blacks. Their data confirm the impression "that Negroes are handicapped at every step in their attempts to achieve economic success, and these cumulative disadvantages are what produces the great inequalities of opportunities under which the Negro American suffers. . . . The multiple handicaps associated with being an American Negro are cumulative in their deleterious consequences for a man's career."

Education, which we have seen opens all sorts of doors to whites, even to those of quite low social origin, does not work the same way for blacks.

The difference in occupational status between Negroes and whites is twice as great for men who have graduated from high school or gone to college as for those who have completed no more than eight years of schooling. In short the careers of well-educated Negroes lag even further behind those of comparable whites than do the careers of poorly educated Negroes. . . . Negroes, as an underprivileged group, must make greater sacrifices to remain in school, but they have less incentive than whites to make these sacrifices, which may well be a major reason why Negroes often exhibit little motivation to continue in school and advance their education.[32]

Given the fact that no European country has had to absorb as large an immigrant population into the lower echelons of an expanding economy, and that none of them have ethnic, racial, religious cleavages, which separate the distribution of occupational advantages along racial lines, as widely and as long as the United States has had, it should be clear that the fact (if it is a fact) of roughly comparable rates of mass social mobility among many different countries should have sharply different consequences on the possibilities for working-class consciousness or political solidarity. For as the data reported here, both for the past and the present, suggest, the opportunities and economic advantages available to the less privileged sectors of the native white population have been much greater than for comparable groups in Europe. Unskilled American blacks have a much lower rate of upward social mobility than Europeans, while when "the upward mobility rate of unskilled [American] white workers is considered separately, it is appreciably higher than the upward mobility rate for the total unskilled group. The assumption that the United States has higher mobility rates than European countries may, then, rest in part on a disregard of a sizeable sector of the society."[33]

Conclusion

Historians such as Thernstrom who have been willing to dig beneath the impressionistic consensus concerning American society by quantifying who did what, who got what, and the like, have severely upset many of our cherished beliefs about the American past. Not only have they challenged the conventional wisdom about mobility rates which assumed that we have moved from greater to lesser equality, but a related group of quantitatively oriented historians have examined the distribution of income and of variations in social class behavior from early times on. And the tentative conclusion which may be reached from a number of these studies is that Jacksonian America, described by Tocqueville and others as an egalitarian social system (which, compared to Europe, it undoubtedly was), was probably characterized by much more severe forms of social and economic inequality, of variations in standards of living among the classes than the society of the 1970s. The assumption that the growth of an industrialized urban society broke up an egalitarian one is simply contrary to the available evidence about Tocqueville's America, including even "agricultural areas and small towns."

The explanation, popular since Karl Marx's time, that it was industrialization that pauperized the masses, in the process transforming a relatively egalitarian social order, appears wanting. Vast disparities between urban rich and poor antedated industrialization [in America].[34]

The evidence concerning the existence of extremely wide disparities in income, property, and consumption styles in pre-Civil War America puts into question the assumptions that industrialization has led to greater inequality, particularly in urban areas. Without entering into the issue of trends in the distribution of income in this century, it is obvious that economic growth has brought with it an almost constant increase in the Gross National Income, that the average per capita income has increased close to six times during this century. And as Bendix and I noted in our earlier work on social mobility, this dramatic growth in income necessarily has meant a wider distribution of various consumption goods, usually more general than in any other country. Thus, a much larger percentage of Americans (over 80) graduate from high school or enter college (close to 50) than is true in any other nation. Almost 80 per cent of the black population now finishes twelve years of school, and over 40 per cent of those of college age enters higher education. The greater wealth of the United States also means that consumer goods such as automobiles, telephones, and the like are more equitably distributed here than elsewhere. A recent effort, using twelve social indicators, at a comparative evaluation of the relative advantages of different countries as places to live by *The* (London) *Economist* placed the United States far in the lead of eight other major non-Communist industrialized states.[35] The wider distribution of consumers' goods that inevitably accompanies greater wealth means that the gap in standards of living between social classes, particularly among the white community, is relatively low by comparative world standards. And as income, as style of life, increases, even men who remain in the same occupational position may experience a sense of gain.

The discussion of rates of social mobility and related aspects of social stratification by Thernstrom and others is clearly premised on the oft repeated suggestion that societies characterized by high rates of social mobility are much less likely to be affected by intense class conflict, by polarized politics, than those in which little opportunity exists. This thesis has been enunciated by Karl Marx seeking to account for weak working-class consciousness in the United States and by a variety of contemporary sociological observers.[36] The most detailed effort to test some of the implications of these assumptions in the context of examining the differences between the mobile, upward and downward, and the non-mobile in different classes in the context of their opinion and voting choices in recent years tends to validate the proposition that mobile individuals are less likely to take strong class positions than the non-mobile. James Barber concludes his study with the assertion: "The influence of mobility on the political system would seem . . . to be a moderating one: lending flexibility to the electoral process, reducing the stakes involved in elections, and diluting the class content of politics."[37]

As a reading of the essays in this volume indicates, there are many factors and social processes which have determined the character of political conflict in America, particularly the weakness of socialist class-based politics. The emphasis here on the possible effects of social mobility is not meant to suggest a belief that the opportunity structure of the society is the main determinant of the state of class consciousness. Elsewhere, in the context of comparing various aspects of the United States and Canada, I have suggested that historical experiences which have sustained more "conservative," traditional, and hierarchical status structures north of the border, reflecting the fact that Canada came into existence as the country of the "counterrevolution," facilitated the emergence of more particularistic (group- and class-related) politics there than in the United States.[38]

Strong socialist movements exist in countries with high rates of mobility and strong emphases on equalitarianism (e.g., Australia and New Zealand). A radical movement may emerge in this country, as it briefly appeared to do in the late 1960s, though rates of mobility had not changed. That movement, however, was almost totally based on the liberal segment of the intelligentsia and the college student population. It had little or no appeal to white workers. Its momentary existence, therefore, does not challenge the contention that the high rate of social mobility existing among native working-class white Americans has adversely affected efforts to foster radical class politics in the United States. Hence, the kind of studies discussed here is of more than academic interest. And thus far, no available data indicate any sign of a decline in the rate of social mobility; if they suggest any trend, it is an opposite one, toward enlargement of opportunity through the combination of increased bureaucratization and a widening of educational facilities.

NOTES

1. A detailed, highly sophisticated methodological critique with references to much of the methodological literature is Karl Ulrich Mayer and Walter Müller, "Progress in Social Mobility Research?" *Quality and Quantity*, 5 (June 1971), pp. 141–77. For discussions of various methodological and theoretical issues in mobility research see the articles in Neil Smelser and S. M. Lipset (eds.), *Social Structure and Mobility in Economic Development* (Chicago: Aldine, 1966), esp. those by O. D. Duncan, H. L. Wilensky, W. E. Moore, and N. R. Ramsøy and the introductory chapter by the editors.

2. P. A. Sorokin, *Social and Cultural Mobility* (New York: The Free Press, 1959). This book was first published in 1927. David V. Glass (ed.), *Social Mobility in Britain* (London: Routledge, 1954); S. M. Lipset and Reinhard Bendix, *Social Mobility in Industrial Society* (Berkeley: University of California Press, 1959); S. M. Miller, "Comparative Social Mobility: A Trend Report and Bibliography," *Current Sociology*, 9, no. 1 (1960), pp. 1–89; Thomas G. Fox and S. M. Miller, "Economic, Political and Social Determinants of Mobility," *Acta Sociologica*, 9 (1965), pp. 76–93; Thomas G. Fox and S. M. Miller, "Intra-Country Variations: Occupational Stratification and Mobility," in Reinhard Bendix and S. M. Lipset (eds.), *Class, Status, and Power: Social Stratification in Comparative Perspective* (New York: The Free Press, 1966), pp. 574–81; Philips Cutright, "Occupational Inheritance: A Cross-national Analysis," *American Journal of Sociology*, 73 (1968), pp. 400–16.

3. Peter M. Blau and Otis Dudley Duncan, *The American Occupational Structure* (New York: John Wiley, 1967), p. 433.

4. Cutright, op. cit. A similar conclusion was reached by K. Svalastoga, *Social Differentiation* (New York: David McKay, 1965), pp. 123–26. He also points to "The pervasiveness of mobility. Even crude measurements produce the finding that in any industrial society the majority is mobile" (p. 141).

5. Joseph Schumpeter, "The Problem of Classes," in Bendix and Lipset (eds.), *Class, Status, and Power*, p. 45.

6. Zdaněk Šaféř, "Different Approaches to the Measurement of Social Differentiation of the Czechoslovak Socialist Society," *Quality and Quantity*, 5 (June 1971), pp. 205–6. See also P. Machonin, "Social Stratification in Contemporary Czechoslovakia," *American Journal of Sociology*, 75 (1970), pp. 725–41. For a detailed report of the large body of empirical research on social mobility and stratification in the Soviet Union, see S. M. Lipset and Richard Dobson, "Social Stratification and Sociology in the Soviet Union," *Survey*, 19 (Summer 1973), pp. 114–85.

7. As cited in I. F. Stone, "Can Russia Change?" *New York Review of Books*, 18 (February 24, 1972), p. 22.

8. From summary of the published Russian report in Z. Katz, *Hereditary Elements in Education and Social Structure in the USSR* (Glascow: Institute of Soviet and East-European Studies, University of Glascow, 1969), p. 4. I am very indebted to Professor Katz for references and comments.

9. As cited in ibid., p. 6 (emphases are by Z. Katz).

10. Cutright, op. cit.

11. Stanislaus Ossowski, "Social Mobility Brought About by Social Revolution" (Paper presented at the Fourth Working Conference on Social Stratification and Social Mobility, International Sociological Association, Geneva, December 1957). (Emphases mine–S.M.L.) This paper is discussed in Lipset and Bendix, *Social Mobility*, pp. 281–82.

12. R. Adorka, "Social Mobility and Economic Development in Hungary," *Acta Oeconomica*, 7, no. 1 (1971), pp. 40–41.

13. Maria Markus, "Quelques problèmes sociologiques du choix de la profession et de son pretige," in Andreas Hegedus (ed.), *Études recherches. sociologues hongrois* (Paris: Éditions Anthropos, 1969), pp. 198–99.

14. Adam Sarapata, "Distance et mobilité sociale dans la société polonaise contemporaine," *Sociologie du travail*, 8 (January–March 1966), p. 19. Joseph R. Fiszman, "Education and Social Mobility in People's Poland," *The Polish Review*, 16 (Summer 1971), pp. 5–31.

15. See Vojin Milić, "General Trends in Social Mobility in Yugoslavia," *Acta Sociologica*, 9, nos. 1–2 (1966), see p. 133, and notes 10 and 12 on p. 135.

16. For a review of the discussion of Soviet sociologists on social stratification, see Z. Katz, "The Soviet Sociologists' Debate on Social Structure in the USSR" (Draft prepared for the Center for International Studies, MIT; Russian Research Center, Harvard University, July 30, 1971), pp. 49–56.

17. "Young Soviet Citizens No Longer Wish to Be Workers" (a summary of an article by the Moscow correspondent of the *Corriere della Sera* [Milan], Giuseppe Josca), *SIPE* (International Student Press Service, Rome), 3 (October–November 1971), pp. 12–14.

18. As cited in Katz, *Hereditary Elements*, p. 41.

19. For a critique of historians, just ten years old, for ignoring the area, see Oscar and Mary Handlin, "Mobility," in Edward Saveth (ed.), *American History and the Social Sciences* (New York: The Free Press, 1964), pp. 215–30.

20. Natalie Rogoff, *Recent Trends in Occupational Mobility* (Glencoe: The Free Press, 1963).

21. Blau and Duncan, op. cit., p. 111.

22. Tom Rishøj, "Metropolitan Social Mobility 1850–1950: The Case of Copenhagen," *Quality and Quantity*, 5 (June 1971), pp. 131–40.

23. Ibid., p. 139.

24. Stephan Thernstrom, "Poverty in Historical Perspective," in D.

P. Moynihan (ed.), *On Understanding Poverty* (New York: Basic Books, 1969), pp. 160–86.

25. *The Big Business Executive/1964 A Study of His Social and Educational Background* (A study sponsored by *The Scientific American,* conducted by Market Statistics Inc. of New York City, in collaboration with Dr. Mabel Newcomer), p. 2. The study was designed to update Mabel Newcomer, *The Big Business Executive—The Factors That Made Him: 1900–1950* (New York: Columbia University Press, 1950). All the comparisons in it are with materials reported in Dr. Newcomer's published work.

26. Ibid., p. 33.

27. For a recent discussion of this factor in the context of American mobility, see Anselm Strauss, *The Contexts of Social Mobility: Ideology and Theory* (Chicago: Aldine, 1971), pp. 79–104.

28. E. P. Hutchinson, *Immigrants and Their Children* (New York: John Wiley, 1956), p. 114.

29. Ibid., pp. 138–39.

30. Ibid., p. 171.

31. Lipset and Bendix, *Social Mobility,* pp. 105–6.

32. Blau and Duncan, op. cit., pp. 404–7. Otis Dudley Duncan, "Inheritance of Poverty or Inheritance of Race," in Moynihan (ed.), op. cit., pp. 103–9.

33. Herbert Goldhammer, "Social Mobility," *International Encyclopedia of the Social Sciences,* vol. 14 (New York: Macmillan and The Free Press, 1968), pp. 434–35.

34. Edward Pessen, "The Egalitarian Myth and the American Social Reality: Wealth, Mobility, and Equality in the 'Era of the Common Man,'" *The American Historical Review,* 76 (October 1971), pp. 1027–28, 1030. Pessen cites many relevant recent historical works bearing on the intense forms of inequality in this period.

35. "Where the Grass Is Greener," *The Economist,* December 25, 1971, p. 15.

36. For a review of some of the literature on this subject see James Alden Barber, Jr., *Social Mobility and Voting Behavior* (Chicago: Rand McNally, 1950), pp. 9–12, 264–66. With respect to problems of developing countries, see Gino Germani, "Social and Political Consequences of Mobility," in Smelser and Lipset (eds.), op. cit., pp. 364–94.

37. Barber, op. cit., p. 267. See also Lipset and Bendix, *Social Mobility,* pp. 261–65, 66–71, 73–74, 268–69; Blau and Duncan, op. cit., pp. 436–41. For citation to the literature of specific studies, see Mayer and Müller, op. cit., p. 148, n. 16.

38. S. M. Lipset, *Revolution and Counterrevolution* (Garden City, N.Y.: Doubleday, Anchor Books, rev. ed., 1970), pp. 37–75; and S. M. Lipset, *Agrarian Socialism: The Cooperative Commonwealth Federation in Saskatchewan* (Berkeley: University of California paperback, rev. ed., 1971), pp. xiv–xv.

REPLY

Stephan Thernstrom

My essay attempted to shed a little light on a large problem—the failure of the American socialist movement. The explanations that can be offered for that failure are of two broad types. Some observers have placed heavy stress upon factors internal to the movement itself—tactical blunders, failures of leadership, and the like. About the precise nature of these internal weaknesses there has been disagreement, with some writers denouncing leaders of the radical movement as unduly opportunistic, and others maintaining that the chief problem was just the opposite—excessive ideological rigidity, sectarianism, an inability to grasp American realities. Both groups assume, however, that better leadership, pursuing a more "correct" strategy, could have brought masses of voters into the socialist camp.

Such internal explanations strike me as dubious on two grounds. First, it has yet to be demonstrated that the tactics of American socialists actually differed dramatically from those of their more successful brethren in other countries like France, Germany, and Britain. The problem, after all, is a problem in comparative history, and the necessary comparative analysis of socialist leadership and socialist tactics has yet to be done.

Second, even if it could be shown that American socialists were indeed distinctively deficient on this count, I would want to ask *why* that was the case. This kind of explanation is all too reminiscent of the now discredited view that the American Civil War erupted because of the mistakes of a "blundering generation" of inept politicians. Possibly Lincoln, Douglas, and other leaders of the 1850s were less talented politicians than the Founding Fathers or even Clay and Calhoun—though it seems doubtful—but the further question is whether this may be taken as an uncaused cause, i.e., a truly independent variable. My prejudice would be that the quality of political leadership available in a given historical context is largely determined by the context. It was the clash of the radically divergent social systems that had developed in the northern and southern states by the 1850s that brought the men of the "blundering generation" to the fore and pushed them toward the actions (and inactions) that led finally to war. Likewise, I would urge, the successes of Samuel Gompers and the failures of Gene Debs and Big Bill Haywood stemmed largely from fundamental features of the social context in which they operated. The failure of American socialism, I believe, was attributable not so much to internal as to external circumstances. Socialism foundered because certain basic structural features of American society were antithetical to the socialist impulse.

The task of defining those features is too large to attempt here. A full answer would certainly take cognizance of Louis Hartz's brilliant discussion of the role of feudalism in creating a politics of class. The absence of a feudal aristocracy in the American past inhibited the formation of a class-conscious bourgeoisie, which in turn dampened the degree of proletarian identification and solidarity. Lipset's comment on my initial essay properly emphasizes another factor—ethnic, racial, and religious cleavages within the American working class, and differentials in access to opportunity for different groups. One obviously must look too at the nature of the American political system itself, which has institutional features (such as the single-member electoral district) that tend to foster the dominance of two centrist parties.

My essay, of course, did not purport to offer a comprehensive discussion of the structural factors that impeded the rise of a socialist movement in the United States. Instead I concentrated on the possible relevance of four closely related circumstances: that American workers were exceptionally mobile geographically; that levels of occupational career mobility were high; that levels of intergenerational occupational mobility were also high; and that strikingly large numbers of American laborers were able to accumulate significant property holdings.

My view at the time the essay was written was that there was dismayingly little in the way of solid comparative evidence concerning levels of mobility of these four kinds in other societies in the nineteenth and early twentieth centuries, but that there were fragments of data pointing to the conclusion that the American social system was more fluid than those of other countries at comparable levels of economic development.

That still seems to me the best generalization that can be made on the basis of the information currently available. In his Comment Lipset has, rather surprisingly, failed to mention three of the four types of mobility I discussed; about them I will say only that the few fragments of new evidence that have come to my attention since my paper was written are consistent with my suggestion that the American social system was unusually fluid in these important respects.[1] Lipset draws bold conclusions about "social mobility" on the basis of evidence that bears upon only one kind of mobility —intergenerational occupational mobility.

On that one issue, I find his contribution provocative. The bulk of his material, of course, refers to the contemporary scene, not to the past. But his data from Eastern Europe does serve to strengthen the conclusion he and Bendix advanced earlier in *Social Mobility in Industrial Society*—that rates of intergenerational mobility display rather striking uniformities in all advanced industrial societies.

The one new long-term historical study he cites, however, Rishøj's *Quality and Quantity* paper on Copenhagen from 1850 to 1950, does not seem to me to provide persuasive support for his position. Rishøj asserts that there was no significant change in the Copenhagen mobility pattern in the course of a century on the basis of summary tables that show that the *total* amount of upward and downward mobility in the community remained roughly constant over the entire period. But the significant question is whether the rate of upward mobility for working-class sons remained similarly constant, and it appears that in Copenhagen it did not.

There was little upward mobility among workers' sons in his 1853–55 sample, and a good deal of downward mobility on the part of men born into the middle class. In 1901 and 1953 samples the reverse was the case.[2] It is not the constancy of over-all mobility ratio but the shift in the opportunity levels for particular social classes that seems most striking and important to me. The mid-nineteenth-century Copenhagen figures for youths of working-class origins do not diverge widely from Sewell's findings for Marseille at about the same time, and they contrast very sharply with the pattern of opportunity in several nineteenth-century American cities. Later, with advancing urbanization and industrialization, the gap between the American and European scene doubtless narrowed, but the common nineteenth-century belief that the social system of the New World offered unique opportunities for upward mobility had some foundation in fact.

It should also be pointed out that there is a serious question whether intergenerational mobility can legitimately be separated from the measurement of career mobility without producing misleading conclusions. Suppose that I am correct in my contention—ignored by Lipset—that there was a uniquely high rate of career mobility in the United States. Suppose, for instance, that 30 per cent of the Americans who began work in blue-collar jobs moved up into white-collar occupations by the time they started to rear children, and that in Denmark the comparable figure was only 10 per cent. In these circumstances, a finding that there were similar rates of upward and downward intergenerational mobility in the United States and Denmark could be quite misleading, for the base line from which intergenerational mobility is normally computed is the occupational rank of the father at some point subsequent to the birth of his son. A larger fraction of the sons of American white-collar workers *should* have been downwardly mobile, because fewer of their fathers were solidly established in the white-collar world for their full careers. Conversely, we would expect to find less upward intergenerational mobility on the part of the sons of American workers, because many of the more ambitious and intelligent workers would have been removed from the working class and drawn up into the middle class, leaving a diminished pool of talent at the working-class level. Identical rates of intergenerational mobility would in this instance obscure very real differences in the fluidity of the two social systems being compared.

Whether or not this hypothetical example corresponds to historical reality, of course, is unknown at present. The work of Lipset has been of immense value in challenging the easy assumptions that have so often been made about the unique fluidity of the American social system. It is not impossible that a wave of future historical mobility studies of a highly refined kind, studies that treat the full range of phenomena that are embraced in a comprehensive conception of social mobility, will show that his skepticism is well founded. But the issue is certainly open at present. I am still inclined to believe that American mobility patterns were in some ways distinctive, and that this distinctiveness did have a good deal to do with another fairly distinctive aspect of the American historical record—the failure of working-class-based protest movements to attract a mass following.

NOTES

1. I have in mind particularly the forthcoming study of the glass-blowers of Carmaux by Jean W. Scott of Northwestern University, and the comparative analysis of mobility in Amsterdam, Frankfurt, and San Francisco being undertaken by Allen Emrich, Jr., of Temple University.

2. So it appears, at least, from Rishøj's Table 5. My own attempt to verify these figures by recomputing the raw data in Tables 1–4, however, shows a different pattern. A more detailed report on this study is badly needed. See Tom Rishøj, "Metropolitan Social Mobility 1850–1950: The Case of Copenhagen," *Quality and Quantity*, 5 (June 1971), pp. 131–40.

Chapter 13

THE LABOR MOVEMENT AND AMERICAN VALUES*

Seymour Martin Lipset

Societal Values and the Union Movement

THE RELATIVE LACK OF CLASS CONSCIOUSNESS AND THE SELF-INTEREST OF INDIVIDUAL UNIONS. The lack of a class-conscious ideology in the American labor movement may be directly traced to the equalitarian, anti-class orientation of the values associated with America's national identity. Thus it may be suggested that one of the reasons unions have had trouble organizing new segments of the employed population as compared to unions in northern Europe is that they have been handicapped by their slightly illegitimate position relative to the value system. "Union" connotes "class" organization.

In an interesting effort to account for the failure of socialism to take root in American society, Leon Samson has suggested that an important cause has been that Americanism is a political ideology with much the same value content as socialism.[1] It endorses the progress of the society toward the more equal distribution of privileges that socialism demands. As a result, the rank and file members of American labor unions have not had to look for an ideology that justified the changes which they desired in the society.

However, the failure of the American labor movement to identify itself as a class movement may be traced more directly to the way in which equalitarianism and achievement orientation permeated the social structure. As Schumpeter has noted, the self-interested orientation of the American labor movement is but the application, in the realm of working-class life and trade unions, of the general value scheme.[2] *Indeed, instead of reducing the individualistic ori-*

* Taken from Chapter 5 of Seymour M. Lipset, *The First New Nation: The United States in Historical and Comparative Perspective* (Garden City, N.Y.: Doubleday, Anchor ed., 1967), pp. 202–33. In the original the chapter was entitled "Trade Unions and the American Value System."

entation that Marxism associates with the early phase of capitalism, increasing industrialization in American society has reinforced the egalitarian-achievement attitudes toward stratification that early became part of the American national character. In a sense, industrialization has lent these attitudes continued legitimacy: industrialization and advancing technology brought about an almost unbroken increase in national wealth on both an absolute and a per capita basis, so that in the nineteenth century America became the wealthiest country in the world, a position it has never relinquished.[3] And as David Potter has well stressed, the fact of increasing abundance, no matter how unequally distributed, has served to permit the majority of the American population, including most trade-unionists, to enjoy a visible living standard roughly comparable among all groups with the exception of the extremely wealthy:

> American social distinctions, however real they may be and however difficult to break down, are not based upon or supported by great disparities in wealth, in education, in speech, in dress, etc., as they are in the old world. If the American class structure is in reality very unlike the classless society which we imagine, it is equally unlike the formalized class societies of former times. . . . the factor of abundance has . . . constantly operated to equalize the overt differences between the various classes. . . .[4]

Within this context the very success of trade unions in improving the relative position of their members *vis-à-vis* other groups in the population has simply contributed to the maintenance of their members' belief in the American value system.

THE MILITANT TACTICS OF UNIONS. Just as ideological conservatism and pursuit of narrow self-interests may be derived from the value system, so may the use of violent and militant tactics.[5] Here the labor movement, like American business, reflects the social system's relatively greater emphasis on ends as contrasted with means. One tries to win economic and social objectives by whatever means are at hand. The fact that American workers are sufficiently dissatisfied with their economic conditions to tolerate relatively frequent, long, and bitter strikes may also be explained by reference to the social structure and its values. In summing up the conclusions of late nineteenth-century foreign visitors to America, Robert Smuts points out that they saw it in this light:

> The frequency and the bitterness of industrial conflict was the most basic fault the foreigners found in American industrial life. . . .
> Most of the European visitors explained industrial conflict as a result rather than a contradiction of the material and social democracy which typified the life of the American worker. The abundance of his life, they pointed out, added to the strength of his ambition for more. His self-reliance made him sensitive to his rights. Industrial conflict in America was a man-to-man fight, with no quarter asked or given, unmitigated by the tradition of subordination on the one hand, or of benevolence and responsibility on the other.[6]

It may also be argued that we should expect more *individual* discontent with income and position among workers in America than within the more rigidly and visibly stratified European countries. The more rigid the stratification of a nation, the more candid the emphasis on the existence of differences among classes, the greater the extent to which lower status individuals will be likely to contrast their lot—*as a class*—with that of the more privileged classes. On the other hand, in a more loosely structured class system, people will be more prone to compare themselves *individually* with other workers who are relatively close to them in income and status. Thus if, in the latter system, groups or individuals improve their status, there will be resentment on the part of those left behind.

In other words, an open-class system leads workers to resent inequalities in income and status between themselves and others more frequently than does an ascriptively stratified system, where the only inequalities that count are class inequalities. America's equalitarian value system, by less clearly defining the range of groups with which workers may legitimately compare themselves, can make for greater individual discontent among workers than is the case in Europe.[7] European social structure, by regarding labor, in the words of Winston Churchill, as "an estate of the realm," makes clear to workers why they are lowly and calls upon them to act collectively; American social structure, by eschewing estates, creating vague and even illegitimate class boundaries, and stressing equality, blames individuals for being lowly and calls upon them to alleviate their resentment by improving their status in as self-interested and narrowly defined terms as possible. John L. Lewis, founder of the Congress of Industrial Organizations, president of the United Mine Workers for nearly forty years, and perhaps the most militant labor leader in the United States since the 1920's was a Republican most of his life and a strong advocate of conservative, *laissez-faire* economics (although he was willing to use state power to bolster his union and the coal industry).

There is some evidence in support of the contention that this self-interested bargaining policy does make sense for *any particular group*. Recent research dealing with the influence of trade unions on wages suggests that the existence of organized labor does not change the national distribution of income between workers and owners through collective bargaining, but it may improve the wage situation of one group of workers relative to others.[8] (As will be noted later, it has been argued, however, that aggressive unionism increases national wealth—and thereby workers' incomes—in absolute terms by creating constant pressure on employers to mechanize and increase productivity so as to readjust any imbalances created by increases in labor costs.) Hence the narrow self-interested policies traditionally pursued by many American unions would seem to be warranted if the objective of unionism is to secure as much as possible for the members of the given union. This is most likely to be its objective if the union movement reflects the values of achievement and individualism.

Conversely, however, there seems to be evidence that government can redistribute income among the classes through welfare, tax, and spending policies.[9] Thus, if the labor movement seeks to improve the situation of an entire class, a goal inherent in the economic conflicts which emerged in the previously aristocratic societies, a policy of concentrating on political action rather than trade union militancy is warranted.

LARGE WAGE DIFFERENTIALS. The approval of the pursuit of self-interest within the American labor movement may also help to account for the fact that wage differentials between skilled and unskilled workers are larger in America than in the other nations. A study of such differentials in six countries indicates that in France, Germany, Italy, the Netherlands, and Norway, "skill differentials are rather narrow, compared, say, with United States averages."[10] And: "Differences in wages between unskilled and skilled jobs in Swedish industry are generally much less than in

America. For example, the head machine operator in an American paper mill will earn at least 50 per cent more than the lowest paid worker in the mill. In Sweden the difference is less than 20 per cent."[11]

There are many factors related to variations in wage differentials, but it seems possible that variations in basic values may play a role. Sturmthal points this out:

Undoubtedly also the notions of what are proper differentials . . . vary a good deal on both sides of the Atlantic. The absence of feudal concepts of the place in society to which a worker may properly aspire may have played a part in allowing the larger wage differentials to arise in the United States, just as the heritage of the feudal concepts may have helped maintain the highly compressed wage structure in Europe.[12]

The very insistence on the "formal" equality of all people in the United States places a higher value on income and conspicuous consumption than in societies in which status and occupation are closely linked. Although comparative studies of occupational status indicate that occupations tend to rank at roughly the same level in all industrial societies,[13] occupation seems to be less important than sheer income as a determinant of status in the United States, as compared with some European nations. Two surveys made at about the same time in the United States and Germany suggest this interpretation (see Table III). Although the differences in results may reflect the variations in the questions that were asked, it seems likely that both surveys touched to some extent on the same basic issue: the relative weight given to occupational prestige as compared with the size of income. In both countries those who had higher status (i.e., those who wore either better educated or who occupied a white-collar position) were more likely than those of lower status to favor white-collar status, even if it meant lower income than that obtained by a skilled worker. But the important result was that the majority of the American respondents, even among the college graduates, preferred the higher paid, lower status job; on the other hand, the majority of the German respondents ranked the lower paid, white-collar job higher.

A report on a similar study in another European country, this time a Communist one, Poland, suggests that in that country, as in Germany, white-collar status is given more weight than income. This study, which was apparently more like the American than the German in its approach, indicates that "passage of the better paid skilled manual workers to the position of the slightly lower paid white-collar workers . . . in the majority of cases is looked on as a promotion . . . [although] from the point of view of the new criteria of prestige, this should not be considered a promotion."[14]

TABLE III

Preference Percentages for White-Collar Status and Low Income or for Manual Position and High Income in Germany and the United States

UNITED STATES—1951

"Which of these two jobs would you personally prefer a son of yours to take, assuming he is equally qualified: a skilled worker's job at $100 a week, or a white-collar desk job at $75 a week?"

		Years of Education			
Answer	*Total Sample*	*0–8*	*9–12*	*13–15*	*16*
White collar	28	22	31	34	42
Skilled laborer	69	72	67	65	52
Don't know	3	6	2	1	6
Total	100.0	100.0	100.0	100.0	100.0
Number interviewed	(658)	(287)	(257)	(62)	(52)

Source: Computed from Gallup data in the files of the Roper Public Opinion Research Center at Williams College.

GERMANY—1952

"Who do you think receives more prestige from the population in general: a bookkeeper who earns 300 marks a month, or a foundry worker who brings home 450 marks a month?"

Answer	*Total Sample*	*Manual Worker Respondents Only*
The bookkeeper	58	56
The foundry worker	24	28
Don't know	18	16
Total	100.0	100.0

Source: Erich Peter Neumann and Elizabeth Noelle, Antworten, Politik im Kraftfeld der öffentlichen Meinung (Allensbach am Bodensee: Verlag für Demoskopie, 1954), p. 107.

Assuming, therefore, that higher occupational status is more of an incentive in countries with relatively formalized status systems than in countries stressing equalitarian behavioral norms, there should be less need in the first group of societies to magnify economic incentives in order to motivate people to prepare for positions requiring long periods of training.[15] As Sturmthal has put it, "incentives that are necessary in one country to produce a certain supply of highly skilled labor may be excessive in another country or *vice versa*. This may be the result of different noneconomic compensations offered to the higher skills—status and prestige—or simply of different 'styles of life' in which lesser financial rewards are sufficient to bring about the desired result."[16]

Differences in behavior of organized labor from country to country seem to reflect in some measure variations in the differentials that are considered morally appropriate. Thus, in the United States, for individuals or groups of individuals to seek to better themselves at the expense of others tends to be encouraged by the dominant achievement orientation. In the past few years, several industrial unions formed by the CIO have had difficulty with skilled workers among their membership who have insisted that the wage differentials be widened. In New York, the most highly skilled groups employed on the city's transportation system tried to break away from the Transport Workers' Union to form separate craft unions. A strike called for this purpose failed, but this relatively old industrial union made important concessions to its skilled workers. In the United Automobile Workers the skilled crafts have been allowed to form separate councils within the union and have forced the union to press their demand for greater differentials. In some old craft unions which accepted unskilled and semi-skilled workers, the latter were often given second-class membership, *i.e.*, no voting rights, to prevent them from inhibiting the bargaining strategy of the skilled group.[17]

In much of Europe, on the other hand, the norms implicit in socialist and working-class ideology have made such behavior difficult. The Swedish labor movement for many years made a reduction of differentials one of its aims.[18] Clark Kerr notes that in Germany one of the forces which explains the greater emphasis on wage equality has been "Socialist theories of standardizing pay. . . ."[19] In Italy after World War II, "for political reasons and under the pressure of left-wing parties, the general trend was in favor of raising as much as possible the wages paid to common laborers. . . ."[20] The Norwegian labor movement followed for many years the policy of "wages solidarity," *i.e.*, the reduction of differentials.[21]

In recent years, under pressure from their skilled members and on the advice of various economists who are disturbed by the possible effects on efficiency of narrow differentials for large variations in skills, many of the European labor movements have formally dropped their insistence on narrowing the gap, and some even advocate widening it. As far as the labor economists can judge, the skill differentials, which began dropping in most countries in the late 1930's and continued falling until around 1952, have been rising slightly since then. For socialists, however, to avowedly seek to benefit a more well-to-do group at the expense of the poorer one would seem to violate essential values.[22] And the greater centralization of the union movement in most of these European countries requires that such a wage policy be an explicit national one, rather than one simply reflecting adjustments to immediate pressures.

The general behavior of American unions in perpetuating wide differentials is congruent with the assumption that Americans remain more narrowly self-interested and that the more powerful groups of workers are able to maintain or occasionally even improve a relatively privileged position at the expense of the less powerful, usually less organized, and less skilled workers.[23]

Societal Values and Union Leadership

Any effort to account for the ways in which American unionism differs from unionism in northern Europe and Australasia necessarily must deal with the behavior of the leaders. As recent congressional investigations and journalistic exposés have made manifest, union officials in this country receive higher salaries, are more wont to engage in practices which violate conventional morality, and show a lesser regard for the mechanisms of democratic procedure than leaders in the other nations discussed here.

UNION LEADERS' JOB ORIENTATION, SALARIES, AND ENTRENCHED POSITIONS. The concept of "business unionism," the dominant ideology of the American labor movement which perceives unions as fighting for more money rather than for any program of social reconstruction, has important consequences in encouraging union leaders to view themselves as bound by the same standards as profit-oriented businessmen.

Usually the leaders of social movements are expected to have a "calling," to feel moved by a moral ethic toward serving certain major social values. In the early days of many American unions, when they were weak, often illegitimate, and could yield few rewards in the form of status, power, or income, their leaders did adhere to some such larger ideology, often a variant of socialism. This ideology prescribed certain standards of ethical behavior and a certain style of life. But as American union leaders shifted from social or socialist unionism to business unionism, they also changed their values and standards of comparisons. To a considerable extent, those unions which have retained important aspects of socialist values, such as the United Automobile Workers or the International Ladies' Garment Workers' Union, are precisely the unions whose leaders, even with great power, still insist upon relatively low officer salaries and show great concern over problems of corruption and civil liberties.[24] To the extent that union office has changed from a "calling" to a "career" as unions have aged and ideology has declined, to that extent have leaders lost their inhibitions about comparing themselves with businessmen or widening the discrepancy between their salaries and those of their members.[25]

The emphasis on pecuniary success, combined with the absence of the kind of class consciousness characteristic of more aristocratic societies, has thus served to motivate workers to use the labor movement itself as an avenue to financial and status gain. The high incomes which many union leaders receive represent their adaptation to the norm of "getting ahead." As long as a union leader has the reputation for "delivering the goods" to his members, they seem willing to allow him a high salary and sometimes the right to engage in private business, or even to be corrupt.[26]

The greater perquisites attached to high union office in America, a seeming consequence of pressure inherent in the achievement-equalitarianism syndrome, may also account for the fact that American union leaders have formally institutionalized dictatorial mechanisms which prevent the possibility of their being defeated for re-election. Although trade-union leaders in all countries have achieved a great deal by moving up from the machine or bench to the union office, this shift has nowhere meant as much in terms of money and consequent style of life as in the United States. Most high status positions carry with them some security of tenure, but political positions in democratic societies are insecure by definition. Politicians in most countries may move from electoral defeat to highly paid positions in private industry or the professions, but union leaders customarily cannot do so. This means, as I have noted elsewhere, that they are under considerable pressure to find means to protect their source of status. Thus the greater the gap between the rewards of union leadership and of those jobs from which the leader came and to which he might return on defeat, the greater the pressure to eliminate democratic rights. Within the American labor movement itself those unions in which the gap between leaders and rank and file is narrow in income or in status seem to be much more democratic than those in which the gap is great. Among the unions which fall in this former category are Actors' Equity, the American Newspaper Guild, and the International Typographical Union.[27] Thus the very forces which press for higher rewards of various types for American labor leaders also support and encourage greater restrictions on democratic politics in the unions.

It may also be argued that in societies in which deferential values are strong, union leaders may maintain an oligarchic structure with less strain than is possible in America. And as I stated in an earlier essay:

> Given the assumption that leaders in both [continents] would seek to make their tenure secure, we would expect that American labor leaders would be under greater pressure to formalize dictatorial mechanisms so as to prevent the possibility of their being overthrown. Or, to put it another way, since the values inherent in American society operate to make American union officers more vulnerable than, say, their German counterparts, they would be obliged to act more vigorously and decisively and dictatorially to stabilize their status.[28]

Some evidence that relatively elite societies are more willing to give tenure to union leaders may be found in Great Britain and Sweden, where the principal officers of many national unions are formally chosen for life.[29] Although similar commitments are much less common elsewhere, actual opposition to the re-election of national leaders is almost non-existent among most European unions. Lower level leaders and convention delegates may and often do oppose top leadership policies, but such opposition—and even successful efforts to change policies by convention vote—are rarely linked to an effort to replace the high-ranking officers.

The logic of the argument presented here is similar to that made by many foreign analysts of American stratification, who have suggested that precisely because of the antagonism to aristocratic values in the United States, upper-class Americans—as contrasted with upper-class Europeans—are more likely to be concerned with the social origins and social backgrounds of those with whom they associate at play, in clubs, in school, and so forth. Insecurity stemming from an equalitarian democracy's denial of permanent status, calls forth defensive reactions on the part of those who would preserve their positions.

The American Political System and the Union Movement

The difference between the American labor movement and those in other modern industrial countries cannot be attributed solely to the direct effect of American values on its ideology. The greater authority and power centered in the hands of American national union presidents, as compared with European leaders,[30] may also be viewed as an outgrowth of the role of the executive and of federalism in American politics.[31]

As a result of its history and size, the United States has adopted two distinct political institutions, the presidential system and the federal system. Our principal elections at the national, state, and local levels are for one man—the president, governor, or mayor. Government is largely viewed as the government of the man who holds the key executive office. His cabinet is responsible to him, not to his party nor to parliamentary colleagues. Hence there is an emphasis on personality and a relative de-emphasis of party or principles. These factors, which have become normative elements in the political sphere, undoubtedly affect the way in which other institutions, such as unions, operate.

The federal system, with its relatively strong local government institutions, has also affected the logic and organization of trade unions, since many of them are involved in various kinds of relations with the centers of political power. If political power for certain major purposes rests on the level of the municipality, this means that unions too must be able to deal with local officials. But probably at least as important as this structural parallelism is the fact that federalism and local self-government have facilitated the maintenance of strong norms of local and regional solidarity and consciousness of difference from other parts of the nation. Business power, also, is comparatively decentralized in the United States. The norms support the institutionalization of competition; this is reflected in the early passage of anti-trust laws and other legislation against unfair restraint of trade. Unions have to deal not only with local political power but with local business power as well. And business groups in various parts of the country often follow different strategies.[32]

The decentralization of authority may be related to other aspects of union behavior discussed earlier. There are fewer organizational restrictions on union militancy when authority is decentralized. National agreements require centralization of union authority and inhibit locally called strikes. Hence American union militancy may be partly a reflection of the prevalence of local agreements, which, as we have seen, may be regarded as an indirect consequence of the overreaching value system.

The militancy of American unions, which has been derived from attributes and consequences of these basic values, may in turn be one of the major factors contributing to the pattern of innovation which characterizes the economy. The editors of the London *Economist* have suggested that the historic propensity of American unions to demand "more" forces employers to find ways to resolve their dilemma by improving productivity.[33] "Thus, there is generated a constant force pushing the employer into installing more labor-saving equipment, into reducing costs in other directions."[34] European unions with their involvement in making national contracts and with their regard for the over-all needs of the polity and economy—concerns which seem in some measure to stem from their political commitments—are less inclined to make "irresponsible" demands or to insist on policies which will adversely affect a sizable part of an industry. Decentralized collective bargaining is in part an *outgrowth* of a dynamic economy in which different portions are advancing at varying rates, and in part a *cause* of that very dynamism.

Decentralization of power also facilitates corruption. Corruption in American unions and other institutions is more prevalent on the local than on the national level. Where lower level officials such as union business agents or municipal inspectors deal directly with businessmen, the possibilities of undetected corruption are much greater than they are in relations among the heads of major organizations.

Political decentralization and strong local governments, as Tocqueville noted well over a century ago, strongly reinforce the norms of individualism. Americans are encouraged to press for their objectives through individual or organized group action, not to accept their lot or to hope for remedy from an established upper class or a strong central government. Over time, of course, changes in technology and the nature of social problems have led to increasing centralization of power within government, business, and labor. But it still remains true that, on a comparative scale, American institutions remain decentralized and local units retain considerable autonomy. Hence one has here another example of interrelated supports and consequences of the dominant value system.

Within the labor movement, the emphasis on strong local organizations has, in turn, facilitated the creation of the large numbers of full-time union positions referred to earlier. Thus in its decentralization, as in its conservative politics and militant strike tactics, the American union may be viewed as an outgrowth of the American social and American value system.

Conclusion

The basic values—equality and achievement—that America acquired from its Revolutionary and Puritan origins have continued to shape American institutions. From early in their histories to the present day, many of the unique features in American institutions may be attributed to them.

Thus the American labor movement has been less class conscious and more militant than those in European countries where there is less emphasis on individual achievement and equality. Since the American emphasis has been upon individual responsibility for success or failure, the American worker has not seen himself as a member of a class. He has felt his lower status as a personal affront, while he has felt that his attempts to better himself, collectively as well as individually, were legitimate. As a result there have been pressures, unchecked by traditional deference relations between classes, to support aggressive union action.

While the principle of equality has thus extended pressures to succeed to all members of the society, regardless of class, the stress on achievement has created inequalities. The difference between the income and status of union leaders and the union rank and file is but one example of the way in which the stress on both equality and achievement may bring about institutional features that appear contradictory to one another.

The ability of American trade unionists calmly to accept such a paradox may be partially explained by the fact that labor unions, like other American associations, tend to play a specific rather than diffuse role in the lives of their members. From time to time union leaders have espoused radical class conscious ideologies, but the members generally have not followed them. Rather they have viewed the union as a means of specifically improving their wages and working conditions, rather than as a means of raising them from their generally "lowly status." These ideologies did not convince them that they were part of an underprivileged class, because they believed that, as individuals, they had as good a chance as anyone else.

The paradox of ideological conservatism and militant tactics parallels, to some extent, the paradox that American society is, at the same time, one of the most religious (moral) and one of the most secular (materialistic) societies in the world. Both paradoxes are made possible by the specificity of the role that these two institutions play in American society. Thus, both the church and the trade union are allowed to express generalizations that people do not necessarily accept because they judge religious and trade-union institutions in terms of their specific roles rather than their ideologies. But whereas, in the area of religion, this has simply meant that Americans limit the degree to which religious principles govern their daily lives, it has deeply affected the structure of the labor movement.

Democracy has divorced religion from political power, and made the organization of its Protestant sects democratic. It is antagonistic to the self-righteous concept of "the elect" in Calvinism. As such, democracy has made religious institutions an inappropriate place to satisfy the individual's ambition to succeed. On the other hand, trade unions deal with money and power, both of which provide very tangible evidence of where one stands in relation to others. In a sense, trade unions represent an organized attempt to achieve individual equality and as such they are permeated by the peculiarly American characteristic, the pressure to succeed.

Much of the behavior which we deplore in the American labor movement is the expression of the tension inherent in valuing both equality and achievement. The American trade union, like the American church, behaves in ways which often displease those whose institutional model is of European origin. True believers in one area desire militant class consciousness and honest unionism, just as, in the other, they desire devout, theologically serious religion with a high level of participation in observances. America gives them some traits which they like, combined with some which they dislike. But such contradictions are seemingly inherent in complex social structures.

NOTES

1. Leon Samson, *Towards a United Front* (New York: Farrar and Rinehart, 1933), pp. 1–90.

2. Joseph A. Schumpeter, *Capitalism, Socialism and Democracy* (New York: Harper & Bros., 1942), pp. 331–36.

3. Between 1869 and 1953 per capita annual income (standardized to 1929 prices) rose from $215 to $1,043. George J. Stigler, *Trends in Employment in the Service Industries* (Princeton, N.J.: Princeton University Press, 1956), p. 25. The gross national product increased five times from 1890 to 1950 as a result of a two-fold increase in population and a three-fold rise in labor productivity. Frederick C. Mills, *Productivity and Economic Progress* (New York: National Bureau of Economic Research, Inc., 1952), p. 2. This increase in the gross national product has, in turn, meant that the average income per consumption unit increased. In 1929, it was $4,190 per year, standardized to 1960 prices; in 1954, it was $6,730. Simon Kuznets, "Income Distribution and Changes in Consumption," in Hoke S. Simpson (ed.), *The Changing American Population* (A Report of the Arden House Conference, jointly sponsored by the Graduate School of Business, Columbia University, and the Institute of Life Insurance, 1962), p. 30.

4. David Potter, *People of Plenty* (Chicago: University of Chicago Press, 1954), p. 102.

5. For data on the greater propensity of North American and Australian unions to strike, see Arthur M. Ross and Paul T. Hartman, *Changing Patterns of Industrial Conflict* (New York: John Wiley, 1960), pp. 141–45, 161–62. See also B. C. Roberts, *Unions in America: A British View* (Princeton, N.J.: Industrial Relations Section, Princeton University, 1959), p. 95.

6. Robert W. Smuts, *European Impressions of the American Worker* (New York: King's Crown Press, 1953), pp. 26–27. On greater violence and bitterness, see also Roberts, op. cit., p. 95; Louis Adamic, *Dynamite: The Story of Class Violence in America* (New York: Viking Press, 1934); and Henry Pelling, *America and the British Left from Bright to Bevan* (New York: New York University Press, 1956), p. 79.

7. See Seymour Martin Lipset and Martin Trow, "Reference Group Theory and Trade-Union Wage Policy," in Mirra Komarovsky (ed.), *Common Frontiers of the Social Sciences* (Glencoe, Ill.: The Free Press, 1957), pp. 391–411.

8. See John Dunlop, *Wage Determination under Trade Unions* (New York: Macmillan, 1944), and *The Theory of Wage Determination* (New York: Macmillan, 1957); George Cyriax and Robert Oakeshott, *The Bargainers* (New York: Praeger, 1960), p. 170; and Melvin W. Reder, "Job Scarcity and the Nature of Union Power," *Industrial and Labor Relations Review*, 13 (1960), pp. 349–62. In a detailed

summary of research on the subject, Clark Kerr concludes that there is no evidence that collective bargaining has increased labor's share of the national income in the United States, and further that there is "no significant relationship between the degree of unionization and labor's share, industry group by industry group." See his "Trade-Unionism and Distributive Shares," *The American Economic Review, Papers and Proceedings,* 44 (1954), p. 289. An opposite conclusion is reached by Robert Ozanne, "Impact of Unions on Wage Levels and Income Distribution," *Quarterly Journal of Economics,* 73 (1959), pp. 177–96.

9. Kerr, op. cit., pp. 279–92.

10. Adolph Sturmthal (ed.), *Contemporary Collective Bargaining in Seven Countries* (Ithaca, N.Y.: Institute of International Industrial and Labor Relations, 1957), p. 335.

11. Charles A. Myers, *Industrial Relations in Sweden* (Cambridge, Mass.: Technology Press, 1951), p. 42.

12. Sturmthal (ed.), op. cit., p. 343.

13. See Alex Inkeles and Peter Rossi, "National Comparisons of Occupational Prestige," *American Journal of Sociology,* 61 (1956), p. 339. These authors compared the results of surveys completed in Japan, Great Britain, the United States, Germany, Australia, and a sample of Russian "defectors." They concluded that the rankings were roughly similar in these countries. Later studies in Brazil, the Philippines, Denmark, and the Netherlands showed similar results. For discussion and references, see S. M. Lipset and R. Bendix, *Social Mobility in Industrial Society* (Berkeley: University of California Press, 1959), pp. 14, 111.

14. S. Ossowski, "Social Mobility Brought About by Social Revolutions," *Fourth Working Conference on Social Stratification and Social Mobility* (International Sociological Association, December, 1957), p. 3.

15. "The function of skill differentials is primarily to provide incentives to embark upon careers requiring longer and arduous training." Sturmthal (ed.), op. cit., p. 340.

16. Ibid., p. 341.

17. The practice is now illegal. For a general discussion of some of these problems, see David Cole, "Union Self-Discipline and the Freedom of Individual Workers," in Michael Harrington and Paul Jacobs (eds.), *Labor in a Free Society* (Berkeley: University of California Press, 1959), pp. 88–101.

18. Myers, op. cit., p. 43.

19. Clark Kerr, "Collective Bargaining in Postwar Germany," in Sturmthal (ed.), op. cit., p. 208.

20. Luisa R. Sanseverino, "Collective Bargaining in Italy," in Sturmthal (ed.), op. cit., p. 224.

21. Sturmthal (ed.), op. cit., p. 339.

22. There has, of course, been tension between the skilled and unskilled sections of the labor movement over such issues in most coun-

tries. The point here, as in the other comparisons, is always a relative rather than an absolute one. Denmark, for example, represents an extreme case of such internecine warfare. The Laborers Union, the union of the unskilled, which contains almost 40 per cent of all organized workers in the country, has had bitter battles with the craft unions over wage systems. However, as Galenson notes, "Acceptance of socialism by Danish workers by no means eliminated or even dampened internecine strife when important economic interests were involved, but it did contribute to prevention of the breaches of labor solidarity sometimes witnessed in American rival union warfare." And in the 1930's, the Danish Federation of Labor adopted "the so-called 'solidaristic' wage policy, whereby lower paid workers were to receive extra wage concessions. . . ." Walter Galenson, *The Danish System of Labor Relations* (Cambridge, Mass.: Harvard University Press, 1952), pp. 50–57, 68, 186.

23. Skill and organized collective bargaining power do not necessarily go together. Among the less skilled groups which have powerful unions are the coal miners, the truck drivers, and the West Coast longshoremen. It may also be suggested that one further reason for widespread skill differentials in the United States has been the constant addition of immigrants, most recently Negroes and Puerto Ricans, to the lowest occupational strata. Such sources of migration may involve downward pressure on the wages of the unskilled.

24. The two unions which have established external boards to review appeals from members who feel that they have been deprived of their rights by union officers are the United Automobile Workers and the Upholsterers International Union. Both organizations are still led by men who show various signs of having retained parts of their early socialist beliefs.

25. For a more elaborate discussion of these concepts, see Lipset, *Political Man* (Garden City, N.Y.: Doubleday, 1960), pp. 383–89. In the United States, "the gap between the members' wages and the salaries of the presidents of the larger unions has increased relatively during the 1940's and 1950's. The heads of the dozen largest unions have salaries ranging from $18,000 to $60,000 a year, plus ample expense accounts and frequently other perquisites." Richard Lester, *As Unions Mature* (Princeton, N.J.: Princeton University Press, 1958), p. 27. For data on union leaders' salaries in three different periods, see C. Wright Mills, *New Men of Power* (New York: Harcourt, Brace, 1948), p. 305; Philip Taft, *Structure and Government of Labor Unions* (Cambridge, Mass.: Harvard University Press, 1954), pp. 104–10; and Harry Cohany and Irving P. Philips, *Union Constitution Provisions: Election and Tenure of International Union Officers*, 1958 (Washington: U.S. Bureau of Labor Statistics, 1958), pp. 21–24. A recent study which yields much information on the salaries of European labor leaders is Walter Galenson, *Trade Union Democracy in Western Europe* (Berkeley: University of California Press, 1961). British salaries are reported in H. A. Clegg, A. J. Killick, and Rex Adams, *Trade Union*

Officers (Cambridge, Mass.: Harvard University Press, 1961), pp. 55–60.

26. Some indication of the extent of corruption may be found in a speech by George Meany, president of the AFL-CIO, in which, discussing the revelations of the Senate Committee, he commented: "We thought we knew a few things about trade union corruption, but we didn't know the half of it, one tenth of it, or the hundredth of it." Reported in the New York *Times,* November 2, 1957, and cited in Sylvester Petro, *Power Unlimited* (New York: Ronald Press, 1959), p. 146; and in Sidney Lens, *The Crisis of American Labor* (New York: Sagamore Press, 1959), p. 105. On corruption in American unions, see also John Hutchinson, "Corruption in American Unions," *Political Quarterly,* 28 (1957), pp. 214–35; Harold Seidman, *Labor Czars— A History of Labor Racketeering* (New York: Liveright, 1938); B. C. Roberts, *Unions in America*, pp. 59–73; Petro, op. cit., especially pp. 144–81; and Lens, op. cit., pp. 70–132.

27. See Seymour Martin Lipset, Martin Trow, and James S. Coleman, *Union Democracy* (Glencoe, Ill.: The Free Press, 1956).

28. Seymour Martin Lipset, "The Political Process in Trade Unions," in Morroe Berger, Theodore Abel, and Charles Page (eds.), *Freedom and Control in Modern Society* (Princeton, N.J.: Van Nostrand, 1954), pp. 116–17. These two pages present my first efforts to suggest a relationship between societal values and variation in union structures.

29. In Great Britain, 86 of 127 general secretaries of unions have permanent status. These unions cover 74 per cent of the total membership of the T.U.C. See V. L. Allen, *Power in Trade Unions* (New York: Longmans, Green, 1954), p. 215. On Sweden, see Galenson, *The Danish System of Labor Relations,* p. 74.

30. The English labor authority B. C. Roberts has commented, "Once elected, the power of an American union president generally far exceeds that of any officer of British or Scandinavian unions." *Unions in America,* p. 36; see also Cyriax and Oakeshott, op. cit., p. 79; Walter Galenson (ed.), *Comparative Labor Movements* (New York: Prentice-Hall, 1952), p. 121; and Leo Bromwich, *Union Constitutions* (New York: Fund for the Republic, 1959), p. 38.

31. American collective bargaining "is perhaps the most decentralized in the world." Ross and Hartman, op. cit., p. 166. See also the ILO Mission Report, *The Trade Union Situation in the United States* (Geneva: ILO, 1960), pp. 24–25; Neil Chamberlain, "Collective Bargaining in the United States," in Sturmthal (ed.), op. cit., p. 259; Roberts, op. cit., p. 78; Lester, op. cit., pp. 23–26.

32. The ILO Mission points out in the conclusion of its report (p. 146): "Much has been said in this report about the different conditions for trade union activity which are found in different parts of the country. . . . The general public attitude towards trade unions may vary from one state, city or locality to another. Relations with the employers vary in the same way. The relations between the unions and

a company may not be the same in all the company's plants in different areas. Unions which are accepted in certain industries in some parts of the country may be opposed in the same industries in other parts."

33. Will Herberg, "When Social Scientists View Labor," *Commentary,* 11 (1951), p. 593.

34. Roberts, op. cit., p. 102. Sumner Slichter pointed to this phenomenon even earlier: "[T]he tendency for collective bargaining to accelerate technological discovery is undoubtedly one of its most useful effects. . . ." *The Challenge of Industrial Relations* (Ithaca, N.Y.: Cornell University Press, 1947), pp. 90–91. American union pressure to raise wages has been a major force "goading management into technical improvement and increased capital investment." Sidney Sufrin, *Union Wages and Labor's Earnings* (Syracuse, N.Y.: Syracuse University Press, 1950), p. 86; see also p. 51.

COMMENT

Gus Tyler

Why has socialism failed to take root with the American working class?

There are traditional responses: Socialism is the outgrowth of proletarian class consciousness. Such *Klassenbewusstsein* is a foreignism to the American worker because in this country the worker (*a*) had no centuries-long heritage of class (caste) struggle preceding the industrial revolution and the use of the franchise; (*b*) enjoyed an unusual upward and outward mobility that allowed him to escape his occupational class or his neighborhood; (*c*) was influenced by the lure and the openness of the frontier; (*d*) found his first *polis* in his ethnicity rather than his employment.

These factors may really boil down to Lipset's "general value scheme" of the culture that conditioned the behavior of the American unions. More specifically, the above factors determined the egalitarianism and the consequent achievement orientation of the society and its workers.

Although I (as others) am in the easy habit of rattling off these reasons that underlie the individualist rather than collectivist bent of the American, including the American worker, I should like to explore additional, if not alternative, explanations. In particular, I should like to examine the attitudes of American workers to authority, to community, and to time. I choose these three because I sense that it is a national trait to want to do your own thing, to do it with your own kind, and to enjoy it NOW!

We are anti-authoritarian: scratch an American and you will find an anarchist. The evidence? Roger Williams, Anne Hutchinson, Leisler, Bacon, the Regulators, Shays, the Whiskey Boys, the Revolution, Dorr, Thoreau, the Molly Maguires, the Hartford Convention, John Brown, secession, the Klan, frontier fighting, lynch law, vigilantism, the McNamaras, Bonnie and Clyde, O'Bannion and Torrio, Jean Lafitte, John Murrel, the way we drive our cars, and the way we cheat the IRS. Reasons? The continent was peopled by runaways from authority. And those who were running hard enough could find places here where there was no authority but a man's fist or gun. On the long frontier, authority was a *posse comitatus* which, in free translation, means a committee-to-do: a terminological contradiction.

Very few, of course, were anarchist by preachment; but many were in practice. In businesslike garb, this practice was called *laissez faire* (do your own thing). In the raw, it was called syndicalism, riot, insurrection, banditry. In either case, it was an innate, even if unspoken, disestablishmentarianism, a visceral kind of anarchism.

Somehow, anarchism and socialism are associated as revolutionary movements with similar origins and purposes. The reason is historical. Marx and Bakunin struggled over the soul and then the corpse of the First International. The movements were contemporaneous, anti-capitalist, and appealed to the same explosively discontented proletariat.

But, logically, these siblings are opposites. Anarchism is individualism carried to the extreme. Marxism is collectivism that, in its Lenin-Stalin-Mao version, is carried to the extreme. Anarchism is anti-institutional and anti-structural; Marxism envisions a cooperative commonwealth that operates on vast long-range, national, and supranational plans. Anarchism is, above all, anti-authority; Marxism assumes central authority and, in its Communist version, becomes downright authoritarian.

In *State and Revolution,* Lenin thought he had resolved the head-on collision between the anarchist and socialist views by "withering away the state" and turning the society over to all those little "soviets." It looked good in print but never worked in practice. The party took over both soviets and state and, in the process, the Russian anarchists were among the first to be snuffed out.

In the United States, the bent of the worker has been toward individualism rather than collectivism. Add militancy and violence to this individualism and the result was the IWW—the first important anarcho-syndicalist movement anywhere in the world.

The sense of Samuel Gompers, ironically, was much closer to that of the anarchists than to that of the socialists. Gompers' resistance to socioeconomic legislation at the federal level was far less an expression of political conservatism than it was a downright distrust of the state. Argued Gompers: If the state passes a minimum wage law with our approval then we have given legitimacy to the passage of a maximum wage law; if a minimum wage law is passed, the bureaucrats won't enforce it; if it is enforced, the Supreme Court will find it unconstitutional. Hence, don't trust the state. If you want something, go get it direct: strike, bargain, put it in the contract, and then enforce that law yourself. Gompers caught the spirit of the American proletarian—a spirit that in its more desperate and angry phase was the syndicalism of the IWW and in its more measured phase was the pure-and-simplism of the AFL. In neither case was it socialism.

If Americans were true anarchists, of course, the society could never have functioned. A social order implies a social contract with lawgivers who enjoy a measure of popular legitimacy. To resolve the dilemma of freedom versus organization, anarchy versus authority, Americans compromised with the concept of local autonomy. You can trust what you can see with your own eyes: a town meeting, a sheriff, a posse, a mayor; maybe even a governor. But the leviathan—the Feds, the system—was a dark, dangerous beast to be kept flabby and toothless.

The evidence: States' rights, home rule, neighborhood control, power to Bergen Avenue between Elm and Poplar. The reason? We just grew up that way. The Pilgrims were a ready-made community—hierarchy and all—transported as such in the Mayflower: their government moved from boat to rock. Those who didn't like it, lumped it: they migrated out with their congregation and set up their own little nation. Later, Mormons, Shakers, Mennonites, Amish, Litvaks, Swedes, Sicilians, Basques, and other assorted tribes set up their little subgovernments across the land in the open air and the stifling ghettos.

Other nations, too, have a history of tribal origins. But in European countries, central authorities were able to establish themselves —church, lord, or state—over centuries. In the United States several factors delayed the maturation of a central authority: lateness of settlement, colonial provincialism, westward migration, the federal form, ethnic pluralism. (When the Depression hit America in 1929, Hoover proposed to rescue the victims with "block aid.")

In the formative years of the United States, it was the conservative rather than the progressive wing of America that pushed for central authority. The Establishment in the colonies conspired to write the Constitution: the "people" resisted and forced through the Bill of Rights. It was Hamilton, not Jefferson, who wanted strong central power.

The notion that the way to solve problems was to do it on a local basis—town, city, state—had its economic counterpart in the idea that the worker could solve his problems by organizing within his occupational community, his work *polis*. Hence, American unionism was set up on a craft, trade, or industrial basis rather than on a universal class basis. Jurisdictions were marked off and possessed jealously. Contracts provided for exclusive bargaining agents. The job was the turf on which the worker would wage and win his war.

Even the exceptions to the rule proved the rule. The *theory* of the Knights of Labor, for instance, was to organize general assemblies across craft and industry lines. But, in practice, where they succeeded in being anything more than a propaganda society, they organized by trade. The Knights were also against the system of wage slavery. But what they meant was a return to self-employment or, where that was no longer possible, to producer co-ops: to the old idea of do-it-yourself, singly or collectively.

The Wobblies, like the Knights, were also going to change the system with "one-big-union." That was the theory. But, again, where they succeeded the practice was to operate on trade lines as a pure and simple trade union—with the revolution postponed sine die. At the founding convention of the Agricultural Workers Organization—the sole solid mass base the Wobblies were able to establish—they "resolved to ban speaking and soap boxing as methods of organization: delegates seemed more interested in members and dues than in propaganda and revolutionary rhetoric."[1] The union promptly "established a $2 initiation fee, high by IWW standards." The AWO organized by demanding "a better deal today—not revolution tomorrow," things like shorter hours (ten a day), a minimum wage, "good board, and clean beds with ample bedding." The working stiffs were shoved into the union: if you tried to ride the rails or live in the hobo jungles without a card (IWW) you were risking your life. At trip's end you were herded into the Wobbly hiring hall—just about the only place the farm operator could find hands. The job delegate—the key union functionary—went out in the field to organize and to enforce the contract. The size of this "burocracy" was impressive. The result was that for the first time "the IWW had ample funds," and the AWO, founded in April 1915, was able eighteen months later to report a membership of 20,000.

For the Knights and the IWW, as for the narrowly craft-minded AFL, the viable community for organizational purposes was the workplace. The "system" was, at best, an abstraction: useful for a rhetorical text but useless for an organizational base.

Up to the Great Depression, the parochial approach—solve your problem in your trade through your union at the local level—seemed to work. Despite the recurrent business cycles, the American worker was doing better than his European counterpart. This was largely due to the relative scarcity of labor in North America. (The native Indian population never was integrated into the work force as in South America.) In the skilled crafts, labor was even more scarce. These workers were in a good bargaining position. Hence, the craft unions that dominated American labor from 1890 to 1930 felt no need to question the system.

The great change in the attitude of both labor and the nation came after the Great Depression. Now the system was shaken. In the attempt to revive the economy, the *federal* government moved in with a series of social measures—minimum wages, PWA, WPA, CWA, FERA, CCC, unemployment insurance, social security, public housing, TVA, medical funding—that might easily have been lifted from the socialist platform of "immediate demands."

But in the transition to permanent political action, to build a labor force (not a party) in the United States, the unions did not abandon their traditional concern with the work *polis*. Politics did not become a substitute for but an addition to collective bargaining: hence, the unions dealt with their separate employers by direct action and with the system by the ballot.

But in dealing with the system the American unions—like the American people—go at the problem with no-nonsense Nowness. For the rank-and-file prole, the proof of the pudding is in the eating not in the rhetoric of the recipe. His expectation is that next year he will live better than this year and will be able to prove it by himself. He wants such tangible gains here and now and will use the strike *or the vote* to get them.

Contrast this insistence upon immediate advance with the attitude of a worker in a country where he knows that he is stuck in a subclass from which he cannot escape and whose circumstance has not improved very much over generations. Such a man becomes a "philosopher," tolerating the present until such time as he can overturn the system, can "grasp this sorry scheme of things," shatter it, and "remold it nearer to the heart's desire." Because the American is no chiliast, he is less inclined to think in terms of any ism. In more stratified nations, a change in the ism is the only change that counts.

These traits of American labor—distrust of authority, the decentralized approach, the pragmatic measure—are all, of course, aspects of the national culture. Each of these may also be seen as facets of Lipset's thoughts on our value system: antiauthoritarianism as an aspect of egalitarianism; decentralization as a phase of federalism; pragmatic push as part of achievement orientation. Taken together, they do, as Lipset suggests, mold not only the objectives but also the structure of the American trade unions.

In the American labor movement, there is no central authority. The AFL-CIO has no real power over its affiliates: it cannot remove leaders, negotiate contracts, compel political allegiance. It can apply moral suasion or expel. The real power of the unions is at a lower level. For a long period, the true strength was with the local union; later with the central labor council; and more recently with the national union. But through it all, the unions—despite occasional jurisdictional aggression—function within a given craft or industry. Finally, because American workers want results the unions are geared to give results, a commitment that requires solid organization and experienced leadership. Hence American unions have relatively high dues and initiation fees; they insist on union or agency shops; they prefer the checkoff; they pay their officers to do a professional job.

Lipset suggests that "decentralization" leads to corruption in American unions. I would suggest that corruption in unions, like other traits, is a derivative of the culture. More bankers than union leaders are sentenced annually for violation of trust; from my experience, business agents are less buyable than the cop on the beat. It should also be pointed out that some of the most flagrant cases of corruption in American unions—as in American business and politics—have taken place on a highly centralized level.

The violence that has characterized unions at certain times and certain places is attributed by Lipset to labor's "relatively greater emphasis on ends as contrasted with means." No doubt, this is partly true, for the ultimate test of the pragmatist is—"does it work?" But I would further suggest that violence has been in the American air from earliest times. This was a rapable land conquered by men who came with an ax in one hand and a weapon in the other. Our history reads like a running riot: white against red, black against white, poor versus rich, backwoodsman versus tidewater aristocrat, immigrant versus native, Catholic versus Protestant, cattleman versus sheepherder, North versus South, street gang versus street gang, town versus town, hippie versus hardhat. Violence, like corruption, has deep socio-historic roots.

Lipset refers—albeit in passing—to the "conservative politics" of American labor. The term "conservatism" is appropriate, in the sense we noted before, if we limit the application to the *official* position of the AFL during *the days of Gompers*. But it was not true before that period: the first labor parties in the world were set up in the United States in the late 1820s; workingmen's associations were behind Jefferson and Jackson; the Greenback-Labor Party; the Populists. Even during Gompers' days, there were highly political unions: some Socialist, some Progressive, some Farmer-Labor, and some Democrat. In the post-Gompers period—especially after the election of FDR—the unions became the mass base of the New Deal, the Fair Deal, and the New Frontier. In these latter developments, the old Marxist elements in the unions have given up some of their millennialism, most of their rhetoric, and all of their political apartheid. Simultaneously, the pure-and-simplers have become more political and are pushing for an ever expanding body of social legislation that recognizes that collective bargaining is not enough and that would have looked strongly "socialistic" to Gompers.

As a result, America—in its step-by-step non-theoretic, non-conceptual, piecemeal, decentralized, anti-authoritarian way—may be drifting toward an autochthonous brand of "mixed economy" that Karl Marx would have called "capitalism" and John Birchers called "socialism." If this is so, then labor has shaped as well as been shaped by the total culture.

NOTE

1. Melvyn Dubofsky, *We Shall Be All* (Chicago: Quadrangle Books, 1969).

REPLY

Seymour Martin Lipset

Gus Tyler's generalizations concerning aspects of American behavior which make anarchist rather than collectivist ideologies more appropriate for American working-class protest make a great deal of sense. Although he draws his examples from American working-class history, the early New Left ideology which stressed decentralization and community control may be cited as a further illustration of his thesis. There are clearly strong links between the orientations of the IWW and the early New Left, both extremely American movements. The reliance on confrontationist tactics and other forms of civil disobedience by the New Left also follows well the traditions of the American labor movement and the Wobblies. One of the most influential professorial influences on the early New Left, the historian William Appleman Williams, whose students started *Studies on the Left,* reflects this orientation in his strong preference for Herbert Hoover rather than Franklin Roosevelt as reflecting the best in the American capitalist tradition. Hoover is to be preferred since his solution for the crisis of capitalism lay not in strengthening the power of the central state, but rather in the proposal "that American capitalism should cope with its economic problems by voluntaristic but nevertheless organized cooperation within and between each major sector of the economy."[1] The ideological congruence between academic spokesmen of the extreme Left and Right may be found in an anthology of articles from *Studies on the Left*. In introducing an essay by laissez-faire economist Murray Rothbard, the New Left editors comment: "He is a free-Market conservative and individualist whose anti-imperialism and proscriptions of bureaucracy and the corporist state coincide with those of the New Left."[2]

Another early academic stimulator of the student New Left, C. Wright Mills, also exhibited a strong admiration for the competitive, free yeoman tradition of American free enterprise and decentralized politics. There is perhaps no more favorable portrait of the operation and consequences of the pre-Civil War American economy and polity than is presented by Mills. He described early-nineteenth-century America as having been an almost perfect utopia, with property widely and almost equitably distributed, with rapid and continuing social mobility, so that few remained propertyless for long, with property ownership providing security against the business cycle, and protection against tyranny.³ And Mills saw the early United States as close to a libertarian society. "Political authority, the traditional mode of social integration, became a loose framework of protection rather than a centralized engine of domination; it too was largely unseen and for long periods very slight."⁴ Mills's strong preferences for a decentralized society went along with a lifelong opposition to Stalinism, orientations which a practicing hard-line communist like Ché Guevara described as reflecting typical impractical North American naïveté.

More recently, the individualist proclivities of the American Left have been reflected in the special role played by anarchist and decentralist socialist intellectuals such as Noam Chomsky, David Dellinger, and Staughton Lynd. Such men have been influential in strengthening the anti-statist components of New Left ideology. Curiously, however, few supporters of this brand of socialism have been sharply critical of recently established authoritarian socialist regimes abroad, e.g., in North Vietnam. Thus, when reporting on life in North Vietnam, New Left visitors have largely ignored the coercive, one-party, "cult of personality" aspects of the system. These led as strong an opponent to American Vietnam policy as the French Indo-Chinese authority Jean Lacouture (who incidentally speaks Vietnamese) to describe the Hanoi regime as the most Stalinist one in the communist world. American New Left articles on North Vietnam never see fit to mention that there, as in China, Joseph Stalin remains a hero figure, that his portraits may occasionally still be seen among the sanctified images along with those of Marx, Lenin, Ho, and Mao.⁵ In restraining their criticisms they shame the precedent set by the anarchist contemporaries of the Russian Revolution such as Emma Goldman and Alexander Berkman, or by libertarian Marxist revolutionaries as Rosa Luxemburg, who vigorously denounced the authoritarian aspects of Bolshevism from the start.

Yet if the American New Left fails to criticize statism and collectivism when present in the context of a new anti-American revolution abroad, it finds a common ground with some whose penchant for individualism first led them to right-wing politics. What was once the "libertarian" faction of the Goldwater-Buckley-oriented Young Americans for Freedom has joined with the decentralizers of the New Left. Both groups have found a common ideology in their rejection of the welfare state, of the war, and of large bureaucratic organizations. Karl Hess, Senator Goldwater's main speech writer in the 1964 presidential campaign, became a "card-carrying" member of the New Left and even served as an editor of *Ramparts,* while insisting that he has not changed his political beliefs in any substantial manner. Indicative of the congruence of ideological concerns is the composition of the Board of the National Taxpayers' Union, an organization formed largely by conservatives and dedicated to "individual liberty and financial security for the American taxpayer," which actively lobbies against high taxes and the big bureaucratic welfare state. The Board not only includes eminent conservatives such as Ludwig von Mises, Henry Lazlitt, and Felix Morley, but also Noam Chomsky, Marc Raskin, the head of the New Left think tank, the Institute for Policy Studies, and co-defendant with Dr. Benjamin Spock in the Boston draft conspiracy trial, and Karl Hess.[6] A comparable lineup of leading *National Review*-type conservatives and New Left worthies could be found on the national committee of the leading organization of the late 1960s dedicated to creating a volunteer Army and abolishing conscription. In commenting on the National Taxpayers' Union, New Left columnist David Deitch has pointed up some of the sources of agreement between the ideological extremes in America.

If the decentralization of government is a key place where New Left and Old Right have touched bases, taxation, the handmaiden of big government, is the arch enemy of libertarians everywhere. . . . Its [the National Taxpayers' Union] board of directors is a left-right alliance of strange bedfellows made comfortable by a single-minded devotion to tax cutting and the social possibilities that might accrue from a less elephantine government.

. . . There is overwhelming agreement [among them] that whether known as the "corporate state" or "big government" the growth of institutions has resulted in a significant loss of freedom.

According to Deitch, the group is concerned that its tax cuts do not hurt "needy recipients such as welfare people." The solution to the problem is "a proposal for a system of tax credits for any individual or group that provides private support for welfare recipients," whether they be other individuals or incorporated communities. "The law now permits charitable contributions to be deducted from gross income, but the new proposal would make it even more attractive to make private support contributions by granting an outright cut."[7] It is difficult to realize that this proposal was made by an organization whose leaders included some of the leading left-wing radicals in America. To find anything resembling it, one must go back at least to the literature in opposition to federal welfare programs presented by the Liberty League in the 1930s.

New Left writers find to their surprise that much of what is said by extreme right-wingers exposing the interlocking activities of the Establishment forces strongly resembles their own outlook. This first became apparent on a wide scale during the 1968 presidential campaign, when many New Leftists found much to identify with in the campaign utterances of George Wallace. Clark Kissinger, a correspondent for the national New Left weekly *The Guardian,* noted his strong populist sentiments (power to the people, local control), and said Wallace by sometimes making "a comment worthy of any new leftist" has been able "to mobilize the very real force of class consciousness in America."[8] More recently William Domhoff, a young New Left faculty member at the University of California at Santa Cruz, who has written a widely used radically oriented textbook, *Who Rules America,* has recommended in a political pamphlet, *How to Commit Revolution in Corporate America,* that left-wing radical students read the *Dan Smoot Report,* as a "right-on" guide to the activities of the Establishment. Smoot, who lives in Dallas and is supported by ultra-rightist millionaire H. L. Hunt, puts out a Birchite-oriented newsweekly which in the words of another New Left writer, Charles Fager, "looks exactly like a right-wing take-off on I. F. Stone's *Bi-Weekly.*"[9] Fager also reported his surprise at the communality of the anti-Establishment views of the pro-Wallace racist Lester Maddox of Georgia and the New Left, and concluded that a man with such opinions cannot "be all bad."

The anti-statist, strongly individualist views of the New Left and

much of the extreme Right in America today offer a sharp contrast
to those of the ideological extremes in Europe. There, the fascist
Right and the communist Left have coincided in their support for
a strongly centralized government. Both extremes attack the democratic Center for its inefficiency, its inability to control the society.
Similarly, the democratic socialist Left and conservative Right have
often shared a belief in the welfare state. European conservatism
with its origins in the interests and values of aristocracy and
monarchy supported the collectivity assumptions inherent in the
noblesse oblige concept of the role of the privileged classes and
the state. Socialist and welfare-state concepts have in fact been
closer to the basic morality of aristocratic conservatism than either
is to the *laissez-faire,* rugged individualist assumptions of bourgeois Manchester liberalism. In the United States, on the other
hand, the national ethos with its emphasis on equality and liberty
has basically gloried in the image of a free decentralized society
of yeoman property holders, the one which C. Wright Mills found
so appealing. Hence, those alienated from the body politic in America, whether from the extreme Right or the extreme Left, insist
on reconstructing a society of small communities.[10]

The strong appeal of liberty, populism, and decentralization to
Americans may explain, in part, the lack of popular support for
traditional European-oriented Marxist socialist efforts. The stress
on the part of the American Socialist Party on the need to expand
the role of government, to widen public ownership on the municipal, state, and federal level, was never appealing in the American social context. Americans had rejected the all-powerful
monarchical state in 1776, and reiterated their objections to it
whenever they commemorated their Revolutionary origins. They
saw the state as an enemy of equality and liberty, not as a force
to enhance them. They would support radical populist movements
which denounced great wealth and economic power, but in the
name of widening the base of property ownership or the strength
of non-statist popular institutions, the trade unions and the co-
operatives. The long-term opposition of the AF of L to socialist
movements and its foot-dragging antagonism until the New Deal
period to various welfare state proposals may also reflect the comparative strength of individualist and decentralist values in America, as contrasted to the strong collectivity orientations of Europe.

Some readers may want to counter this argument by pointing to the obvious fact that the United States, like all other nations, has experienced a steady increase in state power, that it is committed to the welfare state, that the Populist, Progressive, Socialist, and more recently the Democratic parties have each in different ways secured electoral strength for programs which advocated a moderate or considerable enlargement of the functions and power of the central state. Yet these policies in the American context have been presented largely as a way of making the American objective of equality of opportunity, of the competitive race for success, more meaningful, as distinct from the greater stress in Europe on raising the level of the less privileged as a class.

The first party in the world to appeal to workers as a class, the Workingmen's parties of New York and other eastern states which arose in the 1820s, initiated this pattern. The New York party called attention to the fact that the children of the poor were less able to compete with those from well-to-do families because they suffered from what we, today, call cultural deprivation and secured an inadequate education. One solution they proposed was that *all* children be required to attend state boarding schools, that they be taken from their unequal family backgrounds and placed in a common total school environment.[11] This radical proposal, of course, was not stressed or widely backed, but the extension of education was at the heart of their concerns, for many believed "that a sound system of educating the young was not only the surest guarantee that society would be changed but, in itself, the central feature of the good society."[12] Awareness of the existence and electoral strength of this party helped convince Karl Marx that the workers inevitably become politically conscious of their class interests.[13] Yet this radical party, which at times sought to equalize opportunity by proposing to nationalize the children, adhered in the main to a "laissez-faire philosophy," and believed in the competitive race for economic success.[14]

The latter-day agrarian, Populist, and Progressive parties which attained considerable success as third parties between the Civil War and World War I, although advocates of increased state power and nationalization of various utilities and industries, also emphasized the preservation of private property and the extension of opportunity to succeed. They attacked the banks, the railroads, and the "trusts" for undercutting the free enterprise system. But unlike European socialist movements, or even Tory "radicals"

like Disraeli and Bismarck, they rarely stressed the need to use
state power to lift the level of those living in poverty, to transfer
wealth from the wealthy to the poor. Essentially, like the early
Workingmen's parties, they sought to protect individualism and
the opportunity to succeed as an independent entrepreneur against
the restrictions imposed by large concentrations of economic
power.

The pre-World War Socialist Party, which secured 6 per cent
of the vote in the 1912 elections and reached a membership of
over 125,000, cannot be described in the same terms as these
other movements. Whatever criticisms different ideologues may
make of its policies at any given time, there can be little doubt that
it was able to attract the support of a significant minority of Americans for a statist program. Yet Daniel Bell has pointed to a curious
characteristic of the party at its height, the attraction which "get-
rich-quick fantasies" had for its supporters.

One can find regularly in the pages of the *International Socialist
Review*—which labeled itself "the fighting magazine of the working-
class," and of which William D. Haywood was an editor—a large number of advertisements which promised quick returns through land
speculation. In the June 1912 issue, a full-page advertisement proclaimed: "DOUBLING OR TRIPLING YOUR MONEY THROUGH
CLEAN HONEST INVESTMENT." It stated (shades of Henry
George): "Getting in Ahead of the railroad and the resulting rise in
real estate values is the way thousands of people have made fortunes,
especially in Western Canada. The wise real estate buyers of yesterday are wealthy people today." And in the text following: "Lots in
Fort Fraser B.C.—destined to be the hub of the Canadian West." Nor
were these isolated instances. Similar advertisements kept appearing
in the *International Socialist Review* for many years, indicating their
"pulling power." (The cover of the January 1916 issue is a painting
of a hungry man in the snow, the inside half-page has an ad stating
that a salesman could make $300 a month selling a cream separator.)

But this type of get-rich-quick appeal was not limited to the *International Socialist Review*. It was a mania throughout the party. In
1909 the Chicago *Daily Socialist* was carrying page advertisements for
gold-mine stocks, whale-oil stocks, Florida lands, and other speculative
ventures. John M. Crook, a party official and employee of the Chicago
Daily Socialist, sold stock in a floor-surfacing machine company;
Bentall, former state secretary of the party in Illinois, promoted a flying-

machine company; Kaplan, a national executive committee member from Minnesota, had other stock schemes; these as well as Dickson's Matterhorn Goldmine and Insurance and Florida land schemes, were actively promoted by the Chicago *Daily Socialist*.

But perhaps the most spectacular promotions were those of Gaylord Wilshire, millionaire socialist and publisher of *Wilshire's Magazine*, a popular muckraking magazine of the period. After selling subscriptions to his magazine, and then common stock in it by flamboyant premiums (gold watches, pianos, etc., as prizes), Wilshire—whose name today adorns resplendent Wilshire Boulevard in Los Angeles—began the active pushing of blue-sky stocks for gold mines in British Guiana and Bishop Creek, Colorado, promising a 30 per cent dividend. The manager of the Colorado mine was Ernest Untermann, the translator of *Das Kapital* and leading socialist theoretician; various leading party officials, including a leading member of the national executive committee and a noted socialist editor, actively engaged in selling *Wilshire's Magazine* and gold-mining stock.[15]

Most recently, the "war on poverty" (a socialist slogan) initiated by the Kennedy and Johnson administrations was defined basically as an effort to enable the poor to take part in the race for success by eliminating their "personal" handicaps of low levels of education, skill, and achievement motivation. The problem was perceived not as a structural one, resultant from an absence of opportunity or an inequitable distribution of reward, but rather in terms comparable to the old Republican-conservative assumptions that the poor were in their position because they were lazy, immoral, or corrupt. The liberal Democratic alternative has been to say they are not lazy, they are undereducated or undermotivated. Thus, the war on poverty of the 1960s followed in the tradition set by the Workingmen's party of the 1820s.

The various native American radical movements such as the Populist Party, the Socialist Party, the Industrial Workers of the World (IWW), or the early New Left also emphasized in their organizational structure the American concern for individualism and local control. Unlike the European movements, which Robert Michels rightly described as highly centralized and bureaucratic, these American ones resembled the major parties in being decentralized, reflecting the federal pattern of party power being located at the local city, county, and state level, rather than at the national center. Some of the leftist movements went much further than the major groups, in part perhaps because they had less resources, in rejecting tendencies toward bureaucratization, i.e., "machines."

The factors which inhibited support for centralization and strong leadership in much of the American Left must also be added to the list of factors involved in the repeated failure of efforts to build radical movements in America. For however praiseworthy resistance to bureaucratic domination and strong personal direction may be, it would seem true that even protest movements require institutionalization and competent experienced leadership for survival and growth. The IWW failed, in part, because its anarcho-syndicalist anti-bureaucratic ideology dictated reliance on inexperienced leadership, since it required frequent turnover in office (officials could only serve for a year and received the same pay as workers in the trade). It had an unstable organization, because it refused to sign contracts with employers which would have ensured continuity of membership and of dues income.

In different ways, many of the original New Left groupings which emerged in the 1964–68 period also followed organizational practices which limited institutional stability and encouraged factionalism. The national office of SDS, for example, was little more than a mail drop which also published *New Left Notes*. Most members of local chapters did not contribute a cent to the upkeep of the national organization. Organizers, as in the case of the IWW, usually were dependent upon local contributions for a bare sustenance. The enormous funds generated by the movement largely went to support the myriad of underground newspapers and magazines, some of which, like the Los Angeles *Free Press*, the *East Village Other*, the Berkeley *Barb* and later *Tribe*, the *New York Review of Books*, and *Ramparts*, provided a considerable capital gain (or in the case of the various millionaire backers of *Ramparts*, tax loss) or good jobs. (Most, of course, yielded little income for long hours of work.) Following traditional American political practice (accepted by the Socialist Party) and movement ideology, the hundreds of papers remained the private property of their owners, who were free to adopt any political line they wish, and not infrequently to use some of the worst methods of yellow journalism, particularly pornography, to promote circulation and advertising revenue. Yet almost no one within the American New Left of the 1960s saw any incongruity or problem in these practices;

the few who argued the need to convert the chaotic movement into a revolutionary organization met with little response.

The success of the AF of L and CIO trade unions was to some considerable degree a function of their emphasis on organizational stability (strikes for union recognition, long-term contracts with dues checkoff, large, well-paid staffs). Similarly, the repeated ability of small Bolshevik groups to undermine, penetrate, and destroy anarchist, IWW, democratic socialist, and New Left groupings from 1919 to 1974 is a tribute not to their superior ideological approaches (they were usually disastrously wrong in the policies they pursued), but to their effective use of the communist "organizational weapon," a disciplined cadre who give unquestioning obedience to the directives coming from the leadership, including those which require concealment of political objectives and even of political identity in order to penetrate positions of power in various groups and institutions.[16] The American Socialist Party was undermined by such tactics used by Stalinist and Trotskyist groups. The SDS and other New Left and anti-war groups were unable to resist encroachments and take-overs from Maoists and Trotskyists. In brief, the very dedication to individualism, decentralization, weak organization, and turnover in leadership of genuine American radicals has severely hampered efforts to build radical movements.

It may be, of course, that these non-bureaucratic organizational policies are much more an effect rather than a cause of failure. Weak groups are inherently less well organized than strong ones. Yet as I read the history of American leftist movements, I remain convinced that they resisted practices which have been common on the European left in some part because of their greater commitment to the kind of American populist and Jeffersonian values reflected in the writings of a man like C. Wright Mills. There is no way to "prove" an interpretation such as this. It must remain, therefore, as another way of conceptualizing the differences between the American and European Lefts, as a suggestion of another possible component aspect of what was once known in discussions within the Comintern as "American exceptionalism."

NOTES

1. William Appleman Williams, *The Great Evasion* (Chicago: Quadrangle Books, 1964), p. 155.

2. James Weinstein and David W. Eakins (eds.), *For a New America, Essays in History and Politics from Studies on the Left, 1959–1967* (New York: Vintage Books, 1970), p. 162. Rothbard, in his article in the book "The Hoover Myth," takes a very different point of view than Williams.

3. This impression of an egalitarian Jacksonian America has been conclusively refuted by a number of detailed quantitative studies. Thus before the American Revolution, the upper 10 per cent in Boston and Philadelphia owned over half the property. By 1833, 4 per cent owned almost 60 per cent in Boston. "In the year of Andrew Jackson's election to the Presidency the wealthiest four per cent of the population of New York City . . . owned almost half the wealth. . . . By 1845 the disparities had sharply increased." For a comprehensive survey of the evidence demonstrating the patterns of intense social and economic inequality from before the Revolution to the Civil War, see Edward Pessen, "The Egalitarian Myth and the American Social Reality: Wealth, Mobility and Equality in the 'Era of the Common Man,'" *American Historical Review*, 76 (October 1971), pp. 989–1034.

4. C. Wright Mills, *White Collar* (New York: Oxford University Press, 1951), p. 10.

5. Ho's record as a devoted Stalinist who served as the Far Eastern representative of the Comintern and strongly fought the large Indochinese Trotskyist party, ultimately physically destroying it after taking power, is rarely mentioned in New Left discussions. Most histories of Vietnamese communism describe Ho's record as a Comintern agent under Stalin. As Bernard Fall noted, before World War II, Ho and the Indochinese Communist Party were "faithful to the Moscow line in its most minute aberrations." Bernard Fall, *The Two Viet-Nams* (New York: Praeger, 1963), pp. 98, 101. In reporting the negative reaction of the North Vietnamese to President Nixon's visit to Peking in February 1972, a British correspondent for the New York *Times* reported, "Posters and embroideries of Marx, Lenin, Stalin and Ho Chi Minh are displayed in windows and on street kiosks, but Mao Tse-tung . . . has disappeared." David Boulton, "A Different Salute for the President," New York *Times*, February 20, 1972, p. E1.

6. See "What's This?", *Dissent*, 18 (August 1971), p. 395.

7. David Deitch, "Libertarians Unite in Drive to Reduce Tax Burden," Boston *Globe*, April 10, 1971, p. 7.

8. Clark Kissinger, "Who Supports George and Gene?", *The Guardian*, September 21, 1968, p. 7.

9. Charles E. Fager, "Left, Right and Center with Lester Maddox," *Boston After Dark*, March 2, 1971, p. 1.

592 / SEYMOUR MARTIN LIPSET

10. I have elaborated on these basic themes with respect to analyzing American values and political traditions in comparative perspective elsewhere, particularly in *The First New Nation* (Garden City, N.Y.: Doubleday, Anchor Books, 1967) and in *Revolution and Counterrevolution* (Garden City, N.Y.: Doubleday, Anchor Books, rev. ed., 1970), particularly in Chapter 3.

11. Nathan Fine, *Labor and Farmer Parties in the United States, 1828–1928* (New York: Rand School of Social Science, 1928), pp. 13–14; Edward Pessen, *Most Uncommon Jacksonians* (Albany: State University of New York Press, 1967), pp. 183–89; Walter Hugins, *Jacksonian Democracy and the Working Class* (Stanford: Stanford University Press, 1960), pp. 13, 18–20, 132–34.

12. Pessen, *Most Uncommon Jacksonians,* op. cit., p. 185.

13. Lewis S. Feuer, *Marx and the Intellectuals* (Garden City, N.Y.: Doubleday, Anchor Books, 1969), pp. 198–209.

14. Hugins, op. cit., p. 143.

15. Daniel Bell, "The Background and Development of Marxian Socialism in the United States," in Donald D. Egbert and Stow Persons (eds.), *Socialism and American Life,* vol. 1 (Princeton: Princeton University Press, 1952), pp. 298–99.

16. Philip Selznick, *The Organizational Weapon* (New York: McGraw-Hill, 1952).

Chapter 14

AMERICAN CAPITALISM'S ECONOMIC REWARDS*

Werner Sombart

How the Worker Lives

If the American worker receives a money wage two to three times as high as that of the German, but obtains the necessaries of life at no significantly greater cost than with us [i.e., in Germany], then what does the living standard of the American worker actually consist of—what use does he make of his "surplus" income? Does he save more? Does he spend more on essentials, such as food, housing, or clothing? Or does he spend more on luxury items? For certainly these are the three possibilities which are open to him. As far as I can see—and the evidence presented here appears to confirm it—he does all three of these things, perhaps most of all the second.

Here the household budgets come into their own as the most important source. . . . For America we possess the frequently cited enquiry of the Washington Bureau [of Labor Statistics], which compiled its figures from 25,440 workers' budgets. The investigations of the Massachusetts Bureau of Labor [Statistics] in 1902, which covered 152 workers' families, serve to supplement the federal enquiry, and to act as a control on its results. The average [yearly] income of the families investigated by the Washington office was $749.50—that of the 2,567 families for which especially detailed information is available being $827.19. The comparable figures for the 152 families from Massachusetts was $863.37. [For Germany, we have] . . . the following, which I regard as the most valuable among the more recent compilations, and the most

* Taken from Section Two, Parts Four and Five, and Section Three, Parts One, Two, and Three, of Werner Sombart, *Warum gibt es in den Vereinigten Staaten keinen Sozialismus?* (Tübingen, 1906), pp. 112–42. Translated by Howard A. Fleming, Jr. Selected, edited, and revised by John H. M. Laslett.

useful for the purposes of this investigation. [Sombart here cites four German surveys of workers' budgets, the first a general survey of twenty urban and rural household budgets from a variety of areas; the second a survey of budgets in the city of Nuremberg; the third a survey of budgets drawn from seventeen rural communities near Karlsruhe; and the fourth from Berlin. For the full reference, see below.†]

Let us examine first of all how income and expenditure relate to each other in the budgets which are available for comparison, and what the chances of saving [money] are, in one case compared to another:

May [general German survey]: Out of 20 families, 5 save an average of 92 marks [$22] each.

Nuremberg [city]: 32 families have a surplus of 125 marks [$30] each on an average, 12 a deficit of 82 marks [$20] each.

Berlin [city]: 399 budgets have an average surplus of 53 marks [$13] each; 464 a deficit of 79 marks [$19] each.

Massachusetts [state]: For 96 families income exceeds expenditure on an average by $85. For nine they are in balance, so that here forty-seven [families] end up with an average deficit of $77

† 1. *How the Worker Lives: (Twenty) Urban and Rural Workers' Household Budgets* (Collected, Reported in Extracts, and with Comments by Max May, Berlin, 1897). Cited as May. The incomes vary between 647 and 1,957 marks [from $154 to $466], the average income totaling 1,222 marks [$291]. That of the big-city worker varies from 1,445 to 1,957 marks [from $344 to $466]. 2. *Household Budgets of Nuremberg Workers: A Contribution Toward Illuminating the Living Conditions of the Nuremberg Proletariat* (Edited in the Nuremberg Workers' Secretariat, Adolph Braun, ed. November 1901). Cited as Nuremberg. 3. *The Circumstances of Industrial Workers in Seventeen Rural Communities near Karlsruhe* (Presented by Dr. Fuchs, Grand Ducal Factory Inspector, Karlsruhe, 1904). Cited as Karlsruhe. The money incomes in the fourteen workers' budgets investigated vary between 1,065 and 2,285 marks [from $254 to $544]. The average totals 1,762 marks [$420]. 4. *Wage Investigations and Household Budgets of the Less Well-Off Population of Berlin in 1904* (Berlin Statistics, Issued by the Statistical Office of the City of Berlin, Professor Dr. E. Hirschberg, ed., vol. 3, Berlin, 1904). Cited as Berlin. Deals with 908 budgets, the total incomes in which averaged out at 1,751 marks each [$417]. In 221 cases the income was between 1,200 and 1,500 marks [$286 and $357]; in 303 cases, between 1,500 and 1,800 marks [$357 and $429]; in 169 cases, between 1,800 and 2,100 marks [$429 and $500]; and in 693 cases, between 1,200 and 2,100 marks [$285 and $500]. Note that the dollar equivalents for mark values are given to the nearest dollar, at the then current rate of exchange. (Ed.)

each. However, it should be noted in relation to this that two of the deficits alone total $710.85.

Washington [general U.S. survey]: 12,816 families have a surplus of $120.84 each on an average; 4,117 a deficit (averaging $65.58). The remaining 8,507 families have a balance between income and expenditure.

The Americans thus are in a somewhat more favorable position, but not as much by far as one would expect. The number of families that have something left over from their yearly income is not significantly greater than with us [i.e., in Germany]. . . . The American worker also as frequently spends everything that he takes in, and more. Therefore he must live significantly better than the German worker. And that he does so cannot be doubted. . . .

One can assume, [for example], that the American worker's dwelling has an average of four rooms each, whereas the German's does not even have two. After all, the 908 Berlin households, which more likely than not represent an above-average type, had on the average a dwelling area of about 1.4 rooms, while the 25,440 American families [of the general U.S. survey] averaged 4.67 rooms [per family] if they lived in rented houses, and 5.12 rooms if they lived in their own houses. But the interior furnishings of the dwellings are also incomparably more comfortable in America. . . . The better sort of workers' dwellings [in America] resemble those of the middle-class German: they are abundantly furnished with good beds, comfortable chairs, carpets, etc.

We can best measure the differences in *diet* if we know the amounts of food consumed and thus can compare the total consumption. The longer [American, i.e., Washington] inquiry contains useful data on this topic, and of the German investigations two, the Karlsruhe [rural] and the Nuremberg [city] ones, include at least partially comparable figures.

It should be noted that in all cases the size of the families is almost exactly the same: 5.31 members per family in America, 5.36 in Karlsruhe, and 5 in Nuremberg. I have converted the American measurements (bushels, quarts, pounds, and loaves) into kilograms in order to make them comparable to the German figures. For the food items missing no comparable figures were to be found.

On an average, a worker's family consumes yearly:

		In the U.S.	Around Karlsruhe	In Nuremberg
Black bread	kg.	113.2	582	—
White bread	"		132	—
Meat (for Germany, meat and sausage together; for the United States, fresh and salt meat, fish, and poultry together)	"	381.7	112	95 (without
Potatoes	"	376.1	647	267 sausage)
Flour	"	306.4	91	55
Butter	"	52.7	20	5.3
Other fats (for Germany, including chicken fat and edible oils; in the United States, including lard)	"	38.0	32	22.6
Cheese	"	7.2	12	—
Milk	Liters	333.2	737	—
Eggs	"	1,022.0	612	—
Sugar	kg.	120.6	31	—
Rice	"	11.3	—	5.5

According to this, the American worker eats almost three times as much meat, three times as much flour, and four times as much sugar as the German—the high consumption of flour, eggs, and sugar showing ample enjoyment of baked goods such as pies and puddings. . . . To sum it up, the diet of the American worker is much closer to that of our better-off middle-class circles than to that of our class of wage laborers: the American worker dines already, he no longer just eats.

The fact that the American worker ranks much more nearly with our bourgeois middle class than with our working class as far as standard of living is concerned is shown perhaps most clearly in his *clothing*. This strikes everyone who comes to America for the first time. Kolb, for example, noted the following: "Many [workers] even wore starched shirts there (i.e., in the bicycle factory); the collars were unbuttoned during work and the cuffs—all sewed on, without exception, by the way—were rolled back to the elbows. Then, when the whistle blew and the people peeled off their overalls, one could scarcely see that they were workers. Many used their bicycles for the ride home, and several rode off wearing elegant hats, yellow laced boots, and fashionably colored gloves—dressed fit to kill, [and they were] unskilled manual laborers with a daily wage of $1.25." And then the working women! —the "ladies," as they are generally called. Here the clothing is often downright elegant, particularly in the case of the young girls. In more than one factory I have seen working women in brightly colored, even in white silk blouses. A hat is almost never lacking on the way to the factory.

Mrs. [John] Van Vorst reports of a working girls' ball that "white gloves were compulsory," and describes the attire of the "ladies" in the restaurant where they lunch . . . as follows: "They arrived in groups, elegant in a rustle of silk skirts" (just think of that!), "under hats loaded with feathers, garlands of flowers, and a whole mountain of ornaments; with artificial flowers, kid gloves, silver sash purses, embroidered blouses, and embossed belt buckles—completely attired, with everything designed for effect."

The question arises of whether this luxury in clothing may be enumerated statistically, in order to be able to compare it, say, with that of other countries. Peter Roberts, who looks at the modern luxury of the working-class population with a petty and jaundiced eye, to be sure, nonetheless makes some very interesting observations on precisely [this question of comparative] expenditures for clothing, in his investigations into the condition of the coal miners of Pennsylvania. [According to him], while the newly arrived "Slav" woman satisfies her demand for clothing on $25 a year, the average American woman requires $50 to $60, and some up to $100 or $150. He reports as follows on the men: The "Hun" pays $5 for a suit, the "Pole" $10, and the "Lett" $15. The Anglo-Saxon pays $15 to $25, and many wear tailored suits. They [the Anglo-Saxons] never go without a collar and a tie, cuffs and a white shirt, tie pins, buttons, and a gold watch with a chain, and they are seldom without a gold ring. They pay $2 to $3 for a pair of shoes and approximately the same price for their hats. They never shop in a used clothing store. Each has a comfortable topcoat for cold weather. Many of them have two such coats: one for the early part of the year and the autumn, the other for winter. In contrast to recently arrived immigrants—and probably also to the older generation of the native-born—young America changes clothes mighty often. If a suit is somewhat worn, it is discarded. Collars and ties are changed according to the demands of fashion. Much is spent also for linen and underwear. So the average young man of native birth, married or single, must need about $40 to $50 [a year] (or 168 to 210 marks) for clothing.

These assertions are confirmed in the figures of our household budgets. [American] expenditures for clothing, both in absolute and in relative terms [i.e., relative to total income], are high throughout, and significantly higher than in Germany. The Washington [sample of] 2,567 [families] shows the following average expenditures per year:

Husband's
clothing 142 marks [$34] = 4.39% of total income
Wife's
clothing 109   "   [$26] = 3.39% "   "   "
Children's
clothing 202   "   [$48] = 6.26% "   "   "

Total
clothing 453   "   [$108] = 14.04% "   "   "

On an average, the Massachusetts families spend annually, for clothing, 456 marks [$109], i.e., 12.81% of their total income.

In contrast now, the German surveys show the following average expenditure for clothing:

Mays'
families 163 marks [$39] = 13 % of total expenditure
Karlsruhe
families 218   "   [$52] = 12.5% "   "   "
Nuremberg
families 117   "   [$28] = 8.5% "   "   "
Berlin
families 144   "   [$34] = 8.5% "   "   "

Living Standard and World View

It would be risky to attempt to demonstrate in detail the effect which such a different standard of living has upon the American worker. . . .

This much is certain, however: the American worker lives in comfortable circumstances. By and large he does not know the oppression of miserable housing. He is not driven out of his house into the saloon, because his home is not simply a "room," like that of the big-city worker in continental Europe; on the contrary, he can to a considerable degree indulge the "egotistical feelings" which a comfortable domestic life tends to develop. He is well nourished, and he does not know the miseries which necessarily result in the long run from a diet of potatoes and alcohol. He dresses like a gentleman, and the working woman like a lady, so that his outward appearance tends to make him unaware of the distance which separates him from the ruling class.

Small wonder if, in these circumstances, dissatisfaction with the existing social order is only established with difficulty in the mind of the [American] worker—particularly if his tolerable, even comfortable, standard of living appears safe over the long run. And up to this point in time [Sombart is writing in 1906 (Ed.)] he could be certain that it would remain safe. For we must never forget what steady progress, save for short periods, the "economic upswing" in the United States has made during the last two generations—during which socialism should actually have taken root—and this obviously not in spite of capitalism, but because of it.

A glance at the most general statistics is enough to dispel any doubt as to the reality of this "upswing." . . . And as the material condition of the wage worker has improved—and the increasing comfort of his way of life has enabled him to savor the corrupting effects of material wealth—so he has been impelled to love the economic system which has shaped his fate, and to adapt his spirit to the characteristic operations of the capitalist economy. He has fallen under the spell which rapid change and the increasing scale of modern production exert irresistibly on almost everybody in this wondrous age. A dose of patriotism—of the proud consciousness that the United States has led all other peoples along the high road of capitalist "progress"—has confirmed the businesslike character of his mind, and has made him into the sober, calculating, down-to-earth "businessman" that we know today. All socialist utopias have come to grief on roast beef and apple pie.

The Social Position of the Worker

I. THE DEMOCRATIC STYLE OF PUBLIC LIFE IN AMERICA

Not only is the position of the American worker in relation to the world of material goods, his standard of living, more favorable by far than that of his European counterpart. His relationship to other people and to social institutions, and his position both in society and in relation to it—in short what I would call his social position as a whole—is also advantageous compared to the situation [of his counterpart] in Europe. For him "freedom" and "equality" (not only in the legal and political sense, but also in the material and social sense) are not empty concepts, or vague dreams, as they are for the proletariat in Europe. To a great extent they are realities.

The American worker's superior social position results from his political and economic situation: namely from a radical-democratic Constitution, and from a comfortable standard of living, both of them present among rapidly developing population without a separate history, which basically consisted (and still consists) entirely of "immigrants," where the traditions of feudalism—with the exception of some southern states—are lacking. . . .

In his external appearance, the worker does not bear those signs of belonging to a separate class which almost all European workers have. In his approach, in his demeanor, and in his manner of conversation the American worker contrasts strikingly with the European worker. . . . He seems neither oppressed, nor submissive. He treats everyone as "his equal," not just in theory, but in practice. The union leader who goes to a formal banquet handles himself as well on the dance floor as any person of high rank in Germany. In addition, he wears a well-fitting dress suit, patent leather boots, and elegant linen in the latest fashion, so that here again no one can distinguish him outwardly from the President of the Republic.

Cringing and crawling before the "upper classes," which makes such an unpleasant impression in Europe, is absolutely unknown. It would never occur to any waiter, to any streetcar conductor, or to any policeman [in America] to behave any differently toward an "ordinary worker" than he would toward the governor of Pennsylvania. Being able to behave like that gives confidence to these kinds of people, especially if they belong to the poorer segment of the population, just as it does to those who are treated that way. . . .

Snobbery concerning one's social position is also probably less widespread in the United States than it is in Germany. The individual is not valued for what he *is*, still less for what his parents *were*; he is valued for what he *accomplishes*. Hence it is easy to make "work" in its abstract form into something honorable, and thereby also to treat the "worker" respectfully because of rather than in spite of the fact that he is simply a worker. As a result of this, of course, the workingman *feels* differently than his counterpart does in a country where "man" [properly so-called] first begins, if not with the baron, then with the reserve officer, the doctor, or the government official. Due to the factors described above, social distance between individual levels of the population—already smaller in reality as a result of the democratic Constitution, the general diffusion of education, and the workers' higher standard of living—becomes even smaller in the minds of the various classes than it actually is.

II. EMPLOYEES AND WORKERS

This tone of "equal treatment," to which social and public life in the United States is attuned, is also dominant within the capitalist enterprise itself. Here, too, the employer does not treat the worker as if he [the employer] were a "lord" who demands obedience, as the employer did, and still generally does, in "old" Europe, with its feudal traditions. From the beginning a purely business approach became the dominant one in dealing with wage contracts. Formal "equalization" of employers and workers did not have to be won first in a long struggle. Just as the American woman was given special consideration because she was few in numbers, so the employer of labor took care to adopt a polite, obliging attitude toward his workers—who were initially also in short supply—an attitude which naturally found strong support in the democratic atmosphere of the country. Even today, even English workers are astonished at the respectful tone which [American] employers and foremen adopt toward their workers; at the lack of restraints placed on the American worker even at his place of work; and at the "absence of what one might call annoying supervision." . . .

It is also a peculiarity of American factory owners that while on the one hand they do not introduce even the simplest safety precautions into their plants and do not worry in the least about the proper layout of their workshops—which on the contrary are often overcrowded, etc.—on the other hand they are most willing to do everything they can to provide what the workers regard as comforts, such as bathtubs, showers, lockers, and temperature controls in the workrooms, which are cooled by ventilators in the summer and heated in the winter. The English workers of the Mosely Commission could not marvel enough over this arrangement, in particular, which one finds fairly generally in American factories. "You imagine the answer of an English industrialist you asked to take such measures for the well-being of his personnel," said the iron founder Mr. Madison; and all the others were "impressed by the exceptional care taken to assure the comfort and well-being of the personnel."

Certainly these are minor things, but it is true here too that "it's the little things that count." I will try to show later that, seen objectively, in no other country in the world is the worker so exploited by capitalism as in the United States—in no other country is he "rubbed so bloody by the harness of capitalism," or works himself to death as quickly as there. But that is not the important thing when it comes to explaining the feelings of the proletariat. For the only thing which really determines these feelings is what the individual worker does or does not value, or likes or does not like for himself. And it is one of the most brilliant diplomatic feats of the American employer (just like the professional politician in his way) that he understands how to keep the worker in a contented mood in spite of all the actual exploitation, so that workers never become conscious of their actual situation. And being generous in little things has significantly contributed to that.

There is yet another circumstance which works in the same direction, and influences the worker psychologically so that he becomes not an opponent, but even an active supporter of the capitalist system. American employers understand brilliantly how to interest the worker in the success of their enterprise, how to identify his interests—up to a point at least—with their own. This is done not so much through profit sharing (although this does occur in the United States in all its various forms), but rather by means of a small, interrelated series of measures which, taken together, achieve marvelous results. In the first place, all American employers are praised—again, for example, by the people on the Mosely Commission—for not attempting to cut back on the exceptionally high wages which workers occasionally earn as a result of previously agreed-on piece rates, as European employers usually do. As a result of this liberal practice the [American] worker constantly remains in a fever of activity, and is, moreover, kept in a good mood by the possibility of *very* high gains.

A second widespread custom of the American employer is that of directly interesting the worker in technical progress by gladly entertaining every suggestion [his employees make] for improving the machinery, etc., and by letting the worker profit directly or indirectly from the suggestion if it is adopted and proves successful. Thus the organization of which the worker is a member becomes *his* plant, in the fortunes of which he has an interest. This habit of accepting "suggestions" and "complaints" from the workers and always taking them seriously is found in all branches of American industry: in steel production and in shipbuilding, in knife manufacture and in spinning, in leatherwork and in bookbinding, in paper manufacture and in the chemical or optical industry. In most factories there is a so-called "suggestion box," into which the workers put their "proposals" or "suggestions." This system is particularly well developed, like all such methods, in the well-known model works of the [National] Cash Register Co., of Dayton, Ohio. . . . Honorary diplomas and money prizes are distributed semi-annually for noteworthy suggestions. The amount of the prizes is based upon the value of the innovation, the company spending several thousand marks [at that time 4.20 = $1.00] on them annually. All the workers—over 2,000 people—are invited to a meeting for the distribution of the prizes, and the occasion is accompanied by music and speeches. In 1897, 4,000 "suggestions" were received, of which 1,078 were implemented; in 1898 2,500 more; and in 1901 2,000, of which one third were introduced into the plant either wholly or partially.

Finally, capitalists seek to attract the interest of their workers by profit-sharing schemes, through offering them stocks at advantageous rates. In this way the capitalists sometimes kill two birds with one stone. In the first place they draw the worker into the business operations of the company, awakening his lower instincts —his speculative fever, and his striving for gain—thereby attaching him to the system of production they represent. Secondly, though, this also enables them to dispose of their bad stocks, to prevent a threatened fall in prices, or perhaps to influence momentarily the stock market so as to get an extra something for themselves.

This system has been brought into widespread use by the steel trust [i.e., United States Steel]. In 1903 the company first used $2,000,000 of its profits from the previous year in order to buy 25,000 of its own preferred stock. It offered these to its 168,000 employees at $82.50 a share, payable within three years. To induce the workers to hold on to the stocks, an extra dividend of $5 per share per year was promised in the event that the stocks remained in the hands of the original purchaser for longer than five years. The offer found general approval: 48,983 shares were bought by employees of the company. . . . It is clear what at least is the temporary result of such a policy. [As one observer puts it]: "Partners in a great enterprise, the mass of petty shareholders are led more and more to consider economic questions from the employers' standpoint." "The chances of collision [with the employers] . . . will disappear . . ." [writes another observer], "when their differences are merged in a sense of common ownership. . . ." Above all, the worker is permeated with the ethos of capitalism: "The present ambition of the higher wage-earner" [writes a third observer], "seems to incline more to the pecuniary rewards of his work than to the work itself. Doubtless this tendency is due in no small measure to the fact that the wage earner is brought into constant and immediate contact with the money-making class. He sees that the value of the industry is measured chiefly by its profits. Sometimes the profit is flaunted in his face. At all times the thing most in evidence to him is money."

The Escape of the Worker into Freedom

However enticing these temptations may be . . .—and however successfully they may operate on the "weaker souls" among the workers—one may still doubt whether they would have been enough in themselves to turn the worker into the peaceful citizen he is, at almost every level, if he had not been induced in still another way to reconcile himself to the dominant economic system, or at least not to take up a hostile attitude toward it. For American capitalism, too, puts tight chains on a man; it, too, cannot wholly conceal the condition of slavery in which it holds its workers. It, too, has had periods of stagnation with all their ruinous consequences for the worker: unemployment, pressure on wages, etc. With the passage of time a spirit of opposition would almost certainly have developed at least among the best workers, had not an avenue of escape from the capitalist system—or at least from the tight circle of wage labor—been open to the leading elements among them, to those upon whom the fetters [of capitalism] had begun to chafe: to those, in other words, who were the most rebellious, defiant, and troublesome, and to those who were the most enterprising and farsighted.

With this I come to that peculiarity of the American economy which has been of the utmost significance for the development of the proletarian psyche. For there is a kernel of truth in all the chatter of the Carnegies and their clique, who want to lull the rabble to sleep by telling miraculous tales of themselves and others who began as newspaper boys and ended as billionaires: namely, that the chances of the worker rising out of his class were indeed greater than they were in "old" Europe. Anglo-Saxon purposefulness, the newness of the society and its democratic character, the smaller class barriers between employers and employees, the colonial vigor of many of the immigrants—all these and many other factors not infrequently operated to allow the ordinary worker to climb up the ladder of capitalism to the top, or almost to the top. The much greater extent of their savings—at least by European standards—enabled still other workers to become independent as *petits bourgeois,* i.e., shopkeepers, saloonkeepers, etc.

But yet another goal, bringing liberation in the fullest sense of the word, has beckoned the great mass of dissatisfied wage workers—and one which hundreds of thousands, in fact millions of workers have striven for and reached in the course of the past century, freeing them wholly from the burden of capitalism: namely, a free homestead in the unsettled West. In fact, I believe that the explanation for the peculiarly peaceful mood of the American worker lies above all in this fact, that practically any number of people of sound body could make themselves into independent farmers without—or almost without—any capital, by settling on free land. . . .

By means of the Homestead Laws of 1860 [sic] and subsequent years, every person over twenty-one years old who is a citizen, or who declares his intention of becoming one, secures the right to take possession of 80 acres of public land located between reserved railway lands, or 160 acres of public land located elsewhere, if he declares under oath that he actually intends to inhabit and cultivate the site exclusively for his own use, and not use it to bestow any advantage on anyone else, directly or indirectly. Only an insignificant fee has to be paid for this right. The right to [actual] ownership of this "homestead" is granted to the settler after five years, under certain conditions which are easily fulfilled.

It is a universally known fact, for which no proof need be given, that millions of people have settled as farmers in the United States [in this manner] during the last half century. I only cite the number of farms, as determined in each census year, in order to establish the real significance of the figures involved:

1850	1,449,073
1860	2,044,077
1870	2,659,985
1880	4,008,907
1890	4,564,641
1900	5,737,372

And these are all new farms, which have been developed on virgin soil, [shown by the fact that in] the same period of time the area of land under cultivation grew at almost the same rate as the number of farms.

1850	113,032,614 acres
1860	163,110,720
1870	183,921,099
1880	284,771,042
1890	357,616,755
1900	418,498,487

That is to say, in the two decades from 1870 to 1890 an area twice the size of the German Reich was brought under cultivation for the first time.

Americans themselves play the most prominent part in this process of new settlement. That is to say, the free land of the West is as much the goal of residents in other American states, which send their "surplus" population there, as it is of foreign immigrants, if not more so. Internal migration takes on greater dimensions in the United States than it does in any other country, and its character is totally different from the internal migration in European states. With us [i.e., in Germany] it is basically a desire to move out of predominantly agrarian areas into the cities and the industrial districts that sets the population in motion. This trend is by no means lacking in the United States now, particularly in the East, and it becomes stronger from year to year. But next to it, and far surpassing it in strength, there is an opposite movement out of the more densely settled, more industrial areas into non-populated areas with free land. . . .

But other figures, namely the statistics on the number of homesteads distributed each year, show us that these migrations are also to a large degree connected with developments in the capitalist system itself, i.e., that they indicate an escape from the nexus of capitalist organization. For we can clearly trace how the number of homesteads increases rapidly in times of economic depression, without this being explained by rising immigration. This means that it is the "industrial reserve army" which pours out of the industrial districts onto the land and settles there in these [depression] years. This applies especially to the earlier periods in which settlement was easier. Thus, for example, the number of acres given out under the Homestead Act, and since 1875 under the Timber Act as well, rose from 2,698,770 acres in 1877 to 6,288,779 and 8,026,685 in the following two years, respectively—when the industrial crisis reached its high point—while immigration was less in 1878 than in any year since 1863.

The economic depression continued throughout the 1880s. As a result immigration fell by one half, from 669,000 [immigrants] in 1882 and 789,000 in 1883, to 395,000 in 1885 and 334,000 in 1886. But despite this the number of acres given out rose from between seven and eight million at the beginning of the 1880s to over twelve million in the second half of the 1880s. In the middle of the 1880s an upheaval threatened to take place within the American working class due to the continuing depression. In Chicago and other cities anarchism raised its head and the Knights of Labor, which had originally been strongly socialistic, grew from a membership of 52,000 in 1883 to 703,000 in 1886, only to sink to almost one half of that number in 1888, when the force of the storm had been broken. [By this time] the rebellious unemployed popula-

608 / WERNER SOMBART

tion had begun to leave in ever larger numbers for the West, for the areas of *terra libera.*

The importance for the development of the proletarian psyche of the fact that American capitalism has developed in a land with enormous stretches of *terra libera* is by no means exhausted by indicating the number of settlers who have actually ceased being "servants of capitalism" over the years. In addition, one must take into account the fact that the mere awareness that at any time he *could* become an independent farmer must have given the American worker a feeling of security and ease which is foreign to the European worker. One can tolerate any unpleasant situation better if one at least lives under the illusion of being able to escape from it in the event of extreme necessity!

As a result of this, it is clear that the attitude of the proletariat toward future economic developments has of necessity become something very special: the possibility of choosing between capitalism and non-capitalism transforms every budding [movement of] opposition to the economic system from an active to a passive role, and takes the sting out of all anti-capitalist agitation.

COMMENT 1

Adolph Sturmthal

Werner Sombart's case rests, first of all, on the American worker's higher standard of living. Given the exchange rates then and now, and taking account of devaluation and revaluation, we may assert that money wages in the United States, on the average, are undoubtedly and substantially higher than in any other country. International comparisons of real wages—considering, as does Sombart, the relative prices of consumer goods bought by workers —are notoriously difficult, in view of the vast differences in consumption habits from country to country. In principle, such differences exist even within a given country, particularly one as large as the United States, containing various climatic and cultural zones. Still, in a rough estimate most observers agree that average real per capita incomes are, and were for more than a century, significantly higher in the United States than anywhere else.

This is Sombart's main argument. "Socialist utopias," he says, "have been defeated by roast beef and apple pie." As a first approximation, this proposition seems to be true enough. The attractiveness of socialist ideas is, in general, in inverse proportion to living standards. This, however, does not mean that there is a more or less straight monotonic functional relationship between the two.

In the first place, at the lower end of the income scale, the curve seems to reverse itself, flatten out, or become meaningless. At very low living standards, radicalism does not seem to flourish; lethargy prevails. Radical movements, including the early socialist and trade union organizations, have rarely been started by the lowest income group living in misery. The pioneers of such movements were either students and other members of the intelligentsia joining the cause of the workers, or skilled artisans threatened by a more modern industrial technology, or finally, men simply moved by a sense of solidarity with the poorest of the poor.

Second, the degree of inequality of the distribution of incomes can be of vital significance. Given a certain level of the per capita gross national product, the lowest-income groups may be living in misery or not, according to the degree of inequality of the distribution of the GNP. Was—or is—inequality greater in the United States than, say, in Western or Central Europe?[1] It would seem probable, although statistical evidence could hardly be conclusive, that once the social reforms of Bismarck and Lloyd George in Germany and Britain were accomplished, inequality in the United States—at least in the urban areas—was greater than in Europe. As against this, the "frontier" may have put a fairly high floor under wages in this country, even though the impact of this factor may have been less than Sombart assumed. A further complication is introduced by ethnic and racial divisions among the population. The sense of solidarity that caused intellectuals and skilled workers on the Continent and—in a different way—those in Great Britain to take the side of the uneducated and helpless poorest social groups and to organize them failed to operate with similar strength in the United States toward whichever was the most recent ethnic groups of immigrants. Hence the ease with which the skilled workers in the AFL separated themselves from the bulk of the immigrants and the blacks. We shall come back to this topic in due course.

Sombart's general proposition needs further qualification by reference to the rate of economic growth in this country as compared to that of most of Western Europe. There are two aspects to this issue. One is of lesser relevance today in a comparison between the United States and other industrial nations, but matters a good deal when we think of the newly industrializing nations. The first impact of modernization on pre-industrial nations is frequently powerful and revolutionizing. Radicalism has its strongest appeal—and meets its strongest resistance—when the pre-industrial social forms are in acute danger of being ousted. Once these early battles have been fought and the forces of modernization are victorious, the rate of economic growth—the second issue—becomes a primary factor determining the political and social climate. While the industrial revolution destroys the privileges of various social groups, it tends to advance the GNP and personal incomes after a more or less short interval. The fact that in the United States industrial output increased four times between 1870 and 1900 and again more than four times between 1900 and 1940, a period that included the Great Depression of the thirties, created that atmosphere of social optimism in which Marxian socialism had little appeal. Real wages in manufacturing in the United States rose by a yearly average of 1.6 per cent, a rate of advance that contrasted sharply with the almost total stagnation in the British workers' living standard during the quarter century before World War I,[2] and that of France during the period between 1929 and 1950 when the GNP did not grow at all. Even though the benefits of the expansion in the United States were highly unevenly distributed, economic growth was rapid and substantial enough to satisfy the bulk of the working class—by actual achievement or at least by arousing their hopes. The chances of social or economic advancement in an economy expanding in breadth as well as in depth were obviously more substantial than in the older and established countries of Western and Central Europe. Thus opportunities were available for a rapid improvement in working-class living standards without radical institutional reforms.[3]

The Role of Collective Bargaining

If rapid economic growth made rising living standards possible for large numbers of workers, the scarce labor supply in relation to land and other resources, to which Sombart refers only in passing, provided the necessary leverage for the American workers to share in prosperity. In countries with large excess labor supplies, strikes are a weapon of doubtful effectiveness for most workers; indeed, few of those lucky enough to have found a job would be willing to engage in strikes unless driven by despair. True, skilled workers may be successful in using collective action, even if total labor supply is excessive, because their skill may be rare. It is no accident that the separation of the skilled workers from the broad-based organization of the Knights of Labor occurred when it did, i.e., in a period of mass immigration of common labor which coincided with the relatively less prosperous era of the eighties and early nineties of the last century.[4] Once the unions of skilled workers had abandoned their alliance with the unskilled, the economic power which relative scarcity provided for the skilled workers became fully effective.

Collective bargaining was thus a convenient and powerful instrument to let the organized skilled workers share in prosperity. Economic expansion provided the means by which the standard of living of the workers could be raised without radical social change. In very much the same way, the long period of economic growth in Western and Central Europe following the reconstruction period after World War II, accompanied by a labor shortage unequaled in recorded European history, brought collective bargaining to the fore in countries—e.g., France—where earlier it had played only a secondary role even for skilled workers.[5]

Not every one, of course, shared equally in the results of economic progress and collective bargaining. While in the United States large numbers of semi-skilled workers, by way of the CIO, joined the organized labor movement in due course and benefited from its advance, substantial parts of the working population shared only little in economic progress. This was the case of the overwhelming majority of the blacks and Mexicans in the United States, of migratory workers in general, and of large numbers of sharecroppers and agricultural workers. Neither the great majority of the organized trade unions nor the new labor laws concerned themselves at first with the fate of these millions of workers. The gap between the more or less privileged members of the bulk of the trade unions and the poor—including the working poor—became one of the dominant features of the American social scene. On the one hand, a substantial number of workers approached the middle classes in their standard of living, though not in their style of life—in their outlook they had long before done so. On the other hand, large parts of the population continued to live on the fringes of society, separated not only from the upper and middle classes, but also from a large fraction of the working class. Indeed, the very term "working class" became meaningless, if it ever had any meaning in American society. For the gap—in standard of living, in outlook on economic and social problems, though perhaps not in cultural matters—separating the upper working class from the poor became greater than the distance between the bulk of the unionized workers and most of the middle- and higher-income groups, a tiny minority of semi-aristocrats perhaps excepted. While rapid economic growth and long-term labor shortages channeled the main effort of organized labor into collective bargaining, the "liberal"—in the European meaning of the term—industrial relations system had little to offer to a large number of people outside union ranks.

To this internal division of the working population in economic and social status corresponds the lack of class consciousness and class solidarity among American workers. Apart perhaps from brief episodes, the AFL was never a movement expressing common class interests, opposed to those of other classes in society, and it relied only infrequently upon means of action expressing a communality of interests transcending those of individual groups within the working class. Indeed, from its beginnings the AFL was a protest against, or at least a departure from, the vague social reform movement of the Knights of Labor. The craft unions defended the idea that each group best take care of itself without any ambition to change the fate of "the working class." Competitive sectional bargaining was the expression of this state of mind which corresponded to the social situation in the country. By contrast, even during the fifties and sixties of this century when vast labor shortages offered unequaled opportunities for collective bargaining successes to the European workers, interconfederal agreements, concluded by the trade union confederation and the organization of all employers, rather than individual unions and their industry counterparts, and covering all the members of all unions, were a frequent instrument of economic and social advance for French and Italian workers. While this may have been one step away from the traditional class consciousness that had contributed to working-class reliance on uniform law and administrative regulation in the past, the legacy of class solidarity was still strong enough to prevent competitive sectional advances. Occupational, industrial, and even ideological divisions were still secondary to the feeling of solidarity among organized workers. Indeed, in principle, most of these agreements covered all workers, whether unionized or not.

Lack of Class Consciousness

Most of the factors that prevented the development or at least the perpetuation of class consciousness among American workers have already been mentioned. Yet one of the fundamentals must still be added: the absence of a feudal tradition in the United States, i.e., of a social system which ordered life in all its aspects according to the social status of each individual. To rise above one's origins—

the American call to action—is the opposite of the European tradition of "living according to one's station in life," or of the "ridiculous" posture of anyone who pretends to be "better" than he is—both expressions of the ascriptive social order of feudalism. The lack of this tradition is at the root of the informal relationship between employer and workers in the United States which Sombart noticed with considerable surprise.

Further evidence for the importance of the feudal traditions (or of their absence), sometimes long after the feudal institutions themselves had withered away, is the "heroic" age of the European labor movements when they fought for political and social equality, and increased educational opportunities for the members of the working class. Class consciousness thus formed the firm basis for the growth of a socialist movement in all of its ramifications. While the struggle for equal suffrage and free secular primary school education for members of the working class was the most spectacular aspect of this movement, one should not overlook the extent to which socialist-inspired organizations endeavored to meet all the needs of their members which the existing society left unfulfilled—from education to sports and the upbringing of small children. This special class culture which the European—particularly the Continental—radical labor movements developed for their members provides a key for an understanding of the sources of strength of these movements and their appeal to the working class which Sombart unfortunately failed to discern, perhaps because in his days this subculture was still in its infancy.

In current terminology these ideas could be summarized as follows: Marx and following him Sombart put too much emphasis on the economic exploitation of the workers alone and expected the revolutionary movement to arise from increasing misery. They neglected to put equal emphasis on the exclusion of the workers from the political community. This exclusion manifested itself most clearly, though not alone, in the refusal to grant the franchise or equal franchise to the workers. This fact was as important for the appeal of revolutionary class consciousness to the workers on the Continent as the economic distress of the workers. The fact that the issue of equal suffrage was more or less settled in the United States when the modern labor movement arose and this symbol of class discrimination was eliminated made possible an early integration of the workers in the national community. Instead of class divisions, racial, ethnic, and religious issues proved of greater relevance in the consciousness of American workers. In England, too, the gradual extension of the right to vote to the workers during the nineteenth century at least weakened, if not prevented, the development of revolutionary class consciousness.[6]

In the United States social mobility, connected with the rapid economic expansion of the country, also helped prevent the development of a separate class culture. Some of the energies which in Europe found their expression in the organization and the leadership of movements of social protest and emancipation were diverted in the United States into the channels of personal advancement. Neither feudal tradition, nor a powerful sense of class solidarity, nor, finally, an overwhelming sense of scarcity of opportunity stood in the way of a search for individual success.

I am aware that the last remark is in open contradiction to Perlman's well-known theory. According to him, workers have a sense of a scarcity of opportunity, as distinguished from entrepreneurs, for whom the world is full of opportunities. There is little evidence to support this assertion unless his theory is interpreted to apply only to opportunities of a particular occupational kind, i.e., to jobs for carpenters or workers of a particular skill. In the light of technological change and of potentially competitive immigrants, the wish of the skilled trades to restrict access to their occupation is understandable. Yet mass immigration of people of foreign languages and little education provided many opportunities for the social advancement of those who had a higher level of education and were familiar with the language and the institutions of this country. Many a radical of leadership potential has ended up in the United States as a business magnate or at least a successful businessman.

It is in line with the absence of a sense of class belonging and class solidarity that labor organizations have consistently played a far smaller role in the lives of their members than in the European countries of the same period. There is little to be found in American labor of that sense of dedication, that call to achieve the millennium which animated, until fairly recently, the radical leaders of the European working class. Whether the impetus for this missionary sense came out of religious conviction, Marxian philosophy, or an anarchist sense of total rejection of what there is, few counterparts to such men as James Keir Hardie, Wilhelm

Liebknecht, Jean Jaurès, Émile Vandervelde, Anton Hueber, Hjalmar Branting can be found in the United States. And the few that did exist—Eugene Debs, Norman Thomas—rarely if ever succeeded in gaining lasting influence upon the bulk of the organized workers. Walter Reuther, who came closer to this goal than anyone else since Eugene Debs, could only do so by fitting himself within the existing structures in the very attempt to change them. Even so, he failed to achieve that leadership position to which his qualifications would have entitled him. The fact that not even John L. Lewis could "deliver the vote" of union members, while his counterparts in Europe control solid voting blocs is a measure of the more modest role which American labor organizations play in the lives of their members. Moreover, the marriage between radicalism and labor which formed the basis upon which the European socialist organizations were built was never consummated in the United States. There were a few moments when at long last an engagement seemed in sight—the nineties of the last and the thirties of this century—but in fact not even the engagement was ever formalized. And in the sixties, the role of the hardhats in combating the anti-war movement indicated the wide gap that separated at least a significant part of organized labor from the radicals.

NOTES

1. We are speaking, of course, of income after taxes and taking into account various social security measures.

2. Phelps Brown, *The Growth of British Industrial Relations* (London, 1959).

3. Except those required to make collective bargaining possible. Insofar as the latter necessitated governmental intervention to remove legal and other impediments for effective bargaining, the labor movement was compelled to rely upon the government and thus to turn toward political action. In France this involved the sit-down strikes and semi-revolutionary advent to power of the Popular Front government in 1936. In the United States the labor-supported New Deal may have appeared no less revolutionary to tradition-minded contemporaries, but in the end, both events proved evolutionary steps in the modernization of the capitalistic system in the two countries.

4. A declining branch of the Kondratieff cycle. "Less prosperous" means primarily a predominance of recession periods over boom periods. The general trend of production in the United States was of course still upward.

5. It will be noted below that even then collective bargaining largely took forms different from the sectional competitive bargaining of the Anglo-American variety.

6. Harold Wilensky, "Class, Class Consciousness, and American Workers," in William Haber (ed.), *Labor in a Changing America* (New York: Basic Books, 1966); Reinhard Bendix, "The Lower Classes and the 'Democratic Revolution,'" *Industrial Relations*, 1 (October 1961).

Iring Fetscher

A close rereading of Werner Sombart's famous book suggests that he was much less pessimistic as to the future of socialism in the United States than one would expect. At the end of his book, in fact, he forecast (wrongly as it turned out) the end of class harmony in the United States, and the coming of a strong socialist movement.[1] I think it is necessary to begin by reminding the reader of this, for Sombart's reputation—owing to his later alignment with the anti-socialist tendencies of the 1920s, and with Nazism—has by now sunk almost so low, in Europe at least, as to do him an injustice. It should also be remembered that earlier in his career he had been one of the first pro-socialist professors in imperial Germany.

I cannot and will not discuss Sombart's statistics, but assume that on the whole they are accurate. Nevertheless I think something should be said about the theoretical framework of his essay. Sombart bases his argument on three specific characteristics of American life: the political position of the worker and the two-party system; the economic situation of the worker, as compared with his position in European countries; and the social status of the worker. We are here concerned only with the economic and social aspects of his argument, which can be summarized in the following manner. First, that the economic situation of the American worker was superior to that of his European counterpart in respect of his money wages as well as in his general living conditions, particularly as to housing, food, and clothing. Second, the social position of the American worker was less clearly separated from that of the middle classes than it was in Europe, the worker being treated virtually as an equal by both entrepreneurs and business managers. And thirdly, Sombart argues that every American worker has (or at least had, in the 1890s) theoretically (and this is important for his level of consciousness) the possibility of becoming a free settler in the new territories with the help of state grants of land and public loans. According to Sombart, this permits the worker to "cease being a 'servant of capitalism.'" Leaving aside the question of whether or not the western frontier was indeed a "safety valve" for labor during this period—about which there is in America considerable academic debate[2]—I shall come back to this rather peculiar argument, which seems to assume that the settler-farmer drops out of the market society altogether, and becomes a self-supporting non-specialized farmer who thereby ceases to be a member of capitalist society.

Even though some of the statistics which Sombart gives in his general picture of the relative life-styles of the German and American worker might be criticized, I think on the whole the picture he gives is right. But it is not complete and it is therefore theoretically misleading. The principal omissions which I think should not have been made are as follows:

Sombart treats the American working class as a single unity. But in fact this has never been the case, and in the U.S.A. less so than in any other capitalist country. Not only does he not mention the Negro, but he also overlooks the importance of the constant inflow of immigrants and the marked distinctions between immigrants from different parts of Europe and Asia. These national and ethnic distinctions among the working class and their combination with specific strata within that class prevented (and still prevent to a large extent) the creation of a genuine sense of class consciousness and class solidarity. The "poor whites" psychology has many times been examined as a factor in separating the white working class from the black, but the mentality of the English, Dutch, Scandinavian, and German immigrants and the differences between these and the southern and western European immigrants have probably played a somewhat similar role. Another no less important division within the working class was the split between citizens or older immigrants on the one hand, and the most recent generation of newcomers on the other. The newcomers were not allowed to play a leading part in politics and as soon as they had become "citizens," they tended to distinguish themselves as much as they could from the next generation of newcomers "below them," as well as from the Establishment above.

Hand in hand with the integration of the immigrant into American society went his climbing (at least a few steps) up the social ladder, and this experience might well have played a role in the forming of his social consciousness as well. But it should be noted that the lack of class solidarity among workingmen has been a serious obstacle to class consciousness in England as well. In his letter to S. Meyer and A. Vogt in New York[3] of April 9, 1870, for example, Karl Marx wrote: "and what is most important: in all the industrial and commercial centers of England the working-class is now divided into two antagonistic camps: English and Irish proletarians. The average English worker hates the Irish worker as a competitor who depresses his standard of living. He feels himself compared to him [i.e., to the average Irishman] as a member of the ruling nation, and consequently becomes an instrument in the hands of his own aristocrats and capitalists against Ireland—in this way consolidating their rule over himself. He has religious, social and national prejudices against the Irish, and behaves about the same way as the poor white does towards the 'niggers' in the former slave-holding states of the American Union. The Irish 'pays him back,' with interest, in kind. He sees in the English worker someone who is both responsible for, as well as being a stupid instrument of, British dominion over Ireland."[4] So much was Marx convinced of the importance of this question that he even thought that "the decisive blow against the ruling classes in England (and this would be decisive for the labour movement all over the world) could not be made in England, but only in Ireland."[5]

A second omission in Sombart's essay is of lesser practical but of greater theoretical relevance. He writes about high wages and about the possibility of free settlement in the new western territories, but he does not comment on the close link between the two phenomena. The employers had to pay relatively high wages because the possibility of settlement—and of setting oneself up as an independent businessman, such as a small-shop keeper or a bar owner—deprived them of the benefit of an "industrial reserve army." One should perhaps add that at the time of the disappearance of the frontier American craft unions had already won such a strong bargaining position that they could—at least in times of "normal business"—maintain a high level of wages. On the other hand the very high level of wages had been (and is) a strong stimulus to mechanization and automation in industry, which gave some

American industrial products in the long run (i.e., for a period in the twentieth century) predominance on the world market. The reality of high wages was certainly due to the expansion of the American home market which allowed mass production to a much greater extent than in Europe and to the strength of American industry on the world market later on.

A third weak point in Sombart's argument has already been mentioned, namely his contention that the settlers "ceased to be servants of capitalism." I have not the statistical material on hand to prove it, but I am convinced that the settler movement not only served as a safety valve for the American proletariat but also as a means of increasing food production for the market, and of developing agricultural techniques that made food relatively cheap. It is possible that this economic consequence of increased agricultural production was—later on, when the farmers had to fight for their survival—balanced by their political influence, at least in some states. But it would be strange if increased farming should not have made for cheaper products at least in the earlier period. People coming from the cities certainly did not abandon all their habits, and it seems to me quite obvious that the new farmers from the very beginning had to produce for the market in order to get all the consumer goods they needed and were accustomed to. The necessary specialization of the farms certainly further increased this trend. As dairy farmers, crop farmers, or whatever (chicken farmers), the settlers did not "drop out" of capitalist society, but simply served it in another function, i.e., as commodity producers. It may be that in many instances their real income as new farmers did not surpass but even fell below the level which they had reached as industrial workers. The all-prevailing worship of "property" and the presumed "independence" of a "free settler" may have been a myth, but it was a myth which as such was at the same time a social reality.

A fourth point which is not completely overlooked by Sombart, but is not sufficiently stressed, is the size of American territory, with its enormously varied geographical, climatic, social, and cultural conditions. The enormous differences between—let us say Texas and New York, Montana and California—were another strong obstacle against nationwide class solidarity, an obstacle which was aggravated by the federal character of the American Constitution and of its political life.

A last point which should not have been overlooked even in 1906 is the international position of the United States. Sombart passes over the impact of the American position in Asia and Latin America, which began to be built up at the end of the nineteenth century. The role of American nationalism (jingoism) in preventing an internationalist socialist movement from developing into a powerful political force cannot easily be underestimated. (This connection could by the way be established indirectly if one looks at the combination of anti-Vietnam war feelings and growing criticism of American capitalism in the last few years. With the disappearance of pride in national achievements overseas, the possibility of radical social criticism in the United States has been opened once again.) But American imperialist policies overseas did not only have an impact on working-class ideologies (as they have up to our own day). They may also have played a role in the economic prosperity of the country, thus permitting the American entrepreneur to pay the high wages on which Sombart—in somewhat too superficial a manner—bases most of his argument.[6] This imperialistic aspect of American scenery corresponds again to the analogous phenomenon which Karl Marx earlier observed in England. In his address to the General Council of the International Workingmen's Association on January 1, 1870, Marx said: Ireland "is the only pretext the British government has for maintaining a large standing army, which—when necessary, as has been shown—can be used against British workers after having been trained in Ireland. . . ."[7] It would surely not be too difficult to find contemporary parallels to this argument now. And Marx adds: "Finally in England is repeated what we have seen in ancient Rome on a large scale. That people which enslaves another people is forging its own chains."[8] When Martin Luther King, Jr., discovered the connection between the Vietnamese war and the civil rights movement he had rediscovered—probably without knowing it—this century-old observation of Marx.

Sombart's book is—to a European reader—interesting for other reasons as well. Western European societies—above all England, West Germany, Scandinavia, the Netherlands, and Switzerland—are today in very much the same position that the U.S.A. was in in 1906. They are highly industrialized countries with objective antagonistic class structures, but they have no revolutionary socialist movement of any important size. The reason for this absence or weakness of revolutionary socialism may be to a certain extent the same as in the United States at an earlier period: a relatively high standard of living (together with social security measures which were largely absent from the United States in 1906), a new "underproletariat" in the form of foreign workers (from southern Europe above all), ethnic prejudices against these workers among the domestic proletariat, and a privileged international market position which allows for high profits and increased real wages at the same time; and finally also a growing domestic market (the European Economic Community) which may become analogous to the great American market. The differences which seemed so striking to Werner Sombart in 1906 are less prominent in our day. The problems confronting socialism are more and more the same.

NOTES

1. This assertion was not included in the excerpts translated here, but it is worth quoting: "My opinion," says Sombart, "is, however, the following: all these factors which up to now have prevented the development of socialism in the United States will soon disappear, or change into their opposite, so that in the next generation socialism has a very good chance of flourishing." *Warum gibt es in den Vereinigten Staaten keinen Sozialismus?*, pp. 141 et seq.

2. See, for example, Richard Hofstadter and Seymour M. Lipset, *Turner and the Sociology of the Frontier* (New York: Basic Books, 1968), *passim*.

3. Siegfried Meyer (about 1840 to 1872), a co-founder of the Berlin section of the International Workingmen's Association, emigrated in 1866 to the U.S.A., where he was a member of the German Communist Club in New York and one of the organizers of the American section of the IWA. August Vogt (about 1830 to about 1883), shoemaker and member of the League of Communists, participated in the revolution of 1848, emigrated in 1867 to the U.S.A., and became corresponding secretary of the International Workingmen's Association for the U.S.A.

4. Marx-Engels, *Werke*, vol. 32, pp. 668 et seq.

5. Ibid., p. 667.

6. American history—it is true—has only recently been analyzed in the light of economic imperialism. See, among others, the collection by Barton J. Bernstein, *Towards a New Past: Dissenting Essays in American History* (New York: Vintage Books, 1967).

7. Marx-Engels, *Werke*, vol. 16, p. 388.

8. Ibid., p. 389.

Chapter 15

THE ROLE OF INTELLECTUALS*

Adolph Sturmthal

In his *A Theory of the Labor Movement,* published in 1928, Selig Perlman attempted to demonstrate that "job consciousness" was labor's "home-grown philosophy" everywhere; the ideological and political elements in the European labor movement were the results of indoctrination by intellectuals. Having made a not too friendly attempt at classifying the intellectuals operating in and on the labor movement, Perlman ascribes to them the responsibility for having led labor in directions which do not correspond to the inborn trends of the workingmen, nor—it would seem—to their real interests. But, the *Theory* concludes on an optimistic note: European labor is in the process of freeing itself from intellectual leadership. It is particularly the German labor movement on which Perlman bases his main hopes for the delivery of labor from the "intellectual scourge." It was there that the trade union movement during the 1920's "delivered a critical blow to the leadership of the labor movement by the revolutionary intellectual."[1]

This raises a number of questions: Was it, indeed, the intellectual who carried the ideological and political germ into European labor's home-grown philosophy? What is the role of the intellectual in the labor movement? Does the emancipation of labor from intellectual leadership change the ideological and political character of European labor?

An attempt will be made to answer these questions in the light of the experience of the first half of this century and then to proceed to a brief examination of the present relationship between American and European labor.

* Adolph Sturmthal, "Comments on Selig Perlman's *A Theory of the Labor Movement,*" reprinted from the *Industrial and Labor Relations Review,* vol. 4, no. 4, July 1951. Copyright © 1951 by Cornell University. All rights reserved.

Perlman's Precursors

Discussions about the proper role of the intellectual in the labor movement have been frequent in European labor history. No less a man than Lenin was greatly concerned with the question. It is important to understand the circumstances which led him to examine it.

In the early 1890's the Russian Social Democratic Party consisted of small groups of intellectuals and students who had few contacts with the industrial workers; most of the workers were completely untrained in trade union methods and unfamiliar with even the most primitive forms of organized action. In the middle of the 1890's a wave of prosperity led to an upsurge of working class activity. It concerned purely economic demands, mainly for higher wages and shorter hours. This gave the social democratic organizations an opportunity to establish closer contacts with the workers. The Socialists set up "associations for the struggle," to which workers in the factories reported. On the basis of these reports the associations wrote and published leaflets denouncing the employers. These leaflets were distributed in the factories by the workers who co-operated with the associations. The associations helped to formulate the workers' demands to be addressed to the employers. When strikes broke out, the associations supported the strikers morally and intellectually. In this way the social-democratic groups succeeded in gaining influence over larger numbers of workers. The large strike movements in Moscow and St. Petersburg in 1895 and the textile workers' strikes of the following year were led by social democrats.[2]

As a result, a movement arose within the Russian Social Democratic Party which corresponded in some ways to the contemporary "revisionist" movement of Eduard Bernstein in Germany. The struggles for the economic demands of the workers took precedence over the political struggle against Czarism and capitalism. This movement was labeled "economism." Lenin was its bitterest enemy. It is undeniable, however, that it was the activity of the "economists" which first established close co-operation between the social democratic intelligentsia and the workers. In this way, industrial workers in larger numbers were for the first time exposed to the Marxian propaganda of the "associations," while the Party was given its first opportunity to leave the ivory tower of its endless debates and to enter into action.

"Economism," however, was destined to be a brief, though vital, phase in the evolution of the Russian labor movement. The great strike wave petered out at the turn of the century and political issues took first place. It was this evolution which culminated in the revolution of 1905. The Social Democratic Party changed its strategy according to the new circumstances. For this change to succeed it was essential that the influence of the "economists" be overcome. The paper *Iskra,* published by Martov and Lenin—later the leaders of the Menshevik and Bolshevik wings of the Social Democratic Party, respectively, but at this stage still united—was devoted to the struggle against the influence of the "economists." To the same task Lenin dedicated his famous pamphlet "What Is to Be Done."[3] In this work, which is very important for an understanding of the principles of Leninism, Lenin wrote: . . .

The history of all countries shows that the working class, exclusively by its own effort, is able to develop only trade-union consciousness; i.e., it may itself realize the necessity for combining in unions, for fighting against the employers, and for striving to compel the government to press necessary labor legislation, etc. The theory of Socialism, however, grew out of the philosophic, historical and economic theories that were elaborated by the educated representatives of the propertied classes, the intellectuals. According to their social status, the founders of modern scientific Socialism, Marx and Engels, themselves belonged to the bourgeois intelligentsia. Similarly, in Russia, the theoretical doctrine of Social Democracy arose quite independently of the spontaneous growth of the labor movement; it arose as a natural and inevitable outcome of the development of ideas among the revolutionary socialist intelligentsia. . . .

This statement—with one significant difference—could have been written by Professor Perlman. This is essentially the approach of the *Theory* to the problem of the relationship between the workers and the intelligentsia. The difference between the *Theory* and "What Is to Be Done" is, of course, that Lenin used the very same approach for a criticism of the "economists" which Perlman, in the same situation, would have used to support them. . . .

The Intellectuals and Labor

I have referred in footnote 3 to the discussions between Lenin and Plekhanoff regarding the role of the intellectual in the labor movement. The problem, however, is not fully understood unless one takes into account the low level of education of the workers in the early stages of the labor movement and their inherited attitude toward education, widely at variance with American attitudes.

Up to the middle and far into the second half of the nineteenth century an aristocratic view of education dominated in Europe. Its main tenets were that higher education was to be reserved to the children of the upper classes and that education for the children of the poor, if provided at all, ought to be restricted to those skills which would improve their value in work. This spirit was expressed in the famous words of Governor Berkeley of Virginia in the 1670's: "I thank God there are no free schools, and I hope we shall not have them these hundred years; for learning has brought disobedience and heresy and sects into the world."[4] While the "great educational awakening" during the period 1835–1860 brought the common school and the high school to many parts of the United States, educational progress in Europe was slow in developing. Thus in regard to France we are told that "during the eighteenth and early nineteenth century the different monarchic powers were not at all favorable to training the masses, and popular education was badly neglected. It required several revolutions in government and the establishment of a permanent republic, to break the old traditions completely, and to make it evident that universal suffrage should be accompanied by universal education."[5] Free elementary education was introduced only in 1881 and made compulsory the following year. In England, the "nationalization and universalizing of education were delayed even longer than in France," partly because "the House of Lords . . . strove to keep the poor in ignorance and to maintain the authority of the established church."[6] Compulsory attendance laws were enacted in 1876 and 1880.

Thus, at the time of the Chartist movement large parts of the British working class were still illiterate.[7] But there was gradual progress, there were substantial local differences, and some working class groups were far ahead of the great mass. Thus Lovett, writing to his fellow Chartist, Francis Place, in 1834, said: "If I now enter a mixed assembly of workingmen, I find twenty where I formerly met with one who knew anything of society, politics or government. . . ."[8] It was particularly the skilled craftsmen in London who were well educated. "Their influence gave an element of stability to the trade union movement."[9]

Needless to say, universal education was far more backward still in Belgium, Italy, Austria-Hungary, and, of course, Russia. Where —as in Prussia—universal education came at a fairly early date (1808 to 1817), it was accompanied by a class division which kept the children of the lower classes apart from those of the upper classes and reserved to the latter not only higher, but also secondary education and a whole series of privileges attached to graduation from the "reserved" schools.

What this brief survey may indicate is, in the first place, that intellectuals were, under the given conditions, indispensable for the labor movement in its first steps. Without their assistance even the list of demands to be presented to the employers might not have been drawn up in the Russian strikes of the 1890's; nor would it have been possible without their teaching for the Belgian unions to find the required number of workers who—by being able to read and write—had the legally necessary qualifications to become members of the labor courts (*conseils des prud'hommes*), since free universal compulsory education became a fact in Belgium as late as 1919.[10]

Furthermore, the aristocratic view of education has impressed the workers of Europe with a respect for higher education which has no counterpart in the United States. To be sure, there was a good deal of distrust, often enough not without justification, for the intellectual who "offered his services" to the labor movement.[11] But when it came, for instance, to elections, time and again the workers preferred to nominate members of the intelligentsia rather than workers as their candidates, or, given the choice among several candidates of the Socialist Party, voted for the intellectuals. As Michels points out: "The peculiar reluctance of the proletarian to give his vote to his equals, a reluctance which has its origin in his lack of confidence in himself, in his capacities and perhaps also in the strength of his own character has greatly contributed to cause . . . the Party of the Workers to be consistently and for a long time led almost entirely by intellectuals."[12]

From this would follow two important inferences: (1) that the influence of the intellectual on the labor movement in Europe is part and parcel of the very same legacy of feudalism which has given European labor so much of its general outlook on life; and (2) that with the progress of democracy, and particularly of democratic education, the influence of the intellectuals may be expected to diminish. Undoubtedly, this has happened, at least in the form that more and more workers and workers' children themselves turn "intellectual" and that unions develop in professional fields. Surely, the dependency of the workers on intellectuals who can read or write for them has greatly decreased, if not altogether disappeared.

But this evolution has not been accompanied by a turn of European labor away from politics and the reform ideas by which, according to Perlman, the intellectuals "corrupted" the "homegrown" philosophy of labor.[13] Indeed, . . . attempts to lead labor into new ways after World War II have failed, although by now quite clearly the influence of the intellectuals ought to be weakened as a result of the progress of working class education.

Have the intellectuals consistently led European labor into "leftist" ways? It is conceivable that on this point Perlman has been the victim of personal experience. In the United States the intellectual who has approached labor has been typically a radical who has criticized it, from a leftist point of view, as too conservative, as insufficiently ambitious, as showing only a limited interest in wider issues. Perlman's discussion of the role of the intellectuals in European labor[14] gives the impression that he judges the European intellectual in the light of his American counterpart.

The fact is, however, that in Europe intellectuals have been found at least as often on the "right" of the large mass of workers as on their "left." It is true that many trade union leaders supported the revisionists in Germany against the radicals, and even more so against the extreme left which advocated the revolutionary general strike; but many trade union leaders found themselves among the radical majority which defeated the revisionists, and the latter were quite typically led by intellectuals rather than by workers.[15] In other words: *the radical-revisionist division cut across the unions as well as the party, and the most articulate moderates were intellectuals rather than workers.* Indeed, the main trend of the discussions at the decisive Party Conference (Dresden, 1903) leaves no room for doubt that the German workers regarded the conflict as a revolt of moderate intellectuals against radical workers. The belief that the intellectuals were trying to lead the workers into "weak compromises" with capitalism has been at least as widespread in Europe as Perlman's view that intellectuals are attempting to force the workers into radical views and methods. Perlman's attempt to establish a division between the radical intellectuals and the moderate trade unionists clearly does not fit this situation. As I have attempted to show,[16] it was precisely the victory of the radical which for many years blocked the way for effective political action on the part of German labor.

Another example of the inappropriateness of Perlman's analysis as applied to European labor is his discussion of the French labor movement. Perlman's own explanation is limited to a footnote. He writes:

Working-class anarchism, like French Syndicalism, has been a clever working-class stratagem to get rid of the hegemony of the intellectual The intellectual was eliminated from the trade union movement in the name of the very revolutionary class-consciousness which he himself had helped to evoke in labor. But observe how naturally the Confédération Génerale du Travail had slipped during the War into a position of opportunistic unionism. On the whole, the disappointing weakness of French unionism after 1921 exposing a deplorable instability in the movement, goes back to its constant absorption in mere matters of abstract ideology—syndicalism, reformist socialism and communism—largely the result of an earlier indoctrination, directly and indirectly, by intellectuals. Lacking a safe psychic anchorage in a body of "job control" practices, the French labor movement has proved an easy plaything for the gusts of wind blowing from Soviet Russia, until the frail bark has been broken on the rocks of an exceptionally entrenched capitalism.[17]

The phenomenon to be explained is the fact that the most anti-intellectual labor movement of Europe has been far more absorbed by ideological issues than e.g., the labor movements of Germany and Britain, both of which are Perlman's own examples for movements "infected" by intellectual leadership. By any yardstick the French unions have been (and continue to be) more interested in discussions of social philosophies than their far more practical brethren in Great Britain or Germany.[18] But to attempt to explain this by the intellectual influence to which the movement was exposed in the 1880's and 1890's, while intellectuals have been at work in the far more practical British and German movements up to this day, is obviously difficult. Perlman's thesis would lead us to expect that the British and the German unions are the most "ideological," the French the most "practical"; in actual fact, the situation is the exact reverse.[19]

In a certain sense Perlman's thesis might be compared with the theory underlying the War Labor Disputes Act of 1943, which provided that no strike could be called in an industry producing war materials until after the NLRB had taken a secret vote of the union members. The theory behind this was "that the policies of union leaders do not represent the wishes of the rank and file union members."[20] But for the union leaders, the workers would be reasonable and modest. Everyone knows that "the result in almost every case was an overwhelming majority vote in favor of a strike."[21] In somewhat the same way Perlman believes that "the intellectuals" have smuggled ideology as contraband into a labor movement which otherwise would have been eminently "practical" and merely job-conscious. The evidence contradicts this thesis as powerfully as the strike votes during the war were in opposition to the assumptions underlying the War Labor Disputes Act. Thus I doubt whether it could be shown that the demand for the nationalization of industry has been imposed upon the British and French workers by the intellectuals; indeed, in a few specific cases the exactly opposite view could be more readily defended. Similarly the demand for workers' control of industry in France has had its chief protagonists in the unions, while the intellectuals in the Socialist Party reluctantly accepted and modified what they regarded as inevitable.[22] It is quite true that one of the powerful forces behind these demands was the workers' belief—whether an illusion or not—that the attainment of these objectives would be followed by higher wages and better working conditions. But this was, according to all accounts, not the only motivating force, nor can we disregard the "political" and ideological character of the demand itself. It may well be that it was "bad" for the workers to embark upon these policies or that they fail ultimately to implement them; but this is immaterial in our context. What matters is that these demands were carried forward by the workers, often against the doubts of the intellectuals.

NOTES

1. *A Theory of the Labor Movement* (New York, 1949), p. 303.
2. See Isaac Deutscher, *Soviet Trade Unions: Their Place in Soviet Labor Policy* (London; New York, 1950), pp. 2–8. Otto Bauer, *Die illegale Partei* (Paris, 1939), *passim*.
3. Lenin, *Collected Works*, 1929, vol. IV. The following quotation is on p. 114. Part of this is quoted by Perlman himself (p. 8, note) but not the subsequent Lenin-Plekhanoff discussion.
4. F. P. Graves, *A History of Education in Modern Times* (New York, 1928), p. 84.
5. Ibid., p. 292.
6. Ibid., pp. 301–2.
7. "Of a group who were tried in connection with a Chartist outbreak in the manufacturing districts, a large proportion could scarcely read or write." A. E. Dobbs, *Education and Social Movements* 1700–1850 (London, 1919), p. 213.
8. Quoted by Dobbs, op. cit., p. 215.
9. Ibid., p. 216. "Elementary education was aimed not at producing democratic citizens but at fitting the ordinary people for the state in life to which they were called, whereas secondary education was conceived as fitting the potential rulers of the nation to take their rightful places in the state, church, or business world. Whenever American education is compared with European education, this essential difference in social structure and purpose of education should be taken into account." R. Freeman Butts, *A Cultural History of Education* (New York and London, 1947), p. 422. "Whereas most European countries maintained a dual system of schools frankly designed to separate the upper classes from the lower classes, the United States launched a democratic system designed to provide equality of opportunity for everyone to go as far upward as his talents and abilities would take him." Ibid., p. 486.
10. The law was passed in 1913, but implemented only after World War I. I have known personally a senator of Belgium who, for the reason stated above, learned how to read and write as an adult in a school run by the unions.
11. After Lassalle's death his followers, in their struggle against the rival Eisenacher group, boasted that they did not accept intellectuals as members, and above all not Jews. R. Meyer, *Der Emancipationskampf des vierten Standes in Deutschland*" (Berlin, 1874), p. 57. The Workers' Party of Milan declared in its Manifesto of May 17, 1882, that it accepted only manual workers as members; by 1890, however, it welcomed in fact the affiliation of intellectuals. Robert Michels, *Political Parties* (New York, 1915), p. 266.
12. Michels, op. cit., p. 311. This book contains (pp. 87ff.) significant statistics about the proportions of intellectuals in the parliamentary

group of Socialist parties of a number of European countries between 1903 and 1905.

13. This overstates Perlman's case, but only very little. In his contribution to H. A. Marquand's *Organized Labor in Four Continents* (Longmans: New York, Toronto, 1939) Perlman regretfully speaks of American labor's lack of "class consciousness"; and in his *Theory* (p. 33) he asscribes to the intellectual the virtue of having left "upon the labor movement an indelible imprint of idealism and of an unquestioned solidarity . . . which has survived, to the great advantage of the movement." But these are exceptions in a long list of "sins" enumerated by Perlman.

14. *Theory,* pp. 280–303.

15. Charles A. Gulick, *Austria from Habsburg to Hitler,* vol. I: *Labor's Workshop of Democracy* (Berkeley and Los Angeles, 1948), pp. 293–308.

16. In my *The Tragedy of European Labor 1918–1939* (New York, 1943), pp. 18ff.

17. *Theory,* pp. 288–89, note.

18. As one piece of evidence among many: At the founding congress of C.G.T.–F.O. in April 1948 the recorded votes, by name and organization, concerned the following four issues: Preamble of the Statutes, structure of organization, name of organization, affiliation (or disaffiliation) with the World Federation of Trade Unions. None of the votes on labor issues in the accepted meaning of the term was found worthy of being recorded. Of 142 pages of the printed report on the congress proceedings roughly 25 are devoted to labor problems, 117 to "philosophical" questions. This seems to have upset even some of the delegates, for Albert Thomas, delegate of the metal workers of the Paris region, complained: "We hoped that in a trade union congress, the direction the union is to take, the purchasing power of the workers would interest the Congress at least as much as the conflict between two currents about the name of our Confederation. Well, I have discovered . . . that the Congress listened with attention when the 'stars' engaged in speech-making; everyone hung on their lips; but since we started talking about the purchasing power of the worker, the room has become almost empty and our comrades carry on little conversations aside. . . ."

19. An attempt to offer an alternative explanation would clearly far exceed the limits set to this essay, but as a working hypothesis the idea might be put forth that the problem might be connected with the traditional weakness of French unions. This in turn might well be related to the arrested economic development of the country, the relative weakness of its capitalistic spirit, the survival of feudal concepts, etc.; in other words, to national behavior patterns.

20. Lloyd G. Reynolds, *Labor Economics and Labor Relations* (New York, 1949), p. 268.

21. Ibid.

22. Perlman's statement (*Theory,* pp. 246–47) apparently refers to British experience. It surely does not apply to France.

COMMENT

Paul Buhle

The theoretical underpinning of Selig Perlman's *Theory of the Labor Movement* was, as Adolph Sturmthal perceptively noted, polemically misposed. Perlman believed that, in setting out a conception of worker "job consciousness" dominating over political concerns, he was implicitly denying the conclusions of Lenin's *What Is to Be Done?*, the foremost revolutionary political statement of the period. In fact, Perlman had merely agreed with Lenin that workers left to themselves would not create a revolution, and that therefore intellectuals would necessarily have to introduce socialist consciousness "from the outside." Sturmthal might have added that Lenin's view was by no means unique or philosophically original. In the words of situationist theoretician Guy Debord, Lenin was in this respect "a faithful and consistent Kautskyist who applied the revolutionary ideology of this 'orthodox Marxism' to Russian conditions, conditions which did not allow the reformist practice of the Second International."[1] Perlman had, in effect, taken on the central premises of the Second and Third Internationals' "orthodox Marxist" theory and practice. The larger theses of *Theory of the Labor Movement* reveal a similar impreciseness when measured against the subsequent historical experience of working-class movements. In Perlman's view, a matured working class would refuse to be led off to ideological utopias by left-wing intellectuals and politicians. Certainly, Perlman has in this narrow sense been vindicated: in recent decades there has been a widespread disaffection among the Western working classes toward the "parties of labor," self-avowedly revolutionary or reformist. However, what Perlman's central prophecy gains in form, it loses in content, for in throwing off the "ideologists" the workers have not returned to the passivity of mere wages-and-hours bargaining. Rather, while party and union bureaucracies have sought to limit the industrial struggle to wages and hours, workers have frequently demanded changes in the work process itself and occasionally—as in the case of many workers during the May–June 1968 events in France—striven for the transformation of the economic system.² Between the working class and the powers who own the machines of production, no new stratum of successful reform politicians or "social-minded" labor leaders of note has arisen. Indeed, Sturmthal's cautious prediction of reformers rising out of labor, such as Walter Reuther or James Carey in the United States, has proved as illusory as Perlman's view of worker pacification. In truth, no economic or political force—above all in the United States—can claim to represent authentically the newer campfires of industrial militancy, whether in the traditional sectors of labor action (e.g., auto) or those most novel (e.g., postal service).

Thus the predictions of Marxist and anti-Marxist observers a half century ago as to the future course of labor have been proved inadequate. Specifically, the relationship which Leftists hoped would be established between intellectuals and workers has been least prophetic. Within the United States (as compared to Europe), such a relationship has not even a past. The influence of intellectuals has, indeed, at all points been so slight as to be virtually irrelevant to the main course of labor, and insignificant to radicals save in what they choose to believe about their movements' future in guiding the working class. In part, the socialists and communists have denied this reality, or chosen to explain it as a result of the (always "temporary") power of conservative "misleaders" over the ranks of labor. In part, labor's anti-intellectualism has been internalized by the Left and constitutes a major peculiarity of the American radical movement. More than in any European counterpart, American radicals deeply mistrust the expense of time and energies for the reproduction of mere ideas. Similarly, those few exceptional Leftists who as individuals influenced the labor movement from within were more commonly than in other nations openly indifferent to ideological fineries. Even in the short-lived overtly revolutionary wing of American labor, the IWW, politicians and ideologues were suspect where not actually objects of derision.

There have been interrelationships between Left "intellectuals" and labor, and these are worth some detailed consideration. One cannot successfully find clues to the real nature of the implications for both forces, however, in framing the question as instrumentally as Perlman or even Sturmthal. Rather, it is necessary to assess the ways in which the transformation of the labor movement, particularly in the early period of American radicalism, shaped the role of the intellectuals and established the limitations of the formal Marxist movements.

As is well known, the American labor movement emerged in the late nineteenth century as a preeminently "practical" (i.e., nonsocialist) stratum of the working class, removed by skills and to some extent ethnicity from the bulk of workers. External "intellectuals" from the Socialist Labor Party exerted a certain influence upon the collapse of the Knights of Labor and the rise of the American Federation of Labor, but were in no sense decisive to the course of either organization. The case of Daniel De Leon in regard to both has been central to the historical discussion of the intellectuals' role, and has been sufficiently studied that we may draw general conclusions as to the meaning of his efforts.

From his entry into the socialist movement in 1890 until well after the turn of the century, De Leon saw the union as an essentially defensive institution which could *at best* provide socialist indoctrination for workers stripped of their livelihood by the collapse of the capitalist system. With the support of the more politically oriented socialists, De Leon set out to free the workers from the "Labor Fakirs." De Leon's influence manifested itself first nationally with the *coup de grâce* to the faltering Knights at the 1895 convention, where the leadership denied De Leon a seat and the SLP concessions previously promised. Utilizing the socialist forces withdrawn from the hapless labor organization, De Leon sought in 1895 to create an alternative organization to the American Federation of Labor, where socialist influence had also been turned back. De Leon's efforts proved however to be in vain, and by the late 1890s even the leaders of the SLP's pet Socialist Trade and Labor Alliance were denounced by De Leon as crooks and fakirs. De Leon gained real influence within the labor movement only by reversing his tactical position, in assuming and then brilliantly elucidating a quasi-syndicalist position toward unions, in which political organization was to serve only as an educational arm of the revolutionary struggle. Despite the temporary influence he achieved within the IWW, De Leon was doomed again by the indifference of the labor movement toward political chimeras.[3] At the end of his life, De Leon found himself the leader of a mere propaganda sect, frustrated at every point from gaining real influence upon the working class.

The principles De Leon espoused for the IWW were later to be partially vindicated, with the formation of industrial unions. But in a different way than Perlman, De Leon saw only half the truth, for the SLP's revered "socialist industrial unionism" was never to be and the direct influence of De Leon's ideas assumed practical form only where forms of leadership were immediately lacking (as in the first days of the Paterson, New Jersey, strikes of 1912) or where De Leonists functioned essentially like other radical trade unionists (as with some Pennsylvania furniture workers in the late 1930s).[4]

De Leon was indeed prophetic in his understanding that the ascendance of "state socialism" (the ideology of the stratum from the middle class or the skilled working class who saw in the growth of the state a solution to all social problems) within the radical movement would not draw the mass of workers into political struggles. His final alternative, the reshaping of radical forces from below (at the industrial level), was at least a plausible solution for the inability of socialists to organize within the new work force of foreign-speaking immigrants during the Progressive period. Yet at the point of his clearest expression of revolutionary strategy, De Leon pointed toward a theory in which all "outside" forces *including his own SLP* were growingly obsolescent if not already unnecessary.[5] Here the great contradiction of socialist intellectuals was forcefully exposed: the more one sought in objective class forces the actual liberation of workers, the more the intellectual's role seemed relegated to observer or at best respected adviser on the great events of the time.

Mainstream socialists who determined to play a reformist role in the day-to-day life of the working class scarcely escaped this dilemma. Two counterparts to De Leon will serve as an illustration of the opposite side of the contradiction: Max Hayes, editor of the Cleveland *Citizen;* and Victor Berger, "architect of victory" for Milwaukee municipal socialism, power in the local Federated Trades Council, and key ideologist for the Milwaukee *Leader.* Neither of these men qualifies as an "intellectual" in the sense of European theoreticians or even in the sense of De Leon. Hayes and Berger neither wrote nor translated books, nor even used the newspapers they influenced to further Marxist theory. On the contrary, they were commonly regarded among local workers and political activists as they saw themselves, eminently practical men operating within the historical framework of "material determinism" (in Hayes's phrase) toward the achievement of socialist society.

Hayes influenced the labor movement and thereby American socialism in a number of diverse ways. As editor of the *Citizen,* socialist-oriented organ of the Cleveland Central Labor Council, Hayes offered shrewd pronouncements on the political events around the nation and world through the editorial columns. His role during the 1890s was especially important, for he diligently sought to separate the potential working-class socialist movement from the stream of patrician reform organizations and causes that appeared on the scene. Unlike De Leon, Hayes saw no distinction between the immediate needs of the city's skilled workers and the long-run interests of the socialist movement. Hayes remained therefore an "AFL socialist," bitterly denouncing the IWW as "De Leon-dominated" splitters of labor unity. Yet Hayes was not in any simple sense the opportunist De Leon believed him to be: within the AFL, Hayes bitterly decried Gompers' pure-and-simple leadership of the organization and ran for president against the old leader. In later years Hayes left the Socialist Party because of his support of World War I, but returned to radical ranks in principled fashion as candidate for vice-president on the Farmer-Labor ticket in 1920.[6]

Hayes like Berger was prone to see his efforts within the labor movement on two levels. As a good trade unionist, he provided leadership and advice in a day-to-day fashion; and as a socialist, he offered educational opportunities to the most politically advanced workers. Berger elevated this approach to the level of pedestrian theory, conceptualizing a "two-armed labor movement" (one arm organized labor, the other arm socialist-political), the limbs of which were for some reason not coordinated systematically but acted in a merely fraternal manner toward each other. Inevitably, therefore, Hayes like Berger provided himself with a role which was self-limiting: a socialist ideologue could advise or even plead, but he could not direct trade unionist energies toward the capture of the political state. Since Hayes and Berger believed in capitalism's imminent economic decline, they perceived no conflict between their interests. But given American economic prosperity and the relative well-being of the AFL unions, this policy was bound to produce a split between political-ideological ethics and the harsh realities of labor stability.

Berger was never directly dependent upon his position within labor organizations, although labor support was indispensable for the Milwaukee Social Democratic political machine and its daily paper, the *Leader*. Berger's avowed opposition to World War I and the extensive opposition conducted by the Socialist Party for an early peace had an oddly liberating effect upon Berger, even as it destroyed for the last time his hopes to effect a coalition to overturn Gompers' AFL leadership. By 1920 Berger looked to the creation of some force similar to the IWW which could gather the unorganized workers including blacks and recent immigrants.[7] Berger could not, however, provide a socialist political strategy to embrace such workers, and in any case, after having defended the industrial conservatism of the AFL for so long, his reconsideration was mere sentiment.

Hayes's and Berger's relationship to the AFL had all the while been dominated by a *merely* political opposition toward Gompers. Advanced in their own eyes, the AFL socialists were for the most part socially conservative, suspicious of new ideas and new directions for socialist agitation. The major effect of Berger's and Hayes's efforts within the socialist movement was to reinforce the archaism of the party's class perspectives when it had entered into a crucial period for growth or decay. While the industrial proletariat became an increasingly foreign-speaking group born in eastern and southern Europe, the two defended and praised the characteristics of the "real American worker" (of previous migrations), the old-style skilled craftsman who was losing his central role within industry. At best, these men had thrown their considerable energies into developing a solid basis of working-class support for socialism within their communities, and had made at least persistent efforts to spread socialist doctrines throughout the AFL. At worst, Hayes and Berger failed to confront the changing realities of American labor which would render their political strategy shortsighted and their anti-immigrationist, racist bias suicidal for the future of the Left. Unlike De Leon, who had foregone substantive relationships with workers for the sake of a dreamed future, Hayes and Berger gave up the potentialities of the future for the sake of a working-class stratum moving into the past.[8]

The transformation of labor after the Debsian period did nothing to alter intellectuals' most fundamental dilemmas. Individual left-wingers learned that in order to be effective, they had to work in conjunction with the AFL, but that the very operation of that organization drastically limited their potentialities as radical leaders —thus William Z. Foster in the steel strike of 1919, or such lesser figures as A. J. Muste and Louis Budenz of the Brookwood Labor College and the Committee for Progressive Labor Action, ultimately renounced direct linkage to organized workers in order to speak more openly of revolution to the working class. When the CIO arose in the mid-1930s, in response to widespread spontaneous strikes and the opportunities presented by the Wagner Act, Leftists of all sorts rose to union leadership positions. But their predominance was neither gained nor maintained by the strength of a revolutionary political position; rather, they found their efforts frequently (and by the 1940s, often intolerably) dichotomized between "practical" and "political" work. Few ever derived a public formula so simplistic as Berger's "two-armed labor movement," but in practice their efforts remained essentially segregated.[9]

The outcome of the "Red decade" was different than the early period of socialist strength, insofar as labor had surged ahead to industrial organization while Left politics was effectively controlled and directed through the vacillating "line" of the Communist Party. Communists found themselves by dint of hard work and organizational skills near top levels of major CIO unions. Yet when postwar prosperity emerged, radicals of every variety faced the same predicament as socialists a generation or so earlier: they had gambled that capitalism would finally grind to a halt, and that workers would inevitably turn to their friends and guides for the opening political struggle. As American capitalism survived, strengthened— indeed, with a world empire in its grasp—and workers continued to turn away from Left political faiths, radicals again found that their economic and political chores could not be reconciled. They could become able functionaries with little or no political strength; or they could fight rearguard actions against political isolation, and hope for the best. The choice was in any case Hobbesian, for *as radicals* they were bound to lose either way.

Moreover, it should be noted that socialist and communist functionaries of the 1930s were if anything less classical "outside" intellectuals than the Debsian writers and organizers. Rather than being alien to the working class by virtue of their Marxism, they were frequently so close to their origins that political leaders were distressed. Particularly interesting in this regard is the case of the Minneapolis Trotskyists, who by their very persuasion were not as susceptible to charges of personal "opportunism" as communists or socialists. Half a decade after their leadership of the famous Minneapolis general strike, the Trotskyist militants fell under the criticism of Trotsky for their unquestionably sincere adaptation to the "progressive" wing of the Teamster hierarchy.[10] Even the most revolutionary European political formulas could not prevent radicals from succumbing to American reality. Similarly in the case of the communists, the hundreds of young people who left college as "intellectuals" to enter the trade unions did not emerge as leading figures in the left-wing unions. Rather, communists gained leadership where they discovered amenable figures from the rank and file, who for shorter or longer periods cooperated with party strategies.[11] The control of these strategies from the party itself through the "mass leaders" (of unions or political organizations) was so tenuous that in the waves of post-war crisis, when the party demanded leaders gather their forces to support Henry Wallace in 1948, the party's powerlines snapped. Whatever widespread relationships the communists had maintained with millions of workers dissipated rapidly, the strongest possible sign of underlying weakness in the communist union position.

The militancy of American workers two decades later, when there is emphatically no significant Left union leadership, points to the conclusion that the combative trade union movement arose largely independently of the intellectuals' and parties' efforts. The Left—including all the intellectuals worth consideration here—neither provoked the spontaneous strikes of the early 1930s nor did it in any real sense control the aims of the rank and file as the unions were being built. Only for an interim, and largely insofar as they reflected the immediate desires of the organized workers, did organized Leftists exert substantial influences upon the labor movement for the benefit of American radicalism.[12]

In the broad sense we may conclude that American workers' movements at best partially coincided with the efforts of radical parties (whose membership has been, by any standards, disproportionately radical intellectuals). The American situation is certainly unique in degree, but it may, as Perlman suggested, contain universal qualities which still speak to the future of Western labor movements. Attempting during World War II to bring together the lessons of defeats to the workers' movements, Anton Pannekoek noted that the Marx of Marxism had been appropriated by socialists and communists, and that in the new situation workers would have to struggle for social reconstruction *against* the existing parties of socialism. As Pannekoek put the case:

The propaganda of the Socialist doctrine has the tendency to throw doubts into the minds of the workers, to raise or to strengthen distrust in their own powers, and to dim the consciousness of their task and their potentialities. That is the social function of socialism now, and at every moment of workers' success in the coming struggles. From the hard fight for freedom ahead, the workers are to be lured by the soft shine of a mild new servitude. . . . Thus the only role socialism can play in the future will be to act as an impediment standing in the way of the workers' fight for freedom.[13]

Pannekoek's description of the situation and prospects, if perhaps overdrawn, provides at least a more satisfactory analysis of recent events and potential directions within the working classes than the neo-traditional Left views or the conceptions of "labor experts" following Perlman. If such is the case, Perlman will have been proved correct in a most uniquely ironic way: the flight of the working class from the political arena may lead not to quiescence but to invigorated struggle over the very conditions of social relations at the point of production. And this struggle, so long derogated by the Left to a secondary role, may become decisive in the transformation of society as a whole.[14]

NOTES

1. Guy Debord, *Society of the Spectacle* (translation by Black & Red, published in the United States in *Radical America,* vol. IV, #5), paragraph #98. Emphasis omitted.

In passing, it should be noted that some scholars of Lenin have doubted that his attitude in *What Is to Be Done?* prevailed throughout his life or was intended as an all-inclusive formula (although it became so under Stalin). See, for instance, C. L. R. James, *Lenin, Trotsky and the Vanguard Party* (Detroit, 1964); and Raya Dunayevskaya, "The Shock of Recognition and the Philosophic Ambivalence of Lenin," *TELOS,* #5 (Spring 1970), pp. 44–57.

2. In a recent article on the Italian working-class struggles, Bruce Brown notes that

. . . the general strike in France [in 1968 (PB)] was only the culmination of a dynamic of confrontation and industrial ferment whose beginnings can be traced back at least as far as the insurrectionary general strike which shook Belgium in 1960–61, and whose subsequent development has left an almost endless trail of disruptive strikes extending from West Germany to Great Britain. The recurrent characteristics of these struggles have been the spontaneous nature of their development, outside of and sometimes even in opposition to the existing trade-union organizations; their explosive violence, often verging on insurrection; and their emphasis on questions such as working conditions and even workers' control rather than on simple wage issues. "Revolution in Western Europe?", *Liberation,* 15 (Winter 1971), pp. 28–33.

3. In some ways, the best single account of De Leon's activities remains Rudolph Katz's memorial essay, "With De Leon since '89," in *Daniel De Leon: The Man and His Work, a Symposium* (New York: New York Labor News, 1919). See esp. pp. 17–31, 75–78, 150–53.

4. Michael Ebner, "The Paterson Strike of 1912 and the Two I.W.W.s," *Labor History,* 11 (Fall 1970), pp. 452–66; Paul Buhle, "Introduction" to *Labor Power* reprint (Westport, Conn.: Greenwood Press, 1970).

5. See Daniel De Leon, *As to Politics* (New York: New York Labor News, 1956), esp. pp. 57, 61.

6. James Weinstein, *Decline of Socialism in America, 1912–1925* (New York: Monthly Review, 1967), pp. 36, 227, 273–74.

7. James Weinstein, "The IWW and American Socialism," *Socialist Revolution,* I (September–October 1970), p. 28, n. 20.

8. See Charles Leinenweber, "The American Socialist Party and 'New' Immigrants," *Science & Society,* 32 (Winter 1968), pp. 6–16, 22–25, on the content and significance of nativism within the Socialist

Party. John H. M. Laslett's *Labor and the Left* (New York: Basic Books, 1970) suggests but does not comprehensively analyze the peculiar radicalism of the pre-World War I "labor aristocracy" of skilled workers. See esp. pp. 296–97.

9. An extremely valuable recent autobiography, Len DeCaux, *Labor Radical* (Boston: Beacon Press, 1971), indicates the political relations within the CIO which frequently frustrated left-wingers. See, for instance, pp. 315–16, 379–80.

10. Tim Wolhforth, *The Struggle for Marxism in the United States* (New York: Bulletin Publications, 1969), p. 32.

11. See DeCaux, op. cit., for comments on Harry Bridges, Mike Quill, and Joe Curran, pp. 301, 425–29, 422–23.

12. See the suggestive essay by George Rawick, "Working Class Self-Activity," *Radical America*, III (March–April 1969), pp. 23–31; and Staughton Lynd "Rank-and-File Organizing in the 'Thirties'," *Radical America*, V (May–June 1971).

13. Anton Pannekoek, *Workers' Councils* (American edition published in *Root and Branch*, #1, Spring 1970), p. 36.

14. Several texts published since the Second World War have indicated the continuity of such a view with the Marxism of Marx. See particularly the following: C. L. R. James, *State Capitalism and World Revolution* (Detroit: Facing Reality Publishing Committee, 1969); J. R. Johnson, Grace Lee, and Pierre Chaulieu, *Facing Reality* (Detroit: Correspondence, 1958); and Martin Glaberman, *"Be His Payment High or Low": The American Working Class of the Sixties* (Detroit: Facing Reality Publishing Committee, 1966).

REPLY

Adolph Sturmthal

What is a revolutionary transformation of society? Apart from a few references to Lenin, Mr. Buhle's Comment has been limited to the U.S. experience. This is not surprising. In few countries has the discussion about the relationship of intellectuals to the labor movement been as voluminous and intense as in this country. Even in Czarist Russia, the discussion lasted only a short period, to be buried shortly afterward by issues of more momentous significance.

If I read Buhle's Comment correctly—and I am not quite sure that I do—he starts from the assumption that the influence of the intelligentsia on American labor was never very great and, more importantly, that it was this lack of influence which was responsible for the failure of socialist (and other radical) ideas to take hold in the American labor movement. It is of course true that neither De Leon nor Hayes, Berger, et al. exerted any profound or long-lasting influence on American workers. The facts themselves are thus not in dispute. What may be questioned is whether it was this lack of intellectual impact that caused the failure of socialism to establish itself in the ranks of organized labor, or, vice versa, whether outside circumstances were such as to make American workers singularly unreceptive to socialist propaganda. Although it would be difficult to produce conclusive evidence for either sequence of events, it would seem to me that the weakening of socialist consciousness in most Western countries during the long and extraordinary wave of prosperity that followed World War II would make it appear plausible that prosperity was equally at work in limiting socialist influence in the United States. This would be particularly likely to have been the case during the rapid industrial expansion that followed the Civil War.

Somewhat connected with this argument is a further question raised in Buhle's Comment: is there a new wave of militancy among industrial workers and what is the role of the current generation of intellectuals in this phenomenon? It would be difficult, I believe, to produce objective and measurable evidence that there is widespread disaffection with left-wing parties. Election returns in Western countries would not tend to confirm this view. Labour was turned out of office in England, but by a narrow margin, and against this stand socialist successes in West Germany, Austria, and most of the Scandinavian countries. More important: to the extent to which the left-wing parties lost, the benefit did not go to the extreme Left, but rather to conservative groups. More persuasive is the evidence as regards the trade unions. Since the French events in 1968 a large-scale movement of rebellion against union leadership has manifested itself in such traditionally well-disciplined countries as West Germany and Sweden, while in Italy the trade unions themselves have transformed their character so profoundly that they are now expressions of political dissatisfaction of the workers with all the various left-wing parties dotting the political landscape.

The events of the last three years—for which some modest counterparts could, with some effort, be found in the United States— do indeed raise an issue: did this radicalism originate with the workers themselves or did the students and other intellectual groups play a key role in the movements? Has Lenin (first version) come into his own or is Plekhanoff still to be trusted? Has Perlman's interpretation anything to offer for our understanding of recent history? Obviously, in this narrow frame we can only provide hints for an answer.

There is no question that trade union leaders of all kinds of political persuasion are engaged in a self-examination which has few parallels in recent labor history. True, so far few fundamental changes have occurred in union structure or leadership except possibly in Italy but perhaps these are still to come. Large organizations with a substantial history and a long tradition do not change rapidly; but the mere fact of soul-searching cannot be denied. What is doubtful, however, is whether this process is likely to lead any one of the labor organizations into a search for a new relationship to the intelligentsia. In the first place, because—France excepted— there is no evidence that the rebellion of the workers against their leadership was in any way inspired or engineered by students or other groups of intellectuals. The series of West German wildcat strikes, the strike movement in northern Sweden, the endless strike wave in Italy had little or nothing to do with intellectual influences. Second, even in France, where undeniably the student rebellion gave the signal for the vast strike movement and the occupation of plants by the workers, the attempts of the students to establish contact and cooperation with the striking workers ended in total failure. The Communist Party, which for a moment had lost control of the labor movement in the Paris area—the formerly Christian CFTD (Confédération Française du Travail Démocratique) proved quicker in moving along with the workers —rapidly reestablished its influence. It used its power to resist all revolutionary slogans that Leftist student groups were propagandizing, and succeeded in turning the strikes into ordinary bread-and-butter movements. Their main accomplishments were the achievement of old-standing union demands which the employers and the government had so far rejected and in particular the possibility of establishing union sections in the plants themselves— something American unions regard at least since 1936 as a matter of course and distinctly compatible with the functioning of a modern capitalistic society.

It is of course possible to regard these movements as evidence of a new radicalism of labor. But if this is done, it is well to keep in mind that this is still bread-and-butter radicalism, a demand for more of the same, at the most for a larger share in the gross national product. There is no evidence, as far as I can see, that intellectual influence has played a significant part in determining the direction in which the movements have been propelled.

Indeed, a rather careful investigation of the attitudes of the "affluent worker" by a group of British sociologists would tend to indicate that the main change that seems to have occurred among the new, prosperous, geographically mobile workers is a different view of their union and class party; a weakening of the social solidarity element and an inclination to regard first of all the union and to a lesser extent the party as an instrument for the achievement of higher living standards.[1] The crucial factor in this change, according to the authors, is less the affluence of the workers but their more intense social contacts with white-collar workers and middle-class families. In this "instrumental" view of labor organizations, radicalism in the pursuit of bread-and-butter aims would be a fairly obvious implication. This, however, should not be mistaken for a radical desire to change the foundations of the society which has provided these workers with the highest standard of living in history.

If there is any other new element in the picture it is the progressive unionization of white-collar workers, following with some considerable distance upon the growth of the share of white-collar workers in the total labor force. This fact may give increased influence to white-collar workers in determining the direction in which the entire movement is progressing. With some considerable degree of imagination the vigor with which the demand for "participation" (whatever this vague term is intended to signify) has been raised may be related to this new power center within organized labor. It is doubtful whether intellectuals have had any real part in this trend.

That there is a new kind of radicalism in the Western world cannot be denied. It can be traced clearly to blacks and other minority groups in the United States and to student groups all over the Western world. The first need no elaborate explanation in our context. The new radicalism of the youth, however, requires some comment.

In the Marxian perspective the breakdown of the capitalistic system was the result of its increasing failure to "deliver the goods," a view which has entered the English language under the horrible title of the "law of the increasing immiseration of the masses." No elaborate demonstration is required to show that in the Western, i.e., capitalistic world, the evolution has not followed the Marxian prediction. Whatever the still intolerable forms of poverty that exist in advanced industrial nations, it can hardly be denied that per capita incomes have increased tremendously since the days of Marx. Even in the modified version of "relative immiseration" —from which it would anyhow be considerably more difficult to infer the inevitability of an anti-capitalistic revolution—the theory can hardly be defended with any degree of precision. Indeed, apart from the obscure writings of an East German economics professor no such attempt has been made in recent years.

The "new radicals" do not fall into the trap of asserting increasing immiseration in either the absolute or the relative meaning of the term. The facts are too obvious. Instead, they have made a complete turnabout, or to use Marxian terminology, they have turned Marx upside down. The main charge against the contemporary society is not that it produces too little for too many, but on the contrary that it shows an obsessive concern with economic growth and material advancement. It is being accused of neglecting the environment, of being insufficiently concerned with cultural values, with the proper use of leisure. A good deal can be said in favor of these accusations and it is the proper role of intellectuals to bring these issues to public attention. If the forms in which this is done—e.g., by "dropping out"—are often objectionable and self-defeating, this may be regarded by many as the lesser evil compared with the ability of other social groups to live in extreme luxury surrounded by oceans of garbage, both literally and figuratively in the quality of the cultural environment. This criticism, although it often has its origin with left-wing intellectuals, has no ancestry that leads to Marx. Indeed, if anything, it contradicts Marx and is more closely related to some of the utopian socialists for whom Marx had so much disdain.

In this rebellion labor organizations so far have played no significant part. Indeed, it is not unfair to say that they have shown a distinct lack of concern with the issues which the Leftist student groups have emphasized, and sometimes even outright hostility. Yet the need of organized labor for the services of experts in various fields has increased far beyond anything the old craft unions of pre-World War I days could have ever envisaged, and some of the students, a few years later, have become such experts. Now, it is easy to say that these are hired hands which do not determine policy but merely help to produce intellectually respectable arguments to support policies determined by the workers themselves. At first sight, this is indeed a persuasive point often advanced by intellectuals who were deeply involved in the actual operations of labor organizations, especially in this country. Yet I maintain some doubts about its validity.

The difficulty with this kind of reasoning is that it is less and less clear where the boundary between expert advice and policy-making lies. If labor leaders appear before congressional committees and have to argue fine points regarding the international monetary system, are they not completely dependent, even in their policy-making capacity, upon the advice of professionals in the field? Yugoslav observers, friendly toward the system of "workers' management" in that country, are aware of the scarcity of managerial talent among the workers and point toward the danger of technocracy. Obviously, the relationship between labor and the intelligentsia is too complicated to be fitted into the simple rules that were derived from the experience of half a century ago.

This brings me to the last two points I should like to make. Mr. Buhle's Comment refers, rightly I believe, to the "invigorated struggle over the very conditions of social relations at the point of production." He means, I suspect, that in a number of Western countries the actual leadership of working-class protest has passed from the distant union officials to the shop stewards and workers' councils at the plant. The British Donovan Commission has made this one of the central points of its findings and has gone so far as to speak of a dual system of industrial relations, one represented by the nation- or area-wide collective agreements, the other by the more or less formal understandings at the plant level. Other studies of industrial nations have come to similar conclusions, although they are not as sharply articulated as in the Donovan Report. Whether this is in fact a new form of revolutionary development or not remains to be seen. If it were, it would represent, not a new form of Marxist rebellion, but rather a return to the syndicalist ideas which Marx so bitterly opposed in his lifetime. In a peculiar fashion, however, these apparently syndicalist movements of the last few years have managed to combine reliance upon the state with syndicalist forms of movement. It is only a half-truth to assert that there has been "a flight of the working class from the political arena." True: In the great movements of the last few years it was the unions, rather than the political parties, that finally took hold of popular rebellion and negotiated the ultimate settlement. But the fact cannot be overlooked that it was the French government in the *constats de Grenelle* which arranged for the meeting of unions and employers and set the tone for the principles of agreement that were embodied in the document of Grenelle. Nor should one overlook in an analysis of these events the fact that in France and in Italy the political representation of working-class interests is weakened by special circumstances.

The French Communist Party, the dominant working-class party of the country, is outside the system and thus prevented from functioning in any other capacity than as an expression of protest. No serious alternative to conservative governments is possible as long as the Left is prevented, by the very existence of a powerful Communist Party, from throwing its full weight into the political arena.

While the Italian Communist Party, having shown some slight signs of independence from Moscow, is less of an outcast than its French counterpart, the incredible divisions of the non-Communist Left (plus a few splinters on the Communist side) make the political representation of the Italian working class almost as ineffective as is the case in France. The unions have thus been compelled to take on political assignments which elsewhere would have been handled by more effective working-class or popular parties. Whether this is indeed a new form of working-class radicalism of a permanent nature or not is an open question. Nor do the results obtained so far indicate that this development is likely to "become decisive in the transformation of society as a whole." In the main, the workers in both countries have obtained rights which American workers have long enjoyed. Perhaps the main difference is the insistence in Western Europe upon far longer paid vacations than in the United States. This is most probably a wholesome achievement, but whether it can be classified as a transformation of society any more than most other improvements of working-class conditions seems to me doubtful.

NOTE

1. John M. Goldthorpe et al.: *The Affluent Worker: Political Attitudes and Behaviour* (Cambridge University Press, 1968).

Chapter 16

PLURALISM AND POLITICAL PARTIES*

Norman Thomas

No third party [in America] has ever grown like an oak from an acorn. The Republican Party is no exception. It became a second party in its first national election, it was the Whig Party which died. Why has there been this general failure of "third" parties?

The reasons are largely political and are to be found in America's history, and its Constitution. I have sometimes told English friends that had we had a centralized parliamentary government rather than a federal presidential government, we should have had, under some name or another, a moderately strong socialist party.

President Kennedy, reflecting on what a Democratic Congress has done to his program, might, with some justice, challenge my calling ours a presidential government. It is near enough to it in that the choice of the President is the major all-absorbing political issue. He is the man for or against whom everybody votes, or thinks he votes. But in legal form, citizens vote not directly for the presidential candidate, but for a college of electors. Each state has as many electors as it has representatives, plus its two senators. The system is so arranged that voting strength of small states is disproportionately high. In voting for electors, the citizens do not vote under uniform qualifications or rules for getting candidates on the ballot, but under the various laws and procedures of fifty states, some of which make it virtually impossible for a minor party to get or stay on the ballot. To be elected, especially in our times, a candidate must be backed by a party strong enough to raise millions of dollars. A single, hour-long, syndicated television program, costs more than the Socialist Party had in funds during any of my six campaigns.

To win, the candidate must win a majority vote of the electoral

* Chapter 8 from Norman Thomas, *Socialism Re-examined* (New York: Norton, 1963), originally entitled "Socialism in the U.S.A."

college, or, failing that, the election goes to the House of Representatives, in which each state has one vote, thus enormously increasing the already disproportionate electoral weight of the less populous states. Three times the candidate with the popular plurality has lost. In 1948 a small shift in three close states, Ohio, Illinois and California, would have elected Dewey, without destroying Truman's substantial plurality. The average American voter wants to take no chance on this. He may prefer a minor party candidate, but will cast his vote for one of the two major party candidates. His decision is based on how much he likes, or learns to like, one of the candidates, or on how much he dislikes or hates one candidate more actively than the other. Almost up to election day, he may think he will vote for his real preference, a minor party candidate who managed to get on the ballot in his state, but then he will decide that he can't take a chance, "lest that so-and-so get in." (How often I have been told just that!) If the President of the United States could be elected by a popular preferential ballot in which the voters numbered their choices, the Socialist Party would be a force to be reckoned with at the polls.

This opinion is bolstered by many considerations, one of them the fact that Gene Debs got his highest vote—6 per cent of the total—in 1912. Why? Partly, at least, because that year, voters were pretty sure that the winner would be Woodrow Wilson or Theodore Roosevelt, not William H. Taft, and they didn't believe that the difference between these two fairly progressive men was important enough to prevent their voting for their real preference, the outspoken socialist and labor man, the beloved Gene Debs. In 1916, when the Party itself was stronger, they gave no such vote to Allan Benson, the socialist candidate. For one thing, he wasn't Debs, but that is not the whole story.

It is easier to make the sort of choice I have described because of the logical absurdities of our two-party system. Each of them is a federation of state parties, held together by historic and sociological considerations, rather than by ideological principle. The leaders of both parties, especially the Democratic, since 1932, have shown considerable willingness to adopt measures once considered socialist or almost socialist. Within each party, differences are greater than, on the average, between them, so that one asks of a candidate for Federal office not so much whether he is a Democrat or a Republican but what kind of a Democrat or Republican.

Labor, since 1932, is fairly content that it has kept and increased its gains by picking individuals (usually Democrats), who, by conviction or for the sake of labor votes, will come nearest to its demands. It runs its political campaigns on this principle with fair, but far from total success.

The differences between the parties are sociological rather than philosophical. Let an observer find out the sex, geographical location, occupation, national origin, church connection of an American citizen, and, nine times out of ten, he can determine the voter's party preference. However, it by no means follows that the citizen will always vote according to the label.

Insofar as the parties claim to have historic principles, they have swapped them. On the whole, except in the South, the Democratic Party tends to support very strong federal government, while the Republican Party—with exceptions—mourns the continuing decline of state's rights. Alexander Hamilton, Abraham Lincoln, Thomas Jefferson, John C. Calhoun, would all be surprised by today's political parties. So little are the voters accustomed to honest thinking in terms of political preference, that the average Democrat and Republican, if asked to give reasons for voting as he does, wouldn't know what you were talking about.

If this extraordinary irrationality of our parties and lack of sharp division between them made it possible, under strong leadership like Roosevelt's in time of crisis, to work out a pragmatic peaceful near-social revolution, it has also made possible the flouting, not only of the advanced Democratic platform of 1960, but of most of the Democratic President's program by a Democratic Congress in which the generally conservative Southern Democratic senators and representatives hold, by virtue of seniority, most of the important committee chairmanships.

In spite of a political set up in which the cards are stacked against a third party, had Roosevelt's New Deal not given us a welfare state, which was in no way indicated by his 1932 campaign platform, the Socialist Party, the Communist Party, and perhaps some new party compounded of enthusiasts for Huey Long and Father Coughlin, would have acquired political strength. Roosevelt's great public support was not won during his first campaign, but began with his inaugural address in 1933. He was elected the first time simply because he wasn't Mr. Hoover, but that was not the only reason for his popularity. The New Deal averted popular disturbances of a serious sort, without solving the problems it ameliorated or without giving us the improvements in the mechanics of democracy which we needed. . . .

For many years I hoped, sometimes against hope, that the Socialist Party and its campaigns could serve as a catalytic agency to stir up and guide the kind of mass awakening which would give us a new party, basically a consciously farmer-labor party, increasingly socialist, and in the process, bring about an opposing conservative party. As late as 1932, there was nothing in the Republican or Democratic national platforms to indicate that this was impossible.

In 1924, we socialists staked a great deal on our gamble that our coalition with some labor and farm organizations and the Wisconsin Progressives would bring about an American farmer-labor mass party strong enough soon to supplant one of the old parties or bring about their merger. We knew that such a party would not immediately be socialist, but we hoped that the logic of the situation, and our efforts, would soon make it so in fact, if not in name.

The odds were always against us, but they multiplied even before the end of a good campaign because some of the labor organizations originally interested, virtually defected. One of the forces that held down the La Follette vote was the cry: A vote for La Follette is a vote to send the election to the House of Representatives.

Now, while I do not affirm the impossibility of the rise of a new party which, substantially would be backed by labor organizations, I think a major party, controlled by labor to the degree that it is in Britain, would be neither attainable nor desirable for reasons I have repeatedly suggested in discussing labor and its relations to socialism in America. Today I do not think that a new mass party, if it is to emerge at all, will call itself a labor party, nor will it be controlled by the same men who control the unions. While a strong new mass party with a socialist philosophy and program may seem remote, such a party may yet come to birth. If so, it will be concerned largely with the road to peace.

After the establishment of the welfare state under Roosevelt, there emerged the possibility that one of the old parties, probably the Democratic, could be helped to evolve into a party at least as socialist as the British Labor Party or the German Social Democrats. This would require either an honorable democratic political solution of the race problems in the South or a clean-cut break in the Democratic Party. It would also require the development of a decided change in the present climate of political action in the United States. This would begin with an active minority which accepts the revolutionary belief that plenty, peace and freedom for all are attainable by us imperfectly rational men and that to work for them is to find life's deepest meaning. To that minority, a dedicated socialism should furnish driving power and guidance.

Older generations of American socialists would never have used such words to frame their role. In Debs' time they expected the party as such to grow to major strength. After World War I, under Morris Hillquit's intellectual leadership, we hoped socialism would become a prime force in creating a labor or farmer-labor party. Hence, in 1924, the coalition with the La Follette forces, which included the Conference for Progressive Labor Action. With most of us, the hope for such a party, although postponed, still lingered.

Meanwhile, to educate the public, or even to keep socialist ideas alive after the failure of our plans in 1924, we nominated candidates. The 1932 campaign brought us new hope and strength, but after 1933, Roosevelt and the New Deal, communist pressure, and later, fear of nazism abroad and of fascist tendencies at home, greatly changed the external situation and socialist and labor reaction to it. Before 1936, the Party, bedevilled by our internal factions, had lost numerous sympathizers and members of right and left to the Democrats, or rather, to Roosevelt. In 1936, a section of the Party split off, nominally on the question of the way to handle the communist issue. Thereupon, in New York (and only in New York) ardent anti-communists, communists, and others, joined in building the American Labor Party, which could strengthen support of Roosevelt. Some years later that party split over the communist issue, and today the secessionists carry on as the Liberal Party, supported by some unions. The American Labor Party died. The Liberal Party exists only in New York State and usually simply nominates Democratic candidates. For this service it gets occasional recognition in nominations and jobs.

The Socialist Party, which remembered how well its opposition to the first world war was justified by events, also opposed entry into the second world war (but not on isolationist grounds). After Pearl Harbor, it gave critical support to the war, and concerned itself with an approach to peace. It was opposed to Roosevelt's simple slogan of unconditional surrender, and to Anglo-American concessions to Stalin in Central Europe.

I am perhaps prouder of our 1944 campaign and its platform than of any of my six presidential campaigns. Unhappily, it did not build the Socialist Party. I ran again in 1948, against my original intention, because I thought that we socialists should not allow the strange conglomeration of the Wallace Progressives, with a minority of communists rather cleverly playing the dominant role, to represent socialism to the American voters.

All this, while state laws, or the way they were enforced, made it harder and harder to stay on the ballot. The popular vote in 1948 was smaller than the reception accorded to me and to my colleague, Tucker Smith, had led us to expect. Wherefore, around 1950, I began a campaign within the Party to utilize our limited resources of money and manpower in campaigning for socialist ideas rather than for a presidential ticket doomed to little notice and humiliating defeat. By 1960, this became the prevailing opinion of the Party. The majority put its hope on the political front by working for a meaningful political realignment. Socialists are now allowed by their Party not only to vote, but to work for those candidates of other parties who come nearest to the socialist position. The reasoning behind this is that the welfare state has incorporated a great many socialist "immediate demands." In doing so, it has precluded, we hope, the necessity of immediate, if peaceful, internal "revolution." The difference between more or less good or bad political measures might now be very important, perhaps decisive, in terms of war or peace. We dare not hope to have an indefinite number of years free from war during which we can work for our version of a socialist society which can be achieved only by complete victory at the polls.

Neither can we afford to allow ourselves or our fellow citizens to lose sight of the great socialist goal. Within our American political-economic complex, our efforts to build a significant numerical force at the polls have failed as have also our efforts to precipitate a coming of a new mass party, strongly supported by organized labor. Our devoted efforts in 1952 and 1956 were scarcely noticed except sometimes to be pitied. It was time to look for other means, to be more flexible in cooperation, to recognize that the political realignment we wanted could be brought about by more than one method. At present we can contribute more by persuasively presenting well-thought-out programs and by campaigning for candidates of a numerically significant party who might be going our way. We have no intention of following the communist tactics of "boring from within" and denying our true loyalty. The very lack of a principled theoretical basis for either great party makes it possible for an avowed socialist to support those candidates who most accurately represent our ideals, but we must always combine our support with an insistence on the need of better political alignment.

Just how to work out this campaign for realignment is still a subject of much debate within the Socialist Party. I greatly doubt the wisdom of our nominating a presidential candidate. I would like us, however, to be in a position, in congressional campaigns, where old party candidates are very unsatisfactory and we cannot successfully nominate our own, to favor those independent candidates who emphasize our stand on foreign relations. At present, the average Democratic congressman, even one originally well disposed, somehow fails to do this with any vigor because he falls under heavy Administration pressure. Events can change this judgment.

Meanwhile, it is only fair to sympathize with socialists who find it difficult to support any candidate of a "capitalist" or "bourgeois" party. On the practical side they point out the difficulty of maintaining a political party which does not nominate candidates or give voters a chance for a protest vote. They say that it violates our American traditions to call ourselves a party while failing to nominate a presidential candidate. I confess to frequent attacks of nostalgia for those not-so-good old days. It is necessary, however, to change the pattern; to show how a socialist party, under present conditions, can introduce principle and program into political discussion without depleting its limited strength, and without alienating sympathizers by running candidates who would, inevitably, merely draw away votes from the better of the two major party candidates.

COMMENT 1

Michael Harrington

In *Socialism Re-examined,* Norman Thomas unquestionably stated an important truth about why there is no mass socialist movement in America. Yet I believe he overstated his point, turning a problem of socialism in this country into *the* problem. But even though I thus disagree with his analysis—or at least with its emphasis—I am very much in agreement with him on the urgent necessity of a party realignment in this country.

First of all, let me define the area of agreement.

Thomas wrote, "I have sometimes told English friends that had we a centralized parliamentary government rather than a federal presidential government, we would have had, under some name or another, a moderately strong socialist party." And he was quite right to stress the impact of the political structure on American radicalism in this way.

The American government was, of course, designed by the Founding Fathers to frustrate the will of majorities. The intricate system of checks and balances, the tripartite division of power, and the other conservative devices of the Founding Fathers were supposed to minimize conflict, or at least to prevent any single faction, even one representing most of the people, from imposing its will upon the society. To borrow Richard Hofstadter's brilliant phrase (he applied it to Calhoun), some of the *Federalist Papers* seem to have been written by a Marx of the master class.

One consequence of this system was to make the life of the minority party exceedingly difficult. Under a parliamentary system, by voting for the candidate of your choice in a single constituency, even if he were a member of a dissident opposition group, you still had a chance to influence the choice of the Prime Minister. But under the American system there was a logic of either/or which tended to subvert the third party on both the presidential and other levels of politics.

In the case of the presidency, as Thomas knew so well from his six campaigns for that office, the existence of a national constituency puts a premium on broad, amorphous parties which are capable of building a variegated coalition in a vast country. So it was that Thomas' strength invariably declined as the election neared, even though he himself was an extremely attractive leader and effective political speaker. For by November it would have become clear to the voter that the basic choice was between the nominees of the Democratic and Republican parties. And many who actually preferred Thomas—and would have voted for him as a socialist parliamentarian—turned to one of the major party candidates.

On the congressional level the same logic held. There were, at one time or another, various socialist enclaves of considerable strength in the United States: the Lower East Side of New York and Milwaukee, Wisconsin, with socialist members of the House (and in Milwaukee, a socialist mayor), Reading, Pennsylvania, and Bridgeport, Connecticut, with municipal administrations. But those areas could not, in the absence of a parliamentary system, serve as steppingstones to national power. And sooner or later all of them were absorbed by the major parties.

This, I think, explains much about the contrasting fate of socialism in the United States and Canada. Just to the north of this country there are farmers and workers quite like their American neighbors who have given a certain measure of political power to the old Canadian Commonwealth Federation and to the present New Democratic Party. In the case of the NDP the comparison is particularly revealing since many of the AFL-CIO unions in Canada back that social democratic party (it is affiliated to the Socialist International) but stick with the Democrats in the United States. In the Canadian parliamentary system one does not "waste" a vote by casting it for the NDP opposition, because its legislative delegation also has the power to influence the decisions of the executive.

This point, however, should not be made to bear excessive weight. If there are unquestionably advantages to parliamentary rule, in that it favors parties with a certain consistency and program and allows a minority opposition to have its effect, there are also problems in that system. It can lead, as in the French Fourth Republic, to a diffusion of political power which makes stable government impossible. It can tend, as it has been doing for some years in England, toward a covert mechanism of presidential rule, as the Liberal Party in that country can attest. Therefore, in agreeing with part of Norman Thomas' thesis I am not suggesting that a parliament is the answer for all of America's ills. (It will, in any case, never be adopted.) I am simply observing that the lack of one was certainly a factor in the failure of the Socialist Party of the United States.

But, and now I am moving into the area of my disagreement with Thomas, the American political structure was not the crucial element in the socialist defeat.

There was, and is, a class struggle in the United States, and indeed it has been bloodier and more violent here than in Europe. And, beginning with the presidency of Woodrow Wilson, labor has been involved in mainstream politics on a class basis. The peculiarities of American political structure are one reason why this process did not culminate in a mass socialist movement. But there are many other factors. The Debsians had modeled themselves on the pre-World War I German social democracy, in which labor political organization preceded and dominated industrial organization. They therefore expected to become the central organizational expression of working-class political consciousness. But the American reality followed the English model. Unions which were officially pro-capitalist were gradually forced into a political struggle for reforms, often against their will. As a result, and it was fateful that too few socialists understood the fact, the Socialist Party was more often than not counterposed to the actual political organizations of the labor movement.

Some, like Hillquit, understood that it was therefore necessary to amend the Debsian perspective, and he helped bring about formal Socialist participation in the La Follette campaign of 1924. Thomas himself came to recognize this situation and in 1938 proposed that the Socialist Party abandon its electoral emphasis.[1] Had that been done, many of the trade unionists who felt that they were forced to choose between the party and union political action, and opted for the latter, might have been able to remain as active socialists. That would not have created a mass movement, but it would have provided the basis for a much more powerful socialist presence in American politics. Shortly after he came to this conclusion, the imminence of World War II turned Thomas back to the party's traditional stance of intransigent opposition to what were called—wrongly I think—Tweedledum and Tweedledee.

In the last period of his life, Thomas once more adopted the perspective he had briefly held in 1938. He was one of the leaders of the Socialist Party—as was this writer—who argued in 1960 that there was no sense in running a campaign every four years which only revealed the weakness of the movement and took a few votes away from liberal candidates to boot. And yet in my own relations with him, as comrade and friend, I always sensed a certain nostalgia for the old days. Thomas supported Johnson against Goldwater, backed Eugene McCarthy in 1968, and, with considerable reluctance, decided to vote for Hubert Humphrey in the general election of that year. But, as I know from conversations with him in 1967, he was exploring the possibility of an independent antiwar presidential campaign in 1968.

One of the reasons for his ambivalence is obvious from his essay. "Labor," he wrote, "since 1932 is fairly content it has kept and increased its gains by picking individuals (usually Democrats) who, by conviction or for the sake of labor votes, will come nearest to its demands." This is a fairly typical description of the unions as an interest group in the tradition of the Gompers maxim "Reward your friends, punish your enemies." Yet I do not think that it is accurate.

After that La Follette campaign in 1924, American labor veered back to the Gompers "voluntarism" it had abandoned right after World War I. It is quite sobering to remember that John L. Lewis, the architect of the CIO, voted for Herbert Hoover in 1932. But with the Roosevelt campaign of 1936, something unprecedented began to happen. The unions started to build an ongoing political apparatus. That process was marked by the creation of the CIO Political Action Committee and the AFL's League for Political Education in the forties. It was accelerated by the merger in the fifties and the appearance of the Committee on Political Education of the AFL-CIO. And in the campaigns of 1968 and 1970 it was obvious to most observers that union political organization was the single most important factor in the Democrats' effort.

The "English" pattern was unfolding and Thomas missed the fact. The labor commitment to politics was no longer individualistic and episodic, as he thought, but permanent and concerted.[2] And that made it possible to hope that, as in England, the pragmatic trade unionists would come to see the necessity of basic, structural change in the society. In fairness, though, I should add that there is another model which is not so encouraging from a socialist point of view: the Australian. In that country, the unions have been in politics for three quarters of a century, there is a long tradition of labor partyism—and yet the labor parties have never really become socialist.[3]

My criticism, then, is that Norman Thomas, by focusing too much on how the American political structure affected the Debsian perspective of a mass socialist party emerging in its own name, overlooked an alternative possibility: the politicalization of bread-and-butter unions as in the case of the British Labour Party. And yet I would not push that analogy too far, for I agree with Thomas that the Labour Party cannot be the model for American socialists. In what has gone before, my emphasis has been on the way in which a mass socialist movement developed in England—and could develop in America—not upon the actual structure which came into being.

And indeed in the 1960s, the Labour Party probably owed its electoral victories to the fact that it abandoned its narrow "laborite" identification. Harold Wilson projected the party as a modern institution appealing to the college-educated as well as to industrial workers. And that was the meaning of the German Social Democratic Party's change from a "party of the working class" to a "party of all laboring people" at the Bad Godesberg Congress in 1959. For in Europe, as in America, the class structure has evolved so that a party making an exclusively proletarian appeal is doomed to permanent minority status.

Moreover, there are specifically American reasons why the slogan of a "labor party" will not have great appeal. It is a profound tradition in this country to act upon the reality of class differences —the workers, as Seymour Martin Lipset pointed out in *Political Man*, vote more massively for the Democrats than their British counterparts for the Labour Party—but also to pretend that they do not exist. If American socialists want to advance their cause in terms of actual political power I believe that they will have to learn to tolerate a great deal of rhetorical imprecision. A party explicitly based on the working class in this country will not get very far; but a party implicitly based on the working class, but

666 / MICHAEL HARRINGTON

appealing to other groups as well, is the only vehicle for progressive political change.

That is why, finally, I agree with Thomas' political conclusion even though I disagree with elements in his analysis. Our present party counterposition, as I tried to show in *Toward a Democratic Left,* is based upon utopian pragmatism. It is assumed that providence has somehow designed social reality so that those fratricidal coalitions, the Republican and Democratic parties, will stumble down the middle of the road into the best of all possible futures. That is not the case. The invisible hand of Adam Smith will not guide a technology which is now producing more external diseconomies than economies. And a party system proud of its amorphousness will hardly be able to respond to complicated challenges at home and abroad. There must indeed be, as Thomas argues, a realignment.

The way to that realignment is through the liberal wing of the Democratic Party. It will not, in the near future at least, lead to the emergence of a mass socialist movement under its own, or any other, name. But it will finally allow Americans something like a relatively serious choice between conservatism and liberalism, the Right and Left limits of mass politics today. And it is only when such a confrontation has taken place that it will be possible to pose a socialist alternative in terms that tens of millions of Americans can understand.

Norman Thomas devoted a lifetime to the struggle for that alternative. He was not simply the "conscience" of his nation as so many of the obituaries insisted, for that suggests that he stood for principles good for Sunday sermons but not for the real political life of the society. On the contrary. He was profoundly, and practically, right about the necessity of restructuring the American political party system. He made his tactical errors in fighting for that ideal, but if this country ever does adopt the realignment he described in *Socialism Re-examined,* he will be seen as a precursor of a crucial American change, and one which will finally make it possible for this country to face up to its problems. Norman Thomas possessed a very practical conscience.

NOTES

1. Since Thomas rather quickly reverted back to the classic socialist position, many people are not aware of this interlude. It is documented in Bernard K. Johnpoll, *Pacifist's Progress: Norman Thomas and the Decline of American Socialism* (Chicago: Quadrangle Books, 1970), p. 203.

2. J. David Greenstone, *Labor in American Politics* (New York: Knopf, 1969) is a good description of this development.

3. This history is summarized in G. D. H. Cole's *History of Socialist Thought* (London: Macmillan's, 1956), vol. III, pt. 2, ch. XXIII; and vol. IV, pt. 2, ch. XXVIII.

Leon D. Epstein

To ask why there has been no large and durable American socialist party is a conventionally important question in comparative social and political analysis. It is unusual, however, to answer the question with Norman Thomas' emphasis on structural obstacles raised by constitutional and electoral arrangements. Social scientists generally, including historians, prefer broad sociological or economic causes rather than mechanistic political explanations. As must be apparent from the essays of this volume, the preference is not confined to Marxists or other economic determinists.

Understanding Thomas' emphasis is easier after a close look at the question as usually asked and then at Thomas' version of it. The "socialist party" absent in the United States is ordinarily conceived in British and Western European terms as an organization of numerous political activists capable of mobilizing mass electoral support for a program of economic redistribution antithetical, at least in the long run, to a prevailing capitalist system. In the traditional model, mass support as well as some of the leadership derives from industrial workers possessing a class consciousness sufficient for a political cause that is primarily their own. With industrialization, the working class develops not only the requisite consciousness of its interest and so of its political role, but also the numbers and strength of an electoral majority. Hence a socialist party is able to gain effective power in a nation whose policy makers are chosen by mass suffrage. And it is to exercise that power in the name of the majoritarian class that elected it, although, in democratic, non-Leninist socialism, with due regard for minority interests. The politics of socialism thus seem distinct from those of an American pluralism, in which interests are many rather than dichotomous, combined and compromised rather than sharpened as program commitments, and expressed electorally through loose and broad coalitions rather than through cohesive and disciplined forces.

A socialist party is not supposed to resemble the structure of the Republican or Democratic party. It is to have a large, organized, and ideologically recruited membership both for effective campaigning and for making the policy of the leaders whom it recruits and helps elect to public office. As such, a socialist party is the prototype "modern" party that Duverger, among other scholars, has found to exist in Britain and Western Europe but not in the United States.[1] It is also a prime example of the "responsible" party that non-socialist American political scientists like Schattschneider and Burns have advocated to replace the unprogrammatic, uncohesive brokerage structure characteristic of Republicans and Democrats.[2] Since, however, the responsible-party reformers would attempt to create a majoritarian party without reliance on class-conscious socialism, the difficulties of establishing a socialist party in the United States would only be relevant to their advocacy if those difficulties were of such a nature as to stand in the way of any strongly programmatic party seeking to win national power in the United States.

Usual explanations of American socialist party failure have been directed to the conditions uncongenial to socialism rather than to those uncongenial to "responsible" parties in general. Thomas himself, before discussing the structural obstacles, briefly notes the familiar factors (expanding frontiers, immigration, and social mobility) softening the impact of class in the United States. It is common to conclude that the weakness of American socialists, relative to European socialists, results from less class consciousness in the United States.[3] Not everyone would agree that there was less about which to be class-conscious, but the early, virtually pre-industrial "gift of the ballot" to white males seems to have reduced the potential.[4] And so did the nation's total wealth, making for fairly widespread affluence despite gross inequalities. Together these factors are thought to account both for late unionization of American labor and for its unresponsiveness to socialist party politics. And without formal or informal organizational ties to unionized labor, there is no basis for a socialist party on the British or European scale.[5]

Thomas, however, is not primarily concerned with an American socialist party conceived on that scale. Specifically, the British Labour Party, whose heavy trade union orientation has made it one of two major parties, is not his model. Thomas' aspirations seem to have been much more modest. He writes not of a failure to build a socialist party that would, like British Labour, have displaced one of the old parties in two-party competition and so have been able to achieve power as a majoritarian force. Rather he thinks in terms of "a moderately strong socialist party" that would at best be a substantial third or fourth party in a multi-party system, and at worst a consistently strong minor party in a weakened two-party system. It is true that Thomas wants a party whose socialist principles would make it even more cohesive and programmatic than the responsible-party school desires in a reconstituted Republican or Democratic party. Yet Thomas is significantly closer to a crucial assumption of American political practice: that the nation is too large and varied in its interests, regions, and ethnicity to provide a majority for a party committed to a doctrinal program that it will not compromise. Implicitly if not explicitly, Thomas accepts this assumption along with the usual socioeconomic explanation of why there has been no specifically socialist majoritarian party in the United States.

Consequently, in reality, he asks why there has been no substantial third or fourth party of American socialists, capable of regularly winning more votes than a "minor" party in essentially two-party competition. The European model, if there is one, seems to be not British but Continental, and to be limited to those multiparty situations in which socialists have remained well short of majority status. In this light, Thomas' question can be restated as an inquiry into the forces so preserving two-party competition as to discourage effectively the durable development of third parties. Here it is orthodox political science to stress structural features of the American Constitution and of election laws. In particular, Thomas is by no means the first or the last critic to focus attention on the presidential election system as a prime obstacle to those who would convert two-party competition to multi-party competition. Less common except among Anglophiles is Thomas' preference for "a centralized parliamentary government rather than a federalized presidential government." The difficulty here for anyone wanting several major parties rather than two is that there is nothing inherent in parliamentary government, as British experience demonstrates, that always produces multipartism. Combining

proportional-representation elections with parliamentary government is a likelier means of facilitating multipartism, given the
association of these institutions in Continental Europe, but the
direction of the causation is by no means settled.

At any rate, parliamentary government, with or without propor-
tional representation, receives only passing attention from Thomas.
Whatever his preference on this score, he generally accepts the
presidential form as a settled feature of American government
and concentrates on proposing a change in the method by which
Presidents are elected. He urges not only popular direct election,
instead of the electoral college, but also a preferential ballot allowing voters to number their choices. The latter is naturally favored
by the third-party advocate. Preferential voting, by allowing second
choices to be added to first choices, does more than produce a
winner without a runoff election. Simultaneously it encourages
those who like a third- or fourth-party candidate to give him their
first choice knowing that their vote is not thereby wasted just
because he has no chance to win a majority of first choices. Even
if he cannot pick up enough second choices for a majority, those
who voted for him can still affect the outcome by their second
choices—presumably cast for the lesser evil among the potential
winners. Thus the preferential ballot sustains the third-party cause.
Direct popular election of the President, as some of its present-day
advocates understand, might itself work in the same direction.
Even with a prospective runoff, additional party candidacies would
be encouraged by the prospects of trading votes after the first
inconclusive round. But the preferential ballot, Thomas recognizes,
is the straightforward way to seek the multi-party end.

No technique exists for learning whether this tinkering with the
election machinery would in fact produce an American multi-party
voting pattern and along with it the strong socialist party that
Thomas wants. It can be granted that the present election method,
both in its coalition-imposing requirement of an electoral college
majority and in its use of the standard simple-plurality principle
of carrying a state, is well suited to the prevalent two-party competition. But that does not mean that two-party competition persists
only because of the election method, or that it would fail to persist
with a different election method. Nor is there any way to know
that the established election method, however well suited to two-
party competition, has really been crucial in frustrating socialist

or other third-party hopes. Thomas himself ascribes his party's difficulties partly to financial shortages, and these would likely persist under any election method.

It can at least be argued that third-party efforts have been more successful, or less unsuccessful, in presidential elections than in other American contests. George Wallace's campaign is now added to those of Theodore Roosevelt and Robert La Follette as substantial twentieth-century efforts, besides that of Debs in 1912. None, it is true, secured many electoral votes, but their popular vote totals are impressive when compared to even the occasional victories of third-party candidates for Congress and for state offices. And, as George Wallace has been trying to teach us, even a small number of electoral votes might in a close election be transformed into effective bargaining power for the third-party candidate. To be more specific about Thomas' analysis, I cannot believe that difficulty in contesting presidential elections was a principal cause of Socialist Party failure. It cannot explain why the party's state and local electoral strength, peaking before World War I, should have declined instead of reviving in the 1920s and 1930s. Curiously the party faded almost completely at state, local, and congressional levels before Norman Thomas' presidential cause was abandoned.

Thomas is not unaware of the likely reasons, notably of Franklin Roosevelt's success in absorbing potential socialist strength under the banner of the New Deal and the welfare state. Since the absorption was within a coalition, namely a Democratic Party containing many decidedly non-socialist and non-New Dealish elements, Thomas can hardly regard the result as entirely satisfactory. Yet it may be inherently characteristic of American party politics. Each major party is not only ideologically broad but also structurally loose and open. New forces, once large and politically mobilizable, find it easier and more effective to enter an existing party than to start a new party. State and local organizations, when they cannot readily be taken over, are often bypassed. The direct primary is a nearly unique American device facilitating the process. State parties are reshaped and then used to influence national parties. Influence, of course, is not the same as control, and compromise is required as it is not in a new party reconciled to minority status.

To a considerable extent, this process seems to belong to any working two-party pattern and not just to American politics. Each of only two major parties must always be a fairly broad coalition capable of absorbing new interests and forces along with diverse older ones. Obviously it might become so broad as to be an ineffective political means to enact a positive program. That is the charge against American parties of the last few decades. Those who would reform them, within the two-party pattern, rest their hopes on emulating the apparently greater programmatic cohesion of British parties although it is achieved in a much less diverse society more readily permitting the maintenance of parliamentary party solidarity. Rejecting that kind of reform, while agreeing with the charge against American parties, leads, as it did for Norman Thomas, to the search for the means to build a third party. Neither as a political leader nor as a retrospective analyst did Norman Thomas discover the means. But it is likelier now than when he wrote that numerous successors will continue the search. American two-party politics is not presently enjoying its best days.

NOTES

1. Maurice Duverger, *Political Parties,* trans. Barbara and Robert North (New York: John Wiley, 1954).

2. E. E. Schattschneider, *Party Government* (New York: Rinehart, 1942); James MacGregor Burns, *The Deadlock of Democracy* (Englewood Cliffs, N.J.: Prentice-Hall, 1963).

3. David A. Shannon, *The Socialist Party of America* (New York: Macmillan, 1955), p. 263.

4. Selig Perlman, *A Theory of the Labor Movement* (New York: Augustus Kelley, 1949), pp. 167–68.

5. I have tried to explain the difference between American labor politics (in Canada and the United States) and European socialist parties in ch. VI of *Political Parties in Western Democracies* (New York: Praeger, 1967).

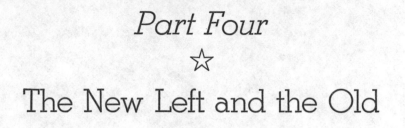

Part Four
☆
The New Left and the Old

Chapter 17

THE FORTUNES OF THE OLD LEFT COMPARED TO THE FORTUNES OF THE NEW*

James Weinstein

I

To make sense of the Old Left and the New Left, of their differences and similarities, the categories themselves have to be rejected except as historical descriptions. Stripped of its ideological content, the New Left is the partial and still self-contradictory re-emergence of a popular revolutionary movement. And the Old Left is the liberal remnant of a once popular movement for democratic socialism in the United States. Much that seemed to be new in the early days of the New Left was, in fact, a return to the early days of the Old Left—to the open revolutionary politics of the old Socialist Party of America (1900–20). The idea of a public revolutionary politics by the New Left and its commitment to a democratic movement for a new society gave it its socialist potential. But the New Left's unconscious acceptance of liberal (and Old Left) social categories—its classless concept of "radical change" and its tendency toward a politics of guilt—was evidence that it was not yet fully a "Left."

Despite its conscious refusal to attempt a comprehensive definition of its politics—a refusal that revealed its acceptance of liberal pragmatism—the movement of the 1960s did develop a genuinely new understanding and practical critique of the liberalism of corporate capitalism. And it has begun to develop a new and more complex understanding of the working class—the proletariat. This process was not completed by Students for a Democratic Society (SDS) or by other New Left organizations because of how the movement emerged, who comprised it, and how they understood themselves. Because they were students who were immersed in traditional sociological ideology, they were not only considered but considered themselves as part of the middle class. And because

* Essay commissioned for this symposium. A somewhat different version appeared in the journal *Socialist Revolution* for July–August 1972.

they rejected the need to develop theory (seeing it as useless sectarian ideological squabbling, which on the part of the Old Left parties and sects it was), they were stuck with the prevailing ideas of class and revolutionary agency. The poor were seen to be the only, or the leading, revolutionary agent by early SDS community organizers. This narrow concept was partially overcome from 1965 to 1968 when SDS and other radical groups were building and leading the peace movement. But once the political leadership of the peace movement was assumed by liberal Democrats—by McCarthy and Kennedy—SDS fell back upon its earlier understanding. Under pressure from Progressive Labor and other sects, building a revolutionary movement came to be understood as aiding and emulating blue-collar workers, revolutionary black organizations (the Black Panthers), or various Third World groups. The breakup of SDS and the splintering of the organized New Left in 1969 expressed the movement's failure to understand itself and the changing nature of the working class in the United States. But the flamboyant posturing of Weatherman and other post-SDS groups did not represent the fate of the movement. It represented only the end of the first stage in the re-emergence of a revolutionary socialist movement in the United States. Hidden from view by the infantile acting out of frustration and despair by Weatherman, the Revolutionary Union, and other such groups, a new process of formation began despite much confusion and demoralization. At issue in this new process is the creation of a modern socialist movement in the United States, one that can comprehend and overthrow capitalist society as a whole. It is within this perspective, for the purpose of trying to understand the limitations and failures of the Left, both Old and New, that this essay is written.

II

Karl Marx understood a socialist movement (party) to be one that consciously seeks to transform capitalist society as a whole. For Marxists, capitalism is a social system that organizes all human activity—"economic," "political," and "social"—around the need to create and realize surplus value, around capitalist commodity production. And, accordingly, revolution requires a change in the principle that now determines all social decision-making. In socialist theory, such a transformation is possible only with the transfer of power over the political economy from the capitalist class to the proletariat, a transformation that establishes the conditions for developing social relations on a new basis.

To make a revolution of this kind the working class must be conscious of itself as a class and must also be aware of its historic possibilities. If the producers are to participate in determining social priorities—if they are to govern themselves—they must want socialism and must join together in a popular movement to attain it. In the United States, of course, no party has come close to building such a movement, although many parties and groups have called themselves socialist or revolutionary. Of these, the old Socialist Party of America came closest to building a popular movement infused with the intention to transform the United States from a capitalist to a socialist society, and in that sense it came closer than any other movement, before or since, to being revolutionary. But the old Socialist Party also had many of the failings that led to reformist politics and to absorption by large-scale corporate capitalism and the "new liberalism" that developed before World War I.

The Socialist Party's revolutionary potential arose from its commitment to democracy and from its strategy of making socialism versus capitalism the central question in all its public activity. Its failures arose from its historical determinism, which blinded it to the differences between the competitive capitalism of the nineteenth century and corporate capitalism of the twentieth, and to the possibility that the ruling class could act as a self-conscious class in its own defense so as to shape history in its own behalf.

The old Socialist Party reached its high point before and during World War I, and then broke up and declined after 1919. From then until the 1960s the popular movement for socialism as an alternative social system consistently dissipated. Socialist history from 1919 to the emergence of the New Left is, in essence, the history of the disintegration of the popular socialist politics created by the old Socialist Party.

The impact of the Russian Revolution and of the Communist International after 1919 and their concepts and forms of organization distinguish the various Communist Parties after 1920 from the old Socialist Party. But despite these differences the Parties formed after 1919 differed little from the old Party in their understanding of capitalist development, the nature of the working class, or the nature of socialism. All the Parties had a perspective rooted in competitive capitalism and unsuited to large-scale corporate capitalism as it has existed in the United States in the twentieth century. Indeed, the Communist Party's strategy, because it was taken directly from the Russian experience, was rooted in the problem of making revolution in a pre-capitalist society. And as a result, both organizationally and theoretically, the Communist Party moved steadily away from the concept of popular movements for socialism. The degree of popularity that the Communist Party attained in its early years was the result of its identification with the Soviets, the first revolutionary socialist state. As a Party of the Third International, the Communist Party shared the prestige of the Russians among Leftists of all kinds in the United States. In particular, this meant that most young revolutionaries gravitated toward the Communists, which, in turn, infused that Party with a sense of vitality that was entirely lacking in the Socialist Party, which was still identified in many ways with the Second International and its wartime collapse. With the initiative in the hands of the Communist Party, the understanding of the need for a popular, self-consciously revolutionary movement lay buried until the 1960s.

III

The limitations of socialist theory followed from the old Party's formation at the time of transition from competitive industrialization to large-scale corporate capitalism. When the Party was organized in 1901 as a coalition of several existing groups and movements, the basis of socialist theory was their common experience of nineteenth-century capitalism. This experience provided the shared understanding within which all tendencies analyzed American politics and acted. At the turn of the century, Socialists believed that competitive capitalism would inexorably lead to a transition to socialism. Competitive industrialization appeared to be the last stage of capitalist development. The emergence of monopoly in all sectors of the economy would create the material basis and social forces for a socialist society, while increasingly severe crises would precipitate the transfer of power to the working class. The conception of socialism prevalent in this period—simply a more efficient and equitable process of industrialization—reflected these beliefs. To members of the old Socialist Party and other Socialists, "socialism" meant above all a more rational, but not qualitatively different, development of productive capacity and a more just distribution of income. The development of capitalism meant the growth of the working class to a majority, and this, along with continuing crises, would provide the basis for a socialist electoral majority.

In general, then, Socialists had a determinist view of capitalist development and an evolutionary optimism about the prospects for a socialist victory. They saw technological development and capitalist integration (through corporate mergers, consolidations, trust agreements, etc.) as steps in a direct path to socialism, and they had a similar understanding of state intervention in the economy. The immediate contradictions between capital and labor, most Socialists believed, would become steadily sharper as conditions of work became more oppressive, as depressions became more frequent, and as workers became radicalized in the futile struggle for the general recognition and acceptance of trade unionism.

Not only would workers more or less automatically become radicalized, but all of society would increasingly be polarized between a small capitalist class and a growing industrial working class. This expectation was based on the constant expansion of capital (through reinvestment of the surplus) that was bringing more and more people into the factories. As Marx put it, 'accumulation of capital entailed increase of the proletariat.[1] The experience of rapid industrialization from the end of the Civil War to the early 1900s appeared to verify the belief that society would eventually be divided between a handful of capitalists and a majority of industrial workers. While more and larger factories and a rapidly growing railroad network required more and more workers, modern machinery and the mechanization of additional kinds of work constantly reduced the number of independent artisans and farmers.

This development, combined with the fierce resistance to unions exhibited by manufacturers competing to cut costs in order to capture more of the market, led Socialists to think that a majority of the population would soon come to be Socialists. And given free suffrage (most workers were white males, and immigrants were expected to become citizens), the electoral machinery of the state seemed the logical instrument to utilize in order to win power.

Thus, secure in the belief that the determined opposition of capitalists to the limited goals of trade unionism would turn struggling workers into revolutionaries, the Socialists looked ahead with confidence to a growing vote and to the prospect of a parliamentary road to ultimate victory for the working class.

Yet the period from 1897 to 1904—in the middle of which the Socialist Party of America was organized—witnessed the most rapid, and decisive, series of mergers and consolidations in American industrial history. When these were over a small number of giant corporations dominated many key sectors of American business. The form of competition known in the nineteenth century was doomed as the large corporations began to transform the political economy from laissez-faire liberalism (free competition and the less government interference the better—except to protect business from attacks by workers or farmers) to corporate liberalism (regulated competition, with the government as a central instrument of social amelioration and control).

The long-term result of these changes in the political economy of American capitalism was to make the Socialist Party program and strategy obsolete, and to create the need for a redefinition of the meaning of socialist revolution in the United States. But this was not immediately apparent—either to Socialists or to business leaders.

The social attitudes and social relations of competitive capitalism persisting beyond the years of their technical necessity thus spurred the growth of the Socialist Party. But by the same token, the growth of the socialist movement forced capitalists to move toward the realization of the humane potential in large-scale industrial production. Fierce trade union struggles had gone on for decades. Ironically, these struggles did not lead to the emergence of a revolutionary movement until after the more sophisticated corporation leaders and financiers were already organizing to reduce overt class antagonism and the threat of conscious class politics that a frustrated trade union movement was producing. Within this political context, the challenge presented by a growing socialist movement helped shape the development of the new liberalism during the Progressive era of 1900–17. But precisely because the development of the new liberalism was in large part a response to the long-term struggles in which the Socialists participated, it was impossible for Socialists fully to understand the changing character of the political economy then taking place. Acting on their view of competitive capitalism, they forced changes in the political economy for which they had no adequate response.

IV

World War I and the Russian Revolution changed the character of the socialist movement in the United States as in the rest of the world. The almost universal support given their wartime governments by European socialist parties in 1914 shocked and disillusioned millions of Party members and sympathizers and made it clear that there was something profoundly wrong with the movement. The result was the collapse of the Second International and a widespread realization of the reformist character of European social democracy.

But the United States did not enter the war until 1917 and by then, for a number of reasons, the Socialist Party firmly opposed American participation. Throughout the war the Party refused support and campaigned for an immediate peace. This was possible partly because the American Party, unlike the major European parties, had a diverse membership with substantial numbers of immigrants or children of immigrants from countries on both sides of the conflict. The Party membership was internationalist not only in its politics, but also in its composition. More important was the independence of the Party from the trade union movement. In Europe, particularly in Germany, the unions were socialist-led and the Party tended more and more to become simply the political expression of trade unionism.[2] When the war began the unions were faced with the choice of opposing it and being smashed by the employers and their government, or of cooperating to ensure wartime production in exchange for increased recognition of the right to organize, and participation in government. With regard to the unions the same situation existed in the United States. The IWW, which neither opposed nor supported the war, was destroyed by wartime prosecutions, while the pro-war AFL unions were given unprecedented recognition. (For the first time, for example, official union representatives sat on various government boards, such as the War Labor Board and War Industries Board.) But few AFL unions were socialist-led, and where they were the union leaders were not also Party leaders. Most of these unions supported the war (needle trades unions officially opposed the war but cooperated in wartime production), with the result that their leaders either quit or were expelled from the Party. During the war, the Party maintained or increased its support among rank-and-file workers but lost its positions of power within the AFL.[3]

The response of the trade unions to the war therefore undermined socialist optimism about the radicalizing function of unionism and about the prospects for gaining control of the unions. Even Victor Berger, right-wing socialist leader from Wisconsin, and one of the strongest advocates of working within the AFL in order to convert it to socialism, believed that the war strengthened *"treason* within the working class." Both publicly and privately, Berger reversed himself with regard to the AFL and the IWW, which he had militantly opposed before the war. To an IWW leader Berger wrote in 1918 that he was "beginning to believe that the IWW (or some labor organization that will succeed it but that will inherit its matchless spirit) is destined to take the place of the AFL in our country and fulfill the mission in which the AFL has failed." And Berger's paper, the Milwaukee *Leader,* editorialized a short time later that the IWW might "have a brilliant future as a labor organization." "Certainly," it added, "there is abundant room for a real labor organization in the industrial field in this country—one that is loyal to the working class—one that will not barter its principles for a few dollars and fishes—one that understands the ultimate as well as the immediate needs of the workers."[4]

The war and the Russian Revolution also undermined the confidence that Socialists had in winning power through the electoral process. Berger still believed that socialism would come in the United States "by means of the ballot." But he believed that millions of people had learned "that it was capitalism that caused the war, and that capitalism is likely to keep on causing wars until it is replaced by socialism." To Berger, this meant that "either before the war is over or soon after, the common people" would "take possession of the various governments *either by means of the ballot or otherwise,* and establish social democracy."[5] If Berger still had a parliamentary perspective, though with far less certainty than before the war, a left-wing Socialist like Charles E. Ruthenberg saw a positive need to break "with American methods and American ideals." This need arose out of the experience of socialist agitators and elected Socialists in Ohio and New York—and even from Berger himself being denied the seat in Congress to which he was elected in 1918. When Socialists tried to educate voters to an understanding of the socialist view of the war at public meetings and in electoral campaigns, Ruthenberg pointed out, "they went to prison by the thousands." And in Cleveland, when the three Socialists elected to city office in 1917 refused to pledge support to the war they were expelled from the council. "If the Socialists are seeking new weapons," Ruthenberg concluded, "it is because the ruling class has taught them the need of new weapons."[6]

Despite the wartime repression of the Party and government destruction of the IWW, the socialist movement emerged from the war with a much wider base of potential support than it had had before the United States entered the conflict. This had been indicated in the elections of 1917, in which the party increased its vote by some 400 per cent in scores of cities, as well as in scattered elections in cities where the Party organization was still intact in 1918.[7] The potential existed because the Party had been the only major political organization to oppose the war, and because in the minds of millions of people its analysis of the war made good sense. For years after 1919, despite its breakup and decline, the Party's wartime stand and activities remained its greatest political asset.

But three things prevented the resurgence of the Socialist Party and of a large-scale popular movement for socialism after World War I. The first, most obvious but least important, was the government attacks on the Party and its press during the war. Over two thousand Socialists were convicted under the wartime Espionage and Sedition Acts, and dozens of newspapers and magazines were denied second-class mailing privileges, or were banned outright from the mails. The latter was the greater blow of the two, since many of these publications had widespread readership in rural areas and small cities throughout the nation. When the war started, socialist publications regularly reached over 2 million people. As a result of removal from the mails most were forced to stop publishing. By 1918 only a few large city newspapers survived.

The second factor was a generally shaken faith in the traditional theory of the Party and in the international movement. The ease with which the immediate interests of the trade unions overcame

any long-range or class-conscious perspective in the unions undermined the Party's optimism about a trade unionist political perspective. Similarly, the ease with which the government used
reforms to weaken support for the radicals—as, for example, when
it simultaneously smashed the IWW in the Northwest and imposed
an eight-hour day (the IWW's central demand) on the lumber industry—brought into question the relationship of immediate demands to ultimate ends.

Finally, in this situation the effect of the Russian Revolution
was sharply to polarize the socialist movement not only in Europe
(where most socialist parties had joined their bourgeois governments during the war) but also in the United States. Among American Socialists, support for the Revolution and opposition to Allied
intervention against the Bolsheviks was never in question. Virtually all American Socialists enthusiastically and joyfully supported
the Bolshevik seizure of power. But the meaning of the Revolution—as enunciated by the newly formed Communist International
in 1919—for socialist politics in the United States did cause a deep
division. By 1919 the old Party had split into three parties and
some smaller groupings.

V

The splitting of the socialist movement in the United States was
not, however, the result of conflicting views about American
corporate capitalism. It was, or appeared to be, the result of differences over the possibility of immediate insurrection. Yet neither
side seriously examined the political basis of this difference. Those
who were to remain Socialists pointed out that conditions in the
United States in 1919 were entirely different from those that made
insurrection possible in Russia in 1917. As Berger argued, Russia
had been "a beaten country" both militarily and economically. Her
army was all but destroyed and was "honeycombed with propaganda." Russian Socialists controlled the trade unions, and the
peasants, who were ready to revolt against their feudal masters,
had no party to turn to except the Bolsheviks. In contrast, various
socialist leaders insisted, the large corporations in the United States
had been strengthened by the war. The trade union movement had
been purged of Socialists, and the Party had been weakened. Although there was considerable post-war disillusionment with the

"war for democracy," there was no indication that any substantial numbers of workers or farmers were ready to revolt.[8]

Those who formed the Communist Party never confronted these arguments. They simply accepted the call of the new International to take up insurrectionary politics. For the Bolsheviks this demand had a compelling logic. Socialist revolution had always been thought to be possible only in the more highly industrialized nations—those that had the industrial base for an economy of abundance. When Lenin had argued that revolution was possible in Russia he meant only that it could set off a revolutionary wave that would sweep rapidly over Western Europe. If that did not happen, Lenin believed, the prospects for the Revolution in Russia were poor. Indeed, as late as 1922 Lenin proclaimed "this elementary truth of Marxism, that the victory of socialism *requires* the joint efforts of workers in a number of *advanced* countries."[9] Thus when the Bolsheviks seized power in Russia it was in the belief that the revolution must spread and that when it did the leadership of the revolutionary movement would pass back to the West, where the proletariat was more highly developed. For two or three years after 1917 the Bolsheviks believed that they themselves were doomed if this did not happen. From this point of view, the International's insistence that affiliation required an insurrectionary politics was not arbitrary. A Party that professed support of the Revolution but did not move toward the seizure of power appeared "objectively" anti-Soviet.

The American Party split over that question. The two Communist parties affiliated with the Third International. The Socialist Party leadership at first opposed affiliation but applied for membership after a Party referendum upheld the "minority" position in favor of joining. But in response to the Socialist Party's application, Gregory Zinoviev replied for the International that it was "not a hotel" where anyone could come with his own baggage. The International was "an army in wartime." Those who joined this "Army of Revolution," Zinoviev explained, "must adopt as their program the program of the Communist International—open and revolutionary mass struggle for Communism through the Dictatorship of the Proletariat by means of the Workers' Soviets." Furthermore, they must "create a strongly centralized form of organization, a military discipline," and all Party members "must be absolutely subject to the full-powered Central Committee of the Party." In addition, they must "prepare for revolutionary action, for merciless civil war."[10]

The debate over immediate insurrection and over affiliation with the Communist International did not advance the socialist movement in the United States. Rather, it diverted Socialists from consideration of the meaning of their wartime experiences and of the increasing stagnation of the Party in the face of a developing liberal corporatism. There was some new thinking among those who became Communists about the narrow parliamentarism of the Socialist Party. This advance, stimulated by the Bolshevik seizure of power, was around the concept of mass action—which according to Louis Fraina, leading left-wing theoretician, meant bringing "mass proletarian pressure on the capitalist state" by shifting the center of activity from the parliaments to the shops and the streets, making electoral activity only one phase of socialist politics.[11]

But Communist leaders, including Fraina, retained the traditional socialist historical determinism. While Fraina understood the necessity of developing new concepts of direct rule, and shared Lenin's vision of the Soviets as a transitional form of the state, he had little else to offer. He believed that the crisis of American capitalism would proceed apace, and that revolutionaries needed simply to wait and prepare themselves for the seizure of power. In less thoughtful hands the limitations of such an understanding were more apparent. William F. Dunne, editor of the Butte *Daily Bulletin* and a founder of the Communist Labor Party, argued in 1919 that "Craft unionism is out of date; it's too late for industrial unionism; mass action is the only thing—mass action." Dunne then predicted that "unemployment will increase, there'll be starvation, and some day the banks will fail and the people will come pouring out on the streets and the revolution will start."[12]

Fraina's and Dunne's views came in part from the euphoria created by the Russian Revolution and the social turmoil in the United States in 1919—the Seattle general strike had already occurred; the Boston police strike and the great steel strike were only months away. But their views were also consistent with the traditional Marxist understanding of the tendencies inherent in capitalism. As a prediction, the first part of Dunne's scenario was fairly accurate—even if ten years premature. But the belief that revolution would be the result of an inevitable unfolding of capitalist contradictions was wrong both empirically and theoretically. As it happened, when the collapse came in 1929 the Communists were unable to turn it to their advantage, except on the pitifully small scale of being able to emerge from the 1930s as the largest of the several socialist sects. Instead, the corporate capitalists and their political and academic allies restored faith in "the system" despite their inability over a ten-year span to pull out of the Great Depression.

Neither the Communists nor the Socialists were prepared for these events because both—particularly the Communists—viewed the Party as a long-term beneficiary of predetermined historical development. The Party was seen as a conduit that contained the vital energies of revolution, which could be released at the appropriate moment to win power for the working class. This elitist concept followed from a mechanistic understanding of Marx's theories of capitalist development, one that left out the conscious activity of both the working class and the capitalist class. Actually, revolution could have followed the events Dunne anticipated only if the Party had helped make history by continuously and publicly examining the meaning of socialism as an alternative to capitalism, only if it attempted to seize the initiative from the capitalists in order to realize the tendencies inherent in the system, rather than allowing these to be thwarted by the defensive actions of the ruling class. For revolution to occur at the time of collapse, the great majority of the population, of the working class, would already have to have had a socialist consciousness. In other words, the collapse would be a genuine crisis for the system only if the working class were already organized into a movement (led by some form of party) to replace capitalism with socialism. In Russia, the demand for bourgeois democratic reforms could precipitate a revolutionary crisis because Russia was a semi-feudal nation. But the only revolutionary program in the United States was the need for socialism embodied in every immediate issue. The increasing integration and self-consciousness of the corporate ruling class, as well as their increasing ability to use the state for planning to achieve social stability, meant that immediate demands could not in themselves lead to a revolutionary crisis.

But the Communists' politics were based immediately on the Russian experience—the seizure of state power by a small Party prepared to take the initiative when the ruling class had com-

690 / JAMES WEINSTEIN

pletely lost control and the nation was disintegrating rapidly. The central importance of the will to take power, and the need in that situation to break with those that did not share that will, enabled the Bolsheviks to triumph in Russia. But in the United States such politics were doomed to the failure they achieved. Within two years of their formation the Communist Parties had squandered 90 per cent of their membership, and by 1921, when a reversal of their initial program was forced on them by the International, they themselves admitted that they did "not exist as a factor in the class struggle."[13]

VI

The last half of the 1920s was a period of continuing stagnation for the Socialist Party and of great internal turmoil for the Communist Party. As organizers of a popular movement for socialism, both Parties reached a dead end in 1924. The Socialist Party had lost its youth and its identification with the world revolutionary movement to the Communists. And it had squandered its few remaining resources in support of La Follette's candidacy for President on an independent ticket in 1924. The Communists, whose major political asset was identification with the Soviet Union, were caught up in the intensive factional struggles between Stalin, Trotsky, Zinoviev, and Bukharin. The various factions within the Communist Party were also so busy during these years trying to keep up with what was going on in Russia—and trying to line up with the winners—that they could pay little attention to developments in the United States. In most cases policy was decided on the basis of its correlation with the policy of the International—in fact it often was decided *by* the International and simply imposed upon the American Party. These years which immediately followed Lenin's death were the period of "Bolshevization" of the International and its constituent Parties. The result was firmly to establish the distinctive forms of organization and modes of work that characterized the Communist Party for the coming decades.

The Socialist Party had developed a form of Party organization that was appropriate to its political perspective, which was parliamentary and based on an alliance between the industrial workers (who were expected to become the largest sector of society) and tenant and small farmers. The Socialist Party structure generally followed that of official political divisions. There were forty-eight state Parties, each with a good deal of autonomy from the national organization. Each city constituted a local, subdivided into branches that usually followed ward lines, or those of other political subdivisions. Party officers were elected at various conventions, and Party programs and policies were subject to approval by membership referendums. In addition, a small number of locals could initiate new policy proposals, and they could also initiate recall of elected officers on a state or national level. The foreign-language federations, made up of Socialists from various European countries, were semi-autonomous. They had their own locals and language press and were represented in the national office by secretaries who functioned as translators and spokesmen for each federation. Members paid monthly dues, and membership was calculated on the basis of the average number of monthly dues payments throughout the year.

The Party structure was a model of formal democracy, and did in fact allow for substantial participation and initiative by the membership. Party bureaucracies developed on the national and state levels, but these were constantly subject to challenge from within, and since the Party press was mostly controlled by individuals or by Party locals (a national Party-owned newspaper did not appear until 1914), it was difficult for any one group to dominate the Party.

When the Communist Parties were established in 1919, they did not immediately change the form of organization inherited from the Socialists. The Communist Labor Party made no changes, the Communist Party added shop nuclei (branches based on the place of work) to the geographical branches. These changes meant little, because both Parties immediately went "underground" and paid little attention to the formal structure, since democratic functioning was not possible, even if it were desirable. While the Parties were underground they adopted some of the forms of the Russian Party, but with the founding of the Workers' Party in late 1921 the Communists returned to an organization that closely resembled the old Socialist Party.

Until mid-1924 this situation was tolerated by the International. Then the Communists came under increasing pressure to Bolshevize their organization—which meant both a change in policy and in organization. Bolshevization was in part designed to bring the

American Party into closer touch with the industrial workers, and accordingly the main demands put upon it by the International were to establish factory branches and to set up "fractions" in non-party organizations. (Fractions were Party caucuses that operated secretly and had no authority to make policy for themselves.) The immediate political implication of this new policy was a shift away from involvement with farmer-labor politics, which was primarily electoral, and into the factories and unions where the fractions operated.

VII

This process ended in 1929. Thereafter the Party moved to an understanding of "monolithism" in which the absence of factions faithfully reflected the state of things in the Soviet Union. In this later period, when the absence of political disagreements within the Party made it possible for all energies to be focused on building the movement, the Communists reached their highest level of popularity. The Party began to emerge from its isolation in late 1929 with the onset of the Great Depression. In the next few years Party members were active in the unemployed movement, helping to organize unemployed councils and militantly leading demonstrations. With American capitalism in collapse and chaos on all sides undermining belief in the system, the Communists could proudly point to the Soviet Union, where the first five-year-plan was under way and unemployment was unknown. Communist militance and leadership of the unemployed brought them into contact with countless thousands who had never heard of the Party. And the Party's approach fitted the mood of the time. The Communists gave voice to a widespread hostility to America's rulers, and pressed for jobs and a return to order.[14]

Even so, it was not until the International changed its line from the "Third Period" to the Popular Front against fascism that the Communists succeeded in gaining virtually uncontested leadership of the American Left. This occurred in 1935, after Hitler had already seized power in Germany and the Nazis had systematically destroyed the Left. Like virtually all the changes in policy of the American Communists, neither the adoption of the Third Period Left line nor the switch to the Popular Front had anything to do with events in the United States. The International imposed the

Left line of the Third Period partly because of Stalin's decision to begin rapid industrialization and collectivization of agriculture, and partly in response to the failure of the Russians' conciliatory foreign policy in the mid-twenties.

In the United States the effects of the Third Period were less disastrous than they were in Europe or in China only because there was so much less at stake. The main result was to continue the isolation of the Party from the organized workers as a result of the dual union policy forced on the Americans by the Comintern. The most striking example of this involved the Communists in the United Mine Workers Union, in which a broad coalition of Progressives and Communists, the Save the Union Committee, had been challenging John L. Lewis' leadership in 1927 and early 1928. The Save the Union Committee had been organized by William Z. Foster's Trade Union Educational League, and Foster, who had quit the IWW in 1911 so that he could work within the AFL and had later been the main organizer of the AFL-led steel strike in 1919, had long been the Party's most militant exponent of "boring from within" the existing trade unions. The Save the Union Committee was his most successful venture in the 1920s, but just when it was gaining strength most rapidly the Comintern issued instructions that "the Left Wing in the UMW and amongst the unorganized miners must prepare to become the basis of a new union."[15] This meant a break with the Progressives in the UMW and led to the formation of the short-lived and isolated National Miners Union—an organization that was abandoned with the adoption of the Popular Front policy in 1935.

At times during the Third Period the Party publicly espoused its own concept of socialism. This was the idea of a Soviet America. It was a vision that could not be, and was not, attractive to American workers, since it was based on emulating a society that was trying desperately to industrialize under extremely harsh conditions. At best, the Soviets offered the prospect of forced industrialization (which meant no unemployment) under undemocratic rule—which was insufficient as a revolutionary inspiration for Americans. Furthermore, during the Third Period the Communists bitterly attacked other Socialists and liberals as "social fascists," despite the similarities of their programs to Communist demands for unemployment insurance, public assistance and work relief, food for school children, and public construction programs. Thus, despite their gains during the late 1920s and early 1930s, the Communists developed little following.

The Third Period ended with Hitler's annihilation of the Communists and Social Democrats, and with the subsequent realization by the Russians that fascism constituted a new and grave threat to the very existence of the Soviet Union. The Russians now desperately sought to prevent the formation of a coalition of capitalist powers aimed at their destruction. To build alliances wherever possible in order to halt the enhancement of fascist power it was necessary to repudiate the view that Social Democrats (Progressives and liberals in the United States) were as much or more the enemy than were the reactionaries. Thus after 1935 the erstwhile "social fascists" became sought-after allies in a front of liberals and Socialists that would defend liberal (bourgeois) democracy against warlike and totalitarian reaction.

This change in the Communist line was most strikingly evident in the change from the early days of Franklin D. Roosevelt's administration, when Communists labeled as fascist both the Agricultural Adjustment Act and the National Recovery Act, to the Popular Front days, when they attacked the Supreme Court as fascist for declaring these acts unconstitutional. Similarly, during the National Miners Union days, John L. Lewis was attacked as a leader of the "fascist AFL." Yet when he set up the Committee for Industrial Organization in the AFL, and later led it out of the AFL to found the Congress of Industrial Organizations as a rival federation, the Communists completely subordinated themselves to his leadership.

It was in this later period, when the CIO was rapidly organizing millions of workers in the mass production industries, that the Party achieved its largest following and its greatest success. Communists were prominent in many CIO unions and controlled several. They were dedicated and effective organizers, skilled in leading militant struggles, and while they were perfectly at home in the bureaucratic hierarchy of the CIO they often appeared as firm supporters of democracy within the unions. This was particularly so in unions like the United Electrical Workers and the United Auto Workers, where the Party had strong influence from the beginning but did not have control, and in which, therefore, they had to rely on popular support (as opposed to support of the CIO leadership) to retain their influence.[16]

The rapid increase of Communist influence and popularity in the second half of the 1930s rested in large part on their identification with the organization of the new industrial unions—the fulfillment of the dream of old-time radicals. But it also rested on the Party's close ties to the Soviet Union. To take oneself seriously as a revolutionary in the years before and immediately after World War II it was necessary to identify with the Soviets—the only embodiment of socialism triumphant. And the Communist Party had the franchise. Thus it had the best of both worlds. It acted the part of the most militant of liberals, defending the highly popular Roosevelt administration (while maintaining a mildly critical stance) and declaring that Communism was nothing less than twentieth-century Americanism carrying on the traditions of Jefferson, Jackson, and Lincoln.[17] While the Party's relationship to the Soviet Union attracted many liberals who were having doubts about the viability or desirability of capitalism in the face of the Great Depression, some Party members only grudgingly accepted the liberal politics of the Popular Front as a necessary expedient to defend the Revolution in Russia. But others greeted the new line as a welcome opening to respectability. As one former Party functionary happily wrote, when Americanization replaced Bolshevization, the "proletarian garb favored by functionaries was replaced by the business suit; our professional revolutionaries could hardly be distinguished from office executives; bus travel was replaced by Pullman . . . and the day Earl Browder stood up in a restaurant to help his wife don her new coat initiated a new standard of deportment."[18]

Looking back on the 1930s from the experience of the 1960s, the Popular Front period often appears to New Leftists as a key turning point in the degeneration of the Old Left. But in fact the Popular Front represented only a change in tactics; the larger political perspective underlying it—the concept of class and of social development, and of the role of the Party—was unchanged from the Third Period. Thus Communists and their liberal followers generally look back on these years as a Golden Age of radicalism. After all, the Party's line during the 1930s had made it popular—more so than ever before or since. And the longer-term strategy had always been implicit in the form of organization that had developed in the 1920s. The Party had acted as if, even in the United States, the revolution would be in two stages, and as if the Party could seize power in a moment of crisis without having conducted any public agitation for socialism beforehand. Socialism itself, in the Communist Party's view, was a public issue neither during the Third Period nor during the Popular Front. Socialist consciousness remained the property of the vanguard, which to Lenin had meant the self-consciously revolutionary workers, but which had come to mean simply the Party. "Mass action," in contrast, was increasingly understood to be around immediate issues.

The refusal of Lenin and the Bolsheviks to acquiesce in the historical determinism of European social democracy, and the Bolshevik Revolution in pre-capitalist Russia, had been a giant step forward in the development of Marxist politics. But mechanically transferred to the United States, Bolshevism became a step backward from parliamentary socialism to militant liberalism—and in the Popular Front to not-so-militant liberalism. Similarly, the worldwide effect of the Russian Revolution was to advance the revolutionary movements in the colonies and semi-colonies and to retard it in the industrialized West. In countries like China, and later Vietnam and Indonesia, it was possible to turn bourgeois goals for national independence and formal democratic rights to the advantage of socialist revolutionaries because the capitalist class had not yet established its hegemony. But in the developed capitalist nations a similar strategy only strengthened the hand of the ruling class.

The only major exception to this rule was in the American Party's relationship to the blacks. Here, the International's emphasis on national liberation and its orientation toward the colonies forced the American Party to make the Negro question a central part of its politics, and thus to make a major advance over all earlier socialist and radical parties. The American Communists themselves at first had no particular interest in blacks. The old Socialist Party had had many more Negro members, and after 1917 had a substantial black following in the North centering around A. Phillip Randolph and Chandler Owen's *Messenger*.[19] In contrast, and despite the prodding from Lenin and other leaders of the International, the Communist Party had only two dozen black members as late as 1927.[20] But there had been a running debate on the Negro question in Moscow, starting at the Second Congress of the Comintern in 1920. This discussion ended in late 1928 at the Sixth Congress of the International, with the adoption of the position that Negroes constituted a nation in the black belt in the South. As the *Daily Worker* then explained, this meant that "while continuing and intensifying the struggle under the slogan of full social and political equality for the Negroes," the "party must come out openly and unreservedly for the right of Negroes to national self-determination in the southern states where Negroes form a majority of the population."[21]

This new "Thesis" of the International was part of its program for building revolutionary movements in the "Colonies and Semi-Colonies," and profoundly changed the attitude of the American Party. Although the call for an independent black republic in the South attracted little support, the Party's concentration on the Negro question and its activity around immediate issues—like unemployment, discrimination in hiring and in the unions—and for welfare quickly gained it considerable following among blacks. The Party was particularly active in Harlem and other northern ghettos, as well as in the black belt, and thousands of blacks joined the Party in the North. By the late 1930s there were 8,000 to 10,000 black Communists, more than 10 per cent of Party membership. This was achieved by militant struggles for civil rights, mostly in the North, while disarming nationalists by proclaiming their support for national self-determination in the South and their intention to fight for it once a Party base could be established there.[22] During the 1930s, for the first time, the Communists succeeded in building a substantially interracial radical movement with the Party at the center.

Yet, largely because of the theory on which the Party acted, the results were not all positive. The basis of the Party's politics was the idea of independence for an agrarian nation of blacks. Thus national liberation for American Negroes would have meant the perpetuation of a majority in the black belt and centered on the demand for land. But the path of development for blacks was already clearly going in another direction. Modernization of agriculture and the rapid growth of cities, north and south, combined to push blacks off the land and into the cities, where they became part of the working class rather than of the peasantry (which is how Communists understood them). But this situation had been ignored by the Communists because the position on American blacks had not come out of an analysis of American conditions, but out of an analogy with Asian and African colonies. As the

Party understood it, the revolutionary content of its program for blacks consisted of the demand for national self-determination in the South, while its day-to-day politics consisted of struggles for civil rights. Given this, it is no surprise that socialism was considered even less an issue for blacks than for whites.

For whites, socialism was at least seen as the conscious goal of Party members. Among blacks even this was not so. As George Blake Charney, the Party's second-in-command in Harlem, writes of this period, "we never quite knew to what degree, if any, the idea of socialism penetrated the minds of the party members" in Harlem. "For most [blacks]," he concludes, "the relationship of the freedom struggle to socialism was nebulous, even irrelevant."[23] It should be no surprise, then, that although the Party espoused a nationalist line for blacks, it always strictly opposed an autonomous black revolutionary movement. Nor was it an accident that some years later, when the Communist Party abandoned the idea of a Negro nation in the South, it returned to a liberal integrationist line and opposed the new proto-socialist revolutionary nationalist movements for as long as it was possible to do so. In the long run, Communist policy toward blacks aided the liberal corporatists of the New Deal in weakening the autonomous black liberation movement in much the same way that Communist policy generally during the 1930s served finally to obliterate the popular movement for socialism in the United States.

By the end of the 1930s, Communists were virtually indistinguishable from left-wing New Dealers except in their loyalty to the Soviet Union—and in their almost purely private commitment to revolution. During the Second World War, with the Soviets as an ally, this identification served the Communists well, so that even as the Party was formally dissolved—as a token of its increasingly explicit liberalism—the new organization (the Communist Political Association) remained popular.[24] But, more than ever after the war, the Communist Party's strength rested on its identification with the Soviets—in other respects, even after the Party was reconstituted in 1945, it was at best militantly liberal. And when the war ended, and along with it the temporary alliance of the Western imperial powers and the Soviet Union against Germany, Italy, and Japan, Communists came under renewed attack as Russian agents. Support of the Cold War and of aggressive postwar American expansion by the CIO leadership and the vast majority of liberal leaders sealed the Party's fate. The result was the collapse of the Left, the rise of Joseph McCarthy and McCarthyism, and what came to be known as the "silent decade" of the 1950s.

VIII

The New Left, which came into being with the 1960s, was a loosely organized movement, made up largely of students, that began with the wave of sit-in demonstrations that started at a North Carolina lunch counter on New Year's Day 1960 and swept throughout the South in the following year. Out of those demonstrations involving both black and white students, the Student Nonviolent Coordinating Committee (SNCC) came into being (April 1960). Largely inspired by SNCC, and by their experience in the southern civil rights demonstrations, a group of white students founded Students for a Democratic Society (SDS) in 1962. When organized, SDS was sponsored and subsidized by the League for Industrial Democracy, a Cold War socialist group that dated back to the early 1920s.

SNCC and SDS, of course, were to be the major national organizations of the student Left, but from the beginning they encompassed only a small part of the new movement. Many *ad hoc* groups sprang up from Berkeley to Cambridge in the early 1960s around immediate issues—such as the Caryl Chessman execution in California, the 1960 HUAC hearings in San Francisco, the plight of union miners in Hazard, Kentucky. Some of these formed into temporary organizations that followed one another as the central issues changed—SLATE, then the Free Speech Movement (FSM), then the Vietnam Day Committee (VDC) at Berkeley. In addition, starting in 1959 with *Studies on the Left* (at Madison, Wisconsin), several new student magazines appeared: *New University Thought* at Chicago, *Root and Branch* at Berkeley, and others at Cornell University, Chapel Hill, etc.

These groups had in common two things that sharply distinguished them from the practice of the Old Left parties. They acted directly against immediately perceived evils in American society, and their central idea was to defend or extend democratic rights. "Participatory democracy," a slogan of SDS, captured these characteristics and gained its great popularity because it so well expressed the general feeling. All the various groups were motivated by the idea of democracy and equality. The president of the SLATE Peace Committee, arguing for Easter peace demonstrations in 1960, insisted that "the power of democracy is a living idea," and that "freedom of speech, equality, self-determination of peoples" were "the most powerful political ideas in the world."[25]

But if this is true, why would a radical Left arise in the United States, the most democratic nation in the world, in a period when the remnants of McCarthyism were receding into the background? And why would the New Left be a student movement, when students were relatively well off and traditionally part of the ruling or middle class, and, therefore, already "participants" in the decision-making process? The answer, in part, lay in the general changes in American corporate capitalism over the previous several decades and the post-war policies designed to prevent a return to the crisis of the 1930s. The Great Depression, which lasted over ten years and was ended only by massive arms expenditures by the government and by the absorption of surplus workers into the armed forces, made it clear that "free market" capitalism could no longer provide enough jobs in industry for workers displaced by developing technology. And it also showed that the corporations could not find enough areas for investment outside of goods manufacturing to maintain a satisfactory level of profits unless the government intervened to protect and subsidize private investment on a massive scale.

Thus, in order to prevent a return to the Depression in the post-war years, the government (with the aid and advice of corporate planners) embarked on a number of programs to make work and secure profits. These policies centered in the Cold War, which served both to justify a policy of massive armaments spending (which created jobs and profits without dumping goods on the market) and to provide an ideological cover (the battle between godless Communism and the Free World) under which the United States assumed global responsibility for the maintenance of an empire. For a time the Cold War, enthusiastically supported by liberals and Socialists, succeeded in hiding the changed nature of American imperialism after World War II. Before the war, although the United States was as involved in overseas trade and investment as other capitalist nations, it had few colonies and generally opposed colonialism in the interest of free trade or the open door—a policy that allowed American corporations to compete, more or less freely, in the markets of "sovereign" nations like China or Argentina. After the war, not only did American corporations push for vastly expanded overseas investment for their surplus capital, but also the United States was the only nation with the power to reimpose the colonial system throughout the world. Germany and Japan were defeated; England, France, and Holland were exhausted and had to rebuild their domestic economies. Only the United States emerged with a vastly expanded productive capacity and the will to take responsibility for capitalist survival throughout the world. So, for example, in 1945 the United States decided to support France's return to Indo-China and for the next nine years provided the great bulk of military supplies used in the unsuccessful attempt to re-establish French colonialism in Vietnam. And when France failed even with that aid, the United States stepped in to prevent Vietnamese escape from imperial domination.

Within this over-all situation, the position of youth and the meaning of being a college student was also rapidly changing. In 1940, just before the war, only 5 per cent of eighteen- to twenty-one-year-olds were in college. By 1970 close to 50 per cent were enrolled. This vast increase in the student population served two purposes: to delay entry into the work force of several million youth for several years, and to train millions of new workers, no longer needed in the direct production of goods, for jobs in sales promotion, social control, and various kinds of research and development. The meaning of being a college student and the nature of work that college-trained people did after graduation changed dramatically with the rapid expansion of higher education. Students, most of whom two decades earlier were from or entering the middle classes (small entrepreneurs, independent professionals, upper-level management), now, by and large, were faced with becoming employees in corporate or government bureaucracies. How students felt about this, what it meant to their lives, was dramatically expressed in the Free Speech Movement in Berkeley, particularly by Mario Savio, whose charisma consisted of faithfully expressing the not yet fully conscious feelings of most students.

Like the vast majority of students in 1964, Savio did not yet understand himself as a revolutionary and was not a Socialist. During the previous summer he had gone to Mississippi to "join the struggle for civil rights." In the fall he was "engaged in another phase of the same struggle" in Berkeley. These were two battlefields where the same rights were at stake: "the right to participate as citizens in a democratic society and the right to due process of law." As Savio explained, the university in the post-war period had become "part and parcel of this particular stage in the history of American society; it stands to serve the needs of American industry; it is a factory that turns out a certain product needed by industry or government." That product was supposed to be an unthinking and unquestioning cog in a vast bureaucratic system. "The 'futures' and 'careers' for which American students now prepare," Savio complained, were "for the most part intellectual and moral wastelands." But Savio was determined to help fight against a future in which men and women would be "standardized, replaceable, and irrelevant."[26]

This commitment to act, to engage in "active dissent," was the common bond among early New Leftists. It was important in that it broke with all the ideological justifications for rejecting joint action, and for the failure to see or take seriously the glaring inequalities in American society, by Old Leftists and liberals in the 1950s. The wide range of actions, the diversity and studied openness of the student movement in its early years led to rapid changes in the activists' understanding of American society. United in activity around their feelings on issues, radical students soon began to see the limitations of the liberal "solutions" to the evils they opposed. Thus, for example, the growing awareness of the systematic oppression of blacks not only in the South but also in the northern ghettos made people question what good the simple attainment of civil rights could do. As one early SDS community organizer observed, " 'civil rights' gets the Negro in the south no more than a Harlem."[27] And events in the early 1960s combined to reveal the inhuman nature of corporate capitalism at a time when liberal ideologues were busy crowing over the virtues and triumphs of the system. For example, the invasion of Cuba by CIA-trained and -financed counterrevolutionaries in 1961—and the exposure of the bald lies of Adlai Stevenson and others in denying complicity—undermined people's faith in the liberal establishment's professions of support for democracy abroad.

The war in Vietnam and the protest movement built around it became the central experience of the New Left in awakening an understanding not only that the "system" was undemocratic, corrupt, and immoral, but also that it was a *system*. And SDS leadership in anti-war actions, starting with the SDS-sponsored march on Washington on April 17, 1965, also led to the new student movement's decisive break with Cold War pacifism and socialism. The march itself had been planned before President Johnson ordered the bombing of North Vietnam and at first SDS invitations to participate had been ignored by the old-line peace groups (SANE, Turn Toward Peace, War Resisters' League, etc.) but accepted by the Trotskyist and Communist youth groups. After the bombing began and SDS was well along with its plans, the old-line groups were forced grudgingly to come along, particularly since it then appeared that the march would draw large numbers of people to Washington. But as it became clear that SDS would not exclude what the Cold War pacifists called "anti-American" groups, and that SDS itself identified with the aspirations of the NLF and the North Vietnamese, such people as Bayard Rustin and Michael Harrington began to red-bait the march and SDS behind its back. Besides being unprincipled, this attack proved a major tactical error. The march drew a then-record crowd for a peace demonstration—some 25,000 people—and the leadership of the anti-war movement passed from the old pacifist organizations to the new student Left.

The April 1965 march on Washington also marked the beginning of a public concern on the part of SDS to come to terms with itself as a movement for "radical social change." This was symbolized in Paul Potter's speech to the rally in Washington when he spoke for the first time of the need to "name the system." In characteristic SDS style, however, he failed to do so, and the question of whether or not "radical social change" meant overthrowing capitalism in favor of socialism remained unexamined.

Thus, despite the rapid spread of radical consciousness among students and a growing awareness that it was the system as a whole and not just particular issues that were at stake, the New Left did not put forward an alternative. It did not develop a revolutionary strategy that posed the existing social structure against a new one. And, of course, it follows that at this stage the student radicals had no conception of themselves as being part of a revolutionary (or potentially revolutionary) class that could speak for a new society. Indeed, in the community-organizing stage of SDS, when student radicals were asked "What do you people want?" (the inevitable but not entirely misplaced question), they insisted that it was not their job to provide answers, but only to make it plain that changes were needed. Most of the community organizers had a sense that they were building a "mass radical movement" with the intention to "transform American institutions."[28] And yet they could argue that "Poor people need to form independent movements if the war-on-poverty is to get anywhere," that, in general, "even 'reforms' require millions of people taking direct action and organizing themselves."[29] Lacking an explicit socialist framework, that view fitted perfectly within the pluralist view of political science, which recognizes the need for pressure groups of dissenters as means of informing the ruling class about what reforms are necessary.

And yet, the New Left was not just another pressure group. For not only did the need for revolutionary change (albeit still undefined) become more and more widespread and explicit among movement people, but there was also the beginning of seeing students as a legitimate social force in their own right, as part of a "new working class" that could fight for a new society in its own interest. So that even though New Left analyses of revolution and of the class role of students were unclear they did represent the beginnings of a new socialist politics in the United States.

The anti-war movement spurred on the development of a new understanding of the class position of students, since unlike the community-organizing days, tens, maybe hundreds, of thousands of students were now engaged in activity in their own behalf. As SDS grew into a movement with hundreds of chapters and many thousands of members the need to understand this experience stimulated thinking about students as part of a "new working class." This development at first centered around Bob Gottlieb, Dave Gilbert, and Gerry Tenney in New York and was further developed by SDS national officers Carl Davidson and Greg Calvert.[30] Its most organized expression was in the attempt to build the movement among college graduates—Movement for a Democratic Society, and Teachers for a Democratic Society (MDS and TDS), both formed in 1968.

Calvert summed up this thinking in a 1967 speech at Princeton. Revolutionary consciousness begins, he said, with an awareness of the gap between what is historically possible, "what one could be," and the ways in which that potential is limited and frustrated —"what is." This awareness becomes revolutionary when one discovers oneself as part of an oppressed group or class, who must unite with others in order to change society so that the historical potential can be realized. For students this meant understanding themselves as part of the oppressed, rather than simply as privileged members of society (which in part they are) who can relate to the underclasses only through feelings of guilt and liberal missionary politics. This was possible through a rejection of the bourgeois sociological definitions of class (definitions based on income levels or on life-styles) and a return to defining class in terms of people's relationship to the process of production. Advanced technology required relatively fewer industrial workers and many more technicians; and mass production required greatly expanded consumption as well as whole new industries to create, sustain, and manage demand for the commodities produced. Furthermore, the social conditions of modern production required whole new industries of social control. All of these workers—technicians, teachers, advertising people, social workers—were now seen as workers rather than as middle class because they had no independent access to productive property and less and less control over the nature of their work or over people in the lower classes. This analysis, which was an extension of the FSM and other such thinking, defined students as trainees for new working-class jobs, as apprentice workers. And Calvert's conclusion was that students should understand themselves as part of a "broad range of social strata" that included the "old" and "new" working class and the "underclass" of racial and ethnic minorities—all of whom must move together to revolutionize the United States.[81]

The attempt to understand students as part of a potentially revolutionary, diversified working class was part of a general tendency within the New Left that saw the anti-theoretical stance of the movement as increasingly unproductive and dangerous. In early 1966 some of the *Studies on the Left* editors had argued that the new movements were at or were fast approaching states of crisis, that "the initial usefulness and success of their anti-ideological stances have worn thin," and that the need was for the development of a socialist movement that would think in terms of a post-industrial socialism.[82] The new working-class theory, to the extent that it placed students within a diverse working class, was a step in that direction. But the anti-theoretical and anti-intellectual currents were too strong in the movement, and the new tendency quickly faded in the face of youth culture advocates on one side and Progressive Labor (PL), with its narrow industrial-working-class perspective, on the other.

Even in the absence of these competing pressures, however, it would have been difficult to translate the newly developing view of the working class into a coherent politics in 1967. The power of traditional Marxism and of pragmatic liberal theory weighed too heavily in the balance against such ideas. Further, the experience of success in the form of a rapidly growing movement and a rapidly developing anti-capitalist consciousness, as well as a widespread acceptance of themselves as middle-class (privileged) students, militated against such a development. In any case, other circumstances were unfavorable.

By 1968, for example, liberal politicians began to emerge as "leaders" of the anti-war movement, most actively through Eugene McCarthy's campaign against Lyndon Johnson. Until then, the absence of a defined socialist politics had not been immediately detrimental to the movement because the anti-war movement itself was constantly radicalizing tens of thousands of people under the leadership of SDS, radical blacks, and various Old Left and radical peace groups. In the pre-1968 days, in fact, many radicals argued that the peace movement was itself a surrogate revolutionary party, which in a narrow sense, and briefly, it was. For those who relied on the continued leftward development of the peace movement the campaigns of McCarthy and Robert Kennedy, and the ease with which they recruited young activists, were a serious blow. This was particularly so within SDS, where the then Maoist oriented Progressive Labor Party had been making steady gains. PL saw the working class as the agent of revolution, but its working class consisted only of industrial workers; students were members of the middle class who could become revolutionaries only by recognizing the leading position of the industrial workers and, ultimately, by becoming either industrial workers or "professional revolutionaries." PL was not a profound threat before 1968 because the anti-war movement was composed of those groups that PL denied were potentially revolutionary—middle-class students and ghetto blacks—while the industrial workers gave no sign of opposing the war. But once the anti-war movement began to stagnate, and especially when the liberals began to take a more active role in opposing the war—aided by the Trotskyist Socialist Workers Party's insistence on eliminating anti-imperialist politics from peace demonstrations—the anti-war movement took on a different meaning. As it became more difficult to equate anti-war and revolutionary activity, as students flocked to support liberal Democrats, especially McCarthy, PL's industrial-working-class theories assumed a more menacing aspect to SDS leaders.

It was at this point that the various groups that coalesced as the Revolutionary Youth Movement tendencies (RYM I and RYM II) began to take shape. The need to combat PL and its idea of the working class (narrowly defined) as revolutionary agent; the idea of youth as a class coupled with the current wave of high school and college militance; and the romantic appeal of the revolutionary guerrilla as exemplified by Ché Guevara—all these factors were present in the formation of Weatherman, the major development to emerge in the New Left during the course of 1969.

Of the different groups that formed during early 1969, Weatherman had the widest appeal because it combined these elements. The Weatherman rejection of older people (workers of various strata) corresponded to the current youth culture rejection of "straights"—anyone who worked for a living. At the same time, their identification with the Third World, and particularly with the Black Panthers, who were at the peak of their influence in mid-1969, gave them a semblance of plausibility as well as a continuity with the missionary side of early SDS "ghetto organizing."

All the post-1969 splinters of SDS, Weatherman, RYM II, Revolutionary Union, PL, based their "politics" on self-repudiation and on the implicit idea of redemption through identification with the one true or key revolutionary agent—ghetto blacks, youth culture "freaks," or industrial workers. And in doing so all the splinter groups of necessity repudiated the two major ideas of the early New Left that had given it its revolutionary impulse and direction: that radicalism was based on an awareness of one's own oppression, and that the question of popular participation in the process of political decision-making was central to radical politics. These two ideas had been responsible for New Leftists steadily moving toward an understanding of the working class as diverse and stratified, and for the necessity of a socialist revolution in order to realize substantial democracy in place of the formal democracy of corporate capitalism. But these ideas were rejected as part of the same process that led various groups to identify with Leninist revolutionary politics. Thus as the student Left moved toward a socialist consciousness it fell back on the existing stock of revolutionary ideas: the need for an elite vanguard; a narrow concept of class; an emphasis on military action. At the same time it continued to accept bourgeois sociological categories of thought in understanding people primarily as consumers and in defining the working class, or the potentially revolutionary class, in terms of income levels and life-styles rather than according to their relationship to the process of production. In short, both the process of events and the failure to develop a theoretical understanding of advanced capitalism combined to produce frustration and an overwhelming sense of crisis. Increasing isolation of the New Left despite its early growth and the ease with which many sectors of society vacillated between the new radicalism and acceptance of liberal anti-war leadership combined to reinforce the already existing elitist tendency within SDS. Weatherman was the result.

Even at its height, Weatherman numbered only a few hundreds while SDS had had upward of 50,000 adherents and many tens of thousands more followers in 1968 and early 1969. But numbers alone are not a true measure of the impact of a political tendency. Within the student and ex-student movement Weatherman ideas predominated for the year after the June 1969 convention. The result was a continued process of breakup and disintegration of the movement, a splintering that briefly reproduced a number of political tendencies from the past or from other social experiences. The Revolutionary Union, Detroit Organizing Committee, and RYM II adopted PL's view of the working class with minor modifications and attempted to "colonize" factories or working-class neighborhoods. Other groups took up guerrilla warfare and engaged in clandestine bombings of banks, utilities, and other installations. Much larger numbers dropped out of "politics" altogether and set up various forms of communes in which they sought at least to change their own lives. The main tendency in these was a rejection of engagement with the existing society and a retreat to pre-industrial life-styles and social relations. And the main difference between these latter-day communes and the historic experiments of a century or more ago was that the process of disillusionment was measured in weeks rather than in decades.

During the years that followed, a new movement has developed based in part on the two central ideas of the New Left. This is the women's liberation movement, which has been both an extension of the New Left and a reaction against the treatment of women within the movement during the 1960s. As an organized autonomous movement, women's liberation has consisted primarily of college-educated women, and is a result of the vast increase in the number of women attending college in recent years. For like male college students who expected college education to allow them to lead creative and self-determining lives and found themselves being prepared to become cogs in bureaucratic machines, women students were receiving training that they thought would allow them to participate in work outside the home. Women went through the same formal process of education as men, but were also instructed that their futures depended on finding a man, to whom they and any possible careers would be subordinated. The women's movement began as caucuses within SDS and other movement groups because despite their protestations of the need for equal participation, movement groups were no better than society at large in their attitudes and behavior toward women. In fact, in effect, they were often worse because they stripped women of the defenses available in bourgeois social relations.

But because the experience of women in the movement so closely paralleled that of those outside, the women's caucuses demanding equality within SDS and other movement groups quickly grew into an autonomous movement to end the systematic oppression of women in all areas of social life, a movement that included many women who had not been part of the New Left. The women's movement emphasized two things in its initial stages: that the personal experience of oppression of women was most often not unique or individual but was common and systematic, part of the social division of labor between men and women, and that therefore the personal was also political. And, second, that every woman had the capacity to discuss and understand the nature of her oppression through participation in a collective effort—the small group. At its best, women's liberation stood for a revolution that would encompass all social relations—those in the family as well as those in the outside workplace—as opposed to the various movement sects after 1969 that understood revolution almost entirely in terms of changing the traditionally understood relations of production.

But the origin of the women's movement in apparent opposition to the New Left, and in real opposition to the treatment of women in it, made it difficult for women to see the connections between women's liberation and the "male Left"—or to appreciate the degree of continuity between the central ideas of the New Left and their own. The major tendency in the women's movement, therefore, was toward a separatism that went beyond autonomy. As with the cultural nationalists in the black movement and the "youth as a class" New Leftists, the women's movement tended to see all men as the enemy and to define the revolution purely in terms of sexual divisions—in terms of the division of labor between the sexes. And, at least partly for this reason, the women's movement has been unable to extend its initial rapid growth into a stable organized movement with a viable political direction. Nor have Socialists within the movement been able to create a coherent socialist tendency as part of the women's movement.

Thus the New Left has not yet fully emerged as a Left—as a coherent revolutionary movement. It has not because (although in both of these respects it is in some ways superior to the Old) it has not yet found the way to connect its understanding of the need for a fully democratic society with its developing understanding of the nature of the working class and of the need for socialism. That synthesis will be the next stage in the development of the Left in the United States.

NOTES

1. *Capital*, I (New York: Modern Library, 1936), p. 673.
2. Carl Schorske, *German Social Democracy, 1905–1917* (New York: John Wiley, 1955).
3. See James Weinstein, *The Decline of Socialism in America, 1912–1925* (New York: Vintage, 1969), pp. 51–53.
4. Berger to Morris Hillquit, Milwaukee, August 20, 1919 (Hillquit Papers, Wisconsin State Historical Society); Weinstein, op. cit., p. 178; Milwaukee *Leader*, September 3, 1918.
5. Milwaukee *Leader*, January 3, 1918, emphasis added.
6. *Ohio Socialist*, April 9, 1919, quoted in Weinstein, op. cit., p. 200.
7. Weinstein, op. cit., ch. III. This was also *reflected* in party membership, which from a low of under 70,000 in 1916 climbed again to 109,000 in 1919.
8. Weinstein, op. cit., ch. IV.
9. Quoted in Moshe Lewin, *Lenin's Last Struggle* (New York: Vintage, 1969), p. 4. Emphasis in the original.
10. See Weinstein, op. cit., ch. IV.
11. The New York *Communist*, 1, 2, April 26, 1919, quoted in James Weinstein, "The Underdevelopment of Socialism in Advanced Industrial Society," *Socialist Revolution*, I, 1, January–February 1970.
12. Quoted in Weinstein, op. cit., p. 206.
13. A. Rafael (Alexander Bittleman), "The Task of the Hour," *The Communist*, October 1921.
14. For a description of Communist activities among the unemployed, see Len DeCaux, *Labor Radical* (Boston: Beacon Press, 1970), pp. 162ff. Also, William Z. Foster, *History of the Communist Party of the United States* (New York: International Publishers, 1952), pp. 182–84.
15. Minutes of the Political Committee of the Communist International, May 16, 1928, cited in Theodore Draper, *American Communism and Soviet Russia* (New York: Viking, 1960), p. 289.
16. Interview with Len DeCaux, February 1972.
17. See, for example, Earl Browder, *The People's Front* (New York: International Publishers, 1938), pp. 153–96.
18. George Blake Charney, *A Long Journey* (New York: Quadrangle Books, 1968), p. 74.
19. Socialists ran several black candidates for state legislative office in New York, and Randolph was the Socialist Party's candidate for state comptroller in 1920. See Weinstein, op. cit., pp. 63–74.
20. Theodore G. Vincent, *Black Power and the Garvey Movement* (Berkeley: Ramparts Press, 1971), p. 82.
21. Draper, op. cit., pp. 349, 351.
22. Vincent, op. cit., pp. 233ff.

23. Charney, op. cit., p. 105.

24. When the war ended in Europe (May 1945) the CPA had about 80,000 members and widespread influence beyond the Party itself. Over a fifth of the membership of the CIO was in unions led by Communists or men close to the Party. The Party could count on one third of the votes in the CIO executive board. In addition, in New York City the Communists elected two Party members to the City Council in 1945, one black, Benjamin Davis, while two others were elected on the American Labor Party line and worked closely with the Party. See David Shannon, *The Decline of American Communism* (New York: Harcourt, Brace, 1959), ch. I.

25. Quoted in Massimo Teodori (ed.), *The New Left: A Documentary History* (Indianapolis: Bobbs-Merrill, 1969), p. 122.

26. Mario Savio, "An End to History," reprinted in Teodori (ed.), op. cit., pp. 159–61.

27. Carl Whitman, "Students and Economic Action," in Teodori (ed.), op. cit., p. 128.

28. Todd Gitlin, "The Radical Potential of the Poor," in Teodori (ed.), op. cit., p. 137.

29. Tom Hayden and Staughton Lynd, "Reply to Herbert Haus," *Studies on the Left,* V, 3 (Summer 1965), p. 136.

30. See Gottlieb, Gilbert, and Tenney, "Toward a Theory of Social Change in America," *New Left Notes,* May 22, 1967. This group had been developing their ideas since 1966.

31. Gregory Calvert, "In White America: Radical Consciousness and Social Change," in Teodori (ed.), op. cit., pp. 412–18.

32. Martin J. Sklar and James Weinstein, "Socialism and the New Left," *Studies on the Left,* VI, 2 (March–April 1966), pp. 62–70.

Chapter 18

THE PROSPECTS OF THE NEW LEFT*

Staughton Lynd

I

The New Left was created by men and women who had lost confidence in the various embodiments of the Old Left (including the Soviet Union) either to lead a socialist revolution or to create a society worthy of man. The Old Left was found wanting on grounds both of effectiveness and of ethics. Hungary's and Khrushchev's denunciation of Stalin, the Montgomery bus boycott and Fidel Castro's landing in Oriente Province, all took place in 1956 and together seemed to make clear the need and possibility for something new.

In retrospect, it is less important to choose sides in the debate between Old and New Lefts than to understand with as much depth as possible why the split occurred. Perhaps the fundamental fact is that post-World War II social reality so little resembled what socialist theory had led one to expect. Writing in *Politics* magazine in April 1946, Dwight Macdonald touched on both the effectiveness and the ethics of the received radicalism. "We are all in the position," he wrote, "of a man going upstairs who thinks there is another step, and finds there is not." And again, on the ethical theme: "The external process is working out, but the inner spirit is the reverse of what Marx expected. The operation is a success, but the patient is dying."[1]

One aspect of the apparent miscarriage of socialist expectations was that the European resistance movements, especially in France and Italy, failed to take state power. A second cardinal fact was that the economic breakdown in the West confidently predicted

* Essay commissioned for this symposium. A somewhat different version, containing a fuller discussion of the 1930s, appeared in *Liberation* magazine for January 1971, and in Staughton Lynd and Gar Alperovitz, *Strategy and Program: Two Essays Toward a New American Socialism* (Boston: Beacon Press, 1973).

as a sequel to the end of World War II defense spending did not take place; American radicals, expecting after 1945 a new economic depression and a continuation of the insurgency of the CIO, were instead confronted with the affluence of a permanent war economy and a relatively lethargic white working class. Trotsky had written just before the war that if World War II did not lead to working-class revolution in the Western capitalist nations, Marxist analysis of the working class and its role would be called into question. The revolution did not happen and the re-examination perforce began.

Opposition movements were widespread in the post-war years but at different places, by different groups, and in different forms than had been anticipated. Geographically the storm center was the Third World of colonies and neo-colonies. Insofar as anything like revolution took place in the advanced capitalist societies, the protagonists were not industrial workers but racial minorities and the young. And whether in China or the United States, Cuba or Algeria, France or Japan, post-World War II insurgencies were directed not only against economic "exploitation" but against an "oppression" at once economic, political, cultural, and psychological. "The originality of the colonial context," Frantz Fanon stated, "is that economic reality, inequality and the immense difference of ways of life never come to mask the human realities. . . . In the colonies the economic substructure is also a superstructure. The cause is the consequence; you are rich because you are white, you are white because you are rich." Young people and women faced similar ambiguities.[2]

The classics were unhelpful and useful new theory failed to appear. Between Walter Oakes's enunciation of the concept of "permanent war economy" in 1944 and André Gorz's ideas about "revolutionary reform" and a "new working class" stretched twenty years (at least in Europe and the United States) of theoretical barrenness. Year after year one read *Monthly Review* editorials predicting imminent economic collapse and essays in *Dissent* which once again explained the quiescence of industrial workers. No one convincingly explained the specific characteristics of post-war capitalism and no one communicated confidence that a socialist revolution was still possible in this kind of society. None of the upheavals of the 1960s appear to have been predicted by socialist scholars. Even spokesmen for the New Left such as Mills and

Marcuse can now be seen to have accepted with too little question the assumption central to the ideology of the 1950s that capitalism had stabilized itself. I can recall the editorial board of *Studies on the Left* sitting together shortly after Lyndon Johnson's election in 1964, unable to imagine any way that Johnson could dissipate his massive electoral support. A few weeks later the United States bombed North Vietnam.

It was action not theory which broke out of the 1950s and made it clear that systemic contradictions (albeit of a new kind) still existed. These were personal exemplary acts, unconnected with an articulated strategy. They were actions which had to be taken without knowing whether they would turn out to be catalysts for a mass movement or gestures with no echo. They were actions in which, as both Goodman and Camus wrote, an individual drew a line and refused to be pushed further.[8] They were acts of "resistance" and "rebellion" rather than revolution, acts such as Rosa Parks refusing to go to the back of the bus, teen-agers hurling bricks at Soviet tanks, four young men sitting-in at a lunch counter, draft resistance in France and the United States.

In country after country New Left intellectuals defended such actions against the charge that they were moralistic, undisciplined, petit-bourgeois. It can help to give us perspective on the continuing wrangles within the radical intellectual community in this country to be aware that our quarrel is a local variant of a debate which took place previously between, for example, Sartre and Camus in France, Perry Anderson and Edward Thompson in England.

Criticism of reality in the name of values and the insistence on action to make those values real are also the themes of American New Left intellectuals, such as Mills and Howard Zinn. Thus Mills defended "utopianism," and Zinn wrote that the theory which the Left most needs is "a vision of what it is working toward —one based on transcendental human needs and not limited by the reality we are so far stuck with." (In this connection one thinks also of the strongest of all concerns in the work of Marcuse, namely, appeal to the latent and unfulfilled potentialities in man.) The appeal to values is never separated from the call to act. "'But it is just some kind of moral upsurge, isn't it?,'" Mills asked rhetorically at the close of his *Letter to the New Left,* and answered:

Correct. But under it: no apathy. Much of it is direct non-violent action, and it seems to be working, here and there. Now we must learn from the practice of these young intellectuals and with them work out new forms of action. . . .

Similarly Zinn, like Camus, criticizes the Marxist claim that the vision of a society in which men are free, equal, creative in their work "springs not from a wish but from an observation—from a scientific plotting of an historical curve." Zinn observes that "we don't have such confidence in inevitability these days" because "we've had too many surprises in this century." Because a desirable future is not inevitable, commitment to action is all the more important. Zinn concludes:

It is very easy to feel helpless in our era. We need, I think, the Existentialist emphasis on our freedom. . . . To stress our freedom . . . is not the result of ignorance that we do have a history, and we do have a present environment. . . . Existentialism, knowing of these pressures on us, is also aware that there is a huge element of indeterminacy in the combat between us and the obstacles around us. We never know exactly the depth or the shallowness of the resistance to our actions. We never know exactly what effect our actions will have.[4]

Even so sketchy a survey makes it clear that the New Left is more than "mindless activism." Whether in France, England, or the United States, common intellectual attitudes recur. There is no general hostility to Marxism but a reaffirmation of certain emphases in Marx: the insistence that theory be tied to the specifics of experience; the thesis that "the philosophers have interpreted the world but the thing is, to change it"; the normative concept of alienation (how can one speak of alienation unless there is an unchanging essence of human nature from which to be estranged?). Theory is not only logical lines connecting conceptual points. It is an intellectual atmosphere, in Edward Thompson's phrase "a tone of voice," a way of going at problems. New Left theory restored to its proper place what had bleakly come to be called the "subjective factor," and paid attention to questions such as whether to trust one's own perception of one's own experience, and whether, in a generally difficult situation, it makes a difference to take personal small steps in faith. The breakthrough actions of the late 1950s and 1960s needed this encouragement.

But this is the 1970s and more is required. To begin with, while the New Left has yet to produce an over-all analysis, particular analyses of particular problems have begun to emerge. Mario Savio, one might say, described the multiversity through his action; when he asked students to throw their bodies on the gears of a heartless machine he implied a critique which at the time he could only formulate in part. Since then a respectable mini-theory has been formulated to explain the explosion of youth. It seems that the rapid expansion of higher education is responsive to the new technology which calls for a university-educated "new working class." Conscription, for its part, serves not only to recruit a flexible supply of military manpower for imperialist wars but also to channel other young men into apprenticeship for the jobs which industry wants. Both in choosing a vocation and in choosing a Selective Service deferment the citizen is subject to "pressurized guidance" while believing himself to be free, exactly as in consuming objects he or she has been induced by advertising to desire. The principle of "repressive tolerance" applies not only to ostentatious permission for harmless demonstrations, but also to the more subtle and pervasive encouragement of pseudo-satisfaction of wants ("repressive desublimation").

All this goes some distance toward understanding the rebellion of the young, the white-collar proletarian, the student. Meantime Old Left theory also has been catching up with the new realities surrounding its old subject, the blue-collar worker. Ernest Mandel, especially, builds a bridge between the permanent war economy, the absence of a catastrophic depression, and the systemic tendency toward erosion of real wages through inflation. From this he goes on to the illuminating notion that because of state intervention in the economy strike action will increasingly pit the worker directly against the generalized employer, the state. Several New Left writers have noted that labor organizations are often most militant and radical in a formative stage, before the signing of a contract with its dues checkoff and no-strike pledge. Old Left theory may now be in a position to respond that the state's effort to restrict strike action will reproduce the situation which existed before collective bargaining was legitimized, and that the characteristics of that situation—tactical aggressiveness, rank-and-file participation in decision-making, concern for the oppression of all workingmen everywhere—will appear again.[5]

Put together these two lines of argument and the student and worker upheavals of May–June 1968 in France begin to make sense. Old and New Left theory join in comprehending the conjuncture of Old and New Left constituencies in practice. May we not, with these arguments and these great events before our eyes, begin to speak of an overcoming of the painful bifurcation between thought and action which has haunted post-war radicalism, of an end to silly discussion as to which of two equally essential constituencies is the "revolutionary vanguard"? Is there not a new possibility of students and workers, in their respective millions, patiently, carefully moving toward a political alliance in which each will speak in its own voice?

The promise of what happened in France contrasts sharply with the disintegration of the American New Left during the past few years. Underlying contradictions have not disappeared and (to quote Todd Gitlin from memory) society continues to make radicals more rapidly than the radical movement turns them off. Yet something clearly has gone wrong. Some say that SNCC and SDS had too little Marxist theory, others that they had too much. In any case one cannot continue to believe, as so many of us used to, that "the movement" was born under a lucky star which would make all its experiments cumulatively fruitful and extract from its experience just the kind and amount of theory and leadership that it required. That too was a kind of inevitabilism, which can no longer be afforded.

Accordingly, in the following pages I do not intend to pursue well-worn themes of controversy between the Old Left and the New (except, by way of reminder, at the very end). The truths to which the New Left testified seem to me as valid and important as they ever were, and moreover in need of frequent restatement. But unless we can move on to a more specific kind of discussion, drawing on what is best in the traditions of both Old Left and New Left, we are not going to build the mass socialist movement in the 1970s which I am convinced is possible.

Especially the need is to combine the best in both traditions practically, in terms useful to the organizer and active citizen. If most of the great debates between the Old and New Lefts can now be recognized as confrontations between two parts of a single larger truth (which it would be sterile to continue endlessly, at least on so abstract a level of discourse), then now is the time to talk again about more prosaic matters lower down on the agenda. Exactly how and why did the Old Left miss the opportunity to create a labor party in the 1930s? What forms of leadership and decision-making do we want in a mass radical movement? And what should be the role of a left wing within it?

No one paper or one person can do justice to these questions. If the New Left is right about anything, it is in believing that what each of us should try to contribute to the common fund of knowledge is his or her own experience. Perhaps, in reporting on my own work as historian and as organizer, I can make a beginning.

II

The New Left "blew the minds" of hundreds of thousands of persons, especially young persons, but failed to create permanent organizations through which those who have been radicalized can express their new consciousness and begin to change the world. Campus-based, it did not reach the home-owning, union-belonging, over-thirty middle American, nor had it had much to offer its own activists once they left the academic world and its environs. The New Left has been strong on vision and weak on organization.

The Old Left had the opposite combination of strengths and weaknesses. It reached hundreds of thousands of ordinary citizens around issues of immediate self-interest and drew them together into stable organizations. But the process dramatically failed to transform the individuals who took part in it or to project a vision which would continue to be compelling after the immediate pinch of a self-interest issue was gone. Particularly in its uncritical support for World War II the Old Left lowered rather than raised consciousness, and left its members and fellow travelers psychologically unprepared for the witch-hunt that followed. (Consider, in contrast, the New Left's insubordination during the Vietnam war and the effect of that wartime resistance in creating what John McDermott calls a "popular resistance culture.") Only in recent years, as the scholarship of Chomsky, Kolko, and others has begun to describe World War II resistance movements which were independent of all Great Powers and continually betrayed by all Great

Powers, has the magnitude of the Communist Party's failure in that period become fully clear.

The most critical failure of the Old Left occurred not during World War II but in the years preceding, 1929–40. It is desperately important to come to grips with that experience, first, because it is the model of radical "mass work" historically closest to us, and second, because so much that is distinctive in the New Left came about by reaction and overreaction to what radicals did during those years. During that decade a number of influential individuals broke with the Old Left in a way that prefigured the mass movement after 1956. Ignazio Silone's novel *Bread and Wine,* for example, is a primer of New Left attitudes: the rejection of dogma and the return to elemental realities (bread, wine, friendship); the celebration of action (one man writing anti-fascist slogans on the wall in the night); the shy courtship with religion (the revolutionary disguised as a priest); the vision of a movement as a band of comrades acting out the future as if it were already here. In the United States during roughly the same period A. J. Muste broke away from Trotskyism, Bayard Rustin left the Young Communist League, Dave Dellinger rejected the contention of socialist friends that prison meant political irrelevance and refused to register for the draft. (Together, in 1957, the three founded *Liberation* magazine; later, Rustin organized the civil rights march on Washington for jobs and freedom in 1963, and Muste and Dellinger the great peace demonstrations of 1967.) Dwight Macdonald, another ex-Trotskyist, put into words a first synthesis of American New Leftism in essays in *Politics* magazine cited by Noam Chomsky twenty years later in "The Responsibility of Intellectuals."

Midway through the 1930s the Seventh Congress of the Comintern adopted the Popular Front perspective, more or less adhered to ever since, which gave Old Leftism the form in which New Leftists rejected it. In America, Hungary's and Khrushchev's denunciation of Stalin was probably less important in stimulating a New Left than the bland and manipulative politics of the Popular Front. Many of the founders of SDS were "Red diaper babies," in the loose sense that older relatives or friends of the family, if not one's own parents, were in or close to the Communist Party. Hence, although too young to have experienced Popular Front politics personally, the political style of Popular Front politics was very real to them (I should say, to us) in the persons of the adults whom they knew best.

How to describe that politics and that style? The central assumption, of course, was that the enemy was fascism rather than capitalism, hence that the so-called liberal wing of the ruling class might be an ally. In the United States from 1936 to 1945 the liberal wing of the ruling class meant Franklin D. Roosevelt and the New Deal, just as in 1964 it meant Lyndon Johnson. The sentimentalizing of FDR, the New Deal, the Democratic Party, and the CIO bureaucracy by the Communist Party in the 1930s and 1940s helps to explain the rage with which New Leftists attacked liberals and sought to unmask liberalism as an ideology which (in Carl Oglesby's words) "performs for the corporate state a function quite like what the Church once performed for the feudal state. It seeks to justify its burdens and protect it from change."[6] The celebrated New Left revolt against authority was especially against paternalistic, indirect authority, against power—whether of parents, university presidents, Selective Service administrators, diplomats—cloaked in liberal words. In its concern to dissolve the alliance between radicalism and New Deal liberalism, the New Left tended to revert to the perspective of the Communist Party before the Popular Front which held that the main enemy was not the reactionary Right but the liberal Center, not fascism but social democracy.

The attempt to build the widest possible coalition against fascism led to a habit of dissembling one's own beliefs. Little was said about socialism and much about democracy, and a certain deferential, ingratiating personal manner became characteristic which is still recognizable when radicals of several generations meet. The tendency was to rely not on one's own strength but on figures of authority whose charisma held the coalition together. I recall arguing as a ripe Marxist of fourteen against the "Browder line" which carried Popular Frontism to the ridiculous extremity of dissolving the Communist Party, declaring the class struggle at an end, supporting a no-strike pledge in industry to help the war effort, and looking forward to an era of international peace on the basis of unity among the Big Three. Apart from all these political particulars, what offended me (if I have not prettified this memory) was an abject dependence on persons in positions of power: Roosevelt in Washington, Earl Browder on Fourteenth Street in New York City.

A second personal experience was in the winter of 1948–49 when, having dropped out of Harvard and journeyed across the country to Oregon, I sat in the Portland Public Library reading the transcript of the Smith Act trials in the New York *Times*. Adrift as I was in my own life, it was peculiarly dismaying to read statements by Foster, Dennis, and the others which declared that communists would defend their country in time of war, that communism would come to the United States by parliamentary means, and so on. I contrasted not just the content but the tone of these statements with Eugene Debs's demeanor on trial for opposition to World War I. I felt ashamed for American radicalism. Much as I might sympathize with the Smith Act defendants, I could not respect them. (This dispraise of the Communist Party is not intended as back-door argument for other variants of Old Leftism. In my experience Trotskyists outdid all others in furious haggling about resolutions which no one was in a position to implement.)

Such were the sorts of encounters with the older radicalism which led one premature New Leftist to look in new directions. I suspect my experience was not untypical.

The Popular Front practice of the Old Left was an important source for the attitudes of the New. Self-imprisoned within the limits of New Deal and CIO politics, the Left sought to salve its ideological conscience by passing resolutions. Little was done about these resolutions, but "one took a position," and that was felt to be significant. Verbal victories were substituted for action which would have split the organizations in which the Old Left worked. Understandably, and exaggeratedly, the New Left swept aside debating as a waste of time and asked everyone to put his body where his mouth was.

III

Up to this point it has been argued:

That a radical mass movement needs both white- and blue-collar workers as strong, independent components.

That it is time to lay aside abstract debate between Old and New Lefts and try to combine what was best in the political work of the 1960s with what was best in the political work of the 1930s.

That like the Old Left we must begin to build radical mass movements, but in a way that avoids the opportunism of the Communist Party in the Popular Front period.

But none of this will happen unless the question of leadership and decision-making is resolved. Organization after organization in which New Leftists have worked has collapsed in a welter of charges and countercharges of "elitism" on the one hand, "anarchism" on the other. Here, of course, both Old and New Left are touched on a most sensitive nerve. The redefinition of authority, including the authority of Old Left parents, is a short way of saying what the movement is all about. Understandably such a movement finds the creation of its own structure of authority traumatic. And as the New Left struggles with this Sisyphean labor Old Left structures stand by ready to welcome tired young radicals into the fold with a murmured "I told you so."

I believe the New Left's attempt to find new forms of decision-making is significant and creative and in keeping with rational concepts of man and how he (or she) learns; I do not believe it should be dismissed as aimless, irrational anti-authoritarianism. Once more, however, the point is not to defend the New Left's intention but to appraise in detail how that intention has misfired, and to propose alternatives.

Some necessary themes of this discussion are familiar to all. There is the matter of consensus and participatory democracy. There is the elitism which participatory democracy was meant to prevent but which in some ways it fostered. There is the question of caucuses, and the New Left's utter inability to deal with them. These themes can be dealt with briefly.

Why consensus prevailed in early meetings of the movement (including SNCC meetings, in the almost underground setting of the southern movement) is something of a historical mystery. It may have had to do with the experimentalism everyone felt because social reality was so different from what anyone's theory had predicted. A journey is planned in one way if there is a road map. If there is no road map, if the country is strange and wild, and hills block off the view in all directions, if previous travelers have not returned or have come back broken and dismayed, then the traveler is likely to move tentatively, stage by stage, surveying the landscape freshly as he tops each ridge. And meetings, under these circumstances, will naturally tend to a sharing of experiences already undergone rather than the abstract resolution of situations not yet encountered in practice.

But there was more to it than that. Consensus is the most natural and human way to make decisions. It is the way families and friends decide things. People who took part in the movements of the early 1960s will recall the fierce resistance to voting group after group displayed, simply because they had found something better. (Sometimes one took "straw votes" to get the sense of a meeting without calling it a decision.) As late as the fall of 1967, consensus was advocated in an article on draft resistance written by Dee Jacobsen of the SDS national office and growing out of discussions in which SDS veterans Vernon Grizzard, Paul Potter, John Maher, and Les Coleman each had a hand. Entitled "We've Got to Reach Our Own People," the article said in part:

> You are a serious resistance: don't vote on issues, discuss them until you can agree. All the pain of long meetings amounts to a group which knows itself well, holds together with a serious, human spirit, and any member of which can step into a role of responsibility if someone else leaves. Fight for that kind of group, because people will want to join with it: there are not many things in this country like that. Stand by each other.[7]

The weakness of consensus decision-making was simply that it worked well only in small groups. Once a group became large, and especially if those who composed it were heterogeneous in background and experience, consensus broke down. A long-time participant in the JOIN community union project in Chicago insists that voting was more democratic even in JOIN's meetings of two or three dozen persons, because the community people intimidated by the verbalism of student organizers felt free to cast ballots as they wished.[8]

If we are talking about a mass movement then we are talking about representative government and voting. This doesn't mean (I shall argue) that small groups taking direct action after consensual discussion must disappear. On the contrary. But there has got to be a way for hundreds and thousands of people to set policy together regarding fundamental issues, and consensus is not it.

This conclusion should be easier to accept for Old New Leftists like myself because it is so clear by now that participatory democracy in large meetings in fact led to elitism. After the inconclusive discussion, a few people went back to the office and decided. This appears to be especially the case in movements which focus on periodic national events, like the peace movement, and was less a problem in early- and middle-period SDS, where the organization's action was the sum of what the local chapters did. Again to be personal for a moment, let me describe how I became a "peace movement leader." The week Johnson began bombing North Vietnam in February 1965 Yale students who had worked with me in the southern civil rights movement asked me to speak at a university protest meeting. This led to an invitation (no doubt because an anti-government Yale professor was a man-bites-dog phenomenon) to chair a protest meeting at Carnegie Hall in New York. Then on the eve of the SDS-sponsored protest march in April 1965 the SDS national secretary (who already knew me) called me and asked that I chair that gathering too. In August several of us, who were besplattered with red paint as the Assembly of Unrepresented People approached the Capitol grounds, were prominently depicted in *Life* magazine. Finally, in September A. J. Muste phoned to ask me to join "a few of us" in a small discussion prior to an anti-war movement conference. I had arrived at the center of peace movement decision-making by co-option rather than election, through a politics of friendship, and a search for leaders by the media. When in December of that year the New York *Times* informed me that I was a "peace movement leader" the process was complete. I submit that this is a profoundly undemocratic way for a movement to select leaders and make top-level decisions.

The New Left would probably have found non-consensual forms for somewhat less participatory decision-making had it not been invaded by Old Left caucuses. A first instance occurred when after April 1965 SDS failed to give continuing leadership to the student anti-war movement. Moving into the vacuum, Communist Party members and sympathizers helped to create a National Coordinating Committee to End the War in Vietnam with themselves in key roles at its national headquarters. Trotskyists responded by a disciplined attempt at take-over at the NCCEWV's first national convention. By the end of the convention a new national organization was being launched in a locked hotel room, the majority of delegates from grass roots *ad hoc* anti-war committees were bewildered and disgusted, and one more organizational effort was in a shambles.

In 1966 the Progressive Labor Party (PLP) dissolved its front group, the May 2nd Movement, and directed its youth to join SDS. The new atmosphere of hairsplitting doctrinal debate frustrated SDS members who were pushing the national organization to involve itself in draft resistance, and led to their going their separate way to form the Resistance. The PLP had much to contribute, particularly in its emphasis on the blue-collar working class, but imbedded this contribution in a style of work so dogmatic and aggressive that the existing SDS leadership took on the manner of the PLP caucus in order to combat it. Overnight everyone became a Marxist, not because this conviction had grown organically from experience (indeed, just at this time SDS efforts at working-class organizing were being given up), but because quotations from Marxism-Leninism-Maoism had become counters of value in an internal struggle for power.

About caucuses, perhaps one should conclude something like the following:

1. Caucuses are inevitable in organizations which grow large or are made up of people with very different backgrounds or experiences.
2. Nevertheless, there are caucuses and caucuses, and an organization can best survive them if all concerned agree:
   a. that all caucus meetings should be open to anyone who wishes to attend;
   b. that, when presenting a position agreed on by a caucus, caucus members should identify themselves as such in workshops and plenary sessions ("speaking as a member of the so-and-so caucus, I favor the following . . .").
3. What is most important is a certain openness and humility which cannot be legislated.

Caucuses I have worked in which practiced points 1 and 2 (such as the radical caucus in the American Historical Association) have tended to transform the larger organizations of which they were parts rather than to destroy them.

The caucus within a larger organization illustrates microcosmically the broader dilemma of the staff of organizers, or party of professional revolutionaries, within a mass movement. New

Leftists objected to the Old Left's failure to make the government of the Soviet Union wither away. But we run into similar problems when we organize. A scenario widely accepted in the early New Left held that the successful staff is that which organizes itself out of existence, that is, which exits from the scene leaving behind it an organization which can continue on its own. We have rarely achieved this, however, and it is important to ask why.

New Left organizational concepts are far better suited to the staff (or to the affinity group, collective, or vanguard party) than to the organization. The staff is smaller and staff members have similar backgrounds and experiences, hence consensus may work well in a staff. The elitism characteristic of staffs which operate consensually is usually an earned elitism: the leader is a Bob Moses whose authority is tacitly recognized on the basis of observed personal achievement. Caucuses may exist for reasons of personal antagonism or political difference within the smallest staff but such caucusing is informal and, however painful, less a built-in problem than in a large and heterogeneous structure. When everything has been said that should be said about male chauvinism and the absence of "criticism and self-criticism" in early New Left staff communities, they can be remembered without the aura of nightmare which attends all memories of late-period SDS.

However, precisely because there was considerable "fit" between staff existence and New Left rhetoric, New Leftists tended to remain in the staff womb and to postpone the creation of large, heterogeneous, in some ways more prosaic and less romantic organizations run by others. Large organizations make imperfect communities. Large organizations probably have less capacity to anticipate the lineaments of a future society than the small staff group in which intellectual and physical labor can be combined, authority and rewards can be made equal, and the quality of life can be humanized more readily than in a large organization. Sensing this, the New Left usually failed to give organizational birth at all, and so failed even to confront the problems of post-partum bureaucracy which the Old Left (in the Soviet Union and elsewhere) so dramatically muffed.

SNCC is a case in point. The Freedom Summer of 1964 left behind it the first off-campus mass organization the New Left had created, the Mississippi Freedom Democratic Party. For the first time it was possible to organize in Mississippi in relative safety. Every organizational instinct should have directed SNCC staff members toward turning the precinct and county MFDP structures which had been jerry-built for the National Democratic Convention into real entities, and running candidates, operating institutions (such as the day care centers which came into being under other auspices), mounting local direct action campaigns, in short, challenging the Mississippi power structure in particular places day by day. Instead, with a few exceptions SNCC organizers left the state. They were exhausted from three years of struggle and made uncomfortable by the presence of white volunteers for the Freedom Summer who stayed on. But another factor, I believe, was that the MFDP was made up of persons older, less radical, and more interested in immediate small gains than the SNCC organizers.

Similarly SDS passed by the opportunity of creating a national student union and the peace movement failed to capitalize organizationally on the broad support it had mobilized by, say, the fall of 1967.

We draw back on the brink of building mass organizations because we fear they will be Frankenstein monsters. Observing what happened to the CIO unions built by communists and socialists, to the community organizations built along similar lines by Saul Alinsky, and to most if not all societies in which socialists have come to power, we shrink from permitting our radical congregations to become bureaucratic, reformist, coopted churches.

In the dead days of the late 1950s this attitude could be justified by the argument: "there are only a few of us ready to act, anyway." No longer! In any profession, the handful of radicals who slunk from pillar to pillar of convention lobbies ten or even five years ago now find themselves spokesmen for a third, a half, a majority of their co-workers. Outside the white-collar world working people cast protest votes for George Wallace or James Buckley because the Left gives them no alternative. If, in the 1970s, we fail to build mass organizations it will not be because we can't but because we don't want to.

The reasons for not wanting to are grave. Large organization does mean representative government, even if the organization does not engage in electoral politics, and all that we have said about the superficiality of voting, the danger of shuffling off responsibility on representatives, the tendency of representative systems to talk rather than act, the possibility electoral politics offers for being a part-time radical who casts his insurgent ballot after a submissive workday—all this remains as true as before. Large organization breeds bureaucracy, internal specialization of labor, the institutionalization of the full-time organizer who now draws a salary from an organizational budget. Large organizations do tend to coalition politics, both within and without the organization's structure, because in large organizations goals have a way of shrinking to specific "interests" which can be traded off, made into composite packages, and compromised. No one in the past has talked about these things more than I and I am unrepentant in insisting on their importance.

Still, if we are serious about changing our own society and about our responsibilities to oppressed people elsewhere, do we have any choice? Can anyone really imagine the coming of a socialist America without the prior creation of people's organizations, institutions of dual power, a labor party? The vogue of guerrilla warfare circa 1967–70 can be partly explained, I suspect, by the fact that it seemed to offer a way of being revolutionary without the tedium of talking to masses of one's fellow citizens. We should open our eyes. No more dogged coalition builders exist than the cadre of the revolutionary movement in Vietnam. There was all the difference in the world between Ché Guevara's experience as a guerrilla in Cuba, where as villages were liberated the transformation of their whole life began and Ché himself set up temporary clinics, and his tragic account of not swimming in the sea of the Bolivian people: gathering villagers together half-forcibly to hear a hurried and abstract account of the revolution before the pursuing government troops forced one to leave, without new recruits. In the Russian Revolution of 1917 there was no attempt to take power until the Bolsheviks had won a majority in the soviets. What all these experiences have in common is the revolutionary's confidence that he speaks to the basic needs of the majority of his own people. Without this feeling of being unalienated, at home, swimming in a supportive sea when among the common people of one's own society, Leftists, whether Old, New, or intermediate, are not going to bring about basic change; and with this feeling, I submit, the natural first step is to begin to build forms of collective struggle which express it.

More concretely, the question is how to work creatively within a mass organization which is somewhat radical (which is why you are in it) but not as radical as you yourself are. The art of radicalizing reformist structures, including structures we have helped to create, requires relearning.

IV

I have attempted to describe how the New Left finds itself suspended between small cadre or communal structures on the one hand, and mass organizations on the other. Conscious of the need to build more broadly than the first we yet have been unable to commit ourselves to the second. The 1930s bequeath models of lowest-common-denominator coalitions and of a Left boring from within and maneuvering behind the scenes in left-of-center mass organizations. Rather than do that, we have usually concluded, it is better to put together something small in which you can speak your whole mind and act without bureaucratic delay.

I want to argue now that such action committees belong within rather than outside of mass organizations. They are the kind of caucus which the New Left can create most naturally, and a far better kind of caucus, in my opinion, than groups thrown together on the occasion of election of officers.

Consider the trade union movement. Old Leftists who remain in industry tend to define their objective as election to union office. Year after year, they patiently inch their way up the hierarchy of the local union, from assistant griever to griever, from secretary of the grievance committee to chairman of the grievance committee, and finally, if all goes well, to president of the local. This strategy has proved no more rewarding than that of national rank-and-file movements which replace McDonalds with Abels. Once elected, the radical president of a local has little power to affect nationally negotiated contracts. I know of one man, first president of a large CIO local in the 1930s, who was elected again in the 1960s after two decades of the dirtiest sort of Red-baiting. Unable to deliver on his campaign promises, he was defeated at the next election by an opponent who reprinted the radical's own platform and asked the voters how many of these changes had come about.

In my opinion a better approach within the unions would be to go for the powers which the Left gave up to the union bureaucracy in the 1930s: the local right to strike, and the shop steward system. The first major CIO contracts, signed in March 1937 with General Motors and United States Steel, took away from the rank and file in those corporations the right to speak effectively through on-the-spot representatives and the right to act effectively through departmental and plant-wide strikes. In place of a shop steward for every twenty-five or fifty workers, authorized by contract to leave his job in order to take up a grievance with the foreman concerned, the GM contract limited the "shop committee" to nine workers per plant and the U. S. Steel contract restricted the "grievance committee" to ten workers per mill. This is the origin of the cumbersome grievance machinery which today compels an aggrieved worker not to take action, at the time, on the spot, but to fill out papers which may take years to process (academics enjoy a strictly analogous opportunity vis-à-vis their own company union, the American Association of University Professors).

Similarly both these precedent-forming contracts forbade strike action initiated from below. Both provided for referral of problems to arbitration by an umpire as a last resort. The GM contract explicitly stated that strike action was forbidden "without the approval of the International officers of the Union." And the unions involved, the United Automobile Workers and the Steel Workers Organizing Committee, rigorously enforced these understandings. Today the worker who wildcats can expect to be dismissed with the assistance, indeed at the insistence, of the union.

So far as I can see, the best thing for a radical in a union is to hold low-level local office (as a griever, committeeman, or whatever) but at the same time to be active in grass roots organizational forms outside the union structure. This might be simply an informal association of the workers in the department he represents as a griever, who could test the limits of their freedom of action under the contract. (For instance, the steel contract permits a worker to refuse to perform a job he considers unsafe. What if a department refused together?) Groupings outside the formal structure of the union need not be limited to the workplace, however. A group of workers battling pollution in a particular part of the factory can establish a direct relation to a community group fighting the same pollution as it affects persons on the outside. In fact, a community group can give workers some protection from the union bureaucracy. Rank-and-file caucuses in different plants may find it easier to explain to the international union their presence at the same meeting if they are able to point to an organization in the community which called them together.

As mass radical organizations develop in the 1970s, therefore, it seems to me the New Left can best operate through groups similar to shop committees or draft resistance unions which, while keeping one foot within the circle of a larger organization, also insist on acting out their convictions. In this way we can both learn from the Old Left in recognizing the necessity for mass organization yet keep faith with the New Left's insight that the best way to communicate a position is by exemplifying it.

Sometimes we will enter existing large organizations like a CIO union. There will also be times when we ourselves build a large organization. In the latter case there are things that can be done in the organizational phase which will make it easier for rank-and-file action committees to function later on. We can avoid operating through the existing leadership of established organizations and seek out the offbeat teachers' local, the small but innovative independent union of oil workers, the emerging caucuses in the International Brotherhood of Teamsters (to draw on my own experience in Gary), or, to go back to Moses' work in Mississippi, we can give recognition to the state president of the NAACP but build especially on the embattled officers of local NAACP chapters. We can also anticipate the substantive issues which will tend to divide the mass organization once it comes into being. If SNCC had done more to emphasize the limitations of winning the right to vote at the time it worked mainly on voter registration, the MFDP might have been more conscious of the need for economic as well as political power and less vulnerable to the Democratic Party. A useful rule of thumb, in my experience, is to avoid easy political targets—the notorious mayor, the corrupt machine boss—and keep the focus on corporations. Last but not least, of course, at all stages in the process radicals must be prepared to say publicly that they are socialists and to take the consequences. Whether the mass organization is prepared to defend them is an issue that must sooner or later be faced.

What is most important, in the context of the perspective I am urging, is to keep clearly in mind from the outset the model of a large organization which has the capacity to make decisions and take actions but which also allows freedom of action to its constituent small groups (committees, caucuses, branches, chapters, locals, affiliated organizations, soviets, or what have you). We need a CORE which will not condemn six members of its East River chapter for sitting-down on the Triborough Bridge at rush hour to protest housing conditions in Harlem. We need an MFDP which will not repudiate young black civil rights workers in McComb, Mississippi, where SNCC's activity in the state began, when they call for draft resistance. We want industrial unions that will defend local work stoppages unauthorized at higher levels. If we recreate a mass socialist party we want it to be different from the pre-World War I Socialist Party which expelled the IWW.

Ultimately, we want mass organizations tolerant of smaller action groups within them because we want this kind of revolution and this kind of good society. The New Left has accurately intuited that an organization is likely to make a revolution in its own image. Democratic centralist vanguard parties, for instance, can be expected to create revolutionary governments which will destroy local soviets. In advocating both representative decision-making in radical mass organizations and small groups within them that act out new demands, risk expulsion, compel the large organizations to remember their original rhetoric, I am also saying that this is how a revolution should happen, and that this is what a new society should look like.

It is an aspect of the radical failure of nerve in this country since World War II that few people dare to talk about how a transition to socialism might actually take place. In our hearts, most of us most of the time don't believe it can happen. I find that if I set aside all the old debates about direct action and electoral politics, and entertain the possibility that both kinds of action could be involved, then I can begin to imagine a realistic scenario. The transition to socialism in the United States, it now seems to me, would require both the election of a socialist government and mass civil disobedience, such as a general strike. Which of the two kinds of action predominates and which comes first and just how they are related seems to me less important than to accept the principle that both are needed. Perhaps the electoral transition would simply formalize a change which had already taken place in the shops and on the streets. Perhaps civil disobedience would be necessary to protect an elected socialist government and to make it do its job.

There are precedents. May–June 1968 in France is important again here, in that there was not only a general strike but very nearly the fall of a quasi-dictatorship. A general strike forestalled a fascist putsch in Germany in 1920. More to the point, in our own experience we have seen direct action cause the government to reverse the direction of its Vietnam policy, cause one presidential candidate to declare and another to withdraw, and cause the government two years later to hasten the conclusion of the Cambodian invasion. It is true that it took another two and a half years before U.S. withdrawal, but it is also true that the Cambodian protests seriously inhibited further escalation. Imagine a bigger, broader movement capable of impeding the off-campus industry of the country as well as the education industry, imagine dozens of candidates running for offices of every kind as declared socialists, imagine regional movements in a number of metropolitan areas which have won the respect of the electorate through gutsy action on behalf of obviously needed programs, imagine these things—none of which, singly, seem to me at all impossible—and one begins to envision a transition which might really happen.

The first step in this direction, it appears to me, is not a political party (at least not a national political party) but the building and rebuilding of regional movements. The "parallel central labor union" or "community union"—which is exactly what the soviets of St. Petersburg and Moscow were—is a more useful model than the party, vanguard or electoral. It is a place to which particular groups of workers can bring problems that need broad support outside a single workplace, such as pollution and taxation problems, but also an organizational form that by definition tends to address itself to the concerns of working people in general. Its members should not be limited to representatives of groups of workers, but should include community representatives, as it were grievance committeemen from neighborhoods. ("Workers" and "community" are not two groups of people, but the same people in their different roles of employees and residents of the community. A single person might vote for a delegate from his local union or rank-and-file caucus and also vote for, or be, a delegate from a parents' group, a conservation club, a writers' workshop, and so on.) Its characteristic form of action, as was the case with the soviets, will be direct action of one kind or another: strikes, boycotts, and the like. But this should not exclude the intelligent use of political forms such as administrative hearings, nor should it exclude discriminating participation in electoral campaigns after the organization is solidly in being. There are many more kinds of election than for alderman, mayor, or congressman, and these others—for union office, school board office, and what have you—are probably the place to begin.

One way such people's councils can originate became clear in the months after President Nixon launched his "new economic policy" in August 1971. Following the precedent of state capitalist societies elsewhere, and of American practice during World War II, the government created a series of control boards to manage wages and prices. All this was done under cover of a resolution comparable in its vagueness to the Tonkin Bay resolution contrived by President Johnson to legitimize escalation in Vietnam. The American public had no say whatsoever in the decision to have economic controls, or in setting any of the guidelines, or in choosing the people to carry out the policies. These people can accurately be described as representatives of the ruling class.

Here, then, was the American version of that late-capitalist confrontation between the state and the worker previously described by Gorz and Mandel. Here was a situation in which working people had to begin to create people's or community control boards for economic problems, not because they abstractly desired people's control of the economy, but because, unless they acted, the economy would be controlled by people whose interest it was to beat down wages, increase "productivity," and outlaw strikes. For the first time, under these circumstances, the New Left philosophy of taking control of the decisions which affect your life began to make sense to the American worker.

By whatever means such movements come into being and begin to grow, they (we) must be serious about being an alternative government. In a period of repression like the present there is the temptation to be so preoccupied with survival and the defense of existing rights that, as in the 1930s, we let the question of socialism slip from view. To the contrary, the fact that the powers that be feel themselves obliged to attack what democracy exists can be used to win recruits for a vision of what a consistently democratic society would be: democracy, we must say again and again, can only survive as libertarian socialism, in which economic as well as political decision makers are elected and the people take more part in decisions of every kind.

We are not planning a conspiracy and we should not hide as if we were. It is not our intention to manipulate people, to put something over on them under an innocent guise. We need to feel about ourselves and act consistently with the belief that we are trying to give substance to those aspirations toward a better life which people know they are being denied.

To be serious about being an alternative government we must be able to talk concretely about how a socialist society would deal with problems which oppress people now. Recognizing that much can only be resolved in the midst of experience; still, we should begin to gather experience from other countries and spell out in specifics what a socialist approach to public health, a socialist system of education (if any), workers' control in particular industries under socialism, and the rest might look like.

It may be said: there is no time. I think I feel the urgency, whether about nuclear war, genocide in Vietnam, or political repression, that others feel. I do not believe in bypassing present crises and organizing (in the old SDS phrase) for the seventh war from now. Yet I cannot see how a few friends pursuing hastily improvised programs by means of one or another single tactic can make a revolution. One thing urgency might lead us to do is to lay aside ancient movement quarrels and be humble enough to start fresh.

V

At the turn of the century Werner Sombart asked his famous and still unanswered question: Why is there no socialist movement in the United States? In asking that question again, we must ask it not as detached spectators but as men and women who will attempt to act out an answer. We must ask, not: Why is there *still* no socialist movement in the United States?, but: Can a socialist movement in the United States be built?

The essential contention of the New Left is that no "scientific" analysis can assure us of a "correct" path to inevitable success, and that, in the absence of such certainty, we must nevertheless act. A number of distinguished Marxists have found ways to agree with this contention in recent years.

Reviewing the lessons of Soviet experience, Paul Sweezy and Leo Huberman wrote in 1967:

> If what has happened in the Soviet Union had to happen, the chances that other socialist countries, present and future, will be able to escape the same fate would, at the very least, have to be rated low. If on the other hand events might have taken a different course in the Soviet Union, then other socialist countries, learning from Soviet experience, can still hope to prove that Marx and Lenin were right after all and that in entering the era of socialism mankind has at last found the key to a new and qualitatively better future.

From this point they go on to distinguish between more and less "deterministic" (as opposed to "voluntaristic") historical periods, and argue that a time of revolution is a time when "the range of possibilities widens, and groups . . . and great leaders come into their own as actors on the stage of history. Determinism recedes into the background, and voluntarism seems to take over."[9]

Reflecting on the experience of Third World revolution, Regis Debray says:

> Fidel once blamed certain failures of the guerrillas on a purely intellectual attitude toward war. The reason is understandable: aside from his physical weakness and lack of adjustment to rural life, the intellectual will try to grasp the present through preconceived ideological constructs and live it through books. He will be less able than others to invent, improvise, make do with available resources, decide instantly on bold moves when he is in a tight spot. Thinking that he already knows, he will learn more slowly, display less flexibility.[10]

Finally, coming to the United States, one finds these words of Gabriel Kolko's:

> The intellectual and political heritage of Marxism did not prepare the left in America and Europe for the complexities of the twentieth century, if only because, exegetical citations notwithstanding, Marxism and all its varieties and schools prior to World War I accepted a paralyzing and debilitating optimism which was inherited from the intellectual tradition of the idea of Progress. Defeat as a possibility of long-term, even permanent duration was never entertained, and a social theory that cannot consider this option is not merely intellectually unsatisfactory but misleading as a basis of political analysis and action.

Ignoring the intellectual issue of possessing an accurate account of past events, mechanistic optimism led socialists to slight the negative consequences of action or inaction in relation to desired goals, and to try to fit every major event of political and economic development into a pattern of inevitable progression that justified optimism. Such determinism led to quietism, even celebration and opportunism, as socialists everywhere welcomed the events that led to their undoing.

To succeed politically, Kolko concludes, the New Left "must find dynamic possibilities and forces of movement in a social order in crisis, forces it must frankly acknowledge may not exist as permanent or decisive factors for social change."[11]

The contradictions of American capitalism are as real now, in the 1970s, as for Debs in the 1890s or CIO organizers during the New Deal. Some of the contradictions are new; for instance, the systemic inflation caused by a permanent war economy. Some are old, such as competition from other capitalist economies now once again able to compete with the American colossus. Even the more technical formulations of Marxist economics, among them the tendency of the rate of profit to fall as industry puts more and more money into fixed investment, reclaim conviction. The objective necessity for socialism is there.

Whether the necessary socialist transformation can be accomplished is uncertain. But no one can demonstrate by analysis that socialism in America is an impossible dream. We will not know whether socialism in America is possible until, once more, we try.

NOTES

1. Dwight Macdonald, "The Root Is Man," *Politics,* April 1946. The continuity between this journal and later New Leftism is suggested by the fact that Macdonald got the idea for its title from a then-obscure sociologist at the University of Maryland, C. Wright Mills (Stephen J. Whitfield, "Dwight Macdonald and the Vagaries of Politics" [unpublished paper], p. 58).

2. I owe the distinction between "exploitation" and "oppression" to Juliet Mitchell of the English women's liberation movement. Fanon's phrase is from *The Wretched of the Earth,* tr. Constance Farrington (New York: Grove Press, 1963), p. 32.

3. Thus the opening passages of *The Rebel:* "What is a rebel? . . . What does he mean by saying, 'no'? He means, for example, that 'this has been going on too long,' 'up to this point yes, beyond it no,' 'you are going too far,' or again, 'there is a limit beyond which you shall not go.' " (Tr. Anthony Brower [New York: Vintage Books, 1956], p. 13.)

4. C. Wright Mills, *Letter to the New Left* (New York: SDS, 1961) and Howard Zinn, "Marxism and the New Left," in Alfred F. Young (ed.), *Dissent: Explorations in the History of American Radicalism,* (De Kalb: Northern Illinois University Press, 1968), pp. 363, 267, 271.

5. Mandel's "Where Is America Going?", widely reprinted in the United States from *New Left Review,* 54 (March–April 1969), pp. 3–15, is less significant than two less well-known titles: "Lessons of May," *New Left Review,* no. 52 (November–December 1968), esp. pp. 10–12, and *Marxist Economic Theory,* tr. Brian Pearce (New York: Monthly Review Press, 1968), esp. vol. II, ch. 14. I have attempted to summarize the elements of Mandel's thought most useful to the practical organizer in "Ernest Mandel's America," *Liberation* (December 1969), reprinted in Mitchell Goodman, *The Movement Toward a New America* (Philadelphia: Pilgrim Press; and New York: Knopf, 1970), pp. 550–52.

6. Carl Oglesby, "Let Us Shape the Future," a speech delivered to an anti-war rally in Washington, D.C., in November 1965, and variously reprinted.

7. This article was published in *The Movement,* November 1967.

8. One of the best historians of the civil rights movement concurs: "Participatory democracy, it was found, worked well in a staff of five but was not quite so efficient in a group of fifty." (Debbie Louis, *And We Are Not Saved: A History of the Movement As People* [Garden City, N.Y.: Doubleday, 1970], p. 249.)

9. Leo Huberman and Paul M. Sweezy, "Lessons of Soviet Experience," *Monthly Review* (November 1967), pp. 18–21.

10. Regis Debray, "Revolution in the Revolution?," *Monthly Review* (July–August 1967), p. 21.

11. Gabriel Kolko, "The Decline of American Radicalism in the Twentieth Century," *Studies on the Left* (September–October 1966), pp. 10, 26.

NOTES ON CONTRIBUTORS

Daniel Bell is Professor of Sociology at Harvard University, having taught formerly at Columbia and the University of Chicago. He also was an editor of *The New Leader* and labor editor of *Fortune* magazine. Bell is the author of, among other works, *Marxian Socialism in the United States* and *The End of Ideology: On the Exhaustion of Political Ideas in the Fifties*. His most recent book is *The Coming of Post-Industrial Society*.

Tom Bottomore is Professor of Sociology at the University of Sussex, in England. A past president of the British Sociological Association, he is the author of *Elites and Society; Classes in Modern Society;* and *Critics of Society* as well as of other works dealing with social conflict. His most recent book is *Karl Marx*.

Henry J. Browne was between 1958 and 1970 active in Catholic socio-political and pastoral activity as Senior Associate of St. Gregory the Great Parish on the west side of New York City. Author of *The Catholic Church and the Knights of Labor,* he recently became Associate Professor of Sociology at Rutgers University, where he is conducting further research into nineteenth-century Catholic social history.

Paul Buhle is founder and editor of *Radical America,* a New Left quarterly. A graduate student at the University of Wisconsin, Buhle has written essays on Marxism, the American Left, and popular culture for *Monthly Review, New Politics* and other journals. He has also prepared several volumes of poetry for publication, and is editor of *Woman Suffrage in America,* forthcoming from the University of Illinois Press.

Martin Diamond received his Ph.D. from the University of Chicago in 1956. He taught for many years at Claremont Men's College and Claremont Graduate School in California, and has recently moved to become Professor of Political Science at Northern Illinois University. He is the co-author of *The Democratic Republic*.

Melvyn Dubofsky is Professor of American History at the State University of New York at Binghamton, having taught previously at the University of Massachusetts and at the Centre for the Study of Social History, at the University of Warwick in England. He has written *When Workers Organize* and *We Shall Be All: A History of the I.W.W.*. Dubofsky is currently working on a biography of John L. Lewis.

Leon Epstein is Professor of Political Science at the University of Wisconsin. In 1971–72 he spent a year as Fellow at the Center for Advanced Study in the Behavioral Sciences at Stanford. Author of *Political Parties in Western Democracies* and of other studies, principally of politics in Britain and the United States, his current interests include the relationship of party organization to the development of social class.

Iring Fetscher is Professor of Sociology at Frankfurt University, in West Germany. He was Theodore Heuss Professor at the New School for Social Research in New York in 1968–69, and has lectured and taught in numerous places on problems of Marxism, political sociology, and political thought. His major works include *Rousseau's Political Philosophy; Karl Marx and Marxism;* and *Great Britain: Society, State, and Ideology*.

Philip S. Foner is the author of numerous books on American labor, radical, and socialist history including *The Fur and Leather Workers Union; Jack London: American Rebel;* and *American Labor and the Indochina War: Growth of Union Opposition.* His best-known work is a *History of the Labor Movement in the United States,* in four volumes. Between 1941 and 1945 Foner was educational director of the International Fur and Leather Workers Union; and from 1945 to 1967 he was publisher of the Citadel Press. Since 1967 he has been Professor of History at Lincoln University in Pennsylvania.

Gerald Friedberg received a Ph.D. in Government from Harvard University in 1965. His thesis topic was *Marxism in the United States: John Spargo and the Socialist Party of America.* He held the position of Assistant Professor of Political Science at the University of California at Davis.

Michael Harrington was until recently one of the national leaders of the League for Industrial Democracy, as well as of the Socialist Party of America. Well known as an activist in socialist circles, he is editor of the *Newsletter of the Democratic Left,* author of *The Other America; The Accidental Century;* and *Socialism,* as well as Professor of Political Science at Queens College in New York City.

Louis Hartz is Professor of Government at Harvard. He has visited at various other universities, and spent a year as a Fellow at the Center for Advanced Study in the Behavioral Sciences at Stanford. In 1948 he published *Economic Policy and Democratic Thought;* and in 1955 *The Liberal Tradition in America,* which attempted to demonstrate why liberalism has been the dominant political ideology in the United States. In 1964 he followed this up with *The Founding of New Societies,* analyzing patterns of political behavior in a number of other countries.

Irving Horowitz is Professor and Chairman of the Department of Sociology at Rutgers University and a noted political sociologist. He is the editor of the important social science journal *Society.* His publications include *The Knowledge Factory, Latin American Radicalism, Masses in Latin America, The Use and Abuse of Social Science, The New Sociology, Professing Sociology,* and *Revolution in Brazil.* He is the literary executor of C. Wright Mills and edited his collected papers under the title of *Power, Politics and People.*

Bernard Johnpoll, formerly a journalist, has taught political science at the State University of New York at Albany since 1966. He has written *The Politics of Futility,* a study of the Jewish Socialist Bund in eastern Europe; and in 1970 he published *Pacifist's Progress: Norman Thomas and the Decline of American Socialism.*

Marc Karson was a student of Harold Laski's at the London School of Economics in the 1950s, and is the author of *American Labor Unions and Politics, 1900–1918* and of a number of other articles on labor and socialist politics. Currently he is Professor and Chairman of the Political Science Department at Mankato State College, in Mankato, Minnesota.

Ann J. Lane is an Associate Professor of History at the John Jay College, City University of New York. She has taught at Rutgers and Sarah Lawrence College, and is a founder of the Socialist Scholars Conference. She is the author of *The Brownsville Affair: National Outrage and Black Reaction*, and the editor of *The Debate Over 'Slavery': Stanley Elkins and His Critics*. She is currently doing research on historian Mary Ritter Beard.

Staughton Lynd, formerly director of freedom schools in the Mississippi Summer Project of 1964 and an instructor at Saul Alinsky's Industrial Areas Foundation Training Institute, is currently associated with the Institute for Policy Studies. He also taught formerly at Yale. He has published *Class Conflict, Slavery, and the United States Constitution*, and *The Intellectual Origins of American Radicalism*. Now, with his wife Alice, he is working in the field of labor history. Their *Rank and File: Personal Histories by Working Class Organizers*, was published in 1973.

Kenneth McNaught is a Canadian-born scholar who is Professor of History at the University of Toronto. He has written widely on both Canadian and American history, his most recent work being *The Winnipeg General Strike* (in collaboration with D. J. Berenson). His current scholarly interests include comparative labor and socialist history in Canada, the United States, and Great Britain.

Michael Rogin has taught political science at Berkeley for the past decade. He was Fulbright Visiting Lecturer at the University of Sussex in 1967–68. Rogin is the author of *The Intellectuals and McCarthy: The Radical Specter; Political Change in California* (with John L. Shover); and "The Indian Question." He is currently completing a book on Andrew Jackson and the destruction of American Indians.

Clinton Rossiter (1917–70) was the John L. Senior University Professor of American Institutions at Cornell University, where he had also been Professor of Government and Chairman of the Department. Among his publications are *Constitutional Dictatorship; Conservatism in America; Parties and Politics in America; The Essential Lippmann;* and *Marxism: The View from America*.

Theodore Saloutos is Professor of History at UCLA and a past president of the Agricultural History Society. He has been Visiting Professor at the University of Freiburg and has held Guggenheim and Fulbright research awards. He is the author of *Farmer Movements in the South, 1865–1933; Agricultural Discontent in the Middle West, 1900–1939;* and has edited *Populism: Reaction or Reform?*

Leon Samson was an active socialist intellectual for much of his life. He was expelled from CCNY in 1917 for anti-war activities. His book *Towards a United Front* had considerable influence as an original interpretation of the obstacles faced by American socialists. Other books by him include *The American Mind* and *The New Humanism*.

Werner Sombart (1863–1941) was a Professor of Political Science at the University of Berlin. His book *Socialism and the Social Movement in the 19th Century*, a severely anti-socialist work, was published in ten revised and enlarged editions and was translated into twenty-four languages. Among his other books are: *A New Social Philosophy; The Quintessence of Capitalism: A Study of the History and Psychology of the Modern Business Man; Die deutsche Volkswirtschaft im 19. Jahrhundert und im Anfang des 20. Jahrhundert;* and *The Jews and Modern Capitalism*.

Adolph Sturmthal has recently retired as Professor of Labor and Industrial Relations at the University of Illinois. Austrian by birth, he has written and lectured widely on problems of economic development and the international labor movement, and has advised both the United States government and the United Nations on these matters. Among other works, he has written *The Tragedy of European Labor, 1918–1939; Workers Councils: A Study of Workplace Organizations on Both Sides of the Iron Curtain;* and, most recently, *The International Labor Movement in Transition: Essays on Africa, Asia, Europe, and South America* (with James G. Scoville).

Warren Susman is Professor of History and Chairman of the Department of History at Rutgers University. A cultural historian interested in the relationship between culture and society, Susman's most recent publication is *Culture and Commitment, 1929–1945.*

Stephan Thernstrom moved in 1973 from UCLA to become Professor of History at Harvard. An urban historian interested in problems of social mobility and social change, he has written *Poverty and Progress: Social Mobility in a Nineteenth Century City* and *The Other Bostonians: Poverty and Progress in the American Metropolis, 1880–1970.*

Norman Thomas had by his death in 1968 become the virtual personification of the American tradition of social democracy. A Presbyterian minister by training and a Christian socialist rather than a Marxist in his politics, Thomas ran for the presidency on the Socialist Party of America ticket in every election between 1928 and 1948. He also wrote numerous books and pamphlets on socialism, besides retaining the respect and affection of numerous elements in the 1960s New Left.

Gus Tyler is an Assistant President of the International Ladies' Garment Workers' Union, and a frequent commentator on the state of the American labor movement. Among his works are *Organized Crime in America; The State of the Unions; The Elements of Revolutionary Socialism; Labor in the Metropolis; The Labor Revolution;* and *The Political Imperative: The Corporate Character of Unions.*

Robert L. Tyler teaches at Southern Connecticut State College. He published *Rebels of the Woods: The I.W.W. in the Pacific Northwest* in 1967, and has written other articles on the Industrial Workers of the World. He is currently researching the problem of generations in psycho-history.

James Weinstein was between 1959 and 1967 editor of *Studies on the Left*, perhaps the most influential of the 1960s New Left journals. Together with David Eakins, he published *For a New America*, a collection of essays from the *Studies* journal. Weinstein is also the author of *The Decline of Socialism in America, 1912–1925;* and of *The Corporate Ideal in the Liberal State, 1900–1918.* He now lives in San Francisco, and helps edit *Socialist Revolution.*

Betty Yorburg is an Associate Professor of Sociology at the College of the City of New York. She is also a visiting lecturer, Graduate Faculty, of the New School for Social Research in New York City. Marriage and the family and social psychology are her special areas of competence. She is the author of *Utopia and Reality: A Collective Portrait of American Socialists; The Changing Family;* and *Sexual Identity: Sex Roles and Social Change* (forthcoming).

INDEX